Lecture Notes in Computer Science 14905

Founding Editors

Gerhard Goos
Juris Hartmanis

AF147395

The series Lecture Notes in Computer Science (LNCS), including its subseries Lecture Notes in Artificial Intelligence (LNAI) and Lecture Notes in Bioinformatics (LNBI), has established itself as a medium for the publication of new developments in computer science and information technology research, teaching, and education.

LNCS enjoys close cooperation with the computer science R & D community, the series counts many renowned academics among its volume editors and paper authors, and collaborates with prestigious societies. Its mission is to serve this international community by providing an invaluable service, mainly focused on the publication of conference and workshop proceedings and postproceedings. LNCS commenced publication in 1973.

Markulf Kohlweiss · Roberto Di Pietro ·
Alastair Beresford
Editors

Cryptology and Network Security

23rd International Conference, CANS 2024
Cambridge, UK, September 24–27, 2024
Proceedings, Part I

 Springer

Editors
Markulf Kohlweiss ⓘ
University of Edinburgh
Edinburgh, UK

Roberto Di Pietro ⓘ
King Abdullah University of Science
and Technology
Thuwal, Saudi Arabia

Alastair Beresford ⓘ
Department of Computer Science
and Technology
University of Cambridge
Cambridge, UK

ISSN 0302-9743 ISSN 1611-3349 (electronic)
Lecture Notes in Computer Science
ISBN 978-981-97-8012-9 ISBN 978-981-97-8013-6 (eBook)
https://doi.org/10.1007/978-981-97-8013-6

Preface

This volume contains the keynote abstracts and papers of the first four sessions presented at CANS 2024. The International Conference on Cryptology and Network Security (CANS) is a premier forum for presenting research in the field of cryptology and network security. The conference seeks academic, industry, and government submissions on theoretical and practical aspects of security and cryptography.

The 23rd International Conference on Cryptology and Network Security (CANS 2024) took place in Cambridge, UK on September 24–27, 2024. The conference was held in cooperation with the International Association for Cryptologic Research (IACR). We received 76 submissions, which were reviewed by 56 security and cryptography experts including the two program chairs and the two publicity chairs. The committee's work was complemented by reviews provided by 64 external reviewers. Each submission received at least 3, and on average 3.5 reviews. Of the 76 submissions, 25 were accepted for publication. Out of these, 10 papers were assigned to a shepherd from the program committee to further improve the quality of articles included in the proceedings. These papers were peer-reviewed and subsequently discussed based on the quality of their scientific contribution, novelty, and impact by the members of the Program Committee. The reviews were double-blind, and in almost all cases there were lively discussions among the members of the Program Committee to decide the merit of reviewed papers. Aside from the paper presentations, we were honored to have three outstanding keynote speakers: Wenjing Lou, Professor at Virginia Tech, IEEE Fellow, Jens Groth, Chief Scientist at Nexus, and George Danezis, Chief Scientist at Mysten Labs and Professor at University College London. Their talks provided interesting insights and research directions in important research areas.

CANS is relatively unique in that it accepts research contributions from the two worlds of cryptography and network security. Thanks to the efforts of the publicity chairs, we attracted a diverse field of submissions, with four out of the eight sessions covering cybersecurity and leakage, machine learning and security, as well as a wide variety of application areas, including anonymity & privacy and blockchain technology. We hope to further encourage this trend in future years.

Acknowledgements. We thank the very professional editors and staff at Springer who guided us in producing these proceedings. We gratefully acknowledge the support of Queens' College, Robinson College, and the Department of Computer Science and Technology at the University of Cambridge for hosting the event as well as KAUST, which supported two best paper awards (student and regular). We also thank the Steering Committee and Organizing Committee as well as the previous Program Chairs for their valuable advice and encouragement. Last, but not least, we thank all the attendees of CANS 2024 for making the event such a success.

August 2024

Markulf Kohlweiss
Roberto Di Pietro
Alastair Beresford

Organization

General Chair

Alastair Beresford   University of Cambridge, UK

Program Committee Chairs

Markulf Kohlweiss   University of Edinburgh, UK
Roberto Di Pietro   King Abdullah University of Science and
           Technology, Saudi Arabia

Publicity Chairs

Nik Sultana   Illinois Institute of Technology, USA
Natalia Stakhanova   University of Saskatchewan, Canada

Steering Committee

Yvo Desmedt   University of Texas at Dallas, USA
Sara Foresti   University of Milan, Italy
Juan Garay   Texas A&M University, USA
Amir Herzberg   University of Connecticut, USA
Atsuko Miyaji   Osaka University, Japan
Panos Papadimitratos   KTH Royal Institute of Technology, Sweden
David Pointcheval   École Normale Supérieure, France
Huaxiong Wang   Nanyang Technological University, Singapore

Organizing Committee

Jungha Lee   University of Cambridge, UK
Matthew Patterson   University of Cambridge, UK
Kata Szabo   University of Cambridge, UK

Program Committee

Cristina Alcaraz	University of Málaga, Spain
Megumi Ando	Tufts University, USA
Thomas Attema	TNO, The Netherlands
Subhadeep Banik	University of Lugano, Switzerland
Emanuele Bellini	Cryptography Research Centre, Technology Innovation Institute, UAE
Alastair Beresford	University of Cambridge, UK
Jan Bobolz	University of Edinburgh, UK
Tamara Bonaci	Northeastern University, USA
Anupam Chattopadhyay	Nanyang Technological University, Singapore
Sherman S. M. Chow	Chinese University of Hong Kong, China
Frédéric Cuppens	Polytechnique Montréal, Canada
Bernardo David	IT University of Copenhagen, Denmark
Pooya Farshim	Durham University, UK
Joaquin Garcia-Alfaro	Institut Polytechnique de Paris, France
Gayathri Garimella	Brown University, USA
Satrajit Ghosh	IIT Kharagpur, India
Dieter Gollmann	Hamburg University of Technology, Germany
Xinlei He	CISPA Helmholtz Center for Information Security, Germany
Ashwin Jha	Ruhr-Universität Bochum, Germany
Dimitris Karakostas	University of Edinburgh, UK
Sokratis Katsikas	Norwegian University of Science and Technology, Norway
Qiqi Lai	Shaanxi Normal University, China
Eysa Lee	Brown University, USA
Shujun Li	University of Kent, UK
Kaitai Liang	Delft University of Technology, The Netherlands
Xiapu Luo	Hong Kong Polytechnic University, China
Rene Mayrhofer	Johannes Kepler University Linz, Austria
Weizhi Meng	Technical University of Denmark, Denmark
Omid Mir	Austrian Institute of Technology, Austria
Johannes Müller	University of Luxembourg, Luxembourg
Sergio Pastrana	Universidad Carlos III de Madrid, Spain
Octavio Pérez Kempner	NTT Social Informatics Laboratories, Japan
Joachim Posegga	University of Passau, Germany
Siddharth Prakash Rao	Nokia Bell Labs, Finland
Somitra Sanadhya	IIT Jodhpur, India
Savio Sciancalepore	Eindhoven University of Technology, The Netherlands

Additional Reviewers

O'Neill, Adam
Ovezik, Christina
Pan, Ying-Yu
Pöhls, Henrich C.
Ramacher, Sebastian
Ricco, Emanuele
Sedaghat, Mahdi
Sha, Kailun
Shen, Yu
Shi, Zeshun
Sijpesteijn, Thom
Singh, Jaspal
Sinha, Sayani
Smith, Dane

Sousa, Pedro
Spini, Gabriele
Sun, Zhen
Talayhan, Abdullah
Tyner, Lakyah
Wang, Lijin
Wang, Rui
Wong, Harry W. H.
Youdom Kemmoe, Victor
Zhang, Heyi
Zhao, Yi
Zheng, Jingyi
Zhou, Wenchang
Zindros, Dionysis

Keynote Abstracts

Zero-Knowledge Virtual Machines and Applications

Jens Groth

Nexus, USA
`jens@nexus.xyz`

Abstract. Zero-knowledge proofs are powering an increasing number of applications. A main driver of adoption is that proofs can be succinct. Succinctness allows users to cheaply verify a computation without having to recompute. In the blockchain space, the Ethereum Foundation is now talking about a zero-knowledge singularity, where the main job of the Ethereum chain no longer is to do computation directly but to order and verify batches of external computation.

Designing proofs directly for applications is cumbersome and error-prone. Zero-knowledge virtual machines in contrast make it easy for developers to express the statements they want to prove. When using a zkVM you compile a program written in a high-level language, e.g., Rust or Solidity, to a VM program. The zkVM then executes the VM program and attaches a succinct proof to the VM output that it has been correctly computed.

Bio Jens Groth is Chief Scientist at Nexus. In the past he has been Professor of Cryptology at UCL and Principal Researcher & Director of Research at DFINITY. Groth's research focus is on zero-knowledge proofs, with notable achievements including the invention of pairing-based SNARKs and co-inventions of pairing-friendly proof systems, logarithmic size proofs in cyclic groups, prover efficient proofs with constant overhead, and usage of lookups in proving correct machine execution. His contributions have been recognized with test-of-time awards in 2021 and 2023 by the International Association for Cryptologic Research.

Private Communication in Public 5G and Beyond Networks

Wenjing Lou

Virginia Tech, USA
`wjlou@vt.edu`

Abstract. While softwarization, cloudification, and advanced radio access network (RAN) technologies have been key enablers of current 5G networks, the focuses of next-generation (nextG) mobile networks are likely to shift—integrating AI/ML into networks, adopting Open-RAN architecture, and enhancing security will likely be the key differentiators. This talk centers on security and privacy protection in nextG mobile networks. We will begin with a general discussion of zero-trust architecture, the O-RAN initiative, and key security and privacy challenges in nextG networks. We will then introduce our recent research on enhancing mobile users' privacy in 5G and beyond networks. I will introduce AAKA, an anonymous authentication and key agreement protocol that allows mobile users to access the mobile network anonymously, effectively thwarting tracking by mobile network operators. I will also introduce UCBlocker, a user-defined, policy-based, end-to-end system to block unwanted calls (e.g., scam and spam calls) in mobile networks. Both works are inspired by emerging decentralized identifiers (DIDs) and anonymous credentials technologies.

Bio Wenjing Lou is the W. C. English Endowed Professor of Computer Science at Virginia Tech and a Fellow of the IEEE and ACM. Her research interests cover many topics in the cybersecurity field, with her current research interest focusing on wireless networks, blockchain systems, trustworthy machine learning systems, and security and privacy problems in the Internet of Things (IoT) systems. Prof. Lou is a highly cited researcher by the Web of Science Group. She received the Virginia Tech Alumni Award for Research Excellence in 2018, the highest university-level faculty research award. She received the INFOCOM Test-of-Time paper award in 2020. She was the TPC chair for IEEE INFOCOM 2019 and ACM WiSec 2020. She was the Steering Committee Chair for IEEE CNS conference from 2013 to 2020. She is currently a steering committee member of IEEE INFOCOM and IEEE CNS. She served as a program director at US National Science Foundation (NSF) from 2014 to 2017.

Modern Blockchains for the Modern Security Engineer

George Danezis

Mysten Labs, USA
jgeorge@mystenlabs.com

Abstract. Modern blockchains are marvels of cryptography and security engineering. They embody the latest advances in language based security, distributed systems security, advanced cryptography, and security economics. They allow unprecedented expressivity for commercial integrity policies, and unparalleled strength of mechanism. Yet they are still largely used for toy applications. In this talk I discuss how modern blockchains have fundamentally different characteristics from early ones in terms of cost, latency, throughput, scaling, expressivity, governance and power consumption. However the evolution from the old to the modern was slow, full of setbacks, and confusion and the significant shift in capabilities was easy to miss. Using the Sui blockchain as an example, I present the current technologies for high-performance consensus, transaction processing, execution and data dissemination. Then, I argue that modern blockchains are particularly useful as a "consistent core" to engineer large open security protocols: from Multi-Party Computations, Private Information Retrieval, Onion Routing to Certificate/Binary transparency. In brief, assuming their modern capabilities, modern blockchains can resolve the hard coordination problems present in large security systems, in a systematic, performant and secure manner. They are a tool every security engineer needs to have in their toolbox.

Bio Prof George Danezis, B.A, M.A (Cantab), Ph.D, FBCS. George Danezis is Professor of Security and Privacy Engineering at the Department of Computer Science, University College London. He co-founded and acts as Chief Scientist at Mysten Labs since 2021. George has conducted research on Privacy Enhancing Technologies (PET) and Decentralised/Distributed Systems Security since 2000. His current research interests focus around secure communications, highintegrity systems to support privacy, blockchains and decentralization. In the past, he co-founded chainspace.io in 2018, and had his team acquired in 2019 by Facebook Novi to help design the Diem payment system. In 2021 he departed and co-founded MystenLabs, to help build the Sui smart contracts platform. He has previously been a Researcher for Microsoft Research, Cambridge; a visiting fellow at K.U. Leuven (Belgium); and a research associate at the University of Cambridge (UK).

Modern Blockchain for the Modern Security Engineer

Contents – Part I

Blockchain Technology

Contents – Part II

Cryptanalysis

Multi-party Computation

Efficient Secure Multi-party Computation for Multi-dimensional Arithmetics and Its Application in Privacy-Preserving Biometric Identification

Dongyu Wu$^{(\boxtimes)}$ (iD), Bei Liang (iD), Zijie Lu (iD), and Jintai Ding (iD)

Beijing Institute of Mathematical Sciences and Applications, Beijing 101408, China
{wudongyu,lbei,luzijie,dinglab}@bimsa.cn

Abstract. Over years of the development of secure multi-party computation (MPC), many sophisticated functionalities have been made practical and multi-dimensional operations occur more and more frequently in MPC protocols, especially in protocols involving datasets of vector elements, such as privacy-preserving biometric identification and privacy-preserving machine learning. In this paper, we introduce a new kind of correlation, called tensor triples, which is designed to make multi-dimensional MPC protocols more efficient. We will discuss the generation process, the usage, as well as the applications of tensor triples and show that it can accelerate privacy-preserving biometric identification protocols, such as FingerCode, Eigenfaces and FaceNet, by more than 1000 times, with reasonable offline costs.

Keywords: Tensor triple · MPC · Beaver triple · VOLE · Privacy-preserving biometric identification · Privacy-preserving machine learning

1 Introduction

1.1 Motivation

Secure multiparty computation (MPC) is one of the central subfields in cryptography. MPC aims to accomplish a joint evaluation of a function over inputs provided by multiple parties without revealing any extra information. Due to its feature on protection of the inputs, it has been widely used in analysis and processing of private or sensitive data held by multiple parties. Starting from Yao's Garbled Circuit [1], numerous advances have been made on the most fundamental circuit-based MPC. Over years of development, circuit-based MPC gradually gains capability of practically computing more and more sophisticated and large-scale functions. Apart from one-dimensional numeric computation, the necessity of handling higher dimensional operations has also become a concern. For instance, people for years have explored the possibility of application of MPC on privacy-preserving biometric identification [2–10], privacy-preserving machine learning [11–15] and many other practical fields that require an intensive use of vector and matrix operations, such as vector tensoring and matrix multiplication. Unlike the straightforward homomorphic encryption methods, which often behave less computationally efficient, it is crucial to find a way to accelerate multi-dimensional arithmetics for circuit-based MPC protocols. For instance, SPDZ framework has been used to boost multi-dimensional MPC protocols [16].

Meanwhile, apart from the classical correlation generation protocols such as OT and Beaver triples, researchers have also attempted to find new kinds of correlations (for example [17]) that can fulfill different needs of MPC protocols and perform more efficiently compared to classical ways [18–21]. Among these variants, VOLE, as an efficient way to provide correlated random vector sharings for two parties, has been widely used as a convenient auxiliary tool to accomplish circuit-based MPC involving multi-dimensional inputs. Therefore, we would like to explore a way to boost MPC protocols involving multi-dimensional objects, such as vectors and matrices, and we would like to take advantage of the correlation properties of VOLE to assist the procedure.

1.2   Our Contribution

The goal of this paper is to explore a more efficient way to fulfill multi-dimensional secure multi-party computation. In this paper, we define a new kind of correlated triples, called tensor triples, which can be generated using VOLE, or alternatively RLWE-based homomorphic encryption. We will also prove that this type of triples can be used to assist the secure multi-party computation on multi-dimensional arithmetics and accelerate MPC protocols involving vectors and matrices. The corresponding protocols will be much more efficient both computationally and communicatively compared to the usual Beaver's method. As a result, we discover several practical applications of tensor triples on classical privacy-preserving biometric identification and privacy-preserving machine learning protocols. As instances, we realize implementations of three privacy-preserving biometric identification protocols, namely FingerCode [22], Eigenfaces [23] and FaceNet [24]. We will also analyze the performance of the implementations and prove our claim that the tensor triple method indeed provides a more efficient way to carry out multi-dimensional MPC protocols. Our implementation results show that the squared Euclidean distance computation in 128 queries of batched Fingercodes against a database of 1024 only takes 0.082 s while the GSHADE takes 176.64 s, which is more than 2000 times faster than previous work. We also show that the squared Euclidean distance computation in 80 queries of batched Eigenface against a database of 1000 only takes 0.032 s while the GSHADE takes 104 s, which is more than 3000 times faster than previous work.

1.3   Related Works

Abspoel et al. in [17] proposed the concept of "outer product triple" through linear secret sharing schemes over Galois rings. The authors have also explained the outer product triples are useful as they can be utilized to assist the secure multiparty computation of outer products between vectors. Also, Boyle et al. in [21] proposed the idea of using subfield VOLE for secure matrix multiplications. The definition of outer product triple in [17] is equivalent to the notion of tensor triple we will define in Sect. 3, and we will introduce protocols involving these triples for secure 2PC of the outer product and matrix multiplication as noted in [21], but we will provide a detailed description of the protocols as well as an application of a broader range of parameters. More precisely, for the parameter setting, we do not require the dimensions of tensor triples equal to the dimensions of target vectors in computation, since the triple generation process is in the preprocessing phase, and making the knowledge of the dimensions of multi-dimensional objects occurred in MPC protocols beforehand is unreasonable. Hence in our definition, the tensor triples can always be generated without any knowledge of the dimensions in advance. For the generation process, we focus on the two-party and (s, s)-additive secret sharing case. We propose efficient methods to generate tensor triples and show in experiments that these methods greatly outperform SPDZ-based methods. For applications, we explicitly provide the protocols for MPC of vector outer products and matrix multiplications.

As pointed out, MPC of matrix multiplication is a crucial functionality in many areas. As we are aware, there exist various works attempting to fulfill this functionality more efficiently. The most seemingly practical way is the realization through the SPDZ framework (for instance [16,25]). On the other hand, our work only uses comparatively lightweight MPC components such as VOLE. As a result, we will show in detailed statistics that our method obtains a high efficiency and greatly outperforms the homomorphic encryption based protocols.

Similarly, there are multiple works aimed to accelerate the privacy-preserving biometric identification process. For FingerCode, Eigenfaces and FaceNet, the three protocols discussed in this paper, we are also aware of the existence of various works and improvements. Nevertheless, we have not discovered any work using VOLE or similar techniques to improve the efficiency. We will still discuss them in the corresponding sections and show a detailed comparison between different implementations.

1.4   Security Model

All protocols involved in the rest of the paper are secure against semi-honest and computationally bounded adversaries.

1.5   Organization of Paper

In Sect. 2, we define necessary notions and primitives in MPC. In Sect. 3, we define the notion of tensor triple and briefly explain the intuition and the idea how it can be used to accelerate multi-dimensional circuit-based MPC protocols. We then proceed to introducing several ways to generate tensor triples. The protocols are focused on resolving the generation of tensor triples for two parties, as is the usual need in most practical applications. In Sect. 4 we explain the usage of tensor triples to accomplish MPC of basic algebraic operations for scalars, vectors and matrices. Matrix operations. In Sect. 5, we discuss possible applications of tensor triples in practice. It should be emphasized that tensor triples can be used to accelerate all multi-dimensional MPC protocols universally, and the applications we list in the section are merely few instances. In Sect. 6 implementations of protocols as well as results of the experiments after the execution are presented. It can been clearly seen that the tensor triple method provide a significant speedup.

2   Preliminaries and Notations

2.1   Oblivious Transfer (OT)

We provide a very brief introduction of oblivious transfer together with its multiple invariants in order to import all possible notations to be used. In an oblivious trnasfer [26], the sender with a pair of messages (m_0, m_1) interacts with the receiver with a choice bit b. The result ensures that the receiver learns m_b but obtains no knowledge of m_{1-b}, while the sender obtains no knowledge of b. In an OT extension protocol OT_l^n, the input of the sender is n message pairs $(m_{i,0}, m_{i,1}) \in \{0, 1\}^{2l}$ and the input of the receiver is a string $\mathbf{b} \in \{0, 1\}^n$. The result allows the receiver to learn $m_{i,\mathbf{b}[i]}$ for $1 \leq i \leq n$. In a Random OT (ROT), the sender inputs nothing beforehand but obtains two random strings in the outputs as the message pair, and the receiver inputs nothing either but obtains the choice bit together with the selected message afterwards. Similiarly, a batched version of ROT (or also known as OT extension, see [27–29]) which generates n message pairs of bit-length l is denoted by ROT_l^n. A correlated OT (COT) [21,30,31] is a variant of ROT that allows the sender to pre-determine a string Δ and obtain two correlated random strings as the message pair with their XOR equal Δ. The extension of COT denoted by COT_m^n allows the sender to choose $\Delta \in \mathbb{F}_{2^m}$. The protocol eventually provides two uniformly distributed vectors $\mathbf{u} \in \mathbb{F}_2^n, \mathbf{v} \in \mathbb{F}_{2^m}^n$ to the receiver, and $\mathbf{v} \oplus (\mathbf{u} \cdot \Delta)$ to the sender. A subfield vector oblivious linear evaluation (sVOLE) protocol is a generalization of COT_m^n to an arbitrary finite base field. A vector oblivious linear evaluation (VOLE) allows one party to obtain two vectors $\mathbf{u}, \mathbf{v} \in \mathbb{F}_p^n$, and the other party a scalar $x \in \mathbb{F}_p$ and the linear evaluation $\mathbf{u}x + \mathbf{v}$.

In further chapters, we will be mainly using the random variants of COT_m^n and sVOLE functionalities defined below in Fig. 1. It is not difficult to see that RCOT_m^n is a special case of $\mathscr{F}_{\text{RsVOLE}}^{p,m,n}$ when $p = 2$.

VOLE protocols with semi-honest and computational security in OT-hybrid model have been defined in [19,21]. Subfield VOLE, as an important variant of VOLE, has also been implemented in various ways (See [20,21,31–34]).

Functionality RCOT_m^n	Functionality $\mathscr{F}_{\text{RsVOLE}}^{p,m,n}$
Players: The sender S and the receiver R.	**Players:** The sender S and the receiver R.
Inputs: $\perp$.	**Inputs:** A dimension pair (n, m).
Outputs:	**Outputs:**
– S outputs $\mathbf{v} \in \mathbb{F}_{2^m}^n, \Delta \in \mathbb{F}_{2^m}$;	– S outputs $x \in \mathbb{F}_{p^m}, \mathbf{v} \in \mathbb{F}_{p^m}^n$;
– R outputs $\mathbf{u} \in \mathbb{F}_2^n, \mathbf{v} \oplus (\mathbf{u} \cdot \Delta) \in \mathbb{F}_{2^m}^n$.	– R outputs $\mathbf{u} \in \mathbb{F}_p^n, x\mathbf{u} + \mathbf{v} \in \mathbb{F}_{p^m}^n$.

Fig. 1. Functionality of RCOT and RsVOLE

2.2 RLWE-Based Additively Homomorphic Encryption (RLWE-AHE)

The notion of an AHE scheme we follow is basically the same as the one in [35], with an addition of a tensorial scalar operation which is needed for further use. Roughly speaking, it is a scheme with "linearity". For brevity, the detailed definition will be introduced in Appendix A.2.

Instances of an AHE scheme which are not based on RLWE are [36–38]. While most RLWE-based instantiations of such a scheme (such as [39,40]) are designed to be fully homomorphic, we emphasize that the additive homomorphicity suffices the scheme. We assume that the parameters of a RLWE-based AHE scheme have been chosen to be large enough to allow evaluation of the circuit for further protocols and prevent leakage through amplified ciphertext noise from homomorphic operations.

3 Tensor Triple

3.1 Definition of Tensor Triple

In this section, we first define the notion of vector sharing.

Definition 1. *An (s,t)-secret sharing of a vector $\boldsymbol{v}$ is a set $\{[\boldsymbol{v}]_1, ..., [\boldsymbol{v}]_s\}$ of s vectors, such that there exists an efficient algorithm to reconstruct $\boldsymbol{v}$ from any t shares $[\boldsymbol{v}]_{i_1}, ..., [\boldsymbol{v}]_{i_t}$, but there is no algorithm that can efficiently reconstruct $\boldsymbol{v}$ from any subset of shares with fewer cardinality. We will denote a share of $\boldsymbol{v}$ by $[\boldsymbol{v}]$ if indices are not particularly involved. The secret sharing is called linear if $[\boldsymbol{u}]_i + [\boldsymbol{v}]_i = [\boldsymbol{u}+\boldsymbol{v}]_i$. A linear (s,t)-vector sharing scheme involves s participants, inputs a vector $\boldsymbol{v}$, and outputs to each participant a linear (s,t)-secret sharing of $\boldsymbol{v}$. A vector sharing scheme is called (information-theoretically) secure, if*

$$Pr(\boldsymbol{v} = \boldsymbol{x} | [\boldsymbol{v}]_{i_1}, ..., [\boldsymbol{v}]_{i_{t-1}}) = Pr(\boldsymbol{v} = \boldsymbol{x}' | [\boldsymbol{v}]_{i_1}, ..., [\boldsymbol{v}]_{i_{t-1}})$$

for any subset $\{i_1, ..., i_{t-1}\} \subset \{1, ..., s\}$ and any $\boldsymbol{x}, \boldsymbol{x}'$ in the ambient space.

Remark 2. *In the rest of the paper, we use $t = s$, and in the ideal setting, a vector sharing scheme over finite fields consists of a trusted party and s participants.*

The trusted party takes the input v, randomly samples vectors $r_1, ..., r_{s-1}$ and sends them to the first $s-1$ participants respectively. It then sends $v - r_1 - ... - r_{s-1}$ to the last participant. The secret vector v is therefore only recoverable by all parties together.

The notion of tensor triple has been proposed in various forms (See [17, 21]) to more efficiently fulfill MPC of vectors. We propose the following definition to better facilitate its properties.

Definition 3. (Tensor triple). *By definition, a tensor triple (u, v, W) consists of data $u \in K^m, v \in K^n, W \in M_{m \times n}(K)$ satisfying $u \otimes v = uv^T = W$.*

Definition 4. (Tensor triple sharing). *Let $P_1, ..., P_s$ be the participants of a secure multi-party computation protocol over an ambient finite field or ring K. By definition, a tensor triple sharing scheme provides two vectors and one matrix $[u]_i \in K^m, [v]_i \in K^n, [W]_i \in M_{m \times n}(K)$ for the participant P_i, such that $[u]_i, [v]_i$ form secret sharings of $u \in K^m, v \in K^n$ respectively, with the relation $u \otimes v = uv^T = \sum_{i=1}^s [W]_i$. Shares of u, v and W will be denoted by $[u], [v]$ and $[W]$ if indices are not particularly involved. For our convenience, such a triple will be called an (m, n)-triple. A tensor triple sharing scheme is called secure if the distribution of u, v to an adversary who obtains $\{([u]_i, [v]_i, [W]_i)\}_{i \neq i^*}$ for any $i^* \in \{1, ..., s\}$ is computationally indistinguishable from the uniform one.*

3.2   Tensor Triple Generation

Now we would like to introduce multiple ways to efficiently generate tensor triples. Figure 5 shows the ideal functionality of tensor triple generation. In practice, the generation process can be fulfilled via Ring-LWE or subfield VOLE. We provide below these protocols in details.

RLWE-Based Two-Party Tensor Triple Generation. A batch generation method for Beaver triples based on RLWE-AHE has been introduced in [35]. It can be modified as dipicted in Fig. 2 to generate tensor triples.

sVOLE-Based Two-Party Tensor Triple Generation. An OT-based protocol for generating Beaver multiplication triples was proposed in [41]. In [42], the authors established a more efficient protocol based on Correlated-OT extension, which has been shown to outperform the AHE based generation method. In this section, we propose an sVOLE-based method to efficiently generate tensor triples.

Observe that under a fixed $\mathbb{F}_p$-vector space isomorphism $\varphi : \mathbb{F}_{p^m} \to \mathbb{F}_p^m$ (for instance, $\varphi(a_0 + a_1\alpha + ... + a_{m-1}\alpha^{m-1}) = (a_0, ..., a_{m-1})$ where $\mathbb{F}_{p^m}$ is realized through an extension $\mathbb{F}_p[\alpha]$ by adding a root of an irreducible monic polynomial of degree m), $\mathscr{F}_{\text{RsVOLE}}^{p,m,n}$ becomes the following functionality $\mathscr{F}_{\text{RsVOLE}'}^{p,m,n}$, as shown in Fig. 3.

RLWE-based tensor triple generation TT.Gen(m, n, λ)

Setup: P_0 generates (pk,sk) $\leftarrow$ AHE.Gen(1^λ) and publish pk.

Interacting Phase:

1. P_0 samples $\mathbf{u}_0 \leftarrow_\$ K^m, \mathbf{v}_0 \leftarrow_\$ K^n$ and encrypts them to obtain the ciphertexts

$$\mathsf{ct_u} \leftarrow \mathsf{AHE.Enc(pk, u_0)}, \mathsf{ct_v} \leftarrow \mathsf{AHE.Enc(pk, v_0)}.$$

   P_1 samples $\mathbf{u}_1, \leftarrow_\$ K^m, \mathbf{v}_1 \leftarrow_\$ K^n, R_u \leftarrow_\$ M_{m \times n}(K), R_v \leftarrow_\$ M_{n \times m}(K)$ and encrypts them to obtain the ciphertexts $\vec{\mathsf{ct}}_{R_u} = \mathsf{AHE.Enc(pk, }R_u), \vec{\mathsf{ct}}_{R_v} = \mathsf{AHE.Enc(pk, }R_v)$.

2. P_0 sends to P_1 the ciphertexts $\mathsf{ct_u}, \mathsf{ct_v}$;

3. By homomorphicity, P_1 computes $\vec{\mathsf{ct}}_1 = \mathbf{u}_1 \otimes \mathsf{ct_v}, \vec{\mathsf{ct}}_2 = \mathbf{v}_1 \otimes \mathsf{ct_u}$ and $\vec{\mathsf{ct}}_{W_u} = \vec{\mathsf{ct}}_1 + \vec{\mathsf{ct}}_{R_u}, \vec{\mathsf{ct}}_{W_v} = \vec{\mathsf{ct}}_2 + \vec{\mathsf{ct}}_{R_v}$ and then sends to P_1 the ciphertexts $\vec{\mathsf{ct}}_{W_u}, \vec{\mathsf{ct}}_{W_v}$;

4. P_0 performs decryption to obtain $W_u = \mathsf{AHE.Dec(sk, }\vec{\mathsf{ct}}_{W_u}), W_v = \mathsf{AHE.Dec(sk, }\vec{\mathsf{ct}}_{W_v})$ and then computes $W_0 = W_u + W_v^T + \mathbf{u}_0 \otimes \mathbf{v}_0$. P_1 computes $W_1 = \mathbf{u}_1 \otimes \mathbf{v}_1 - R_u - R_v^T$.

Outputs: P_0 outputs $(\mathbf{u}_0, \mathbf{v}_0, W_0)$, P_1 outputs $(\mathbf{u}_1, \mathbf{v}_1, W_1)$.

Fig. 2. RLWE-based tensor triple generation

Functionality $\mathscr{F}_{\mathrm{RsVOLE}'}^{p,m,n}$

Players: Participants S, R.

Functionality: Receive (sender, sid) from S and (receiver, sid) from R, sample $\mathbf{x} \in_r \mathbb{F}_p^m, V \in_r \mathbb{F}_p^{mn}, \mathbf{y} \in_r \mathbb{F}_p^n$, compute $U = \mathbf{x} \otimes \mathbf{y} + V \in \mathbb{F}_p^{mn}$, return $(\mathbf{x}, V)$ to S and $(\mathbf{y}, U)$ to R.

Fig. 3. Functionality of RsVOLE'

Given a protocol RsVOLE(m, n, λ) realizing $\mathscr{F}_{\mathrm{RsVOLE}'}^{p,m,n}$, we can easily formulate many ways to generate a tensor multiplication triple. Figure 4 shows a straightforward method.

In particular, when $p = 2$, one may also use COT protocols in an analogous way to generate tensor triples over fields with even characteristics.

We use two ways to materialize RsVOLE(m, n, λ). The first method is to use COT for the case when $p = 2$, as shown in Fig. 6. The idea is similar to the one implemented in [21], and we simply adapt it in tensor form to suit our need.

The second way is to use Silent OT (SOT). SOT procotol can be directly used to fulfill RsVOLE(m, n, λ). We omit the details and refer to [21] for brevity.

4   Secure Multi-dimensional Arithmetic Evaluations

In this section we will discuss various vector operations which may be performed securely using Beaver's method. When $m = n = 1$, tensor triples are simply usual Beaver triples. Therefore they can also be used for basic arithmetics. We mainly discuss the multi-dimensional computations below.

Functionality $\mathscr{F}_{\text{TTGen}}^{p,m,n}$

Players: Participants $P_1, ..., P_k$.

Functionality: Receive (sid, i) from P_i, sample $\mathbf{u} \in_r \mathbb{F}_p^m, \mathbf{v} \in_r \mathbb{F}_p^n$, compute $W = \mathbf{u} \otimes \mathbf{v}$, securely secret share $\mathbf{u}, \mathbf{v}, W$ into $[\mathbf{u}]_i, [\mathbf{v}]_i, [W]_i$ and return to P_i the share $([\mathbf{u}]_i, [\mathbf{v}]_i, [W]_i)$.

Fig. 4. sVOLE-based tensor triple generation

---

sVOLE-based tensor triple generation $\text{TT.Gen}(m, n, \lambda)$

Inputs: None.

Primitive: A random subfield VOLE protocol $\text{RsVOLE}(m, n, \lambda)$.

Interacting Phase:

1. P_0 and P_1 launch the protocol $\text{RsVOLE}(m, n, \lambda)$ where P_0 acts as the sender and P_1 acts as the receiver. P_0 obtains $\mathbf{x} \in_r \mathbb{F}_p^m, V \in_r \mathbb{F}_p^{mn}$ and P_1 obtains $\mathbf{y} \in_r \mathbb{F}_p^n, U = \mathbf{x} \otimes \mathbf{y} + V \in \mathbb{F}_p^{mn}$;

2. P_0 and P_1 launch the protocol $\text{RsVOLE}(m, n, \lambda)$ where P_0 acts as the receiver and P_1 acts as the sender. P_1 obtains $\mathbf{x}' \in_r \mathbb{F}_p^m, V' \in_r \mathbb{F}_p^{mn}$ and P_0 obtains $\mathbf{y}' \in_r \mathbb{F}_p^n, U' = \mathbf{x}' \otimes \mathbf{y}' + V' \in \mathbb{F}_p^{mn}$;

Outputs: P_0 outputs $(\mathbf{u}_0 = \mathbf{x}, \mathbf{v}_0 = \mathbf{y}', W_0 = -V + U' + \mathbf{x} \otimes \mathbf{y}')$, P_1 outputs $(\mathbf{u}_1 = \mathbf{x}', \mathbf{v}_1 = \mathbf{y}, W_1 = U - V' + \mathbf{x}' \otimes \mathbf{y})$.

Fig. 5. Functionality of tensor triple generation

4.1 Linear Operations and Dot Product

As expected, additions and operations involving constants may all be computed locally without any interaction by the homomorphicity. More specifically, the following operations are securely multi-party computable and the computation can be done locally without any interaction:

- $[\mathbf{a}] + [\mathbf{b}] = [\mathbf{a} + \mathbf{b}]$;
- Given a public constant vector $\mathbf{c}$, $[\mathbf{a} + \mathbf{c}]_1 = [\mathbf{a}]_1 + \mathbf{c}$, $[\mathbf{a} + \mathbf{c}]_i = [\mathbf{a}]_i$ for $i \neq 1$.
- $c[\mathbf{a}] = [c\mathbf{a}]$, where $c \in K$ is a constant number;
- $\mathbf{c} \cdot [\mathbf{a}] = [\mathbf{c} \cdot \mathbf{a}]$, where $\mathbf{a} \in K^n$, and $\mathbf{c} \in K^n$ is a constant vector;
- $\mathbf{c} \otimes [\mathbf{a}] = [\mathbf{c} \otimes \mathbf{a}]$, where $\mathbf{c}$ is a constant vector.

Now let us consider the dot product of two vectors $\mathbf{a}, \mathbf{b}$ in the same dimension n. Suppose we have a (n, n)-triple. First we denote $\mathbf{a} - \mathbf{u} = \mathbf{s}, \mathbf{b} - \mathbf{v} = \mathbf{t}$. By Beaver's method, each party may annouce its share of $\mathbf{s}$ and $\mathbf{t}$ to recover the two vectors. Then they could securely compute the shares as $[\mathbf{a} \cdot \mathbf{b}] = \mathbf{s} \cdot \mathbf{t} + [\mathbf{u}] \cdot \mathbf{t} + [\mathbf{v}] \cdot \mathbf{s} + \text{tr}([W])$. Note that the last term uses the fact that the trace function is linear. The correctness can easily be verified by a direct computation.

4.2 Outer Product and Matrix Product

Figure 7 shows the ideal functionality for secure multi-party outer product computation. One can use exactly the same method to fulfill the need of an outer

---

COT-based $\mathsf{RsVOLE}(m, n, \lambda)$

Inputs: None.
Primitive: A random OT extension protocol and a pre-determined pseudorandom generator PRG.
Interacting Phase:

1. The receiver R and the sender S invoke the ROT extension protocol (preferably with extension). ROT protocol outputs to S a family of pairs $\{\mathsf{seed}_{i,0}, \mathsf{seed}_{i,1}\}_{i=1,...,n}$ and to R its choices $\{y_i, \mathsf{seed}_{i,y_i}\}_{i=1,...,n}$. We denote $\mathbf{y} = (y_1, ..., y_n)$. Additionally S samples a string $\mathbf{x} \leftarrow_\$ \{0,1\}^m$;
2. S computes $\mathbf{s}_i = \mathsf{PRG}(\mathsf{seed}_{i,0}) \oplus \mathsf{PRG}(\mathsf{seed}_{i,1}) \oplus \mathbf{x}$ for $i = 1, ..., n$ and sends all $\mathbf{s}_i$ to R;
3. R computes $\mathbf{u}_i = \mathsf{PRG}(\mathsf{seed}_{i,y_i}) \oplus y_i \mathbf{s}_i$ and formulates the matrix $U = (\mathbf{u}_1^T, ..., \mathbf{u}_n^T)$. S formulates the matrix $V = (\mathsf{PRG}(\mathsf{seed}_{i,0}))_{i=1,...,n}^T$.

Outputs: R outputs $(\mathbf{y}, U)$, S outputs $(\mathbf{x}, V)$.

Fig. 6. COT-based RsVOLE

Functionality $\mathscr{F}_{\mathsf{Out}}$

Players: Participants $P_1, ..., P_k$.
Functionality: Receive $(\mathsf{sid}, i, [\mathbf{u}]_i, [\mathbf{v}]_i)$ from P_i, recover $\mathbf{u}, \mathbf{v}$ from shares $(i, [\mathbf{u}]_i, [\mathbf{v}]_i)$, abort if the recovery fails, securely secret share $\mathbf{u} \cdot \mathbf{v}$ into $[\mathbf{u} \otimes \mathbf{v}]_i$ and return to P_i the share $[\mathbf{u} \otimes \mathbf{v}]_i$.

Fig. 7. Functionality of secure outer product

product. Let us suppose all parties would like to compute the outer product $\mathbf{a} \otimes \mathbf{b}$ of two vectors $\mathbf{a} \in K^m$ and $\mathbf{b} \in K^n$ with the help of an (m, n)-triple $(\mathbf{u}, \mathbf{v}, W)$. First we denote $\mathbf{a} - \mathbf{u} = \mathbf{s}, \mathbf{b} - \mathbf{v} = \mathbf{t}$. Then similarly we could compute

$$\mathbf{a} \otimes \mathbf{b} = (\mathbf{s} + \mathbf{u}) \otimes (\mathbf{t} + \mathbf{v}) = \mathbf{s} \otimes \mathbf{t} + \mathbf{u} \otimes \mathbf{t} + \mathbf{s} \otimes \mathbf{v} + W.$$

Therefore we could similarly make a protocol described below in Fig. 8.

As a direct application of the outer product, we could now introduce a way to securely compute a matrix product of two matrices. Figure 9 shows the functionality of secure multi-party matrix multiplication. In practice, we consider $A \in M_{m \times k}(K)$, $B \in M_{k \times n}(K)$. First denote the columns of A by $A = (\mathbf{a}_1, ..., \mathbf{a}_k)$, and the rows of B by $B = (\mathbf{b}_1, ..., \mathbf{b}_k)^T$. As is well-known, the matrix product has the following outer product expansion formula: $AB = \sum_{i=1}^k \mathbf{a}_i \otimes \mathbf{b}_i$. Therefore, it is easy to formulate a way to compute the matrix product from the outer product primitive. All the parties may simultaneously perform k primitives to compute each summand in the formula above and then individually add the results together without any further interaction. A protocol is described as follows in Fig. 10.

4.3   Security

On the security of all protocols proposed above, the proofs are somehow evident from the simple observation that the triple always hides perfectly the input vectors and in none of the protocols the third matrix share is published in any sense. This also illustrates the correct and secure usage of tensor triples, namely to randomize the input vectors to announce, while always keeping the third matrix share secret. The precise statements of the security are given below.

Theorem 5. ([35]). *The RLWE-based tensor triple generation protocol (Fig. 2) realizes the functionality $\mathscr{F}_{TTGen}^{p,m,n}$ in the two-party setting and is semi-honest secure.*

Theorem 6. ([21]). *The COT-based RsVOLE protocol (Fig. 6) realizes the functionality $\mathscr{F}_{RsVOLE'}^{p,m,n}$ in the two-party setting and is semi-honest secure.*

Theorem 7. *The sVOLE-based tensor triple generatio protocol TT.Gen() realizes the functionality $\mathscr{F}_{TTGen}^{p,m,n}$ in the two-party setting and is semi-honest secure in the $\mathscr{F}_{RsVOLE'}^{p,m,n}$-hybrid model.*

Theorem 8. *The secure outer product protocol Out() realizes the functionality $\mathscr{F}_{Out}$ and is semi-honest secure in the $\mathscr{F}_{TTGen}^{p,m,n}$-hybrid model.*

Theorem 9. *The secure matrix product protocol MatProd() realizes the functionality $\mathscr{F}_{MatProd}$ and is semi-honest secure in the $\mathscr{F}_{Out}$-hybrid model.*

Secure Multi-Party Outer Product Out($\mathbf{a}, \mathbf{b}$)

Input: P_i inputs shares $[\mathbf{a}]_i, [\mathbf{b}]_i$ of two vectors $\mathbf{a} \in K^m, \mathbf{b} \in K^n$.
Primitive: A tensor triple generation protocol TT.Gen(m, n, λ)
Pre-processing Phase: The participants perform a TT.Gen(m, n, λ) protocol. P_i outputs $[\mathbf{u}]_i \in K^m, [\mathbf{v}]_i \in K^n, [W]_i \in M_{m \times n}(K)$.
Initial Phase: P_i computes $[\mathbf{s}]_i \leftarrow [\mathbf{a}]_i - [\mathbf{u}]_i$ and $[\mathbf{t}]_i \leftarrow [\mathbf{b}]_i - [\mathbf{v}]_i$.
Interacting Phase:

1. P_i annouces publicly to all parties $[\mathbf{s}]_i$ and $[\mathbf{t}]_i$;
2. All parties recover $\mathbf{s}$ and $\mathbf{t}$ from the annoucement;
3. Each party P_i secretly computes $[\mathbf{a} \otimes \mathbf{b}]_i \leftarrow \mathbf{s} \otimes \mathbf{t} + [\mathbf{u}]_i \otimes \mathbf{t} + \mathbf{s} \otimes [\mathbf{v}]_i + [W]_i$

Outputs: P_i outputs $[\mathbf{a} \otimes \mathbf{b}]_i$.

Fig. 8. Secure Multi-Party Outer Product

Functionality $\mathscr{F}_{MatProd}$

Players: Participants $P_1, ..., P_k$.
Functionality: Receive $(\mathsf{sid}, i, [A]_i, [B]_i)$ from P_i, recover A, B from shares $(i, [A]_i, [B]_i)$, abort if the recovery fails or A, B are not multiplicable, securely secret share $A \cdot B$ into $[AB]_i$ and return to P_i the share $[AB]_i$.

Fig. 9. Functionality of secure matrix product

Secure Multi-Party Matrix Product MatProd(A, B)

Input: P_i inputs shares $[A]_i, [B]_i$ of two matrices $A \in M_{m \times k}(K), B \in M_{k \times n}(K)$.
Primitive: A tensor triple generation protocol TT.Gen(m, n, λ), secure outer product Out$(\mathbf{a}, \mathbf{b})$.
Pre-processing Phase: The participants perform k times of a TT.Gen(m, n, λ) protocol. P_i outputs $([\mathbf{u}]_i^{(j)}, [\mathbf{v}]_i^{(j)}, [W]_i^{(j)})$ $(j = 1, ..., k)$.
Initial Phase: Each party P_i pairs columns of A and transposes of rows of B by indices and obtains k pairs of vectors $(\mathbf{a}_l, \mathbf{b}_l), l = 1, ..., k$.
Interacting Phase: All parties perform Out$(\mathbf{a}_l, \mathbf{b}_l)$ for $l = 1, ..., k$. Each P_i obtains $[\mathbf{a}_l \otimes \mathbf{b}_l]_i$.
Outputs: P_i outputs $[AB]_i \leftarrow \sum_{l=1}^{k}[\mathbf{a}_l \otimes \mathbf{b}_l]_i$.

Fig. 10. Secure Multi-Party Matrix Product

Proof. The proofs of the three theorems 7,8,9 are given in details in Appendix A.1. □

4.4   Advantages of Tensor Triple

Secure multi-party matrix multiplication can also be realized using Beaver triples. For a matrix multiplication of size (m, k) by (k, n), we need k of (m, n)-triples or mnk Beaver triples. While the cost may not seem to differ much in low dimensions, the cost of Beaver triples will increase quadratically as the size of matrices increases. As an example, to carry out a secure multi-party matrix multiplication between two 1024×1024 matrices, we need 2^{30} Beaver triples in total. Even the generation process of this many Beaver triples is a burden to all the parties. For instance, if we use RLWE-based method [35] for Beaver triple generation, the communication cost reaches an astonishing 256TB. Meanwhile, the parties only need to consume 1024 tensor triples to accomplish the computation. Due to the batch generation nature of sVOLE, it is much easier to generate tensor triples of the required amount.

On the other hand, the tensor multiplication triples are more flexible and applicable for matrix operations. As mentioned in previous sections, any (n, n)-triple can be trimmed to serve as two triples of size (s, t) and $(n - s, n - t)$ respectively, for any $s, t < n$. Therefore, secure multi-party matrix operations with different matrix sizes can be achieved using tensor triples of a universal size.

More importantly, when tensor triple technique is applied to achieve the secure multi-party matrix multiplication $A \cdot B$, the number of columns of A (which equals the number of rows of B) can be arbitrary. This is extremely convenient in some applications, for example the ones we will introduce in Sect. 5. For instance, if the parties choose to generate"matrix triples" $([X], [Y], [Z] = [X \cdot Y])$ to assist the computation of matrix multiplication, since the size of matrices may not be determined beforehand by the nature of "pre"-computation process, the parties must choose the dimensions of X, Y, Z large enough to satisfy all possible needs, and this may turn out to become an overkill when the protocol is executed. Hence it is convenient to use tensor triples, as the method does not require the parties to know anything about k while still being able to accomplish 100% utilization of the pre-computed triples.

5   Applications

5.1   Batched Squared Euclidean Distance Computing

Squared Euclidean distance is a widely-used and crucial function in biometric identification and machine learning. In biometric identification, it is often the case the client needs to launch multiple queries, and the server needs to compute the squared Euclidean distance between each query with all references in its own dataset. This type of batched queries essentially portraits a matrix multiplication functionality. Therefore one can use tensor triple to accelerate this process. We will explain by presenting concrete examples as follows.

5.2   Batched Privacy-Preserving Biometric Identification

In this chapter we show applications for vector triples on privacy-preserving biometric identification protocols. Biometric identification, such as face recognition and fingerprint recognition, often involves computation between biometric samples and references in a dataset. In this scenario, Euclidean distance computing between a vector and a fixed family of vectors is implemented each time a query is launched. We demonstrate tensor triples can be used for batched queries in privacy-preserving biometric identification protocols to extremely increase the efficiency.

FingerCode. FingerCode [4,22] is a fingerprint recognition algorithm. In the setting of FingerCode, the server holds a dataset of references $Y = (\mathbf{y}_1^T, ..., \mathbf{y}_n^T) \in M_{k \times n}(K)$. The client would like to securely make a batch of queries $X = (\mathbf{x}_1^T, ..., \mathbf{x}_m^T)^T \in M_{m \times k}(K)$ for recognition. The protocol should proceed as described below.

1. The parties securely compute $D = D_X + D_Y - XY \in M_{m \times n}(K)$, where $D_X = (\mathbf{x}_1 \mathbf{x}_1^T, ..., \mathbf{x}_m \mathbf{x}_m^T) \otimes (1, 1, ..., 1)$ and $D_Y = (1, 1, ..., 1) \otimes (\mathbf{y}_1 \mathbf{y}_1^T, ..., \mathbf{y}_n \mathbf{y}_n^T)$.
2. The parties securely compare entries of D with the predetermined threshold d. Recognize $\mathbf{x}_i$ as $\mathbf{y}_j$ if $D_{ij} \le d$;

Note D_X and D_Y can be computed locally. Therefore the first step can be fulfilled by implementing $\mathsf{MatProd}(X, Y)$ using tensor triples. The second step can be done using any regular implementation of the secure comparison protocol.

Eigenfaces. Eigenfaces [23] is a classical face recognition algorithm. In the setting of Eigenfaces, the server holds a dataset of Eigenfaces $U = (\mathbf{u}_1^T, ..., \mathbf{u}_n^T) \in M_{k \times n}(K)$, an average face $\bar{\mathbf{u}} \in K^k$, and a dataset of N projected faces $Y = (\mathbf{y}_1^T, ..., \mathbf{y}_N^T) \in M_{n \times N}(K)$. The client would like to securely make a batch of queries $X = (\mathbf{x}_1^T, ..., \mathbf{x}_m^T)^T \in M_{m \times k}(K)$ for recognition. The protocol should proceed as described below.

1. The parties securely compute $\bar{X} = (X - \bar{U})U \in M_{m \times n}(K)$, where $\bar{U} = (\bar{\mathbf{u}}^T, ..., \bar{\mathbf{u}}^T)^T \in M_{m \times k}(K)$;
2. The parties securely compute $D = D_X + D_Y - 2\bar{X}Y \in M_{m \times N}(K)$, where $D_X = (\bar{\mathbf{x}}_1\bar{\mathbf{x}}_1^T, ..., \bar{\mathbf{x}}_m\bar{\mathbf{x}}_m^T) \otimes (1, 1, ..., 1)$ and $D_Y = (1, 1, ..., 1) \otimes (\mathbf{y}_1\mathbf{y}_1^T, ..., \mathbf{y}_N\mathbf{y}_N^T)$. More specifically, they use Beaver triple to compute $\langle \bar{\mathbf{x}}_i, \bar{\mathbf{x}}_i \rangle$ and tensor triple to compute $\bar{X}Y$. Also note D_Y can be computed locally;
3. The parties securely compare entries of D with the predetermined threshold d. Recognize $\mathbf{x}_i$ as $\mathbf{y}_j$ if $D_{ij} \leq d$;

FaceNet. FaceNet [24] is a more recent facial recognition system based on deep learning. It was proposed in 2015 and successfully provided a way to generate a very high-quality mapping from face images to their vector representatives. In its setting, the server holds a dataset of references $Y = (\mathbf{y}_1^T, ..., \mathbf{y}_n^T) \in M_{k \times n}(K)$. The client would like to securely make a batch of queries $X = (\mathbf{x}_1^T, ..., \mathbf{x}_m^T)^T \in M_{m \times k}(K)$ for recognition. We assume all the data have been pre-processed through a well-trained network. The protocol should proceed as described below.

1. The parties securely compute $D = D_X + D_Y - XY \in M_{m \times n}(K)$, where $D_X = (\mathbf{x}_1\mathbf{x}_1^T, ..., \mathbf{x}_m\mathbf{x}_m^T) \otimes (1, 1, ..., 1)$ and $D_Y = (1, 1, ..., 1) \otimes (\mathbf{y}_1\mathbf{y}_1^T, ..., \mathbf{y}_n\mathbf{y}_n^T)$.
2. The parties securely compare entries of D with the predetermined threshold d. Recognize $\mathbf{x}_i$ as $\mathbf{y}_j$ if $D_{ij} \leq d$;

Here again, D_X and D_Y can be computed locally. The MPC part of the overall protocol proceeds exactly the same as in the FingerCode case.

As a remark, the flexibility of tensor triples allows us to apply all protocols above on a dataset of vectors in an arbitrary dimension. This is extremely useful as dimensions of data points many vary in different settings.

6   Implementation and Performance

In this chapter, our implementations are based on C++. The experiments are run on desktop with AMD 3950X CPU and 48GB RAM. We considered both simulated LAN and WAN environments with 500 mbps bandwidth and 20 ms one-way latency. The protocols are suitable for multi-threading by parallel computation, but we measure the performance in single thread setting. The experiments are executed 10 times and the medians of the results are presented in the following tables. Source codes have been provided at https://github.com/lzjluzijie/triple.

6.1 Tensor Triple Generation

We mainly choose to use the subfield VOLE method to generate triples as it generally have a better performance than the RLWE method. We implement both Correlated OT based protocol and silent OT based protocol for RsVOLE. We also use libOTe library to fulfill basic functionalities such as COT and OT extension. For silent OT, we used the expand-convolute code from [34] with expander weight 7 and convolution state size 24. The hamming weight of the sparse vector in this setting is 400, which means each silent VOLE requires an execution of an OT extension based subfield VOLE of size 400.

We present the performance as well as the corresponding communication cost for each method in Tables 1, 2, and 3. It can be seen from the tables that COT method is more efficient when tensor triples of small sizes are needed, while SOT method allows generation of tensor triples of large sizes with moderate communication cost.

Table 1. Performance of COT-based 32-bit (m, n)-tensor triple generation (in milliseconds). For each size we generate $1, 2^5, 2^{10}$ number of triples (arranged in rows).

$m \backslash n$	2^3		2^8		2^{10}		2^{14}	
	LAN	WAN	LAN	WAN	LAN	WAN	LAN	WAN
	10	188	10	312	12	394	53	985
2^3	14	317	23	649	60	1596	748	19153
	287	5836	567	15354	1771	45577	22378	597527
			29	654	108	1603	3906	22553
2^8			409	9356	1737	37379	85391	602922
			12603	309499	57274	1181690		
					638	5530	22323	92565
2^{10}					14003	149363	567917	2665457
					425520	4732780		

We present here also a high-level analysis of the two methods. In small cases, COT-based generation method is straightforward and faster, while it may take a considerable amount of time for SOT-based method to finish the structure building for the protocol. When one deals with matrices of large dimensions or needs a large amount of tensor triples, since there is a linear overhead in the communication cost of COT-based generation method, the data transfer may become intolerable for the parties to generate these triples. While on the other hand, as the communication cost of the SOT-based generation method is sublinear asymptotically, it requires much less communication to generate all the necessary tensor triples.

Table 2. Performance of SOT-based 32-bit (m, n)-tensor triple generation (in milliseconds). For each size we generate $1, 2^5, 2^{10}$ number of triples (arranged in rows).

$m \backslash n$	2^3		2^8		2^{10}		2^{14}	
	LAN	WAN	LAN	WAN	LAN	WAN	LAN	WAN
	104	529	93	528	93	576	193	691
2^3	3865	4554	3765	4651	3840	4690	7922	7972
	123127	143559	122763	143203	122937	140101	257346	267526
			593	1603	591	1646	763	1733
2^8			24532	33195	24534	32774	31096	37629
			786790	1047499	788486	1052955	1006983	1193853
					2271	4850	2647	5252
2^{10}					92154	137287	104976	142970
					2991083	4441299	3395699	4606848

Table 3. Communication cost of 32-bit (m, n)-tensor triple generation (in megabytes). For each size we test the cost for $1, 2^5, 2^{10}$ number of triples (arranged in rows).

$m \backslash n$	2^3		2^8		2^{10}		2^{14}	
	COT	SOT	COT	SOT	COT	SOT	COT	SOT
	0.032	1.00	0.52	1.00	2.02	1.00	32.02	1.23
2^3	0.76	32.86	16.26	32.86	64.26	32.86	1024.26	39.31
	12.10	525.82	260.10	525.82	1028.10	525.82	16388.08	628.95
			16.26	28.79	64.26	28.79	1024.26	28.99
2^8			520.01	921.21	2056.01	921.21	32776.01	927.65
			8320.08	14739.36	32896.08	14739.36	-	14842.48
					257.01	114.76	4097.02	114.96
2^{10}					8224.01	3672.21	131104.04	3678.65
					130969.60	58755.36	-	58858.48

As a brief comparison, based on the performance tables provided by [35], it takes approximately 2300 milliseconds to generate one $(2^{10}, 2^{10})$-triple RLWE-based tensor triple generation method, with a communication cost of 256MB. We see from the example that VOLE-based generation method indeed performs better.

6.2   Matrix Multiplication

Table 4 shows the performance and the communication cost of the online phase for our implementation of the tensor triple based secure multi-party matrix multiplication protocol.

Table 4. Performance and communication cost of tensor triple-based 32-bit $(m, k) \times (k, n)$ matrix multiplication time (in milliseconds and megabytes, resp.).

$k\backslash(m,n)$	$(2^3, 2^3)$			$(2^5, 2^5)$			$(2^8, 2^8)$			$(2^{10}, 2^{10})$		
	LAN	WAN	Com.	LAN	WAN	Com.	LAN	WAN	Com.	LAN	WAN	Com.
2^3	1	26	0.001	1	26	0.004	1	27	0.031	11	44	0.125
2^8	1	26	0.031	1	37	0.125	22	62	1	292	323	4
2^{10}	1	37	0.125	2	44	0.5	71	128	4	1062	1289	16

As a comparison with previous works [16,25,43], we also provide the following table on the performance of secure multiparty square matrix multiplication protocols. Due to a lack of source codes or problems in code running, we were not able to individually launch experiments in these previous works under the same environment, but we believe the statistics in the table already implies the high efficiency of the tensor triple method. Note that our experiments are executed with a single thread, and matrix multiplication is known to be highly parallelizable. The computation can be fulfilled easily using parallel computation. Although not given explicitly in the performance tables, parallel computation is capable of significantly reducing the overall computational cost. Hence our performance significantly outperforms all previous works listed in the table. This is reasonable as in these previous works homomorphic encryption is heavily used, while in our work we have mainly applied VOLE which is somewhat lightweight comparatively (Table 5).

Table 5. Comparison of our performance with previous works on 128-bit sqaure matrix multiplication of size $d \times d$ (Single thread by default, LAN environment, in seconds)

Size d	[16] (16 threads)	[16]	SPDZ [43]	[25] (16 threads)	Ours	Ours (Offline)
128	5.9	36.1	128	3.09	**0.007**	0.51
256	25.5	214.5	900	13.49	**0.049**	2.82
384	68.3	653.6	2808	33.6	**0.158**	9.22
512	138	1470	6300	67.39	**0.402**	18.94
1024	870	10380	44100	395.2	**4.324**	143.36

6.3   Batched Privacy-Preserving Biometric Identification

In this section we present performance of tensor triple based implementations of batched queries of FingerCode [22] and Eigenfaces [23] protocols with a comparison of the efficiency with the GSHADE [7] protocol, and FaceNet [24] with a comparison with the [44] protocol. For FingerCode, we use 640-dimensional vectors of 8-bit elements, and we use 32 bits to record each square Euclidean

Table 6. Performance of secure squared Euclidean distance computation in batched FingerCode protocol (128 queries, LAN environment)

	$n = 128$			$n = 1024$		
Protocol	[7]	Ours	Ours (Offline)	[7]	Ours	Ours (Offline)
Time (s)	154.37	**0.016**	1.90	176.64	**0.082**	15.54
Comm. (MB)	1688.71	**1.25**	2640.02	5379.24	**5.63**	20560

Table 7. Performance of Eigenfaces protocol without the secure comparison step (80 queries, LAN environment)

	$N = 320$		$N = 1000$	
Protocol	Ours	Ours (Offline)	Ours	Ours (Offline)
Time (s)	0.029	41.44	0.032	124.24
Communication (MB)	14.57	65207	14.69	202057

distance. For EigenFaces, we use 10304-dimensional vectors of 8-bit elements, and we use 32 bits to record each square Euclidean distance. For FaceNet, the database consists of 128-dimensional vectors of elements with floating point precision, but a truncation will be applied to all of the elements to map them into 8-bit strings, and each final square Euclidean distance consumes 64 bits. It can be seen from the comparison the tensor triple significantly accelerates the identification process. The data for the performance of FingerCode and FaceNet protocols are collected individually according to our experiments. The experiments for all implementations are run in the same environment introduced at the beginning of this chapter.

Table 6 shows a comparison between the performances of our FingerCode implementation with COT-based triple generation and the one in [7]. Clearly, tensor triple method achieves a much better online performance according to the comparison.

Table 7 shows the performance of our implementation for Eigenfaces protocol with COT-based triple generation. As a comparison to the performance in [7], a single query for the $N = 320$ case would take 0.6 s to fulfill, and the corresponding communication cost is 7.7MB. When $N = 1000$, a single query takes 1.6 s and costs 9.4MB. Although the performance in [7] takes also the secure comparison step into consideration, it can still clearly be seen that the tensor triple method behaves much better for batched queries.

Table 8 shows a comparison between the performances of our FaceNet implementation and the one in [44]. We achieve a significant speedup by around 10000 times.

One may argue that there is a pre-computation cost for the tensor triple method. We shall elaborate here with two points. First, even if one considers the generation step, the tensor triple method still performs faster under almost

Table 8. Performance (time in seconds, LAN environment) of secure squared Euclidean distance computation in batched FaceNet protocol for m queries against a database of n references

(m,n)	[44]	Ours (Online)	Ours (Offline, COT)	Ours (Offline, SOT)
$(2^4, 2^4)$	2.58	**0.00068**	0.02	-
$(2^4, 2^{10})$	165.95	**0.0055**	0.378	12.00
$(2^{10}, 2^{10})$	10559.68	**0.25**	19.456	1219.05

all circumstances, as shown in the tables. Second, as we have pointed out, the tensor triple method truly enables the possibility of pre-computation process in secure multi-party matrix computation. Compared to other protocols, for instance GSHADE for the FingerCode protocol, there is no valid way to split the protocol into online and offline process, as the dimensions of the matrices is already involved in its fundamental components, such as OT. Therefore, it should be considered fair for such comparisons in the tables we listed.

7 Conclusion

Tensor triple is a new kind of correlation which is very suitable for multi-dimensional MPC. It can be used to accelerate many existing privacy-preserving biometric idenfication protocols and privacy-preserving machine learning protocols which mainly involve vector and matrix operations.

Acknowledgement. This work is supported by National Key R&D Program of China No. 2021YFB2701304.

A Appendix

A.1 Security

In this chapter we give the detailed proofs for the security of the protocols.

Theorem. *The sVOLE-based tensor triple generatio protocol* TT.Gen() *realizes the functionality* $\mathscr{F}_{TTGen}^{p,m,n}$ *in the two-party setting and is semi-honest secure in the* $\mathscr{F}_{RsVOLE'}^{p,m,n}$*-hybrid model.*

Proof. Due to symmetry, it suffices to consider a semi-honest adversary P_0. The simulator plays the role of $\mathscr{F}_{RsVOLE'}^{p,m,n}$ and provides P_0 with $\mathbf{x} \in_r \mathbb{F}_p^m, \mathbf{y}' \in_r \mathbb{F}_p^n, V \in_r \mathbb{F}_p^{mn}, U' \in_r \mathbb{F}_p^{mn}$, and itself as P_1 with $\mathbf{x}' \in_r \mathbb{F}_p^n, \mathbf{y} \in_r \mathbb{F}_p^n$. Then it computes $U = V + \mathbf{x} \otimes \mathbf{y}$ and $V' = U' - \mathbf{x}' \otimes \mathbf{y}'$. Since in the original interaction $\mathbf{x}, \mathbf{y}, V, U'$ are uniformly distributed over the corresponding ambient spaces, this hybrid is indistinguishable from the original interaction. Thus the protocol is secure against semi-honest P_0. The proof goes exactly the same way for a semi-honest adversary P_1. $\square$

Theorem. *The secure outer product protocol* Out() *realizes the functionality* $\mathscr{F}_{Out}$ *and is semi-honest secure in the* $\mathscr{F}^{p,m,n}_{TTGen}$-*hybrid model.*

Proof. This is obvious as the vector shares are perfectly rerandomized by the tensor triples and thus uniformly distributed over the corresponding ambient spaces. We emphasize the matrix share $[W]$ is never published in any of the protocols throughout the paper as it shall not be, hence not affecting the protocol security. □

Theorem. *The secure matrix product protocol* MatProd() *realizes the functionality* $\mathscr{F}_{MatProd}$ *and is semi-honest secure in the* $\mathscr{F}_{Out}$-*hybrid model.*

Proof. As pointed out in the earlier sections, $\mathscr{F}_{MatProd}$ can be seen as a repetitive application of $\mathscr{F}_{Out}$. Therefore MatProd() as an application of multiple Out() individually realizes $\mathscr{F}_{MatProd}$. □

A.2 Additively Homomorphic Encryption (AHE)

In this section we give a detailed defintion of an AHE scheme.

Definition 10. *An AHE scheme is a tuple of algorithms AHE=(Gen, Enc, Dec, Add, ScMult, ScTensor) described as follows:*

- *Gen(1^λ) → (pk,sk): Key Generation is a randomized algorithm that outputs a pair of keys (pk,sk), with public key pk and secret key sk.*
- *Enc(pk, m) → ct: Encryption is a randomized algorithm that takes a message $m \in PT_{n,\lambda}$ and the public key pk as input, and outputs a ciphertext ct $\in CT_{n,\lambda}$, where $PT_{n,\lambda}$ denotes the plaintext space of AHE for security parameter λ and rank n, and $CT_{n,\lambda}$ the corresponding ciphertext space.*
- *Dec(sk,ct) → m: Decryption is a deterministic algorithm that takes the secret key sk and a ciphertext ct and outputs the plaintext m.*
- *Add(pk, ct$_1$, ct$_2$) → ct$_+$: Addition takes two ciphertexts ct$_1$, ct$_2$ and the public key pk as input, and outputs a ciphertext ct$_+ \in CT_{n,\lambda}$. This binary operation with respect to ct$_1$, ct$_2$ will be denoted by +.*
- *ScMult(pk,ct, s) → ct$_\bullet$: Scalar Multiplication takes a ciphertext ct $\in CT_{n,\lambda}$, a plaintext $s \in PT_{n,\lambda}$ and the public key pk as input, and outputs a ciphertext ct$_\bullet \in CT_{n,\lambda}$. This binary operation with respect to ct and s will be denoted by $\bullet$.*
- *ScTensor(pk,ct, s) → ct$_\otimes$: Scalar Tensor takes a ciphertext ct $\in CT_{n,\lambda}$, a constant vector s of dimension l and the public key pk as input, and outputs an array of ciphertexts ct$_\otimes \in CT^l_{n,\lambda}$. This binary operation with respect to ct and s will be denoted by $s \otimes$ ct.*

The algorithms should satisfy the following properties:

1. *Correctness:*
    - *For a generic pair of keys (pk,sk) ← Gen(1^λ) and any message m, with an overwhelming probability we have*

$$Dec(sk, Enc(pk, m)) = m$$

- *For a generic pair of keys* (*pk,sk*) ← *Gen*(1^λ) *and any two ciphertexts* $\mathrm{ct}_1, \mathrm{ct}_2$, *with an overwhelming probability we have*

$$Dec(sk, Add(\mathrm{pk}, \mathrm{ct}_1, \mathrm{ct}_2)) = Dec(sk, \mathrm{ct}_1) + Dec(sk, \mathrm{ct}_2)$$

- *For a generic pair of keys* (*pk,sk*) ← *Gen*(1^λ), *a ciphertext* ct *and a plaintext scalar* s, *with an overwhelming probability we have*

$$Dec(sk, ScMult(\mathrm{pk}, \mathrm{ct}, s)) = s\,Dec(sk, \mathrm{ct})$$

- *For a generic pair of keys* (*pk,sk*) ← *Gen*(1^λ), *a ciphertext* ct *and a scalar vector* s, *with an overwhelming probability we have*

$$Dec(sk, ScTensor(\mathrm{pk}, \mathrm{ct}, s)) = s \otimes Dec(sk, \mathrm{ct}),$$

where the decryption procedure is applied to each row of the ciphertext array.

2. *Security: The scheme is required to be IND-CPA secure.*

A.3   Third-Party Tensor Triple Generation

A third-party with computational power may be eligible to provide triples for multiple parties in a much more efficient way. This idea has been explored by many people, such as [45,46]. The protocol described in all these papers can be used almost directly to generate tensor triples for multiple parties (not necessarily only two). The flexibility of tensor triple allows the server to provide triples of fixed dimensions while fulfilling the needs for all lower dimensional computations. More specifically, the dimensions of the triples may be predetermined, as a generic (n, n)-triple could be tailored to serve as a pair of triples of dimensions (s, t) and $(n - s, n - t)$ for any $s, t < n$. this means the parties may not need to know the precise dimensions in advance for the preprocessing procedure. A great advantage is that a specialized server may serve as the triple generator for multiple sets of multiple parties in order to speed up all preprocessing procedure. The detail of the third-party generation will be provided in a follow-up paper.

References

1. Yao, A.C.C.: How to generate and exchange secrets. In: 27th Annual Symposium on Foundations of Computer Science (SFCS 1986), pp. 162–167 (1986)
2. Erkin, Z., Franz, M., Guajardo, J., Katzenbeisser, S., Lagendijk, I., Toft, T.: Privacy-preserving face recognition. In: Goldberg, I., Atallah, M.J. (eds.) Privacy Enhancing Technologies, pp. 235–253. Springer, Berlin, Heidelberg (2009). https://doi.org/10.1007/978-3-642-03168-7_14
3. Blanton, M., Gasti, P.: Secure and efficient protocols for Iris and fingerprint identification. In: Atluri, V., Diaz, C. (eds.) ESORICS 2011. LNCS, vol. 6879, pp. 190–209. Springer, Heidelberg (2011). https://doi.org/10.1007/978-3-642-23822-2_11

4. Evans, D., Huang, Y., Katz, J., Malka, L.: Efficient privacy-preserving biometric identification. In: Network and Distributed System Security Symposium (2011)
5. Shahandashti, S.F., Safavi-Naini, R., Ogunbona, P.: Private fingerprint matching. In: Susilo, W., Mu, Y., Seberry, J. (eds.) ACISP 2012. LNCS, vol. 7372, pp. 426–433. Springer, Heidelberg (2012). https://doi.org/10.1007/978-3-642-31448-3_32
6. Bringer, J., Chabanne, H., Patey, A.: Privacy-preserving biometric identification using secure multiparty computation: an overview and recent trends. IEEE Sign. Process. Mag. **30**(2), 42–52 (2013)
7. Bringer, J., Chabanne, H., Favre, M., Patey, A., Schneider, T., Zohner, M.: GSHADE: faster privacy-preserving distance computation and biometric identification. In: Proceedings of the 2nd ACM Workshop on Information Hiding and Multimedia Security, pp. 187–198 (2014)
8. Hahn, C., Hur, J.: Efficient and privacy-preserving biometric identification in cloud. ICT Express **2**(3), 135–139 (2016)
9. Gomez-Barrero, M., Galbally, J., Morales, A., Fierrez, J.: Privacy-preserving comparison of variable-length data with application to biometric template protection. IEEE Access **5**, 8606–8619 (2017)
10. Ma, Z., Liu, Y., Liu, X., Ma, J., Ren, K.: Lightweight privacy-preserving ensemble classification for face recognition. IEEE Internet Things J. **6**(3), 5778–5790 (2019)
11. Nikolaenko, V., Weinsberg, U., Ioannidis, S., Joye, M., Boneh, D., Taft, N.: Privacy-preserving ridge regression on hundreds of millions of records. In: IEEE Symposium on Security and Privacy, pp. 334–348 (2013)
12. Bonawitz, K.: Practical secure aggregation for privacy-preserving machine learning. In: Proceedings of the 2017 ACM SIGSAC Conference on Computer and Communications Security, pp. 1175–1191 (2017)
13. Mohassel, P., Rindal, P.: ABY3: a mixed protocol framework for machine learning. In: Proceedings of the 2018 ACM SIGSAC Conference on Computer and Communications Security, pp. 35–52 (2018)
14. Mohassel, P., Rosulek, M., Trieu, N.: Practical privacy-preserving k-means clustering. In: Proceedings on Privacy Enhancing Technologies, pp. 414–433 (2020)
15. Koti, N., Pancholi, M., Patra, A., Suresh, A.: SWIFT: super-fast and robust privacy-preserving machine learning. In: 30th USENIX Security Symposium (USENIX Security 21), pp. 2651–2668 (2021)
16. Chen, H., Kim, M., Razenshteyn, I., Rotaru, D., Song, Y., Wagh, S.: Maliciously secure matrix multiplication with applications to private deep learning. In: Moriai, S., Wang, H. (eds.) ASIACRYPT 2020. LNCS, vol. 12493, pp. 31–59. Springer, Cham (2020). https://doi.org/10.1007/978-3-030-64840-4_2
17. Abspoel, M., et al.: Asymptotically good multiplicative LSSS over Galois Rings and applications to MPC over $\mathbb{Z}/p^k\mathbb{Z}$. In: Moriai, S., Wang, H. (eds.) ASIACRYPT 2020. LNCS, vol. 12493, pp. 151–180. Springer, Cham (2020). https://doi.org/10.1007/978-3-030-64840-4_6
18. Naor, M., Pinkas, B.: Oblivious polynomial evaluation. SIAM J. Comput. **35**(5), 1254–1281 (2006)
19. Applebaum, B., Damgård, I., Ishai, Y., Nielsen, M., Zichron, L.: Secure arithmetic computation with constant computational overhead. In: Katz, J., Shacham, H. (eds.) CRYPTO 2017. LNCS, vol. 10401, pp. 223–254. Springer, Cham (2017). https://doi.org/10.1007/978-3-319-63688-7_8
20. Boyle, E., Couteau, G., Gilboa, N., Ishai, Y.: Compressing vector ole. In: Proceedings of the 2018 ACM SIGSAC Conference on Computer and Communications Security, pp. 896–912 (2018)

21. Boyle, E., et al.: Efficient two-round OT extension and silent non-interactive secure computation. In: Proceedings of the 2019 ACM SIGSAC Conference on Computer and Communications Security, pp. 291–308 (2019)
22. Jain, A.K., Prabhakar, S., Hong, L., Pankanti, S.: FingerCode: a filterbank for fingerprint representation and matching. In: Proceedings. 1999 IEEE Computer Society Conference on Computer Vision and Pattern Recognition (Cat. No PR00149), vol. 2, pp. 187–193 (1999)
23. Turk, M., Pentland, A.: Eigenfaces for recognition. J. Cogn. Neurosci. 3(1), 71–86 (1991)
24. Schroff, F., Kalenichenko, D., Philbin, J.: Facenet: a unified embedding for face recognition and clustering. In: 2015 IEEE Conference on Computer Vision and Pattern Recognition (CVPR), pp. 815–823 (2015)
25. Mono, J., Güneysu, T.: Implementing and optimizing matrix triples with homomorphic encryption. In: Proceedings of the 2023 ACM Asia Conference on Computer and Communications Security, pp. 29–40 (2023)
26. Rabin, M.O.: How to exchange secrets with oblivious transfer, TR-81 Edition (1981)
27. Ishai, Y., Kilian, J., Nissim, K., Petrank, E.: Extending oblivious transfers efficiently. In: Advances in Cryptology - CRYPTO, pp. 145–161 (2003)
28. Kolesnikov, V., Kumaresan, R.: Improved OT extension for transferring short secrets. In: Canetti, R., Garay, J.A. (eds.) CRYPTO 2013, pp. 54–70. Springer, Berlin, Heidelberg (2013). https://doi.org/10.1007/978-3-642-40084-1_4
29. Kolesnikov, V., Kumaresan, R., Rosulek, M., Trieu, N.: Efficient batched oblivious PRF with applications to private set intersection. In: Proceedings of the 2016 ACM SIGSAC Conference on Computer and Communications Security, pp. 818–829 (2016)
30. Asharov, G., Lindell, Y., Schneider, T., Zohner, M.: More efficient oblivious transfer and extensions for faster secure computation. In: Proceedings of the 2013 ACM SIGSAC Conference on Computer and Communications Security, pp. 535–548 (2013)
31. Yang, K., Weng, C., Lan, X., Zhang, J., Wang, X.: Ferret: fast extension for correlated OT with small communication. In: Proceedings of the 2020 ACM SIGSAC Conference on Computer and Communications Security, pp. 1607–1626 (2020)
32. Schoppmann, P., Gascón, A., Reichert, L., Raykova, M.: Distributed vector-OLE: improved constructions and implementation. In: Proceedings of the 2019 ACM SIGSAC Conference on Computer and Communications Security, pp. 1055–1072 (2019)
33. Couteau, G., Rindal, P., Raghuraman, S.: Silver: silent VOLE and oblivious transfer from hardness of decoding structured LDPC codes. In: Malkin, T., Peikert, C. (eds.) CRYPTO 2021. LNCS, vol. 12827, pp. 502–534. Springer, Cham (2021). https://doi.org/10.1007/978-3-030-84252-9_17
34. Raghuraman, S., Rindal, P., Tanguy, T.: Expand-convolute codes for pseudorandom correlation generators from LPN. In: Advances in Cryptology - CRYPTO, pp. 602–632 (2023)
35. Rathee, D., Schneider, T., Shukla, K.K.: Improved multiplication triple generation over rings via RLWE-based AHE. In: Mu, Y., Deng, R.H., Huang, X. (eds.) CANS 2019. LNCS, vol. 11829, pp. 347–359. Springer, Cham (2019). https://doi.org/10.1007/978-3-030-31578-8_19
36. Paillier, P.: Public-key cryptosystems based on composite degree Residuosity classes. In: Stern, J. (ed.) EUROCRYPT 1999. LNCS, vol. 1592, pp. 223–238. Springer, Heidelberg (1999). https://doi.org/10.1007/3-540-48910-X_16

37. Damgård, I., Jurik, M.: A generalisation, a simplification and some applications of Paillier's probabilistic public-key system. In: Kim, K. (ed.) PKC 2001. LNCS, vol. 1992, pp. 119–136. Springer, Heidelberg (2001). https://doi.org/10.1007/3-540-44586-2_9
38. Damgård, I., Geisler, M., Krøigaard, M.: Efficient and secure comparison for online auctions. In: Pieprzyk, J., Ghodosi, H., Dawson, E. (eds.) ACISP 2007. LNCS, vol. 4586, pp. 416–430. Springer, Heidelberg (2007). https://doi.org/10.1007/978-3-540-73458-1_30
39. Brakerski, Z., Gentry, C., Vaikuntanathan, V.: (Leveled) fully homomorphic encryption without bootstrapping. In: Proceedings of the 3rd Innovations in Theoretical Computer Science Conference, pp. 309–325 (2012)
40. Fan, J., Vercauteren, F.: Somewhat practical fully homomorphic encryption. In: IACR Cryptology ePrint Archive, p. 144 (2012)
41. Gilboa, N.: Two party RSA key generation. In: Wiener, M. (ed.) CRYPTO' 99. LNCS, pp. 116–129. Springer, Berlin, Heidelberg (1999). https://doi.org/10.1007/3-540-48405-1_8
42. Demmler, D., Schneider, T., Zohner, M.: ABY - a framework for efficient mixed-protocol secure two-party computation. In: Network and Distributed System Security Symposium (2015)
43. Damgård, I., Pastro, V., Smart, N., Zakarias, S.: Multiparty computation from somewhat homomorphic encryption. In: Advances in Cryptology - CRYPTO, pp. 643–662 (2012)
44. Boddeti, V.N.: Secure face matching using fully homomorphic encryption. In: 2018 IEEE 9th International Conference on Biometrics Theory, Applications and Systems (BTAS), pp. 1–10 (2018)
45. Smart, N.P., Tanguy, T.: TaaS: Commodity MPC via triples-as-a-service. In: Proceedings of the 2019 ACM SIGSAC Conference on Cloud Computing Security Workshop (2019)
46. Muth, P., Katzenbeisser, S.: Assisted MPC. Cryptology ePrint Archive, Paper 2022/1453 (2022)

Cryptographic Cryptid Protocols
How to Play Cryptid with Cheaters

Xavier Bultel[1](✉) [ID], Charlène Jojon[1] [ID], and Pascal Lafourcade[2] [ID]

[1] LIFO, Université d'Orléans, INSA Centre Val de Loire, Inria, Bourges, France
{xavier.bultel,charlene.jojon}@insa-cvl.fr
[2] Université Clermont-Auvergne, CNRS, Mines de Saint-Étienne,
Clermont-Auvergne-INP, LIMOS, 63000 Clermont-Ferrand, France
pascal.lafourcade@uca.fr

Abstract. Cryptid is a board game in which the goal is to be the first player to locate the cryptid, a legendary creature, on a map. Each player knows a secret clue as to which cell on the map contains the cryptid. Players take it in turns to ask each other if the cryptid could be on a given cell according to their clue, until one of them guesses the cryptid cell. This game is great fun, but completely loses its interest if one of the players cheats by answering the questions incorrectly. For example, if a player answers negatively on the cryptid cell, the game continues for a long time until all the cells have been tested, and ends without a winner. We provide cryptographic protocols to prevent cheating in Cryptid. The main idea is to use encryption to commit the players' clues, enabling them to show that they are answering correctly in accordance with their clue using zero-knowledge proofs. We give a security model which captures soundness (a player cannot cheat) and confidentiality (the protocol does not leak more information than the players' answers about their clues), and prove the security of our protocols in this model. We also analyze the practical efficiency of our protocols, based on an implementation of the main algorithms in Rust. Finally, we extend our protocols to ensure that the game designer has correctly constructed the cryptid games, *i.e.*, that the clues are well formed and converge on at least one cell.

Keywords: Provable security · Board game · Cryptid · Zero Knowledge Proof

1 Introduction

Cryptid is a deduction game designed by Hal Duncan and Ruth Veevers, and edited by Osprey Games. This game is based on the theme of cryptozoology: players are in search of a cryptid, a legendary creature, and try throughout the game to glean information to locate it on a map. The map is divided into cells, each with its own type (forest, desert, etc.) and several properties (close to a hut, animal territory, etc.). Each player receives a secret clue as to where the

M. Kohlweiss et al. (Eds.): CANS 2024, LNCS 14905, pp. 26–48, 2025.
https://doi.org/10.1007/978-981-97-8013-6_2

cryptid is located, which can take one of two forms: the cell of the cryptid is one of several given types, or the cell is at a given distance from something. The players then take it in turns to ask each other whether a given cell corresponds to their secret clue or not. As the game progresses, each player accumulates more and more information about the cryptid's cell, until one player deduces it and wins the game.

First released in 2018, the game has since enjoyed international success with a great reception from the player community and has been translated into multiple languages, which has earned it numerous festival nominations and even an award (Palme d'Or 2020 for Best Family Game). An online version of the game is also available for free on https://www.playcryptid.com/. However, the game loses all interest if one of the players lies. Accumulating and processing information involves a considerable mental effort, and discovering that the game has been spoiled because a player has answered incorrectly is very frustrating. For instance, if a cheater answers negatively on the cryptid's cell, the game can last until all the cells have been invalidated before the other players become aware of the cheating, which is long. Worse still, the cheater can get away with winning the game without being discovered by the others, giving them a substantial advantage and encouraging dishonest players to cheat. Aware of the problem, the authors of the game have included a paragraph on honesty in the rulebook:

"Cryptid allows room for misdirection, but the game is completely dependent on all players [answering] honestly. If that doesn't sound like your gaming group, then this might not be the game for you."

It can be interpreted as an open problem left to cryptographers. In this paper we address this open problem by proposing a cryptographic version of cryptid to prevent cheating. We also extend the question to cases where the game designer is not honest and tries to give an advantage to one player or to design games where no player can win.

Motivation. Our work offers the possibility to play online such that players no longer have to trust other players, the game designer, or the server that manages the games. In addition to this direct application, our motivation is also pedagogical. Cryptography makes it possible to secure protocols in which entities interact with sensitive data, even if they do not behave as expected. The game analogy illustrates this concept: Entities play a game in which each player has secret values, and cryptography ensures that everyone respects the rules of the game (*i.e.,* does not cheat) without exposing the secret values. The playful nature of the games makes it easier to interest the general public in these topics, and to introduce counterintuitive concepts such as zero-knowledge proofs. Discovering these powerful tools through fun applications then opens the way to presenting similar protocols with more concrete societal applications, such as e-voting [11] or e-cash [9]. Although the general public will be able to understand the concepts used to secure Cryptid, they will not necessarily have the knowledge to understand the technical part of our work, but it can attract and stimulate a more experienced audience (*e.g.,* computer science students who enjoy playing board games) to discover cryptographic protocols, security models, and security proofs through a playful and relatable example.

Contributions. We begin by giving a formal treatment to the cryptid game and its security. We define what a cryptographic cryptid protocol is and model two security properties: soundness, which ensures that a player cannot lie when answering a question, and confidentiality, which ensures that players learn nothing more than what they are supposed to know according to the rules of the game through the protocol. We then propose two instantiations of this protocol based on two ways of encoding the clues. The first requires a large storage capacity for each clue (linear in the number of cells, *i.e.*, 108 in the original game) but little computational power from the players, while the second requires moderate storage capacity and computational power (linear in the number of properties a cell can have, *i.e.*, 14 in the original game).

We then address the case where the game master (who constructs the maps and clues) is not honest. Indeed, the game must be designed in such a way that the clues respect the structure given in the game rules (which allows the clues to be deduced from the answers to the questions), and that the clues converge on at least one cell on the board (which ensures that the game can end when this cell is discovered). In the physical version of the game, players cannot verify this without knowing each other's clues. So they have to trust the game designers, who may have built impossible games to confuse them. Thus, we extend our model and our second protocol to take into account security against malicious game masters.

Our three protocols use the same paradigm: the clues are encrypted by the game master, then we use zero-knowledge proofs on these encrypted clues to allow the master to prove that the game is well designed and to allow the users to prove they answer correctly. For each protocol, we prove the security properties by reduction in our security model, under the assumption that the encryption scheme we use is IND-CPA and that the proofs are zero-knowledge and sound. The third protocol additionally requires the use of a partially homomorphic encryption scheme (we use ElGamal) and the hash function proposed in [5], which is collision resistant under the discrete logarithm assumption. We also provide a Rust implementation of the main algorithms used in our protocol, then we evaluate in practice the size of the cryptographic data generated and exchanged during a game and the computation time required to produce them.

Related Works. The first cryptographic protocol to enable a secure electronic version of a board game was mental poker, proposed by Shamir, Rivest, and Adelman [20]. This protocol enables remote users to play poker with the same properties as a classic card game. Numerous works have extended this result to card games in general [1,16,19,22], proposing different security models. However, these protocols make it possible to play online games that are usually physical, guaranteeing only the same properties as those of the physical version.

Another line of work focuses specifically on trick-taking games (like Whist or Bridge), and guarantees more security than the physical version of the game [2,7]:

in trick-taking games, a player cannot always play any of the cards in their hand, and if the player decides to cheat, the cheating will only be detected much later, when the player plays a card they are not supposed to have. Cryptographic trick-taking game protocols force the player to prove that they are playing correctly without leaking any information about the player's cards, thus preventing cases of cheating that would not have been detected immediately with real cards. Our work has a similar objective since we aim to play Cryptid while avoiding the cheating problems that are unavoidable in the physical version, but concerns a game with a very different structure.

Finally, we could have used generic tools to easily reach our goal, such as multi-party computation protocols [13] or zero-knowledge proofs for circuits [15]. However, these tools are heavy due to their genericity (in short, they require the implementation of the function to be evaluated by a boolean or arithmetic circuit, and the evaluation of each of the operations of this circuit on encrypted data), and would have been much less efficient than our solutions.

2   Rules of Cryptid

We briefly explain the rules of the Cryptid game. A full version of the rules, including a description of the physical material of the game, can be found in the appendix of the full version of this paper [6].

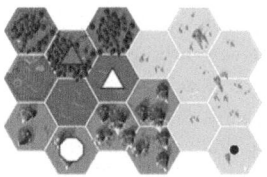

Fig. 1. A section of a cryptid map.

Cryptid is played on a map consisting of hexagonal tiles called "*cells*". Each cell has a type among "*forest*", "*mountain*", "*swamp*", "*water*", and "*desert*", represented by a color. In addition to its type, a cell may contain a "*bear territory*" (the cell is circled in dotted lines), a "*cougar territory*" (the cell is circled in red), and/or a "*structure*". A structure has one color and can be an "*abandoned shack*" (represented by a triangle) or a "*standing stone*" (represented by an octagon). For instance, Fig. 1 shows a portion of the map with "*forest*" cells in green, "*desert*" cells in yellow, "*mountain*" cells in gray, and "*water*" cells in blue. The two cells at the top left contain a cougar territory. Three cells contain structures: a white standing stone, a white abandoned shack, and a green abandoned shack.

Each player is secretly given a clue. This clue can take two forms:

- the type of cell in which the cryptid is located is one of two given types (there are therefore $10 = \binom{5}{2}$ such clues),
- the cell where the cryptid is located is n cells away from a cell with a specific property.

In the second case, there are 14 different possible clues:

- one cell or less from a cell of a given type (among 5), or of the territory of any animal (6 cases)
- two cells or less from a stone, a shack, a cougar territory, or a bear territory (4 cases)
- three cells or less from a blue, white, green, or black structure (4 cases).

The game also offers a *difficult mode* in which clues can be the negation of one of the 20 clues mentioned above (we do not consider the difficult mode in this paper and leave it for future works).

For the sake of formalism, we consider these 14 neighborhood properties as cell properties directly. For example, the cell at bottom left in Fig. 1 is considered to have the 8 following neighborhood properties: one cell from a mountain, water, and animal territory, two cells from a stone, shack, and cougar territory, and three cells from a white and green structure.

Each player in turn asks another player a question as follows: the player points to a cell, and ask one other player to say whether that cell could be the cryptid's or not, according to its clue. When the player thinks they know which cell the cryptid is on, they can instead ask all the other players to take turns answering on that cell. If all players answer affirmatively, then the player has found the cryptid cell and wins the game. However, after each negative answer, the player must leak a little of their clue by pointing to another cell that has never been invalidated and revealing that it cannot be the cryptid's cell.

In its physical version, the game contains material to build 180 maps of 108 cells for 3 to 5 players. With a booklet system, each player can secretly find their clue for a given map. The 180 game setups are constructed in such a way that only one of the cells corresponds to the clues of all players. Note that to ensure that each game ends correctly, it is sufficient to ensure that at least one cell matches all player's clues.

3   Cryptographic Background

First of all, here are the notations we will be using throughout this paper. We denote by $[\![n]\!]$ the set $\{0, \ldots, n\}$ and $[\![n]\!]^*$ the set $\{1, \ldots, n\}$ where $n \in \mathbb{N}$. By $x \leftarrow y$ we mean that the variable x takes a value y, by $x \leftarrow \mathsf{Algo}(y)$ that the variable x takes a value outputted by the algorithm Algo on input y, and by $r \xleftarrow{\$} S$ that r is chosen from the uniform distribution on S. We use the acronym p.p.t. for *probabilistic polynomial time*, and s.t. for *such that*.

We now recall the definition of negligible function, public-key encryption scheme, ElGamal encryption scheme, and non-interactive proof systems.

Definition 1 (Negligible Function). *A function $\epsilon : \mathbb{N} \to \mathbb{R}$ is said to be negligible if for any positive polynomial t, there exists an integer n s.t. for all integer $x > n$, $|\epsilon(x)| < \frac{1}{t(x)}$.*

Definition 2 (Public-Key Encryption Scheme). *A public-key encryption scheme $\mathcal{E}_\lambda$ is a tuple of three algorithms* (Gen, Enc, Dec) *defined as follows:*

Gen(λ): *takes as input a security parameter λ and returns a public/private key pair* (pk, sk).

Enc$_{pk}(m)$: *takes as input the public key* pk *and a message m, and returns a ciphertext c.*

Dec$_{sk}(c)$: *takes as input the secret key* sk *and a ciphertext c, and returns a message m.*

The IND-CPA experiment $Exp_{\mathcal{E}_\lambda, \mathcal{A}, b}^{IND\text{-}CPA}(\lambda)$ of a public-key encryption $\mathcal{E}_\lambda$ is defined as follows, where $\mathcal{A} = (\mathcal{A}_1, \mathcal{A}_2)$ is a pair of p.p.t. algorithms: the experiment generates (pk, sk) $\leftarrow$ Gen(λ), *runs $(m_0, m_1) \leftarrow \mathcal{A}_1(pk)$, computes $c \leftarrow$ Enc$_{pk}(m_b)$, runs $b' \leftarrow \mathcal{A}_2(c)$, and returns $b = b'$. $\mathcal{E}_\lambda$ is said to be IND-CPA if for any pair of p.p.t. algorithms $\mathcal{A}$, there exists a negligible function $\epsilon_{IND\text{-}CPA}$ s.t.:*

$$\left| \Pr\left[0 \leftarrow Exp_{\mathcal{E}_\lambda, \mathcal{A}, 0}^{IND\text{-}CPA}(\lambda) \right] - \Pr\left[1 \leftarrow Exp_{\mathcal{E}_\lambda, \mathcal{A}, 1}^{IND\text{-}CPA}(\lambda) \right] \right| \leq \epsilon_{IND\text{-}CPA}(\lambda).$$

Definition 3 (ElGamal Encryption Scheme). *Let λ be a security parameter. The ElGamal encryption* ElGamal $=$ (Gen, Enc, Dec) *instanciated by a group $\mathbb{G}$ of prime order p generated by g s.t. $p > 2^\lambda$ is defined as follows:*

Gen(λ): *picks* sk $\xleftarrow{\$} \mathbb{Z}_p^*$, *computes* pk $\leftarrow g^{sk}$, *and returns* (pk, sk).

Enc$_{pk}(m)$: *picks $r \xleftarrow{\$} \mathbb{Z}_p^*$, computes $c_1 \leftarrow g^r$, computes $c_2 = pk^r m$, and returns $c = (c_1, c_2)$.*

Dec$_{sk}(c)$: *computes $m \leftarrow c_2/(c_1^{sk})$ and returns it.*

The ElGamal encryption is known to be IND-CPA [21] under the Decisional Diffie-Hellman assumption [4]. Moreover, by defining the binary operation $\cdot$ between two ciphertexts $c = (c_1, c_2)$ and $c' = (c_1', c_2')$ as $c \cdot c' = (c_1 c_1', c_2 c_2')$, the following property holds: if $m =$ Dec$_{sk}(c)$ and $m' =$ Dec$_{sk}(c')$, then $mm' =$ Dec$_{sk}(c \cdot c')$. ElGamal is said to be partially homomorphic.

Definition 4 (Non-interactive Proof System (NIP) [3]). *Let $\mathcal{R}$ be a binary relation and $\mathcal{L}$ a language depending on a security parameter λ s.t. $s \in \mathcal{L} \Leftrightarrow (\exists\, w, (s, w) \in \mathcal{R})$. A Non-Interactive Proof system (NIP) for the language $\mathcal{L}$ is a couple of algorithms* (NIP, Ver) *defined as follows:*

NIP $\{w : (s, w) \in \mathcal{R}\}$: *takes as input a witness w and a statement s s.t. $(s, w) \in \mathcal{R}$, and returns a proof π.*

Ver(s, π): *takes as input a statement s and a proof π, returns a bit b.*

A NIP has the following security properties:

Soundness. A NIP is *sound* if there is no p.p.t. algorithm $\mathcal{A}$ s.t. $\mathcal{A}(\mathcal{L})$ outputs (s, π) s.t. $\mathsf{Ver}(s, \pi) = 1$ and $s \notin \mathcal{L}$ with non-negligible probability.

Extractability. A NIP is *extractable* if for any algorithm $\mathcal{A}$ and any statement s s.t. $\mathcal{A}(\mathcal{L})$ outputs π s.t. $\mathsf{Ver}(s, \pi) = 1$ with non-negligible probability, there exists a negligible function ϵ and a p.p.t. algorithm Ext having access to $\mathcal{A}(\mathcal{L})$ as an oracle that outputs w s.t. $(s, w) \in \mathcal{R}$ with probability $1 - \epsilon(\lambda)$.

Zero-knowledge. A NIP is *zero-knowledge* if the proof π leaks no information, *i.e.*, there exists a p.p.t. algorithm Sim (called the simulator) s.t. for any $(s, w) \in \mathcal{R}$, the outputs of the algorithms $\mathsf{NIP}\{w : (s, w) \in \mathcal{R}\}$ and $\mathsf{Sim}(s)$ follow the same distribution.

4   Cryptographic Cryptid

4.1   Formal Definitions

We begin by giving a formal treatment of a cryptid game, defining the required algorithms and elements. We define the clues, the map and the algorithm for answering a question on a cell of the map in accordance with a clue.

Definition 5 (Cryptid Encoding). *A cryptid encoding is a tuple* $(n, \mathcal{C}, N, \mathcal{M}, \mathsf{Answer})$ *where n is an integer called the* number of players, *$\mathcal{C}$ is a set called the* clue set, *N is an integer called the* size of the map, *$\mathcal{M}$ is a set called the* map set *(where each* map $\in \mathcal{M}$ *is a vector of N elements* map $= (\mathrm{cell}_i)_{i \in [\![N]\!]}$ *and each* cell$_i$ *is called a* cell *of the map), and* Answer *is a p.p.t. algorithm defined as follows:*

Answer(map, clue, j): *takes as input a map* map $\in \mathcal{M}$, *a clue* clue $\in \mathcal{C}$ *and an index $j \leq N$ of a cell. It returns $A \in \{\mathtt{maybe}, \mathtt{no}\}$ the correct answer for the cell j according to the rules of Cryptid ("$\mathtt{maybe}$" corresponds to bit 1 and "$\mathtt{no}$" to 0).*

We define a cryptographic cryptid as a tuple of algorithms. In particular, a cryptographic cryptid contains an algorithm GenClue for committing a clue, and an algorithm Play for proving that the answer of a player on a cell is correct according to the committed clue. These algorithms can be used in a cryptid game to provide some security properties.

Definition 6 (Cryptographic Cryptid). *A cryptographic cryptid for a cryptid encoding* $(n, \mathcal{C}, N, \mathcal{M}, \mathsf{Answer})$ *is a tuple of p.p.t. algorithms* (Setup, GenClue, OpenClue, Play, Verify) *defined as follows:*

Setup(λ): *takes as input the security parameter λ and returns a setup set. This setup is implicitly used as input in the other algorithms.*

GenClue(clue): *takes as input* clue $\in \mathcal{C}$ *and returns the pair of public/secret clue key* (pc, sc).

OpenClue(pc, sc): *takes as input the pair of public/private clue key* (pc, sc) *and returns* clue $\in \mathcal{C}$.

Play(pc, sc, map, j, A): *takes as input a public/private clue key pair* (pc, sc), *a map* map $\in \mathcal{M}$, *an index* j, *and an answer* $A \in \{0, 1\}$ *for the cell* j *in* map. *It returns a proof* π.

Verify(π, pc, map, j, A): *takes as input a proof* π, *a public clue key* pc, *a map* map $\in \mathcal{M}$, *an index* j, *an answer* A, *and returns* $b \in \{\texttt{accept}, \texttt{reject}\}$ *("*accept*" corresponds to bit* 1 *and "*reject*" to* 0*)*.

To play the game using cryptographic algorithms, the players use the following protocol.

Definition 7 (Cryptid Protocol). *Let* λ *be a security parameter. The cryptid protocol for* n *players is a protocol between* $n + 1$ *parties, called the players (denoted* Player$_\alpha$ *for* $\alpha \in [\![n]\!]^*$) *and the game master (denoted* Master*). This protocol is instantiated by a cryptid encoding* $(n, \mathcal{C}, N, \mathcal{M}, \mathsf{Answer})$, *a cryptographic cryptid* (Setup, GenClue, OpenClue, Play, Verify), *a map* map $\in \mathcal{M}$, *and* n *clues (denoted* clue$_\alpha \in \mathcal{C}$ *for* $\alpha \in [\![n]\!]^*$). *This protocol is defined as follows (where the setup* set *used has been generated by the algorithm* Setup(λ)).

Cryptid $\langle \{\text{Player}_\alpha(\text{set}, \text{map})\}_{\alpha \in [\![n]\!]^*}, \text{Master}(\text{set}, \text{map}, (\text{clue}_\alpha)_{\alpha \in [\![n]\!]^*}) \rangle$:

– *For each* $\alpha \in [\![n]\!]^*$, Master *runs* $(\text{pc}_\alpha, \text{sc}_\alpha) \leftarrow \text{GenClue}(\text{set}, \text{clue}_\alpha)$. Master *then sends* sc_α, *and* $(\text{pc}_{\alpha'})_{\alpha' \in [\![n]\!]^*}$ *to each* Player$_\alpha$ *where* $\alpha \in [\![n]\!]^*$.
– *Each player* Player$_\alpha$ *computes* clue$_\alpha \leftarrow \text{OpenClue}(\text{pc}_\alpha, \text{sc}_\alpha)$.
– *Players then play among themselves following ther rules. At the* i^{th} *play:*
  • *One* Player$_{\alpha_i}$ *for some* $\alpha_i \in [\![n]\!]^*$ *receives an index* $j < N$ *from another player.* Player$_{\alpha_i}$ *runs* $A_i \leftarrow \text{Answer}(\text{clue}_{\alpha_i}, \text{map}, j_i)$, *and* $\pi_i \leftarrow \text{Play}(\text{pc}_{\alpha_i}, \text{sc}_{\alpha_i}, \text{map}, j_i, A_i)$, *then sends* (A_i, π_i) *to everyone.*
  • *For each* $\alpha \neq \alpha_i$, Player$_\alpha$ *checks that* $\text{Verify}(\pi_i, \text{pc}_{\alpha_i}, \text{map}, j_i, A_i) = 1$ *(if not,* Player$_\alpha$ *aborts the protocol).*
– *At the end of the game, each* Player$_\alpha$ *for* $\alpha \in [\![n]\!]^*$ *returns* view$_\alpha = (\text{clue}_\alpha, \text{sc}_\alpha, (\text{pc}_{\alpha'})_{\alpha' \in [\![n]\!]^*}, \{(\alpha_i, A_i, j_i, \pi_i)\}_{i \in [\![t]\!]^*})$, *where* t *is the number of plays.* Master *returns nothing.*

We now formally define the two required security properties, namely soundness and confidentiality. Soundness must ensure that players cannot cheat, *i.e.*, that they cannot make a valid proof π if they do not answer a question correctly.

Definition 8 (Soundness). *Let* λ *be a security parameter and* $\Pi = ($Setup, GenClue, OpenClue, Play, Verify$)$ *be a cryptographic cryptid for a cryptid encoding* $(n, \mathcal{C}, N, \mathcal{M}, \mathsf{Answer})$. Π *is said to be* sound *if for any pair of p.p.t. algorithms* $\mathcal{A} = (\mathcal{A}_1, \mathcal{A}_2)$, *the probability of success of the following experiment is negligible in* λ:

$\mathbf{Exp}_{\Pi, \mathcal{A}}^{\mathsf{Soundness}}(\lambda)$:
set $\leftarrow$ Setup(λ)
clue $\leftarrow \mathcal{A}_1(\text{set})$
(pc, sc) $\leftarrow$ GenClue(clue)
$(\pi, \text{map}, j, A) \leftarrow \mathcal{A}_2(\text{pc}, \text{sc})$
$A' \leftarrow$ Answer(map, clue, j)
return $((\text{clue} \in \mathcal{C}) \wedge (\text{map} \in \mathcal{M}) \wedge (A' \neq \perp)$
     $\wedge (A = 1 - A') \wedge \text{Verify}(\pi, \text{pc}, \text{map}, j, A))$

Confidentiality ensures the protection of players' clues. More precisely, an adversary must not be able to deduce any more information about players' clues in the cryptographic version than in the physical version of Cryptid. Note that each answer leaks some information about the secret clue; this leakage is inherent to the game and must be taken into account in our definition. Thus, confidentiality must ensure that, at any point in the game, a player has no more information about the clues of others than can be deduced from their answers.

We propose a simulation-based security definition [17]: a cryptographic cryptid is confidential if there exists a polynomial-time simulator that simulates for a player the cryptid protocol until play t, using only the values known by that player and the answers of the other players until play t. So, as the player could have simulated the whole protocol with their own data, we show that they learn nothing more than they already know during the game.

Definition 9 (Confidentiality). *Let λ be a security parameter and $\Pi = $ (Setup, GenClue, OpenClue, Play, Verify) be a cryptographic cryptid for a cryptid encoding $\mathsf{CE} = (n, \mathcal{C}, N, \mathcal{M}, \mathsf{Answer})$. Let $\mathsf{Cryptid}_{\alpha^*, t}$ be a protocol defined as the cryptid protocol instantiated by Π and CE (Definition 7) except that it aborts after t plays and returns view_{α^*} only.*

We define a cryptid simulator Sim instantiated by Π and CE as an algorithm that takes as input a setup set, an integer t, a map $\mathsf{map} \in \mathcal{M}$, an integer $\alpha^* \in [\![n]\!]^*$, a clue $\mathsf{clue} \in \mathcal{C}$, and a set of t triplets $\{(\alpha_i, A_i, j_i)\}_{i \in [\![t]\!]^*}$ each containing an integer $\alpha_i \in [\![n]\!]^*$, a bit A_i and an integer $j_i \in [\![N]\!]^*$, and that returns a tuple $(\mathsf{sc}_{\alpha^*}, (\mathsf{pc}_\alpha)_{\alpha \in [\![n]\!]^*}, \{\pi_i\}_{i \in [\![t]\!]^*})$.

Π is said to be confidential if there exists a negligible function ϵ s.t. for any p.p.t. algorithms $\mathcal{D}$, any integer t, any $\alpha^* \in [\![n]\!]^*$, any map $\mathsf{map} \in \mathcal{M}$, and any tuple of clues $(\mathsf{clue}_\alpha)_{\alpha \in [\![n]\!]^*} \in \mathcal{C}^n$, there exists a p.p.t. cryptid simulator Sim s.t., considering the following experiment:

$\mathsf{Exp}^{\mathsf{Confidentiality}}_{\Pi, \mathcal{D}, b}(\lambda):$
$\mathsf{set} \leftarrow \mathsf{Setup}(\lambda)$
$\mathsf{view}_{\alpha^*} \leftarrow \mathsf{Cryptid}_{\alpha^*, t} \langle \{\mathsf{Player}_\alpha(\mathsf{set}, \mathsf{map})\}_{\alpha \in [\![n]\!]^*},$
$\qquad\qquad \mathsf{Master}(\mathsf{set}, \mathsf{map}, (\mathsf{clue}_\alpha)_{\alpha \in [\![n]\!]^*}) \rangle$
parse view_{α^*} *as* $(\mathsf{sc}^0_{\alpha^*}, (\mathsf{pc}^0_\alpha)_{\alpha \in [\![n]\!]^*}, \{(\alpha_i, A_i, j_i, \pi^0_i)\}_{i \in [\![t]\!]^*})$
$(\mathsf{sc}^1_{\alpha^*}, (\mathsf{pc}^1_\alpha)_{\alpha \in [\![n]\!]^*}, \{\pi^1_i\}_{i \in [\![t]\!]^*}) \leftarrow \mathsf{Sim}(\mathsf{set}, t, \mathsf{map}, \alpha^*, \mathsf{clue}_{\alpha^*},$
$\qquad\qquad\qquad\qquad\qquad \{(\alpha_i, A_i, j_i)\}_{i \in [\![t]\!]^*})$
$b' \leftarrow \mathcal{D}(\mathsf{set}, t, \mathsf{map}, \alpha^*, \mathsf{clue}_{\alpha^*}, \mathsf{sc}^b_{\alpha^*}, (\mathsf{pc}^b_\alpha)_{\alpha \in [\![n]\!]^*}, \{(\alpha_i, A_i, j_i, \pi^b_i)\}_{i \in [\![t]\!]^*})$
return $b = b'$
we have: $\left| \Pr\left[0 \leftarrow \mathsf{Exp}^{\mathsf{Confidentiality}}_{\Pi, \mathcal{D}, 0}(\lambda)\right] - \Pr\left[1 \leftarrow \mathsf{Exp}^{\mathsf{Confidentiality}}_{\Pi, \mathcal{D}, 1}(\lambda)\right] \right| \leq \epsilon(\lambda).$

4.2   Our Cryptographic Cryptid

We build two cryptographic cryptid schemes based on two different cryptid encodings. These two schemes provide two different trade-offs between the size of the committed clues and the size/efficiency of the proofs generated during the game. Both schemes are based on the same paradigm: the clues are committed in ElGamal ciphertexts, and the proofs are built from NIP of correct/incorrect decryption of these ciphertexts.

The first encoding we propose, called *map-based clue cryptid encoding*, frees the clue encoding from its actual structure (based on cell types and properties): it gives only the answer the user must give for each of the map cells.

Definition 10 (MBC Cryptid Encoding). *The* Map-Based Clue *(MBC) cryptid encoding for n players is a tuple* $(n, \mathcal{C}, N, \mathcal{M}, \mathsf{Answer})$ *where* $N = 108$, $\mathcal{C} = \{0, 1\}^N$, $\mathrm{map} = (\mathrm{cell}_i)_{i \in [\![N]\!]^*}$ *where each* cell_i *describes the properties of the corresponding cell (however this information is encoded), and* Answer *is defined by:*

Answer$(\mathrm{map}, \mathrm{clue}, j)$: *parses* $\mathrm{clue} = (\mathrm{clue}_i)_{i \in [\![N]\!]^*}$ *and returns* $A = \mathrm{clue}_j$.

Based on this encoding, we can commit the clue by encrypting each of the answers for each of the cells. So, when a player answers a question concerning a given cell, they can prove with a NIP that their answer corresponds to the one encrypted in the ciphertext corresponding to the cell in their committed clue.

Definition 11 (CC1 scheme). *The cryptographic cryptid scheme* CC1 *for the MBC cryptid encoding* $(n, \mathcal{C}, N, \mathcal{M}, \mathsf{Answer})$ *is defined by the following algorithms:*

Setup(λ): *generates a group* $\mathbb{G}$ *of prime order* p *generated by* g *s.t.* $p > 2^\lambda$ *and instanciated the ElGamal encryption* ElGamal $= (\mathsf{Gen}, \mathsf{Enc}, \mathsf{Dec})$ *by* $\mathbb{G}$, *and returns* set $\leftarrow (\lambda, \mathsf{ElGamal})$.

GenClue(clue): *parses* clue *as* $(\mathrm{clue}_i)_{i \in [\![N]\!]^*}$, *generates* $(\mathsf{pk}, \mathsf{sk}) \leftarrow \mathsf{Gen}(\lambda)$, *computes* $E_i \leftarrow \mathsf{Enc}_{\mathsf{pk}}(\mathrm{clue}_i)$ *for each* $i \in [\![N]\!]^*$, *sets* $E \leftarrow (E_i)_{i \in [\![N]\!]^*}$, pc $\leftarrow (\mathsf{pk}, E)$ *and* sc $\leftarrow$ sk, *then returns* $(\mathsf{pc}, \mathsf{sc})$.

OpenClue$(\mathsf{pc}, \mathsf{sc})$: *parses* pc *as* $(\mathsf{pk}, (E_i)_{i \in [\![N]\!]^*})$, *checks that* pk $= g^{\mathsf{sc}}$ *(otherwise aborts), computes* $\mathrm{clue}_i \leftarrow \mathsf{Dec}_{\mathsf{sc}}(E_i)$ *for each* $i \in [\![N]\!]^*$, *then returns* clue $= (\mathrm{clue}_i)_{i \in [\![N]\!]^*}$.

Play$(\mathsf{pc}, \mathsf{sc}, \mathrm{map}, j, A)$: *parses* $(\mathsf{pc}, \mathsf{sc})$ *as* $((\mathsf{pk}, (E_i)_{i \in [\![N]\!]^*}), \mathsf{sk})$, *computes the proof* $\pi \leftarrow \mathsf{NIP}\{\mathsf{sk} : (\mathsf{Dec}_{\mathsf{sk}}(E_j) = A)\}$, *then returns* π.

Verify$(\pi, \mathsf{pc}, \mathrm{map}, j, A)$: *parses* $(\mathsf{pc}, \mathsf{sc})$ *as* $((\mathsf{pk}, (E_i)_{i \in [\![N]\!]^*}), \mathsf{sk})$, *verifies the proof* π *on the statement* (pk, E_j, A), *then returns* 1 *if the proof is valid,* 0 *otherwise.*

Theorem 1 and 2 claim that CC1 is sound and confidential.

Theorem 1. *If the* NIP *used in* CC1 *is sound, then* CC1 *is sound.*

Theorem 2. *If the* NIP *used in* CC1 *is zero-knowledge and* ElGamal *is* IND-CPA, *then* CC1 *is confidential.*

Proofs are given in appendix of the full version of the paper [6]. The computation time of the algorithm Play and the size of the proof π are in $O(1)$. In return, the computation time of the algorithm GenClue and the size of each public clue key pc it generates are in $O(N)$, where $N = 108$ in the original cryptid game. As these public clue keys must be produced a priori for each player (between 3 and

5) for each possible game (180 in the original cryptid game) before acquiring the game, it seems worthwhile to reduce the size of these elements.

   To this end, we propose another cryptid encoding, called the property-based clue cryptid encoding, which is closer to the clue structure as presented in the original game. Each cell is encoded by its type (desert, forest, *etc.*) and neighborhood properties (one cell from a desert, two cells from a bear's territory, etc.). Clues are divided into two kinds: (*i*) those indicating that the type of the cell is one of two given types, and (*ii*) those indicating one of the cell's neighborhood properties. We encode them with a triplet (C_1, C_2, C_3) s.t. if the clue is of kind (*i*), then C_1 and C_2 are the two types given by the clue and C_3 is undefined, else if the clue is of kind (*ii*), then C_3 is the neighborhood property, and C_1 and C_2 are undefined.

Definition 12 (PBC Cryptid Encoding). *We denote the set containing the 5 cell types (desert, forest,* etc.*) by* $\mathcal{T} = \{\bar{T}_l\}_{l \in [\![5]\!]}*$ *and the set containing the 14 neighboring properties (one cell from a desert, two cells from a bear's territory, etc.) by* $\mathcal{P} = \{\bar{P}_l\}_{l \in [\![14]\!]}*$. *In what follows, for any set S, $S_\perp$ denotes* $S \cup \{\perp\}$, *and* $\mathfrak{P}(S)$ *denotes the power set of S. The* Property-Based Clue *(PBC) cryptid encoding for n players is the tuple* $(n, \mathcal{C}, N, \mathcal{M}, \text{Answer})$ *where* $N = 108$, $\mathcal{C} = \mathcal{T}_\perp \times \mathcal{T}_\perp \times \mathcal{P}_\perp$, $\mathcal{M}$ *is the set of all the maps* $\text{map} = (\text{cell}_i)_{i \in [\![N]\!]}*$ *s.t. each* $\text{cell}_i \in \mathcal{T} \times \mathfrak{P}(\mathcal{P})$, *and* Answer *is defined as follows:*

Answer(map, clue, j): *parses each* cell_j *in* map *as* $(T_j, \mathcal{P}_j)$ *and the clue as* (C_1, C_2, C_3). *If* $(C_1, C_2) = (\perp, \perp)$, *then if* $C_3 \in \mathcal{P}_j$ *returns 1, otherwise 0. Else if* $C_3 = \perp$, *then if* $C_1 = T_j$ *or* $C_2 = T_j$ *returns 1, otherwise 0. Else, aborts.*

   We build a scheme based on this encoding where each element of the clue triplet (C_1, C_2, C_3) is committed in a ciphertext. Given a cell on the map, the type and neighborhood properties of that cell, and their answer on that cell, a player can prove the validity of this answer based on their committed clue as follows. If the answer is *yes*, then they show using a NIP that the type of the cell is one of the two types C_1 or C_2 encrypted in the committed clue, or that the property C_3 encrypted in the committed clue is one of the properties of the cell. Else, if the answer is *no*, then they show using a NIP that the type of the cell is not one of C_1 and C_2 encrypted in the committed clue, and that the property C_3 encrypted in the committed clue is not one of the properties of the cell.

Definition 13 (CC2 scheme). *The cryptographic cryptid scheme CC2 for the PBC cryptid encoding* $(n, \mathcal{C}, N, \mathcal{M}, \text{Answer})$ *is defined by the following algorithms:*

Setup(λ): *generates a group* $\mathbb{G}$ *of prime order p generated by g s.t. $p > 2^\lambda$ and instantiates the ElGamal encryption* ElGamal $=$ (Gen, Enc, Dec) *by* $\mathbb{G}$. *We denote the set containing the 5 cell types by* $\mathcal{T}$ *and the set containing the 14 neighboring properties by* $\mathcal{P}$. *This algorithm associates a group element picked in the uniform distribution on* $\mathbb{G}$ *with each element in* $\mathcal{T} \cup \mathcal{P} \cup \{\perp\}$ *(it will repeat this process if two different elements are associated with the same group element, which happens with negligible probability* $\leq |\mathcal{T} \cup \mathcal{P} \cup \{\perp\}|^2/p$).

In the following, by abuse of notation, each $X \in \mathcal{T}$ (resp. $X \in \mathcal{P}$ and $\perp$) will denote both the cell type (resp. the neighboring property and the bottom symbol) and the group element associated with it, and so $\mathcal{T}$ (resp. $\mathcal{P}$) will denote both the cell type set (resp. the neighboring property set) and the set of the group elements associated with all cell types (resp. neighboring properties). It returns set $= (\lambda, \mathsf{ElGamal}, \mathcal{T}, \mathcal{P}, \perp)$.

GenClue(clue): *parses* clue *as* (C_1, C_2, C_3), *generates* $(\mathsf{pk}, \mathsf{sk}) \leftarrow \mathsf{Gen}(\lambda)$, *computes* $E_i \leftarrow \mathsf{Enc}_{\mathsf{pk}}(C_i)$ *for each* $i \in [\![3]\!]^*$, *sets* $\mathsf{pc} \leftarrow (\mathsf{pk}, E_1, E_2, E_3)$ *and* $\mathsf{sc} \leftarrow \mathsf{sk}$, *then returns* $(\mathsf{pc}, \mathsf{sc})$.

OpenClue(pc, sc): *parses* pc *as* $(\mathsf{pk}, E_1, E_2, E_3)$, *checks that* $\mathsf{pk} = g^{\mathsf{sc}}$ *(otherwise aborts), computes* $C_i \leftarrow \mathsf{Dec}_{\mathsf{sc}}(E_i)$ *for each* $i \in [\![3]\!]^*$, *then returns* clue $= (C_1, C_2, C_3)$.

Play(pc, sc, map, j, A): *parses the public/private clue key pair* $(\mathsf{pc}, \mathsf{sc})$ *as* $((\mathsf{pk}, E_1, E_2, E_3), \mathsf{sk})$, map *as* $(\mathsf{cell}_i)_{i \in [\![N]\!]^*}$ *and* cell_j *as* $(T_j, \mathcal{P}_j)$. *If* $A = 1$, *this algorithm computes and returns:*

$$\pi \leftarrow \mathsf{NIP}\left\{\mathsf{sk} : \mathsf{Dec}_{\mathsf{sk}}(E_1) = T_j \vee \mathsf{Dec}_{\mathsf{sk}}(E_2) = T_j \vee \left(\bigvee_{P \in \mathcal{P}_j} \mathsf{Dec}_{\mathsf{sk}}(E_3) = P\right)\right\}.$$

Else, if $A = 0$ *it computes and returns:*

$$\pi \leftarrow \mathsf{NIP}\left\{\mathsf{sk} : \mathsf{Dec}_{\mathsf{sk}}(E_1) \neq T_j \wedge \mathsf{Dec}_{\mathsf{sk}}(E_2) \neq T_j \wedge \left(\bigwedge_{P \in \mathcal{P}_j} \mathsf{Dec}_{\mathsf{sk}}(E_3) \neq P\right)\right\}.$$

Verify(π, pc, map, j, A): *parses the public/private clue key pair* $(\mathsf{pc}, \mathsf{sc})$ *as* $((\mathsf{pk}, E_1, E_2, E_3), \mathsf{sk})$, map *as* $(\mathsf{cell}_i)_{i \in [\![N]\!]^*}$, *and* cell_j *as* $(T_j, \mathcal{P}_j)$. *Depending on* A, *this algorithm verifies the proof* π *on the statement* $(\mathsf{ElGamal}, \mathsf{pk}, E_1, E_2, E_3, T_j, \mathcal{P}_j)$, *it returns* 1 *if the proof is valid,* 0 *otherwise.*

Theorem 3 and 4 claim that CC2 is sound and confidential.

Theorem 3. *If the* NIP *used in* CC2 *are sound, then* CC2 *is sound.*

Theorem 4. *If the* NIP *used in* CC2 *are zero-knowledge and* ElGamal *is* IND-CPA, *then* CC2 *is confidential.*

Proofs are given in appendix of the full version of the paper [6]. The complexity of the proof size and computation time is linear in the number of neighborhood properties $|\mathcal{P}|$ (we will explain how this proof is instantiated and why its complexity is so later in this section). Thus, the computation time of the algorithm Play and the size of the proof π it generates are in $O(|\mathcal{P}|)$, where $|\mathcal{P}| = 14$ in the original cryptid game. In return, the computation time of the GenClue algorithm and the size of each committed clue pc it generates are in $O(1)$. We therefore obtain much smaller commitments, at the cost of proofs requiring moderate computing capacity for the players. Depending on the power of the players' devices and their storage capacity, one can choose the most suitable scheme between CC1 and CC2.

4.3 NIP Instantiation

Let $\mathbb{G}$ be a group of prime order p and let $g \in \mathbb{G}$ be a generator. Let $(g_1, g_2) \in \mathbb{G}^2$ and $x \in \mathbb{Z}_p^*$ be. We set $y_1 = g_1^x$ and $y_2 = g_2^x$. An instantiation of the (interactive) proof of discrete logarithms equality $\mathsf{IP}\{x : y_1 = g_1^x \wedge y_2 = g_2^x\}$ is given in [10], and an instantiation of the (interactive) proof of discrete logarithms inequality $\mathsf{IP}\{x : y_1 = g_1^x \wedge y_2 \neq g_2^x\}$ is given in [8]. These proofs are correct, sound, and zero-knowledge. Moreover, these proofs are *sigma protocols*, which means that these protocols consist of three interactions: the prover sends a commitment, the verifier sends a challenge chosen at random in a given set, and the prover sends a response. Consider now an ElGamal public key $\mathsf{pk} = g^{\mathsf{sk}}$ and an ElGamal ciphertext $c = (c_1, c_2) = (g^r, \mathsf{pk}^r m)$. The relation $\mathsf{Dec}_{\mathsf{sk}}(c) = m$ is equivalent to the relation $(\mathsf{pk} = g^{\mathsf{sk}} \wedge c_2/(c_1^{\mathsf{sk}}) = m)$, which is equivalent to $(\mathsf{pk} = g^{\mathsf{sk}} \wedge (c_2/m) = c_1^{\mathsf{sk}})$. Similarly, the relation $\mathsf{Dec}_{\mathsf{sk}}(c) \neq m$ is equivalent to the relation $(\mathsf{pk} = g^{\mathsf{sk}} \wedge (c_2/m) \neq c_1^{\mathsf{sk}})$. Thus, the proofs $\mathsf{IP}\{\mathsf{sk} : \mathsf{Dec}_{\mathsf{sk}}(c) = m\}$ and $\mathsf{IP}\{\mathsf{sk} : \mathsf{Dec}_{\mathsf{sk}}(c) \neq m\}$ can be instantiated by the discrete logarithms equality proof in [10] and the discrete logarithms equality proof in [8].

Now let us consider two relations $\mathcal{R}_1$ and $\mathcal{R}_2$ and two associated proofs $\mathsf{IP}\{w_1 : (s_1, w_1) \in \mathcal{R}_1\}$ and $\mathsf{IP}\{w_2 : (s_2, w_2) \in \mathcal{R}_2\}$ for some pairs of statement/witness (s_1, w_1) and (s_2, w_2), s.t. these two proofs are sigma protocols and use the same challenge set. The proof $\mathsf{IP}\{(w_1, w_2) : (s_1, w_1) \in \mathcal{R}_1 \wedge (s_2, w_2) \in \mathcal{R}_2\}$ can be easily obtained by using the same challenge for the two relations in the two previous proofs. This method can be generalized for any number of relations, and can therefore be used to prove several correct/incorrect decryptions of ciphertexts (note that if the ciphertexts use the same public key, it also proves that the secret keys used to decrypt the ciphertexts are all the same). On the other hand, the generic transformation given in [12] allows us to build a proof $\mathsf{IP}\{w : (s_1, w) \in \mathcal{R}_1 \vee (s_2, w) \in \mathcal{R}_2\}$ under the same hypothesis (the challenge used in the resulted proof comes from the same challenge set as for $\mathcal{R}_1$ or $\mathcal{R}_2$, and the method can be generalized for any number of relations). Thus, this method can be used to prove one correct/incorrect decryption of ciphertext out of several ciphertext decryptions.

These two methods can be used together to produce proofs for boolean relations of correct/incorrect ciphertext decryptions, and thus instantiate all the proofs used in the schemes CC1 and CC2. Note that the size of these proofs and the computation time increase linearly with the number of correct/incorrect ciphertext decryptions in the relation. Finally, since these proofs are also sigma protocols, they can be turned into non-interactive proofs using the Fiat-Shamir transformation [14].

4.4   Implementation

To demonstate the practicality of our schemes, we implement the algorithms GenClue, OpenClue, Play, and Verify in Rust. We use the prime order group Ristretto with the curve25519_dalek [18] library and we use 255 bits secret keys. The source code for our implementation is available at [6]. Table 1 describes the average computation time, measured in milliseconds, of each algorithm for our two cryptographic crytid schemes, and Table 2 illustrates the average size of the public clue key pc and the size of the proof π generated by the players. The averages are based on 1000 runs and we used the optimized release mode of Cargo.

Our measurements depend on the player's answer {maybe, no}, moreover for the scheme CC2, we differentiate between the two forms of clue. Our experiments are not based on the real maps proposed in the original game, but on randomly generated cells and clues. We have chosen to evaluate our algorithms on cells that match all the properties together (or all but one in the case where the clue concerns a neighbouring property and the answer is no), as this maximises the generation time and the size of the proof in CC2 (it makes no difference for CC1). The times given are therefore worst-case.

As we had predicted in the theoretical analysis of our schemes, the computation time and the size of the public clues are higher in CC1 than in CC2, conversely the computation time and the size of the proofs are higher in CC2. The generation of all public clues is done once by the game editor, and each occurrence of OpenClue, Play, and Verify is done by the players. Generating a clue or building a proof takes less than 7 milliseconds in all cases, which is reasonable for playing the game in real time. Opening a clue takes longer in CC1 (less than 4 milliseconds versus 0.11 milliseconds in CC2), but is still efficient and only needs to be done once per player at the start of the game. On the other hand, a Cryptid game consists of 180 game setup for 3 to 5 players, so its cryptographic version requires the download of $180 \times 4 = 720$ public clue keys, *i.e.*, about $7 \times 720 = 5040$ kilobytes for CC1 and $0.25 \times 720 = 180$ kilobytes for CC2. In summary, CC1 requires more memory to download and store when acquiring the game, but has a lower latency during gameplay.

Table 1. Running time in milliseconds for our two cryptographic cryptid scheme. The results are an average over 1000 executions.

Scheme	CC1		CC2			
Answer	no	maybe	no		maybe	
clue	$(\text{clue}_i)_{i\in[\![N]\!]^*} \in \{0,1\}^N$		$(\bar{T}_1,\bar{T}_2,\bot)$	$(\bot,\bot,\bar{P})$	$(\bar{T}_1,\bar{T}_2,\bot)$	$(\bot,\bot,\bar{P})$
GenClue	6.27	6.27	0.20	0.20	0.20	0.20
OpenClue	3.38	3.38	0.11	0.11	0.11	0.11
Play	0.10	0.10	2.46	2.31	1.26	1.49
Verify	0.20	0.20	2.02	1.90	1.33	1.31

Table 2. Size in bytes for our two cryptographic cryptid scheme. The results are an average over 1000 executions.

Scheme	CC1		CC2			
Answer	no	maybe	no		maybe	
clue	$(\text{clue}_i)_{i\in[\![N]\!]^*} \in \{0,1\}^N$		$(\bar{T}_1,\bar{T}_2,\bot)$	$(\bot,\bot,\bar{P})$	$(\bar{T}_1,\bar{T}_2,\bot)$	$(\bot,\bot,\bar{P})$
pc	6944	6944	224	224	224	224
π	96	96	1696	1600	1600	1600

5   Cryptographic Cryptid with Dishonest Game Master

We extend our model to check that the game designer (called the game master) has prepared the clues and the map correctly (*i.e.*, they are honest). The aim is to allow players to check from the start of the game that their clues are correctly formed and that they converge on at least one cell of the map, which guarantees that the game will end. To do this, we also need to extend our formalism and security properties. We call this new primitive *verifiable cryptographic cryptid*.

5.1   Formal Model

We start by giving a new definition of cryptid encoding by adding the algorithm CorrectClue, which decides whether a clue is well formed.

Definition 14 (Verifiable Cryptid Encoding). *A verifiable cryptid encoding is a tuple* $(n, \mathcal{C}, N, \mathcal{M}, \mathsf{Answer}, \mathsf{CorrectClue})$ *where* $(n, \mathcal{C}, N, \mathcal{M}, \mathsf{Answer})$ *is a cryptid encoding and* CorrectClue *is defined as follows:*

CorrectClue(map, clue): *takes as input a map* map $\in \mathcal{M}$ *and a clue* clue $\in \mathcal{C}$. *It returns* **true** *or* **false** *depending on whether the clue is well-formed or not according to the rules ("**true**" corresponds to bit 1 and "**false**" to 0).*

For instance, in the original version of the game, CorrectClue will test whether the encoded clue corresponds to a clue of the form "the cell is of this or that type" or of the form "the cell is n cells away from a cell with such-and-such a property". We now define verifiable cryptographic cryptids. This primitive extends cryptographic cryptids by adding a pair of algorithms to prove/verify that the game (the committed clues and the map) has been built correctly by the game master.

Definition 15 (Verifiable Cryptographic Cryptid). *A verifiable cryptographic cryptid for a verifiable cryptid encoding* $(n, \mathcal{C}, N, \mathcal{M}, \mathsf{Answer}, \mathsf{CorrectClue})$ *is a tuple of polynomial time algorithms* (Setup, GenClue, OpenClue, ProveGame, VerifyGame, Play, Verify) *where* (Setup, GenClue, OpenClue, Play, Verify) *is a cryptographic cryptid and* ProveGame *and* VerifyGame *are defined as follows:*

ProveGame$(j, (\mathsf{pc}_\alpha, \mathsf{sc}_\alpha)_{\alpha \in [\![n]\!]^*}, \mathrm{map})$: *takes as input the index* j *of the cryptid habitat, the clue keys* $(\mathsf{pc}_\alpha, \mathsf{sc}_\alpha)_{\alpha \in [\![n]\!]^*}$ *of the players, a map* map, *and returns a proof* ρ.

VerifyGame$(\rho, (\mathsf{pc}_\alpha)_{\alpha \in [\![n]\!]^*}, \mathrm{map})$: *takes as input a proof* ρ, *the public clue keys of the players, the map* map *and returns* $b \in \{\texttt{accept}, \texttt{reject}\}$ *("accept" corresponds to bit 1 and "reject" to 0).*

It is therefore necessary to extend the notion of the cryptid protocol to include a phase where the game master proves to the players via the algorithm ProveGame that the public clue keys have been constructed correctly and that the game ends. This phase takes place between the clue key distribution phase and the start of the game phase.

Definition 16 (Verifiable Cryptid Protocol). *Let λ be a security param-eter. The* verifiable cryptid protocol *for n players instantiated by a verifi-able cryptid encoding $(n, \mathcal{C}, N, \mathcal{M}, \mathsf{Answer}, \mathsf{CorrectClue})$ and a verifiable cryp-tographic cryptid $(\mathsf{Setup}, \mathsf{GenClue}, \mathsf{OpenClue}, \mathsf{ProveGame}, \mathsf{VerifyGame}, \mathsf{Play}, \mathsf{Verify})$ is defined as the verifiable cryptid protocol except that after that each player Player_α has computed $\mathrm{clue}_\alpha \leftarrow \mathsf{OpenClue}(\mathrm{pc}_\alpha, \mathrm{sc}_\alpha)$:*

- *Master runs $\rho \leftarrow \mathsf{ProveGame}(j, (\mathrm{pc}_\alpha, \mathrm{sc}_\alpha)_{\alpha \in [\![n]\!]^*}, \mathrm{map})$, then sends ρ to each Player_α where $\alpha \in [\![n]\!]^*$ and j is the index of the cell where the cryptid is.*
- *Each player Player_α checks that $\mathsf{VerifyGame}(\rho, (\mathrm{pc}_\alpha)_{\alpha \in [\![n]\!]}, \mathrm{map}) = 1$ (if not, Player_α aborts the protocol).*
- *The other steps are identical to those of the cryptographic cryptid protocol.*

At the end of the game, each Player_α for $\alpha \in [\![n]\!]^*$ returns $\mathrm{view}_\alpha = (\mathrm{clue}_\alpha, \mathrm{sc}_\alpha, (\mathrm{pc}_{\alpha'})_{\alpha' \in [\![n]\!]^*}, \rho, \{(\alpha_i, A_i, j_i, \pi_i)\}_{i \in [\![t]\!]^*})$, where t is the number of plays.

A verifiable cryptid protocol must verify the same properties as a cryptid protocol (soundness and confidentiality). These properties do not need to be redefined. In addition, the security model must capture cases where a dishonest game master tries to give players incorrect clues, or clues that do not converge on at least one cell of the map. We call this security property *game soundness*. More specifically, a verifiable cryptid protocol is game-sound if no adversary is able to forge a valid proof, even if some clues are incorrect or there is no cell that matches all the clues. To verify that the adversary has succeeded in its attack, we need to extract the clues from the players' public clue keys. To do this, we need to define an algorithm, not necessarily in polynomial time, to retrieve the clues from the public keys, but without the secret keys. Note that the fact that this algorithm is not polynomial time is not a problem, since it will only be used in the experiment to test the adversary's success, never by a player.

Definition 17 (Game Soundness). *Let λ be a security parameter and let $\Pi = (\mathsf{Setup}, \mathsf{GenClue}, \mathsf{ProveGame}, \mathsf{VerifyGame}, \mathsf{OpenClue}, \mathsf{Play}, \mathsf{Verify})$ be a verifi-able cryptid for a verifiable cryptid encoding $(n, \mathcal{C}, N, \mathcal{M}, \mathsf{Answer}, \mathsf{CorrectClue})$. Π is said to be* game sound *if there is a (not necessary p.p.t.) algorithm $\mathsf{OpenClue}^*$ s.t. $\mathsf{OpenClue}(\mathrm{pc}, \mathrm{sc}) = \mathsf{OpenClue}^*(\mathrm{pc})$ for any $(\mathrm{pc}, \mathrm{sc}) \leftarrow \mathsf{GenClue}(\mathrm{clue})$ and the probability that the following experiment returns 1 is negligible in λ for any p.p.t. algorithm $\mathcal{A}$.*

$\mathbf{Exp}_{\Pi, \mathcal{A}}^{\mathsf{Game\text{-}Soundness}}(\lambda):$
$\mathrm{set} \leftarrow \mathsf{Setup}(\lambda)$
$(\rho, \mathrm{map}, (\mathrm{pc}_\alpha)_{\alpha \in [\![n]\!]^*}) \leftarrow \mathcal{A}(\mathrm{set})$
$\forall \alpha \in [\![n]\!]^*, \mathrm{clue}_\alpha \leftarrow \mathsf{OpenClue}^*(\mathrm{pc}_\alpha)$
$return ((\mathrm{clue}_\alpha)_{\alpha \in [\![n]\!]^*} \in \mathcal{C}) \wedge (\mathrm{map} \in \mathcal{M}) \wedge \mathsf{VerifyGame}(\rho, (\mathrm{pc}_\alpha)_{\alpha \in [\![n]\!]^*}, \mathrm{map})$
$\qquad \wedge ((\exists \alpha \in [\![n]\!]^* \ s.t. \ 0 \leftarrow \mathsf{CorrectClue}(\mathrm{map}, \mathrm{clue}_\alpha))$
$\qquad \vee (\forall i \in [\![N]\!]^*, \exists \alpha \in [\![n]\!]^* \ s.t. \ 0 \leftarrow \mathsf{Answer}(\mathrm{map}, \mathrm{clue}_\alpha, i)))$

5.2 Our Verifiable Cryptographic Cryptid

We are now going to build a verifiable cryptographic cryptid. To do this, we will extend the PBC encoding and the CC2 scheme. Note that the PBC encoding is much more suitable than the MBC encoding for building a verifiable cryptographic cryptid: indeed, the MBC encoding is not based on the actual structure of the clue, but on the answers it gives for each cell, and it is tedious to prove that the structure of the clue is correct just by looking at the answers it gives for each cell on the map. Note also that even if the game master has proven that the game ends, it is also very important for the smooth running of the game to prove that the clues are well constructed, as this could give a player a huge advantage and be very difficult for other players to guess. For example, with MBC encoding in the CC1 scheme, a malicious game master could give a clue to a player that only answers true on the cryptid cell.

Definition 18 (VPBC Cryptid Encoding). *By using the same notation as in Definition 12, we define the* Verifiable Property-Based Clue *(VPBC) verifiable cryptid encoding for n players as the tuple* $(n, \mathcal{C}, N, \mathcal{M}, \mathsf{Answer}, \mathsf{CorrectClue})$, *where* $(n, \mathcal{C}, N, \mathcal{M}, \mathsf{Answer})$ *is the PBC and* CorrectClue *is defined as follows:*

CorrectClue(map, clue): *takes as input a map* map $\in \mathcal{M}$ *and a clue* clue $\in \mathcal{C}$, *and parses* clue *as* (C_1, C_2, C_3). *If* $(((C_1, C_2) \in \mathcal{T}^2 \wedge C_1 \neq C_2 \wedge C_3 = \bot) \vee (C_1 = C_2 = \bot \wedge C_3 \in \mathcal{P}))$, *then it returns 1 ("**true**"), else it returns 0 ("**false**").*

Naive Solution to Prove that the Game Ends. A first idea is to prove that the game ends directly from the public clues and the map. The game ends when there is a cell s.t. each player's clue returns the answer 1 on that cell. We already know how to show that a player's clue returns 1 on a cell (see the Play algorithm of CC2), so we just need to extend this proof to check that a cell in the map verifies this property for each of the clues. Using the methods given in Sect. 4.2, we can build the following proof:

$$\mathsf{NIP}\left\{(\mathsf{sk}_\alpha)_{\alpha \in [\![n]\!]^*} : \bigvee_{i=1}^{N}\left(\bigwedge_{\alpha=1}^{n}\left(\begin{array}{c}\mathsf{Dec}_{\mathsf{sk}_\alpha}(E_{\alpha,1}) = T_i \vee \mathsf{Dec}_{\mathsf{sk}}(E_{\alpha,2}) = T_i \\ \vee \left(\bigvee_{P \in \mathcal{P}_i} \mathsf{Dec}_{\mathsf{sk}_\alpha}(E_{\alpha,3}) = P\right)\end{array}\right)\right)\right\},$$

where $\mathsf{pc}_\alpha = (\mathsf{pk}_\alpha, E_{\alpha,1}, E_{\alpha,2}, E_{\alpha,3})$ for each $\alpha \in [\![n]\!]^*$ and where map $= \{(T_i, \mathcal{P}_i)\}_{i \in [\![N]\!]^*}$. However, the time and size complexity of this proof is $O(nN|\mathcal{P}|)$, which is not very efficient, especially since the full Cryptid game contains 180 games, and so its cryptographic version will contain 180 of such proofs, which must be downloaded when the game is acquired.

Efficient Game Proof. We propose a solution where the size complexity of the proof that the game ends and the clues are correct is in $O(N + n(|\mathcal{P}| + |\mathcal{T}|))$. The time complexity is in $O(N|\mathcal{P}| + n(|\mathcal{P}| + |\mathcal{T}|))$, but if we neglect the computation time of a multiplication in $\mathbb{G}$ (a multiplication is much less computationally expensive than an exponentiation in a prime order group), it goes down to $O(N +$

$n(|\mathcal{P}|+|\mathcal{T}|))$. Since N is the largest parameter, this solution is more efficient than the previous one, as N has no factors in the time and size complexity expression.

The main idea is to first commit the cryptid cell. To do this, the game master encrypts the type and each of the neighbourhood properties of the cell in different ciphertexts. More precisely, they encrypt the type in a ciphertext E_0, and if the cryptid cell verifies the ith property in $\mathcal{P}$ then they encrypt this property in E_i, otherwise they encrypt the neutral element $1_{\mathbb{G}}$. The game master constructs a NIP ρ_1 that each E_i correctly encrypts either the ith property or $1_{\mathbb{G}}$ (with time/size complexity in $O(|\mathcal{P}|)$). The game master then hashes each cell of the map by computing the product of the group elements corresponding to the type and properties of each cell (this operation requires $N|\mathcal{P}|$ group element multiplications but no exponentiation). This hash function is known to be collision resistant under the discrete logarithm assumption. This result has been proved in [5] and is recalled in the following theorem.

Theorem 5. *Let n be an integer, λ be a security parameter, and $\mathbb{G}$ be a group of prime order p s.t. $p > 2^{\lambda}$ and the discrete logarithm assumption holds in $\mathbb{G}$ (i.e., given a random pair $(g, h) \xleftarrow{\$} \mathbb{G}^2$, the probability that any p.p.t. algorithm outputs $\log_g(h)$ is negligible). For any p.p.t. algorithm $\mathcal{A}$, there exists a negligible function $\epsilon_{n\text{-col}}(\lambda)$ s.t.:*
$$\Pr\left[g \xleftarrow{\$} \mathbb{G}^n; (x, y) \leftarrow \mathcal{A}(g);\ :\ x, y \in \{0, 1\}^n \wedge x \neq y \wedge \prod_{i=0}^{n-1} g_i^{x_i} = \prod_{i=0}^{n-1} g_i^{y_i}\right] \leq \epsilon_{n\text{-col}}(\lambda).$$

Using the ElGamal homomorphism property, any user can compute the encryption of the hash of the cell committed in the E_i. The game master can then build a NIP ρ_0 that the hash of the committed cell corresponds to one of the cells on the map (with time/size complexity in $O(N)$). To prove that the game ends, the game master just has to prove in $\rho_{2,\alpha}$ using a NIP that each player's clue (indexed by α) answers 1 on the committed cryptid cell (with time/size complexity in $O(|\mathcal{P}|)$ for each of the n proofs), in a similar way to the proof of the Play algorithm.

Finally, the game master proves that each of the n clues is well formed by showing that either the first two elements of the clue encrypt two different types in $\mathcal{T}$ and the third element encrypts $\perp$, or that the first two elements encrypt $\perp$ and the last element encrypts one of the properties of $\mathcal{P}$ (with time/size complexity in $O(|\mathcal{T}| + |\mathcal{P}|)$ for each of the n proofs).

Definition 19 (VCC scheme). *The verifiable cryptographic cryptid scheme VCC = (Setup, GenClue, ProveGame, VerifyGame, OpenClue, Play, Verify) for the VPBC cryptid encoding $(n, \mathcal{C}, N, \mathcal{M}, \text{Answer}, \text{CorrectClue})$ is defined as CC2 except that Setup, ProveGame and VerifyGame are defined as follows:*

Setup(λ): *same as in CC2, except that it will repeat the association between the elements of $\mathcal{T} \cup \mathcal{P} \cup \{\perp\}$ and the random elements of $\mathbb{G}$ process if at least one element is associated with $1_{\mathbb{G}}$, which happens with negligible probability $\leq |\mathcal{T} \cup \mathcal{P} \cup \{\perp\}|/p$.*

$\mathsf{ProveGame}(j, (\mathsf{pc}_\alpha, \mathsf{sc}_\alpha)_{\alpha \in [\![n]\!]^*}, \mathsf{map})$: *parses* $(\mathsf{pc}_\alpha)_{\alpha \in [\![n]\!]^*}$ *as* $(\mathsf{pk}_\alpha, E_{\alpha,1}, E_{\alpha,2},$
$E_{\alpha,3})_{\alpha \in [\![n]\!]^*}$, $(\mathsf{sc}_\alpha)_{\alpha \in [\![n]\!]^*}$ *as* $(\mathsf{sk}_\alpha)_{\alpha \in [\![n]\!]^*}$, map *as* $(\mathsf{cell}_i)_{i \in [\![N]\!]^*}$ *and each* cell_i
as $(T_i, \mathcal{P}_i)$, *generates* $(\mathsf{pk}, \mathsf{sk}) \leftarrow \mathsf{Gen}(\lambda)$, *computes* $E_0 \leftarrow \mathsf{Enc}_{\mathsf{pk}}(T_j)$, *and for*
all $l \in [\![14]\!]^*$:

$$E_l = \begin{cases} \mathsf{Enc}_{\mathsf{pk}}(\bar{P}_l) \; \textit{if} \; \bar{P}_l \in \mathcal{P}_j \\ \mathsf{Enc}_{\mathsf{pk}}(1_{\mathbb{G}}) \; \textit{else} \end{cases},$$

For all $i \in [\![N]\!]^*$, *it sets* $H(\mathsf{cell}_i) = \prod_{P \in \mathcal{P}_i} P$. *It generates the following* NIP:

$$\rho_0 \leftarrow \mathsf{NIP} \left\{ \mathsf{sk} : \bigvee_{i \in [\![N]\!]^*} \mathsf{Dec}_{\mathsf{sk}} \left(\prod_{l \in [\![14]\!]^*} E_l \right) = H(\mathsf{cell}_i) \wedge \mathsf{Dec}_{\mathsf{sk}}(E_0) = T_i \right\},$$

$$\rho_1 \leftarrow \mathsf{NIP} \left\{ \mathsf{sk} : \bigwedge_{l \in [\![14]\!]^*} \mathsf{Dec}_{\mathsf{sk}}(E_l) = \bar{P}_l \vee \mathsf{Dec}_{\mathsf{sk}}(E_l) = 1_{\mathbb{G}} \right\}.$$

Then for each $\alpha \in [\![n]\!]^*$, *it generates the two following* NIP:

$$\rho_{2,\alpha} \leftarrow \mathsf{NIP} \left\{ \mathsf{sk}, \mathsf{sk}_\alpha : \begin{matrix} \mathsf{Dec}_{\mathsf{sk}_\alpha}(E_{\alpha,1}) = \mathsf{Dec}_{\mathsf{sk}}(E_0) \\ \vee \mathsf{Dec}_{\mathsf{sk}_\alpha}(E_{\alpha,2}) = \mathsf{Dec}_{\mathsf{sk}}(E_0) \\ \vee \left(\bigvee_{l \in [\![14]\!]^*} \mathsf{Dec}_{\mathsf{sk}_\alpha}(E_{\alpha,3}) = \mathsf{Dec}_{\mathsf{sk}}(E_l) \right) \end{matrix} \right\},$$

$$\rho_{3,\alpha} \leftarrow \mathsf{NIP} \left\{ \mathsf{sk}_\alpha : \begin{matrix} \left(\begin{matrix} \mathsf{Dec}_{\mathsf{sk}_\alpha}(E_{\alpha,3}) = \bot \wedge \mathsf{Dec}_{\mathsf{sk}_\alpha}(E_{\alpha,1}) \neq \mathsf{Dec}_{\mathsf{sk}_\alpha}(E_{\alpha,2}) \\ \wedge \left(\bigvee_{\bar{T} \in \mathcal{T}} \mathsf{Dec}_{\mathsf{sk}_\alpha}(E_{\alpha,1}) = \bar{T} \right) \\ \wedge \left(\bigvee_{\bar{T} \in \mathcal{T}} \mathsf{Dec}_{\mathsf{sk}_\alpha}(E_{\alpha,2}) = \bar{T} \right) \end{matrix} \right) \\ \vee \left(\begin{matrix} \mathsf{Dec}_{\mathsf{sk}_\alpha}(E_{\alpha,1}) = \mathsf{Dec}_{\mathsf{sk}_\alpha}(E_{\alpha,2}) = \bot \\ \wedge \left(\bigvee_{\bar{P} \in \mathcal{P}} \mathsf{Dec}_{\mathsf{sk}_\alpha}(E_{\alpha,3}) = \bar{P} \right) \end{matrix} \right) \end{matrix} \right\}.$$

Finally, it returns $\rho \leftarrow (\mathsf{pk}, (E_l)_{l \in [\![14]\!]^*}, \rho_0, \rho_1, (\rho_{2,\alpha})_{\alpha \in [\![n]\!]^*}, (\rho_{3,\alpha})_{\alpha \in [\![n]\!]^*})$.

$\mathsf{VerifyGame}(\rho, (\mathsf{pc}_\alpha)_{\alpha \in [\![n]\!]^*}, \mathsf{map})$: *parses* ρ *as* $(\mathsf{pk}, (E_l)_{l \in [\![14]\!]^*}, \rho_0, \rho_1, (\rho_{2,\alpha})_{\alpha \in [\![n]\!]^*},$
$(\rho_{3,\alpha})_{\alpha \in [\![n]\!]^*})$, $(\mathsf{pc}_\alpha)_{\alpha \in [\![n]\!]^*}$ *as* $(\mathsf{pk}_\alpha, E_{\alpha,1}, E_{\alpha,2}, E_{\alpha,3})_{\alpha \in [\![n]\!]^*}$, *the map* map *as*
$(\mathsf{cell}_i)_{i \in [\![N]\!]^*}$ *and each* cell_i *as* $(T_i, \mathcal{P}_i)$. *Verifies the proofs* ρ_0 *on the state-*
ment $(\mathsf{ElGamal}, \mathsf{pk}, \prod_{l \in [\![14]\!]^*} E_l, (T_i, H(\mathsf{cell}_i))_{i \in [\![N]\!]^*}, E_0)$, ρ_1 *on the statement*
$(\mathsf{ElGamal}, \mathsf{pk}, (E_l)_{l \in [\![14]\!]^*}, \mathcal{P}, 1_{\mathbb{G}})$, *and for all* $\alpha \in [\![n]\!]^*$, $\rho_{2,\alpha}$ *on the state-*
ment $(\mathsf{ElGamal}, \mathsf{pk}_\alpha, E_{\alpha,1}, E_{\alpha,2}, E_{\alpha,3}, \mathsf{pk}, (E_l)_{l \in [\![14]\!]})$ *and* $\rho_{3,\alpha}$ *on the statement*
$(\mathsf{ElGamal}, \mathsf{pk}_\alpha, E_{\alpha,1}, E_{\alpha,2}, E_{\alpha,3}, \mathcal{T}, \mathcal{P}, \bot)$. *It returns 1 if proofs are valid, 0 oth-*
erwise.

The following theorems claim that VCC is sound, game-sound, and confidential.

Theorem 6. *If the* NIP *used in VCC are sound, then* VCC *is sound.*

Theorem 7. *If the* NIP *used in VCC are extractable, then* VCC *is game-sound*
under the discrete logarithm assumption.

Theorem 8. *If the* NIP *used in VCC are zero-knowledge and ElGamal is*
IND-CPA, *then* VCC *is confidential.*

Theorem 6 is a direct implication of Theorem 3. The proof of the two other theorems are given in appendix of full version of this paper [6].

5.3 NIP Instantiation

NIP of VCC can be instantiated using the same tools as described in Sect. 4.2, except for the proofs that involve the equivalence of two decryptions, *i.e.*, those that contain expressions such as $\mathsf{Dec}_{\mathsf{sk}}(c) = \mathsf{Dec}_{\mathsf{sk}'}(c')$ (the proofs $\rho_{2,\alpha}$). Consider two ElGamal public keys $\mathsf{pk} = g^{\mathsf{sk}}$ and $\mathsf{pk}' = g^{\mathsf{sk}'}$, and two ElGamal cipher-texts $c = (c_1, c_2) = (g^r, \mathsf{pk}^r m)$ and $c' = (c_1', c_2') = (g^{r'}, \mathsf{pk}'^{r'} m)$. The relation $\mathsf{Dec}_{\mathsf{sk}}(c) = \mathsf{Dec}_{\mathsf{sk}'}(c')$ is equivalent to the relation $(\mathsf{pk} = g^{\mathsf{sk}} \wedge \mathsf{pk}' = g^{\mathsf{sk}'} \wedge c_2/(c_1^{\mathsf{sk}}) = c_2'/(c_1'^{\mathsf{sk}'}))$, which is equivalent to $(\mathsf{pk} = g^{\mathsf{sk}} \wedge \mathsf{pk}' = g^{\mathsf{sk}'} \wedge (c_2/c_2') = c_1^{\mathsf{sk}}(c_1'^{-1})^{\mathsf{sk}'})$. By renaming the variables, we obtain the relation $(y_1 = g_1^{x_1} \wedge y_2 = g_2^{x_2} \wedge y = g^{x_1} h^{x_2})$. We give an extractable zero-knowledge sigma-protocol NIP for this relation, which can therefore be used in relations containing "or" and "and" operators as it is the case in $\rho_{2,\alpha}$.

NIP $\{x_1, x_2 : y_1 = g_1^{x_1} \wedge y_2 = g_2^{x_2} \wedge y = g^{x_1} h^{x_2}\}$: picks $r_1, r_2 \xleftarrow{\$} \mathbb{Z}_p^*$, sets $R_1 \leftarrow g_1^{r_1}$, $R_2 \leftarrow g_2^{r_2}$, $R \leftarrow g^{r_1}$, and $S \leftarrow h^{r_2}$, then hashes $(g_1, g_2, g, h, y_1, y_2, y, R_1, R_2, R, S)$ using a random oracle in order to obtain a challenge $c \in \mathbb{Z}_p^*$, and computes $z_1 \leftarrow r_1 + cx_1$, and $z_2 \leftarrow r_2 + cx_2$. It returns $\pi \leftarrow (R_1, R_2, R, S, z_1, z_2)$.

Ver(s, π): parses s as $(g_1, g_2, g, h, y_1, y_2, y, R_1, R_2, R, S)$ and π as $(R_1, R_2, R, S, z_1, z_2)$, and verifies that $g_1^{z_1} = R_1 y_1^c$ and $g_2^{z_2} = R_2 y_2^c$ and $g^{z_1} h^{z_2} = RS y^c$.

This NIP is extractable (so sound). Indeed, we can build the following extrac-tor: runs the prover and simulates the random oracle to the prover in order to obtain a valid transcript $(R_1, R_2, R, S, z_1, z_2)$ for a challenge c, then rewinds the prover to the challenge step in order to obtain a second valid transcript $(R_1, R_2, R, S, z_1', z_2')$ having the same commitments (R_1, R_2, R, S) for another challenge c' outputted by the random oracle (tries again if the prover fails). The witness (x_1, x_2) can be efficiently extracted from these values by computing $(x_1, x_2) = ((z_1 - z_1')/(c - c')^{-1}, (z_2 - z_2')(c - c')^{-1})$.

This NIP is also zero-knowledge. Indeed, we can build the follow-ing simulator: picks $c, z_1, z_2 \xleftarrow{\$} \mathbb{Z}_p^*$ and $S \xleftarrow{\$} \mathbb{G}$, and computes $R_1 = g_1^{z_1} y_1^{-c}$ and $R_2 = g_2^{z_2} y_2^{-c}$ and $R = g^{z_1} h^{z_2} S^{-1} y^{-c}$. Set c as the hash of $(g_1, g_2, g, h, y_1, y_2, y, R_1, R_2, R, S)$ and returns the transcript $(R_1, R_2, R, S, z_1, z_2)$.

5.4 Implementation

We have extended our Rust implementation of CC2 by adding the algorithms ProveGame and VerifyGame in order to analyse the practicality of VCC. The Table 3 provides an overview of an average computation time, in milliseconds, of the algorithms ProveGame and VerifyGame of the scheme VCC, and the Table 4 describes an average size, in kilobytes, of the proof of the correct game. Our measurements are based on 1000 runs and depend on the number of players: 3, 4, and 5. Again, we did not evaluate efficiency on real games, but on randomly generated maps and clues. Since clues of the form "one of two types" are less common than clues of the form "so many cells away from something", we decide to use $\lfloor n/2 \rfloor$ clues of the first type and $\lceil n/2 \rceil$ clues of the second type, where n is the number of players.

The proof that the game is correct takes less than 50 milliseconds and must be done for the 180 game setups by the game editor. It will therefore take less than 9 seconds for the whole Cryptid game, bearing in mind that this operation is only performed once, a priori, before the game distribution. The verification of the game takes also less than 50 milliseconds. This operation must be performed by each player, we remind the reader that it is only done once before the start of the game.

The size of the proof of each game setup is less than 50 kilobytes, knowing that these proofs must be downloaded at the same time as the public clue keys when the game is acquired. Downloading the full game will therefore require less than $180 + 180 \times 50 = 9180$ kilobytes of storage.

Table 3. Running time in milliseconds for our verifiable cryptographic cryptid scheme. The results are an average over 1000 executions.

Scheme	VCC		
Number of player	3	4	5
ProveGame	38.88	45.34	46.18
VerifyGame	28.94	31.15	35.11

Table 4. Size in kilobytes for our verifiable cryptographic cryptid scheme. The results are an average over 1000 executions.

Scheme	VCC		
Number of player	3	4	5
ρ	34.05	39.52	44.99

6   Conclusion

We have proposed cryptographic protocols to prevent cheating in the game Cryptid. We have formally defined and proved two security properties for these protocols: soundness and confidentiality. We give an implementation to show that they can be used in a practical context. We have also extended one of these protocols to allow the game designer to prove that the clues are well formed and converge on at least one cell of the map.

However, the cryptid game has a feature that we did not consider. If the players get impatient and all agree, they can consult a booklet to get an extra clue for their game. This clue does not have the same structure as the player's clues; for instance, the general clue might be "there is no clue indicating that the type of the cryptid cell is one of two given types". It would be interesting to add a system for committing these clues, so that if the players agree, they can open these commitments. It would then be necessary for the game designer to prove that these hidden clues are also well formed and consistent with the other clues and the map. We leave the design of a protocol that takes these general clues and the difficult mode (described in Sect. 2) into account as future works.

Acknowledgments. This study was supported by the ANR France 2030 project "CyberINSA" (ANR-23-CMAS-0019), the ANR France 2030 project "TracIA" (22-PESN-0006), the ANR project MobiS5 (ANR-18-CE39-0019), the ANR project SEVERITAS (ANR-20-CE39-0009) and the ANR Project PRIVA-SIQ (ANR-23-CE39-0008).

References

1. Barnett, A., Smart, N.P.: Mental poker revisited. In: Paterson, K.G. (ed.) Cryptography and Coding 2003. LNCS, vol. 2898, pp. 370–383. Springer, Heidelberg (2003). https://doi.org/10.1007/978-3-540-40974-8_29
2. Bella, R., Bultel, X., Chevalier, C., Lafourcade, P., Olivier-Anclin, C.: Practical construction for secure trick-taking games even with cards set aside. In: FC2023-Twenty-Seventh International Conference Financial Cryptography and Data Security (2023)
3. Blum, M., Feldman, P., Micali, S.: Non-interactive zero-knowledge and its applications. In: Proceedings of the Twentieth Annual ACM Symposium on Theory of Computing, STOC '88, pp. 103–112. Association for Computing Machinery, New York, NY, USA (1988). https://doi.org/10.1145/62212.62222
4. Boneh, D.: The decision Diffie-Hellman problem. In: Buhler, J.P. (ed.) ANTS 1998. LNCS, vol. 1423, pp. 48–63. Springer, Heidelberg (1998). https://doi.org/10.1007/BFb0054851
5. Brands, S.A.: An efficient off-line electronic cash system based on the representation problem (1993)
6. Bultel, X., Jojon, C., Lafourcade, P.: Cryptographic cryptid protocols: how to play cryptid with cheaters (full version and implementation) (2024). https://github.com/charlene-j/cryptidscheme
7. Bultel, X., Lafourcade, P.: Secure trick-taking game protocols: how to play online spades with cheaters. In: Goldberg, I., Moore, T. (eds.) Financial Cryptography and Data Security, pp. 265–281. Springer, Cham (2019). https://doi.org/10.1007/978-3-030-32101-7_17
8. Camenisch, J., Shoup, V.: Practical verifiable encryption and decryption of discrete logarithms. In: Boneh, D. (ed.) CRYPTO 2003. LNCS, vol. 2729, pp. 126–144. Springer, Heidelberg (2003). https://doi.org/10.1007/978-3-540-45146-4_8

9. Canard, S., Pointcheval, D., Sanders, O., Traoré, J.: Divisible e-cash made practical. In: Katz, J. (ed.) PKC 2015. LNCS, vol. 9020, pp. 77–100. Springer, Heidelberg (2015). https://doi.org/10.1007/978-3-662-46447-2_4

10. Chaum, D., Pedersen, T.P.: Wallet databases with observers. In: Brickell, E.F. (ed.) CRYPTO 1992. LNCS, vol. 740, pp. 89–105. Springer, Heidelberg (1993). https://doi.org/10.1007/3-540-48071-4_7

11. Cortier, V., Gaudry, P., Glondu, S.: Belenios: a simple private and verifiable electronic voting system. In: Guttman, J.D., Landwehr, C.E., Meseguer, J., Pavlovic, D. (eds.) Foundations of Security, Protocols, and Equational Reasoning. LNCS, vol. 11565, pp. 214–238. Springer, Cham (2019). https://doi.org/10.1007/978-3-030-19052-1_14

12. Cramer, R., Damgård, I., Schoenmakers, B.: Proofs of partial knowledge and simplified design of witness hiding protocols. In: Desmedt, Y.G. (ed.) CRYPTO 1994. LNCS, vol. 839, pp. 174–187. Springer, Heidelberg (1994). https://doi.org/10.1007/3-540-48658-5_19

13. Evans, D., Kolesnikov, V., Rosulek, M.: A Pragmatic Introduction to Secure Multi-Party Computation, vol. 2, issue 2–3, pp. 70–246. Foundations and Trends®in Privacy and Security (2018). https://doi.org/10.1561/3300000019

14. Fiat, A., Shamir, A.: How to prove yourself: practical solutions to identification and signature problems. In: Odlyzko, A.M. (ed.) CRYPTO 1986. LNCS, vol. 263, pp. 186–194. Springer, Heidelberg (1987). https://doi.org/10.1007/3-540-47721-7_12

15. Giacomelli, I., Madsen, J., Orlandi, C.: ZKBoo: faster zero-knowledge for Boolean circuits. In: 25th USENIX Security Symposium (USENIX Security 16), pp. 1069–1083. USENIX Association, Austin, TX (2016). https://www.usenix.org/conference/usenixsecurity16/technical-sessions/presentation/giacomelli

16. Golle, P.: Dealing cards in poker games. In: International Conference on Information Technology: Coding and Computing (ITCC'05) - Volume II, vol. 1, pp. 506–511 (2005).https://doi.org/10.1109/ITCC.2005.119

17. Lindell, Y.: How to simulate it – a tutorial on the simulation proof technique. In: Tutorials on the Foundations of Cryptography Dedicated to Oded Goldreich. ISC, pp. 277–346. Springer, Cham (2017). https://doi.org/10.1007/978-3-319-57048-8_6

18. Lovecruft, I.A., de Valence, H.: curve25519_dalek. https://docs.rs/curve25519-dalek/latest/curve25519_dalek/

19. Schindelhauer, C.: A Toolbox for Mental Card Games. Medizinische Universität Lübeck. (1998)

20. Shamir, A., Rivest, R.L., Adleman, L.M.: Mental poker. In: Klarner, D.A. (ed.) The Mathematical Gardner. Springer, US, Boston, MA (1981). https://doi.org/10.1007/978-1-4684-6686-7_5

21. Shoup, V.: Sequences of games: a tool for taming complexity in security proofs. Cryptology ePrint Archive, Paper 2004/332 (2004). https://eprint.iacr.org/2004/332

22. Stamer, H.: Efficient electronic gambling: an extended implementation of the toolbox for mental card games. In: Western European Workshop on Research in Cryptology (2005). https://api.semanticscholar.org/CorpusID:976197

MaSTer: Maliciously Secure Truncation for Replicated Secret Sharing Without Pre-processing

Martin Zbudila$^{(\boxtimes)}$, Erik Pohle , Aysajan Abidin , and Bart Preneel

COSIC, KU Leuven, Leuven, Belgium
martin.zbudila@esat.kuleuven.be

Abstract. Secure multi-party computation (MPC) in a three-party, honest majority scenario is currently the state-of-the-art for running machine learning algorithms in a privacy-preserving manner. For efficiency reasons, fixed-point arithmetic is widely used to approximate computation over decimal numbers. After multiplication in fixed-point arithmetic, truncation is required to keep the result's precision. In this paper, we present an efficient three-party truncation protocol secure in the presence of an active adversary without pre-processing and improve on the current state-of-the-art in MPC over rings using replicated secret sharing (RSS). By adding an efficient consistency check, we lift the efficient but only passively secure three-party truncation protocol from the ABY3 framework by Mohassel and Rindal into the malicious setting without pre-processed data. Our benchmark indicates performance improvements of an order of magnitude in the offline phase for a single batch training. Finally, we apply our protocol to a real-world application for diagnostic prediction based on publicly available ECG heartbeat data. We achieve an improvement by a factor of two in the total throughput for both LAN and WAN settings.

Keywords: truncation · fixed-point arithmetic · replicated secret sharing · privacy-preserving machine learning

1 Introduction

The advancements in artificial intelligence (AI) and machine learning (ML) have brought about significant changes, ranging from predictive analytics to personalised recommendations, reshaping our interaction with the digital world. Because these technologies rely on substantial amounts of potentially sensitive data, ensuring data privacy has become a critical concern during the training of AI/ML models and the execution of AI/ML model inference. This has prompted the need for efficient privacy-enhancing tools to address these privacy challenges. Secure multi-party computation (MPC), a cryptographic technique that enables multiple distrustful parties to collaborate on computations without

© The Author(s), under exclusive license to Springer Nature Singapore Pte Ltd. 2025
M. Kohlweiss et al. (Eds.): CANS 2024, LNCS 14905, pp. 49–73, 2025.
https://doi.org/10.1007/978-981-97-8013-6_3

exposing their input data, stands out as a promising privacy-enhancing solution in the fast evolving field of ML. As long as the adversary corresponds to the threat model for the MPC protocol, data privacy can be ensured. Indeed, privacy-preserving ML (or PPML) based on MPC has been an active area of research in recent years, see for example [11,23,28,29,31,35] and the references therein. Note that in MPC-based PPML, the data owners do not necessarily participate in the computation. There are scenarios where the computing parties are independent of the data owners, allowing the incorporation of data from an arbitrary number of data owners. The state-of-the-art in MPC-based PPML in the three-party setting considers security in an honest majority setting.

One of the key components for high-performance evaluation of PPML algorithms over MPC is the efficient computation on secret-shared decimal numbers. Since accurate floating point arithmetic is expensive, an approximation, namely fixed-point arithmetic, is employed. Here, one encodes a decimal number with fixed precision as an integer of size large enough to accommodate the expected range. Multiplication of two fixed-point integers doubles the length of the fractional part and thus requires efficient truncation afterwards to retain the original precision. Since computation over the ring $\mathbb{Z}_{2^\ell}$, $\ell \geq 1$ allows for efficient utilisation of native instructions in modern processors, secret sharing over $\mathbb{Z}_{2^\ell}$ enables efficient MPC where one considers the fixed-point integers as ring elements.

Truncation is an essential part when working with fixed-point arithmetic. Since it allows retaining the original precision by discarding the least significant bits, one does not need to choose a large ring to accommodate the doubling of the length of the fractional part, allowing us to limit the ring size. SecureML [29] first proposed a technique allowing *probabilistic* truncation by local operations on the shares in a two-party setting in semi-honest security. Here, "probabilistic" means that the value reconstructed from the truncated shares is offset by at most 1 from the correct value with high probability.

The current state-of-the-art three-party maliciously secure truncation is the ABY3 protocol by Mohassel and Rindal [28], adopted by follow-up works such as the Falcon protocol [35]. In the online phase, this truncation requires only one round of communication and one ring element to be sent per party. The pre-processing phase for truncation involves a costly evaluation of subtraction circuits, resulting in lower combined throughput. However, in the context of real-time applications such as diagnostic disease prediction based on sensitive data (cf. Sect. 7), the bottleneck caused by the pre-processing phase can be more pronounced. Real-time users would require immediate responses and queries with batches of small sizes. Such real-time application scenarios underscore the inefficiency of the offline phase and call for the elimination of the pre-processing.

In this paper, we design and implement a replicated secret sharing (RSS) based protocol that computes the truncation of fixed-point numbers without pre-processing securely in the presence of one malicious adversary in the three-party setting. Our protocol achieves an overall low cost of one amortised round of communication and one ring element sent per party. Our protocol augments the truncation method from SecureML [29] and is inspired by its extension to a three-party RSS environment in the semi-honest setting from the ABY3 framework [28]. We benchmark our proposal in MP-SPDZ [22] and compare its performance with that of ABY3 [28]. We also report on the PPML training of MNIST data in the SecureML (3-layer dense) and LeNet-5 network architectures and the training of the CIFAR-10 dataset on the AlexNet architecture.

Contributions. We make the following contributions:

- We propose a novel maliciously secure truncation protocol designed specifically for replicated secret-sharing (RSS) for three parties. Our secure truncation protocol builds upon the SecureML [29] probabilistic truncation method and its subsequent extension to a three-party RSS environment in the semi-honest setting using the ABY3 framework [28]. Unlike other truncation protocols for malicious security, our truncation protocol does not require pre-processing.
- We provide detailed error analysis on the errors occurring in the SecureML truncation, expanding on the correctness analysis provided by [29, Theorem 1]. We further provide a thorough security analysis of our proposed protocol and prove its security against a static malicious adversary with abort. Our protocol gives the adversary a bit more power which is appropriately captured in the functionality. We show that a model evaluated with sufficiently high fixed-point precision is robust to this adversarial influence.
- To assess the practical performance of our protocol, we conduct benchmarking experiments using the MP-SPDZ [22] framework and compare the efficiency of our truncation protocol against the state-of-the-art ABY3 malicious truncation. We make our implementation public on GitHub[1]. By eliminating the pre-processing phase for truncation due to our protocol, the execution time of the offline phase for training one epoch is improved by up to an order of magnitude. Similarly, by removing the pre-processing phase of the truncation protocol, the total communication of the offline phase for training is lowered by an order of magnitude.
- To illustrate the practical relevance of our truncation protocol, we present an application in the context of privacy-preserving neural network inference for the classification of ECG heartbeat signals. Our neural network identifies the occurrence of arrhythmia in a heartbeat signal, and classifies the signal into one of five classes, in accordance to the AAMI EC57 standard, as described by Kachuee et al. [21]. We achieve an accuracy of 95.9%. We improve the total running time, and thus the overall throughput by up to a factor of three in both LAN and WAN settings.

The remainder of the paper is organised as follows. After an overview of the related works in Sect. 2, we introduce the preliminary background necessary to understand the paper in Sect. 3. Section 4 presents our maliciously secure three-party truncation protocol. We prove the security of the protocol in the UC framework in Sect. 5. We benchmark our protocol in the MP-SPDZ [22]

---

[1] https://github.com/KULeuven-COSIC/master-truncation.

framework and compare it to ABY3 malicious truncation in Sect. 6. We discuss a concrete use-case for PPML in Sect. 7 and conclude the paper in Sect. 8.

2 Related Work

Machine learning operations involve arithmetic on decimal numbers expressed in a fixed-point representation to achieve maximal efficiency in MPC. Therefore, truncation is a crucial component when designing an MPC framework for machine learning. Currently, the most efficient protocols for evaluating ML models are based on three-party replicated secret sharing in the semi-honest security setting. For practical deployments, semi-honest security might not be sufficient as a security guarantee, however, only a few works focus on malicious security.

Regarding truncation in MPC over rings, we distinguish between relatively efficient approaches achieving probabilistic truncation and approaches focusing on a faithful truncation result that are much more heavy in communication. A faithful, sometimes called precise truncation, denotes a truncation protocol that outputs a secret-sharing of an arithmetic right shift of the value with probability 1. Some prior works achieving faithful truncation allow an error of ± 1 on the least significant bit (LSB), which we will refer to as "small". On the other hand, probabilistic truncation fails to output a correct truncation result (accounting for the small error) with a non-zero probability, we will call such error "big".

The probabilistic approaches follow the line of work proposed by Catrina et al. [9], with ABY3 [28] formalising the approach for three-party RSS admitting one malicious adversary. Multiple follow-up works adapted these truncation protocols, including Astra [10] and Falcon [35]. Trident [11] builds on the approach of ABY3 by proposing optimisations to the pre-processing phase. Blaze [31] and SWIFT [23] similarly adopt the optimisations proposed by Trident [11] elevating the security to guaranteed output delivery (GOD) in both the three and four-party settings. Taking a different approach to the pre-processing phase, Escudero et al. [15] propose a protocol inspired by the online phase of ABY3 that removes the big error by handling overflow using edaBits (extended daBits [33]). These pre-processed shared bits help with arithmetic-to-Boolean conversions between sharings and are directly applicable to comparison and truncation protocols, compatible with any corruption setting.

Our protocol is also designed for three-party RSS in a malicious setting. However, we take a different approach to achieve malicious security compared to the above-mentioned works. Instead, our protocol utilises the semi-honest three-party truncation that was proposed by the ABY3 framework.

Following the line of work of edaBits [15], Baccarini et al. [3] propose an improved generation of these pre-processed bits, designing multiple protocols for n-party RSS. However, while their pre-processing phase for the truncation triples improves on the approach of Escudero et al., they achieve probabilistic truncation with a constant number of rounds in the semi-honest setting with high communication cost (see Table 1). Finally, Piranha [36] and Fantastic Four [14] build a truncation protocol on a combination of SWIFT [23] and the work of

Dalskov et al. [13]. Similar to SWIFT, Fantastic Four [14] also achieves malicious security with GOD in the four-party setting.

In the two-party scenario, SecureML [29] proposed a local probabilistic truncation, requiring no communication, with similar error probabilities as in the three-party case. Subsequently, a line of works focusing on faithful truncation emerged, with the most recent ones including Cryptflow2 [32] or the work of Zou et al. [39]. Furthermore, Cheetah [20] reduces the communication cost compared to the previous works at the cost of admitting the small error. Bicoptor 2.0 [38] modifies the SecureML truncation protocol to obtain a faithful truncation. However, their resulting shares are in a smaller ring and thus would require an additional modulo switch protocol for compatibility with subsequent protocols in the circuit. Our protocol directly uses the SecureML truncation, in combination with the three-party semi-honest protocol from ABY3 [28], achieving security with abort.

A different approach for truncation uses function secret sharing (FSS) [18, 19] in a 2-online-party computation model admitting a semi-honest adversary. This approach relies on a trusted third party (dealer) that pre-computes and distributes large function shares (keys), in order to avoid an expensive offline phase. For a single truncation, $\mathcal{O}(\ell)$ AES calls are required in the online phase, while the communication cost is similar to the RSS-based schemes, with ℓ bits communicated in one round. Here ℓ denotes the size of the ring $\mathbb{Z}_{2^\ell}$, and k denotes the fixed-point precision.

Hence, to the best of our knowledge, the current state-of-the-art in truncation protocols for three-party RSS with malicious security are protocols based on the proposal of ABY3. While many follow-up works adapt the ABY3 truncation and its optimisations for pre-processing, the online phase remains identical. Nevertheless, creating the required pre-processed truncation triples remains a major bottleneck. The line of works of [11,23,31] try to minimise the communication cost in the offline phase by incorporating protocols with lower offline cost but increasing the communication cost in the online phase. We give an overview of the communication cost, round complexity, and security model of the most relevant works for truncation and our protocol in Table 1.

3   Preliminaries

In this section, we explain our security model, then introduce fixed-point arithmetic and the notation used throughout the paper. Later, we describe three-party replicated secret sharing for which our truncation is designed, and revisit the two main building blocks of our protocol, the two-party probabilistic truncation of SecureML [29], and the three-party truncation of ABY3 [28].

3.1   Security Setting

We consider a setting consisting of three servers, $P = \{P_1, P_2, P_3\}$, with pairwise secure, authenticated channels. We work in the honest majority setting, i.e., tolerating up to one corrupted party. In this paper, we consider security with abort

Table 1. Semi-honest and maliciously secure truncation protocols in the two and three-party setting over a ring $\mathbb{Z}_{2^\ell}$. The communication is in bits per party, κ is a security parameter and k denotes the fixed-point precision.

	Parties	Comm.	Rounds	Result	Security
SecureML [29]	2	-	-	Probabilistic	Semi-honest
Cryptflow2 [32]	2	$\kappa\ell + \kappa k + \kappa + \ell$	$\lceil log(\ell) \rceil + 1$	Faithful	Semi-honest
Cheetah [20]	2	13ℓ	$\lceil log(\ell) \rceil$	Faithful	Semi-honest
Zou et al. [39]	2	$\kappa\ell + \kappa + \ell + m^*$	$\lceil log(\ell) \rceil + 1$	Faithful	Semi-honest
Llama [19]	2	$\ell + k(\kappa + \ell + 2) + \kappa + \ell$	2	Faithful	Semi-honest
Sigma [18]	2	$\mathcal{O}(\kappa\ell)$	3	Faithful	Semi-honest
Baccarini et al. [3]	n	$2\ell^2 - 3\ell - 2$	2	Probabilistic	Semi-honest
Dalskov et al. [13]	2	ℓ	1	Probabilistic	Semi-honest
	3	2ℓ	2	Probabilistic	Semi-honest
edaBits [15]	n	$\mathcal{O}(\ell \cdot log(\ell))$	$\mathcal{O}(log(\ell))$	Probabilistic	Malicious
SWIFT [23]	3	13ℓ	2	Probabilistic	Malicious
ABY3 [28]	3	ℓ	1	Probabilistic	Semi-honest
	n	$20(2\ell - k) + 2\ell$	$\mathcal{O}(\ell)$	Probabilistic	Malicious
MaSTer	3	ℓ	1	Probabilistic	Malicious

$^*m \in [0, 2\kappa\lceil log\lceil \frac{k-1}{4} \rceil \rceil)$

against one malicious static adversary and prove the security of our protocol in the UC framework [7].

3.2   Fixed-Point Arithmetic

Many of the currently most efficient MPC frameworks for privacy-preserving machine learning are based on integer arithmetic in a ring $\mathbb{Z}_{2^\ell}$, e.g., [23,35,36], or a field $\mathbb{F}_p$ [2]. For efficiency, fixed-point arithmetic is adopted to run ML models. A real number $\tilde{x} \in \mathbb{R}$ is transformed to a fixed-point approximation x by setting $x = \lfloor \tilde{x} \cdot 2^k \rfloor \in \mathbb{Z}$, where k denotes the fixed precision and $\lfloor \cdot \rfloor$ denotes the floor function. After multiplication, the precision is doubled, i.e., let $x, y \in \mathbb{Z}$ be fixed-point encodings with precision k, then $w = x \cdot y$ has a precision of $2k$, and hence we need to truncate to preserve the fixed-point arithmetic. Truncation denotes a division by 2^k, or equivalently a logical right shift by k bits.

3.3   Notation

Given a fixed-point encoded secret $x \in (-2^{\ell_x}, 2^{\ell_x})$ with precision k, where ℓ_x denotes the length of the input x and $k < \ell_x < \ell - 1$, we define z to be the encoding in the ring $\mathbb{Z}_{2^\ell}$.

Definition 1 (Encoding of x). *Let x be an integer, the encoding z of x in $\mathbb{Z}_{2^\ell}$ is $z = x$, if $x \geq 0$, and $z = 2^\ell - |x|$, if $x < 0$.*

We use the notation $[\![z]\!]$ to denote a 2-out-of-3 replicated secret sharing (RSS), where $[\![z]\!] = (s_1, s_2, s_3)$, such that $s_1 + s_2 + s_3 = z$. We use $[\![z]\!]_i = (s_i, s_{i+1})$ for $1 \leq i \leq 3$, where $P_0 = P_3$, $P_1 = P_4$ etc., to denote the shares of individual parties. Further, we use $\langle z \rangle$ to denote a 2-out-of-2 additive sharing of z, i.e., $\langle z \rangle_1 + \langle z \rangle_2 = z$ and $\langle z \rangle_i$ denotes the share of party i. Similarly, we use $[z]$ to denote a 3-out-of-3 additive sharing of z. Moreover, we use the notation $[z]^B$ to denote a binary sharing of z, i.e., $z = \bigoplus_{i=1}^{3}[z]_i^B$. Further, $\mathsf{rshift}(z, k)$ denotes logical right shift of z by k bits, and $\lfloor z \rfloor$ denotes probabilistic truncation of SecureML [29] (see Sect. 3.5). We use the notation $\leftarrow_\$ A$ to denote uniformly random sampling from a finite set A. More specifically, $r \leftarrow_{\$ i,j} \mathbb{Z}_{2^\ell}$ denotes a uniformly random sampling of $r \in \mathbb{Z}_{2^\ell}$ from shared randomness between parties i and j (see Fig. 1). In the context of pseudo-random functions (PRFs), we use κ to denote the security parameter. We write $\leftarrow$ to denote assignment from probabilistic algorithms and $:=$ for deterministic assignment. Finally, we use the notation $\mathbb{E}[X]$ to denote the expected value of a random variable X.

Functionality $\mathcal{F}_{\mathsf{cr}}$

Let $F : \{0,1\}^\kappa \times \{0,1\}^\kappa \mapsto \mathbb{Z}_{2^\ell}$ be a keyed pseudo-random function. The functionality generates correlated randomness between a pair (P_i, P_j)

Setup The adversary sends a key $k_{\mathcal{A}}$ and the functionality samples $k \leftarrow_\$ \{0,1\}^\kappa$ uniformly at random and sends $F_{k_{\mathcal{A}}}(0) \oplus k$ to P_i and P_j.
Sample On input cnt of P_i and P_j, the functionality computes $r := F_k(cnt)$ and sends r to P_i and P_j.

Fig. 1. Functionality $\mathcal{F}_{\mathsf{cr}}$.

3.4   Three-Party Replicated Secret Sharing

In this work, we use a 3-party replicated secret sharing scheme, meaning an additive secret sharing, so any two parties can reconstruct the secret as explained in Sect. 3.3. Below, we briefly describe arithmetic operations using RSS. For more details, we refer the reader to Araki et al. [1] for the semi-honest setting and to Furukawa et al. [16] for the malicious setting.

Let $a, b \in \mathbb{Z}_{2^\ell}$ be public constants. Let $[\![x]\!] = (x_1, x_2, x_3)$ and $[\![y]\!] = (y_1, y_2, y_3)$.

Linear operations. $a \cdot [\![x]\!] + b = (ax_1 + b, ax_2, ax_3)$.
Addition of two secret values. $[\![x + y]\!] = (x_1 + y_1, x_2 + y_2, x_3 + y_3)$.
Multiplication of two secret values. $[\![z]\!] = [\![x]\!] \cdot [\![y]\!]$ is obtained by

$$s_i := x_i y_i + x_i y_{i+1} + x_{i+1} y_i + \alpha_i, \qquad \text{for } i \in \{1,2,3\},$$

where $\alpha_1 + \alpha_2 + \alpha_3 = 0$, i.e., α_i is a random share of zero that can be obtained locally by a call to a pseudo-random function (PRF) with pre-shared keys (see Fig. 2). Note that party i can obtain s_i locally. To transfer the 3-out-of-3 sharing of xy to RSS, party i sends s_i to P_{i-1}. In the presence of a malicious adversary, the multiplication result is checked for correctness in a post-processing phase as described by Furukawa et al. [16]. The protocol for generating randomness α_i is based on [16, Protocol 2.5] elevated to a ring setting as in [28]. We provide more details in the full paper [37].

Protocol Π_{cr0}

Let $F : \{0,1\}^\kappa \times \{0,1\}^\kappa \mapsto \mathbb{Z}_{2^\ell}$ be a keyed pseudo-random function.

Setup Each party P_i samples a key $k_i \leftarrow\!\!\$ \{0,1\}^n$ uniformly at random. Then, P_i sends k_i to P_{i+1} and thus obtains k_{i-1}.

Sample Upon input cnt, P_i locally computes $F_{k_i}(cnt) - F_{k_{i-1}}(cnt)$ and outputs the result of the PRF as random element in $\mathbb{Z}_{2^\ell}$.

Fig. 2. The protocol Π_{cr0}.

3.5 Two-Party Probabilistic Truncation

The main building block of our protocol relies on the two-party semi-honest probabilistic truncation proposed by SecureML [29]. The authors observe that the following local operations on a two-party additive sharing of z amount to a truncation by k bits with an error limited to the least significant bit (LSB) with a large probability. If party P_1 computes $\langle \lfloor z \rfloor \rangle_1 := \mathsf{rshift}(\langle z \rangle_1, k)$ and party P_2 computes $\langle \lfloor z \rfloor \rangle_2 := 2^\ell - \mathsf{rshift}(2^\ell - \langle z \rangle_2, k)$ locally, then the result is a sharing of $\lfloor x \rfloor = \mathsf{trc}(x) \pm 1$ with probability $1 - 2^{\ell_x + 1 - \ell}$ (see [29, Theorem 1]), where $\mathsf{trc}(x)$ is defined in Definition 2. As previously mentioned, we will refer to the error of ± 1 as a small error. However, with probability of $2^{\ell_x + 1 - \ell}$ an error of magnitude $2^{\ell - k}$ can occur. Here k denotes the fixed-point precision. We will refer to this error as large/big. We provide a thorough analysis of the errors in Theorem 1, expanding on the results presented in SecureML [29]. For the proof we refer the reader to the full paper [37].

Definition 2 (Truncation). *Let $x \in \mathbb{Z}$ be a fixed point encoding of $\tilde{x} \in \mathbb{R}$, with fixed-point precision of k bits, as described in Sect. 3.2. Then, we can write $x = x_1 2^k + x_2$, with $x_2 \in [0, 2^k)$. We define the truncation of x as $\mathsf{trc}(x) = x_1$.*

Theorem 1 (SecureML truncation error). *Let $R \in [0, 2^\ell)$, and let z be the encoding of x (cf. Definition 1). We decompose $x = x_1 2^k + x_2$ with $0 \le x_1 < 2^{\ell - k}$,*

$0 \leq x_2 < 2^k$, and $R = R_1 2^k + R_2$ with $0 \leq R_1 < 2^{\ell-k}$, $0 \leq R_2 < 2^k$. Then, $\mathsf{rshift}(z+R,k) + 2^\ell - \mathsf{rshift}(R,k) = \mathsf{trc}(x) + c_1 + c_2 2^{\ell-k}$, where

$$c_1 = \begin{cases} 1 & \text{if } x \geq 0 \wedge x_2 + R_2 \geq 2^k \\ -1 & \text{if } x < 0 \wedge |x_2| > R_2 \\ 0 & \text{else} \end{cases} , c_2 = \begin{cases} 1 & \text{if } x < 0 \wedge x_1 + R_1 \geq 2^{\ell-k} \\ -1 & \text{if } x \geq 0 \wedge |x_1| > R_1 \\ 0 & \text{else} \end{cases} .$$

Furthermore, note that when $R \in [2^{\ell_x}, 2^\ell - 2^{\ell_x})$, $c_2 = 0$ *for all such* R. *The probability of a uniformly random* R *being in this range is* $1 - 2^{\ell_x+1-\ell}$. *Thus, with probability* $1 - 2^{\ell_x+1-\ell}$, $\mathsf{rshift}(z+R,k) + 2^\ell - \mathsf{rshift}(R,k) = \mathsf{trc}(x) + c_1$.

The truncation error c_1 in Theorem 1 is therefore formally given by the following function $e_k(z,k)$ in Definition 3.

Definition 3 (SecureML small truncation error). *Let* z *be the encoding of* x *(see Definition 1) and* $0 \leq R < 2^\ell$. *The truncation error* $e_k(z,k)$ *when truncating* z *by* k *bits having randomness* R *in the shares (i.e.* $\langle z \rangle = (z+R, -R)$), *is defined as*

$$e_k(z,R) = \begin{cases} 1 & \text{if } z < 2^{\ell-1} \wedge (z \mod 2^k) + (R \mod 2^k) \geq 2^k \\ -1 & \text{if } z > 2^{\ell-1} \wedge (R \mod 2^k) < (2^\ell - z \mod 2^k) . \\ 0 & \text{else} \end{cases}$$

3.6 Three-Party Probabilistic Truncation

ABY3 [28] introduces two truncation methods for three-party RSS schemes. The authors note that the two-party local truncation of SecureML [29] fails when naively extended to three parties. Nevertheless, assuming semi-honest security and at most one corrupted party, two parties can transform a RSS sharing $[\![z]\!]$ to a 2-out-of-2 sharing $\langle z \rangle$, perform the SecureML truncation with local operations and re-share the result to obtain shares of $[\![\lfloor z \rfloor]\!]$. This extended truncation Π_{trunc1} is formally described in [28, Fig. 2] and is another building block of our protocol. We use this protocol combined with the SecureML truncation to achieve a secure truncation protocol against a malicious adversary, as described in Sect. 4.

The approach described above on its own is not secure in the presence of a malicious adversary. ABY3, therefore, proposes another technique to achieve a maliciously secure truncation based on the line of works started by [9]. The protocol requires a pre-processed pair of shares of a random $r \in \mathbb{Z}_{2^\ell}$, $[\![r]\!]$ and $[\![\lfloor r \rfloor]\!]$, from which the parties can compute $[\![z]\!] = [\![r]\!] + \lfloor(z-r)\rfloor$. The online phase consists of a single round where ℓ bits are sent to reveal $z-r$. In the offline phase, the parties generate random Boolean shares $[r]^B \in \mathbb{Z}_2^\ell$ in replicated secret sharing form and locally compute the k-bit truncation $[r']^B \in \mathbb{Z}_2^\ell$ on the Boolean shares. To convert the shares into arithmetic shares in $\mathbb{Z}_{2^\ell}$, ABY3 proposes that the parties compute two subtraction circuits, one to obtain shares of r and one for r', to emulate $\mathbb{Z}_{2^\ell}$ arithmetic on the Boolean shares using a protocol of Furukawa et al. [16]. Note that this entails evaluating two subtraction circuits per truncation triple. The line of works started by Trident [11] optimises this approach by applying conversion of a binary to arithmetic sharing and then trivially obtaining the difference. The latest work SWIFT [23] following this approach achieves the cost of twelve ring elements sent over one round in the offline phase with the same online cost as ABY3.

4   MaSTer

When we investigate the suitability of the semi-honest ABY3 truncation (Π_{trunc1}, see Sect. 3.6) in the malicious setting, the only leverage the adversary has is corrupting P_1 and modifying the result share of $\lfloor z \rfloor$ when re-sharing. All other operations are local. Consequently, in order to employ Π_{trunc1}, we only need to check if the re-sharing was done correctly. Furthermore, parties P_2 and P_3 have sufficient information about z due to the RSS. In an abstract sense, we run Π_{trunc1} among all three parties and the two-party SecureML truncation protocol among P_2 and P_3 in parallel. We, therefore, obtain *unchecked* RSS shares $[\![\lfloor z \rfloor]\!]$ of the result for all parties. We then use the shares $\langle \lfloor z \rfloor \rangle$ of P_2 and P_3 to verify the correctness of the RSS shares that were dealt by P_1. This is illustrated in Fig. 3. A corrupt P_1 cannot modify $[\![\lfloor z \rfloor]\!]$ without being detected by P_2 and P_3 while corrupt P_2/P_3 cannot influence the creation of $[\![\lfloor z \rfloor]\!]$. Note that an adversary controlling P_2/P_3 can force an abort by wrongfully claiming that P_1 modified the result shares.

We can check the consistency of the RSS shares by checking the difference of $[\![\lfloor z \rfloor]\!]$ and $\langle \lfloor z \rfloor \rangle$. However, due to the probabilistic error in the LSB of the truncation protocols, the difference may not be zero even with correctly created shares. We analyse the error and show that for an honest execution, the difference is ± 1 with high probability (see Sect. 4.3).

Note that the correctness of the truncation (disregarding malicious influence) relies on the correctness of Π_{trunc1}, which is an extension of SecureML, and thus requires the input z to be a valid encoding of $x \in (-2^{\ell_x}, 2^{\ell_x})$ (see Definition 1) to produce a correct truncation $\lfloor z \rfloor$. Hence, it is challenging to use MaSTer to generate pre-processed random truncations $(r, \lfloor r \rfloor)$, where $r \leftarrow_\$ \mathbb{Z}_{2^\ell}$, used in other maliciously secure truncation protocols such as [9,11,23,28]. As in Π_{trunc1}, we require $\ell_x < \ell - 1$.

4.1   Protocol

We employ a similar approach as Furukawa et al. [16] does for multiplication, with an optimistic execution of a semi-honest protocol in the online phase and a check in the post-processing phase (cf. Sect. 3.4). The protocol (see Fig. 4) hence consists of two phases. The first phase is analogous to the semi-honest truncation with re-sharing afterwards and results in *unchecked* shares of the truncated multiplication result in RSS. A cheating P_1 must send $s_2' + \Delta$ in the first round, where Δ is an additive error. In order to detect this potential malicious behaviour in the first phase, we introduce a second phase where parties P_2 and

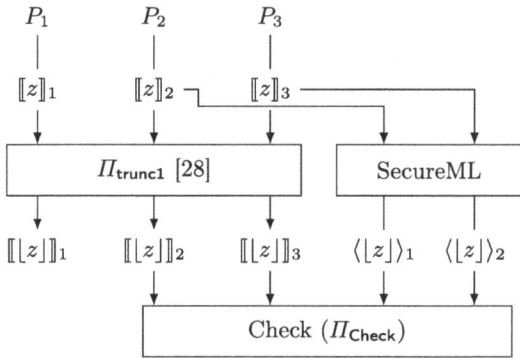

Fig. 3. MaSTer truncation protocol visualised.

P_3 compute the two-party truncation where P_1 does not contribute. Therefore, P_2 and P_3 now hold two independently created sharings of the truncated value, allowing them to compute the difference and hence verifying the correctness of the value sent by P_1, up to an error of ± 1. Concretely, P_2 and P_3 compute $\gamma_i := s_i' - s_i''$, $i \in \{1, 2\}$ and $\gamma_3 := s_3'$, where s_j', $j \in \{1, 2, 3\}$ are components of the RSS share dealt by P_1 and s_i'' is the sharing of the two-party truncation. P_2 stores $\gamma_{2,m}$ and $\gamma_{3,m}$ of the m-th truncation and P_3 stores $\gamma_{1,m}$ and $\gamma_{3,m}$. After M truncations (or at the output phase), P_2 and P_3 use one communication round to send $\gamma_{2,1}, \ldots, \gamma_{2,M}$ and $\gamma_{1,1}, \ldots, \gamma_{1,M}$, respectively, and then check $\forall 1 \leq j \leq M \, | \sum_{i=1}^{3} \gamma_{i,j} | \leq 1$. The second phase thus consists of a batched check of the optimistically executed truncations. The batched consistency check (Fig. 5 requires one round of communication among P_2 and P_3 to check M truncations in parallel. Our protocol therefore achieves an amortised cost of one round of communication. We outline optimisations of the consistency check in Sect. 4.2.

4.2 Further Communication Cost Reduction

We now aim to reduce the communication cost in the parallel consistency check. By computing $a_1 := \gamma_1$ (P_3) and $a_2 := \gamma_2 + \gamma_3$ (P_2), the two parties now hold a two-party additive sharing and wish to check whether $a_1 + a_2 \in \{-1, 0, 1\}$. First note that if the check were $a_1 + a_2 = 0$, P_2 could hash all of its shares $H(a_2^{(1)} || \ldots || a_2^{(m)})$ and P_3 hashes the negation of its shares $H(2^\ell - a_1^{(1)} || \ldots || 2^\ell - a_1^{(m)})$. The parties would only need to share the hash and compare. However, this is no longer feasible since, for example, P_3 needs to check $1 + 2^\ell - a_1^{(i)}$, $2^\ell - a_1^{(i)}$ or $2^\ell - a_1^{(i)} - 1$ without knowing which of the three options yields the same hash. Instead, each party adds their share of a to a Bloom filter [5, 34] and sends the Bloom filter to the other party. Then, each party performs set membership tests of $1 + 2^\ell - a_1^{(i)}$, $2^\ell - a_1^{(i)}$ and $2^\ell - a_1^{(i)} - 1$, and aborts the consistency check if none of the three elements are in the filter. Since Bloom filters are probabilistic, there is a probability of ϵ of a false positive, i.e., in our context, a value $a^{(j)}$ does not reconstruct to $\{-1, 0, 1\}$. Dimensioned such that $\epsilon \leq \min(2^{-\sigma}, 2^{\ell_x + 2 - \ell})$ where σ is the statistical security parameter and $2^{\ell_x + 2 - \ell}$ is the failure probability of the consistency check due to large errors happening (see Theorem 2), the size of the Bloom filter is about $c \log_2(1/\epsilon) = c \cdot \min(40, \ell - \ell_x - 2)$ bits per element where $1 \leq c \leq 1.44$ depends on the exact type of filter. For our parameters where $\ell = 96, \ell_x = 16$, employing Bloom filters saves roughly 58% communication in that phase. Further, one may choose a larger filter to reduce ϵ and compress the filter during transit [27]. However, filling the filter and querying for membership requires additional local computation.

Truncation protocol Π_{Trunc}

P_1	P_2	P_3
$[\![z]\!]_1 = (s_1, s_2)$	$[\![z]\!]_2 = (s_2, s_3)$	$[\![z]\!]_3 = (s_3, s_1)$

$s_1' := r' \leftarrow_{\$1,3} \mathbb{Z}_{2\ell}$ $s_1' := r' \leftarrow_{\$1,3} \mathbb{Z}_{2\ell}$

$s_2' := \mathsf{rshift}(s_1 + s_2, k) - r' \xrightarrow{s_2'} s_3' := 2^\ell - \mathsf{rshift}(2^\ell - s_3, k)$ $s_3' := 2^\ell - \mathsf{rshift}(2^\ell - s_3, k)$

$ s_2'' := 2^\ell - \mathsf{rshift}(2^\ell - s_2, k)$ $s_1'' := \mathsf{rshift}(s_3 + s_1, k)$

$ \gamma_2 := s_2' - s_2''$ $\gamma_1 := s_1' - s_1''$

$ \gamma_3 := s_3'$ $\gamma_3 := s_3'$

Output $[\![\lfloor z \rfloor]\!]_1 := (s_1', s_2')$ Output $[\![\lfloor z \rfloor]\!]_2 := (s_2', s_3')$ Output $[\![\lfloor z \rfloor]\!]_3 := (s_3', s_1')$

 Store γ_2, γ_3 Store γ_1, γ_3

Post-processing $\vdots$ $\vdots$

 Π_{Check} Π_{Check}

Fig. 4. The truncation protocol Π_{Trunc} to truncate z by k bits.

4.3   Error Analysis

In this section, we detail the truncation errors and their role in the consistency check (see Theorem 2). Later, we expand on the probability of detected malicious behaviour and provide more details on the relation between the protocol parameters and the multiplicative depth of the computed circuit.

In the following theorem, we show the correctness of the consistency check. We provide a proof of the theorem in the full version of the paper [37].

Theorem 2 (Correctness of consistency check). *Let x_1 be the result of a truncated value $x \in X$. Let $\mathbb{E}[x_1]$ denote the expected value of x_1. In an honest execution of Π_{Trunc} (see Fig. 4), the consistency check holds with probability* $\Pr\left[\sum_{i=1}^{3} \gamma_i \in \{0, \pm 1\}\right] \geq 1 - 2^{k+2-\ell} \cdot \mathbb{E}[x_1] \geq 1 - 2^{\ell_x + 2 - \ell}$.

A variety of works focusing on precise or faithful truncation [20, 32, 39] motivate their work by arguing that the probability of a large error occurring in a large neural network is rather high. In our protocol this large error would lead

---

Consistency check protocol Π_{Check}

P_2

$\gamma_{2,1}, \ldots, \gamma_{2,M}, \; \gamma_{3,1}, \ldots, \gamma_{3,M}$

$\forall 1 \leq j \leq M$
  $\gamma_{2,j} := s'_{2,j} - s''_{2,j}$
  $\gamma_{3,j} := s'_{3,j}$

P_3

$\gamma_{1,1}, \ldots, \gamma_{1,M}, \; \gamma_{3,1}, \ldots, \gamma_{3,M}$

$\forall 1 \leq j \leq M$
  $\gamma_{1,j} := s'_{1,j} - s''_{1,j}$
  $\gamma_{3,j} := s'_{3,j}$

$\xrightarrow{\gamma_{2,1}, \ldots, \gamma_{2,M}}$

$\xleftarrow{\gamma_{1,1}, \ldots, \gamma_{1,M}}$

$\forall 1 \leq j \leq M$
  Check $|\sum_{i=1}^{3} \gamma_{i,j}| \leq 1$

$\forall 1 \leq j \leq M$
  Check $|\sum_{i=1}^{3} \gamma_{i,j}| \leq 1$

Fig. 5. The consistency check protocol to check a batch of M unchecked truncations.

to an abort even if no malicious error was introduced. We therefore stress the necessity of a mindful selection of the input size ℓ_x in relation to the ring size ℓ, based on the expected distribution of values to be truncated $\mathbb{E}[x]$. We note that for large networks with a number of multiplications exceeding the order of 10^{12}, the usual ring size of $\ell = 64$ bits would not be sufficient, assuming a uniformly distributed x. However, in ML applications x is expected to be rather small, resulting in $\mathbb{E}[x_1] \ll 2^{\ell_x - k}$. Therefore a concrete model and ML network analysis is required for a secure choice of parameters. To achieve statistical security with parameter σ, the parameters would be required to satisfy $n \cdot 2^{k+2-\ell} \cdot \mathbb{E}[x_1] \leq 2^{-\sigma}$, where n denotes the total number of multiplications in the computed circuit and $\mathbb{E}[x_1] \leq 2^{\ell_x - k}$. Recall x_1 here denotes the result of a truncation.

5 Security

We now turn to proving security of our proposed probabilistic truncation protocol. Importantly, and as many other PPML protocols, we require secure, i.e., confidential and mutually authenticated, channels between the parties. We assume these are set up in advance before the protocol runs. This can be achieved with, e.g., client- and server-side authentication in TLS.

5.1 Faithful and Probabilistic Truncation

At USENIX Security '23, Li et al. [26] advocated for precise truncation protocols as opposed to the line of work on probabilistic truncation protocols that introduce errors on the result. They showed that truncation with a truncation tuple $[\![r]\!], [\![\lfloor r \rfloor]\!]$ with $r \leftarrow_\$ \mathbb{Z}_{2^\ell}$ in the style of [9,28] does not securely realise a truncation functionality that adds the probabilistic truncation error in the ideal world solely based on the plaintext value to be truncated. In the real world, the error distribution also depends on r. In fact, the authors show that in the real protocol the adversary learns some function of r and can thus distinguish the worlds based on the reconstructed result. This result highlights the importance of a properly defined functionality and rigorous proofs even for small sub-protocols in a PPML framework. Therefore, we give a formal definition of our desired functionality $\mathcal{F}_{\text{Trunc}}$ (see Fig. 6) and provide a detailed proof. To prevent these issues, our functionality has to extract the randomness in the share and therefore takes all randomness into account when sampling the truncation error. Unfortunately, this results in a less simple description of the ideal behaviour of truncation.

Functionality $\mathcal{F}_{\text{Trunc}}$

The functionality receives $[\![z]\!]_j, k$ from all parties P_j and receives the adversaries output share (s_i', s_{i+1}'). If the adversary corrupts P_1, it also receives an additive error Δ.

- $\mathcal{F}_{\text{Trunc}}$ unpacks the RSS sharing as (s_1, s_2, s_3).
- $\mathcal{F}_{\text{Trunc}}$ reconstructs $z := s_1 + s_2 + s_3$ and sets $r_1 := 2^\ell - s_3$ and $r_2 := 2^\ell - s_2$.
- $\mathcal{F}_{\text{Trunc}}$ computes $b := e_k(z, r_1)$ and $b' := e_k(z, r_1) - e_k(z, r_2)$ (see Def. 3).
- $\mathcal{F}_{\text{Trunc}}$ truncates z by k bits, $\lfloor z \rfloor_k$ and sets $s_{i-1}' := \lfloor z \rfloor_k + \Delta + b - s_i' - s_{i+1}'$.
- If $|b' + \Delta| \leq 1$, the functionality outputs (s_j', s_{j+1}') to party P_j, else the functionality sends abort to the adversary, waits for continue and then sends abort to all honest parties.

Fig. 6. MaSTer truncation functionality $\mathcal{F}_{\text{Trunc}}$.

5.2   Soundness

First, we investigate the soundness of the consistency check, i.e., the probability that it detects cheating when cheating occurred. For this setting, we assume P_1 is corrupted by the adversary and sends $s_{2,\mathcal{A}}' = s_2' + \Delta$ for $\Delta \neq 0$. Modifying the expressions of Theorem 1, we get $\sum_{i=1}^3 \gamma_i + \Delta = c_1' - c_1'' + \Delta$ with probability $\geq 1 - 2^{k+2-\ell} \cdot \mathbb{E}[x_1] \geq 1 - 2^{\ell_x + 2 - \ell}$, since $\mathbb{E}[x_1] \leq 2^{\ell_x - k}$. The adversary can therefore set the truncation error to $c' + \Delta$ under the constraint that $|c' - c'' + \Delta| \leq 1$. Since $|c' - c''| \leq 1$ with probability $\geq 1 - 2^{\ell_x + 2 - \ell}$, any additive error $|c' + \Delta| > 2$ added by a malicious P_1 will be detected with the same probability $\geq 1 - 2^{\ell_x + 2 - \ell}$. We note that an adversary can therefore add an additive error $|\Delta| \leq 2$ without getting detected. This adversarial influence opens up a new attack surface for the adversary. We expand on the attacker possibilities in Sect. 5.4. Further analysis of the $\Delta = \pm 2$ can be found in the full paper [37].

5.3 Security of MaSTer

We prove security of the truncation protocol in the UC framework [7]. For this, we define an ideal functionality $\mathcal{F}_{\mathsf{Trunc}}$ (see Fig. 6) and a simulator $\mathcal{S}$. A protocol Π securely realises the ideal functionality $\mathcal{F}$ if for every adversary $\mathcal{A}$, there is a simulator $\mathcal{S}$ such that all environments $\mathcal{Z}$ cannot distinguish between the ideal world and the real world. We use a pairwise shared PRF between the three parties, formalised as $\mathcal{F}_{\mathsf{cr}}$ in Fig. 1, and give a protocol Π_{cr} implementing the functionality for completeness in the full paper [37]. We use the simplified UC framework [8] that takes care of authenticated channels, message scheduling, etc. The main security theorem for the MaSTer protocol is as follows.

Theorem 3. *The protocol Π_{Trunc} (see Fig. 4) securely realises $\mathcal{F}_{\mathsf{Trunc}}$ (see Fig. 6) in the $\mathcal{F}_{\mathsf{cr}}$-hybrid model against a static malicious adversary with abort who corrupts a single party.*

Proof. We setup a simulator $\mathcal{S}$ that internally runs $\mathcal{A}$ and passes along all communication between $\mathcal{A}$ and $\mathcal{Z}$. Therefore, we can assume $\mathcal{A}$ is a dummy adversary that acts and reports back as told by $\mathcal{Z}$. Thus, in the following, $\mathcal{Z}$ and $\mathcal{A}$ are used interchangeably. The goal of the proof is to show that the simulated view of $\mathcal{A}$ (that is run internally by $\mathcal{S}$) of the protocol in the ideal world is indistinguishable for $\mathcal{Z}$ from the view of $\mathcal{A}$ in the real world. Note that in the $\mathcal{F}$-hybrid model, both in the real and in the ideal world, the protocol parties interact with the $\mathcal{F}$ hybrids when needed. In the real world, these functionalities are proper ideal functionalities. In the ideal model, the simulator also plays the role of the hybrid functionalities towards the adversary.

In the following, we describe a simulator $\mathcal{S}$ that simulates the honest parties towards the adversary $\mathcal{A}$ in an ideal execution with access to $\mathcal{F}_{\mathsf{Trunc}}$. Notably, $\mathcal{S}$ does not know the inputs of the honest parties it simulates. However, $\mathcal{S}$ knows the inputs of the corrupted parties, i.e., in this case the input share of the value to be truncated. This allows $\mathcal{S}$ to replicate and track all computation results of $\mathcal{A}$ if it follows the protocol. Let i be the index of the corrupted party, i.e., $\mathcal{A}$ controls P_i. The index j denotes the honest parties.

In the first step, the simulator $\mathcal{S}$ obtains access to the PRF F_k since it simulates $\mathcal{F}_{\mathsf{cr}}$ towards $\mathcal{A}$, and knows $\mathcal{A}$'s share (s_i, s_{i+1}).

If $P_i = P_1$, $\mathcal{S}$ receives $s'_{2,\mathcal{A}}$ from $\mathcal{A}$. Since the simulator knows s_1, s_2 and r' (from F_k), it computes $s'_{2,\mathcal{S}} := \mathsf{rshift}(s_1 + s_2, k) - r'$, and sets $\Delta := s'_{2,\mathcal{A}} - s'_{2,\mathcal{S}}$. The simulator calls $\mathcal{F}_{\mathsf{Trunc}}(P_i, (s_1, s_2), \Delta)$ and sends $(r', s'_{2,\mathcal{A}})$ as the output share. If the functionality sends abort, the simulator sends abort to the adversary and sends continue to the functionality, else it outputs what $\mathcal{A}$ outputs.

If $P_i = P_2$, the simulator samples $r \leftarrow\!\!\$\ \mathbb{Z}_{2^\ell}$ uniformly at random, and sends r as s'_2 to the adversary on behalf of P_1. The simulator computes $s'_3 := 2^\ell - \mathsf{rshift}(2^\ell - s_3, k)$. The simulator calls $\mathcal{F}_{\mathsf{Trunc}}(P_i, (s_2, s_3), *)$ and sends (r, s'_3) as the adversary's output share. If the functionality sends abort, the simulator sends abort to the adversary, waits for continue and then sends continue to the functionality. Else, $\mathcal{S}$ obtains b' from $\mathcal{F}_{\mathsf{Trunc}}$ and computes γ_3, s''_2 and sends

$\gamma_1 := 2^\ell - \gamma_3 + s_2'' - r + b'$ to the adversary on behalf of P_3. The simulator receives γ_2' from the adversary. Note that if the adversary computes the γ-check, it obtains $\sum \gamma_i = (2^\ell - \gamma_3 + s_2'' - r + b') + (r - s_2'') + \gamma_3 = b'$.
The simulator checks $|b' + \gamma_2' - r + s_2''| \leq 1$. If this holds, the simulator continues and outputs what $\mathcal{A}$ outputs. If not, the simulator sends abort to the adversary and then aborts.

If $P_i = P_3$, the simulator computes s_3', s_1', γ_1 and γ_3. The simulator calls $\mathcal{F}_{\mathsf{Trunc}}(P_i, (s_3, s_1), *)$ and sends (s_3', s_1') as output shares. If the functionality sends abort, the simulator sends abort to the adversary, waits for continue and then sends continue to the functionality. Else, $\mathcal{S}$ obtains b' and sends $2^\ell - \gamma_1 - \gamma_3 + b'$ as γ_2 to the adversary on behalf of P_2. The simulator receives γ_1' from the adversary and checks if $|\gamma_1' - \gamma_1 + b'| \leq 1$. If this holds, the simulator continues and outputs what $\mathcal{A}$ outputs. If not, the simulator sends abort to the adversary and then aborts.

We now show that for each case, $\mathcal{S}$ creates a view for $\mathcal{A}$ that is indistinguishable to the real world execution. Note that the (reconstructed) output is identical in the real and ideal world since $\mathcal{F}_{\mathsf{Trunc}}$ adds the same truncation error on the least significant bit. Further, the adversary's view of the input and output shares fully determines the input and output shares of the honest parties if the adversary also knows the shared value (cf. [16, Def. 2.3]). Therefore, the truncation error and abort conditions in the ideal world must exactly match the side-effects in the real protocol. Since the randomness in the input shares is known by the adversary, the functionality extracts it and bases the abort condition (for a $\Delta = 0$) and truncation error on the extracted randomness. This way, the abort behaviour due to the adversarially added Δ, and the sign and value of the truncation error are identical to the real world execution.

Note that the protocol also aborts with probability $2^{\ell_x + 2 - \ell}$ independent of the adversarial influence. This bound stems from the correctness probability of SecureML (cf. Sect. 3.5 and [29, Theorem 1]). As done in previous works, e.g., SecureML and ABY3, the ring parameters can be adapted to be large enough so that this event becomes negligible, so we will not consider this case further on.

If $P_i = P_1$, since $\mathcal{A}$ does not receive data in this step, the only possibility to distinguish the two worlds is by sending a non-zero additive error Δ in s_2', by observing the reconstructed output or the abort behaviour. Since in this case, $\mathcal{S}$ does not abort, output and abort behaviour with $\Delta = 0$ is already handled as described above. For $\Delta \neq 0$, the abort probability is the same in both worlds since $c' - c'' = b'$ by construction and thus the checks in the real world and in $\mathcal{F}_{\mathsf{Trunc}}$ evaluate to the same value.

If $P_i = P_2$, $\mathcal{A}$ receives s_2' and γ_1. Further by sending different γ_2, it can influence abort behaviour. Let $\alpha_1 = \mathsf{rshift}(s_1 + s_2, k)$, $\alpha_2 = 2^\ell - \mathsf{rshift}(2^\ell - s_3, k)$, $\beta_1 = \mathsf{rshift}(s_3 + s_1, k)$ and $\beta_2 = 2^\ell - \mathsf{rshift}(2^\ell - s_2, k)$ be shorthand notation for the terms, then $\mathcal{A}$ sees $(\alpha_1 - r', r - \beta_1)$ with $r' := F_k(cnt)$ in the real world while the ideal view is $(r, -\alpha_2 + \beta_2 - r + b')$ with $r \leftarrow_\$ \mathbb{Z}_{2^\ell}$. In the ideal world, we now sample r as $\alpha_1 - r'$ where $r' := F_k(cnt)$. Clearly, r and $\alpha_1 - r'$

are identically distributed (under the PRF assumption). Now the ideal world view is

$$(\alpha_1 - r', -\alpha_2 + \beta_2 - (\alpha_1 - r') + b')$$
$$= (\alpha_1 - r', -\alpha_2 + \beta_2 - \alpha_1 + r' + (\alpha_1 + \alpha_2 - \beta_1 - \beta_2)) = (\alpha_1 - r', r' - \beta_1),$$

which is identical to the real world view. Note that $\sum \gamma_i = \alpha_1 + \alpha_2 - \beta_1 - \beta_2 + (r' - r') = b'$. $\mathcal{A}$ can influence the abort behaviour only when sending a different $\gamma_2' = \gamma_2 + \Delta$, $\Delta \neq 0$. In the real world, the protocol aborts if $|\gamma_1 + \gamma_2 + \Delta + \gamma_3| > 1$, more precisely if $|b' + \Delta| > 1$. In the ideal world, the simulator aborts if $|b' + \gamma_2' - r + s_2''| > 1$, which is $|b' + (\gamma_2 + \Delta) - r + s_2''| = |b' + (r - s_2'' + \Delta) - r + s_2''| = |b' + \Delta|$. The abort behaviour in both worlds is therefore the identical.

If $P_i = P_3$, $\mathcal{A}$ receives γ_2 and sends $\gamma_1' = \gamma_1 + \Delta$. In the real world, $\mathcal{A}$ receives γ_2 and in the ideal world it receives $2^\ell - \gamma_1 - \gamma_3 + b' = \gamma_2$ since $\sum \gamma_i = b'$. Thus both worlds yield identical distributions. In the real world, the protocol aborts if $|\gamma_1' + \gamma_2 + \gamma_3| > 1$, and in the ideal world the simulator aborts if $|\gamma_1' - \gamma_1 + b'| > 1$, clearly $|\gamma_1' - \gamma_1 + b'| = |b' + \Delta|$ and thus exhibits the same abort behaviour.

Note that a corrupted P_1 can send an arbitrary value instead of s_2' to P_2. In this case the protocol would continue with the computation using the corrupted shares. However, note that s_3' remains uniformly random in the view of P_1, hence P_1 cannot infer any further information about the secret z. Moreover, before revealing any shares, the parties would run the check to verify correctness (cf. Fig. 5). Thus a corrupted value would be detected and honest parties abort.

5.4   Implications of Δ Introduced by an Adversary

From the soundness results in Sect. 5.2 and $\mathcal{F}_{\text{Trunc}}$ (Fig. 6), it follows that the consistency check detects malicious behaviour up to a small error Δ that can be introduced by an adversary with high probability. It is therefore crucial to demonstrate the effect of the error Δ. We perform an analysis of the error impact by running a forward pass of a dense neural network (DNN) described in Sect. 7 without the error as a baseline and with the error introduced in each truncation. Fig. 7 depicts the absolute value of the difference between the two cases. We find that the effect of the adversary influencing the result with $\Delta = \pm 1$ and $\Delta = \pm 2$ is in the order of 10^{-3} for precision of 16 bits, and 10^{-2} for 13-bit precision, thus has no impact for this particular network. While the impact for $\Delta = \pm 2$ is larger, the probability of detection grows exponentially (cf. Sect. 5.2). Still, the new adversarial capability requires more study in future work. The attack can be viewed as an instance of an adversarial example attack, where, in addition to the query sample, the client also sets noise to the model weights. As such, this scenario can be studied separately outside the scope of this paper. Nevertheless, we believe that a careful choice of fixed-point precision lowers the impact any attacker might have.

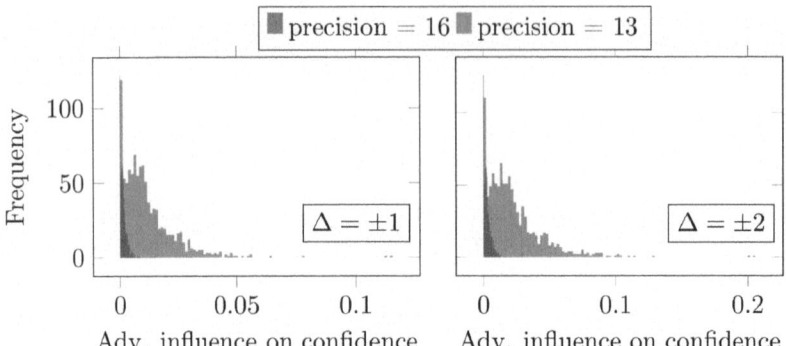

Fig. 7. Illustration of the impact on the predicted confidence levels of a 5-layer network inference when adding truncation errors of ±1 and ±2.

6   Benchmarks

We benchmark our protocol Π_{Trunc} (see Fig. 4) against the generic maliciously secure truncation protocol of ABY3 [28] in replicated secret sharing. We omit a direct comparison to optimised versions of ABY3 pre-processing due to a significant implementation effort required as the source code of neither [11,23] is available. We do however implement the online and offline phases separately, to demonstrate performance of both parts individually. The optimised truncation protocols such as the one of SWIFT [23] are based on the same online phase as ABY3, hence our online phase is directly comparable to these. ABY3 uses the same offline phase for truncation triple generation as the maliciously secure protocol of Furukawa et al. [16], which is implemented in MP-SPDZ. Our experimental setup is detailed in Sect. 6.1. The pre-processing phase of the ABY3 truncation is run separately to accommodate the specified protocol requirements by [28]. Due to its high cost we only benchmark the creation of fewer triples. The numbers reported for the ABY3 truncation pre-processing are then scaled accordingly. Table 2 demonstrates that for the creation of one million pre-processed triples onwards, the execution time and the data sent scale linearly. To be conservative, all of the data reported in the experiments is scaled according to pre-processing for 10^8 multiplications. This is to mitigate any inaccuracy caused by scaling from smaller values.

6.1   Experimental Setup

We implement our and the ABY3 truncation protocols in the MP-SPDZ [22] framework and benchmark on three servers with a 4-core 2.40 GHz Intel Xeon CPU and 16 GB of RAM. We simulate a LAN setting with 0.1ms latency and 10 Gbps bandwidth, and a WAN setting with 40 ms round trip time and 100 Mbps bandwidth. We modify the implementation of the MPC protocol for three-party malicious security in the ring $\mathbb{Z}_{2^\ell}$ in MP-SPDZ by inserting both our protocol

Table 2. Performance data of the pre-processing for ABY3 truncation tuples in the LAN and WAN setting. In our setup, the performance starts to scale linearly from 10^6 tuples onwards.

	Mult.	10^3	10^4	10^5	10^6	10^7	10^8
Time (s)	LAN	0.03	0.07	0.24	2.07	22.92	237.73
	WAN	2.36	3.77	14.42	87.73	834.77	8309.08
Data sent (MB)		2.66	11.65	106.51	1015.25	10092.70	100926.90

and the ABY3 truncation in the online phase. The protocol implemented in MP-SDPZ is based on the pre-processing of Cramer et al. [12] and re-sharing of Araki et al. [1]. The pre-processing of the ABY3 truncation triples is run separately in an MPC protocol for Boolean three-party RSS based on Furukawa et al. [16] as specified in [28], however with Beaver multiplication [4] instead of their post-sacrifice method. Similarly to previous works in PPML [28,29,35], we run experiments in three commonly benchmarked networks. For training on the MNIST dataset (one epoch of training: forward and backward pass with batch size 128), we run a three-layer dense neural network introduced by SecureML [29] with ReLU and Softmax activation functions, and also run the widely known 7-layer CNN LeNet-5 [25]. Further, we run the same training setup with a smaller batch size of 16 due to RAM constraints with the CIFAR-10 dataset on an 11-layer CNN AlexNet [24]. We omit benchmarks of training in the WAN setting due to significant time required for their completion. For inference results in the WAN setting we refer the reader to Sect. 7. We run the ABY3 benchmark in a 64-bit ring, with $k = 7$, $\ell_x = 17$. In order to satisfy parameter analysis outlined in Sect. 4.3, we benchmark MaSTer in a 96-bit ring. We set $\sigma = 40$ and we note that the number of truncations for all experiments is $n < 2^{36}$. Therefore, it is satisfied that $2^{36} \cdot 2^{17+2-96} \leq 2^{-40}$. We further note the choice of k is subjected to the MP-SPDZ framework implementation of probabilistic truncations, which requires $k + 9 \leq \ell_x$ and $\ell_x + k \leq \ell - \sigma$. We stress that the choice of k is for benchmarking only, and while it has no effect on the performance, as mentioned in Sect. 5.4 the choice of k possibly determines an impact of a malicious attacker.

6.2   Results

We showcase the performance results in Table 3. We report the results of the offline and online phases separately. The pre-processing of ABY3 truncation triples is run separately using the protocol of Furukawa et al. [16] and the performance numbers are then added to the offline phase of ABY3 benchmark. The data sent represents the total data sent among all the parties.

For network training using our truncation, the online phase takes marginally more time, but we improve significantly in the offline phase. The increased runtime in the online phase occurs mainly due to computation in a larger ring, which is also reflected in the sent data. In the offline phase, by removing the

Table 3. Training of MNIST and CIFAR-10 datasets with different networks. We run a forward and a backward pass in each network, with 1 batch and full dataset (60000 samples), respectively.

	Network	Protocol	Offline		Online	
			Time(s)	Comm.(MB)	Time(s)	Comm.(MB)
	MNIST	ABY3	$3.29 \cdot 10^2$	$1.13 \cdot 10^5$	$2.50 \cdot 10^1$	$2.25 \cdot 10^3$
	(SecureML)	**MaSTer**	$7.62 \cdot 10^1$	$5.95 \cdot 10^3$	$3.19 \cdot 10^1$	$3.37 \cdot 10^3$
	MNIST	ABY3	$6.17 \cdot 10^3$	$2.32 \cdot 10^6$	$2.54 \cdot 10^2$	$2.85 \cdot 10^4$
1 batch	(LeNet-5)	**MaSTer**	$9.75 \cdot 10^2$	$8.95 \cdot 10^4$	$3.52 \cdot 10^2$	$4.28 \cdot 10^4$
	CIFAR-10	ABY3	$5.17 \cdot 10^4$	$1.84 \cdot 10^7$	$2.91 \cdot 10^3$	$2.32 \cdot 10^5$
	(AlexNet)	**MaSTer**	$9.97 \cdot 10^3$	$7.58 \cdot 10^5$	$3.53 \cdot 10^3$	$3.44 \cdot 10^5$
Full	MNIST	ABY3	$1.48 \cdot 10^5$	$5.37 \cdot 10^7$	$9.19 \cdot 10^3$	$8.43 \cdot 10^5$
	(SecureML)	**MaSTer**	$3.07 \cdot 10^4$	$2.71 \cdot 10^6$	$1.19 \cdot 10^4$	$1.26 \cdot 10^6$

need to compute expensive subtraction circuits, we improve the offline run-time by up to an order of magnitude and we lower the communication overhead by two orders of magnitude. We note that our implementation is for demonstration purposes only and has not been optimised for the best performance.

7 Application: Privacy-Preserving ECG Diagnostic

Consider a scenario concerning diagnostic prediction using sensitive medical data. In this case, MPC would be a desirable tool to perform ML inference to preserve the privacy of both the data and the model owners. We therefore consider inference of small batch sizes, as this resembles queries of individual users in a real-world system. Further, we note that a lighter pre-processing phase increases the overall throughput for small batch sizes, which is desirable for applications with real-time response requirement.

Most frameworks designed for privacy-preserving ML consider the offline-online paradigm [4] where a substantial part of the computational load can be moved to the input-independent pre-processing phase. For this approach to be efficient, the clients are assumed to request computations occasionally (e.g., an organisation running inference at the end of every day). This then creates the time for the MPC servers to perform pre-processing when they don't engage in input-dependent computations. This results in major improvements of the online phase. However, in the scenario described above, the servers are constantly active, responding to queries of both individual users and large organisations. This reduces the time of low load and pre-processing, thus increases the latency of a prediction. Consequently, it is important to maximise the overall throughput.

Given the example of medical data, we run classification of ECG heartbeat data over a dense neural network. We run experiments on the same setup as described in Sect. 6, evaluating the DNN model trained on the MIT-BIH

Arrhythmia dataset [30] together with PTB Diagnostic ECG database [6], both available at [17]. The trained model comprises five dense layers with a ReLU activation function on the first four and the Softmax function on the last layer.

We demonstrate the overall performance in the LAN setting in Table 4 and WAN setting in Table 5. As before, we run ABY3 in the 64-bit ring and MaSTer in a 96-bit ring, with $k = 8$, $\ell_x = 16$. We report the execution time of the online and offline phase separately. The data sent denotes the data sent by all parties collectively. Finally, we showcase the total throughput of classifications per minute. We compare the performance when running inference with a different number of samples per inference query, ranging from a single sample, through a batch size of 128 samples to the whole dataset. We observe an improvement between a factor of two and three for both LAN and WAN settings, depending on the query size. When running the inference on a trained model, we achieve a classification accuracy of 95.9%, same as ABY3 and plaintext.

Table 4. Performance of high-throughput use-case inference with different number of samples per query in the LAN setting. Throughput is denoted in samples per minute.

Number of samples	Number of truncations	Protocol	Offline	Online	Total	Data Sent	Throughput
			Time (s)			(MB)	
1	$2.36 \cdot 10^4$	ABY3	0.21	0.08	0.29	33.79	206.90
		MaSTer	0.07	0.07	0.14	9.55	428.57
128	$3.02 \cdot 10^6$	ABY3	9.73	0.86	10.60	3621.68	724.53
		MaSTer	4.36	1.10	5.46	780.22	1406.59
21892	$5.16 \cdot 10^8$	ABY3	1811	142	1953	716386	672.46
		MaSTer	729	167	896	132892	1465.98

Table 5. Performance of high-throughput use-case inference with different number of samples per query in the WAN setting. Throughput is denoted in samples per minute.

Number of samples	Number of truncations	Protocol	Offline	Online	Total	Data Sent	Throughput
			Time (s)			(MB)	
1	$2.36 \cdot 10^4$	ABY3	10.21	3.55	13.76	33.79	4.36
		MaSTer	7.98	6.30	14.28	9.55	4.21
128	$3.02 \cdot 10^6$	ABY3	326.17	58.11	384.28	3621.68	19.99
		MaSTer	103.67	80.19	183.86	780.22	41.78
21892	$5.16 \cdot 10^8$	ABY3	53267	9889	63157	716386	20.80
		MaSTer	17091	13567	30658	132892	42.84

8   Conclusion

We presented a maliciously secure truncation protocol combining the two-party semi-honest truncation protocol of SecureML with a consistency check. Unlike previous works for malicious security, we do not require pre-processing. We prove our protocol is secure with abort against one malicious corrupted party in the UC framework. In the end, we demonstrate the improvement of our truncation experimentally by comparing training on the commonly used benchmarking networks, namely SecureML, LeNet-5, and AlexNet. We improve the performance of the offline phase by an order of magnitude, achieving higher total throughput. We also show a potential application where overall throughput needs to be maximised, and hence advocate for an efficient protocol without a heavy pre-processing phase.

Acknowledgments. This work was supported by the Flemish Government through FWO SBO project MOZAIK S003321N and by CyberSecurity Research Flanders with reference number VR20192203.

References

1. Araki, T., Furukawa, J., Lindell, Y., Nof, A., Ohara, K.: High-throughput semi-honest secure three-party computation with an honest majority. In: Weippl, E.R., Katzenbeisser, S., Kruegel, C., Myers, A.C., Halevi, S. (eds.) Proceedings of the 2016 ACM SIGSAC Conference on Computer and Communications Security, Vienna, Austria, 24–28 October 2016, pp. 805–817. ACM, New York, NY, USA (2016). https://doi.org/10.1145/2976749.2978331

2. Attrapadung, N., et al.: Adam in private: secure and fast training of deep neural networks with adaptive moment estimation. Proc. Priv. Enhancing Technol. **2022**(4), 746–767 (2022). https://doi.org/10.56553/popets-2022-0131

3. Baccarini, A.N., Blanton, M., Yuan, C.: Multi-party replicated secret sharing over a ring with applications to privacy-preserving machine learning. Proc. Priv. Enhancing Technol. **2023**(1), 608–626 (2023). https://doi.org/10.56553/popets-2023-0035

4. Beaver, D.: Efficient multiparty protocols using circuit randomization. In: Feigenbaum, J. (ed.) CRYPTO 1991. LNCS, vol. 576, pp. 420–432. Springer, Heidelberg (1992). https://doi.org/10.1007/3-540-46766-1_34

5. Bloom, B.H.: Space/time trade-offs in hash coding with allowable errors. Commun. ACM **13**(7), 422-426 (1970). https://doi.org/10.1145/362686.362692

6. Bousseljot, R., Kreiseler, D., Schnabel, A.: Nutzung der EKG-Signaldatenbank CARDIODAT der PTB über das Internet. Biomed. Eng./Biomedizinische Technik **40**(s1), 317–318 (1995)

7. Canetti, R.: Universally composable security: a new paradigm for cryptographic protocols. In: 42nd Annual Symposium on Foundations of Computer Science. FOCS 2001, 14–17 October 2001, pp. 136–145. IEEE Computer Society (2001). https://doi.org/10.1109/SFCS.2001.959888

8. Canetti, R., Cohen, A., Lindell, Y.: A simpler variant of universally composable security for standard multiparty computation. In: Gennaro, R., Robshaw, M. (eds.) CRYPTO 2015. LNCS, vol. 9216, pp. 3–22. Springer, Heidelberg (2015). https://doi.org/10.1007/978-3-662-48000-7_1

9. Catrina, O., de Hoogh, S.: Improved primitives for secure multiparty integer computation. In: Garay, J.A., De Prisco, R. (eds.) SCN 2010. LNCS, vol. 6280, pp. 182–199. Springer, Heidelberg (2010). https://doi.org/10.1007/978-3-642-15317-4_13

10. Chaudhari, H., Choudhury, A., Patra, A., Suresh, A.: ASTRA: High throughput 3PC over rings with application to secure prediction. In: Sion, R., Papamanthou, C. (eds.) Proceedings of the 2019 ACM SIGSAC Conference on Cloud Computing Security Workshop. CCSW@CCS 2019, 11 November 2019, pp. 81–92. ACM (2019). https://doi.org/10.1145/3338466.3358922

11. Chaudhari, H., Rachuri, R., Suresh, A.: Trident: efficient 4pc framework for privacy preserving machine learning. In: 27th Annual Network and Distributed System Security Symposium, NDSS 2020, San Diego, California, USA, 23–26 February 2020. The Internet Society (2020). https://www.ndss-symposium.org/ndss-paper/trident-efficient-4pc-framework-for-privacy-preserving-machine-learning/

12. Cramer, R., Damgård, I., Escudero, D., Scholl, P., Xing, C.: SPDZ$_{2^k}$: efficient MPC mod 2^k for dishonest majority. In: Shacham, H., Boldyreva, A. (eds.) CRYPTO 2018. LNCS, vol. 10992, pp. 769–798. Springer, Cham (2018). https://doi.org/10.1007/978-3-319-96881-0_26

13. Dalskov, A.P.K., Escudero, D., Keller, M.: Secure evaluation of quantized neural networks. Proc. Priv. Enhancing Technol. **2020**(4), 355–375 (2020). https://doi.org/10.2478/popets-2020-0077

14. Dalskov, A.P.K., Escudero, D., Keller, M.: Fantastic four: honest-majority four-party secure computation with malicious security. In: Bailey, M., Greenstadt, R. (eds.) 30th USENIX Security Symposium, USENIX Security 2021, 11–13 August 2021, pp. 2183–2200. USENIX Association (2021). https://www.usenix.org/conference/usenixsecurity21/presentation/dalskov

15. Escudero, D., Ghosh, S., Keller, M., Rachuri, R., Scholl, P.: Improved primitives for MPC over mixed arithmetic-binary circuits. In: Micciancio, D., Ristenpart, T. (eds.) CRYPTO 2020. LNCS, vol. 12171, pp. 823–852. Springer, Cham (2020). https://doi.org/10.1007/978-3-030-56880-1_29

16. Furukawa, J., Lindell, Y., Nof, A., Weinstein, O.: High-throughput secure three-party computation for malicious adversaries and an honest majority. In: Coron, J.-S., Nielsen, J.B. (eds.) EUROCRYPT 2017, Part II. LNCS, vol. 10211, pp. 225–255. Springer, Cham (2017). https://doi.org/10.1007/978-3-319-56614-6_8

17. Goldberger, A.L., et al.: Physiobank, physiotoolkit, and physionet: components of a new research resource for complex physiologic signals. Circulation **101**(23), E215-20 (2000)

18. Gupta, K., et al.: SIGMA: secure GPT inference with function secret sharing. IACR Cryptology ePrint Archive, p. 1269 (2023). https://eprint.iacr.org/2023/1269

19. Gupta, K., Kumaraswamy, D., Chandran, N., Gupta, D.: Llama: a low latency math library for secure inference. Proc. Priv. Enhancing Technol. **2022**(4), 274–294 (2022). https://doi.org/10.56553/popets-2022-0109

20. Huang, Z., Lu, W., Hong, C., Ding, J.: Cheetah: lean and fast secure two-party deep neural network inference. In: Butler, K.R.B., Thomas, K. (eds.) 31st USENIX Security Symposium, USENIX Security 2022, Boston, MA, USA, 10–12 August 2022, pp. 809–826. USENIX Association (2022). https://www.usenix.org/conference/usenixsecurity22/presentation/huang-zhicong

21. Kachuee, M., Fazeli, S., Sarrafzadeh, M.: ECG heartbeat classification: a deep transferable representation. CoRR abs/1805.00794 (2018). http://arxiv.org/abs/1805.00794

22. Keller, M.: MP-SPDZ: a versatile framework for multi-party computation. In: Ligatti, J., Ou, X., Katz, J., Vigna, G. (eds.) CCS '20: 2020 ACM SIGSAC Conference on Computer and Communications Security, Virtual Event, USA, 9–13 November 2020, pp. 1575–1590. ACM (2020). https://doi.org/10.1145/3372297.3417872

23. Koti, N., Pancholi, M., Patra, A., Suresh, A.: SWIFT: super-fast and robust privacy-preserving machine learning. In: Bailey, M., Greenstadt, R. (eds.) 30th USENIX Security Symposium, USENIX Security 2021, 11–13 August 2021, pp. 2651–2668. USENIX Association (2021). https://www.usenix.org/conference/usenixsecurity21/presentation/koti

24. Krizhevsky, A., Sutskever, I., Hinton, G.E.: Imagenet classification with deep convolutional neural networks. In: Bartlett, P.L., Pereira, F.C.N., Burges, C.J.C., Bottou, L., Weinberger, K.Q. (eds.) Advances in Neural Information Processing Systems 25: 26th Annual Conference on Neural Information Processing Systems 2012. Proceedings of a meeting held 3–6 December 2012, pp. 1106–1114 (2012). https://proceedings.neurips.cc/paper/2012/hash/c399862d3b9d6b76c8436e924a68c45b-Abstract.html

25. LeCun, Y., Bottou, L., Bengio, Y., Haffner, P.: Gradient-based learning applied to document recognition. Proc. IEEE **86**(11), 2278–2324 (1998)

26. Li, Y., Duan, Y., Huang, Z., Hong, C., Zhang, C., Song, Y.: Efficient 3PC for binary circuits with application to maliciously-secure DNN inference. In: Calandrino, J.A., Troncoso, C. (eds.) 32nd USENIX Security Symposium, USENIX Security 2023, Anaheim, CA, USA, 9–11 August 2023. USENIX Association (2023). https://www.usenix.org/conference/usenixsecurity23/presentation/li-yun

27. Mitzenmacher, M.: Compressed bloom filters. In: Proceedings of the Twentieth Annual ACM Symposium on Principles of Distributed Computing. PODC '01, pp. 144–150. Association for Computing Machinery, New York, NY, USA (2001). https://doi.org/10.1145/383962.384004

28. Mohassel, P., Rindal, P.: ABY^3: a mixed protocol framework for machine learning. In: Lie, D., Mannan, M., Backes, M., Wang, X. (eds.) Proceedings of the 2018 ACM SIGSAC Conference on Computer and Communications Security. CCS 2018, Toronto, ON, Canada, 15–19 October 2018, pp. 35–52. ACM (2018). https://doi.org/10.1145/3243734.3243760

29. Mohassel, P., Zhang, Y.: SecureML: a system for scalable privacy-preserving machine learning. In: 2017 IEEE Symposium on Security and Privacy. SP 2017, San Jose, CA, USA, 22–26 May 2017, pp. 19–38. IEEE Computer Society (2017). https://doi.org/10.1109/SP.2017.12

30. Moody, G.B., Mark, R.G.: The impact of the mit-bih arrhythmia database. IEEE Eng. Med. Biol. Mag. **20**(3), 45–50 (2001)

31. Patra, A., Suresh, A.: BLAZE: blazing fast privacy-preserving machine learning. In: 27th Annual Network and Distributed System Security Symposium, NDSS 2020, San Diego, California, USA, 23–26 February 2020. The Internet Society (2020). https://www.ndss-symposium.org/ndss-paper/blaze-blazing-fast-privacy-preserving-machine-learning/

32. Rathee, D., et al.: CrypTFlow2: practical 2-party secure inference. In: Ligatti, J., Ou, X., Katz, J., Vigna, G. (eds.) CCS '20: 2020 ACM SIGSAC Conference on Computer and Communications Security, 9–13 November 2020, pp. 325–342. ACM (2020). https://doi.org/10.1145/3372297.3417274

33. Rotaru, D., Wood, T.: MArBled circuits: mixing arithmetic and boolean circuits with active security. In: Hao, F., Ruj, S., Sen Gupta, S. (eds.) INDOCRYPT 2019. LNCS, vol. 11898, pp. 227–249. Springer, Cham (2019). https://doi.org/10.1007/978-3-030-35423-7_12

34. Tarkoma, S., Rothenberg, C.E., Lagerspetz, E.: Theory and practice of bloom filters for distributed systems. IEEE Commun. Surv. Tutor. **14**(1), 131–155 (2012). https://doi.org/10.1109/SURV.2011.031611.00024

35. Wagh, S., Tople, S., Benhamouda, F., Kushilevitz, E., Mittal, P., Rabin, T.: Falcon: honest-majority maliciously secure framework for private deep learning. Proc. Priv. Enhancing Technol. **2021**(1), 188–208 (2021). https://doi.org/10.2478/popets-2021-0011

36. Watson, J., Wagh, S., Popa, R.A.: Piranha: a GPU platform for secure computation. In: Butler, K.R.B., Thomas, K. (eds.) 31st USENIX Security Symposium, USENIX Security 2022, 10–12 August 2022, pp. 827–844. USENIX Association (2022). https://www.usenix.org/conference/usenixsecurity22/presentation/watson

37. Zbudila, M., Pohle, E., Abidin, A., Preneel, B.: MaSTer: maliciously secure truncation for replicated secret sharing without pre-processing. Cryptology ePrint Archive, Paper 2024/1026 (2024). https://eprint.iacr.org/2024/1026

38. Zhou, L., Song, Q., Zhang, S., Wang, Z., Wang, X., Li, Y.: Bicoptor 2.0: addressing challenges in probabilistic truncation for enhanced privacy-preserving machine learning. CoRR abs/2309.04909 (2023). https://doi.org/10.48550/ARXIV.2309.04909

39. Zou, H., Xiao, Y., Zhang, R.: Semi-honest 2-party faithful truncation from two-bit extraction. IACR Cryptology ePrint Archive, p. 1159 (2023), https://eprint.iacr.org/2023/1159

Post-quantum Security

Compact Adaptor Signature from Isogenies with Enhanced Security

Pratima Jana[✉], Surbhi Shaw[✉], and Ratna Dutta

Department of Mathematics, Indian Institute of Technology Kharagpur,
Kharagpur 721302, India
pratimajanahatiary@kgpian.iitkgp.ac.in, surbhi_shaw@iitkgp.ac.in,
ratna@maths.iitkgp.ac.in

Abstract. Blockchain technology has revolutionized decentralized transactional data storage, fostering trustless interactions via consensus mechanisms involving miners. The security of these systems hinges on digital signatures, predominantly elliptic curve cryptography, which is at risk from quantum computing advancements. To tackle scalability and cost issues of on-chain transactions, off-chain solutions, notably payment channel networks (PCNs), have been introduced. Among these solutions, *adaptor signatures* (AS) have emerged as a pivotal cryptographic tool, allowing secure and efficient off-chain interactions by extending conventional signature schemes with additional hard relations tailored for payment channels. Existing post-quantum secure AS schemes, such as LAS and SQI-AS, face challenges ranging from high off-chain communication costs to security vulnerabilities. These schemes often lack consideration for the unlinkability notion of AS and may fail to deliver promised security guarantees. In response to these challenges, our contribution aims to bridge the gap in practical and secure post-quantum AS solutions. Our work introduces an isogeny-based adaptor signature utilizing the CSI-FiSh signature scheme. We define a variant, *Modified* CSI-FiSh (MCSI-FiSh), which incorporates a strong random self-reducible relation derived from CSIDH. Our proposed adaptor signature scheme for MCSI-FiSh not only verifies a valid signature but also ensures the release of a witness. We provide rigorous security proofs, demonstrating our scheme's resilience against *pre-signature adaptability*, *strong-full extractability* and *unlinkability*. Our scheme is the first post-quantum adaptor signature offering *unlinkability* and *strong-full extractability*. We remark that the overhead of our scheme is also minimal in terms of communication cost and signature size compared to the existing post-quantum adaptor signature.

Keywords: Post-quantum cryptography · Isogenies · Adaptor signature · Unlinkability · Blockchain

1 Introduction

Blockchain technology, originating from Bitcoin, offers a decentralized and secure platform for storing transactional data, fostering trustless interactions among

© The Author(s), under exclusive license to Springer Nature Singapore Pte Ltd. 2025
M. Kohlweiss et al. (Eds.): CANS 2024, LNCS 14905, pp. 77–100, 2025.
https://doi.org/10.1007/978-981-97-8013-6_4

participants [15]. In a blockchain system, transactions undergo verification by a majority consensus of nodes, commonly known as miners. This consensus mechanism ensures that transactions are legitimate and that the sender possesses the claimed amount. Miners, incentivized by transaction fees, uphold the integrity of the ledger, which consists of a chain of blocks. Each block stores a set of transactions and the hash of the previous block. This structure fosters a linear progression of blocks, making it computationally prohibitive for malicious actors to alter past transactions. The security of blockchain systems heavily relies on digital signatures to authenticate transactions. Public key cryptography, specifically elliptic curve cryptography, is used to digitally sign users' transactions. However, with the rapid advancements in quantum computing, concerns have arisen regarding the long-term security of elliptic curve cryptography. Quantum algorithms, such as Shor's algorithm [17], threaten to undermine the security provided by these classical cryptographic schemes, potentially exposing blockchain systems to quantum attacks in the future. To address the scalability and cost challenges associated with on-chain transactions, various off-chain solutions have been proposed. Payment channel networks, in particular, have gained traction for enabling faster and more cost-effective transactions off the main blockchain. Within these off-chain solutions, *adaptor signatures* emerge as a noteworthy cryptographic primitive.

Adaptor signatures (AS) allow for secure and efficient off-chain interactions, facilitating transactions without the need to broadcast every detail to the entire network, thus reducing congestion and costs. At its core, an AS extends the conventional signature scheme by integrating an additional hard relation. In an adaptor signature, for any statement, Y, a signer holding a secret key can produce a pre-signature on any message m. This pre-signature can be adapted into a full signature on m if and only if the user has the witness to Y, a concept formally modeled by *pre-signature adaptability*. Additionally, anyone with access to the pre-signature, full signature and statement Y, is able to extract the witness. This security notion is formally modeled by *full extractibility*. *Unlinkability* of an adapted signature guarantees indistinguishability from a standard signature, even if one knows the statement and witness pair used to derive the adapted signature. These features have established AS as a key component in numerous blockchain applications, especially in off-chain payment systems like payment-channel networks (PCNs) [13], payment-channel hubs (PCHs) [18], atomic swaps [13] and discrete log contracts.

Related Works. The notion of adaptor signatures was first introduced by Poelstra [16]. However, adaptor signature was first formally defined by Aumayr et al. [1] in 2020, leveraging signature schemes with classical security. In 2021, Erwig et al. [7] proposed a generic construction of an AS from any signature scheme that satisfies certain homomorphic properties. However, not all post-quantum signatures satisfy these criteria. In support of the efforts towards migration to post-quantum cryptography, Esgin et al. [8] proposed in 2020 the first post-quantum adaptor signature, named LAS. It relies on standard lattice assumptions such as Module-LWE and Module SIS and uses a simplified version of Dilithium as its underlying signature scheme. However, their AS requires zero-knowledge proof [10] to ensure that the extracted witness is of the desired norm and satisfies the hard relation, resulting in significant off-chain communication costs. This makes it challenging for practical deployment of their LAS scheme. From a privacy standpoint, when LAS is employed in specific applications like constructing PCNs, it can disclose significant information, compromising the overall privacy of the system. In a subsequent work [11] in 2022, Gilchrist proposed a construction of an AS, named SQI-AS, in the isogeny realm. Their construction of the AS is based on the isogeny-based signature scheme SQISign [6] and is associated with the SIDH based hard relation. However, due to severe attacks [3] [12] on SIDH, the security of SQI-AS was jeopardized. Another attempt to construct an isogeny-based adaptor signature was proposed by Tairi et al. [19] in 2021, which relies on the signature scheme CSI-FiSh. However, their construction is not efficient in terms of the signature size and key size due to the use of non-interactive zero-knowledge proof. Moreover, the authors have not taken into consideration the unlinkability notion of an adaptor signature. In 2022, Dai et al. [4] identified gaps in existing security formulations of adaptor signatures. They developed security notions that strictly imply previous notions and formalized the concept of unlinkability for adaptor signatures.

Our Contribution. The existing proposals for AS are undesirable for practical applications. While some scheme involves expensive communication costs, others are broken and fail to provide the claimed security guarantees. Also, the majority of the existing schemes did not consider the unlinkability notion of AS. The somewhat unsatisfactory state of the art motivates our search for a post-quantum secure AS with compact key and signature sizes providing advanced security guarantees. In this work, we propose an *isogeny-based adaptor signature* using CSI-FiSh as the underlying signature scheme and exploiting the *hard relation R* from Commutative Supersingular Isogeny Diffie-Hellman (CSIDH) key exchange. We first define a variant of the CSI-FiSh signature scheme, named *Modified* CSI-FiSh (MCSI-FiSh), which is defined against the relation R derived from CSIDH. The *Modified* CSI-FiSh (MCSI-FiSh) additionally verifies the release of a witness alongside a valid signature. We then propose an adaptor signature scheme for MCSI-FiSh and provide rigorous security proof proving our scheme is secure against *pre-signature adaptability*, (strong)-*full extractability* and *unlinkability* following the security model of [4]. We have also demonstrated that the relation R derived from CSIDH exhibits the property of *strong random self-reducible relation*. Leveraging this characteristic of R, we furnish the proof of unlinkability of our AS. We emphasize that our scheme is the first AS in the isogeny setting that exhibits unlinkability property and strong full extractability.

In Table 1, we compare our proposed isogeny-based adaptor signature [8,19] with existing post-quantum secure adaptor signatures in terms of key size, pre-signature size and signature size. Our isogeny-based scheme as well as that of Tairi et al. [19] outperforms LAS [8] in terms of key size. Moreover, both pre-signature and signature sizes are smaller in our proposed scheme compared to LAS [8]. While our signature size is slightly larger than that of Tairi et al. [19],

Table 1. Comparative analysis of existing post-quantum secure adaptor signature schemes with respect to key size, pre-signature size and signature size.

Scheme	Key Size		Pre-signature	Signature
	$\|sk\|$	$\|pk\|$	$\|\hat{\sigma}\|$	$\|\sigma\|$
Esgin et al. [8]	$(n+\ell)$ in $\mathbb{P}_1$	n in $\mathcal{R}_q$	1 in $\mathcal{R}$, $(n+\ell)$ in $\mathbb{P}_{\gamma-\kappa}$, $\|\pi\|$	1 in $\mathcal{R}$, $(n+\ell)$ in $\mathbb{P}_{\gamma-\kappa-1}$, $\|\pi\|$
Tairi et al. [19]	$(S-1)$ in $\mathbb{Z}_N$	$(S-1)$ in $\mathbb{F}_p$	$2T$ in $\mathbb{Z}_N$, T in $\mathbb{F}_p$, $T\|\pi\|$	$2T$ in $\mathbb{Z}_N$
Our		$(S-1)$ in $\mathbb{Z}_N$	$(S-1)$ in $\mathbb{F}_p$	$(2T+1)$ in $\mathbb{Z}_N$, 1 in $\mathbb{F}_p$	$(2T+1)$ in $\mathbb{Z}_N$, 1 in $\mathbb{F}_p$.

$\|pk\|$ = size of public key, $\|sk\|$ = size of secret key, $\|\sigma\|$ = size of signature, $\|\pi\|$ = size of the zero-knowledge proof, N = class number of $Cl(\mathcal{O})$ and S, T are integers with $T < S$ and $\mathbb{F}_p$ is the field with p elements where p is an prime number. Let $n, q, \kappa, \gamma, \ell$ and d be positive integers. $\mathcal{R}_q = \frac{\mathbb{Z}_q[X]}{(X^d+1)}$ is the cyclotomic ring of power-of-2 degree d for an odd modulus q, $\mathcal{R} = \frac{\mathbb{Z}[X]}{(X^d+1)}$ and $\mathbb{P}_c$ the set of polynomials in $\mathcal{R}_q$ whose maximum absolute coefficient is at most c where c is a positive integer.

Table 2. Comparison of security property of existing post-quantum secure adaptor signature schemes

Scheme	Property			
	Adaptability	$FEXT$	$SFEXT$	Unlinkability
Esgin et al. [8]	✓	✓	✗	✗
Tairi et al. [19]	✓	✓	✗	✗
Our	✓	✓	✓	✓

FEXT : full extractability, SFEXT : strong full strong full extractability.

our pre-signature size demonstrates significantly improved efficiency. The lattice-based scheme LAS [8] necessitates a zero-knowledge proof for verifying that the extracted witness belongs to the required norm and satisfies the hard relation. However, the most efficient variant of such a proof is 53KB in size, as outlined in [9], leading to notable communication costs to the applications using LAS. The isogeny-based adaptor signature scheme of [19] also utilizes zero-knowledge proof. In contrast, our proposed isogeny-based adaptor signature scheme eliminates the need for zero-knowledge proof, thereby enhancing efficiency without any security breach. We summarize the security properties attained by existing post-quantum secure adaptor signature schemes in Table 2. Each scheme meets the requirements of adaptability and full extractability (FEXT). Notably, our scheme stands out as the sole one to achieve strong full extractability (SFEXT) and unlinkability, distinguishing it from others in consideration.

2   Preliminaries

Notation. Throughout the paper, we adopt the following notations. Let $\lambda \in \mathbb{N}$ denote the security parameter. We use $\#S$ to denote the cardinality of the set S. By $s_1\|s_2$ we denote the concatenation of strings s_1 and s_2. The notation

$\mathsf{sign}(x)$ represents the sign of the integer x. The notation $\forall i \in [T]$ means for all $i = 1, 2, \ldots, T$. By $[0, I]^n$, we denote the set of n-length integer vectors over the alphabet from $\{0, 1, \ldots, I\}$. A function $\epsilon(\cdot)$ is called *negligible* if, for every positive integer c, there exists an integer k such that for all $\lambda > k$, $|\epsilon(\lambda)| < 1/\lambda^c$.

Elliptic Curves and Isogenies [5]. Let K be a finite field and $\overline{K}$ be its algebraic closure. An elliptic curve E over K is a non-singular, projective, cubic curve having genus one with a special point O, called the point at infinity. The set of K-rational points of the elliptic curve E form an additive abelian group with O as the identity element. A *Montgomery elliptic curve* E is of the form $E : By^2 = x^3 + Ax^2 + x$ where $B(A^2 - 4) \neq 0$ for some $A, B \in K$. The quadratic twist of a curve $E : y^2 = f(x)$ defined over the field K is given by $E^{\mathsf{twist}} : dy^2 = f(x)$ where $d \in K$ is not a square. Let E_1 and E_2 be two elliptic curves over a field K. An *isogeny* from E_1 to E_2 is a non-constant morphism $\varphi : E_1 \longrightarrow E_2$ over $\overline{K}$ preserving the point at infinity O. The *degree* of the isogeny φ, denoted by $\deg(\varphi)$ is its degree as a rational map. A non-zero isogeny φ is called *separable* if and only if $\deg(\varphi) = \#\mathsf{ker}(\varphi)$ where $\mathsf{ker}(\varphi) = \varphi^{-1}(O_{E_2})$.

Endomorphism Ring. The set of all isogenies from E to itself defined over $\overline{K}$ forms a ring under pointwise addition and composition. This ring is called the *endomorphism ring* of the elliptic curve E and is denoted by $\mathsf{End}(E)$. By $\mathsf{End}_K(E)$, we mean the set of all isogenies from E to itself defined over K. If $\mathsf{End}(E)$ is isomorphic to an order in a quaternion algebra, the curve E is said to be *supersingular*. On the other hand, if $\mathsf{End}(E)$ is isomorphic to an order in an imaginary quadratic field, we say the curve E is *ordinary*.

Theorem 1. [21] *Let E_1 be a curve and G be its finite subgroup. Then there is a unique (up to isomorphism) curve E_2 and a separable isogeny $\varphi : E_1 \longrightarrow E_2$ with $\mathsf{ker}(\varphi) = G$ such that $E_2 \cong E_1/G$ which can be computed using Vélu's formulae [20].*

Ideal Class Group. [14] Let $\mathcal{O}$ be an order in an imaginary quadratic field F. A fractional ideal $\mathfrak{a}$ of $\mathcal{O}$ is a finitely generated $\mathcal{O}$-submodule of F. Let $\mathcal{I}(O)$ be a set of invertible fractional ideals of $\mathcal{O}$. Then $\mathcal{I}(\mathcal{O})$ is an abelian group derived from the multiplication of ideals with the identity $\mathcal{O}$. Let $\mathcal{P}(\mathcal{O})$ be a subgroup of $\mathcal{I}(\mathcal{O})$ defined by $\mathcal{P}(O) = \{\mathfrak{a} | \mathfrak{a} = \alpha\mathcal{O}$ for some $\alpha \in F \setminus \{0\} \}$. The abelian group $\mathsf{Cl}(\mathcal{O})$ defined by $\mathcal{I}(\mathcal{O})/\mathcal{P}(\mathcal{O})$ is called the *ideal class group* of $\mathcal{O}$. An element of $\mathsf{Cl}(\mathcal{O})$ denoted by $[\mathfrak{a}]$ is the equivalence class of $\mathfrak{a}$.

The Class Group Action. Let $\mathsf{Ell}_p(\mathcal{O})$ denote the set of $\mathbb{F}_p$-isomorphic classes of supersingular curves E, whose $\mathbb{F}_p$-endomorphism ring $\mathsf{End}_{\mathbb{F}_p}(E) \cong \mathcal{O} = \mathbb{Z}[\sqrt{-p}]$. The ideal class group $\mathsf{Cl}(\mathcal{O})$ acts freely and transitively on $\mathsf{Ell}_p(\mathcal{O})$. For the curve $E \in \mathsf{Ell}_p(\mathcal{O})$, the *action* $*$ of $[\mathfrak{a}] \in \mathsf{Cl}(\mathcal{O})$ on E is defined as follows:

- Consider all the endomorphisms α in $\mathfrak{a}$.
- Compute the subgroup $E[\mathfrak{a}] = \bigcap_{\alpha \in \mathfrak{a}} \mathsf{ker}(\alpha)$.
- Compute the elliptic curve $E/E[\mathfrak{a}]$ and an isogeny $\varphi_{\mathfrak{a}} : E \longrightarrow E/E[\mathfrak{a}]$ using Velu's formula. (See Theorem 1) and return the elliptic curve $E/E[\mathfrak{a}]$.

Henceforth, we will use the notation $[\mathfrak{a}]E$ instead of $[\mathfrak{a}] * E$ to denote the elliptic curve $E/E[\mathfrak{a}]$ obtained by the action of class group element $[\mathfrak{a}] \in \mathsf{Cl}(\mathcal{O})$ on the elliptic curve $E \in \mathsf{Ell}_p(\mathcal{O})$.

Theorem 2. [21] *Let $\mathcal{O}$ be an order of an imaginary quadratic field and E be an elliptic curve defined over $\mathbb{F}_p$. If $\mathsf{Ell}_p(\mathcal{O})$ contains the $\mathbb{F}_p$-isomorphism class of supersingular elliptic curves, then the action of the ideal class group $\mathsf{Cl}(\mathcal{O})$ on $\mathsf{Ell}_p(\mathcal{O})$, defined by*

$$\mathsf{Cl}(\mathcal{O}) \times \mathsf{Ell}_p(\mathcal{O}) \longrightarrow \mathsf{Ell}_p(\mathcal{O})$$
$$([\mathfrak{a}], E) \longrightarrow E/E[\mathfrak{a}]$$

is free and transitive where $\mathfrak{a}$ is an integral ideal of $\mathcal{O}$ and $E[\mathfrak{a}]$ is the intersection of the kernels of elements in $\mathfrak{a}$.

Definition 3. (Group Action Inverse Problem (GAIP) [2]). Given two elliptic curves E_1 and E_2, both having the same endomorphism ring $\mathcal{O}$, the GAIP is to find an element $[\mathfrak{a}] \in \mathsf{Cl}(\mathcal{O})$ such that $E_1 = [\mathfrak{a}]E_2$.

Definition 4. (Multi-target Group Action Inverse Problem (MT-GAIP) [2]). Given k elliptic curves $E_1, \ldots, E_k$, each having the same endomorphism ring $\mathcal{O}$, the MT-GAIP is to find an element $[\mathfrak{a}] \in \mathsf{Cl}(\mathcal{O})$ such that $E_i = [\mathfrak{a}]E_j$ some $i, j \in \{0, \ldots, k\}$ with $i \neq j$.

3   Signature Scheme

Definition 5. (Signature scheme). A *signature scheme* Sig is a quadruple of probabilistic polynomial time (PPT) algorithms associated with a message space $\mathcal{M}$ satisfying the following requirements:

– Sig.Setup(λ) on $\rightarrow$ pp: A trusted party p input λ outputs the public parameter pp.
– Sig.KeyGen(pp) $\rightarrow$ (sk, pk): On input pp, this algorithm generates a signing and verification key pair (sk, pk).
– Sig.Sign(pp, sk, m) $\rightarrow \sigma$: Taking input pp, sk and a message $m \in \mathcal{M}$, this algorithm returns a signature σ of message m.
– Sig.Verify(pp, pk, m, σ) $\rightarrow$ Valid/Invalid: On input pp, pk, m and signature σ, this algorithm returns Valid or Invalid indicating the validity of signature σ.

Definition 6. (Correctness). For all pp $\leftarrow$ Sig.Setup(λ), all (sk, pk) $\leftarrow$ Sig.KeyGen(pp) and all signature $\sigma \leftarrow$ Sig.Sign(pp, sk, m), it must hold that Sig.Verify(pp, pk, m, σ) = Valid.

Definition 7. (sEUF-CMA). A signature scheme Sig is secure against *strong existential unforgeability under chosen-message attacks* (sEUF-CMA) if the advantage $\mathsf{Adv}_{\mathsf{Sig}, \mathcal{A}}^{\mathsf{sEUF\text{-}CMA}}(\lambda)$ of any PPT adversary $\mathcal{A}$ defined as $\mathsf{Adv}_{\mathsf{Sig}, \mathcal{A}}^{\mathsf{sEUF\text{-}CMA}}(\lambda) = \Pr[\mathsf{Exp}_{\mathsf{Sig}, \mathcal{A}}^{\mathsf{sEUF\text{-}CMA}}(\lambda) = 1]$ is negligible, where the experiment $\mathsf{Exp}_{\mathsf{Sig}, \mathcal{A}}^{\mathsf{sEUF\text{-}CMA}}(\lambda)$ between an adversary $\mathcal{A}$ and a challenger $\mathcal{C}$ is depicted in Fig. 1.

- **Setup:** The challenger $\mathcal{C}$ computes pp $\leftarrow$ Sig.Setup(λ) and secret-public key pair (sk, pk) $\leftarrow$ Sig.KeyGen(pp). It forwards pp and pk to the adversary $\mathcal{A}$ while keeps sk secret to itself. It also sets the list SList to ϕ.
- **Query Phase:** The adversary $\mathcal{A}$ issues polynomially many adaptive signature queries to the following oracle $\mathcal{O}_{\mathsf{Sign}}(m)$.
  - $\mathcal{O}_{\mathsf{Sign}}(m)$: Upon receiving a query on the message m, the challenger $\mathcal{C}$ checks if $m \notin \mathcal{M}$. If the check succeeds, it returns $\perp$. Else it computes a signature $\sigma \leftarrow$ Sig.Sign(pp, sk, m) on the message m under the secret key sk and sets SList = SList $\cup$ $\{m, \sigma\}$. It returns the computed signature σ to $\mathcal{A}$.
- **Forgery:** The adversary $\mathcal{A}$ eventually submits a forgery (m^*, σ^*). If Valid $\leftarrow$ Sig.Verify(pp, pk, m^*, σ^*) and $(m^*, \sigma^*) \notin$ SList the experiment $\mathsf{Exp}_{\mathsf{Sig}, \mathcal{A}}^{\mathsf{sEUF\text{-}CMA}}(\lambda)$ returns 1; otherwise, returns 0.

Fig. 1. $\mathsf{Exp}_{\mathsf{Sig}, \mathcal{A}}^{\mathsf{sEUF\text{-}CMA}}(\lambda)$: Strong existential unforgeability under chosen-message attacks

We also define *existential unforgeability under chosen-message attacks* which is a slightly weaker security property of a signature scheme. It is modeled using the experiment $\mathsf{Exp}_{\mathsf{Sig}, \mathcal{A}}^{\mathsf{EUF\text{-}CMA}}(\lambda)$ which is the same as the experiment $\mathsf{Exp}_{\mathsf{Sig}, \mathcal{A}}^{\mathsf{sEUF\text{-}CMA}}(\lambda)$ subject to the condition that the adversary $\mathcal{A}$ needs to submit a valid signature-message pair (σ^*, m^*) in the forgery phase in order to win the experiment $\mathsf{Exp}_{\mathsf{Sig}, \mathcal{A}}^{\mathsf{EUF\text{-}CMA}}(\lambda)$ such that m^* has never been queried before to the signing oracle $\mathcal{O}_{\mathsf{Sign}}(\cdot)$.

Definition 8. (EUF-CMA). A signature scheme Sig satisfies *existential unforgeability under chosen-message attacks* (EUF-CMA) if the advantage $\mathsf{Adv}_{\mathsf{Sig}, \mathcal{A}}^{\mathsf{UF\text{-}CMA}}(\lambda)$ of any PPT adversary $\mathcal{A}$ defined as $\mathsf{Adv}_{\mathsf{Sig}, \mathcal{A}}^{\mathsf{UF\text{-}CMA}}(\lambda) = \mathsf{Pr}[\mathsf{Exp}_{\mathsf{Sig}, \mathcal{A}}^{\mathsf{UF\text{-}CMA}}(\lambda) = 1]$ is negligible.

3.1 CSI-FiSh: A Signature Scheme Based on Isogeny

For a 512 bits prime $p = 4\ell_1\ell_2 \ldots \ell_n - 1$ where ℓ_i's are small distinct odd primes with $n = 74$, $\ell_1 = 3$, $\ell_{73} = 373$ and $\ell_{74} = 587$, Beullens et al. [2] computed the class group structure and the relation lattice. The knowledge of the class group structure and relation lattice allows one to sample random elements from $\mathbb{Z}_{\#\mathsf{Cl}(\mathcal{O})}$ and transform them into vectors by solving easy instances of the closest vector problem using the relation lattice. This ensures that the entire class group is covered uniformly and also allows efficient computation via low-degree isogenies. The ideal class group $\mathsf{Cl}(\mathbb{Z}[\sqrt{-p}])$ is shown to be a cyclic group with generator $\mathfrak{g} = <3, \pi - 1>$ where π is the Frobenius endomorphism and the class number of $\mathsf{Cl}(\mathbb{Z}[\sqrt{-p}])$ is also computed which we denote by N.
We use the following notations for the sake of simplicity.

- Write $[a]E$ instead of $[\mathfrak{a}]E$ for any element $[\mathfrak{a}] = [\mathfrak{g}^a] \in \mathsf{Cl}(\mathbb{Z}[\sqrt{-p}])$.
- Write $[a + b]E$ instead of $[\mathfrak{a}][\mathfrak{b}]E$ for any two elements $[\mathfrak{a}] = [\mathfrak{g}^a]$, $[\mathfrak{b}] = [\mathfrak{g}^b] \in \mathsf{Cl}(\mathbb{Z}[\sqrt{-p}])$.

The *Commutative Supersingular Isogeny based Fiat-Shamir signature* (CSI-FiSh) [2] comprises of four PPT algorithms detailed below:

CSI-FiSh.Setup(λ) $\rightarrow$ pp: A trusted party executes this algorithm on input λ and returns the public parameter pp. It proceeds as follows:

i. Chooses a large prime $p = 4\ell_1\ell_2\ldots\ell_n - 1$ where ℓ_i's are small distinct odd primes with $n = 74$, $\ell_1 = 3$, $\ell_{73} = 373$ and $\ell_{74} = 587$.
ii. Sets a base curve $E_0 : y^2 = x^3 + x \in \mathsf{Ell}_p(\mathbb{Z}[\sqrt{-p}])$ over $\mathbb{F}_p$ and the generator $\mathfrak{g} = \langle 3, \pi - 1 \rangle$ of the class group $\mathcal{G} = \mathsf{Cl}(\mathbb{Z}[\sqrt{-p}])$ with class number N.
iii. Samples a keyed hash functions $\mathcal{H}_1 : \{0,1\}^* \rightarrow \{-S+1,\ldots,0,\ldots,S-1\}^T$ where S, T are positive integers with $T < S$.
iv. Returns $\mathsf{pp} = (p, \mathfrak{g}, N, E_0, \mathcal{H}_1, S, T)$.

$\mathsf{CSI\text{-}FiSh.KeyGen(pp)} \rightarrow (\mathsf{sk}, \mathsf{pk})$: On input pp, a user executes this algorithm to generate a secret key sk and the corresponding public key pk as follows:

i. Uniformly samples $S - 1$ elements a_i from $\mathbb{Z}_N$ and sets $[\mathfrak{a}_i] = [\mathfrak{g}^{a_i}] \in \mathcal{G}$ for $i \in [S-1]$.
ii. Computes the elliptic curve $E_{A_i} = [a_i]E_0 \forall i \in [S-1]$.
iii. Sets $\mathsf{sk} = \{a_i\}_{i=1}^{S-1}$ and $\mathsf{pk} = \{E_{A_i}\}_{i=1}^{S-1}$.
iv. Publishes pk and keeps sk secret to himself.

$\mathsf{CSI\text{-}FiSh.Sign(pp, sk, }m) \rightarrow \sigma$: In this algorithm, a signer generates a signature σ on the message $m \in \mathcal{M}$ using pp and his secret key $\mathsf{sk} = \{a_i\}_{i=1}^{S-1}$ as follows:

i. Sets $a_0 \leftarrow 0$.
ii. Uniformly samples b_i from $\mathbb{Z}_N$ and $[\mathfrak{b}_i] = [\mathfrak{g}^{b_i}] \in \mathcal{G}$ for $i \in [T]$.
iii. Computes the curves $E_{B_i} = [b_i]E_0$, the challenge bits $(h_1,\ldots,h_T) = \mathcal{H}_1(E_{B_1}||\ldots||E_{B_T}||m) \in \{-S+1,\ldots,0,\ldots,S-1\}^T$ and the response $z_i = (b_i - \mathrm{sign}(h_i)a_{|h_i|}) \mod N \forall i \in [T]$.
iv. Returns the signature $\sigma = (\mathsf{h}, \mathsf{z})$ where $\mathsf{h} = \{h_i\}_{i=1}^T$ and $\mathsf{z} = \{z_i\}_{i=1}^T$.

$\mathsf{CSI\text{-}FiSh.Verify(pp, pk, }m, \sigma) \rightarrow \mathsf{Valid/Invalid}$: Employing the signer's public key $\mathsf{pk} = \{E_{A_i}\}_{i=1}^{S-1}$, a verifier executes the following steps to verify σ on m.

i. Parses $\sigma = (\mathsf{h}, \mathsf{z})$ where $\mathsf{h} = \{h_i\}_{i=1}^T$ and $\mathsf{z} = \{z_i\}_{i=1}^T$.
ii. Defines $E_{A_{-i}} = E_{A_i}^{\mathrm{twist}} \forall i \in [S-1]$
iii. Extracts the curves $E_{A_{|h_i|}}$ from pk and computes the curves

$$E_{B_i} = [z_i]E_{A_{h_i}} = \begin{cases} [z_i]E_{A_{|h_i|}} & \text{if } h_i \geq 0 \\ [z_i]E_{A_{|h_i|}}^{\mathrm{twist}} & \text{if } h_i < 0 \end{cases}$$

for $\forall i \in [T]$ and the challenge bits $(h_1',\ldots,h_T') = \mathcal{H}_1(E_{B_1}||\ldots||E_{B_T}||m)$.
iv. If $(h_1,\ldots,h_T) = (h_1',\ldots,h_T')$ returns Valid, else returns Invalid.

Correctness. For all $\mathsf{pp} \leftarrow \mathsf{CSI\text{-}FiSh.Setup}(\lambda)$, all key pair $(\mathsf{sk}, \mathsf{pk}) \leftarrow \mathsf{CSI\text{-}FiSh.KeyGen(pp)}$ and all honestly generated signature $\sigma \leftarrow \mathsf{CSI\text{-}FiSh.Sign(pp, sk, }m)$, it holds that $\mathsf{CSI\text{-}FiSh.Verify(pp, pk, }m, \sigma) = \mathsf{Valid}$ since $E_{B_i} = [b_i]E_0$ is recovered by computing $[z_i]E_{A_{h_i}}$ for $i \in [T]$ as:

$$[z_i]E_{A_{h_i}} = [b_i - \mathrm{sign}(h_i)a_{|h_i|}]E_{A_{h_i}} = [b_i - \mathrm{sign}(h_i)a_{|h_i|}][\mathrm{sign}(h_i)a_{|h_i|}]E_0 = [b_i]E_0.$$

Theorem 9. *The isogeny-based signature scheme* CSI-FiSh *is EUF-CMA secure under the hardness of* MT-GAIP *problem defined in Definition 4, if the hash function $\mathcal{H}_1$ is modeled as a (quantum) random oracle.*

4   Hard Relation

Definition 10 (Relation). Let $R \subseteq \mathcal{D}_s \times \mathcal{D}_w$ be a relation with the statement-witness pair $(Y, y) \in \mathcal{D}_s \times \mathcal{D}_w$ and let the language $L_R \subseteq \mathcal{D}_s$ associated to R be defined as $L_R = \{Y \in \mathcal{D}_s \mid \exists y \in \mathcal{D}_w \text{ such that } (Y, y) \in R\}$. For an NP relation R following holds:

- There exists a PPT sampling algorithm $R.\mathsf{Gen}(\lambda)$ that on input of the security parameter λ outputs a pair $(Y, y) \in R$;
- The relation R is poly-time decidable;

Definition 11 (Hard Relation). A relation R is said to be a *hard relation* if for all q, polynomially dependent on λ and for all PPT adversaries $\mathcal{A}$, there exists a negligible function ϵ such that $\mathsf{Adv}_{R, \mathcal{A}}^{\mathsf{q\text{-}OW}}(\lambda) = \Pr[\mathsf{Exp}_{R, \mathcal{A}}^{\mathsf{q\text{-}OW}}(\lambda) = 1] < \epsilon$ where q-one wayness (q-ow) of R is modeled via the experiment $\mathsf{Exp}_{R, \mathcal{A}}^{\mathsf{q\text{-}OW}}(\lambda)$ between an adversary $\mathcal{A}$ and a challenger $\mathcal{C}$ as shown in Fig. 2.

- **Setup:** For $i = 1, \ldots, q$, the challenger $\mathcal{C}$ generates $(Y_i, \cdot) \leftarrow R.\mathsf{Gen}(\lambda)$ and provides $(Y_1, \ldots, Y_q)$ to the adversary $\mathcal{A}$.
- **Final Phase:** The adversary $\mathcal{A}$ submits (I, y') to the challenger $\mathcal{C}$ and if $(Y_I, y') \in R$ then the $\mathsf{Exp}_{R, \mathcal{A}}^{\mathsf{q\text{-}OW}}(\lambda)$ outputs 1; otherwise, it outputs 0.

Fig. 2. $\mathsf{Exp}_{R, \mathcal{A}}^{\mathsf{q\text{-}OW}}(\lambda)$: q-one wayness of hard relation R

Definition 12 (Unique-Witness). A relation R is said to have *unique-witness* property if for all PPT adversaries $\mathcal{A}$, there exists a negligible function ϵ such that $\mathsf{Adv}_{R, \mathcal{A}}^{\mathsf{UWIT}}(\lambda) = \Pr[(Y, y) \in R \wedge (Y, y') \in R \wedge y \neq y' | (Y, y, y') \leftarrow \mathcal{A}] < \epsilon$.

Definition 13 (Random Self-reducible (RSR)). Let $R \subseteq \mathcal{D}_s \times \mathcal{D}_w$ be a hard relation with the generator algorithm $R.\mathsf{Gen}(\lambda)$. The relation R is said to be RSR if there exists a tuple of deterministic algorithms $(R.\mathsf{Rand}, R.\mathsf{St}, R.\mathsf{Wit}, R.\mathsf{Rec})$ associated with a randomness space $\mathcal{D}_r$ satisfying the following requirements for any $(Y, y) \in R$ generated by $R.\mathsf{Gen}(\lambda)$:

- $R.\mathsf{Rand}(\lambda) \to r$: On input of the security parameter λ, the algorithm $R.\mathsf{Rand}$ outputs a random value r from the set $\mathcal{D}_r$.
- $R.\mathsf{St}(Y, r) \to Y'$: If $Y \in L_R$ and $r \in \mathcal{D}_r$, this algorithm on input (Y, r) where $(Y, \cdot) \leftarrow R.\mathsf{Gen}(\lambda)$ outputs $Y' \in L_R$ which is identically distributed to Y.
- $R.\mathsf{Wit}(y, r) \to y'$: This algorithm on input $(y, r) \in \mathcal{D}_w \times \mathcal{D}_r$ outputs $y' \in \mathcal{D}_w$ which satisfies $(Y', y') \in R$ where $Y' \leftarrow R.\mathsf{St}(Y, r)$ for some $Y \in L_R$.
- $R.\mathsf{Rec}(y', r) \to y$: This algorithm on input $(y', r) \in \mathcal{D}_w \times \mathcal{D}_r$ outputs y such that $(Y, y) \in R$ for some $Y \in \mathcal{D}_s$ satisfying $y' \leftarrow R.\mathsf{Wit}(y, r)$.

Definition 14 (Strong RSR (SRSR)). An RSR relation R is said to be *strong* RSR (SRSR) if for all PPT adversaries $\mathcal{A}$, there exists a negligible function ϵ such that $\mathsf{Adv}_{R, \mathcal{A}}^{\mathsf{SRSR}}(\lambda) = |\Pr[\mathsf{Exp}_{R, \mathcal{A}}^{\mathsf{SRSR}}(\lambda) = 1] - \frac{1}{2}| < \epsilon$ where SRSR is modeled via the experiment $\mathsf{Exp}_{R, \mathcal{A}}^{\mathsf{SRSR}}(\lambda)$ between an adversary $\mathcal{A}$ and a challenger $\mathcal{C}$ presented in Fig. 3.

- **Challenge Phase:** On input of the statement-witness pair (Y, y) from the adversary $\mathcal{A}$, the challenger $\mathcal{C}$ checks if $(Y, y) \in R$. If $(Y, y) \notin R$ then $\mathcal{C}$ aborts the process. If the check succeeds, $\mathcal{C}$ generates $(Y', y') \leftarrow R.\mathsf{Gen}(\lambda)$ and $r \leftarrow R.\mathsf{Rand}(\lambda)$ and computes $Y_0 \leftarrow R.\mathsf{St}(Y', r)$, $y_0 \leftarrow R.\mathsf{Wit}(y', r)$, $Y_1 \leftarrow R.\mathsf{St}(Y, r)$ and $y_1 \leftarrow R.\mathsf{Wit}(y, r)$. Finally, $\mathcal{C}$ samples a random bit $b \leftarrow \{0, 1\}$ and return (Y_b, y_b).
- **Final Phase:** The adversary $\mathcal{A}$ eventually submits a bit b' to $\mathcal{C}$ and if $b = b'$ then the $\mathsf{Exp}_{R, \mathcal{A}}^{\mathsf{SRSR}}(\lambda)$ outputs 1; otherwise, it outputs 0.

Fig. 3. $\mathsf{Exp}_{R, \mathcal{A}}^{\mathsf{SRSR}}(\lambda)$: Strong Random Self-Reducible

4.1   Isogeny-Based Hard Relation

Let us consider a relation $R \subseteq \mathsf{Ell}_p(\mathbb{Z}[\sqrt{-p}]) \times \mathbb{Z}_N$ such that $R = \{(E_Y, y) \in \mathsf{Ell}_p(\mathbb{Z}[\sqrt{-p}]) \times \mathbb{Z}_N \mid E_Y = [y]E_0\}$ with the following generator algorithm where $\mathcal{D}_s = \mathsf{Ell}_p(\mathbb{Z}[\sqrt{-p}])$, $\mathcal{D}_w = \mathbb{Z}_N$ and $E_0 : y^2 = x^3 + x \in \mathsf{Ell}_p(\mathbb{Z}[\sqrt{-p}])$.

- $R.\mathsf{Gen}(\lambda)$: On input of security parameter this algorithm uniformly samples y from $\mathbb{Z}_N$, computes $E_Y = [y]E_0$ and returns (E_Y, y).
- It can be decided in polynomial time if $(E_Y, y) \in R$ or not by checking $E_Y = [y]E_0$.

The relation R defines the language $L_R = \{E_Y \in \mathsf{Ell}_p(\mathbb{Z}[\sqrt{-p}]) \mid \exists\, y \in \mathbb{Z}_N\, \mathrm{s.t.}\, (E_Y, y) \in R\}$. We now show that the relation R associated with the set $\mathbb{Z}_N$ satisfies the properties of random self reducibility as per Definition 13 for any $(E_Y, y) \in R$ generated by $R.\mathsf{Gen}(\lambda)$.

- $R.\mathsf{Rand}(\lambda) \to r$: On input of the security parameter λ, this algorithm randomly samples $r \xleftarrow{\$} \mathbb{Z}_N$ and outputs r.
- $R.\mathsf{St}(E_Y, r) \to Y'$: If $E_Y \in L_R$ and $r \in \mathbb{Z}_N$, then this algorithm computes $E_{Y'} = [r]E_Y$ and returns $E_{Y'} \in L_R$ which is identically distributed to E_Y generated by $R.\mathsf{Gen}(\lambda)$
- $R.\mathsf{Wit}(y, r) \to y'$: On input $(y, r) \in \mathbb{Z}_N \times \mathbb{Z}_N$, outputs $y' = y + r \pmod N \in \mathbb{Z}_N$ such that $(E_{Y'}, y') \in R$. Note that, $E_{Y'} = [y']E_0$ as

$$[y']E_0 = [y + r]E_0 = [r + y]E_0 = [r][y]E_0 = [r]E_Y = E_{Y'}$$

- $R.\mathsf{Rec}(y', r) \to y$: On input (y', r), this algorithm outputs $y = y' - r \pmod N \in \mathbb{Z}_N$ such that $(E_Y, y) \in R$ and also satisfying $y' \leftarrow R.\mathsf{Wit}(y, r)$, i.e. $y' = y + r \pmod N$. Observe that, $E_Y = [y' - r]E_0$ as

$$E_Y = [y]E_0 = [y + r - r]E_0 = [y' - r]E_0$$

Theorem 15. *The relation $R = \{(E_Y, y) \in \mathsf{Ell}_p(\mathbb{Z}[\sqrt{-p}]) \times \mathbb{Z}_N \mid E_Y = [y]E_0\}$ is a hard relation (i.e. $\mathsf{Adv}_{R, \mathcal{A}}^{\mathsf{q\text{-}OW}}(\lambda)$ is negligible) under the hardness of* GAIP *problem defined in Definition 3.*

Theorem 16. *The relation $R = \{(E_Y, y) \in \mathsf{Ell}_p(\mathbb{Z}[\sqrt{-p}]) \times \mathbb{Z}_N \mid E_Y = [y]E_0\}$ satisfies unique-witness property (i.e. $\mathsf{Adv}_{R, \mathcal{A}}^{\mathsf{UWIT}}(\lambda)$ is negligible) as the class group action is transitive as given in Theorem 2.*

Theorem 17. *The relation* $R = \{(E_Y, y) \in Ell_p(\mathbb{Z}[\sqrt{-p}]) \times \mathbb{Z}_N \mid E_Y = [y]E_0\}$ *is* SRSR, *(i.e.* $\mathsf{Adv}_{R,\mathcal{A}}^{\mathsf{SRSR}}(\lambda)$ *is negligible).*

Proof. Let the adversary $\mathcal{A}$ outputs $(E_Y, y) \in R$ i.e. $E_Y = [y]E_0$ and $(E_Y, y) \in Ell_p(\mathbb{Z}[\sqrt{-p}]) \times \mathbb{Z}_N$. Now, consider the challenger $\mathcal{C}$, which computes (E_{Y_0}, y_0) and (E_{Y_1}, y_1) as follows:

– $(E_{Y'}, y') \leftarrow R.\mathsf{Gen}(\lambda)$ and $r \leftarrow R.\mathsf{Rand}(\lambda)$,
– $E_{Y_0} \leftarrow R.\mathsf{St}(E_{Y'}, r)$, $y_0 \leftarrow R.\mathsf{Wit}(y', r)$,
– $E_{Y_1} \leftarrow R.\mathsf{St}(E_Y, r)$ and $y_1 \leftarrow R.\mathsf{Wit}(y, r)$.

We claim that both (E_{Y_0}, y_0) and (E_{Y_1}, y_1) are indistinguishable. Because $y_0 = y' + r \pmod{N}$ and $y_1 = y + r \pmod{N}$ where r is uniformly chosen from $\mathbb{Z}_N$. This implies that both y_0 and y_1 are uniform in $\mathbb{Z}_N$. Therefore, the adversary $\mathcal{A}$ cannot distinguish (E_{Y_0}, y_0) and (E_{Y_1}, y_1) as both y_0 and y_1 are uniformly distributed in $\mathbb{Z}_N$. Hence $\mathsf{Adv}_{R,\mathcal{A}}^{\mathsf{SRSR}}(\lambda)$ is negligible.

5   Adaptor Signatures

In this section, we describe the adaptor signature which enables two parties, say a signer and a publisher to trade a signature in exchange for a secret.

An *adaptor signature scheme* with respect to a hard relation $R \subseteq \mathcal{D}_s \times \mathcal{D}_w$ (See Defn. 10), a signature scheme $\mathsf{Sig} = (\mathsf{Setup}, \mathsf{KeyGen}, \mathsf{Sign}, \mathsf{Verify})$ (See Sect. 3) and a message space $\mathcal{M}$ consists of a tuple $\mathsf{AS}_{R,\mathsf{Sig}} = (\mathsf{PreSign}, \mathsf{PreVerify}, \mathsf{Adapt}, \mathsf{Ext})$ of four PPT algorithms which meet the following requirements:

– $\mathsf{AS}_{R,\mathsf{Sig}}.\mathsf{PreSign}(\mathsf{pp}, \mathsf{sk}, m, Y) \rightarrow \widehat{\sigma}$: This is a probabilistic algorithm that is run by a signer on the input of the public parameter $\mathsf{pp} \leftarrow \mathsf{Sig}.\mathsf{Setup}(\lambda)$, a secret key sk generated by $\mathsf{Sig}.\mathsf{KeyGen}(\mathsf{pp})$, message $m \in \mathcal{M}$ and statement $Y \in L_R$. It outputs a pre-signature $\widehat{\sigma}$.
– $\mathsf{AS}_{R,\mathsf{Sig}}.\mathsf{PreVerify}(\mathsf{pp}, \mathsf{pk}, m, Y, \widehat{\sigma}) \rightarrow \mathsf{Valid/Invalid}$: On input of the public parameter pp, a public key pk generated by $\mathsf{Sig}.\mathsf{KeyGen}(\mathsf{pp})$, message $m \in \mathcal{M}$, statement $Y \in L_R$ and a pre-signature $\widehat{\sigma}$, this deterministic algorithm outputs $\mathsf{Valid/Invalid}$.
– $\mathsf{AS}_{R,\mathsf{Sig}}.\mathsf{Adapt}(\mathsf{pp}, \widehat{\sigma}, y) \rightarrow \sigma$: This a deterministic algorithm executed by a publisher on the input of the public parameter pp, a pre-signature $\widehat{\sigma}$ and witness y. It outputs a full signature σ.
– $\mathsf{AS}_{R,\mathsf{Sig}}.\mathsf{Ext}(\mathsf{pp}, \sigma, \widehat{\sigma}, Y) \rightarrow y'$: The signer executes this deterministic algorithm on the input of the public parameter pp, a full signature σ, pre-signature $\widehat{\sigma}$ and statement $Y \in L_R$ to either extract a witness y' such that $(Y, y') \in R$ or outputs $\bot$.

Correctness. An adaptor signature scheme $\mathsf{AS}_{R,\mathsf{Sig}}$ is correct if it satisfies:

i. *Signature correctness*: For all $\mathsf{pp} \leftarrow \mathsf{Sig}.\mathsf{Setup}(\lambda)$, all $(\mathsf{sk}, \mathsf{pk}) \leftarrow \mathsf{Sig}.\mathsf{KeyGen}(\mathsf{pp})$ and all signature $\sigma \leftarrow \mathsf{Sig}.\mathsf{Sign}(\mathsf{pp}, \mathsf{sk}, m)$, it must hold that $\mathsf{Sig}.\mathsf{Verify}(\mathsf{pp}, \mathsf{pk}, m, \sigma) = \mathsf{Valid}$.

- **Setup:** The challenger $\mathcal{C}$ generates the public parameter pp $\leftarrow$ Sig.Setup(λ) and a secret-public key pair (sk, pk) $\leftarrow$ Sig.KeyGen(pp). It forwards pp and pk to the adversary $\mathcal{A}$ while keeps sk secret to itself. It also maintains two lists CList,QList and T, initially set to ϕ.
- **Oracle Access:** The adversary $\mathcal{A}$ issues polynomially many adaptive signature queries to the oracles $\mathcal{O}_{\mathsf{NewY}}()$, $\mathcal{O}_{\mathsf{Sign}}(m)$ and $\mathcal{O}_{\mathsf{PreSign}}(m, Y)$ described below.
  - $\mathcal{O}_{\mathsf{NewY}}()$: The challenger generates a statement $(Y, \cdot) \leftarrow R.\mathsf{Gen}(\lambda)$ and sets CList = CList $\cup \{Y\}$. It returns the computed statement Y to the adversary $\mathcal{A}$.
  - $\mathcal{O}_{\mathsf{Sign}}(m)$: On receiving a signature query on a message $m \in \mathcal{M}$, the challenger $\mathcal{C}$ computes a signature $\sigma \leftarrow$ Sig.Sign(pp, sk, m) on the message m under the secret key sk and sets QList = QList $\cup \{(m, \sigma)\}$. It returns the computed signature σ to the adversary $\mathcal{A}$.
  - $\mathcal{O}_{\mathsf{PreSign}}(m, Y)$: On receiving a pre-signature query on a message $m \in \mathcal{M}$ and statement Y, the challenger $\mathcal{C}$ computes a pre-signature $\widehat{\sigma} \leftarrow \mathsf{AS}_{R,\mathsf{Sig}}.\mathsf{PreSign}(\mathsf{pp}, \mathsf{sk}, m, Y)$ on the message m and returns the computed pre-signature $\widehat{\sigma}$ to the adversary $\mathcal{A}$. It also stores $(Y, \widehat{\sigma})$ in a table $\mathsf{T}[m]$ indexed by message m which is initialized by $\emptyset$.
- **Forgery:** The adversary $\mathcal{A}$ eventually submits a forgery (m^*, σ^*).
- **Final:** If $(m^*, \sigma^*) \notin$ QList, Valid $\leftarrow$ Sig.Verify(pp, pk, m^*, σ^*) and $\forall\ (Y, \widehat{\sigma}) \in \mathsf{T}[m^*]$ such that $Y \notin$ CList we have $(Y, \mathsf{AS}_{R,\mathsf{Sig}}.\mathsf{Ext}(\mathsf{pp}, \sigma^*, \widehat{\sigma}, Y) \notin R$ the experiment $\mathsf{Exp}^{\mathsf{SFEXT}}_{\mathsf{AS}_{R,\mathsf{Sig}}, \mathcal{A}}(\lambda)$ return 1; otherwise, return 0.

Fig. 4. $\mathsf{Exp}^{\mathsf{FEXT}}_{\mathsf{AS}_{R,\mathsf{Sig}}, \mathcal{A}}(\lambda)$: Full extractibility

ii. *Pre-signature correctness*: For all λ and $m \in \mathcal{M}$, it must hold that

$$\Pr \begin{bmatrix} \mathsf{AS}_{R,\mathsf{Sig}}.\mathsf{PreVerify}(\mathsf{pp}, \mathsf{pk}, m, Y, \widehat{\sigma}) \to \mathsf{Valid} \\ \mathsf{Sig}.\mathsf{Verify}(\mathsf{pp}, \mathsf{pk}, m, \sigma) \to \mathsf{Valid} \\ (Y, y') \in R \end{bmatrix} \left| \begin{array}{l} (Y, y) \leftarrow R.\mathsf{Gen}(\lambda), \mathsf{pp} \leftarrow \mathsf{Sig}.\mathsf{Setup}(\lambda) \\ (\mathsf{sk},\ \mathsf{pk}) \leftarrow \mathsf{Sig}.\mathsf{KeyGen}(\mathsf{pp}) \\ \widehat{\sigma} \leftarrow \mathsf{AS}_{R,\mathsf{Sig}}.\mathsf{PreSign}(\mathsf{pp}, \mathsf{sk}, m, Y) \\ \sigma \leftarrow \mathsf{AS}_{R,\mathsf{Sig}}.\mathsf{Adapt}(\mathsf{pp}, \widehat{\sigma}, y) \\ y' \leftarrow \mathsf{AS}_{R,\mathsf{Sig}}.\mathsf{Ext}(\mathsf{pp}, \sigma, \widehat{\sigma}, Y) \end{array} \right] = 1$$

To demonstrate the security of our scheme, we adopt the security model proposed by Dai et al. [4], which is outlined below.

Definition 18. (FEXT.) An adaptor signature scheme $\mathsf{AS}_{R,\mathsf{Sig}}$ is said to be secure against *full extractability* (FEXT) if for all PPT adversaries $\mathcal{A}$, there exists a negligible function ϵ such that $\mathsf{Adv}^{\mathsf{FEXT}}_{\mathsf{AS}_{R,\mathsf{Sig}}, \mathcal{A}}(\lambda) = \Pr[\mathsf{Exp}^{\mathsf{FEXT}}_{\mathsf{AS}_{R,\mathsf{Sig}}, \mathcal{A}}(\lambda) = 1] < \epsilon$ where full extractability is modeled via the experiment $\mathsf{Exp}^{\mathsf{FEXT}}_{\mathsf{AS}_{R,\mathsf{Sig}}, \mathcal{A}}(\lambda)$ between an adversary $\mathcal{A}$ and a challenger $\mathcal{C}$ given in Fig. 4.

Definition 19. (SFEXT). An adaptor signature scheme $\mathsf{AS}_{R,\mathsf{Sig}}$ is said to be secure against *(strong) full extractability* (SFEXT) if for all PPT adversaries $\mathcal{A}$, there exists a negligible function ϵ such that $\mathsf{Adv}^{\mathsf{SFEXT}}_{\mathsf{AS}_{R,\mathsf{Sig}}, \mathcal{A}}(\lambda) = \Pr[\mathsf{Exp}^{\mathsf{SFEXT}}_{\mathsf{AS}_{R,\mathsf{Sig}}, \mathcal{A}}(\lambda) = 1] < \epsilon$ where (strong) full extractability is modeled via the experiment $\mathsf{Exp}^{\mathsf{SFEXT}}_{\mathsf{AS}_{R,\mathsf{Sig}}, \mathcal{A}}(\lambda)$ between an adversary $\mathcal{A}$ and a challenger $\mathcal{C}$ described in Fig. 5.

Definition 20. (Pre-signature adaptability). An adaptor signature scheme $\mathsf{AS}_{R,\mathsf{Sig}}$ satisfies *pre-signature adaptability* if for any $\lambda \in \mathbb{N}$, any message $m \in \mathcal{M}$, any statement-witness pair $(Y, y) \in R$, any key pair (sk, pk) $\leftarrow$ Sig.KeyGen(pp) and any pre-signature $\widehat{\sigma} \leftarrow \{0,1\}^*$ with $\mathsf{AS}_{R,\mathsf{Sig}}.\mathsf{PreVerify}(\mathsf{pp}, \mathsf{pk}, m, Y, \widehat{\sigma}) = 1$, it must hold that $\Pr[\mathsf{Sig}.\mathsf{Verify}(\mathsf{pp}, \mathsf{pk}, m, \mathsf{AS}_{R,\mathsf{Sig}}.\mathsf{Adapt}(\mathsf{pp}, \widehat{\sigma}, y)) = \mathsf{Valid}] = 1$.

- **Setup:** The challenger $\mathcal{C}$ generates the public parameter $\text{pp} \leftarrow \text{Sig.Setup}(\lambda)$ and a secret-public key pair $(\text{sk}, \text{pk}) \leftarrow \text{Sig.KeyGen}(\text{pp})$. It forwards pp and pk to the adversary $\mathcal{A}$ while keeps sk secret to itself. It also maintains two lists CList, QList and T, initially set to ϕ.
- **Oracle Access:** The adversary $\mathcal{A}$ issues polynomially many adaptive signature queries to the oracles $\mathcal{O}_{\text{NewY}}()$, $\mathcal{O}_{\text{Sign}}(m)$ and $\mathcal{O}_{\text{PreSign}}(m, Y)$ described below.
    - $\mathcal{O}_{\text{NewY}}()$: The challenger generates a statement $(Y, \cdot) \leftarrow R.\text{Gen}(\lambda)$ and sets $\text{CList} = \text{CList} \cup \{Y\}$. It returns the computed statement Y to the adversary $\mathcal{A}$.
    - $\mathcal{O}_{\text{Sign}}(m)$: On receiving a signature query on a message $m \in \mathcal{M}$, the challenger $\mathcal{C}$ computes a signature $\sigma \leftarrow \text{Sig.Sign}(\text{pp}, \text{sk}, m)$ on the message m under the secret key sk and sets $\text{QList} = \text{QList} \cup \{m\}$. It returns the computed signature σ to the adversary $\mathcal{A}$.
    - $\mathcal{O}_{\text{PreSign}}(m, Y)$: On receiving a pre-signature query on a message $m \in \mathcal{M}$ and statement Y, the challenger $\mathcal{C}$ computes a pre-signature $\widehat{\sigma} \leftarrow \text{AS}_{R,\text{Sig}}.\text{PreSign}(\text{pp}, \text{sk}, m, Y)$ on the message m and returns the computed pre-signature $\widehat{\sigma}$ to the adversary $\mathcal{A}$. It also stores $(Y, \widehat{\sigma})$ in a table $T[m]$ indexed by message m which is initialized by $\emptyset$.
- **Forgery:** The adversary $\mathcal{A}$ eventually submits a forgery (m^*, σ^*).
- **Final:** If $m^* \notin \text{QList}$, $\text{Valid} \leftarrow \text{Sig.Verify}(\text{pp}, \text{pk}, m^*, \sigma^*)$ and $\forall \, (Y, \widehat{\sigma}) \in T[m^*]$ such that $Y \notin \text{CList}$ satisfy $(Y, \text{AS}_{R,\text{Sig}}.\text{Ext}(\text{pp}, \sigma^*, \widehat{\sigma}, Y) \notin R$ then the experiment $\text{Exp}^{\text{FEXT}}_{\text{AS}_{R,\text{Sig}}, \mathcal{A}}(\lambda)$ return 1; otherwise, return 0.

Fig. 5. $\text{Exp}^{\text{SFEXT}}_{\text{AS}_{R,\text{Sig}}, \mathcal{A}}(\lambda)$: Strong full extractability

Definition 21. (Unlinkability). An adaptor signature scheme $\text{AS}_{R,\text{Sig}}$ is said to be secure against *unlinkability* (UNL) if for all PPT adversaries $\mathcal{A}$, there exists a negligible function ϵ such that $\text{Adv}^{\text{UNL}}_{\text{AS}_{R,\text{Sig}}, \mathcal{A}}(\lambda) = |\text{Pr}[\text{Exp}^{\text{UNL}}_{\text{AS}_{R,\text{Sig}}, \mathcal{A}}(\lambda) = 1] - \frac{1}{2}| < \epsilon$ where unlinkability is modeled via the experiment $\text{Exp}^{\text{UNL}}_{\text{AS}_{R,\text{Sig}}, \mathcal{A}}(\lambda)$ between an adversary $\mathcal{A}$ and a challenger $\mathcal{C}$ described in Fig. 6.

6 Our Adaptor Signature Scheme

In this section, we describe our isogeny-based adaptor signature using CSI-FiSh ([2]) as the underlying signature scheme and with respect to the hard relation $R \subseteq \text{Ell}_p(\mathbb{Z}[\sqrt{-p}]) \times \mathbb{Z}_N$ given as follows:

$$R = \{(E_Y, y) \in \text{Ell}_p(\mathbb{Z}[\sqrt{-p}]) \times \mathbb{Z}_N \, | \, E_Y = [y]E_0\}$$

Before presenting the construction of the adaptor signature scheme, we will modify the CSI-FiSh signature and our adaptor signature will be built on top of the modified CSI-FiSh(MCSI-FiSh) signature.

6.1 Modified CSI-FiSh (MCSI-FiSh)

In MCSI-FiSh, the MCSI-FiSh.Setup and MCSI-FiSh.KeyGen will remain same as CSI-FiSh.Setup and CSI-FiSh.KeyGen respectively i.e. MCSI-FiSh.Setup $\rightarrow \text{pp} = (p, \mathfrak{g}, N, E_0, \mathcal{H}_1, S, T)$ and CSI-FiSh.KeyGen $\rightarrow (\text{sk}, \text{pk})$ with $\text{sk} = \{a_i\}_{i=1}^{S-1}$ and $\text{pk} = \{E_{A_i}\}_{i=1}^{S-1}$ where $p, \mathfrak{g}, N, E_0, \mathcal{H}_1, S, T, E_0$ and E_{A_i} for $i \in [S-1]$ are as defined in CSI-FiSh.Setup and CSI-FiSh.KeyGen respectively. The MCSI-FiSh uses the hard relation $R = \{(E_Y, y) \in \text{Ell}_p(\mathbb{Z}[\sqrt{-p}]) \times \mathbb{Z}_N \, | \, E_Y = [y]E_0\}$ in signature generation and sends the witness through signature which is later used during the signature verification.

- **Setup:** The challenger $\mathcal{C}$ generates the public parameter pp ← Sig.Setup(λ) and a secret-public key pair (sk, pk) ← Sig.KeyGen(pp). It forwards pp and pk to the adversary $\mathcal{A}$ while keeps sk secret to itself.
- **Oracle Access:** The adversary $\mathcal{A}$ issues polynomially many adaptive signature queries to the oracles $\mathcal{O}_{\text{Sign}}(m)$ and $\mathcal{O}_{\text{PreSign}}(m, Y)$ described below.
  - $\mathcal{O}_{\text{Sign}}(m)$: On receiving a signature query on a message $m \in \mathcal{M}$, the challenger $\mathcal{C}$ computes a signature σ ← Sig.Sign(pp, sk, m) on the message m under the secret key sk. It returns the computed signature σ to the adversary $\mathcal{A}$.
  - $\mathcal{O}_{\text{PreSign}}(m, Y)$: On receiving a pre-signature query on a message $m \in \mathcal{M}$ and statement Y, the challenger $\mathcal{C}$ computes a pre-signature $\widehat{\sigma}$ ← $\text{AS}_{R,\text{Sig}}$.PreSign(pp, sk, m, Y) on the message m. It returns the computed pre-signature $\widehat{\sigma}$ to the adversary $\mathcal{A}$.
- **Challenge Phase:** The adversary $\mathcal{A}$ submits a message and a statement-witness pair $(m, (Y, y))$ to the challenger $\mathcal{C}$. The challenger $\mathcal{C}$ samples a random bit b ← $\{0, 1\}$. If $b = 0$, it computes the pre-signature $\widehat{\sigma}$ ← $\text{AS}_{R,\text{Sig}}$.PreSign(pp, sk, m, Y) on m and returns the full-signature $\sigma_0 = \text{AS}_{R,\text{Sig}}$.Adapt(pp, $\widehat{\sigma}$, y) to the adversary $\mathcal{A}$. If $b = 1$, it returns the signature $\sigma_1 = $ Sig.Sign(pp, sk, m) to the adversary $\mathcal{A}$
- **Final Phase:** The adversary $\mathcal{A}$ eventually submits a bit b' to the challenger $\mathcal{C}$ and if $b = b'$ then the $\text{Exp}^{\text{UNL}}_{\text{AS}_{R,\text{Sig}}, \mathcal{A}}(\lambda)$ returns 1; otherwise, returns 0.

Fig. 6. $\text{Exp}^{\text{UNL}}_{\text{AS}_{R,\text{Sig}}, \mathcal{A}}(\lambda)$: Unlinkability

MCSI-FiSh.Sign(pp, sk, m) → σ: A signer generates a signature σ on the message $m \in \mathcal{M}$ as follows using the public parameter pp and its secret key sk = $\{a_i\}_{i=1}^{S-1}$:

i. Generates (E_Y, y) ← R.Gen(1^λ) where $E_Y = [y]E_0$.
ii. Sets a_0 ← 0 and uniformly samples b_i from $\mathbb{Z}_N$, $\forall i \in [T]$.
iii. Computes the curves $E_{B_i} = [b_i]E_0$, the challenge bits $(h_1, \ldots, h_T) = \mathcal{H}_1(E_{B_1}||\ldots||E_{B_T}||m||E_Y) \in \{-S+1, \ldots, 0, \ldots, S-1\}^T$ and the response $z_i = (b_i - \text{sign}(h_i)a_{|h_i|}) \mod N \forall i \in [T]$.
iv. Returns the signature $\sigma = (\mathsf{h}, \mathsf{z}, E_Y, y)$ where $\mathsf{h} = \{h_i\}_{i=1}^T$ and $\mathsf{z} = \{z_i\}_{i=1}^T$.

MCSI-FiSh.Verify(pp, pk, m, σ) → Valid/Invalid: Any user can run this algorithm by using the signer's public key pk = $\{E_{A_i}\}_{i=1}^{S-1}$ and verify the signature σ on m by executing the following steps.

i. Parses $\sigma = (\mathsf{h}, \mathsf{z}, E_Y, y)$ where $\mathsf{h} = \{h_i\}_{i=1}^T$ and $\mathsf{z} = \{z_i\}_{i=1}^T$.
ii. Defines $E_{A_{-i}} = E_{A_i}^{\text{twist}} \forall i \in [S-1]$
iii. Extracts the curves $E_{A_{|h_i|}}$ from pk and computes the curves

$$E_{B_i} = [z_i]E_{A_{h_i}} = \begin{cases} [z_i]E_{A_{|h_i|}} & \text{if } h_i \geq 0 \\ [z_i]E_{A_{|h_i|}}^{\text{twist}} & \text{if } h_i < 0 \end{cases}$$

for $\forall i \in [T]$ and the challenge bits $(h'_1, \ldots, h'_T) = \mathcal{H}_1(E_{B_1}||\ldots||E_{B_T}||m||E_Y)$.
iv. Returns Valid, if $(h_1, \ldots, h_T) = (h'_1, \ldots, h'_T)$ and $E_Y = [y]E_0$, else returns Invalid.

Correctness. It follows from the correctness of the signature scheme CSI-FiSh described in Sect. 3.1.

6.2   Our Construction of Adaptor Signature Scheme IAS

We now present our second construction of an isogeny-based adaptor signature IAS with respect to the hard relation $R = \{(E_Y, y) \in \mathsf{Ell}_p(\mathbb{Z}[\sqrt{-p}]) \times \mathbb{Z}_N \,|\, E_Y = [y]E_0\}$ and the signature scheme MCSI-FiSh presented in Sect. 6.1.

IAS.PreSign(pp, sk, m, E_Y) $\rightarrow \widehat{\sigma}$: On input of the public parameter pp $= (p, \mathfrak{g}, N, E_0, \mathcal{H}_1, S, T)$, a secret key sk $= \{a_i\}_{i=1}^{S-1}$, message $m \in \{0,1\}^*$ and a statement $E_Y \in L_R$, the signer computes the pre-signature $\widehat{\sigma}$ as follows:

i. Sample $r \leftarrow R.\mathsf{Rand}$
ii. Computes the curve $E_{Y'} = [r]E_Y$.
iii. Sets $a_0 \leftarrow 0$ and samples $[\mathfrak{b}_i] = [\mathfrak{g}^{b_i}] \in \mathcal{G}$ for some $b_i \in \mathbb{Z}_N \forall i \in [T]$.
iv. Computes the curves $E_{B_i} = [b_i]E_0$, the challenge bits $(h_1, \ldots, h_T) = \mathcal{H}_1(E_{B_1}||\ldots||E_{B_T}||m||E_{Y'}) \in \{-S+1, \ldots, 0, \ldots, S-1\}^T$ and the response $z_i = (b_i - \mathsf{sign}(h_i)a_{|h_i|}) \mod N \forall i \in [T]$.
v. Returns the pre-signature $\widehat{\sigma} = (\sigma' = (\mathsf{h}, \mathsf{z}), E_Y, r)$ where $\mathsf{h} = \{h_i\}_{i=1}^T$ and $\mathsf{z} = \{z_i\}_{i=1}^T$.

IAS.PreVerify(pp, pk, m, E_Y, $\widehat{\sigma}$) $\rightarrow$ Valid/Invalid: On input of the public parameter pp $= (p, \mathfrak{g}, N, E_0, \mathcal{H}_1, S, T)$, a public key pk $= \{E_{A_i}\}_{i=1}^{S-1}$, message $m \in \{0,1\}^*$, statement E_Y and a pre-signature $\widehat{\sigma} = (\sigma' = (\mathsf{h}, \mathsf{z}), E_Y)$, the verifier executes the following steps:

i. Extracts r from $\widehat{\sigma}$ and computes $E_{Y'} = [r]E_Y$
ii. Parses $\widehat{\sigma} = (\sigma' = (\mathsf{h} = \{h_i\}_{i=1}^T, \mathsf{z} = \{z_i\}_{i=1}^T), E_Y)$.
iii. Defines $E_{A_{-i}} = E_{A_i}^{\mathsf{twist}} \forall i \in [S-1]$
iv. Extracts the curves $E_{A_{|h_i|}}$ from pk and computes the curves

$$E_{B_i} = [z_i]E_{A_{h_i}} = \begin{cases} [z_i]E_{A_{|h_i|}} & \text{if } h_i \geq 0 \\ [z_i]E_{A_{|h_i|}}^{\mathsf{twist}} & \text{if } h_i < 0 \end{cases}$$

for $\forall i \in [T]$ and the challenge bits $(h'_1, \ldots, h'_T) = \mathcal{H}_1(E_{B_1}||\ldots||E_{B_T}||m||E_{Y'})$.
v. If $(h_1, \ldots, h_T) = (h'_1, \ldots, h'_T)$ returns Valid, else returns Invalid.

IAS.Adapt(pp, $\widehat{\sigma}$, y) $\rightarrow \sigma$: On input of the public parameter pp $= (p, \mathfrak{g}, N, E_0, \mathcal{H}_1, S, T)$, a pre-signature $\widehat{\sigma} = (\sigma' = (\mathsf{h}, \mathsf{z}), E_Y)$ and witness y such that $E_Y = [y]E_0$, the publisher outputs the signature σ as follows:

i. Extracts r from $\widehat{\sigma}$ and compute $y' = y + r$.
ii. Computes the curve $E_{Y'} = [r]E_Y$.
iii. Returns the signature $\sigma = (\sigma' = (\mathsf{h}, \mathsf{z}), E_{Y'}, y')$.

IAS.Ext(pp, σ, $\widehat{\sigma}$, Y) $\rightarrow y$: The signer takes as input the public parameter pp $= (p, \mathfrak{g}, N, E_0, \mathcal{H}_1, S, T)$ a signature $\sigma = (\sigma' = (\mathsf{h}, \mathsf{z}), E_Y, y)$, pre-signature $\widehat{\sigma} = (\sigma' = (\mathsf{h}, \mathsf{z}), E_Y)$ and statement $Y = E_Y$ and runs this algorithm to extract the witness y such that $(E_Y, y) \in R$ in the following manner:

i. Extract r from $\widehat{\sigma}$ and y' from σ.

ii. Computes the witness $y = y' - r$.

Correctness. Our adaptor signature scheme IAS is correct as the following conditions hold:

i. *Signature correctness*: Follows from the correctness of MCSI-FiSh described in Sect. 6.1.
ii. *Pre-signature correctness*: Follows from the fact that since $E_{B_i} = [b_i]E_0$ is recovered by computing $[z_i]E_{A_{h_i}}$ for $i \in [T]$ as:

$$[z_i]E_{A_{h_i}} = [b_i - \mathsf{sign}(h_i)a_{|h_i|}]E_{A_{h_i}} = [b_i - \mathsf{sign}(h_i)a_{|h_i|}][\mathsf{sign}(h_i)a_{|h_i|}]E_0 = [b_i]E_0.$$

7 Security Analysis

Theorem 22. *Our proposed adaptor signature scheme* IAS $=$ (PreSign, PreVerify, Adapt, Ext) *satisfies pre-signature adaptability as per Definition 20.*

Proof. Let $m \in \{0,1\}^*$ be a message and $(E_Y, y) \in R$ statement-witness pair. The public parameter is generated by $\mathsf{pp} = (p, \mathfrak{g}, N, E_0, \mathcal{H}_1, S, T) \leftarrow$ MCSI-FiSh.Setup(λ) and a secret-public key pair is generated by ($\mathsf{sk} = \{a_i\}_{i=1}^{S-1}$, $\mathsf{pk} = \{E_{A_i}\}_{i=1}^{S-1}) \leftarrow$ MCSI-FiSh.KeyGen(pp). Assume that, a pre-signature $\widehat{\sigma} = (\sigma' = (\mathsf{h} = \{h_i\}_{i=1}^T, \mathsf{z} = \{z_i\}_{i=1}^T), E_Y, r) \in \{-S+1, \ldots, 0, \ldots, S-1\}^T \times \mathbb{Z}_N^T \times \mathsf{Ell}_p(\mathbb{Z}[\sqrt{-p}]) \times \mathbb{Z}_N$ satisfies IAS.PreVerify($\mathsf{pp}, \mathsf{pk}, m, E_Y, \widehat{\sigma}$) = Valid.
Also note that, checking the validity of MCSI-FiSh.Verify($\mathsf{pp}, \mathsf{pk}, m, \sigma = (\sigma_1, E_{Y_1}, y_1)$) is equivalent to checking CSI-FiSh.Verify($\mathsf{pp}, \mathsf{pk}, (m, E_{Y_1}), \sigma_1$) = Valid and $E_{Y_1} = [y_1]E_0$. We have, IAS.Adapt($\mathsf{pp}, \widehat{\sigma}, y$) = $\sigma = (\sigma', [r]E_Y, y + r)$ and the validity of IAS.PreVerify($\mathsf{pp}, \mathsf{pk}, m, E_Y, \widehat{\sigma}$) implies CSI-FiSh.Verify($\mathsf{pp}, \mathsf{pk}, (m, [r]E_Y), \sigma'$) = Valid. Hence, MCSI-FiSh.Verify($\mathsf{pp}, \mathsf{pk}, m, \mathsf{IAS.Adapt}(\mathsf{pp}, \widehat{\sigma}, y)$) = Valid as CSI-FiSh.Verify($\mathsf{pp}, \mathsf{pk}, (m, [r]E_Y), \sigma'$) = Valid and $[r]E_Y = [y + r]E_0$.

Theorem 23. *Our proposed isogeny-based adaptor signature* IAS *is unlinkable as per Definition 21 as the relation R (presented in Sect. 4.1) is* SRSR.

Proof. We can construct an adversary $\mathcal{A}_{\mathsf{srsr}}$ to break the SRSR security of the relation R described in Sect. 4.1 by leveraging an adversary $\mathcal{A}$'s ability to win in $\mathsf{Exp}_{\mathsf{IAS}, \mathcal{A}}^{\mathsf{UNL}}(\lambda)$. Let $\mathcal{C}$ be the challenger in the experiment $\mathsf{Exp}_{\mathsf{IAS}, \mathcal{A}_{\mathsf{srsr}}}^{\mathsf{SRSR}}(\lambda)$ and the adversary $\mathcal{A}_{\mathsf{srsr}}$ plays the role of challenger in the experiment $\mathsf{Exp}_{\mathsf{IAS}, \mathcal{A}}^{\mathsf{UNL}}(\lambda)$.

- **Setup:** The adversary $\mathcal{A}_{\mathsf{srsr}}$ generates the public parameter $\mathsf{pp} = (p, \mathfrak{g}, N, E_0, \mathcal{H}_1, S, T) \leftarrow$ CSI-FiSh.Setup(λ) and a secret-public key pair ($\mathsf{sk} = \{a_i\}_{i=1}^{S-1}$, $\mathsf{pk} = \{E_{A_i}\}_{i=1}^{S-1}) \leftarrow$ CSI-FiSh.KeyGen(pp). It forwards pp and pk to the adversary $\mathcal{A}$ while keeps sk secret to itself.
- **Simulation of the oracle query:** In the following, we will show that $\mathcal{A}_{\mathsf{srsr}}$ simulates all oracles perfectly for $\mathcal{A}$.

- $\mathcal{O}_{\mathsf{Sign}}(m)$: On receiving a signature query on a message $m \in \mathcal{M}$, the adversary generates $(E_Y, y) \leftarrow R.\mathsf{Gen}(\lambda)$ and computes signature by running $\sigma \leftarrow \mathsf{CSI\text{-}FiSh.Sign}(\mathsf{pp}, \mathsf{sk}, (m, E_Y))$. It returns (σ, E_Y, y) to the adversary $\mathcal{A}$.

- $\mathcal{O}_{\mathsf{PreSign}}(m, E_Y)$: After receiving a pre-signature query on a message $m \in \mathcal{M}$ and statement E_Y, the adversary $\mathcal{A}_{\mathsf{srsr}}$ generates $r \leftarrow R.\mathsf{Rand}(\lambda)$ and computes signature $\sigma \leftarrow \mathsf{CSI\text{-}FiSh.Sign}(\mathsf{pp}, \mathsf{sk}, (m, E_{Y'}))$. Returns $\widehat{\sigma} = (\sigma', E_Y, r)$ to $\mathcal{A}$.

- **Challenge Phase:** Eventually the adversary $\mathcal{A}$ submits a message and a statement-witness pair outputs $(m, (E_Y, y))$ to the challenger $\mathcal{A}_{\mathsf{srsr}}$. Subsequently, the adversary $\mathcal{A}_{\mathsf{srsr}}$ submits (E_Y, y) to the challenger $\mathcal{C}$ of the $\mathsf{Exp}_{\mathsf{IAS}, \mathcal{A}}^{\mathsf{UNL}}(\lambda)$. Then, the challenger $\mathcal{C}$ returns the challenge (E_{Y_b}, y_b) to $\mathcal{A}_{\mathsf{srsr}}$ where $b \in \{0, 1\}$. Following this, the adversary $\mathcal{A}_{\mathsf{srsr}}$ computes $\sigma' \leftarrow \mathsf{CSI\text{-}FiSh.Sign}(\mathsf{pp}, \mathsf{sk}, (m, E_{Y_b}))$ and sends $\sigma = (\sigma', E_{Y_b}, y_b)$ to $\mathcal{A}$.

- **Extracting the Forgery:** After receiving the forgery b' is submitted by the adversary $\mathcal{A}$, the adversary $\mathcal{A}_{\mathsf{srsr}}$ submits b' to $\mathcal{C}$.

Note that,

- $b = 0$: $y_0 = y + r \pmod{N}$ where $r \xleftarrow{\$} \mathbb{Z}_N$ and $E_{Y_0} = [r]E_Y$. In this case, the signature $\sigma = (\sigma', E_{Y_0}, y_0)$ where $\sigma' \leftarrow \mathsf{CSI\text{-}FiSh.Sign}(\mathsf{pp}, \mathsf{sk}, (m, E_{Y_0}))$ is equivalent to $\widehat{\sigma} = (\sigma', E_Y, r) \leftarrow \mathsf{IAS.PreSig}(\mathsf{pp}, \mathsf{sk}, (m, E_Y))$ and $\sigma = (\sigma', E_{Y_0} = [r]E_Y, y_0 = y + r) \leftarrow \mathsf{IAS.Adapt}(\mathsf{pp}, \widehat{\sigma} = (\sigma', E_Y, r), y))$.

- $b = 1$: $y_1 = y' + r \pmod{N}$ where $y', r \xleftarrow{\$} \mathbb{Z}_N$. The signature $\sigma = (\sigma', E_{Y_1}, y_1)$ where $\sigma' \leftarrow \mathsf{CSI\text{-}FiSh.Sign}(\mathsf{pp}, \mathsf{sk}, (m, E_{Y_1}))$ is equivalent to $\sigma = (\sigma', E_{Y_1} = [y_1]E_0, y_1) \leftarrow \mathsf{MCSI\text{-}FiSh.Sign}(\mathsf{pp}, \mathsf{sk}, m)$.

If the adversary $\mathcal{A}$ correctly distinguishes between (σ', E_{Y_0}, y_0) and (σ', E_{Y_1}, y_1) then $\mathcal{A}_{\mathsf{srsr}}$ can distinguish between (E_{Y_0}, y_0) and (E_{Y_1}, y_1). Hence, if the adversary $\mathcal{A}$ wins in $\mathsf{Exp}_{\mathsf{IAS}, \mathcal{A}}^{\mathsf{UNL}}(\lambda)$ then the adversary $\mathcal{A}_{\mathsf{srsr}}$ wins in $\mathsf{Exp}_{\mathsf{IAS}, \mathcal{A}_{\mathsf{srsr}}}^{\mathsf{SRSR}}(\lambda)$. Therefore, $\mathsf{Adv}_{\mathsf{IAS}, \mathcal{A}}^{\mathsf{UNL}}(\lambda) \leq \mathsf{Adv}_{R, \mathcal{A}_{\mathsf{srsr}}}^{\mathsf{SRSR}}(\lambda)$.

Theorem 24. *Our proposed isogeny-based adaptor signature* IAS *is* FEXT *secure as per Definition 18 as* CSI-FiSh *is* EUF-CMA *secure (described in Sect. 3.1) and the relation* R *(presented in Sect. 4.1) is a hard relation. More concretely, if there exists an adversary* $\mathcal{A}$ *of the* FEXT *game in Fig. 4 for* IAS *then there exists an adversary* $\mathcal{A}_{\mathsf{uf\text{-}cma}}$ *of* EUF-CMA *game for* CSI-FiSh *signature and an adversary* $\mathcal{A}_{\mathsf{ow}}$ *of the one-wayness game in Fig. 2 for the relation* R *such that*

$$\mathsf{Adv}_{\mathsf{IAS}, \mathcal{A}}^{\mathsf{FEXT}}(\lambda) \leq \mathsf{Adv}_{\mathsf{CSI\text{-}FiSh}, \mathcal{A}_{\mathsf{uf\text{-}cma}}}^{\mathsf{EUF\text{-}CMA}}(\lambda) + \mathsf{Adv}_{R, \mathcal{A}_{\mathsf{ow}}}^{\mathsf{q\text{-}OW}}(\lambda)$$

Proof. Let $\mathcal{A}$ be an adversary playing in the experiment $\mathsf{Exp}_{\mathsf{IAS}, \mathcal{A}}^{\mathsf{FEXT}}(\lambda)$ as described in Fig. 4. The challenger $\mathcal{C}$ in the experiment $\mathsf{Exp}_{\mathsf{IAS}, \mathcal{A}}^{\mathsf{FEXT}}(\lambda)$ generates $\mathsf{pp} = (p, \mathfrak{g}, N, E_0, \mathcal{H}_1, S, T) \leftarrow \mathsf{MCSI\text{-}FiSh.Setup}(\lambda)$ and $(\mathsf{sk} = \{a_i\}_{i=1}^{S-1}, \mathsf{pk} = \{E_{A_i}\}_{i=1}^{S-1}) \leftarrow \mathsf{MCSI\text{-}FiSh.KeyGen}(\mathsf{pp})$ where $p, \mathfrak{g}, N, E_0, \mathcal{H}_1, S, T, E_0$ and E_{A_i} for $i \in [S-1]$ are defined in Sect. 3.1. It provides the public parameter pp and public key pk

to $\mathcal{A}$ and keeps sk secret to itself. This theorem is proven via a hybrid argument based on a sequence of security games. The transition between the games is detailed below:

The experiments $\mathsf{Exp}^0_{\mathsf{IAS},\,\mathcal{A}}(\lambda)$, $\mathsf{Exp}^1_{\mathsf{IAS},\,\mathcal{A}}(\lambda)$, $\mathsf{Exp}^2_{\mathsf{IAS},\,\mathcal{A}}(\lambda)$, $\mathsf{Exp}^3_{\mathsf{IAS},\,\mathcal{A}}(\lambda)$ and $\mathsf{Exp}^4_{\mathsf{IAS},\,\mathcal{A}}(\lambda)$ are described in Fig. 8 and $\mathsf{Exp}^{\mathsf{EXT}}_{\mathsf{IAS},\,\mathcal{A}_{\mathsf{ext}}}(\lambda)$ is detailed in Fig. 7. The experiment $\mathsf{Exp}^0_{\mathsf{IAS},\,\mathcal{A}}(\lambda)$ is identical to $\mathsf{Exp}^{\mathsf{FEXT}}_{\mathsf{IAS},\,\mathcal{A}}(\lambda)$. We assert the following claims:

Claim 1. $\Pr[\mathsf{Exp}^1_{\mathsf{IAS},\,\mathcal{A}}(\lambda) = 1] = \Pr[\mathsf{Exp}^0_{\mathsf{IAS},\,\mathcal{A}}(\lambda) = 1]$.

Claim 2. $\Pr[\mathsf{Exp}^2_{\mathsf{IAS},\,\mathcal{A}}(\lambda) = 1] = \Pr[\mathsf{Exp}^1_{\mathsf{IAS},\,\mathcal{A}}(\lambda)]$.

Claim 3. $\Pr[\mathsf{Exp}^2_{\mathsf{IAS},\,\mathcal{A}}(\lambda) = 1] \leq \Pr[\mathsf{Exp}^3_{\mathsf{IAS},\,\mathcal{A}}(\lambda) = 1] + \Pr[\mathsf{Exp}^4_{\mathsf{IAS},\,\mathcal{A}}(\lambda) = 1]$

Claim 4. $\Pr[\mathsf{Exp}^3_{\mathsf{IAS},\,\mathcal{A}}(\lambda) = 1] \leq \Pr[\mathsf{Exp}^{\mathsf{EXT}}_{\mathsf{IAS},\,\mathcal{A}_{\mathsf{ext}}}(\lambda) = 1]$.

Claim 5. $\Pr[\mathsf{Exp}^{\mathsf{EXT}}_{\mathsf{IAS},\,\mathcal{A}_{\mathsf{ext}}}(\lambda) = 1] \leq \mathsf{Adv}^{\mathsf{EUF\text{-}CMA}}_{\mathsf{CSI\text{-}FiSh},\,\mathcal{A}_{\mathsf{uf\text{-}cma}}}(\lambda)$.

Claim 6. $\Pr[\mathsf{Exp}^4_{\mathsf{IAS},\,\mathcal{A}}(\lambda) = 1] \leq \mathsf{Adv}^{\mathsf{q\text{-}OW}}_{R,\,\mathcal{A}_{\mathsf{ow}}}(\lambda)$.

We can deduce from the claims made above that,

$$\mathsf{Adv}^{\mathsf{FEXT}}_{\mathsf{IAS},\,\mathcal{A}}(\lambda) = \Pr[\mathsf{Exp}^0_{\mathsf{IAS},\,\mathcal{A}}(\lambda) = 1]$$
$$= \Pr[\mathsf{Exp}^1_{\mathsf{IAS},\,\mathcal{A}}(\lambda)] \text{ (By using Claim 1)}$$
$$= \Pr[\mathsf{Exp}^2_{\mathsf{IAS},\,\mathcal{A}}(\lambda) = 1] \text{ (By using Claim 2)}$$
$$\leq \Pr[\mathsf{Exp}^3_{\mathsf{IAS},\,\mathcal{A}}(\lambda) = 1] + \Pr[\mathsf{Exp}^4_{\mathsf{IAS},\,\mathcal{A}}(\lambda) = 1] \text{ (By using Claim 3)}$$
$$\leq \Pr[\mathsf{Exp}^{\mathsf{EXT}}_{\mathsf{IAS},\,\mathcal{A}_{\mathsf{ext}}}(\lambda) = 1] + \mathsf{Adv}^{\mathsf{q\text{-}OW}}_{R,\,\mathcal{A}_{\mathsf{ow}}}(\lambda) \text{ (By using Claim 4 and Claim 6)}$$
$$\leq \mathsf{Adv}^{\mathsf{EUF\text{-}CMA}}_{\mathsf{CSI\text{-}FiSh},\,\mathcal{A}_{\mathsf{uf\text{-}cma}}}(\lambda) + \mathsf{Adv}^{\mathsf{q\text{-}OW}}_{R,\,\mathcal{A}_{\mathsf{ow}}}(\lambda) \text{ (By using Claim 5)}$$

$\mathsf{Exp}^{\mathsf{EXT}}_{\mathsf{IAS},\,\mathcal{A}_{\mathsf{ext}}}(\lambda)$

1: Generates $\mathsf{pp} \leftarrow \mathsf{MCSI\text{-}FiSh.Setup}(\lambda)$ and $(\mathsf{sk} = \{a_i\}^{S-1}_{i=1}, \mathsf{pk} = \{E_{A_i}\}^{S-1}_{i=1}) \leftarrow \mathsf{MCSI\text{-}FiSh.KeyGen}(\mathsf{pp})$;

2: Initializes $T = \phi$;

3: $(m^*, \sigma^* = (\{h_i^*\}^T_{i=1}, \{z_i^*\}^T_{i=1}, E_Y^*, y^*)) \leftarrow \mathcal{A}^{\mathcal{O}_{\mathsf{PreSign}}}_{\mathsf{ext}}(\mathsf{pk})$;

4: Set b=0;

5: **if** (Valid $\leftarrow \mathsf{MCSI\text{-}FiSh.Verify}(\mathsf{pp}, \mathsf{pk}, m^*, \sigma^*))$ **then**

6:     **if** $(\forall\, (E_Y, \widehat{\sigma}) \in T[m^*] \mid (E_Y, \mathsf{IAS.Ext}(\mathsf{pp}, \sigma^*, \widehat{\sigma}, E_Y) \notin R)$ **then**

7:         b=1;

8:     **endif**

9: **endif**

10: **return** b;

$\mathcal{O}_{\mathsf{PreSign}}(m, E_Y)$

1: $\widehat{\sigma} \leftarrow \mathsf{IAS.PreSign}(\mathsf{pp}, \mathsf{sk}, m, E_Y)$;

2: $T[m] = T[m] \cup \{(E_Y, \widehat{\sigma})\}$;

3: **return** $\widehat{\sigma}$;

Fig. 7. The experiment $\mathsf{Exp}^{\mathsf{EXT}}_{\mathsf{IAS},\,\mathcal{A}_{\mathsf{ext}}}(\lambda)$

$\mathsf{Exp}^0_{\mathsf{IAS},\,\mathcal{A}}(\lambda)$, $\mathsf{Exp}^1_{\mathsf{IAS},\,\mathcal{A}}(\lambda)$, $\mathsf{Exp}^2_{\mathsf{IAS},\,\mathcal{A}}(\lambda)$, $\mathsf{Exp}^3_{\mathsf{IAS},\,\mathcal{A}}(\lambda)$, $\mathsf{Exp}^4_{\mathsf{IAS},\,\mathcal{A}}(\lambda)$

1 :	Generates $\mathsf{pp} \leftarrow \mathsf{MCSI\text{-}FiSh.Setup}(\lambda)$ and $(\mathsf{sk} = \{a_i\}^{S-1}_{i=1}$, $\mathsf{pk} = \{E_{A_i}\}^{S-1}_{i=1}) \leftarrow \mathsf{MCSI\text{-}FiSh.KeyGen(pp)}$;
2 :	Initializes $\mathsf{CList} = \phi$, $\mathsf{QList} = \phi$, $U = \phi$ and $T = \phi$;
3 :	$(m^*, \sigma^* = (\{h^*_i\}^T_{i=1}, \{z^*_i\}^T_{i=1}, E^*_Y, y^*)) \leftarrow \mathcal{A}^{\mathcal{O}_{\mathsf{NewY}}, \mathcal{O}_{\mathsf{Sign}}, \mathcal{O}_{\mathsf{PreSign}}}(\mathsf{pk})$;
4 :	Sets $b_1 = 0, b_2 = 0$ and $b_3 = 0$;
5 :	**if** $(m^* \notin \mathsf{QList} \land \mathsf{Valid} \leftarrow \mathsf{MCSI\text{-}FiSh.Verify(pp, pk,} m^*, \sigma^*))$ **then**
6 :	**if** $(\forall\, (E_Y, \widehat{\sigma}) \in T[m^*] \land E_Y \notin \mathsf{CList}\ |\ (E_Y, \mathsf{IAS.Ext(pp,} \sigma^*, \widehat{\sigma}, E_Y) \notin R)$ **then**
7 :	$b_1 = 1$;
8 :	**endif**
9 :	**if** $(\forall\, (E_Y, \widehat{\sigma}) \in U[m^*] \land E_Y \notin \mathsf{CList}\ |\ (E_Y, \mathsf{IAS.Ext(pp,} \sigma^*, \widehat{\sigma}, E_Y) \notin R)$ **then**
10 :	$b_2 = 1$;
11 :	**endif**
12 :	**if** $(\forall\, (E_Y, \widehat{\sigma}) \in T[m^*] \cup U[m^*] \land E_Y \in \mathsf{CList}\ |\ (E_Y, \mathsf{IAS.Ext(pp,} \sigma^*, \widehat{\sigma}, E_Y) \notin R)$ **then**
13 :	$b_3 = 1$;
14 :	**endif**
15 :	**endif**
16 :	$\mathsf{Exp}^0_{\mathsf{IAS},\,\mathcal{A}}(\lambda) : $ **return** b_1;
17 :	$\mathsf{Exp}^1_{\mathsf{IAS},\,\mathcal{A}}(\lambda) : $ **return** b_1;
18 :	$\mathsf{Exp}^2_{\mathsf{IAS},\,\mathcal{A}}(\lambda) : $ **return** $b_1 \land b_2$;
19 :	$\mathsf{Exp}^3_{\mathsf{IAS},\,\mathcal{A}}(\lambda) : $ **return** $b_1 \land b_2 \land b_3$;
20 :	$\mathsf{Exp}^4_{\mathsf{IAS},\,\mathcal{A}}(\lambda) : $ **return** $\neg b_3$;

$\mathcal{O}_{\mathsf{Sign}}(m)$ // For $\mathsf{Exp}^i_{\mathsf{IAS},\,\mathcal{A}}(\lambda)$, i=1,2,3,4

1 :	$(E_Y, y) \leftarrow R.\mathsf{Gen}(\lambda)$;
2 :	$\widehat{\sigma} \leftarrow \mathsf{IAS.PreSign(pp, sk,} m, E_Y)$;
3 :	$U[m] = U[m] \cup \{(E_Y, \widehat{\sigma})\}$;
4 :	$\sigma \leftarrow \mathsf{IAS.Adapt(pp,} \widehat{\sigma}, y)$;
5 :	$\mathsf{QList} = \mathsf{QList} \cup \{m\}$;
6 :	**return** σ;

$\mathcal{O}_{\mathsf{Sign}}(m)$ // For $\mathsf{Exp}^0_{\mathsf{IAS},\,\mathcal{A}}(\lambda)$

1 :	$\sigma \leftarrow \mathsf{MCSI\text{-}FiSh.Sign(pp, sk,} m)$;
2 :	$\mathsf{QList} = \mathsf{QList} \cup \{m\}$;
3 :	**return** σ;

$\mathcal{O}_{\mathsf{PreSign}}(m, E_Y)$

1 :	$\widehat{\sigma} \leftarrow \mathsf{IAS.PreSign(pp, sk,} m, E_Y)$;
2 :	$T[m] = T[m] \cup \{(E_Y, \widehat{\sigma})\}$;
3 :	**return** $\widehat{\sigma}$;

$\mathcal{O}_{\mathsf{NewY}}()$

1 :	$(E_Y, \cdot) \leftarrow R.\mathsf{Gen}(\lambda)$;
2 :	$\mathsf{CList} = \mathsf{CList} \cup \{E_Y\}$;
3 :	**return** E_Y;

Fig. 8. The experiment $\mathsf{Exp}^i_{\mathsf{IAS},\,\mathcal{A}}(\lambda)$ for $i = 0, 1, 2, 3, 4$

Here is the substantiation of the aforementioned claims.

Claim 1. $\Pr[\mathsf{Exp}^1_{\mathsf{IAS},\,\mathcal{A}}(\lambda)] = \Pr[\mathsf{Exp}^0_{\mathsf{IAS},\,\mathcal{A}}(\lambda) = 1]$

Proof. In $\mathsf{Exp}^1_{\mathsf{IAS},\,\mathcal{A}}(\lambda)$ (see Fig. 8), the sign oracle is answered using $\mathsf{IAS.PreSign}$ and $\mathsf{IAS.Adapt}$. Let us consider a modified signature scheme mSign as described in Fig. 9. We note that the signature generated by the algorithm mSign and the signature generated by the $\mathsf{MCSI\text{-}FiSh.Sign}$ are identically distributed. Consequently, both experiments are indistinguishable to the adversary $\mathcal{A}$. Hence, $\Pr[\mathsf{Exp}^1_{\mathsf{IAS},\,\mathcal{A}}(\lambda)] = \Pr[\mathsf{Exp}^0_{\mathsf{IAS},\,\mathcal{A}}(\lambda) = 1]$.

mSign(pp, sk, m)
1 : $(E_Y, y) \leftarrow R.\text{Gen}(\lambda)$;
2 : $\widehat{\sigma} \leftarrow \text{IAS.PreSign}(\text{pp}, \text{sk}, m, E_Y)$;
3 : $\sigma \leftarrow \text{IAS.Adapt}(\text{pp}, \widehat{\sigma}, y)$;
4 : **return** σ;

Fig. 9. The algorithm mSign

Claim 2. $\Pr[\text{Exp}^2_{\text{IAS}, \mathcal{A}}(\lambda) = 1] = \Pr[\text{Exp}^1_{\text{IAS}, \mathcal{A}}(\lambda) = 1]$

Proof. The experiment $\text{Exp}^2_{\text{IAS}, \mathcal{A}}(\lambda)$ in addition to checking whether for all $(E_Y, \widehat{\sigma}) \in T[m^*]$ and $E_Y \notin \text{CList}$ the forgery σ^* does not extract valid witness (line 6 in Fig. 8) also checks that for all $(E_Y, \widehat{\sigma}) \in U[m^*]$ and $E_Y \notin \text{CList}$ the forgery σ^* does not extract valid witness (line 9 in Fig. 8). We argue that this change does not change the probability of the experiment returning 1 because $U[m^*]$ is empty as $m^* \notin \text{QList}$. Thus, the flag b_2 is trivially 1. Hence, $\Pr[\text{Exp}^1_{\text{IAS}, \mathcal{A}}(\lambda)] = \Pr[\text{Exp}^2_{\text{IAS}, \mathcal{A}}(\lambda) = 1]$.

Claim 3. $\Pr[\text{Exp}^2_{\text{IAS}, \mathcal{A}}(\lambda) = 1] \leq \Pr[\text{Exp}^3_{\text{IAS}, \mathcal{A}}(\lambda) = 1] + \Pr[\text{Exp}^4_{\text{IAS}, \mathcal{A}}(\lambda) = 1]$

Proof.

$$
\begin{aligned}
\Pr[\text{Exp}^2_{\text{IAS}, \mathcal{A}}(\lambda) = 1] &= \Pr[b_1 \wedge b_2] \\
&= \Pr[(b_1 \wedge b_2) \wedge (b_3 \vee \neg b_3)] \\
&= \Pr[(b_1 \wedge b_2 \wedge b_3) \vee (b_1 \wedge b_2 \wedge \neg b_3)] \\
&= \Pr[(b_1 \wedge b_2 \wedge b_3)] + \Pr[(b_1 \wedge b_2 \wedge \neg b_3)] \\
&\leq \Pr[(b_1 \wedge b_2 \wedge b_3)] + \Pr[\neg b_3] \\
&= \Pr[\text{Exp}^3_{\text{IAS}, \mathcal{A}}(\lambda) = 1] + \Pr[\text{Exp}^4_{\text{IAS}, \mathcal{A}}(\lambda) = 1]
\end{aligned}
$$

Claim 4. $\Pr[\text{Exp}^3_{\text{IAS}, \mathcal{A}}(\lambda) = 1] \leq \Pr[\text{Exp}^{\text{EXT}}_{\text{IAS}, \mathcal{A}_{\text{ext}}}(\lambda) = 1]$.

Proof. We will show that if the adversary $\mathcal{A}$ wins in $\text{Exp}^3_{\text{IAS}, \mathcal{A}}(\lambda)$ then we can construct an adversary $\mathcal{A}_{\text{ext}}$ (say) using the adversary $\mathcal{A}$ that can win in $\text{Exp}^{\text{EXT}}_{\text{IAS}, \mathcal{A}_{\text{ext}}}(\lambda)$.

The challenger $\mathcal{C}$ in the experiment $\text{Exp}^{\text{EXT}}_{\text{IAS}, \mathcal{A}_{\text{ext}}}(\lambda)$ generates the public parameter $\text{pp} = (p, \mathfrak{g}, N, E_0, \mathcal{H}_1, S, T) \leftarrow \text{MCSI-FiSh.Setup}(\lambda)$ and a secret-public key pair $(\text{sk} = \{a_i\}_{i=1}^{S-1}, \text{pk} = \{E_{A_i}\}_{i=1}^{S-1}) \leftarrow \text{MCSI-FiSh.KeyGen}(\text{pp})$. It forwards pp and pk to the adversary $\mathcal{A}_{\text{ext}}$, along with access to $\mathcal{O}_{\text{PreSign}}(\cdot, \cdot)$ oracle and keeps sk secret to itself. The adversary $\mathcal{A}_{\text{ext}}$ simulates the $\text{Exp}^3_{\text{IAS}, \mathcal{A}}(\lambda)$ to the $\mathcal{A}$ in the following way.

Setup: The adversary $\mathcal{A}_{\text{ext}}$ forwards pp and pk to the adversary $\mathcal{A}$ and initializes four lists CList, QList, T and U to ϕ.

Simulation of the oracle query In the following, we will show that $\mathcal{A}_{\text{ext}}$ simulates all oracles perfectly for $\mathcal{A}$.

- $\mathcal{O}_{\text{NewY}}()$: The adversary $\mathcal{A}_{\text{ext}}$ runs $(E_Y, \cdot) \leftarrow R.\text{Gen}(\lambda)$ and sets $\text{CList} = \text{CList} \cup \{E_Y\}$. It returns the statement E_Y to the adversary $\mathcal{A}$.

- $\mathcal{O}_{\text{Sign}}(m)$: On receiving a signature query on a message $m \in \mathcal{M}$ from $\mathcal{A}$, the adversary $\mathcal{A}_{\text{ext}}$ runs $R.\text{Gen}(\lambda)$ and generates (E_Y, y). By calling its own oracle $\mathcal{O}_{\text{PreSign}}(m, E_Y)$ the adversary $\mathcal{A}_{\text{ext}}$ generates pre-signature $\widehat{\sigma}$, generates a full signature σ by running $\text{IAS.Adapt}(\text{pp}, \widehat{\sigma}, y)$ and update the sets $\text{QList} = \text{QList} \cup \{m\}$ and $U[m] = U[m] \cup \{(E_Y, \widehat{\sigma})\}$. It returns the computed signature σ to the adversary $\mathcal{A}$.

- $\mathcal{O}_{\text{PreSign}}(m, E_Y)$: On receiving a pre-signature query on a message $m \in \mathcal{M}$ from $\mathcal{A}$ and statement $E_Y \in L_R$, the adversary $\mathcal{A}_{\text{ext}}$ generates a pre-signature $\widehat{\sigma}$ by calling its own oracle $\mathcal{O}_{\text{PreSign}}(m, E_Y)$ which is simulated by the $\mathcal{C}$. The adversary $\mathcal{A}_{\text{ext}}$ updates the table $T[m] = T[m] \cup \{(E_Y, \widehat{\sigma})\}$ and returns $\widehat{\sigma}$ to $\mathcal{A}$.

Extracting the Forgery: After receiving the forgery (m^*, σ^*) submitted by the adversary $\mathcal{A}$ the adversary $\mathcal{A}_{\text{ext}}$ returns (m^*, σ^*) to the challenger $\mathcal{C}$.

If $\mathcal{A}$ wins in the experiment $\text{Exp}_{\text{IAS}, \mathcal{A}}^{3}(\lambda)$ then $m^* \notin \text{QList}$, $\text{Valid} \leftarrow \text{MCSI-FiSh.Verify}(\text{pp}, \text{pk}, m^*, \sigma^*)$ and the flag b_1, b_2 and b_3 are 1. Hence, $\text{Valid} \leftarrow \text{MCSI-FiSh.Verify}(\text{pp}, \text{pk}, m^*, \sigma^*)$ and the flag b is 1. Therefore, (m^*, σ^*) will be a valid forgery. This implies that the probability of winning in $\text{Exp}_{\text{IAS}, \mathcal{A}_{\text{ext}}}^{\text{EXT}}(\lambda)$ is greater or equal to $\text{Exp}_{\text{IAS}, \mathcal{A}}^{3}(\lambda)$.

Claim 5. $\Pr[\text{Exp}_{\text{IAS}, \mathcal{A}_{\text{ext}}}^{\text{EXT}}(\lambda) = 1] \leq \text{Adv}_{\text{CSI-FiSh}, \mathcal{A}_{\text{uf-cma}}}^{\text{UF-CMA}}(\lambda)$.

Proof. We will show that if the adversary $\mathcal{A}_{\text{ext}}$ wins in $\text{Exp}_{\text{IAS}, \mathcal{A}_{\text{ext}}}^{\text{EXT}}(\lambda)$ then we can construct an adversary $\mathcal{A}_{\text{uf-cma}}$ (say) using the adversary $\mathcal{A}_{\text{ext}}$ that can win in $\text{Exp}_{\text{Sig}, \mathcal{A}}^{\text{UF-CMA}}(\lambda)$ given in Definition 8.

The challenger $\mathcal{C}$ of the experiment $\text{Exp}_{\text{Sig}, \mathcal{A}}^{\text{UF-CMA}}(\lambda)$ generates the public parameter $\text{pp} = (p, \mathfrak{g}, N, E_0, \mathcal{H}_1, S, T) \leftarrow \text{CSI-FiSh.Setup}(\lambda)$ and a secret-public key pair $(\text{sk} = \{a_i\}_{i=1}^{S-1}, \text{pk} = \{E_{A_i}\}_{i=1}^{S-1}) \leftarrow \text{CSI-FiSh.KeyGen}(\text{pp})$. It forwards pp and pk to the adversary $\mathcal{A}_{\text{ext}}$, along with providing access to $\mathcal{O}_{\text{CSI-FiSh.Sign}}(\cdot)$ oracle of CSI-FiSh and keeps sk secret to itself. The challenger $\mathcal{C}$ also maintains a list SList, initially set to ϕ.

Setup: The adversary $\mathcal{A}_{\text{uf-cma}}$ forwards pp and pk to the adversary $\mathcal{A}_{\text{ext}}$. The adversary $\mathcal{A}_{\text{uf-cma}}$ also maintains a table T indexed by message m, initially set to ϕ.

Simulation of the oracle query: In the following, we will show that $\mathcal{A}_{\text{uf-cma}}$ simulates the oracle $\mathcal{O}_{\text{PreSign}}(\cdot, \cdot)$ perfectly for $\mathcal{A}_{\text{ext}}$.

- $\mathcal{O}_{\text{PreSign}}(m, E_Y)$: On receiving a pre-signature query from the adversary $\mathcal{A}_{\text{ext}}$ on a message $m \in \mathcal{M}$ and statement E_Y, the adversary $\mathcal{A}_{\text{uf-cma}}$ generates $r \leftarrow R.\text{Rand}(\lambda)$ and computes $E_{Y'} = [r]E_Y$. Then, it computes a signature σ on the message $(m, E_{Y'})$ by invoking its own oracle $\sigma \leftarrow \mathcal{O}_{\text{CSI-FiSh.Sign}}((m, E_{Y'}))$. It also updates the table $T[m] = T[m] \cup \{(E_Y, (\sigma, E_Y, r))\}$ and returns $\widehat{\sigma} = (\sigma, E_Y, r)$.

Extracting the Forgery: After receiving the forgery $(m^*, \sigma^* = (\sigma_1^*, E_Y^*, y^*)))$ where $\sigma_1^* = (\{h_i^*\}_{i=1}^T, \{z_i^*\}_{i=1}^T)$ from $\mathcal{A}_{\text{ext}}$ the adversary $\mathcal{A}_{\text{uf-cma}}$ returns $((m^*, E_Y^*), \sigma_1^*)$.

We claim that if $(m^*, \sigma^* = (\{h_i^*\}_{i=1}^T, \{z_i^*\}_{i=1}^T, E_Y^*, y^*)))$ is a valid forgery in $\text{Exp}_{\text{IAS}, \mathcal{A}_{\text{ext}}}^{\text{EXT}}(\lambda)$ then $(m^*, E_Y^*) \notin$ SList i.e. $\mathcal{A}_{\text{uf-cma}}$ has not queried $\mathcal{O}_{\text{CSI-FiSh.Sign}}((m^*, E_Y^*))$.

Suppose that adversary $\mathcal{A}_{\text{uf-cma}}$ has incurred a query $\mathcal{O}_{\text{CSI-FiSh.Sign}}((m^*, E_Y^*))$ i.e. $(m^*, E_Y^*) \in$ SList. Then this query must have come from some query $\mathcal{O}_{\text{PreSign}}(m^*, E_{Y_0})$ where the adversary $\mathcal{A}_{\text{uf-cma}}$ has sampled some r_0 such that $E_Y^* = [r_0]E_{Y_0}$. Also note that, $(E_{Y_0}, \hat{\sigma}_0 = (\sigma_0, E_{Y_0}, r)) \in T[m^*]$ where $\sigma_0 \leftarrow \mathcal{O}_{\text{CSI-FiSh.Sign}}((m^*, E_Y^*))$

The validity of the forgery $(m^*, \sigma^* = (\{h_i^*\}_{i=1}^T, \{z_i^*\}_{i=1}^T, E_Y^*, y^*)))$ implies

- Valid $\leftarrow$ MCSI-FiSh.Verify(pp, pk, m^*, σ^*) and
- $(E_Y, \text{IAS.Ext}(\text{pp}, \sigma^*, \hat{\sigma}, E_Y)) \notin R$ for all $(E_Y, \hat{\sigma}) \in T[m^*]$,

  The validity of the MCSI-FiSh.Verify(pp, pk, m^*, σ^*) implies that

- Valid $\leftarrow$ CSI-FiSh.Verify(pp, pk, $(m^*, E_Y^*), \sigma_1^*$) where $\sigma_1^* = (\{h_i^*\}_{i=1}^T, \{z_i^*\}_{i=1}^T)$
- $(E_Y^*, y^*) \in R$, i.e. $E_Y^* = [y^*]E_0$.

  Now $(E_Y, \text{IAS.Ext}(\text{pp}, \sigma^*, \hat{\sigma}, E_Y)) \notin R$ for all $(E_Y, \hat{\sigma}) \in T[m^*]$ and $(E_{Y_0}, \hat{\sigma}_0 = (\sigma_0, E_{Y_0}, r)) \in T[m^*]$ implies $(E_{Y_0}, y_0) \notin R$ where $y_0 \leftarrow \text{IAS.Ext}(\text{pp}, \sigma^*, \hat{\sigma}_0, E_{Y_0})$. But, $y_0 = y^* - r_0$ and $y^* - r_0$ is the witness of E_{Y_0}. Hence $(E_{Y_0}, y_0) \in R$, which is a contradiction. Therefore, $(m^*, E_Y^*) \notin$ SList and $((m^*, E_Y^*), \sigma_1^*)$ will be a valid forgery. Consequently, we can conclude that $\Pr[\text{Exp}_{\text{IAS}, \mathcal{A}_{\text{ext}}}^{\text{EXT}}(\lambda) = 1] \leq \text{Adv}_{\text{CSI-FiSh}, \mathcal{A}_{\text{uf-cma}}}^{\text{UF-CMA}}(\lambda)$.

Claim 6. $\Pr[\text{Exp}_{\text{IAS}, \mathcal{A}}^4(\lambda) = 1] \leq \text{Adv}_{R, \mathcal{A}_{\text{ow}}}^{\text{q-OW}}(\lambda)$.

Proof. We will show that if the adversary $\mathcal{A}$ wins in $\text{Exp}_{\text{IAS}, \mathcal{A}}^4(\lambda)$ then we can construct an adversary $\mathcal{A}_{\text{ow}}$ (say) using the adversary $\mathcal{A}$ that can win in $\text{Exp}_{R, \mathcal{A}_{\text{ow}}}^{\text{q-OW}}$ given in Fig. 2.

The challenger $\mathcal{C}$ in the $\text{Exp}_{R, \mathcal{A}_{\text{ow}}}^{\text{q-OW}}$ generates $(E_{Y_i}, \cdot) \leftarrow R.\text{Gen}(\lambda)$ for $i = 1, \ldots, q$ and forwards $(E_{Y_1}, \ldots, E_{Y_q})$ to $\mathcal{A}_{\text{ow}}$. The adversary $\mathcal{A}_{\text{ow}}$ simulates the $\text{Exp}_{\text{IAS}, \mathcal{A}}^4(\lambda)$ to the $\mathcal{A}$ in the following way.

Setup: The adversary $\mathcal{A}_{\text{ow}}$ generates the public parameter pp = $(p, \mathfrak{g}, N, E_0, \mathcal{H}_1, S, T) \leftarrow$ MCSI-FiSh.Setup(λ) and a secret-public key pair (sk = $\{a_i\}_{i=1}^{S-1}$, pk = $\{E_{A_i}\}_{i=1}^{S-1}) \leftarrow$ MCSI-FiSh.KeyGen(pp). It forwards pp and pk to the adversary $\mathcal{A}$ while keeps sk secret to itself. It maintains two lists QList and T, initializes to ϕ and an index ind = 1.

Simulation of the oracle query: In the following, we will show that $\mathcal{A}_{\text{ow}}$ simulates all oracles perfectly for $\mathcal{A}$.

- $\mathcal{O}_{\text{NewY}}()$: The adversary $\mathcal{A}_{\text{ow}}$ returns $E_{Y_{\text{ind}}}$ and updates ind = ind + 1.

- $\mathcal{O}_{\mathsf{Sign}}(m)$: On receiving a signature query on a message $m \in \mathcal{M}$ from $\mathcal{A}$, the adversary $\mathcal{A}_{\mathsf{ow}}$ generates $(E_Y, y) \leftarrow R.\mathsf{Gen}(\lambda)$ and computes pre-signature $\widehat{\sigma} \leftarrow \mathsf{IAS.PreSign}(\mathsf{pp}, \mathsf{sk}, m, E_Y)$ and a full signature σ by running $\mathsf{IAS.Adapt}(\mathsf{pp}, \widehat{\sigma}, y)$ and update the sets $\mathsf{QList} = \mathsf{QList} \cup \{m\}$ and $T[m] = T[m] \cup \{(E_Y, \widehat{\sigma})\}$. It returns σ to the adversary $\mathcal{A}$.
- $\mathcal{O}_{\mathsf{PreSign}}(m, E_Y)$: On receiving a pre-signature query on a message $m \in \mathcal{M}$ and statement $E_Y \in L_R$ from $\mathcal{A}$, the adversary $\mathcal{A}_{\mathsf{ow}}$ computes pre-signature $\widehat{\sigma} \leftarrow \mathsf{IAS.PreSign}(\mathsf{sk}, m, E_Y)$. It updates the set $T[m] = T[m] \cup \{(E_Y, \widehat{\sigma})\}$ and returns $\widehat{\sigma}$ to $\mathcal{A}$.

Extracting the Forgery: After receiving the forgery (m^*, σ^*) submitted by the adversary $\mathcal{A}$ the adversary $\mathcal{A}_{\mathsf{ow}}$ verify $m^* \notin \mathsf{QList}$, $\mathsf{Valid} \leftarrow \mathsf{MCSI}$-$\mathsf{FiSh.Verify}(\mathsf{pp}, \mathsf{pk}, m^*, \sigma^*)$. The validity of the forgery also guarantees there exists a $(E_Y, \widehat{\sigma}) \in T[m^*]$ with $E_Y = E_{Y_I}$ for some $I \in \{1, \ldots, q\}$ such that $E_Y = [y]E_0$ where $y = \mathsf{IAS.Ext}(\mathsf{pp}, E_Y, \widehat{\sigma}, \sigma^*)$. Then the adversary $\mathcal{A}_{\mathsf{ow}}$ submits the forgery (I, y). This implies that $\mathsf{Adv}_{R, \mathcal{A}_{\mathsf{ow}}}^{\mathsf{q\text{-}OW}}(\lambda)$ is greater or equal to the probability of winning in $\mathsf{Exp}_{\mathsf{IAS}, \mathcal{A}}^4(\lambda)$.

Theorem 25. *Our proposed isogeny-based adaptor signature* IAS *is* SFEXT *secure as per Definition 19 as* $\mathsf{CSI\text{-}FiSh}$ *is* $\mathsf{sEUF\text{-}CMA}$ *secure and the relation* R *is a hard relation and satisfies unique witness property. More concretely, if there exists an adversary* $\mathcal{A}$ *of the* SFEXT *game in Fig. 5 for* IAS *then there exists an adversary* $\mathcal{A}_{\mathsf{suf\text{-}cma}}$ *of* $\mathsf{sEUF\text{-}CMA}$ *game in Fig. 1 for* $\mathsf{CSI\text{-}FiSh}$, *an adversary* $\mathcal{A}_{\mathsf{ow}}$ *of the one-wayness game in Fig. 2 and an adversary* $\mathcal{A}_{\mathsf{uwit}}$ *to break unique witness property (described in Definition 12) for the relation* R *such that*

$$\mathsf{Adv}_{\mathsf{IAS}, \mathcal{A}_{\mathsf{sfext}}}^{\mathsf{SFEXT}}(\lambda) \leq 2\mathsf{Adv}_{\mathsf{CSI\text{-}FiSh}, \mathcal{A}_{\mathsf{suf\text{-}cma}}}^{\mathsf{sEUF\text{-}CMA}}(\lambda) + \mathsf{Adv}_{R, \mathcal{A}_{\mathsf{ow}}}^{\mathsf{q\text{-}OW}}(\lambda) + \mathsf{Adv}_{R, \mathcal{A}_{\mathsf{uwit}}}^{\mathsf{UWIT}}(\lambda)$$

Proof. The proof of the Theorem 25 will appear in the full version of the paper.

References

1. Aumayr, L., et al.: Generalized bitcoin-compatible channels (2020)
2. Beullens, W., Kleinjung, T., Vercauteren, F.: CSI-FiSh: efficient isogeny based signatures through class group computations. In: Galbraith, S.D., Moriai, S. (eds.) ASIACRYPT 2019. LNCS, vol. 11921, pp. 227–247. Springer, Cham (2019). https://doi.org/10.1007/978-3-030-34578-5_9
3. Castryck, W., Decru, T.: An efficient key recovery attack on SIDH. In: Hazay, C., Stam, M. (eds.) Annual International Conference on the Theory and Applications of Cryptographic Techniques, vol. 14008, pp. 423–447. Springer, Cham (2023). https://doi.org/10.1007/978-3-031-30589-4_15
4. Dai, W., Okamoto, T., Yamamoto, G.: Stronger security and generic constructions for adaptor signatures. In: International Conference on Cryptology in India, pp. 52–77. Springer (2022). https://doi.org/10.1007/978-3-031-22912-1_3
5. De Feo, L.: Mathematics of isogeny based cryptography. arXiv preprint arXiv:1711.04062 (2017)

6. De Feo, L., Kohel, D., Leroux, A., Petit, C., Wesolowski, B.: SQISign: compact post-quantum signatures from quaternions and isogenies. In: Moriai, S., Wang, H. (eds.) ASIACRYPT 2020. LNCS, vol. 12491, pp. 64–93. Springer, Cham (2020). https://doi.org/10.1007/978-3-030-64837-4_3

7. Erwig, A., Faust, S., Hostáková, K., Maitra, M., Riahi, S.: Two-party adaptor signatures from identification schemes. In: Garay, J.A. (ed.) PKC 2021. LNCS, vol. 12710, pp. 451–480. Springer, Cham (2021). https://doi.org/10.1007/978-3-030-75245-3_17

8. Esgin, M.F., Ersoy, O., Erkin, Z.: Post-quantum adaptor signatures and payment channel networks. In: Chen, L., Li, N., Liang, K., Schneider, S. (eds.) ESORICS 2020. LNCS, vol. 12309, pp. 378–397. Springer, Cham (2020). https://doi.org/10.1007/978-3-030-59013-0_19

9. Esgin, M.F., Nguyen, N.K., Seiler, G.: Practical exact proofs from lattices: new techniques to exploit fully-splitting rings. In: Moriai, S., Wang, H. (eds.) ASIACRYPT 2020. LNCS, vol. 12492, pp. 259–288. Springer, Cham (2020). https://doi.org/10.1007/978-3-030-64834-3_9

10. Esgin, M.F., Steinfeld, R., Sakzad, A., Liu, J.K., Liu, D.: Short lattice-based one-out-of-many proofs and applications to ring signatures. In: Deng, R.H., Gauthier-Umaña, V., Ochoa, M., Yung, M. (eds.) ACNS 2019. LNCS, vol. 11464, pp. 67–88. Springer, Cham (2019). https://doi.org/10.1007/978-3-030-21568-2_4

11. Gilchrist, V.: An isogeny-based adaptor signature using SQIsign. Master's thesis, University of Waterloo (2022)

12. Maino, L., Martindale, C., Panny, L., Pope, G., Wesolowski, B.: A direct key recovery attack on SIDH. In: Hazay, C., Stam, M. (eds.) Annual International Conference on the Theory and Applications of Cryptographic Techniques, vol. 14008, pp. 448–471. Springer, Cham (2023). https://doi.org/10.1007/978-3-031-30589-4_16

13. Malavolta, G., Moreno-Sanchez, P., Schneidewind, C., Kate, A., Maffei, M.: Anonymous multi-hop locks for blockchain scalability and interoperability. Cryptology ePrint Archive (2018)

14. Moriya, T., Onuki, H., Takagi, T.: SiGamal: a supersingular isogeny-based PKE and its application to a PRF. In: Moriai, S., Wang, H. (eds.) ASIACRYPT 2020. LNCS, vol. 12492, pp. 551–580. Springer, Cham (2020). https://doi.org/10.1007/978-3-030-64834-3_19

15. Nakamoto, S.: Bitcoin: A peer-to-peer electronic cash system (2008)

16. Poelstra, A.: Scriptless scripts. Presentation Slides (2017)

17. Shor, P.W.: Polynomial-time algorithms for prime factorization and discrete logarithms on a quantum computer. SIAM Rev. **41**(2), 303–332 (1999)

18. Tairi, E., Moreno-Sanchez, P., Maffei, M.: A 2 L: anonymous atomic locks for scalability in payment channel hubs. In: 2021 IEEE Symposium on Security and Privacy (SP), pp. 1834–1851. IEEE (2021)

19. Tairi, E., Moreno-Sanchez, P., Maffei, M.: Post-quantum adaptor signature for privacy-preserving off-chain payments. In: Borisov, N., Diaz, C. (eds.) FC 2021. LNCS, vol. 12675, pp. 131–150. Springer, Heidelberg (2021). https://doi.org/10.1007/978-3-662-64331-0_7

20. Vélu, J.: Isogénies entre courbes elliptiques. CR Acad. Sci. Paris, Séries A **273**, 305–347 (1971)

21. Waterhouse, W.C.: Abelian varieties over finite fields. In: Annales Scientifiques de L'École Normale Supérieure, vol. 2, pp. 521–560 (1969)

Compact Post-quantum Bounded-Collusion Identity-Based Encryption

Shingo Sato[1(✉)] and Junji Shikata[1,2]

[1] Institute of Advanced Sciences, Yokohama National University, Yokohama, Japan
{sato-shingo-zk,shikata-junji-rb}@ynu.ac.jp
[2] Graduate School of Environment and Information Sciences, Yokohama National
University, Yokohama, Japan

Abstract. Bounded-collusion identity-based encryption (BC-IBE) is a variant of identity-based encryption, where an adversary obtains at most d secret user-keys for a collusion-parameter d. From results of existing work, there are generic constructions of BC-IBE, which starts from public key encryption (PKE) schemes with several properties. In particular, we consider BC-IBE schemes constructed from post-quantum PKE schemes submitted to the NIST-PQC competition (denoted by NIST-PQC PKE schemes). Although it is possible to construct a post-quantum BC-IBE scheme by applying a NIST-PQC PKE scheme to an existing generic construction, the public parameter-size of the resulting scheme is not compact. In this paper, we propose a post-quantum BC-IBE scheme whose public parameter-size is more compact. To this end, we construct a new generic construction of the objective BC-IBE by employing probabilistic group testing techniques, while existing BC-IBE schemes are constructed by using error-correcting codes or cover-free families. As a result, we can obtain post-quantum BC-IBE schemes with more compact public parameters by applying NIST-PQC PKE schemes to our generic construction.

Keywords: Bounded-collusion identity-based encryption ·
Post-quantum cryptography · Probabilistic group testing

1 Introduction

1.1 Background and Related Work

Identity-based encryption (IBE) is one of the fundamental and important cryptographic primitives. A trusted party called a key generation center generates a public parameter and a master secret key. Any user can encrypt a message by using the public parameter and the user's identity. To decrypt a ciphertext, a user must obtain the secret key for his/her identity generated by the key generation center. Furthermore, IBE is also used to construct cryptosystems with

M. Kohlweiss et al. (Eds.): CANS 2024, LNCS 14905, pp. 101–122, 2025.
https://doi.org/10.1007/978-981-97-8013-6_5

desirable security or advanced functionalities, such as public key encryption (PKE) secure against chosen ciphertext attacks [7], searchable encryption [1], and so on. Hence, there are many researches on IBE such as pairing-based IBE schemes (e.g., [6,8,38]) and lattice-based IBE schemes (e.g., [2,10,19]). As a variant of IBE, Dodis et al. introduced the notion of *bounded-collusion IBE* (BC-IBE) [15]. BC-IBE ensures security in the (security) model where an adversary obtains secret keys associated with at most d identities. Even though BC-IBE is a weak variant of IBE, this cryptographic primitive is effective in terms of practicality. This is because BC-IBE schemes can be constructed from PKE schemes (with several properties) due to results of [13,15,20,36], while there is no existing black-box construction of IBE from PKE. Hence, it is possible to convert an elaborated PKE scheme into a BC-IBE scheme. Furthermore, unlike the standard IBE, we can obtain BC-IBE schemes based on various computational assumptions. There are the following existing BC-IBE schemes constructed from PKE schemes: Dodis et al. proposed the first BC-IBE scheme constructed from any PKE scheme satisfying *indistinguishability against chosen plaintext attacks* (denoted by IND-CPA security) [15]. Goldwasser, Lewko, and Wilson introduced PKE's properties: *linear hash proof* property and *key homomorphism*, and presented a generic construction starting from any PKE scheme satisfying these properties [20]. Tessaro and Wilson provided two BC-IBE schemes. One is constructed from a PKE scheme satisfying key homomorphism and weak multi-key malleability, and the other is constructed from a PKE scheme satisfying multi-key malleability [36]. Choi et al. introduced the notion of *power of message-and-key* property and proposed a generic construction of BC-IBE which starts from any IND-CPA secure PKE scheme with key homomorphism, weak multi-key malleability, and power of message-and-key property [13].

In particular, we focus on post-quantum PKE and BC-IBE. Post-quantum cryptography (PQC) is one of the most important research areas, due to advancement of quantum computers. In order to develop cryptosystems resistant to attacks using quantum computation, many researchers have paid much attention to post-quantum cryptosystems. Furthermore, there are many researches on PKE/KEM algorithms submitted to the NIST-PQC standardization competition (e.g., [21,28,39]). The lattice-based PKE/KEM scheme CRYSTALS-Kyber (Kyber, for short) [9] has already been selected in this competition, as a standard of post-quantum PKE/KEM. In addition, the following three code-based PKE/KEMs are the 4th round candidates of that competition: BIKE [5], HQC [29], and Classic McElicece [3]. Therefore, it is reasonable to consider post-quantum cryptosystems such as post-quantum PKE and BC-IBE.

Importance of Constructing BC-IBE from PKE. Developing post-quantum IBE and BC-IBE schemes is important in a quantum era. As existing post-quantum IBE schemes, there are only lattice-based ones (e.g., [2,10,19])[1]. Although there is no existing direct construction of post-quantum BC-IBE, we

---

[1] As candidates of post-quantum IBE, code-based IBE schemes were proposed in [11, 18]. However, these schemes are broken under the parameters chosen in [11,18], due to attacks proposed in [14].

can obtain a post-quantum BC-IBE scheme by applying a suitable post-quantum PKE scheme to one of generic constructions of [10, 15, 36]

We stress that it is meaningful to consider efficient generic constructions of BC-IBE starting from NIST-PQC PKE, even though there are several post-quantum IBE schemes. In the future, NIST-PQC PKE schemes will be implemented widely for many systems/devices. By employing generic constructions of [13, 15, 36], post-quantum BC-IBE can be constructed from a post-quantum PKE scheme without changing the underlying PKE's algorithms. Hence, generic constructions of BC-IBE derived from PKE is compatible with NIST-PQC PKE schemes, in a real world. On the other hand, techniques employed for existing post-quantum IBE schemes are not compatible with existing post-quantum PKE schemes. This is because all the existing post-quantum (lattice-based) IBE schemes employ inefficient cryptographic tools such as lattice-trapdoors [10, 30], and its methodologies are different from those of practical post-quantum PKE schemes including NIST-PQC PKE. Hence, we focus on presenting simple and efficient generic constructions of BC-IBE, which starts from (NIST-PQC) PKE.

1.2 Our Contribution

Our goal is to convert NIST-PQC PKE schemes into adaptively secure BC-IBE schemes with compact public parameters. In particular, we aim at proposing a generic construction with $O(d \log n)|\mathsf{pk}|$-size public parameters, so that we can construct NIST-PQC BC-IBE schemes with compact public parameters. Here, NIST-PQC BC-IBE means BC-IBE constructed from NIST-PQC PKE, d is the collusion-parameter, n is the size of the identity space, and $|\mathsf{pk}|$ is the bit-length of the public keys of the underlying PKE scheme.

Table 1 shows the generic constructions of adaptively secure BC-IBE. From this table, we see that there is no existing NIST-PQC BC-IBE scheme with a compact public parameter. We discuss this fact by using the parameters $|\mathsf{pk}|, |\mathsf{ct}|, d, n$ defined in Table 1. Although the BC-IBE scheme of [15] can be constructed from any IND-CPA secure PKE, its public parameter-size and ciphertext-size are $O(d^2 \log n)|\mathsf{pk}|$ and $O(d \log n)|\mathsf{ct}|$, respectively. Although the public parameter-size of the generic construction of [20] is $O(d \log n)|\mathsf{pk}|$, there is no post-quantum PKE scheme which can be applied to this generic construction. This is because it is required that the underlying PKE scheme satisfies the linear hash proof property introduced in [20]. Unfortunately, there is no post-quantum PKE scheme satisfying this property. Regarding the generic constructions of [36], we can apply only the PKE scheme of [19] (denoted by GPV-PKE) and a variant of NTRU [35] to these generic constructions, and the public parameter-sizes of the resulting BC-IBE schemes are $O(d^2 \log n)|\mathsf{pk}|$. Although the public parameter-size of the generic construction of [13] is $O(d)|\mathsf{pk}|$, only the GPV-PKE scheme [19] can be applied to this construction. This is because (weak) multi-key homomorphism ensures indistinguishability between an encryption of a message m under a public key pk and an encryption of m under multiple public keys including pk, and algorithms which generate such an encryption under multiple

Table 1. Generic Constructions of Adaptively secure BC-IBE starting from PKE

Scheme	Requirements for PKE	CT-Size	PP-Size	StdM?
[15]	IND-CPA security	$O(d\log n)|\mathsf{ct}|$	$O(d^2\log n)|\mathsf{pk}|$	✓
[20]	IND-CPA security Linear Hash Proof Key Homomorphism	$|\mathsf{ct}|$	$O(d\log n)|\mathsf{pk}|$	✓
[36]	IND-CPA security Key Homomorphism Weak Multi-Key Malleability	$|\mathsf{ct}|$	$O(d^2\log n)|\mathsf{pk}|$	✓
	IND-CPA security Multi-Key Malleability			
[13]	IND-CPA security Key Homomorphism Weak Multi-Key Malleability Power of Message-and-key	$|\mathsf{ct}|$	$O(d)|\mathsf{pk}|$	ROM
Our work (Sect. 4)	IND-CPA security	$O(\log n)|\mathsf{ct}|$	$O(d\log n)|\mathsf{pk}|$	ROM

"CT-Size" and "PP-Size" mean ciphertext-size and public parameter-size, respectively. d is the collusion-parameter (i.e., the maximum number of queries issued to the key extraction oracle). n is the size of an identity space. $|\mathsf{ct}|$ and $|\mathsf{pk}|$ are the bit-lengths of ciphertexts and public keys of the underlying PKE, respectively. "StdM" means the standard model (i.e., the model without any idealized oracles). "ROM" means the random oracle model. Note that the CT-Size of our work is obtained by Proposition 1.

public keys are not known for most post-quantum PKE schemes such as NIST-PQC PKE schemes. Hence, when constructing a NIST-PQC BC-IBE scheme by using these existing results, its public parameter-size is $O(d^2\log n)|\mathsf{pk}|$ and non-compact.

In order to achieve our goal, we utilize a test matrix used in a probabilistic group testing algorithm (e.g., [12,23,25]), while the existing schemes [15,20, 36] implicitly employ test matrices used in combinatorial group testing (e.g., [24,25,31]). Details on group testing appear in Sect. 3. By using a test matrix used in probabilistic group testing, we can construct a BC-IBE scheme with a $O(d\log n)|\mathsf{pk}|$-size public parameter. Details on our contribution are as follows:

1. We introduce a new notion of error-probability for probabilistic group testing, called *random subset error-probability*, in order to give a security proof for our BC-IBE scheme. Because the upper bound of this probability for probabilistic group testing is not clear, we estimate this bound for existing probabilistic group testing algorithms [12,23]. One may think that the error-probability of existing probabilistic group testing algorithms is small enough in terms of practicality, because the bound of error-probability is strictly analyzed in existing work related to group testing. However, it is unclear whether such a bound of error-probability is sufficient to prove the security of cryptographic

primitives[2]. Hence, it is necessary to analyze the introduced error-probability in order to give a security proof for our BC-IBE scheme.

2. We propose a generic construction of BC-IBE (in Sect. 4), which starts from any IND-CPA secure PKE scheme. Namely, it is possible to apply most NIST-PQC PKE schemes to this construction. Although this scheme is similar to the BC-IBE scheme of [15], we utilize a test matrix used in a probabilistic group testing algorithm so that its public parameter-size becomes $O(d \log n)|\mathsf{pk}|$. On the other hand, the existing ones [15,20,36] employ a test matrix used in combinatorial group testing, whose notion is identical to that of error-correcting codes or cover-free families. Notice that just replacing combinatorial group testing with probabilistic group testing does not ensure the security of the BC-IBE scheme, and a random oracle is necessary. We discuss this in Sect. 1.3.

From the results above, it is possible to obtain a NIST-PQC BC-IBE scheme with $O(d \log n)|\mathsf{pk}|$-size public parameters by applying a NIST-PQC PKE scheme to our generic construction. Furthermore, we stress that we can apply any NIST-PQC PKE scheme (such as Kyber [9], BIKE [5], HQC [29], or a slight variant[3] of Classic McEliece [3]) to our generic construction in Sect. 4.

Remark 1. The size of the identity space of our BC-IBE scheme is subexponential in a security parameter, in order to ensure its security. However, users do not have to store a subexponential-size matrix, because there exists a test matrix used in probabilistic group testing, such that the matrix is constructed in a deterministic way; namely, by setting several parameters beforehand, it is possible to construct a suitable test matrix without employing large-size values, when running encryption and decryption procedures.

Comparison of Post-quantum BC-IBE Schemes. We show that it is possible to obtain a NIST-PQC BC-IBE scheme with compact pubic parameters by using our generic construction. To show this fact, we compare post-quantum BC-IBE schemes constructed by applying suitable existing (lattice-based) PKE schemes to generic constructions of BC-IBE. We have chosen the generic constructions of [13,15,36] and our proposed construction in Sect. 4, since it is possible to apply lattice-based PKE schemes to these constructions. Recall that there is no existing post-quantum PKE scheme which can be applied to the construction of [20]. Table 2 shows the comparison of the lattice-based instantiations of the generic constructions. Remark that in this table, we have modified these instantiations secure under the module-learning with errors (MLWE) assumption with dimension k in order to fairly compare the resulting post-quantum BC-IBE schemes. From this table, we observe that the public parameter-size

---

[2] For example, if we apply a test matrix of probabilistic group testing with error-probability depending only on the collusion-parameter d (d implies the maximum number of defective items in the sense of group testing) to our generic construction, the resulting scheme cannot achieve the security of BC-IBE.

[3] It is possible to transform the Classic McEliece PKE scheme into an IND-CPA secure one, by replacing parts of a message string with randomness. For example, see [32].

Table 2. Comparison of Adaptively secure Post-Quantum BC-IBE schemes

Generic Construction	Underlying PKE	Computational Assumption	PK-Size used in PP (under MLWE)	#PK used in PP
[15]	Kyber [9]	MLWE	$O(k^2 N \log \mathsf{poly}(\lambda))$	$O(d^2 \log n)$
[36]	GPV-PKE [19]	SubExp. LWE	$O(k^2 \lambda^{2\epsilon} N)$	$O(d^2 \log n)$
[36]	NTRU variant [35]	SubExp. RLWE	$O(k^2 \lambda^{\epsilon} N)$	$O(d^2 \log n)$
[13]	GPV-PKE [19]	SubExp. LWE	$O(k^2 \lambda^{2\epsilon} N)$	$O(d)$
Our work	Kyber [9]	MLWE	$O(k^2 N \log \mathsf{poly}(\lambda))$	$O(d \log n)$

MLWE means the module-LWE (module-learning with errors) assumption, and SubExp. (R)LWE means the (R)LWE assumption with subexponential modulus. "PK-Size used in PP" means the bit-length of a public key of an underlying PKE scheme under the MLWE assumption with dimension k, and "#PK used in PP" means the number of underlying PKE's public keys used as a public parameter of a BC-IBE scheme. λ is a security parameter, $\epsilon < 1$ is some positive constant, and the parameters $d, n, |\mathsf{pk}|$ are defined in the same as Table 1. For simplicity, we have estimated $|\mathsf{pk}|$ asymptotically, by assuming that subexponential modulus is $2^{\lambda^{\epsilon}}$, $N = \mathsf{poly}(\lambda)$ is a dimension of a ring such as $\mathbb{Z}_q[X]/(X^N + 1)$, and the other parameters are $\mathsf{poly}(\lambda)$.

of our work is asymptotically smaller than those of the other schemes. This is because our work is based on the MLWE assumption with polynomial modulus, and the public parameter-size of our generic construction is $O(d \log n)$. On the other hand, the instantiations of the generic constructions of [13, 36] are based on the (M)LWE or RLWE assumption with subexponential modulus since (weak) multi-key malleability is required for the underlying PKE schemes in the generic constructions of [13, 36]. In addition, the public parameter-size of the generic construction of [15] is $O(d^2 \log n)$. Therefore, our proposed generic construction is the most suitable in order to obtain NIST-PQC BC-IBE schemes with compact public parameters.

1.3   Technical Overview

In order to describe technical aspects on our BC-IBE scheme, we briefly explain the existing BC-IBE schemes [15, 36], because our proposed scheme is based on these existing ones. For the collusion-parameter d, the existing schemes [15, 36] implicitly employ d-disjunct matrices of combinatorial group testing, whose notion is identical to those of cover-free families or error-correcting codes. Group testing is a methodology to efficiently detect d particular items (called defective items) among n items ($d \ll n$), and a canonical combinatorial group testing algorithm for u tests and n items employs a test matrix $\boldsymbol{M} = [\boldsymbol{M}_1 \| \cdots \| \boldsymbol{M}_n] \in \{0, 1\}^{u \times n}$ satisfying the d-disjunct property (see Definition 9).

Then, the public parameter pp of an existing generic construction (e.g., [15, 36]) using a d-disjunct matrix $\boldsymbol{M} = [\boldsymbol{M}_1 \| \cdots \| \boldsymbol{M}_n] \in \{0, 1\}^{u \times n}$ is $(\mathsf{pk}_1, \ldots, \mathsf{pk}_u)$, and each public key pk_i is assigned to the i-th row of $\boldsymbol{M}$, where $\mathsf{pk}_1, \ldots, \mathsf{pk}_u$ are public keys of the underlying PKE scheme. We suppose that the set $\{\mathsf{id}_1, \ldots, \mathsf{id}_n\}$ is the identity space, and the identity id_i corresponds to the column vector $\boldsymbol{M}_i$ for every $i \in \{1, \ldots, n\}$. Then, the secret key of an identity id_i is $(\mathsf{sk}_j)_{j \in \phi_{\boldsymbol{M}}(\mathsf{id}_i)}$, where let $M := (m_{j,i}) \in \{0,1\}^{u \times n}$, let $\phi_M(\text{id}_i) := \{j \in [u] \mid m_{j,i} = 1\}$, and a secret key sk_i corresponds to pk_i for every $i \in \{1, \ldots, n\}$.

Here, the d-disjunct property of M ensures that the union of any d column vectors cannot cover any other vector. Due to this property, the adversary cannot know all the secret keys $(\text{sk}_j)_{j \in \phi_M(\text{id}_i)}$ for a target identity id_i, even if the secret keys for at most d identities are compromised. That is, the adversary cannot break the challenge ciphertext for the target identity id_i if this ciphertext is generated by using the public keys $(\text{pk}_j)_{j \in \phi_M(\text{id}_i)}$. In addition, for a d-disjunct matrix, the bound of the number u of rows is $O(d^2 \log n)$ (e.g., [17,25]). Hence, the public parameter-size of the existing BC-IBE schemes [15,36] is $O(d^2 \log n)|\text{pk}|$.

Difficulty of Employing Probabilistic Group Testing. One may think that it is possible to reduce a public parameter-size by replacing a d-disjunct matrix with a test matrix used in probabilistic group testing, for the BC-IBE schemes [15,36]. This is because the number of rows of such a test matrix is bounded by $O(d \log(n/d))$ [27], and there exist nearly optimal test matrices with $O(d \log n)$ rows (e.g., [12,23,24]). However, we cannot give a security proof for such a BC-IBE scheme in the straightforward way. In a model of probabilistic group testing, the set of defective items (corresponding to corrupted identities) is distributed at random. On the other hand, the distribution of defective items of combinatorial group testing is not necessarily random. Hence, we cannot replace a d-disjunct test matrix used in the schemes [15,36] with a test matrix of probabilistic group testing, straightforwardly.

Our Technique to Resolve the Problem. We employ a random oracle so that a set of corrupted identities (corresponding to defective items) is distributed at random. However, there is another problem to give a security proof even though we use a random oracle. The adversary $\mathcal{A}$ can issue queries to not only the key extraction oracle but also the random oracle, in the security game of BC-IBE. Thus, there is a possibility that this adversary issues q_H queries to the random oracle ($q_H \geq d$) before invoking the key extraction oracle. In a test matrix used in probabilistic group testing, there are a few column vectors covered by the union of d other column vectors, unlike a d-disjunct matrix. Hence, $\mathcal{A}$ may be able to find d column vectors among q_H vectors, whose union covers the column vector of the target identity of the challenge ciphertext. Then, it may be possible to obtain the secret keys corresponding to the target identity, by issuing d queries to the key extraction oracle.

In order to ensure that this event does not occur, we need to estimate the upper bound of the error-probability that, for any random subset $\mathcal{S}$ of column vectors of M such that $|\mathcal{S}| = q_H$, there exists a set $\mathcal{J} \subseteq \mathcal{S}$ such that $|\mathcal{J}| \leq d$ and the union of the column vectors in $\mathcal{J}$ covers any other vector in $\mathcal{S} \backslash \mathcal{J}$. There is no notion identical to this error-probability though there are notions of error-probability related to probabilistic group testing. Hence, we newly formalize the error-probability for probabilistic group testing. Then, we estimate the upper bound of this probability for concrete group testing algorithms, the Monte-Carlo-based construction [12] and Kautz-Singleton construction [23]. In the setting of BC-IBE, these test-designs of M can be determined in deterministic ways. Thus, we do not have to store an exponential-size test matrix when constructing BC-IBE schemes. Hence, we have chosen the probabilistic group testing algorithms [12, 23].

Organization. Section 2 contains the notation used in this paper and definitions of several cryptographic primitives. In Sect. 3, we describe definitions of (non-adaptive) group testing and formalize a new notion of error-probability of probabilistic group testing (i.e., random subset error-probability). In Sect. 3.2, we analyze the bounds of random subset error-probability for existing two algorithms of probabilistic group testing. In Sect. 4, we propose a generic construction of BC-IBE and give a security proof for this construction.

2   Preliminaries

Throughout this paper, we use the following notation: For a positive integer n, let $[n] := \{1, \ldots, n\}$. For values $x_1, \ldots, x_n$ and a subset $S \subseteq [n]$, let $\{x_i\}_{i \in S}$ (resp. $(x_i)_{i \in S}$) be the set (resp. sequence) of values whose indexes are in S. For some value v, let $|v|$ be the bit-length of v. For a positive integer n, let 0^n be the zero-string with bit-length n. For a function $f : \mathbb{N} \to \mathbb{R}$, f is negligible in λ (denoted by $f(\lambda) \leq \mathsf{negl}(\lambda)$) if $f(\lambda) = o(\lambda^{-c})$ for any constant $c > 0$ and sufficiently large $\lambda \in \mathbb{N}$. A probability is an overwhelming probability if it is $1 - \mathsf{negl}(\lambda)$. "Probabilistic polynomial-time" is abbreviated as PPT. For a positive integer λ, let $\mathsf{poly}(\lambda)$ be a universal polynomial of λ.

Matrices and Vectors. For consistency, we use capital bold letters for matrices, non-capital letters for scalars, and bold letters for (column) vectors. For a (binary) matrix $\boldsymbol{M} \in \{0,1\}^{u \times n}$, we use the standard notation $\boldsymbol{M} = (m_{i,j})$. For a n-dimensional vector $\boldsymbol{v}$, v_i is the i-th entry, namely $\boldsymbol{v} = (v_1, \ldots, v_n)^\top$. For matrices $\boldsymbol{M}_1, \ldots, \boldsymbol{M}_n$, $[\boldsymbol{M}_1 \| \cdots \| \boldsymbol{M}_n]^\top$ is defined as the vertical concatenation of $\boldsymbol{M}_1, \ldots, \boldsymbol{M}_n$. For a binary matrix $\boldsymbol{x} \in \{0,1\}^n$, let $\mathsf{supp}(\boldsymbol{x}) := \{i \in [n] \mid x_i = 1\}$. For a binary matrix $\boldsymbol{M} = (m_{i,j}) \in \{0,1\}^{u \times n}$ and a binary vector $\boldsymbol{x} \in \{0,1\}^n$, the binary vector $\boldsymbol{y} = \boldsymbol{M} \odot \boldsymbol{x} \in \{0,1\}^u$ is defined as $\forall i \in [u], y_i = \bigvee_{j \in [n] \text{ s.t. } m_{i,j}=1} x_j$, where $\bigvee$ is the bitwise-OR. For a binary matrix $\boldsymbol{M} = (m_{i,j}) \in \{0,1\}^{u \times n}$ and $c \in [n]$, let $\phi_{\boldsymbol{M}}(c) := \{i \in [u] \mid m_{i,c} = 1\}$.

Furthermore, we describe definitions of some cryptographic primitives.

2.1   Public Key Encryption

We describe the syntax and a security definition of public key encryption (PKE).

Definition 1 (PKE). *A PKE scheme consists of three polynomial-time algorithms* (KGen, Enc, Dec): *For a security parameter* λ, *let* $\mathcal{M} = \mathcal{M}(\lambda)$ *be the message space.*

- (pk, sk) $\leftarrow$ KGen(1^λ): *The randomized algorithm* KGen *takes as input a security parameter* 1^λ *and outputs a public key* pk *and a secret key* sk.

- ct ← Enc(pk, m): *The randomized or deterministic algorithm* Enc *takes as input a public key* pk *and a message* m ∈ $\mathcal{M}$, *and outputs a ciphertext* ct.
- m ← Dec(sk, ct): *The deterministic algorithm* Dec *takes as input a secret key* sk *and a ciphertext* ct, *and outputs a message* m ∈ $\mathcal{M}$.

Definition 2 (Correctness). *A PKE scheme* (KGen, Enc, Dec) *is* correct *if for every* (pk, sk) ← KGen(1^λ) *and every* m ∈ $\mathcal{M}$, *it holds that* Dec(sk, ct) = m *with overwhelming probability, where* ct ← Enc(pk, m).

As a security notion of PKE, we describe the definition of *indistinguishability against chosen plaintext attacks* (denoted by IND-CPA security).

Definition 3 (IND-CPA security). *A PKE scheme* Π_{PKE} = (KGen, Enc, Dec) *is* IND-CPA *secure, if for any PPT adversary* $\mathcal{A}$ *against* Π_{PKE}, *its advantage* $\mathsf{Adv}^{\mathrm{ind\text{-}cpa}}_{\Pi_{\mathsf{PKE}},\mathcal{A}}(\lambda) := |\Pr[\mathcal{A}\ wins] - 1/2|$ *is negligible in* λ, *where* [$\mathcal{A}$ wins] *is the event that* $\mathcal{A}$ *wins in the following game:*

Setup. *The challenger generates* (pk, sk) ← KGen(1^λ) *and gives* pk *to* $\mathcal{A}$.
Challenge. *When* $\mathcal{A}$ *submits* ($\mathsf{m}_0^*, \mathsf{m}_1^*$) ∈ $\mathcal{M}^2$ *such that* $|\mathsf{m}_0^*| = |\mathsf{m}_1^*|$, *the challenger chooses* $b \xleftarrow{\$} \{0,1\}$ *and returns* ct* ← Enc(pk, m_b^*).
Output. $\mathcal{A}$ *outputs the guessing bit* $b' \in \{0,1\}$. $\mathcal{A}$ *wins if* $b = b'$.

2.2 Bounded-Collusion Identity-Based Encryption

Following [36], we describe the syntax of bounded-collusion identity-based encryption (BC-IBE).

Definition 4 (BC-IBE). *A BC-IBE scheme consists of four polynomial-time algorithms* (Setup, Extract, Enc, Dec): *For a security parameter* λ, *let* $\mathcal{ID} = \mathcal{ID}(\lambda)$ *be the identity space and let* $\mathcal{M} = \mathcal{M}(\lambda)$ *be the message space.*

- (pp, msk) ← Setup(1^λ): *The randomized algorithm* Setup *takes as input a security parameter* 1^λ *and outputs a public parameter* pp *and a master secret key* msk.
- $\mathsf{sk}_{\mathsf{id}}$ ← Extract(msk, id): *The randomized or deterministic algorithm* Extract *takes as input a master secret key* msk *and an identity* id ∈ $\mathcal{ID}$, *and outputs a secret key* $\mathsf{sk}_{\mathsf{id}}$.
- ct ← Enc(pp, id, m): *The randomized or deterministic algorithm* Enc *takes as input a public parameter* pp, *an identity* id ∈ $\mathcal{ID}$, *and a message* m ∈ $\mathcal{M}$, *and it outputs a ciphertext* ct.
- m ← Dec($\mathsf{sk}_{\mathsf{id}}$, ct): *The deterministic algorithm* Dec *takes as input a secret key* $\mathsf{sk}_{\mathsf{id}}$ *and a ciphertext* ct, *and outputs a message* m ∈ $\mathcal{M}$.

Definition 5 (Correctness). *A BC-IBE scheme* (Setup, Extract, Enc, Dec) *is* correct *if for every* (pp, msk) ← Setup(1^λ), *every* id ∈ $\mathcal{ID}$, *every* $\mathsf{sk}_{\mathsf{id}}$ ← Extract(msk, id), *and every* m ∈ $\mathcal{M}$, *it holds that* Dec($\mathsf{sk}_{\mathsf{id}}$, ct) = m *with overwhelming probability, where* ct ← Enc(pp, id, m).

As a security notion of BC-IBE, we describe the definition of *adaptive security against chosen plaintext attacks* (denoted by d-adaptive CPA security) for the collusion-parameter d, as follows:

Definition 6 (d-adaptive CPA security). *A BC-IBE scheme* $\Pi_{\text{BC-IBE}} = $ (Setup, Extract, Enc, Dec) *is d-adaptive CPA secure, if for any PPT adversary $\mathcal{A}$ against* $\Pi_{\text{BC-IBE}}$, *its advantage* $\text{Adv}^{\text{adaptive}}_{\Pi_{\text{BC-IBE}},\mathcal{A}}(\lambda) := |\Pr[\mathcal{A} \ wins] - 1/2|$ *is negligible in λ, where $[\mathcal{A} \ wins]$ is the event that $\mathcal{A}$ wins in the following security game:*

Setup. *The challenger generates* (pp, msk) $\leftarrow$ Setup(1^λ) *and gives* pp *to $\mathcal{A}$.*
Phase 1. *$\mathcal{A}$ is allowed to issue queries to the key extraction oracle* $\mathsf{O}_{\text{Extract}}$ *which, on input a key extraction query* id $\in \mathcal{ID}$, *returns* $\text{sk}_{\text{id}} \leftarrow$ KGen(msk, id).
Challenge. *$\mathcal{A}$ submits* $(\text{id}^*, \mathsf{m}_0^*, \mathsf{m}_1^*) \in \mathcal{ID} \times \mathcal{M}^2$ *such that* $|\mathsf{m}_0^*| = |\mathsf{m}_1^*|$, *and* id* *has never been issued to* $\mathsf{O}_{\text{Extract}}$. *The challenger chooses* $b \overset{\$}{\leftarrow} \{0,1\}$ *and returns* ct$^* \leftarrow$ Enc(pp, id*, m_b^*).
Phase 2. *$\mathcal{A}$ can issue queries to* $\mathsf{O}_{\text{Extract}}$. *Notice that $\mathcal{A}$ is forbidden to issue* id* *to this oracle.*
Output. *$\mathcal{A}$ outputs* $b' \in \{0,1\}$. *$\mathcal{A}$ wins if $b = b'$.*

Here, $\mathcal{A}$ is allowed to issue at most d queries to $\mathsf{O}_{\text{Extract}}$.

2.3   All-or-Nothing Transform

An all-or-nothing transform (AONT) splits a message X into v secret shares $x_1, \ldots, x_v$ and a public share z, and the corresponding inverse function recovers X from the shares $(x_1, \ldots, x_v, z)$.

Following [15], we describe the definition of AONTs, as follows:

Definition 7 (AONT). *An efficient randomized algorithm* Trans *is* $(\mu, \bar{\mu}, v)$-*AONT if all the following conditions hold:*

1. *Given $X \in \{0,1\}^\mu$,* Trans *outputs $v + 1$ blocks* $(x_1, \ldots, x_v, z) \in (\{0,1\}^{\bar{\mu}})^{v+1}$, *where for $i \in [v]$, x_i is a secret share, and z is a public share.*
2. *There exists an efficient inverse function* Inverse *which, on input* $(x_1, \ldots, x_v, z) \in (\{0,1\}^{\bar{\mu}})^{v+1}$, *outputs $X \in \{0,1\}^\mu$.*
3. *For any PPT algorithm $\mathcal{A}$ against* Trans, *its advantage*

$$\text{Adv}^{\text{ind}}_{\text{Trans},\mathcal{A}}(\lambda) := \left| \Pr\left[b = b' \mid b \overset{\$}{\leftarrow} \{0,1\}; b' \leftarrow \mathcal{A}^{\mathsf{O}_{\text{LR}}}(1^\lambda) \right] - \frac{1}{2} \right|$$

is negligible in λ, where O_{LR} is the left-or-right oracle which, on input $(j, X_0, X_1) \in [v] \times (\{0,1\}^\mu)^2$, *computes* $(x_1, \ldots, x_v, z) \leftarrow$ Trans(X_b) *and returns* $(x_1, \ldots, x_{j-1}, x_{j+1}, \ldots, x_v, z)$.

3   Non-adaptive Group Testing

In this section, we describe a system model of group testing and introduce a new notion of error-probability of probabilistic group testing.

3.1   System Model of Non-adaptive Group Testing

Dorfman introduced the notion of group testing in order to efficiently detect blood samples contaminated by syphilis during the World War II [16]. Group testing (e.g., [4,16,17]) is methodology of detecting positive items called *defective items* among many whole items with a smaller number of tests than individually testing each item.

The group testing techniques are classified into two types: Non-adaptive setting (e.g., [12,33,37]) and adaptive setting (e.g., [16,22,26]). The test-design of non-adaptive group testing is pre-determined, and its tests are performed in parallel. On the other hand, each test of adaptive group testing depends on the previous test-results. As described in Sect. 1.2, we focus on non-adaptive group testing (probabilistic or combinatorial group testing), in this paper.

Non-adaptive Group Testing. We consider a model where $[n]$ is the set of n tested items, $\mathcal{J} \subset [n]$ is a set of defective items included in $[n]$, and the size of $\mathcal{J}$ is at most d. A binary support vector $\boldsymbol{x} = (x_i)_{i \in [n]}$ such that $|\mathsf{supp}(\boldsymbol{x})| \leq d$ represents the (correct) test outcomes of all items $[n]$. Namely, for $i \in [n]$, $x_i = 1$ indicates that i is defective and $i \in \mathcal{J}$, and $x_i = 0$ indicates that i is non-defective and $i \notin \mathcal{J}$. In addition, we assume that if at least one defective item is included in a test, then the test outcome shows defective; otherwise, the test outcome shows non-defective.

For a support vector $\boldsymbol{x} = (x_i)_{i \in [n]}$ (such that $|\mathsf{supp}(\boldsymbol{x})| \leq d$), the test outcome obtained by using a test matrix $\boldsymbol{M} = (m_{i,j}) \in \{0,1\}^{u \times n}$ is represented by $\boldsymbol{y} = \boldsymbol{M} \odot \boldsymbol{x} \in \{0,1\}^u$. The goal of non-adaptive group testing is to determine $\mathcal{J}$ from $\boldsymbol{y} = \boldsymbol{M} \odot \boldsymbol{x}$, under the model above. As an example, in order to detect $\mathcal{J}$ from $\boldsymbol{y} = \boldsymbol{M} \odot \boldsymbol{x}$, we can use the following *naive decoder*: Given $\boldsymbol{y} = \boldsymbol{M} \odot \boldsymbol{x}$, the naive decoder declare i defective if and only if $y_j = 1$ for every j such that $m_{j,i} = 1$. To describe the combinatorial and probabilistic settings of non-adaptive group testing, we describe the definition of error-probability of decoders.

Definition 8 (Error-Probability of Recovery). *When a decoder estimates $\widehat{\mathcal{J}}$ of $\mathcal{J}$ in the model above, the error-probability is defined as $P_e := \Pr[\widehat{\mathcal{J}} \neq \mathcal{J}]$.*

Combinatorial Group Testing. From existing results, it is widely known that, if a test matrix $\boldsymbol{M} \in \{0,1\}^{u \times n}$ is d-disjunct, then the non-adaptive group testing with $\boldsymbol{M}$ is called *combinatorial group testing* and guarantees that the set $\widehat{\mathcal{J}}$ recovered by the (naive) decoder is always equal to $\mathcal{J}$ (i.e., $P_e = 0$). The definition of d-disjunct matrix is described as follows:

Definition 9 (Disjunct Matrices). *A binary matrix $\boldsymbol{M} = (m_{i,j}) \in \{0,1\}^{u \times n}$ is d-disjunct if for every distinct $s_1, \ldots, s_d \in [n]$ and every $j \in [n] \backslash \{s_1, \ldots, s_d\}$, there exists a row $q \in [u]$ such that $m_{q,j} = 1$ and $\forall j' \in \{s_1, \ldots, s_d\}$, $m_{q,j'} = 0$.*

The number of tests required in combinatorial non-adaptive group testing using d-disjunct matrices is bounded by $u = O(d^2 \log n)$ (e.g., see [17]).

Probabilistic Group Testing. *Probabilistic group testing* can also employ a test matrix $\boldsymbol{M}$ (which is not d-disjunct), and the decoder determines the set $\widehat{\mathcal{J}}$

such that $\widehat{\mathcal{J}} = \mathcal{J}$, with high probability. Namely, unlike combinatorial group testing, $\mathcal{J}$ is correctly determined from $\boldsymbol{y} = \boldsymbol{M} \odot \boldsymbol{x}$ with average probability $1 - P_e$. Due to results of [12,23], the following proposition holds regarding probabilistic group testing:

Proposition 1 ([23, Theorem 1] and [12, Theorem 3.10]). *There exists a randomized or explicit construction of a matrix* $\boldsymbol{M} = (m_{i,j}) \in \{0,1\}^{u \times n}$ *with* $u = O(d \log n)$ *satisfying the following:*

- *For all* $j \in [n]$, *it holds that* $|\mathsf{supp}([m_{1,j}, \ldots, m_{u,j}]^\top)| = O(\log n)$;
- *Given* $\boldsymbol{y} = \boldsymbol{M} \odot \boldsymbol{x}$ *such that* $|\mathsf{supp}(\boldsymbol{x})| \le d$, *it is possible to find* $\boldsymbol{x}$ *with failure probability* $P_e = 1/\mathsf{poly}(n,d)$, *under the system model of non-adaptive group testing.*

Furthermore, in order to prove the security of our BC-IBE scheme, we formalize a new notion of error-probability for probabilistic non-adaptive group testing, called *random subset error-probability*, as follows:

Definition 10 (Random Subset Error-Probability). *Let* ℓ_s *be a positive integer such that* $d \le \ell_s \le n$. *Let* $\boldsymbol{M} = [\boldsymbol{M}_1 \| \cdots \| \boldsymbol{M}_n] \in \{0,1\}^{u \times n}$ *be the test matrix used in a probabilistic non-adaptive group testing system for* u *tests,* n *items, and at most* d *defective items. We suppose that a subset* $\mathcal{S} \subset [n]$ *such that* $|\mathcal{S}| = \ell_s$ *is sampled uniformly at random. When a decoder given only* $(\boldsymbol{M}_i)_{i \in \mathcal{S}}$ *(instead of* $\boldsymbol{M}$*) recovers* $\widehat{\mathcal{J}}$ *of the defective set* $\mathcal{J}$, *its error-probability is called* random subset error-probability *and defined as* $P_e^{(\ell_s)} = \Pr[\widehat{\mathcal{J}} \neq \mathcal{J}]$.

3.2   Upper Bounds on Random Subset Error-Probability

In this section, we estimate the random subset error-probability for the Monte-Carlo-based construction [12] and the Kautz-Singleton construction [23] of probabilistic group testing. Although the rows of both matrices [12,23] are $O(d \log n)$, there are the following differences: In the Kautz-Singleton construction, it is unnecessary to store any hash functions while the Monte-Carlo-based construction needs $O(\log n)$ hash functions. In addition, the maximum number d of defective items in the Kautz-Singleton construction is restricted as $d = \Omega(\log^2 n)$ while the Monte-Carlo-based construction does not have such restrictions. Hence, we have chosen these constructions of test matrices.

<u>Monte-Carlo-Based Construction</u>. A Monte-Carlo-based test matrix used in probabilistic group testing was presented in [12, Theorem 3.10]. Algorithm 1 shows the construction of this test matrix. The matrix $\overline{\boldsymbol{M}}$ is the vertical concatenation of $\log(n/d)$ matrices $\overline{\boldsymbol{M}}^{(\log d)}, \ldots, \overline{\boldsymbol{M}}^{(\log n)} \in \{0,1\}^{\overline{C} d \times n}$ for some constant $\overline{C} > 0$. To construct each $\overline{\boldsymbol{M}}^{(\ell)}$ for $\ell \in \{\log d, \ldots, \log n\}$, the function bPref_ℓ and a hash function $\overline{H}_\ell$, in order to group all $j \in \{0,1\}^{\log n}$, where $\mathsf{bPref}_\ell(j)$ maps $j \in \{0,1\}^{\log n}$ to the first ℓ bits of j, and $\overline{H}_\ell$ (e.g., a $O(d \log(n/d))$-wise independent hash function) is used to map (the first ℓ bits of) j to a row.

Algorithm 1. Construction of the test matrix M

1: **for** $\ell = \log d$ to $\log n$ **do**
2:     Initialize $\overline{M}^{(\ell)} \leftarrow 0$.
3:     Choose a hash function $\overline{H}_\ell : \{0,1\}^\ell \rightarrow \{0, \ldots, \overline{C}d - 1\}$.
4:     **for** $j \in \{0,1\}^{\log n}$ **do**
5:         Set $i \leftarrow \overline{H}_\ell(\mathsf{bPref}_\ell(j))$.
6:         Set $\overline{m}_{i,j}^{(\ell)} \leftarrow 1$.
7:     **end for**
8: **end for**
9: Set $\overline{M} \leftarrow [\overline{M}^{(\log d)} \| \cdots \| \overline{M}^{(\log n)}]^\top$.
10: Initialize $\widehat{M} \leftarrow 0, \widetilde{M} \leftarrow 0$.
11: Choose a hash function $\widehat{H} : [n] \rightarrow [\widehat{C}d \log (n/d))]$.
12: **for** $j \in [n]$ **do**
13:     Set $i \leftarrow \widehat{H}(j)$.
14:     Set $\widehat{m}_{i,j} \leftarrow 1$.
15: **end for**
16: **for** $\ell \in [\log n]$ **do**
17:     Choose a hash function $\widetilde{H}_\ell : [n] \rightarrow [\widetilde{C}d]$
18:     **for** $j \in [n]$ **do**
19:         Set $i \leftarrow \widetilde{H}_\ell(j)$.
20:         Set $\widetilde{m}_{i,j}^{(\ell)} \leftarrow 1$.
21:     **end for**
22: **end for**
23: Set $\widetilde{M} \leftarrow [\widetilde{M}^{(1)} \| \cdots \| \widetilde{M}^{(\log n)}]^\top$.
24: Return $M = [\overline{M} \| \widehat{M} \| \widetilde{M}]^\top$.

In addition, each column of the matrix $\widehat{M}$ with $\widehat{C}d \log (n/d) = O(d \log (n/d))$ rows (and n columns) has exactly one 1 in a random position, where $\widehat{C} > 0$ is some constant. The matrix $\widetilde{M}$ has $O(d \log n)$ rows and it is the vertical concatenation of $O(\log n)$ matrices, each one with $\widetilde{C}d = O(d)$ rows for some constant $\widetilde{C} > 0$. These matrices are also represented by using hash functions, namely, it is possible to determine M if several hash functions are set up beforehand.

Intuitively, by using the outcome $\overline{M} \odot x$, it is possible to determine a $O(d \log (n/d))$-size set $\mathcal{L}$ that includes all defective items and several non-defective items. In order to exclude the non-defective items included in $\mathcal{L}$ with high probability, the matrices $\widehat{M}, \widetilde{M}$ are necessary.

Regarding the random subset error-probability of the construction in Algorithm 1, the following theorem shows the bound of this error-probability.

Theorem 1. *Suppose* $u = \overline{C}d \log (n/d) + \widehat{C}d \log (n/d) + \widetilde{C}d \log n$ *for constants* $\overline{C}, \widehat{C}, \widetilde{C} > 0$. *The Monte-Carlo-based construction of the test matrix* $M \in \{0,1\}^{u \times n}$ *for probabilistic group testing has the random subset error-probability* $P_e^{(\ell_s)} \leq e^{-\ell_s \log (nd/\ell_s^2)}(e^{-\Omega(d)} + 1/\mathsf{poly}(n))$ *for* $d \leq \ell_s \ll n$.

Proof. Let $M_{[\ell_s]}$ denote a matrix which consists of ℓ_s column vectors in M chosen uniformly at random. For $\overline{M}, \widehat{M},$ and $\widetilde{M}$, three matrices $\overline{M}_{[\ell_s]}, \widehat{M}_{[\ell_s]},$

and $\widetilde{M}_{[\ell_s]}$ are also defined in the same way as this, respectively. For each defective vector included in the matrix $\overline{M}_{[\ell_s]}^{(i)}$ ($i \in \{\log d, \ldots, \log n\}$), there exist $O(1)$ non-defective vectors in the same matrix, which is identical to the defective vector. Thus, in $\overline{M}_{[\ell_s]}$, it is possible to identify a set $\mathcal{L}$ of $O(d \log (n/d))$ column vectors (or items) including all defective vectors and several non-defective vectors (i.e., $\mathcal{J} \subseteq \mathcal{L}$).

Regarding the matrix $\widehat{M}_{[\ell_s]}$, the probability that a non-defective vector included in $\widehat{M}_{[\ell_s]}$ is the same as a defective vector included in $\widehat{M}_{[\ell_s]}$ is $O(1/\log (n/d))$. Thus, by using the additive form of the Chernoff bound, $O(d)$ non-defective items in $\mathcal{L}$ are correctly regarded as non-defective ones with probability $1 - e^{-td}$ for some constant $t > 0$. That is, $O(d)$ non-defective vectors in $\widehat{M}_{[\ell_s]}$ are covered by the union of defective vectors, with probability $e^{-\Omega(d)}$. In the same way, we cannot identify the defective vectors (or items) with probability $1/\text{poly}(n)$, when using $\widetilde{M}_{[\ell_s]}$. Furthermore, by using the fact $\binom{a}{b} = e^{b \log (ea/b)}$ for positive integers a, b ($a > b$), the union of any d vectors in $M_{[\ell_s]}$ covers any other vectors, with at most probability $P_e^{(\ell_s)} \leq (\binom{\ell_s}{d}/\binom{n}{\ell_s})(e^{-\Omega(d)} + 1/\text{poly}(n)) < e^{-\ell_s \log (nd/\ell_s^2)}(e^{-\Omega(d)} + 1/\text{poly}(n))$. $\quad\square$

Kautz-Singleton Construction. The Kautz-Singleton construction is based on the Reed-Solomon (RS) code [34]. Following [23], we describe the definition of this error-correcting code, as follows:

Definition 11 (RS code [34]). *Let $\mathbb{F}_q$ be a finite field and $\alpha_1, \ldots, \alpha_{n_u}$ be distinct elements from $\mathbb{F}_q$. Let $k \leq n_u \leq q$. The Reed-Solomon code of dimension k over $\mathbb{F}_q$ with evaluation pairs $\alpha_1, \ldots, \alpha_{n_u}$ is defined with the following encoding function. The encoding of a message $m = (m_0, \ldots, m_{k-1})$ is the evaluation of the corresponding $k-1$ degree polynomial $f_m(X) = \sum_{i \in \{0, \ldots, k-1\}} m_i \cdot X^i$ at all the α_i' s: $RS(m) = (f_m(\alpha_1), \ldots, f_m(\alpha_{n_u}))$.*

The Kautz-Singleton construction for probabilistic group testing is an RS code with $q = 4d$, $n_u = \Theta(\log n)$, and $n = q^k$. Each q-ary symbol is replaced by a unit weight binary vector in $\{0,1\}^q$, by using identity mapping which, given a symbol $i \in [q]$, maps i to the vector (in $\{0,1\}^q$) that has 1 at the i-th position and zero everywhere else. Then, we can obtain a $u \times n$ test matrix of probabilistic group testing with $u = n_u q = O(d \log n)$ tests. Regarding this optimality of the Kautz-Singleton construction, the following result was proved in [23]:

Proposition 2 ([23, Theorem 1]). *Let $\delta > 0$. The Kautz-Singleton construction $M \in \{0,1\}^{u \times n}$ with parameters $u = n_u q$, $q = c_1 d$ for any $c_1 \geq 4$, and $n_u = (1 + \delta) \log n$ has average probability of error $P_e \leq n^{-\Omega(\log q)} + n^{-\delta}$ under the naive decoder in the regime $d = \Omega(\log^2 n)$.*

Regarding the random subset error-probability of Kautz-Singleton, the following theorem shows the bound of this error-probability:

Theorem 2. *Let $\delta > 0$. If $d = \Omega(\log^2(n))$, the Kautz-Singleton construction of a test matrix $M \in \{0,1\}^{u \times n}$ for probabilistic group testing with parameters $u = n_u q$, $q \geq 4d$, and $n_u = (1 + \delta) \log(n - \ell_s + 1)$ has the random subset error-probability $P_e^{(\ell_s)} \leq \frac{\ell_s - d}{n - \ell_s + 1} \left(2^{-n_u} + n^{-c \log q}\right)$ for $d \leq \ell_s \ll n$ and some constant $c > 0$.*

Proof. Let $M := [M_1 \| \cdots \| M_n] \in \{0,1\}^{u \times n}$, where $M_i \in \{0,1\}^u$ is the i-th column vector of M for $i \in [n]$. For $\mathcal{L}_s \subset [n]$ and $\mathcal{J} \subseteq \mathcal{L}_s$, $D^{\mathcal{J}, \mathcal{L}_s}$ is defined as the event that there exists a non-defective column vector in $\mathcal{L}_s$ which is covered by the union of defective items in $\mathcal{J}$. In addition, $D_j^{\mathcal{J}, \mathcal{L}_s}$ is defined as the event that the non-defective column vector M_j is covered by the union of the defective items in $\mathcal{J}$. For an event E, let $1(\mathsf{E})$ denote the indicator function of an event E. We bound the probability $P_e^{(\ell_s)}$ as follows:

$$P_e^{(\ell_s)} \leq \sum_{\mathcal{L}_s \subset [n], |\mathcal{L}_s| = \ell_s} \sum_{\mathcal{J} \subseteq \mathcal{L}_s, |\mathcal{J}| = d} 1(D^{\mathcal{J}}) \cdot \Pr[J = \mathcal{J}] \cdot \Pr[L_s = \mathcal{L}_s]$$

$$\leq \frac{1}{\binom{n}{\ell_s}} \cdot \frac{1}{\binom{\ell_s}{d}} \sum_{\mathcal{L}_s \subset [n], |\mathcal{L}_s| = \ell_s} \sum_{\mathcal{J} \subseteq \mathcal{L}_s, |\mathcal{J}| = d} \sum_{j \in \mathcal{L}_s \setminus \mathcal{J}} 1(D_j^{\mathcal{J}, \mathcal{L}_s})$$

$$= \frac{1}{\binom{n}{\ell_s}} \cdot \frac{1}{\binom{\ell_s}{d}} \sum_{\mathcal{L}_s \subset [n], |\mathcal{L}_s| = \ell_s} \sum_{j \in \mathcal{L}_s} \sum_{\mathcal{J} \subseteq \mathcal{L}_s \setminus \{j\}, |\mathcal{J}| = d} 1(D_j^{\mathcal{J}, \mathcal{L}_s})$$

$$= \frac{1}{\binom{n}{\ell_s}} \cdot \frac{1}{\binom{\ell_s}{d}} \sum_{\substack{j \in [n] \\ }} \sum_{\substack{\mathcal{L}_s \subset [n], |\mathcal{L}_s| = \ell_s \\ j \in \mathcal{L}_s}} \sum_{\mathcal{J} \subseteq \mathcal{L}_s \setminus \{j\}, |\mathcal{J}| = d} 1(D_j^{\mathcal{J}, \mathcal{L}_s})$$

$$= \frac{\binom{n}{\ell_s - 1}}{\binom{n}{\ell_s}} \cdot \frac{\binom{\ell_s - 1}{d}}{\binom{\ell_s}{d}} \sum_{j \in [n]} \frac{1}{\binom{n}{\ell_s - 1}} \sum_{\substack{\mathcal{L}_s \subset [n], |\mathcal{L}_s| = \ell_s \\ j \in \mathcal{L}_s}} \frac{1}{\binom{\ell_s - 1}{d}} \sum_{\mathcal{J} \subseteq \mathcal{L}_s \setminus \{j\}, |\mathcal{J}| = d} 1(D_j^{\mathcal{J}, \mathcal{L}_s})$$

$$= \frac{\ell_s - d}{n - \ell_s + 1} \sum_{j \in [n]} \Pr\left[D_j^{J_{\mathcal{L}_s \setminus \{j\}}}\right],$$

where the subset $J_{\mathcal{L}_s \setminus \{j\}}$ is uniformly distributed on the sets of size is $d - 1$. Notice that $\binom{n}{\ell_s - 1} / \binom{n}{\ell_s} = \ell_s / (n - \ell_s + 1)$ and $\binom{\ell_s - 1}{d} / \binom{\ell_s}{d} = (\ell_s - d) / \ell_s$.

We have $\Pr\left[D_j^{J_{\mathcal{L}_s \setminus \{j\}}}\right] \leq 2^{-n_u} + n^{-c \log q}$ for some constant $c > 0$, in the same way as the proof of [23, Theorem 1]. Hence, we obtain

$$P_e^{(\ell_s)} \leq \frac{\ell_s - d}{n - \ell_s + 1} \left(\frac{1}{2^{n_u}} + \frac{1}{n^{c \log q}}\right),$$

and complete the proof. $\qquad\square$

4   BC-IBE Construction by Probabilistic Group Testing

We propose a BC-IBE scheme with $O(d \log n)|\mathsf{pk}|$-size public parameters, which is constructed from any IND-CPA secure PKE with $|\mathsf{pk}|$-size public keys. We can employ a construction of a test matrix $M \in \{0,1\}^{u \times n}$ in Sect. 3.2. Due to Proposition 1, these constructions of test matrices have $|\phi_M(j)| = O(\log n)$ rows (for each $j \in [n]$), and thus the ciphertext-size of our BC-IBE is $O(\log n)|\text{ct}|$.

The proposed BC-IBE scheme $\Pi_{\text{BC-IBE}} = (\text{Setup}, \text{Extract}, \text{Enc}, \text{Dec})$ is constructed as follows: For a security parameter λ, let $n = n(\lambda)$, $u = u(\lambda)$, $\mu = \mu(\lambda)$, $\bar{\mu} = \bar{\mu}(\lambda)$, $v = v(\lambda)$ be positive integers. Let $\mathcal{ID} = \mathcal{ID}(\lambda)$ be the identity space such that $|\mathcal{ID}| = n$ and $\mathcal{M} = \{0,1\}^{\mu}$ be the message space. Let $H : \mathcal{ID} \to [n]$ be a random oracle. We employ a PKE scheme $\Pi_{\text{PKE}} = (\Pi_{\text{PKE}}.\text{KGen}, \Pi_{\text{PKE}}.\text{Enc}, \Pi_{\text{PKE}}.\text{Dec})$ with the message space $\mathcal{M}_{\Pi_{\text{PKE}}} = \{0,1\}^{\bar{\mu}}$ and a $(\mu, \bar{\mu}, v)$-AONT Trans with an efficient inverse function Inverse. As one of the system parameters of $\Pi_{\text{BC-IBE}}$, $M \in \{0,1\}^{u \times n}$ is used as a test matrix in a probabilistic group testing algorithm.

- $(\text{pp}, \text{msk}) \leftarrow \text{Setup}(1^{\lambda})$: Generate $(\text{pk}_i, \text{sk}_i) \leftarrow \Pi_{\text{PKE}}.\text{KGen}(1^{\lambda})$ for every $i \in [u]$, and output $\text{pp} = (\text{pk}_1, \ldots, \text{pk}_u)$ and $\text{msk} = (\text{sk}_1, \ldots, \text{sk}_u)$.
- $\text{sk}_{\text{id}} \leftarrow \text{Extract}(\text{msk}, \text{id})$:
  Parse $\text{msk} = (\text{sk}_1, \ldots, \text{sk}_u)$ and output $\text{sk}_{\text{id}} = (\text{sk}_i)_{i \in \phi_M(H(\text{id}))}$.
- $\text{ct} \leftarrow \text{Enc}(\text{pp}, \text{id}, m)$:
  1. Parse $\text{pp} = (\text{pk}_1, \ldots, \text{pk}_u)$.
  2. Compute $(x_1, \ldots, x_v, z) \leftarrow \text{Trans}(m)$.
  3. Compute $c_i \leftarrow \Pi_{\text{PKE}}.\text{Enc}(\text{pk}_{\sigma_i}, x_i)$ for every $i \in [v]$, where $\phi_M(H(\text{id})) = \{\sigma_1, \ldots, \sigma_v\}$.
  4. Output $\text{ct} = (c_1, \ldots, c_v, z)$.
- $m \leftarrow \text{Dec}(\text{sk}_{\text{id}}, \text{ct})$:
  1. Parse $\text{sk}_{\text{id}} = (\text{sk}_i)_{i \in \phi_M(H(\text{id}))}$ and $\text{ct} = (c_1, \ldots, c_v, z)$.
  2. Compute $x_i \leftarrow \Pi_{\text{PKE}}.\text{Dec}(\text{sk}_{\sigma_i}, c_i)$ for every $i \in [v]$, where $\phi_M(H(\text{id})) = \{\sigma_1, \ldots, \sigma_v\}$.
  3. Output $m' \leftarrow \text{Inverse}(x_1, \ldots, x_v, z)$.

It is clear that the BC-IBE scheme $\Pi_{\text{BC-IBE}}$ is correct if the underlying PKE scheme Π_{PKE} and AONT Trans are correct. Furthermore, the following theorem shows the security of $\Pi_{\text{BC-IBE}}$:

Theorem 3. *Suppose that the number of queries issued to the random oracle H is at most q_H, and the collusion-parameter of BC-IBE is d.*

If the PKE scheme Π_{PKE} is IND-CPA secure, the randomized transformation Trans with the inverse function Inverse is a $(\mu, \bar{\mu}, v)$-AONT, and the matrix M is a test matrix of probabilistic group testing with random subset error-probability $P_e^{(q_H + d + 1)}$, then the resulting BC-IBE scheme $\Pi_{\text{BC-IBE}}$ is d-adaptive CPA secure in the random oracle model.

Proof. Let $\mathcal{A}$ be a PPT adversary against the d-adaptive CPA security of $\Pi_{\text{BC-IBE}}$ and let T_H be the table of query-response pairs of the H oracle. We define $\text{ct}^* = (c_1^*, \ldots, c_v^*, z^*)$ as the challenge ciphertext in the d-adaptive CPA security game. We consider a security game $\widetilde{\text{Game}}$. This game is the same as the ordinary d-adaptive CPA game except for the procedure of the challenger, as follows: At the beginning of the game, the challenger chooses $(q_H + d + 1)$

hash values $h^{(1)}, \ldots, h^{(q_H+d+1)} \in [n]$ uniformly at random. If the matrix $[\mathbf{M}_{h^{(1)}} \| \ldots \| \mathbf{M}_{h^{(q_H+d+1)}}]$ constructed by the corresponding column vectors of $\mathbf{M} = [\mathbf{M}_1 \| \cdots \| \mathbf{M}_n]$ are not d-disjunct, then the challenger aborts. When $\mathcal{A}$ issues a query id to the H oracle, then this oracle returns h_{id} if $\mathsf{T}_H[\text{id}] = h_{\text{id}}(\neq \emptyset)$ holds; otherwise it chooses $h_{\text{id}} \in \{h^{(i)}\}_{i \in [q_h+d+1]}$ such that $\mathsf{T}_H[\text{id}'] \neq h_{\text{id}}$ holds for all previous queries $\text{id}' \neq \text{id}$, returns h_{id}, and sets $\mathsf{T}_H[\text{id}] \leftarrow h_{\text{id}}$.

In order to estimate the probability of distinguishing between the two games, we define Abort as the event that the challenger aborts when choosing the random values $h^{(1)}, \ldots, h^{(q_H+d+1)} \in [n]$. In order to bound the probability that Abort occurs, we can employ the random subset error-probability of the underlying test matrix $\mathbf{M}$ of probabilistic group testing. This is because the aborting condition corresponds to the condition of Definition 10. Hence, we have $\Pr[\text{Abort}] \leq P_e^{(q_H+d+1)}$, and the probability of distinguishing between the two games is at most $P_e^{(q_H+d+1)}$.

Furthermore, in order to bound the winning probability in the modified game $\widehat{\text{Game}}$, we define an experiment $\mathcal{B}$ simulating $\widehat{\text{Game}}$ and an additional event $\widehat{\text{Abort}}$. $\mathcal{B}$ chooses $i^* \xleftarrow{\$} [u]$ at the beginning of the game and runs the adversary $\mathcal{A}$. This experiment simulates the environment of $\widehat{\text{Game}}$ except for the following: If $i^* \in \phi_M(H(\text{id}))$ holds for some $\mathcal{A}$'s query id issued to the $\mathsf{O}_{\text{Extract}}$ oracle, then $\mathcal{B}$ aborts and outputs a random bit. Then, $\widehat{\text{Abort}}$ is defined as the event that $i^* \in \phi_M(H(\text{id}))$ holds and $\mathcal{B}$ aborts. If $\widehat{\text{Abort}}$ does not occur and $\mathcal{A}$ finally outputs $b' \in \{0, 1\}$, then $\mathcal{B}$ also outputs b'.

We define $W_{\mathcal{B}}$ as the event that $\mathcal{B}$ outputs a bit b' such that $b = b'$, and analyze the probability $\Pr[W_{\mathcal{B}}]$. Then, the following equation holds in the straightforward way:

$$\Pr[W_{\mathcal{B}}] = \Pr\left[W_{\mathcal{B}} \wedge \widehat{\text{Abort}}\right] + \Pr\left[W_{\mathcal{B}} \wedge \neg\widehat{\text{Abort}}\right]$$
$$= \Pr\left[\widehat{\text{Abort}}\right] \cdot \Pr\left[W_{\mathcal{B}} \mid \widehat{\text{Abort}}\right] + \Pr\left[\neg\widehat{\text{Abort}}\right] \cdot \Pr\left[W_{\mathcal{B}} \mid \neg\widehat{\text{Abort}}\right]$$

Since we have $\Pr\left[\widehat{\text{Abort}}\right] = 1 - \Pr\left[\neg\widehat{\text{Abort}}\right]$, $\Pr\left[\neg\widehat{\text{Abort}}\right] \geq 1/u$, and $\Pr\left[W_{\mathcal{B}} \mid \widehat{\text{Abort}}\right] = 1/2$, it holds that

$$\Pr[W_{\mathcal{B}}] \geq \left(1 - \frac{1}{u}\right)\frac{1}{2} + \frac{1}{u}\Pr\left[W_{\mathcal{B}} \mid \neg\widehat{\text{Abort}}\right] = \frac{1}{2} + \frac{1}{u}\left(\Pr\left[W_{\mathcal{B}} \mid \neg\widehat{\text{Abort}}\right] - \frac{1}{2}\right).$$

The $\mathcal{A}$'s advantage $\varepsilon_{\mathcal{A}}$ in $\widehat{\text{Game}}$ is equal to $\left|\Pr\left[W_{\mathcal{B}} \mid \neg\widehat{\text{Abort}}\right] - 1/2\right|$. Hence, the advantage $\varepsilon_{\mathcal{B}} := |\Pr[W_{\mathcal{B}}] - 1/2|$ is at least $\varepsilon_{\mathcal{A}}/u$. Here, let $\phi_M(H(\text{id}^*)) := \{\sigma_1^*, \ldots, \sigma_v^*\}$ and $\sigma_{j^*}^* := i^*$ (where $\sigma_1^*, \ldots, \sigma_v^* \in [u]$). In order to bound $\varepsilon_{\mathcal{B}}$, we change the environment of $\mathcal{A}$. In this environment, the j^*-th share $x_{j^*}^*$ generated by Trans is replaced with the all-zero string $0^{|x_{j^*}^*|}$, when producing the challenge ciphertext. The probability $\Pr[W_{\mathcal{B}}]$ is defined as $p^{(0)}$, and the probability that $W_{\mathcal{B}}$ occurs in the modified environment is defined as $p^{(1)}$. In order to bound

$|p^{(0)} - p^{(1)}|$, we construct a PPT algorithm $\mathcal{B}_1$ against the IND-CPA security of Π_{PKE}. At the beginning of the security game, $\mathcal{B}_1$ on input a public key pk^* chooses $i^* \overset{\$}{\leftarrow} [u]$ and sets $\mathsf{pk}_{i^*} = \mathsf{pk}^*$. In order to simulate the H and $\mathsf{O}_{\mathsf{Extract}}$ oracles in $\widehat{\mathsf{Game}}$, $\mathcal{B}_1$ chooses random hash values $h^{(1)}, \ldots, h^{(q_H + d + 1)} \in [n]$. If the matrix $[M_{h^{(1)}} \| \ldots \| M_{h^{(q_H + d + 1)}}]$ is not d-disjunct, then $\mathcal{B}_1$ aborts and outputs a random bit. In order to simulate the **Setup** phase, this algorithm generates $(\mathsf{pk}_i, \mathsf{sk}_i) \leftarrow \Pi_{\mathsf{PKE}}.\mathsf{KGen}(1^\lambda)$ for $i \in [u] \setminus \{i^*\}$, initializes the table $\mathsf{T}_H \leftarrow \emptyset$, and gives $\mathsf{pp} = (\mathsf{pk}_1, \ldots, \mathsf{pk}_u)$ to $\mathcal{A}$. The H and $\mathsf{O}_{\mathsf{Extract}}$ oracles are simulated as follows:

- $H(\mathsf{id})$: $\mathcal{B}_1$ returns h_{id} if $\mathsf{T}_H[\mathsf{id}] = h_{\mathsf{id}}(\neq \emptyset)$. If $\mathsf{T}_H[\mathsf{id}] = \emptyset$ holds, this algorithm randomly chooses $h_{\mathsf{id}} \in \{h^{(i)}\}_{i \in [q_H + d + 1]}$ such that $h_{\mathsf{id}} \neq \mathsf{T}_H[\mathsf{id}']$ holds for all previous queries $\mathsf{id}' \neq \mathsf{id}$. Then, $\mathcal{B}_1$ returns h_{id} and sets $\mathsf{T}_H[\mathsf{id}] \leftarrow h_{\mathsf{id}}$
- $\mathsf{O}_{\mathsf{Extract}}(\mathsf{id})$: $\mathcal{B}_1$ obtains h_{id} by calling $H(\mathsf{id})$. This algorithm aborts and returns a random bit if $i^* \in \phi_M(H(\mathsf{id}))$ holds; otherwise, $\mathcal{B}_1$ returns $\mathsf{sk}_{\mathsf{id}} = (\mathsf{sk}_i)_{i \in \phi_M(h_{\mathsf{id}})}$.

When $\mathcal{A}$ submits $(\mathsf{id}^*, \mathsf{m}_0^*, \mathsf{m}_1^*)$ in the **Challenge** phase, $\mathcal{B}_1$ does the following:

1. Obtain h_{id^*} by invoking $H(\mathsf{id}^*)$ and let $\phi_M(h_{\mathsf{id}^*}) = \{\sigma_1^*, \ldots, \sigma_v^*\}$, where $\sigma_1^*, \ldots, \sigma_v^* \in [u]$. If $i^* \notin \phi_M(h_{\mathsf{id}^*})$, then abort and output a random bit.
2. Choose $b \overset{\$}{\leftarrow} \{0, 1\}$ and compute $(x_1^*, \ldots, x_v^*, z^*) \leftarrow \mathsf{Trans}(\mathsf{m}_b^*)$.
3. Compute $c_j^* \leftarrow \Pi_{\mathsf{PKE}}.\mathsf{Enc}(\mathsf{pk}_{\sigma_j^*}, x_j^*)$ for $j \in [v] \setminus \{j^*\}$, where $\sigma_{j^*}^* = i^*$.
4. Obtain $c_{j^*}^*$ by submitting $(x_{j^*}^*, 0^{|x_{j^*}^*|})$ to the IND-CPA game.
5. Return $\mathsf{ct}^* = (c_1^*, \ldots, c_v^*, z^*)$.

When $\mathcal{B}_1$ does not abort and $\mathcal{A}$ outputs the guessing bit $b' \in \{0, 1\}$, then $\mathcal{B}_1$ outputs 1 if $b = b'$, and 0 otherwise.

Regarding the challenge ciphertext ct^*, $\widehat{\mathsf{Game}}$ is simulated if $c_{j^*}^* \leftarrow \Pi_{\mathsf{PKE}}.\mathsf{Enc}(\mathsf{pk}_{\sigma_{j^*}^*}, x_{j^*}^*)$; otherwise, the modified environment of $\mathcal{A}$ is simulated. In addition, it is clear that $\mathcal{B}_1$ breaks the IND-CPA security of Π_{PKE} by using the output of $\mathcal{A}$. Hence, $\mathcal{B}_1$ wins the IND-CPA security game with probability at least $|p^{(0)} - p^{(1)}|$.

In order to bound $|p^{(1)} - 1/2|$, we show that there exists a PPT algorithm $\mathcal{B}_2$ breaking the security of $(\mu, \bar{\mu}, v)$-AONT. By using $\mathcal{A}$, we construct $\mathcal{B}_2$ against $(\mu, \bar{\mu}, v)$-AONT, as follows: $\mathcal{B}_2$ is given the O_{LR} oracle in the game of AONT. At the beginning of the game, $\mathcal{B}_2$ randomly chooses $i^* \in [u]$ and $h^{(1)}, \ldots, h^{(q_H + d + 1)} \in [n]$, in the same way as $\mathcal{B}_1$. This algorithm generates $(\mathsf{pk}_i, \mathsf{sk}_i) \leftarrow \Pi_{\mathsf{PKE}}.\mathsf{KGen}(1^\lambda)$ for all $i \in [u]$, sets $\mathsf{T}_H \leftarrow \emptyset$, and gives $\mathsf{pp} = (\mathsf{pk}_1, \ldots, \mathsf{pk}_u)$ to $\mathcal{A}$. The H and $\mathsf{O}_{\mathsf{Extract}}$ oracles are simulated in the same way as $\mathcal{B}_1$. When $\mathcal{A}$ submits $(\mathsf{id}^*, \mathsf{m}_0^*, \mathsf{m}_1^*)$ in the **Challenge** phase, $\mathcal{B}_2$ does the following:

1. Obtain h_{id^*} by invoking $H(\mathsf{id}^*)$, let $\phi_M(h_{\mathsf{id}^*}) = \{\sigma_1^*, \ldots, \sigma_v^*\}$, and let $j^* \in [v]$ be an index such that $i^* = \sigma_{j^*}^*$.
2. Obtain $(x_1^*, \ldots, x_{j^*-1}^*, x_{j^*+1}^*, \ldots, x_v^*, z^*)$ by issuing $(j^*, \mathsf{m}_0^*, \mathsf{m}_1^*)$ to the given oracle O_{LR}.

3. Compute $c_{j^*} \leftarrow \Pi_{\mathsf{PKE}}.\mathsf{Enc}(\mathsf{pk}_{i^*}, 0^{|x^*_{j^*}|})$, and for $i \in [v] \backslash \{j^*\}$, compute $c^*_i \leftarrow \Pi_{\mathsf{PKE}}.\mathsf{Enc}(\mathsf{pk}_{\sigma^*_i}, x^*_i)$.

4. Return $\mathsf{ct}^* = (c^*_1, \ldots, c^*_v, z^*)$.

When $\mathcal{A}$ outputs the guessing bit $b' \in \{0, 1\}$, $\mathcal{B}_2$ also outputs b'.

The H and $\mathsf{O}_{\mathsf{Extract}}$ oracles are simulated correctly, in the same way as the analysis of $\mathcal{B}_1$. The **Challenge** phase is also simulated correctly since $\mathcal{B}_2$ can generate the challenge ciphertext without knowledge of $x^*_{j^*}$. Hence, the advantage of $\mathcal{B}_2$ is at least $\left| p^{(1)} - 1/2 \right|$. Therefore, we have $\mathsf{Adv}^{\mathsf{ind\text{-}cpa}}_{\Pi_{\mathsf{PKE}}, \mathcal{B}_1}(\lambda) + \mathsf{Adv}^{\mathsf{ind}}_{\mathsf{Trans}, \mathcal{B}_2}(\lambda) \geq \varepsilon_{\mathcal{A}}/u$.

From the discussion above, we obtain

$$\mathsf{Adv}^{\mathsf{adaptive}}_{\Pi_{\mathsf{BC\text{-}IBE}}, \mathcal{A}}(\lambda) \leq u \cdot \mathsf{Adv}^{\mathsf{ind\text{-}cpa}}_{\Pi_{\mathsf{PKE}}, \mathcal{B}_1}(\lambda) + u \cdot \mathsf{Adv}^{\mathsf{ind}}_{\mathsf{Trans}, \mathcal{B}_2}(\lambda) + P^{(q_H + d + 1)}_e,$$

and complete the proof. $\qquad\qquad\square$

5   Conclusion

Our goal is to convert NIST-PQC PKE schemes into adaptively secure BC-IBE scheme with compact public parameters. To this end, we proposed a generic construction of BC-IBE via probabilistic group testing. More concretely, we introduced a new notion of error probability of probabilistic group testing, estimated this error probability bounds for two group testing constructions, and presented a generic construction of BC-IBE via probabilistic group testing. Then, it is possible to instantiate our generic construction (in Sect. 4) starting from any IND-CPA secure PKE, by employing any NIST-PQC PKE scheme (such as Kyber [9], BIKE [5], HQC [29], or a slight variant of Classic McEliece [3]). Additionally, by comparing lattice-based instantiations of the generic constructions of [13,15,36] and that proposed construction, we see that the public parameter of ours is more compact than those of the other instantiations (see Table 2 in Sect. 1.2). As a result, our proposed construction starting from IND-CPA secure PKE can transform NIST-PQC PKE schemes into NIST-PQC BC-IBE schemes with compact public parameters.

Acknowledgements. This research was in part conducted under a contract of "Research and development on new generation cryptography for secure wireless communication services" among "Research and Development for Expansion of Radio Wave Resources (JPJ000254)", which was supported by the Ministry of Internal Affairs and Communications, Japan. This work was in part supported by JSPS KAKENHI Grant Number JP22K19773. The authors would like to thank the CANS 2024 anonymous referees for their helpful comments.

References

1. Abdalla, M., et al.: Searchable encryption revisited: consistency properties, relation to anonymous IBE, and extensions. J. Cryptol. **21**(3), 350–391 (2008)
2. Agrawal, S., Boneh, D., Boyen, X.: Efficient lattice (H)IBE in the standard model. In: Gilbert, H. (ed.) EUROCRYPT 2010. LNCS, vol. 6110, pp. 553–572. Springer, Heidelberg (2010). https://doi.org/10.1007/978-3-642-13190-5_28
3. Albrecht, M.R., et al.: Classic McEliece (2024). https://csrc.nist.gov/Projects/post-quantum-cryptography/round-4-submissions
4. Aldridge, M., Johnson, O., Scarlett, J.: Group testing: an information theory perspective. Found. Trends Commun. Inf. Theory **15**(3–4), 196–392 (2019)
5. Aragon, N., et al.: BIKE (2024). https://csrc.nist.gov/Projects/post-quantum-cryptography/round-4-submissions
6. Boneh, D., Boyen, X.: Secure identity based encryption without random oracles. In: Franklin, M. (ed.) CRYPTO 2004. LNCS, vol. 3152, pp. 443–459. Springer, Heidelberg (2004). https://doi.org/10.1007/978-3-540-28628-8_27
7. Boneh, D., Canetti, R., Halevi, S., Katz, J.: Chosen-ciphertext security from identity-based encryption. SIAM J. Comput. **36**(5), 1301–1328 (2007)
8. Boneh, D., Franklin, M.: Identity-based encryption from the weil pairing. In: Kilian, J. (ed.) CRYPTO 2001. LNCS, vol. 2139, pp. 213–229. Springer, Heidelberg (2001). https://doi.org/10.1007/3-540-44647-8_13
9. Bos, J.W., et al.: CRYSTALS - Kyber: a CCA-secure module-lattice-based KEM. In: EuroS&P, pp. 353–367. IEEE (2018)
10. Cash, D., Hofheinz, D., Kiltz, E., Peikert, C.: Bonsai trees, or how to delegate a lattice basis. In: Gilbert, H. (ed.) EUROCRYPT 2010. LNCS, vol. 6110, pp. 523–552. Springer, Heidelberg (2010). https://doi.org/10.1007/978-3-642-13190-5_27
11. Chang, D., Chauhan, A.K., Kumar, S., Sanadhya, S.K.: Revocable identity-based encryption from codes with rank metric. In: Smart, N.P. (ed.) CT-RSA 2018. LNCS, vol. 10808, pp. 435–451. Springer, Cham (2018). https://doi.org/10.1007/978-3-319-76953-0_23
12. Cheraghchi, M., Nakos, V.: Combinatorial group testing and sparse recovery schemes with near-optimal decoding time. In: FOCS, pp. 1203–1213. IEEE (2020)
13. Choi, K.Y., Kim, E., Yoon, H., Moon, D., Cho, J.: Generic construction of bounded-collusion IBE via table-based id-to-key map. In: Mu, Y., Deng, R.H., Huang, X. (eds.) CANS 2019. LNCS, vol. 11829, pp. 457–469. Springer, Cham (2019). https://doi.org/10.1007/978-3-030-31578-8_25
14. Debris-Alazard, T., Tillich, J.-P.: Two attacks on rank metric code-based schemes: RankSign and an IBE scheme. In: Peyrin, T., Galbraith, S. (eds.) ASIACRYPT 2018. LNCS, vol. 11272, pp. 62–92. Springer, Cham (2018). https://doi.org/10.1007/978-3-030-03326-2_3
15. Dodis, Y., Katz, J., Xu, S., Yung, M.: Key-insulated public key cryptosystems. In: Knudsen, L.R. (ed.) EUROCRYPT 2002. LNCS, vol. 2332, pp. 65–82. Springer, Heidelberg (2002). https://doi.org/10.1007/3-540-46035-7_5
16. Dorfman, R.: The detection of defective members of large populations. Ann. Math. Stat. **14**(4), 436–440 (1943)
17. Du, D.Z., Hwang, F.K.: Combinatorial Group Testing and Its Applications. Series on Applied Mathematics, 2nd edn, vol. 12. World Scientific (2000)
18. Gaborit, P., Hauteville, A., Phan, D.H., Tillich, J.-P.: Identity-based encryption from codes with rank metric. In: Katz, J., Shacham, H. (eds.) CRYPTO 2017. LNCS, vol. 10403, pp. 194–224. Springer, Cham (2017). https://doi.org/10.1007/978-3-319-63697-9_7

19. Gentry, C., Peikert, C., Vaikuntanathan, V.: Trapdoors for hard lattices and new cryptographic constructions. In: STOC, pp. 197–206. ACM (2008)
20. Goldwasser, S., Lewko, A., Wilson, D.A.: Bounded-collusion IBE from key homomorphism. In: Cramer, R. (ed.) TCC 2012. LNCS, vol. 7194, pp. 564–581. Springer, Heidelberg (2012). https://doi.org/10.1007/978-3-642-28914-9_32
21. Grubbs, P., Maram, V., Paterson, K.G.: Anonymous, robust post-quantum public key encryption. In: Dunkelman, O., Dziembowski, S. (eds.) EUROCRYPT 2022. LNCS, vol. 13277, pp. 402–432. Springer, Cham (2022). https://doi.org/10.1007/978-3-031-07082-2_15
22. Hwang, F.K.: A method for detecting all defective members in a population by group testing. J. Am. Stat. Assoc. **67**(339), 605–608 (1972)
23. Inan, H.A., Kairouz, P., Wootters, M., Özgür, A.: On the optimality of the Kautz-singleton construction in probabilistic group testing. IEEE Trans. Inf. Theory **65**(9), 5592–5603 (2019)
24. Indyk, P., Ngo, H.Q., Rudra, A.: Efficiently decodable non-adaptive group testing. In: SODA, pp. 1126–1142. SIAM (2010)
25. Kautz, W.H., Singleton, R.C.: Nonrandom binary superimposed codes. IEEE Trans. Inf. Theory **10**(4), 363–377 (1964)
26. Li, C.H.: A sequential method for screening experimental variables. J. Am. Stat. Assoc. **57**(298), 455–477 (1962)
27. Malyutov, M.B.: The separating property of random matrices. Math. Notes Acad. Sci. USSR **23**(1), 84–91 (1978)
28. Maram, V., Xagawa, K.: Post-quantum anonymity of Kyber. In: Boldyreva, A., Kolesnikov, V. (eds.) PKC 2023. LNCS, vol. 13940, pp. 3–35. Springer, Cham (2023). https://doi.org/10.1007/978-3-031-31368-4_1
29. Melchor, C.A., et al.: HQC (2024), https://csrc.nist.gov/Projects/post-quantum-cryptography/round-4-submissions
30. Micciancio, D., Peikert, C.: Trapdoors for lattices: simpler, tighter, faster, smaller. In: Pointcheval, D., Johansson, T. (eds.) EUROCRYPT 2012. LNCS, vol. 7237, pp. 700–718. Springer, Heidelberg (2012). https://doi.org/10.1007/978-3-642-29011-4_41
31. Ngo, H.Q., Porat, E., Rudra, A.: Efficiently decodable error-correcting list disjunct matrices and applications - (extended abstract). In: Aceto, L., Henzinger, M., Sgall, J. (eds.) ICALP 2011. LNCS, vol. 6755, pp. 557–568. Springer, Heidelberg (2011). https://doi.org/10.1007/978-3-642-22006-7_47
32. Nojima, R., Imai, H., Kobara, K., Morozov, K.: Semantic security for the McEliece cryptosystem without random oracles. Des. Codes Cryptogr. **49**(1–3), 289–305 (2008)
33. Porat, E., Rothschild, A.: Explicit non-adaptive combinatorial group testing schemes. In: Aceto, L., Damgård, I., Goldberg, L.A., Halldórsson, M.M., Ingólfsdóttir, A., Walukiewicz, I. (eds.) ICALP 2008. LNCS, vol. 5125, pp. 748–759. Springer, Heidelberg (2008). https://doi.org/10.1007/978-3-540-70575-8_61
34. Reed, I.S., Solomon, G.: Polynomial codes over certain finite fields. J. Soc. Ind. Appl. Math. **8**(2), 300–304 (1960)
35. Stehlé, D., Steinfeld, R.: Making NTRU as secure as worst-case problems over ideal lattices. In: Paterson, K.G. (ed.) EUROCRYPT 2011. LNCS, vol. 6632, pp. 27–47. Springer, Heidelberg (2011). https://doi.org/10.1007/978-3-642-20465-4_4
36. Tessaro, S., Wilson, D.A.: Bounded-collusion identity-based encryption from semantically-secure public-key encryption: generic constructions with short ciphertexts. In: Krawczyk, H. (ed.) PKC 2014. LNCS, vol. 8383, pp. 257–274. Springer, Heidelberg (2014). https://doi.org/10.1007/978-3-642-54631-0_15

37. Thierry-Mieg, N.: A new pooling strategy for high-throughput screening: the shifted transversal design. BMC Bioinform. **7**, 28 (2006)
38. Waters, B.: Dual system encryption: realizing fully secure IBE and HIBE under simple assumptions. In: Halevi, S. (ed.) CRYPTO 2009. LNCS, vol. 5677, pp. 619–636. Springer, Heidelberg (2009). https://doi.org/10.1007/978-3-642-03356-8_36
39. Xagawa, K.: Anonymity of NIST PQC round 3 KEMs. In: Dunkelman, O., Dziembowski, S. (eds.) EUROCRYPT 2022. LNCS, vol. 13277, pp. 551–581. Springer, Cham (2022). https://doi.org/10.1007/978-3-031-07082-2_20

1-Out-of-N Oblivious Transfer
from MLWE

Jingting Xu[1,2] and Yanbin Pan[1,2(✉)]

[1] Academy of Mathematics and Systems Science, Chinese Academy of Sciences,
Beijing 100190, China
{xujingting,panyanbin}@amss.ac.cn

[2] School of Mathematical Sciences, University of Chinese Academy of Sciences,
Beijing 100049, China

Abstract. We construct a 1-out-of-N oblivious transfer (OT) protocol based on the Module-Learning with Errors assumption, which considers the scenario where the sender has N private values $x_1, ..., x_N$, the receiver holds a chosen index i and is allowed to obtain x_i but nothing else, and the sender cannot know the receiver's choice. Under the semi-honest model, our protocol achieves statistical sender security and computational receiver security, which means such protocol guarantees sender's security against computationally unbounded adversaries. In terms of communication cost, our protocol achieves the minimal interaction between the sender and the receiver, which is two-round.

Our main technical contribution is breaking away from the traditional framework of OTs based on public key encryption. Specifically, such traditional framework of (1-out-of-2) OTs either requires the receiver to generate two different public keys and the sender to encrypt messages under these two public keys separately, or it requires the sender to encrypt messages using two different encryption ways under the same public key generated by the receiver. In contrast, our work only involves one pair of keys and one "packed" encryption way, thereby directly achieving 1-out-of-N OTs.

Keywords: Lattice · Oblivious Transfer · Module-Learning with Errors

1   Introduction

Oblivious Transfer (OT), introduced by Rabin [27], is a cryptographic primitive between a sender and a receiver, where the sender has two messages m_0, m_1, the receiver holds a chosen bit b and is allowed to obtain m_b but nothing else, and the sender cannot know the receiver's choice. Oblivious transfer is a powerful and fundamental tool for secure multi-party computation (SMPC). For example, in Yao's garbled circuits protocol [29], an OT is needed for every input bit of one party; the GMW protocol [13] requires OT for every AND gate of the circuit; OT is a basic component for achieving a coin-flipping protocol [4,14].

© The Author(s), under exclusive license to Springer Nature Singapore Pte Ltd. 2025
M. Kohlweiss et al. (Eds.): CANS 2024, LNCS 14905, pp. 123–143, 2025.
https://doi.org/10.1007/978-981-97-8013-6_6

There are some types of OT protocols such as base OT protocols, OT extension (OTE) protocols that focus on executing multiple OT protocols efficiently [2,5,6,15], randomized OT (ROT) protocols [1,9], where neither of the parties have any inputs, etc. Base OT protocols are core cryptographic primitives in both SMPC protocols and OTE protocols. Moreover, 1-out-of-N OT [17,24], where the sender has N private values $x_1, ..., x_N$, the receiver holds a chosen index i and is allowed to obtain x_i but nothing else, and the sender cannot know the receiver's choice, is a type of base OT and is widely used, e.g. Symmetrically-Private Information Retrieval [12,23].

One aspect of OT that we are concerned about is its round complexity. We desire the minimal interaction between the sender and the receiver. Specifically, two-round OT [7,16], where the receiver sends a message to the sender, and the sender sends a reply to the receiver, is what we want.

Another aspect of OT that we focus on is its security. In this paper, we consider the semi-honest (passive) security, where the corrupted party follows the protocol but attempts to learn additional information through the transcripts of the honest party he observes. We desire security against adversaries with unbounded computational power, i.e., OTs simultaneously ensure statistical security for either the receiver or the sender.

Furthermore, it is desirable to have post-quantum OT protocols based on standard assumptions. Recently, Ring-LWE based [28] and ideal lattice based [19] post-quantum 1-out-of-N OT protocols are proposed respectively.

1.1   Our Contributions

In this work, we construct a two-round and statistical sender-private (SSP) in the semi-honest model (computational receiver-private) 1-out-of-N OT from the Module-Learning with Errors (MLWE) assumption with polynomial noise-ratio. Since MLWE problems are widely believed to be hard even with a quantum computer, our protocol is plausibly post-quantum secure.

Regarding efficiency, our work has achieved the minimal round complexity of OT and has improved efficiency compared to OTs based on LWE (e.g. [7,25,26]) in particular. This is because in our protocol based on MLWE, after selecting a specific ring, each private element becomes a polynomial, which allows it to carry more messages. Additionally, compared to protocols based on Ring Learning with Errors (RLWE), protocols based on MLWE have more flexible parameter selection. Regarding security, our OT protocol is computational receiver-private and statistical sender-private in the semi-honest setting. This means our protocol guarantees sender's security against computationally unbounded and honest-but-curious adversaries who will not deviate from the protocol but will attempt to learn all possible information from received messages.

Our idea started from an observation that OT is a special case of private linear function evaluation, where N messages from the sender are considered as the linear function to be privately evaluated, and the receiver is constrained to generate an input of the form $(0, ..., 0, 1, 0, ..., 0)$ (the position of 1 corresponds to the index chosen by the receiver). The output of this linear function precisely corresponds to the message the receiver wants. Additionally, we introduced an extractor to enhance security.

Informally, the receiver in our protocol hides its private index i in a MLWE instance $(A, \boldsymbol{b} = A^\top(2\boldsymbol{s}' + \boldsymbol{e}^i) + 2\boldsymbol{e})$, where $\boldsymbol{e}^i$ is an N-dimensional unit vector over ring $\mathcal{R}$ with its i-th element being 1, $\boldsymbol{s}'$ is a small secret, and $\boldsymbol{e}$ is an error term. The sender computes $\boldsymbol{c_0} := A\boldsymbol{r} + \boldsymbol{v} + 2\boldsymbol{e_1}$ in order to hide his randomness $\boldsymbol{v} = (v_1, ..., v_N)$ with sufficiently high entropy used as inputs to the extractor $\mathrm{Ext}(\cdot)$ in a packed way. $\boldsymbol{c_0}$ is statistically indistinguishable from a uniform N-dimensional vector, with appropriate parameter selection. To ensure correctness, the sender (without knowing $\boldsymbol{s}', \boldsymbol{e}$) needs to compute $c_1 := \boldsymbol{b}^\top \boldsymbol{r} + 2e_2$ additionally. Upon receiving $\boldsymbol{c_0}$ and c_1, the receiver (without knowing $\boldsymbol{r}, \boldsymbol{e_1}$) can compute $\left((2\boldsymbol{s}' + \boldsymbol{e}^i)^\top \boldsymbol{c_0} - c_1\right) \bmod q\mathcal{R} \bmod 2\mathcal{R}$ to recover v_i and $\mathrm{Ext}(v_i)$, which can serve as the key for one-time pad encryption of m_i. We emphasize that introducing an extractor is necessary. If the sender computes $\boldsymbol{c_0} := A\boldsymbol{r} + \boldsymbol{m} + 2\boldsymbol{e_1}$ hiding message vector $\boldsymbol{m}$ directly, the receiver would obtain knowledge of $\boldsymbol{m}$, i.e. $\langle \boldsymbol{s}', \boldsymbol{m} \rangle + 2\langle \boldsymbol{s}', \boldsymbol{e_1} \rangle - \langle \boldsymbol{e}, \boldsymbol{r} \rangle - e_2$, meaning that if e_2 is not large enough to cover $\langle \boldsymbol{s}', \boldsymbol{m} \rangle$, then the receiver would get leakage about messages he did not choose. In contrast, if $\boldsymbol{c_0}$ conceals a random vector $\boldsymbol{v}$ and v_j has sufficiently large min-entropy conditioned on the leakage about $\boldsymbol{v}$, the extractor $\mathrm{Ext}(v_j)$ can securely hide the message.

Our main technical contribution is breaking away from the mainstream frameworks of lattice-based (1-out-of-2) OTs. One of these frameworks is based on lattice-based public key encryption. Specifically, such framework either requires the receiver to generate two different public keys and the sender to encrypt messages under these two public keys separately, or it requires the sender to encrypt messages using two different encryption ways under the same public key generated by the receiver. By contrast, our work requires the receiver to only public an "encryption" related to the index he has chosen, and requires the sender to hide his input based on this public item, implying that the sender needs to conceal his input in only one specific, packed way.

1.2   Related Work

Comparison with Two-Message SSP OTs from LWE ([7,26]).

– Brakerski et.al. ([7], TCC'18) proposed a two-message SSP OT protocol without setup that guarantees security against malicious receivers. This work exploits the property that either a lattice or its dual must have short vectors. Specifically, the sender, based on the chosen index $b \in \{0, 1\}$, either generates a matrix $A \in \mathbb{Z}_q^{2k \times m}$ with a trapdoor or generates a matrix $A := \begin{pmatrix} A_1 \\ SA_1 + E \end{pmatrix}$ concatenated with LWE instances. Then, the receiver sends A to the sender. Next, the sender encrypts two messages m_0, m_1 in two different ways. The above description implies that the receiver needs to send all the elements of A, as A may be sampled with trapdoor. In contrast, in our scheme, the matrix A is uniformly random, so the receiver only needs to send a λ-bit seed for generating A.

The transmission of the matrix A becomes the main communication cost of [7] protocol, reaching $\widetilde{O}(k^2)$ bits, where $k(\lambda)$ is the dimension of LWE instances, k is greater than the message length n, $\widetilde{O}$ hides polynomial factors in $\log q$, and $q \in \text{Poly}(\lambda)$ is the modulus. By contrast, our protocol from MLWE requires communication of $\widetilde{O}(k)$ bits, where $\widetilde{O}$ hides polynomial factors in $\log q'$, and $q' \in \text{Poly}(\lambda)$ is the modulus in our protocol.

- Willy Quach ([26], SCN'20) instantiated the dual-mode encryption framework from LWE problems with sub-exponential noise-ratio, which implies two-round OTs in the common reference string (CRS) model. This protocol either provides statistical receiver security and computational sender security or statistical sender security and computational receiver security. It has two setup modes, corresponding to statistical receiver-private (SRP) and SSP. Here we consider the latter. Under this mode, the receiver needs to generates two public keys pk_0, pk_1 corresponding to two indices and send pk_0, pk_1 to the sender. Then the sender encrypts $m_0, m_1 \in \{0, 1\}$ under pk_0, pk_1 respectively. This scheme can encrypt only 1-bit messages each time.

  By contrast, in our protocol, the sender hides n-bit randomness $v_1, ..., v_N$ in a packed way, where n is usually set to be 256. After using the extractor, it yields a uniformly random bit string of length $l \approx n - 2\omega(1)$ to mask the l-bit message. Furthermore, our protocol does not have a setup phase.

Compared to the two protocols mentioned above, our scheme has a simpler construction. Furthermore, our construction avoids trapdoor sampling.

For computational efficiency, due to the properties of MLWE, we can adjust the dimension of MLWE (denoted as N) to directly achieve 1-out-of-N OT ($N \geq 2$). Both parties can use NTT algorithm [3] to reduce the cost of multiplication. Additionally, not involving trapdoor sampling will also increase computational efficiency.

In conclusion, according to the above comparison, our scheme is more efficient in both computation and communication. However, [7,26] are secure against malicious receivers, while our protocol guarantees security in the semi-honest model.

Comparison with the VOLE from RLWE [8]. Leo de Castro et.al. ([8], WAHC'21) proposed a Ring-LWE-based vector oblivious linear function evaluation (VOLE) protocol, which allows a sender, holding an affine function $f(x) = ax + b$ over a ring, to make a receiver learn $f(x)$ for a x of the receiver's choice. Such primitives can be used to derive 1-out-of-2 OTs, where $a := m_0, b := m_1 - m_0$ and $x := \sigma \in \{0, 1\}$. This protocol achieved computational receiver-security and computational sender-security in the semi-honest model. Roughly speaking, the receiver encrypts index σ under the packed additively homomorphic encryption scheme, and the sender performs a homomorphic evaluation on the ciphertext, where the messages $m_0, m_1 - m_0$ can be seen as a function.

By contrast, in our protocol, the way the sender hides the messages (randomness) is independent of what the receiver sends. This implies that the sender can preprocess in the CRS model. We move the evaluation part to the offline phase, and the evaluation is done by the receiver, where the function being evaluated is related to the receiver's input.

Comparison with the Ring-LWE Based 1-out-of-N OT [28]. In [28], Yadav et al. proposed a 1-out-of-N OT based on the *NewHope Key Exchange Scheme*. In fact, the idea can be generalized to any LWE-based public key encryption scheme. Roughly speaking, the user generates N random polynomials a_i but only one polynomial b, satisfying that there is exactly one j such that (a_j, b) is an RLWE instance, or the legal public key. Then the sender encrypts N messages with every pair (a_i, b) as the public key. It can be easily seen that the user can only recover one message.

We can also construct the MLWE-based 1-out-of-N OT directly, but a better way we think is to combine our technique and the idea in [28], which will lead a more efficient OT. For example, when employing $R_q = \mathbb{Z}_q[x]/(x^{1024} + 1)$ in NewHope in [28], the user has to generate N a_i's, and the sender has to generate N groups of ciphertexts, which consists of two polynomials in R_q. However, when replacing NewHope with our new MLWE-based OT with the parameter $R_q = \mathbb{Z}_q[x]/(x^{256}+1)$ and $N = k_2$ (dimension of the error vector) $= 4$, since our protocol is already a 1-out-of-4 OT, the user just needs to generate $N/4$ public keys, and it is enough for the sender to generate $N/4$ groups of ciphertexts, which reduces the communication and computational complexity.

Roadmap. The remainder of this paper is organized as follows. In Sect. 2, we give some notations and preliminaries needed. In Sect. 3, we describe our 1-out-of-N OT protocol and we prove that it is statistical sender-private and computational receiver-private in the semi-honest model, if the HNF-MLWE assumption hold. The conclusions are summarized in Sect. 4.

2   Notations and Preliminaries

2.1   Notations

Throughout this paper, denote by bold lower-case letters the vectors. For a vector a we write a_j to denote its jth entry. By default, all vectors will be column vectors, and $\| \cdot \|$ denotes the l_2 norm. For a string x over some alphabet, $|x|$ denotes the length of x. For a positive integer k, $[k]$ denotes the set $\{0, ..., k-1\}$, and $[k] + 1$ denotes the set $\{1, ..., k\}$. For real x , $\lfloor x \rceil$ denotes the integer closest to x with ties broken upward. We use $\mathrm{negl}(n)$ to denote that a function in n is negligible.

For a set S, we write $x \xleftarrow{\$} S$ to denote that x is chosen uniformly at random from S and let U_S denote the uniform distribution over S. For arbitrary distribution $\mathcal{D}$ over a set S, sampling x from S according to $\mathcal{D}$ is denoted by $x \leftarrow \mathcal{D}$.

The statistical distance between two distributions $\mathcal{X}$ and $\mathcal{Y}$ over a countable domain D, denoted as $\boldsymbol{SD}(\mathcal{X}, \mathcal{Y})$, is defined to be $\frac{1}{2} \sum_{d \in D} |\mathcal{X}(d) - \mathcal{Y}(d)|$.

Two ensembles of distributions $\{X_n\}$ and $\{Y_n\}$ are computationally indistinguishable if for every probabilistic poly-time machine $\mathcal{A}$, $|\Pr[\mathcal{A}(1^n, X_n) = 1] - \Pr[\mathcal{A}(1^n, Y_n) = 1]|$ is negligible in n. We mark it with $\{X_n\} \overset{c}{\approx} \{Y_n\}$.

2.2   Oblivious Transfer in the Semi-Honest Model

Before introducing the definition of a private oblivious transfer, we list the following notations:

- Let $f = (f_S, f_R) : \{0,1\}^* \times \{0,1\}^* \to \{0,1\}^* \times \{0,1\}^*$ be a polynomial-time functionality and let $\mathcal{OT}$ be a two-party probabilistic polynomial-time protocol. Specifically, $f_S : \sigma \times (m_1, ..., m_N) \mapsto \perp$ and $f_R : \sigma \times (m_1, ..., m_N) \mapsto m_\sigma$.
- The view of the receiver (respectively, the sender) during an execution of $\mathcal{OT}$ on $(\sigma, (m_1, ..., m_N))$ and security parameter λ, denoted as $\mathbf{view}_R^{\mathcal{OT}}(\sigma, (m_1, ..., m_N), \lambda)$ (respectively, $\mathbf{view}_S^{\mathcal{OT}}(\sigma, (m_1, ..., m_N), \lambda)$), is defined as $(\sigma, r^R, c_1^R, ..., c_t^R)$ (respectively, $((m_1, ..., m_N), r^S, c_1^S, ..., c_t^S)$), where r^R (respectively, r^S) denotes the contents of the receiver (respectively, the sender) internal random tape, and c_i^R (respectively, c_i^S) represents the i-th message that the receiver (respectively, the sender) received.

Definition 1 (Oblivious Transfer). *A two-party probabilistic polynomial-time protocol $\mathcal{OT}$ is said to be a private 1-out-of-N oblivious transfer in the presence of static semi-honest adversaries if the following holds:*

- *If the sender and the receiver follow the protocol then after an execution in which the sender has for input any N strings $m_1, ..., m_N \in \{0,1\}^*$, and the receiver has for input any index $\sigma \in [N]$, the output of the receiver is m_σ.*
- *there exist probabilistic polynomial-time algorithms, denoted S_R and S_S, such that*

$$\left\{ \left(S_R(1^\lambda, \sigma, f_R(\sigma, (m_1, ..., m_N))) \right) \right\}_{\sigma, (m_1, ..., m_N), \lambda} \overset{c}{\approx} \left\{ \mathbf{view}_R^{\mathcal{OT}}(\sigma, (m_1, ..., m_N), \lambda) \right\}_{\sigma, (m_1, ..., m_N), \lambda},$$

$$\left\{ \left(S_S(1^\lambda, (m_1, ..., m_N), f_S(\sigma, (m_1, ..., m_N))) \right) \right\}_{\sigma, (m_1, ..., m_N), \lambda} \overset{c}{\approx} \left\{ \mathbf{view}_S^{\mathcal{OT}}(\sigma, (m_1, ..., m_N), \lambda) \right\}_{\sigma, (m_1, ..., m_N), \lambda}.$$

2.3   Rings and Embeddings

Power Basis. For a cyclotomic field $K = \mathbb{Q}(\zeta)$ with $\zeta = \zeta_m$ the primitive m-th root of unity, its minimal polynomial is $\Phi(m) = \prod_{i \in \mathbb{Z}_m^*} (X - \omega_m^i) \in \mathbb{Z}[x]$ with degree $n := \varphi(m)$, where $\omega_m \in \mathbb{C}$ is any primitive m-th root of unity in $\mathbb{C}$ and $\varphi(\cdot)$ denotes the Euler's totient function. We can view K as a vector space of degree n over $\mathbb{Q}$ which has the power basis $\boldsymbol{p} := (\zeta_m^i)_{i \in [n]} = (1, \zeta_m, ..., \zeta_m^{n-1})$.

Throughout this paper, we set m to be a power of 2, $\mathcal{R} := \mathcal{O}_K = \mathbb{Z}[\zeta]$, which is the ring of integers of K. Then $\mathcal{R} \cong \mathbb{Z}[x]/(X^n + 1)$. Additionally, we use $\mathcal{R}_q$ to denote $\mathcal{R}/\langle q \rangle$.

Canonical Embedding. Set $\text{Gal}(K/\mathbb{Q}) = \{\sigma_i : i = 1, ..., n\}$. The canonical embedding $\sigma : K \to \mathbb{C}^{\mathbb{Z}_m^*}$ is defined as $\sigma(a) = (\sigma_i(a))_{i \in \{1,...,n\}}$, where $\overline{\sigma_i(a)} = \sigma_{n+1-i}(a)$ for all $a \in K, i \in \{1, ..., n\}$.

For any $a \in K$, its l_2 norm is $\|a\| = \|\sigma(a)\| = (\Sigma_i|\sigma_i(a)^2|)^{1/2}$ and its l_∞ norm is $\max_i |\sigma_i(a)|$. The trace of a is defined as $\text{Tr}(a) = \sum_i \sigma_i(a)$. For all $a, b \in K, c \in \mathbb{Q}$, $\text{Tr}(ab) = \sum_i \sigma_i(a)\sigma_i(b)$, $\text{Tr}(c \cdot a) = c\text{Tr}(a)$.

Embedding into $\mathbb{R}^n$. Define an embedding $h : \sigma(K) \to \mathbb{R}^n$ as $h(\sigma(x)) = \boldsymbol{y}$, where for $1 \leq i \leq \frac{n}{2}$,

$$\begin{cases} y_i & = \frac{1}{\sqrt{2}}(\sigma_i(x) + \sigma_{n+1-i}(x)) \\ y_{n+1-i} & = \frac{\sqrt{-1}}{\sqrt{2}}(\sigma_i(x) - \sigma_{n+1-i}(x)). \end{cases}$$

2.4 Min-Entropy and Extractors

Definition 2 (Min-Entropy). *The min-entropy of a random variable X, denoted as $\boldsymbol{H}_\infty(X)$, is defined as $\boldsymbol{H}_\infty(X) = -\log(\max_x \Pr[X = x])$.*

Definition 3 (Extractors [10]). *Let* $\text{Ext} : \{0,1\}^n \to \{0,1\}^l$ *be a polynomial time probabilistic function which uses d bits of randomness. We say that Ext is an efficient (n, m, l, ϵ)-strong extractor if for all min-entropy m distributions X on $\{0,1\}^n$, $\boldsymbol{SD}((\text{Ext}(X; s), s), (U_l, s)) \leq \epsilon$, where s is uniform on $\{0,1\}^r$.*

Note 1. For all $v \in \mathcal{R}_2$, we use the notation $\text{Ext}(v; s)$, where v denotes a concatenation of coefficients of polynomial $v \in \mathcal{R}_2$ that can be seen as an n-bit string.

2.5 Lattice Background

Lattice. Given m linearly independent basis vectors $B = [\boldsymbol{b_1}, ..., \boldsymbol{b_m}] \in \mathbb{R}^{n \times m}$, the lattice generated by B is $\Lambda =: \mathcal{L}(B) = \mathcal{L}(\boldsymbol{b_1}, ..., \boldsymbol{b_m}) = \{\sum_{i=1}^m x_i \cdot \boldsymbol{b_i}, x_i \in \mathbb{Z}\}$. Such an n-dimensional lattice of rank m is a discrete additive subgroup of $\mathbb{R}^n$. Let $\widetilde{B} = \{\widetilde{\boldsymbol{b_1}}, ..., \widetilde{\boldsymbol{b_m}}\}$ denote the Gram-Schmidt orthogonalization of B.

Furthermore, in a number field K of degree n, a lattice in K is the $\mathbb{Z}$-span of a $\mathbb{Q}$-basis (i.e. the power basis) of K.

Duality. For a lattice $\Lambda \in \mathbb{R}^n$ its dual lattice is $\Lambda^\vee = \{y \in \mathbb{R}^n : \forall x \in \Lambda, \langle x, y \rangle \in \mathbb{Z}\}$. For a lattice L in K, its dual lattice is $L^\vee = \{a \in K : \text{Tr}(aL) \in \mathbb{Z}\}$.

According to the above choice of $\mathcal{R}$, the dual basis of the power basis is $(d_i)_{i \in [n]}$, where $d_i = \frac{1}{n}\zeta_m^{m-i}$. In this paper, we write $\mathcal{R}_q^\vee = \mathcal{R}^\vee/(q\mathcal{R}^\vee)$.

Gaussian on Lattices. For any $\sigma > 0$ define the Gaussian function on $\mathbb{R}^n$ centered at $\boldsymbol{c}$ with parameter σ: $\forall \boldsymbol{x} \in \mathbb{R}^n, \rho_{\sigma,\boldsymbol{c}}(\boldsymbol{x}) = e^{-\pi\|\boldsymbol{x}-\boldsymbol{c}\|^2/\sigma^2}$. For any $\boldsymbol{c} \in \mathbb{R}^n$, real $\sigma > 0$, and n-dimensional lattice Λ, define the discrete Gaussian distribution over Λ as: $\forall \boldsymbol{x} \in \Lambda, D_{\Lambda,\sigma,\boldsymbol{c}}(\boldsymbol{x}) = \frac{\rho_{\sigma,\boldsymbol{c}}(\boldsymbol{x})}{\sum_{x \in \Lambda} \rho_{\sigma,\boldsymbol{c}}(\boldsymbol{x})} = \frac{\rho_{\sigma,\boldsymbol{c}}(\boldsymbol{x})}{\rho_{\sigma,\boldsymbol{c}}(\Lambda)}$. The subscripts $\boldsymbol{c}$ is taken to be $\mathbf{0}$ when omitted. Further more, the Gaussian function has the following property: For any $s > 0$ and any $\boldsymbol{u} \in \mathbb{R}^n$ it holds that $\rho_s(\Lambda + \boldsymbol{u}) \leq \rho_s(\Lambda)$.

Any non-singular matrix B yields the Gaussian function: $\forall \boldsymbol{x} \in \mathbb{R}^n, \rho_B(\boldsymbol{x}) = \rho(B^{-1}\boldsymbol{x}) = e^{-\pi\langle B^{-1}\boldsymbol{x}, B^{-1}\boldsymbol{x}\rangle} = e^{-\pi \cdot \boldsymbol{x}^\top \Sigma^{-1}\boldsymbol{x}}$, where $\Sigma = BB^\top > 0$. We usually refer to ρ_B as $\rho_{\sqrt{\Sigma}}$. For any $\boldsymbol{c} \in \mathbb{R}^n$, positive definite matrix $\Sigma > 0$, and n-dimensional lattice Λ, define the discrete Gaussian distribution over Λ as: $\forall \boldsymbol{x} \in \Lambda, D_{\Lambda,\boldsymbol{c},\sqrt{\Sigma}}(\boldsymbol{x}) = \frac{\rho_{\sqrt{\Sigma}}(\boldsymbol{x}-\boldsymbol{c})}{\rho_{\sqrt{\Sigma}}(\Lambda-\boldsymbol{c})}$.

Throughout this paper, sampling discrete Gaussian over $\mathcal{R}$ is equivalent to sampling discrete Gaussian over $h \circ \sigma(\mathcal{R}) \subset \mathbb{R}^n$.

Definition 4 (Smoothing Parameter). *For a lattice Λ and positive real $\epsilon > 0$, the smoothing parameter $\eta_\epsilon(\Lambda)$ is the smallest real $s > 0$ such that $\rho_{1/s}(\Lambda^\vee \setminus \{\mathbf{0}\}) \leq \epsilon$.*

Let $\Sigma > 0$ be any positive definite matrix. We say that $\sqrt{\Sigma} \geq \eta_\epsilon(\Lambda)$ if $\eta_\epsilon(\sqrt{\Sigma}^{-1} \cdot \Lambda) \leq 1$, i.e., if $\rho(\sqrt{\Sigma}^\top \cdot \Lambda^\vee \setminus \{\mathbf{0}\}) = \rho_{\sqrt{\Sigma^{-1}}}(\Lambda^\vee \setminus \{\mathbf{0}\}) \leq \epsilon$.

Corollary 1. *When the covariance matrix $\Sigma > 0$ and the lattice Λ is full-rank, if the minimum eigenvalue of Σ, $\lambda_{\min}(\Sigma)$ is at least $\eta_\epsilon^2(\Lambda)$ then $\sqrt{\Sigma} \geq \eta_\epsilon(\Lambda)$.*

Proof. Recall Σ's eigendecomposition, i.e. $\Sigma = Q^\top DQ \in \mathbb{R}^{n \times n}$, where $D = \text{diag}(\lambda_1, ..., \lambda_n)$ is the diagonal matrix containing Σ's all eigenvalues and $Q \in \mathbb{R}^{n \times n}$ is an orthogonal matrix. Then we have

$$
\begin{aligned}
\rho(\sqrt{\Sigma}^\top \cdot \Lambda^\vee \setminus \{\mathbf{0}\}) &= \sum_{\boldsymbol{x} \in \Lambda^\vee \setminus \{\mathbf{0}\}} \exp(-\pi \cdot \boldsymbol{x}^\top \Sigma \boldsymbol{x}) = \sum_{\boldsymbol{x} \in \Lambda^\vee \setminus \{\mathbf{0}\}} \exp(-\pi \cdot \boldsymbol{x}^\top Q^\top DQ\boldsymbol{x}) \\
&\leq \sum_{\boldsymbol{x} \in \Lambda^\vee \setminus \{\mathbf{0}\}} \exp(-\pi \cdot \lambda_{\min}(\boldsymbol{x}^\top Q^\top Q\boldsymbol{x})) \\
&= \sum_{\boldsymbol{x} \in \Lambda^\vee \setminus \{\mathbf{0}\}} \exp(-\pi \cdot \lambda_{\min}\|\boldsymbol{x}\|^2) = \rho_{1/\sqrt{\lambda_{\min}}}(\Lambda^\vee).
\end{aligned}
$$

Since $\sqrt{\lambda_{\min}(\Sigma)} \geq \eta_\epsilon(\Lambda)$, we can conclude that $\rho_{1/\sqrt{\lambda_{\min}}}(\Lambda^\vee) \leq \epsilon$ by definition.

Lemma 1 (Smooth over the cosets). *Let Λ, Λ' be n-dimensional lattices such that $\Lambda' \subset \Lambda$. Then for any $\epsilon > 0$, $\sqrt{\Sigma} \geq \eta_\epsilon(\Lambda')$, and any $\boldsymbol{c} \in \mathbb{R}^n$, we have*

$$
\boldsymbol{SD}(D_{\Lambda,\boldsymbol{c},\sqrt{\Sigma}} \bmod \Lambda', U(\Lambda \bmod \Lambda')) < 2\epsilon.
$$

Lemma 2 ([11], [22]). *Let B be a basis of an n-dimensional lattice Λ, and let $s \geq \|\widetilde{B}\| \cdot \omega(\sqrt{\log(n)})$, where $\|\widetilde{B}\| = \max_{i \in [m]} \|\widetilde{\boldsymbol{b}}_i\|$, then $\Pr_{\boldsymbol{x} \leftarrow D_{\Lambda,s}}[\|\boldsymbol{x}\| \geq s \cdot \sqrt{n}] \leq \text{negl}(n)$.*

Definition 5 (Subgaussian). *For any $\delta \geq 0$, we say that a distribution $\mathcal{D}$ over $\mathbb{R}$ is δ-subgaussian with parameter $s > 0$ if for all $t \in \mathbb{R}, X \leftarrow \mathcal{D}$, the moment-generating function satisfies $\mathbb{E}[\exp(2\pi tX)] \leq \exp(\delta) \cdot \exp(\pi s^2 t^2)$.*

Claim 1 (Tail Bound). If $\mathcal{D}$ is δ-subgaussian with parameter s, then for all $t \geq 0, X \leftarrow \mathcal{D}, \Pr[|X| \geq t] \leq 2\exp(\delta - \pi t^2/s^2)$.

Claim 2 ([20]). If X is δ-subgaussian with parameter s, then cX is δ-subgaussian with parameter $|c|s$ for any real c. If X_i is δ_i-subgaussian with parameter s_i for $i = 1, ..., n$, then $\sum_{i=1}^n X_i$ is $\sum_{i=1}^n \delta_i$-subgaussian with parameter $(\sum_{i=1}^n s_i^2)^{1/2}$.

Claim 3 ([21]). Let $\Lambda \subset \mathbb{R}^n$ be a lattice. For any $s > 0$, $D_{\Lambda,s}$ is 0-subgaussian with parameter s.

Module Learning with Errors. The decision $\mathrm{MLWE}_{q,\psi}^{\mathcal{R}^k}$ problem is to distinguish between the distribution $A_{q,s,\psi}$ for uniformly random secret $\boldsymbol{s} \in (\mathcal{R}^\vee)^k$ and the uniform distribution over $\mathcal{R}_q^k \times K_{\mathbb{R}}/(q\mathcal{R}^\vee)$, where $A_{q,s,\psi}$ is the distribution on $\mathcal{R}_q^k \times K_{\mathbb{R}}/(q\mathcal{R}^\vee)$ obtained by choosing a vector $\boldsymbol{a} \xleftarrow{\$} \mathcal{R}_q^k$, $e \leftarrow \psi$ (some distribution over $K_{\mathbb{R}}/(q\mathcal{R}^\vee)$) and outputting $(\boldsymbol{a}, b =: \langle \boldsymbol{a}, \boldsymbol{s} \rangle + e \bmod q\mathcal{R}^\vee)$.

MLWE Assumption. The original MLWE assumption says that it is hard for any probabilistic polynomial time algorithm to solve the $\mathrm{MLWE}_{q,\psi}^{\mathcal{R}^k}$ problem. The following theorem demonstrates that solving $\mathrm{MLWE}_{q,D_\xi}^{\mathcal{R}^k}$ implies an equally efficient solution to a lattice problem (in the worst case, with high probability).

Theorem 1 ([18]). *Let K be the m-th cyclotomic number field having dimension $n = \varphi(m)$ and $R = \mathcal{O}_k$. Let $\alpha \in (0,1)$ and $q \leq 2$ prime, with $q \leq Poly(nk)$ and $q = 1 \bmod m$ such that $\alpha q > 2\sqrt{k} \cdot \omega(\sqrt{\log(n)})$. There is a quantum reduction from solving $\mathrm{Mod} - \mathrm{GIVP}_\gamma^{\eta_\epsilon}$ with $\epsilon = (nk)^{-\omega(1)}, \gamma = \sqrt{8nk^2} \cdot \omega(\sqrt{\log(n)})/\alpha$ in polynomial time to solving $\mathrm{MLWE}_{q,D_\xi}^{\mathcal{R}^k}$, given only l samples, in polynomial time with non-negligible advantage with $\xi = \alpha(nl/\log(nl))^{1/4}$.*

If the above e, s_i $(i = 1, .., k) \leftarrow D_{\mathcal{R}^\vee, \alpha q}$ (any valid discretization of ψ to $\mathcal{R}^\vee$) ,it is called the Hermite Normal Form of MLWE (HNF-MLWE) problem which is still hard [18]. Slightly modify the HNF-MLWE problem by sampling e, s_i $(i = 1, .., k)$ from χ, which is a valid discretizaion of $p\psi$ to $p\mathcal{R}^\vee$ (p and q are coprime). According to [20], it can be shown that this variant of the MLWE problem is still hard.

Since the ring $\mathcal{R}$ our chosen satisfies $\mathcal{R}^\vee = \frac{1}{n}\mathcal{R}$, we can scale the above output b by n. Then $\boldsymbol{s} \in \mathcal{R}^k, e \in \mathcal{R}$.

3   1-Out-of-N Oblivious Transfer from MLWE

In this section, we present the construction of a 1-out-of-N OT protocol based on MLWE. This OT protocol is two-round and statistical sender-private (computational receiver-private) in the semi-honest setting. Our constructions are parameterized by the security parameter λ, the modulus $q = q(\lambda)$, the number of sender's messages N, and the length of each message l. Let (n, n, l, λ)-strong extractor $\text{Ext} : \{0, 1\}^n \to \{0, 1\}^l$ which uses d bits of randomness.

In the following, let k be a positive integer, m be a power of 2, $n = \varphi(m)$, q be an odd prime such that $q = 1 \bmod m$, and $q >> 2$. Let $\mathcal{R}$ be the ring $\mathbb{Z}[X]/(X^n + 1)$. Finally, let α, β, r, τ be parameters for discrete Gaussians.

We use $\mathbf{S}$ and $\mathbf{R}$ to represent the sender and receiver respectively, and the construction of the protocol is as follows:

- **SENDER INPUT:** $\boldsymbol{m} := (m_1, ..., m_N)$, where $m_i \in \{0, 1\}^l$, $\forall i \in [N]$.
- **RECEIVER INPUT:** $\sigma \in [N]$. Let e^σ be an N-dimensional unit vector over ring $\mathcal{R}$, with its σ-th element being 1.
- $\mathbf{R}$ samples $A \xleftarrow{\$} \mathcal{R}_q^{N \times k}$, $\boldsymbol{s}' \leftarrow D_{\mathcal{R}^N, \alpha q}$, $\boldsymbol{e} \leftarrow D_{\mathcal{R}^k, \alpha q}$, and computes $\boldsymbol{b}^\top := \boldsymbol{s}^\top A + 2\boldsymbol{e}^\top \bmod q\mathcal{R}$, where $\boldsymbol{s} = 2\boldsymbol{s}' + \boldsymbol{e}^\sigma$. $\mathbf{R}$ sends $A, \boldsymbol{b}$ to $\mathbf{S}$.
- $\mathbf{S}$ gets $A, \boldsymbol{b}$ from $\mathbf{R}$, then chooses $\boldsymbol{v} \leftarrow D_{\mathcal{R}^N, \beta}$, $\boldsymbol{r} \leftarrow D_{\mathcal{R}^k, r}$, $e_1 \leftarrow D_{\mathcal{R}^N, r}$, $e_2 \leftarrow D_{\mathcal{R}, \tau r}$, $s \xleftarrow{\$} \{0, 1\}^d$ and computes $\boldsymbol{c_0} = A\boldsymbol{r} + \boldsymbol{v} + 2e_1 \bmod q\mathcal{R}$, $c_1 = \boldsymbol{b}^\top \boldsymbol{r} + 2e_2 \bmod q\mathcal{R}$, $\{c_{2,i} = \text{Ext}(v_i \bmod 2\mathcal{R}; s) \bigoplus m_i\}_{i \in [N]}$. $\mathbf{S}$ sends $s, \boldsymbol{c_0}, c_1, \{c_{2,i}\}_{i \in [N]}$ to $\mathbf{R}$.
- $\mathbf{R}$ gets $s, \boldsymbol{c_0}, c_1, \{c_{2,i}\}_{i \in [N]}$ from $\mathbf{S}$, then computes $v'_\sigma := (\boldsymbol{s}^\top \boldsymbol{c_0} - c_1) \bmod q\mathcal{R} \bmod 2\mathcal{R}$ and outputs $m'_\sigma := \text{Ext}(v'_\sigma; s) \bigoplus c_{2,\sigma}$.

Note 2. In our protocol, $\mathbf{R}$ can send a λ-bits seed ρ instead of a matrix, and then both $\mathbf{R}$ and $\mathbf{S}$ can make use of a pseudorandom function to generate an uniformly random matrix A described above in the semi-honest model.

Note 3. We give a version of this protocol in the common random string (CRS) model. More precisely, we additionally include a trusted setup phase before the protocol begins, where the setup procedure is as follows.

Setup$(1^\lambda) \to (crs)$: Sample $A \xleftarrow{\$} \mathcal{R}_q(\lambda)^{N \times k}$ (respectively, $\rho \xleftarrow{\$} \{0, 1\}^\lambda$). Output $crs := A$ (respectively, $crs := \rho$).

Theorem 2 (Correctness.). *If $D_{\mathcal{R}, \alpha q}$ is δ-subgaussian with parameter $q/2 - \beta - 2r - 2\tau r > 2 \cdot \alpha q \cdot \sqrt{\frac{\beta^2 N}{n} + \frac{r^2 k}{n} + \frac{4r^2 N}{n}} \cdot \omega(\sqrt{\log(\lambda)})$, then $\mathbf{R}$ outputs m_σ with overwhelming probability.*

Before proving the theorem, we introduce a relevant lemma.

Lemma 3. *Let $a \in \mathcal{R}$. If a is δ-subgaussian with parameter s and $b \in \mathcal{R}$, and we rewrite $ab = \sum_{i \in [n]} c_i \zeta_m^i$, then each integral coefficient c_i is δ-subgaussian with parameter $\frac{1}{n} \|b\| \cdot s$.*

Proof. Recall the dual basis of the power basis $\boldsymbol{p} := (\zeta_m^i)_{i \in [n]}$ is $(d_i)_{i \in [n]}$, where $d_i = \frac{1}{n} \zeta_m^{m-i}$. It satisfies that $\text{Tr}(p_i \cdot d_i) = 1$ for all $i \in [n]$ and $\text{Tr}(p_i \cdot d_j) = 0$ for all $i, j \in [n], i \neq j$. Notice that

$$\text{Tr}(d_i \cdot ab) = \sum_{i \in [n]} c_i \text{Tr}(d_i \cdot p_i) = c_i.$$

By the Cauchy-Schwarz inequality and the definition of the l_2 norm of elements in $\mathcal{R}$, we have

$$c_i = \mathrm{Tr}(d_i \cdot ab) \leq \|d_i b\| \|a\| \leq \|d_i\|_\infty \|b\| \|a\| = \frac{1}{n} \|b\| \|a\|$$

for all $i \in [n]$. Since a is δ-subgaussian with parameter s, we can conclude that c_i is δ-subgaussian with parameter $\frac{1}{n}\|b\| \cdot s$ by the Definition 5 and Claim 2.

Proof (proof of theorem 2). Recall that $\mathbf{R}$ computes $(\boldsymbol{s}^\top \boldsymbol{c_0} - c_1) \bmod q\mathcal{R} \bmod 2\mathcal{R}$, where $\boldsymbol{s}^\top \boldsymbol{c_0} - c_1 = 2\langle \boldsymbol{s'}, \boldsymbol{v} \rangle + v_\sigma + 2\langle \boldsymbol{s}, \boldsymbol{e_1} \rangle - 2\langle \boldsymbol{e}, \boldsymbol{r} \rangle - 2e_2 = 2\langle \boldsymbol{s'}, \boldsymbol{v} \rangle + v_\sigma + 4\langle \boldsymbol{s'}, \boldsymbol{e_1} \rangle + 2\langle \boldsymbol{e}^\sigma, \boldsymbol{e_1} \rangle - 2\langle \boldsymbol{e}, \boldsymbol{r} \rangle - 2e_2$.

We use X to denote $2\langle \boldsymbol{s'}, \boldsymbol{v} \rangle + 4\langle \boldsymbol{s'}, \boldsymbol{e_1} \rangle - 2\langle \boldsymbol{e}, \boldsymbol{r} \rangle$ and Y to denote $v_\sigma + 2\langle \boldsymbol{e}^\sigma, \boldsymbol{e_1} \rangle - 2e_2$. Since each element of $\boldsymbol{s'}, \boldsymbol{e}$ is sampled from discrete Gaussian distribution $D_{\mathcal{R}, \alpha q}$, which is also 0-subgaussian with parameter αq. Representing X with the power basis, we know that each coefficient of X is 0-subgaussian with parameter $\frac{2}{n} \cdot \sqrt{\|\boldsymbol{v}\|^2 + \|\boldsymbol{r}\|^2 + 4\|\boldsymbol{e_1}\|^2} \cdot \alpha q$ by Lemma 3, Claim 2 and Claim 3. In addition, $\boldsymbol{r}, \boldsymbol{e_1}$ and $\boldsymbol{v}$ are respectively sampled from discrete Gaussian distribution with parameter r, r and β, hence using Lemma 2 we have $\|\boldsymbol{r}\| \leq r\sqrt{kn}, \|\boldsymbol{e_1}\| \leq r\sqrt{Nn}, \|\boldsymbol{v}\| \leq \beta\sqrt{Nn}$. Therefore, each coefficient of X is 0-subgaussian with parameter $2\sqrt{\frac{\beta^2 N}{n} + \frac{r^2 k}{n} + \frac{4r^2 N}{n}} \cdot \alpha q$ and it is bounded by $2\sqrt{\frac{\beta^2 N}{n} + \frac{r^2 k}{n} + \frac{4r^2 N}{n}} \cdot \alpha q \cdot \omega(\sqrt{log(\lambda)})$ with an overwhelming probability (use Claim 1).

Analogously, each coefficient of $2\langle \boldsymbol{e}^\sigma, \boldsymbol{e_1} \rangle$ when represented in the power basis is bounded by $2\frac{\|e_{1\sigma}\| \|1\|}{n} \leq 2\frac{r\sqrt{n} \cdot \sqrt{n}}{n} = 2r$. In addition, each coefficient of v_σ and $2e_2$ are respectively bounded by β and $2\tau r$, since $\|v_\sigma\| \leq \beta\sqrt{n}, \|e_2\| \leq \tau r\sqrt{n}$ w.h.p.

In summary, if $q/2 - \beta - 2r - 2\tau r > 2 \cdot \alpha q \cdot \sqrt{\frac{\beta^2 N}{n} + \frac{r^2 k}{n} + \frac{4r^2 N}{n}} \cdot \omega(\sqrt{log(\lambda)})$, then the absolute value of each coefficient of $X + Y$ when represented in the power basis is at most $q/2$. This yields that

$$
\begin{aligned}
&(\boldsymbol{s}^\top \boldsymbol{c_0} - c_1) \bmod q\mathcal{R} \bmod 2\mathcal{R} \\
=&(2\langle \boldsymbol{s'}, \boldsymbol{v} \rangle + \langle \boldsymbol{e}^\sigma, \boldsymbol{v} \rangle + 2\langle \boldsymbol{s}, \boldsymbol{e_1} \rangle - 2\langle \boldsymbol{e}, \boldsymbol{r} \rangle - 2e_2) \bmod q\mathcal{R} \bmod 2\mathcal{R} \\
=&(2\langle \boldsymbol{s'}, \boldsymbol{v} \rangle + v_\sigma + 2\langle \boldsymbol{s}, \boldsymbol{e_1} \rangle - 2\langle \boldsymbol{e}, \boldsymbol{r} \rangle - 2e_2) \bmod 2\mathcal{R} \\
=&v_\sigma \bmod 2\mathcal{R}
\end{aligned}
$$

Then $\boldsymbol{R}$ can recover m_σ by computing $m_\sigma := c_{2,\sigma} \bigoplus \mathrm{Ext}(v_\sigma \bmod 2\mathcal{R}; s)$

Next we demonstrate that our protocol is secure in the semi-honest model and can be proven statistical private for the sender and computational private for the receiver through simulation. More precisely, we illustrate the indistinguishability between the sender's view and the simulator S_S by using the HNF-MLWE assumption (Sect. 2.5). In addition, when illustrating the sender's privacy, we exploit the Regularity Lemma [20], which is useful in Ring-based cryptosystems.

We formally state its security as follows:

Theorem 3. *If* $\mathrm{HNF} - \mathrm{MLWE}_{q,k,D_{\mathcal{R},\alpha q}}^{\mathcal{R}^N}$ *assumption (2.5) holds, where* $\alpha q > 2\sqrt{N} \cdot (\frac{\log(nk)}{nk})^{1/4} \cdot \omega(\sqrt{\log(n)}), \tau = 2t\sqrt{N+k} \cdot \alpha q \cdot \omega(\sqrt{\log(\lambda)}), r > 2\sqrt{\frac{t}{t-1}}n \cdot q^{N/(N+k)+2/(nN+nk)}, \beta^2(1 - \frac{\beta^2}{r^2}\sqrt{\frac{2}{N+k}} \cdot \frac{\beta}{\alpha q}) > 4n, r > \beta, \mathcal{R} = \mathbb{Z}[X]/(X^n+1), n \in \Omega(\lambda), N, k \in Poly(\lambda), q \in \lambda^{\omega(1)},$ *and* $t > 1$ *is a constant, then our protocol securely realizes the functionality* (f_S, f_R) *mentioned in Sect. 2.2 in the presence of static semi-honest adversaries.*

Proof. It can be derived from the following Lemma 4 and Lemma 5.

we first display functionalities simulators S_R and S_S as follows.

S_R takes as input $(1^\lambda, \sigma, m_\sigma)$. First, S_R samples some random tapes $\hat{A} \xleftarrow{\$} \mathcal{R}_q^{N \times k}, \hat{s}' \leftarrow D_{\mathcal{R}^N, \alpha q}, \hat{e} \leftarrow D_{\mathcal{R}^k, \alpha q}$. Then it chooses vectors $v \leftarrow D_{\mathcal{R}^N, \beta}, r \leftarrow D_{\mathcal{R}^k, r}, e_1 \leftarrow D_{\mathcal{R}^N, r}, e_2 \leftarrow D_{\mathcal{R}, \tau r}, s \xleftarrow{\$} \{0,1\}^d$ and generates a vector $\hat{m} \in \{0,1\}^{Nl}$ such that $\hat{m}_\sigma = m_\sigma$. Next, S_R computes $\hat{c}_0 = \hat{A}r + v + 2e_1, \hat{c}_1 = \left((2\hat{s}' + e^\sigma)^\top \hat{A} + 2\hat{e}^\top\right)r + 2e_2, \{c\hat{2},_i = \mathrm{Ext}(v_i \bmod 2\mathcal{R}; s) \bigoplus \hat{m}_i\}_{i \in [N]}$ and treats them as the messages that **R** received. Ultimately, S_R outputs $(\sigma, \hat{s}', \hat{e}, \hat{c}_0, \hat{c}_1, \{c\hat{2},_i\}_{i \in [N]}, s)$.

S_S takes as input $(1^\lambda, (m_1, ..., m_N), \bot)$ and uniformly chooses random tapes $v' \leftarrow D_{\mathcal{R}^N, \beta}, r' \leftarrow D_{\mathcal{R}^k, r}, e_1' \leftarrow D_{\mathcal{R}^N, r}, e_2' \leftarrow D_{\mathcal{R}, \tau r}, s' \xleftarrow{\$} \{0,1\}^d$. Then it uniformly samples $A' \xleftarrow{\$} \mathcal{R}_q^{N \times k}, b' \xleftarrow{\$} \mathcal{R}_q^k$ and uses them to simulate the messages received by **S**. Finally S_S outputs $(m, v', r', e_1', e_2', s', A', b')$.

Lemma 4 (Computational Receiver Security). $\mathbf{view}_S^{\mathcal{OT}}(\sigma, (m_1, ..., m_N), \lambda)$ *and* $\{(S_S(1^\lambda, (m_1, ..., m_N), \bot))\}_{\sigma,(m_1,..,m_N),\lambda}$ *are computationally indistinguishable if the HNF-MLWE assumption holds and* $\alpha q > 2\sqrt{N} \cdot (\frac{\log(nk)}{nk})^{1/4} \cdot \omega(\sqrt{\log(n)})$, *where* $\mathcal{OT}$ *denotes the above protocol.*

Proof. If there exists $\mathcal{A}$ having non-negligible advantage in distinguishing between $\{(S_S(1^\lambda, (m_1, ..., m_N), \bot))\}_{\sigma,(m_1,...,m_N),\lambda}$ and $\mathbf{view}_S^{\mathcal{OT}}(\sigma, (m_1, ..., m_N), \lambda)$, then we can use $\mathcal{A}$ to construct an algorithm $\mathcal{B}$ for solving HNF-MLWE problems.

First, we describe experiment **REAL** and experiment **IDEAL** in Fig. 1. Notice that for any adversary $\mathcal{A}$, its advantage in distinguishing between $\{(S_S(1^\lambda, (m_1, ..., m_N), \bot))\}_{\sigma,(m_1,...,m_N),\lambda}$ and $\mathbf{view}_S^{\mathcal{OT}}(\sigma, (m_1, ..., m_N), \lambda)$ is equal to the advantage in distinguishing between experiment **REAL** and experiment **IDEAL**. Hence, we suppose that $\mathcal{A}$ has non-negligible advantage in distinguishing between experiment **REAL** and experiment **IDEAL** in Fig. 1. Then we can use $\mathcal{A}$ to construct a HNF-MLWE algorithm $\mathcal{B}$ as follows:

$\mathcal{B}$ takes the decision-HNF-MLWE problem $(A^\top, b) \in \mathcal{R}_q^{k \times N} \times \mathcal{R}_q^k$ as input. Then it invokes algorithm $\mathcal{A}$. Specifically, $\mathcal{A}$ sends a vector $m \in \{0,1\}^{Nl}$ to $\mathcal{B}$. $\mathcal{B}$ samples an index $\sigma \in [N], v \leftarrow D_{\mathcal{R}^N, \beta}, r \leftarrow D_{\mathcal{R}^k, r}, e_1 \leftarrow D_{\mathcal{R}^N, r}, e_2 \leftarrow D_{\mathcal{R}, \tau r}, s \xleftarrow{\$} \{0,1\}^d$ and computes $b'^\top := (e^\sigma)^\top A + 2b^\top$. Next, $\mathcal{B}$ forwards

$(\boldsymbol{m}, \boldsymbol{v}, \boldsymbol{r}, \boldsymbol{e_1}, e_2, s, A, \boldsymbol{b'})$ to $\mathcal{A}$. Subsequently, $\mathcal{A}$ guesses whether the received inputs belong to experiment **REAL** or experiment **IDEAL** in Fig. 1. Ultimately, $\mathcal{B}$ outputs $\mathcal{A}$'s guess as the answer to the HNF-MLWE challenge it is trying to solve.

If $(A^\top, \boldsymbol{b})$ is uniform in $(\mathcal{R}_q^{k \times N}, \mathcal{R}_q^k)$, then $\boldsymbol{b'}$ is uniform in $\mathcal{R}_q^k$. Thus $(\boldsymbol{m},$ $\boldsymbol{v}, \boldsymbol{r}, \boldsymbol{e_1}, e_2, s, A, \boldsymbol{b'})$ can be viewed as the output of $\{(S_S(1^\lambda, (m_1, ..., m_N), \bot))\}_{\sigma, (m_1, ..., m_N), \lambda}$, i.e., they belong to experiment **IDEAL** in Fig. 1.

If $(A^\top, \boldsymbol{b})$ is a HNF-MLWE instance, $(\boldsymbol{m}, \boldsymbol{v}, \boldsymbol{r}, \boldsymbol{e_1}, e_2, s, A, \boldsymbol{b'})$ can be treated as real sender's view, i.e., they belong to experiment **REAL** in Fig. 1.

Experiment $\mathbf{REAL}_{\mathrm{Adv}}(1^\lambda)$	Experiment $\mathbf{IDEAL}_{\mathrm{Adv}, S_S}(1^\lambda)$
$\sigma \leftarrow [N]$. Let $\boldsymbol{e}^{\vec{\sigma}}$ be an N-dimensional unit vector over ring $\mathcal{R}$, with its σ − th element being 1;	$S_S \leftarrow 1^\lambda$;
$\mathrm{Adv} \rightarrow (m_1, ..., m_N) \in \mathcal{R}_p^N$;	$\mathrm{Adv} \rightarrow (m_1, ..., m_N) \in \mathcal{R}_p^N$;
$\boldsymbol{s'} \leftarrow D_{\mathcal{R}^N, \alpha q}, \boldsymbol{e} \leftarrow D_{\mathcal{R}^k, \alpha q}, A \xleftarrow{\$} \mathcal{R}_q^{N \times k}, \boldsymbol{v} \leftarrow D_{\mathcal{R}^N, \beta}, \boldsymbol{r} \leftarrow D_{\mathcal{R}^k, r}, \boldsymbol{e_1} \leftarrow D_{\mathcal{R}^N, r},$	$S_S(1^\lambda, (m_1, ..., m_N), \bot)$ does the following:
$e_2 \leftarrow D_{\mathcal{R}, \tau r}, s \xleftarrow{\$} \{0,1\}^d,$ computes $\boldsymbol{b}^\top := (2\boldsymbol{s'} + \boldsymbol{e})^\top A + 2\boldsymbol{e}^\top \in \mathcal{R}_q^k;$	$A' \xleftarrow{\$} \mathcal{R}_q^{N \times k}, \boldsymbol{b'} \xleftarrow{\$} \mathcal{R}_q^k, \boldsymbol{v} \leftarrow D_{\mathcal{R}^N, \beta}, \boldsymbol{r} \leftarrow D_{\mathcal{R}^k, r},$
$\mathrm{Adv} \leftarrow (m_1, ..., m_N), A, \boldsymbol{b}, \boldsymbol{v}, \boldsymbol{r}, \boldsymbol{e_1}, e_2, s$	$\boldsymbol{e_1} \leftarrow D_{\mathcal{R}^N, r}, e_2 \leftarrow D_{\mathcal{R}, \tau r}, s \xleftarrow{\$} \{0,1\}^d$
$\mathrm{Adv} \rightarrow b' \in \{0,1\};$ Output b'	$\mathrm{Adv} \leftarrow (m_1, ..., m_N), \boldsymbol{b'}, \boldsymbol{v}, \boldsymbol{r}, \boldsymbol{e_1}, e_2, s$
	$\mathrm{Adv} \rightarrow b' \in \{0,1\};$ Output b'

Fig. 1. Sender's simulated-based experiment

Next, we describe the sender's simulated-based experiment in Fig. 2.

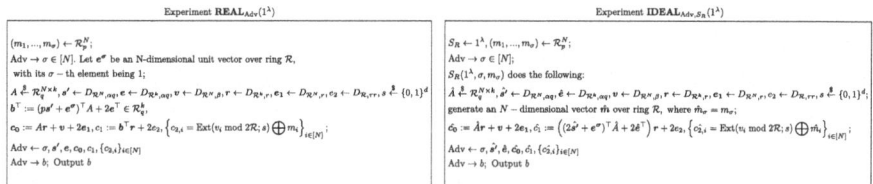

Fig. 2. Receiver's simulated-based experiment

Lemma 5 (Statistical Sender Security). $\{(S_R(1^\lambda, \sigma, m_\sigma))\}_{\sigma, (m_1, ..., m_N), \lambda}$ and $\mathbf{view}_R^{\mathcal{OT}}(\sigma, (m_1, ..., m_N), \lambda)$ *are statistically indistinguishable if the standard deviations* $\tau = 4t\sqrt{N+k} \cdot \alpha q \cdot \omega(\sqrt{\log(\lambda)}), r > 2\sqrt{\frac{t}{t-1}}n \cdot$ $q^{N/(N+k)+2/(nN+nk)}, \beta^2(1 - \frac{\beta^2}{r^2}\sqrt{\frac{2}{N+k}} \cdot \frac{\beta}{\alpha q}) > 4n, r > \beta,$ *where* $n \in \Omega(\lambda), N, k \leq Poly(n), t > 1$ *is a constant, and* $\mathcal{OT}$ *denotes the above protocol.*

First, we consider the following hybrid experiment.

$\mathcal{H}_0$: This is the original experiment, which asks adversary to distinguish between experiment **REAL** and experiment **IDEAL** in Fig. 2.

$\mathcal{H}_1$: This experiment is identical to $\mathcal{H}_0$ expect that in experiment **REAL**, the values $c_0 = Ar + v + 2e_1$, $c_1 = ((2s' + e^\sigma)^\top A + 2e^\top)\, r + 2e_2$ computed during the above protocol are substituted by $c_0 = y + v$, $c_1 = (2s' + e^\sigma)^\top y - 2(2s' + e^\sigma)^\top e_1 + 2e^\top r + 2e_2$, where $y \xleftarrow{\$} \mathcal{R}_q^N$. Similarly in experiment **IDEAL**.

For any adversary $\mathcal{A}$, the advantage of $\mathcal{A}$ can be rewritten as

$$\mathrm{Adv}_{\mathcal{A}} = |\Pr[b' \leftarrow \mathcal{A} \text{ in case } b,\, b \xleftarrow{\$} \{0,1\}] - \frac{1}{2}|$$

$$= |\Pr[b' = b \text{ in } \mathcal{H}_0 : b' \leftarrow \mathcal{A}] - \frac{1}{2}|$$

$$\leq |\Pr[b' = b \text{ in } \mathcal{H}_0 : b' \leftarrow \mathcal{A}] - \Pr[b' = b \text{ in } \mathcal{H}_1 : b' \leftarrow \mathcal{A}]|$$

$$+ |\Pr[b' = b \text{ in } \mathcal{H}_1 : b' \leftarrow \mathcal{A}] - \frac{1}{2}|.$$

In $\mathcal{H}_1$, since the extractor Ext is statistically secure, it is sufficient to prove that the following conditional distributions satisfy:

$$(v_i \bmod 2\mathcal{R} | y + v, 2\langle s', v\rangle + v_\sigma + 2\langle s, e_1\rangle - 2\langle e, r\rangle - 2e_2) \underset{s}{\approx} U_{\mathcal{R}_2}, \forall i \in [N]\backslash\{\sigma\},$$

i.e.

$$(v_i \bmod 2\mathcal{R} | 2\langle s', v\rangle + v_\sigma + 2\langle s, e_1\rangle - 2\langle e, r\rangle - 2e_2) \underset{s}{\approx} U_{\mathcal{R}_2}, \forall i \in [N]\backslash\{\sigma\}.$$

This indicates that for any $i \in [N]\backslash\{\sigma\}$, the minimal entropy of $v_i \bmod 2\mathcal{R}$ is n. Therefore, $\mathrm{Ext}(v_i \bmod 2\mathcal{R}; s)$ is statistically uniformly random, and consequently, $c_{2,i}$ is statistically uniformly random. Then we can conclude that $\Pr[b' = b \text{ in } \mathcal{H}_1 : b' \leftarrow \mathcal{A}] = \frac{1}{2}$. We prove this in Lemma 8 later.

To prove $\mathcal{H}_0 \underset{s}{\approx} \mathcal{H}_1$, it suffices to prove that $Ar + 2e_1$ is uniformly random under the given leakage $\langle 2s', v\rangle + \langle 2s, e_1\rangle - \langle 2e, r\rangle + v_\sigma - 2e_2$. Before proving, we first display the following lemmas.

Lemma 6 (Regularity Lemma [20]). *Let $\mathcal{R}$ be the ring of integers in the m-th cyclotomic field K of degree n, and $q \geq 2$ an integer. For positive integers $k_1, k_2 \leq Poly(n)$, let $A = [I_{k_1} | \overline{A}] \in \mathcal{R}_q^{k_1 \times (k_1 + k_2)}$, where $I_{k_1} \in \mathcal{R}_q^{k_1 \times k_1}$ is the identity matrix and $\overline{A} \in \mathcal{R}_q^{k_1 \times k_2}$ is uniformly random. Then for all $r > 2n$*

$$\mathbb{E}[\rho_{1/r}(\Lambda^\perp(A)^\vee)] \leq 1 + 2(r/n)^{-n(k_1+k_2)} q^{k_1 n + 2} + 2^{-\Omega(n)},$$

where $\Lambda^\perp(A)^\vee = \{z \in \mathcal{R}^{k_1 + k_2} : Az = 0 \bmod q\mathcal{R}\}$.
In particular, if $r > 2n \cdot q^{k_1/(k_1+k_2)+2/(nk_1+nk_2)}$ then $\mathbb{E}[\rho_{1/r}(\Lambda^\perp(A)^\vee)] \leq 1 + 2^{-\Omega(n)}$, and so by Markov's inequality, $\eta_{2^{-\Omega(n)}}(\Lambda^\perp(A)) \leq r$ except with probability at most $2^{-\Omega(n)}$.

Corollary 2. *Let $\mathcal{R}, n, q, k_1, k_2$ be as in Lemma 6. Assume that $A = [pI_{k_1} | \overline{A}] \in \mathcal{R}_q^{k_1 \times (k_1 + k_2)}$, where p is a prime, $q >> p$, and $\overline{A} \in \mathcal{R}_q^{k_1 \times k_2}$ is uniformly random. Then, with probability $1 - 2^{-\Omega(n)}$ over the choice of $\overline{A}$, the distribution of $A\boldsymbol{x} \in \mathcal{R}_q^{k_1}$ where each coordinate of $\boldsymbol{x} \in \mathcal{R}_q^{k_1 + k_2}$ is chosen from a discrete Gaussian distribution with covariance matrix Σ such that $\sqrt{\Sigma} > 2n \cdot q^{k_1/(k_1 + k_2) + 2/(nk_1 + nk_2)}$ over $\mathcal{R}$, satisfies that the probability of each of the q^{nk_1} possible outcomes is in the interval $[1 \pm 2^{-\Omega(n)}]q^{-nk_1}$, i.e. $\boldsymbol{SD}\left(A\boldsymbol{x}, U(\mathcal{R}_q^{k_1})\right) \in 2^{-\Omega(n)}$.*

Proof. Notice that $\Lambda^{\perp}(A) = \Lambda^{\perp}(A')$ where $A' = p^{-1}A \in \mathcal{R}_q^{k_1 \times (k_1 + k_2)}$, and A' and the matrix in Lemma 6 are identically distributed. Hence, $\eta_{2^{-\Omega(n)}}(\Lambda^{\perp}(A)) < 2n \cdot q^{k_1/(k_1 + k_2) + 2/(nk_1 + nk_2)}$ except with probability at most $2^{-\Omega(n)}$. This indicates that $\sqrt{\Sigma} > \eta_{2^{-\Omega(n)}}(\Lambda^{\perp}(A))$.

On the other hand, consider the probability

$$\Pr[A\boldsymbol{x} = \boldsymbol{c} \in \mathcal{R}_q^{k_1}, \boldsymbol{x} \leftarrow D_{\mathcal{R}^{k_1 + k_2}, \sqrt{\Sigma}}] = \Pr[\boldsymbol{x} = \boldsymbol{x_0} \bmod \Lambda^{\perp}(A), \boldsymbol{x} \leftarrow D_{\mathcal{R}^{k_1 + k_2}, \sqrt{\Sigma}}]$$

where $\boldsymbol{x_0}$ can be viewed as a particular solution such that $A\boldsymbol{x_0} = \boldsymbol{c} \bmod q\mathcal{R}$. Because $\sqrt{\Sigma} > \eta_{2^{-\Omega(n)}}(\Lambda^{\perp}(A))$, the probability

$$\Pr[A\boldsymbol{x} = \boldsymbol{c} \in \mathcal{R}_q^{k_1}, \boldsymbol{x} \leftarrow D_{\mathcal{R}^{k_1 + k_2}, \sqrt{\Sigma}}] \in [1 \pm 2^{-\Omega}] \cdot \frac{\det(\mathcal{R}^{k_1 + k_2})}{\det(\Lambda^{\perp}(A))} = [1 \pm 2^{-\Omega}] \cdot q^{-nk_1}.$$

This is followed from Lemma 1.

Back to the leakage scenario where the adversary can know the value of $\langle 2\boldsymbol{s}', \boldsymbol{v} \rangle + \langle 2\boldsymbol{s}, \boldsymbol{e_1} \rangle - \langle 2\boldsymbol{e}, \boldsymbol{r} \rangle + v_{\sigma} - 2e_2$ yielded from executing our protocol. Although our goal is to analyze the distribution of $A\boldsymbol{r} + 2\boldsymbol{e_1} = [2I_N | A]\left(\begin{smallmatrix} \boldsymbol{e_1} \\ \boldsymbol{r} \end{smallmatrix}\right)$ conditioned on $\langle 2\boldsymbol{s}', \boldsymbol{v} \rangle + \langle 2\boldsymbol{s}, \boldsymbol{e_1} \rangle - \langle 2\boldsymbol{e}, \boldsymbol{r} \rangle + v_{\sigma} - 2e_2$ where $\boldsymbol{v}, \boldsymbol{e_1}, \boldsymbol{r}, e_2$ are random variables, the following lemma shows that this conditional distribution of $\left(\begin{smallmatrix} \boldsymbol{e_1} \\ \boldsymbol{r} \end{smallmatrix}\right)$ is still a Gaussian and implies that we can directly use the Regularity Lemma to derive the distribution of $A\boldsymbol{r} + 2\boldsymbol{e_1}$.

Lemma 7. *Let random variable $\boldsymbol{X} := (x_1, ..., x_{N+k})^{\top}$ denote $\left(\begin{smallmatrix} \boldsymbol{e_1} \\ \boldsymbol{r} \end{smallmatrix}\right)$ where each element of them is sampled from the Gaussian distribution with parameter r. Let random variable Y denote $\langle \boldsymbol{s}', 2\boldsymbol{v} \rangle + \langle \boldsymbol{s}, 2\boldsymbol{e_1} \rangle - \langle \boldsymbol{e}, 2\boldsymbol{r} \rangle + v_{\sigma} - 2e_2$, a linear combination of random variable $(\boldsymbol{X}, \boldsymbol{v}, e_2)$. Then we have the the distribution of $\boldsymbol{X}$ conditioned on Y is also a Gaussian that is not centered at $\boldsymbol{0}$ and with a covariance matrix $\Sigma > 0$. Furthermore, if $\tau = 4t\sqrt{N+k} \cdot \alpha q \cdot \omega(\sqrt{\log(\lambda)})$ where $t > 1$ is a constant, then the minimum eigenvalue of Σ, $\lambda_{\min} > r^2(1 - 1/t)$.*

Proof. First we can rewrite $Y = \langle \boldsymbol{s}'^{\top} | \boldsymbol{s}^{\top} | - \boldsymbol{e}^{\top}, 2\boldsymbol{v}^{\top} | 2\boldsymbol{X}^{\top} \rangle - Z$, where $\boldsymbol{X}$ is defined as above, and $Z := v_{\sigma} + 2e_2$, where $v_{\sigma} \leftarrow D_{\mathcal{R}, \beta}, e_2 \leftarrow D_{\mathcal{R}, \tau r}$.

Recall that sampling Gaussian over $\mathcal{R}^l$ is equivalent to sampling Gaussian over $h \circ \sigma(\mathcal{R}^l) \subset \mathbb{R}^{nl}$. Hence, consider that

$$h \circ \sigma((\boldsymbol{s}'^{\top} | \boldsymbol{s}^{\top} | - \boldsymbol{e}^{\top}, \boldsymbol{v}^{\top} | \boldsymbol{X})) = U \begin{pmatrix} \sigma_1(s_1') & & \cdots & \sigma_1(-e_k) \\ & \ddots & & & \ddots & \\ & & \sigma_n(s_1') & \cdots & & \sigma_n(-e_k) \end{pmatrix} \begin{pmatrix} \sigma(v_1) \\ \vdots \\ \sigma(x_{N+k}) \end{pmatrix}.$$

where $U = \frac{1}{\sqrt{2}} \begin{pmatrix} 1 & & & & & \\ & \ddots & & & & \\ & & \frac{1}{\sqrt{-1}} & -\frac{1}{\sqrt{-1}} & & \\ & & & & \ddots & \\ & \sqrt{-1} & & & & -\sqrt{-1} \end{pmatrix} \in \mathbb{C}^{n \times n}.$

Let $(v_{1,1}, ..., v_{N,n}, x_{1,1}, ..., x_{N+k,n})^{\top}$ denotes $h \circ \sigma(\boldsymbol{v}^{\top}|\boldsymbol{X}^{\top}) \in \mathbb{R}^{(2N+k)n}$, then

$$\sigma(\boldsymbol{v}^{\top}|\boldsymbol{X}^{\top}) = \begin{pmatrix} U^* & & & \\ & U^* & & \\ & & \ddots & \\ & & & U^* \end{pmatrix} \begin{pmatrix} v_{1,1} \\ \vdots \\ v_{1,n} \\ \vdots \\ x_{N+k,1} \\ \vdots \\ x_{N+k,n} \end{pmatrix}$$

where U^* is the conjugate transpose of U and also the inverse of U.

Denote $h \circ \sigma(\boldsymbol{s}') =: (s'_{1,1}, ..., s'_{1,n}, ..., s'_{N,1}, ...s'_{N,n})^{\top}$. $(h \circ \sigma(-\boldsymbol{s}), h \circ \sigma(-\boldsymbol{e}), h \circ \sigma(-Z)$ follow this pattern.) Then $h \circ \sigma(\langle \boldsymbol{s'}^{\top}|\boldsymbol{s}^{\top}\rangle - \boldsymbol{e}^{\top}, 2\boldsymbol{v}^{\top}|2\boldsymbol{X}^{\top}\rangle - Z)$ equals

$$\frac{2}{\sqrt{2}} \cdot \text{Diag} \left[\begin{pmatrix} s'_{1,1} & & & & -s'_{1,n} \\ & \ddots & & & \\ & & s'_{1,\frac{n}{2}} & -s'_{1,\frac{n}{2}+1} & \\ & & s'_{1,\frac{n}{2}+1} & s'_{1,\frac{n}{2}} & \\ & & & & \ddots \\ s'_{1,n} & & & & s'_{1,1} \end{pmatrix} , ..., \begin{pmatrix} e_{k,1} & & & & -e_{k,n} \\ & \ddots & & & \\ & & e_{k,\frac{n}{2}} & -e_{k,\frac{n}{2}+1} & \\ & & e_{k,\frac{n}{2}+1} & e_{k,\frac{n}{2}} & \\ & & & & \ddots \\ e_{k,n} & & & & e_{k,1} \end{pmatrix} \right] \begin{pmatrix} v_{1,1} \\ \vdots \\ v_{1,n} \\ \vdots \\ x_{N+k,1} \\ \vdots \\ x_{N+k,n} \end{pmatrix}$$

$$+ \begin{pmatrix} z_1 \\ \vdots \\ z_n \end{pmatrix} = \frac{1}{\sqrt{2}} \begin{pmatrix} 2(s'_{1,1}v_{1,1} - s'_{1,n}v_{1,n} + ... + e_{k,1}x_{N+k,1} - e_{k,n}x_{N+k,n}) + \sqrt{2}z_1 \\ \vdots \\ 2(s'_{1,\frac{n}{2}}v_{1,\frac{n}{2}} - s'_{1,\frac{n}{2}+1}v_{1,\frac{n}{2}+1} + ... + e_{k,\frac{n}{2}}x_{N+k,\frac{n}{2}} - e_{k,\frac{n}{2}+1}x_{N+k,\frac{n}{2}+1}) + \sqrt{2}z_{\frac{n}{2}} \\ 2(s'_{1,\frac{n}{2}+1}v_{1,\frac{n}{2}} + s'_{1,\frac{n}{2}}v_{1,\frac{n}{2}+1} + ... + e_{k,\frac{n}{2}+1}x_{N+k,\frac{n}{2}} + e_{k,\frac{n}{2}}x_{N+k,\frac{n}{2}+1}) + \sqrt{2}z_{\frac{n}{2}+1} \\ \vdots \\ 2(s'_{1,n}v_{1,1} + s'_{1,1}v_{1,n} + ... + e_{k,n}x_{N+k,1} + e_{k,1}x_{N+k,n}) + \sqrt{2}z_n \end{pmatrix}. \quad (1)$$

Notice that each element of the vector in Eq. 1 can be viewed as a sum of some independent Gaussians and is still a Gaussian. Moreover, it is centered at $\boldsymbol{0}$.

Observe that the joint distribution of $\boldsymbol{X}$ and Y can be written as $\begin{bmatrix} Y \\ X \end{bmatrix} = \begin{bmatrix} 2s^{\top}|-2e^{\top} & -1 & s'^{\top} \\ I_{N+k} & 0 & 0 \end{bmatrix} \begin{bmatrix} X \\ Z \\ v \end{bmatrix}$. Since $\boldsymbol{X}$ and $Z\|\boldsymbol{v}^{\top}$ are Gaussian random variables, this joint distribution, a linear transformation of $\begin{bmatrix} X \\ Z \\ v \end{bmatrix}$, is also a Gaussian. Then we can exploit the property of the conditional Gaussian distribution: If the joint distribution of $\begin{bmatrix} Y \\ X \end{bmatrix}$ is a Gaussian, then the distribution of $\boldsymbol{X}$ conditioned on Y is also a Gaussian where the center is equal to $\boldsymbol{\mu_1} + \Sigma_{12}\Sigma_{22}^{-1}(Y - \mu_2)$, and the covariance matrix $\Sigma = \Sigma_{11} - \Sigma_{12}\Sigma_{22}^{-1}\Sigma_{21}$. Here $\boldsymbol{\mu_1}, \mu_2$ are the centers of $\boldsymbol{X}, Y$ respectively, Σ_{11}, Σ_{22} give variances and covariances for $\boldsymbol{X}, Y$ respectively, and Σ_{12} gives covariances between variables in $\boldsymbol{X}$ and Y.

According to $\boldsymbol{X}, Y$ described above, we have

$$\Sigma_{11} = \begin{bmatrix} r^2 & & & \\ & r^2 & & \\ & & \ddots & \\ & & & r^2 \end{bmatrix}, \Sigma_{22} = r^2 \cdot \text{diag}(w_1, ..., w_n),$$

$$\Sigma_{12} = \sqrt{2}r^2 \cdot \begin{bmatrix} s_{1,1} & & & & & & & s_{1,n} \\ & \ddots & & & & & & \\ & & s_{1,\frac{n}{2}} & s_{1,\frac{n}{2}+1} & & & & \\ & & -s_{1,\frac{n}{2}+1} & s_{1,\frac{n}{2}} & & & & \\ & & & & \ddots & & & \\ -s_{1,n} & & & & & & & s_{1,1} \\ \vdots & & & & \vdots & & & \vdots \\ e_{k,1} & & & & & & & e_{k,n} \\ & \ddots & & & & & & \\ & & e_{k,\frac{n}{2}} & e_{k,\frac{n}{2}+1} & & & & \\ & & -e_{k,\frac{n}{2}+1} & e_{k,\frac{n}{2}} & & & & \\ & & & & \ddots & & & \\ -e_{k,n} & & & & & & & e_{k,1} \end{bmatrix},$$

where $w_i = \sum_{j=1}^{N} 2\left(s_{j,i}^2 + s_{j,n-i+1}^2\right) + \sum_{j=1}^{k} 2\left(e_{j,i}^2 + e_{j,n-i+1}\right) + 4\tau^2 + \left[\sum_{j=1}^{N} 2\left(s_{j,i}'^2 + s_{j,n-i+1}'^2\right) + 1 + \sqrt{2}s_{\sigma,i}'\right] \cdot \frac{\beta^2}{r^2} =: w_i' + \sqrt{2}s_{\sigma,i}' \cdot \frac{\beta^2}{r^2}, \forall i = 1, ..., n.$

This can be obtained from properties that the covariance $\text{Cov}(aX + bY, Z) = a \cdot \text{Cov}(X, Z) + b \cdot \text{Cov}(Y, Z)$, and $\text{Cov}(X, Y) = 0$ if X, Y are independent. Since all elements of $\boldsymbol{X}$ are sampled from the Gaussian with the same parameter r, the element in the ith row and $(n - i + 1)$-th column of Σ_{22} is offset, for all $i = 1, ..., n$.

Because the minimum eigenvalue of Σ is equal to $r^2 - \lambda_{\max}(\Sigma_{12}\Sigma_{22}^{-1}\Sigma_{21})$, we now analyze the upper bound of $\lambda_{\max}(\Sigma_{12}\Sigma_{22}^{-1}\Sigma_{21})$. For convenience, instead of presenting matrix $\Sigma_{12}\Sigma_{22}^{-1}\Sigma_{21}$, we present a matrix $(\Sigma_{12}\Sigma_{22}^{-1}\Sigma_{21})'$ as follows, where each element of $(\Sigma_{12}\Sigma_{22}^{-1}\Sigma_{21})'$ is greater in absolute value than the corresponding element of $\Sigma_{12}\Sigma_{22}^{-1}\Sigma_{21}$ in absolute value.

$(\Sigma_{12}\Sigma_{22}^{-1}\Sigma_{21})'$ equals

$$4r^2 \cdot \begin{vmatrix} \frac{s_{1,1}^2 + s_{1,n}^2}{w_1'} & \frac{-s_{1,1}s_{1,n} + s_{1,1}s_{1,n}}{w_1'} & \cdots & \frac{s_{1,1}e_{k,1} + s_{1,n}e_{k,n}}{w_1'} & \frac{-s_{1,1}e_{k,n} + s_{1,n}e_{k,1}}{w_1'} \\ \frac{-s_{1,1}s_{1,n} + s_{1,n}s_{1,1}}{w_n'} & \frac{s_{1,n}^2 + s_{1,1}^2}{w_n'} & \cdots & \frac{-s_{1,n}e_{k,1} + s_{1,1}e_{k,n}}{w_n'} & \frac{s_{1,n}e_{k,n} + s_{1,1}e_{k,1}}{w_n'} \\ \vdots & & & & \vdots \\ \frac{e_{k,1}s_{1,1} + e_{k,n}s_{1,n}}{w_1'} & \frac{-e_{k,1}s_{1,n} + e_{k,n}s_{1,1}}{w_1'} & \cdots & \frac{e_{k,1}^2 + e_{k,n}^2}{w_1'} & \frac{-e_{k,1}e_{k,n} + e_{k,n}e_{k,1}}{w_1'} \\ \frac{-s_{1,1}e_{k,n} + s_{1,n}e_{k,1}}{w_n'} & \frac{s_{1,n}e_{k,n} + s_{1,1}e_{k,1}}{w_n'} & \cdots & \frac{-e_{k,n}e_{k,1} + e_{k,1}e_{k,n}}{w_n'} & \frac{e_{k,n}^2 + e_{k,1}^2}{w_n'} \end{vmatrix}$$

In fact, the spectral radius of $\Sigma_{12}\Sigma_{22}^{-1}\Sigma_{21} =: \rho(\Sigma_{12}\Sigma_{22}^{-1}\Sigma_{21})$ equals its maximum eigenvalue. Using the property of the spectrm radius, we have $\rho(\Sigma_{12}\Sigma_{22}^{-1}\Sigma_{21}) \le \|\Sigma_{12}\Sigma_{22}^{-1}\Sigma_{21}\|_\infty$, where $\|\cdot\|_\infty$ denotes the matrix norm such that for any n-dimensional matrix A, $\|A\|_\infty = \max_i \sum_{j=1}^{n}|a_{ij}| \le \max_i \sqrt{T}\sqrt{\sum_{j=1}^{n} a_{ij}^2}$, T is the number of elements in this row that are not equal to 0. Then we have

$$\frac{\|\Sigma_{12}\Sigma_{22}^{-1}\Sigma_{21}\|_\infty}{r^2}$$

$$\leq \sqrt{16(N+k)} \cdot \max_{\substack{i\in[N]+1\\ j\in[k]+1\\ m\in[n]+1}} \left\{ \sqrt{\frac{2(s_{i,m}^2+s_{i,n-m+1}^2)(w_m'-4\tau^2)}{w_m'^2}}, \sqrt{\frac{2(e_{j,m}^2+e_{j,n-m+1}^2)(w_m'-4\tau^2)}{w_m'^2}} \right\}$$

$$< \sqrt{16(N+k)} \cdot \max_{\substack{i\in[N]+1\\ j\in[k]+1\\ m\in[n]+1}} \left\{ \sqrt{\frac{2(s_{i,m}^2+s_{i,n-m+1}^2)}{w_m'}}, \sqrt{\frac{2(e_{j,m}^2+e_{j,n-m+1}^2)}{w_m'}} \right\},$$

$$< \sqrt{8(N+k)} \cdot \max_{\substack{i\in[N]+1\\ j\in[k]+1\\ m\in[n]+1}} \left\{ \sqrt{\frac{1}{2\tau^2/(s_{i,m}^2+s_{i,n-m+1}^2)}}, \sqrt{\frac{1}{2\tau^2/(e_{j,m}^2+e_{j,n-m+1}^2)}} \right\}$$

where $w_i' = \sum_{j=1}^N 2\left(s_{j,i}^2+s_{j,n-i+1}^2\right) + \sum_{j=1}^k 2\left(e_{j,i}^2+e_{j,n-i+1}\right) + 4\tau^2 + \left[\sum_{j=1}^N 2\left(s_{j,i}'^2+s_{j,n-i+1}'^2\right)+1\right]\cdot\frac{\beta^2}{r^2} = w_{n-i+1}'$.

Notice that

$$\max_{\substack{i\in[N]+1\\ j\in[k]+1\\ m\in[n]+1}} \left\{ s_{i,m}^2+s_{i,n-m+1}^2, e_{j,m}^2+e_{j,n-m+1}^2 \right\} \leq \max_{\substack{i\in[N]+1\\ j\in[k]+1\\ m\in[n]+1}} \left\{ 2(s_{i,m}+s_{i,n-m+1})^2, 2(e_{j,m}+e_{j,n-m+1})^2 \right\}$$

and is at most $4(\alpha q)^2 \omega(\log(\lambda))$, since for all $i\in[N]+1, j\in[k]+1, m\in[n]+1$, $s_{i,m}+s_{i,n-m+1}, e_{j,m}+e_{j,n-m+1}$ are 0-subgaussian with parameter $\sqrt{2}\alpha q$.

Because $\tau = 4t\sqrt{N+k}\cdot\alpha q\cdot\omega(\sqrt{\log(\lambda)})$, we have $\lambda_{\max}(\Sigma_{12}\Sigma_{22}^{-1}\Sigma_{21}) < \frac{r^2}{t}$. Then $\lambda_{\min}(\Sigma) > r^2(1-1/t)$.

Lemma 8. *The conditional distribution $(v_i \bmod 2\mathcal{R}|\boldsymbol{y} + \boldsymbol{v}, 2\langle\boldsymbol{s}',\boldsymbol{v}\rangle + v_\sigma + 2\langle\boldsymbol{s},\boldsymbol{e_1}\rangle - 2\langle\boldsymbol{e},\boldsymbol{r}\rangle - 2e_2)$ is statistically uniform on $\mathcal{R}_2$ for all $i\in[N]\backslash\{\sigma\}$, where $\boldsymbol{v} \leftarrow D_{\mathcal{R}^N,\beta}$, $\boldsymbol{r} \leftarrow D_{\mathcal{R}^k,r}$, $\boldsymbol{e_1} \leftarrow D_{\mathcal{R}^N,r}$, $e_2 \leftarrow D_{\mathcal{R},\tau r}$.*

Proof. Analogously, the conditional distribution $(v_i|2\langle\boldsymbol{s}',\boldsymbol{v}\rangle + v_\sigma + 2\langle\boldsymbol{s},\boldsymbol{e_1}\rangle - 2\langle\boldsymbol{e},\boldsymbol{r}\rangle - 2e_2) =: W$ is also a Gaussian, where we denote its covariance matrix as Σ. Due to space limitations, we omit the calculation process and present the estimate directly: $\lambda_{\min}(\Sigma) > \beta^2(1 - \frac{\beta^2}{r^2}\sqrt{\frac{2}{N+k}}\cdot\frac{\beta}{\alpha q})$. On the other hand, we denote that $\Lambda := \mathcal{R}, \Lambda' := 2\mathcal{R}$. By using the inequality $\rho_{s^{-1}}(\Lambda'^\vee) \leq \max(1, \mathcal{N}(\Lambda'^\vee)^{-1}s^{-n})(1+2^{-2n}) \leq (\frac{2n}{s})^n$ in [20], we can estimate that $\eta_\epsilon(\Lambda') \leq 4n$. If $\beta^2(1 - \frac{\beta^2}{r^2}\sqrt{\frac{2}{N+k}}\cdot\frac{\beta}{\alpha q}) > 4n$, then $\sqrt{\Sigma} > \eta_\epsilon(\Lambda')$, as stated by Corollary 1. This implies that $(v_i \bmod 2\mathcal{R}|2\langle\boldsymbol{s}',\boldsymbol{v}\rangle + v_\sigma + 2\langle\boldsymbol{s},\boldsymbol{e_1}\rangle - 2\langle\boldsymbol{e},\boldsymbol{r}\rangle - 2e_2) \overset{s}{\approx} U(\mathcal{R} \bmod 2\mathcal{R})$ for all $i\in[N]\backslash\{\sigma\}$.

Next, based on Lemma 7, 8, we can give the proof of Lemma 5.

Proof (Lemma 5). Let $\boldsymbol{W}$ be random variables over $\mathcal{R}^{N+k}$ following the same distribution as the conditional distribution of $\boldsymbol{X}$ given knowledge of Y, where $\boldsymbol{X}, Y$ are as described above.

If $\tau = 4t\sqrt{N+k}\cdot\alpha q\cdot\omega(\sqrt{\log(\lambda)})$, then it can deduced from the above analysis that $\boldsymbol{W}$ is a Gaussian with a covariance matrix Σ where its minimum eigenvalue is greater than $r^2(1 - 1/t)$. Because $r > 2\sqrt{\frac{t}{t-1}} n \cdot q^{N/(N+k)+2/(nN+nk)}$, we have that $\sqrt{\lambda_{\min}(\Sigma)} > 2n \cdot q^{N/(N+k)+2/(nN+nk)}$. From Corollary 1, we know that $\sqrt{\Sigma} > 2n \cdot q^{N/(N+k)+2/(nN+nk)}$. Using the Regularity Lemma and Corollary 2 we have that $[2I_N|A]W \approx_s U(\mathcal{R}_q^N)$, which means that $[2I_N|A]\binom{e}{r}$ given knowledge of $2\langle s', v \rangle + 2\langle s, e_1 \rangle - 2\langle e, r \rangle + v_\sigma - 2e_2$ is within statistical distance $2^{-\Omega(n)}$ of the uniform distribution over $\mathcal{R}_q^N$.

Then two hybrid experiments $\mathcal{H}_0$ and $\mathcal{H}_1$ are statistically indistinguishable. Furthermore, Lemma 8 implies that in Experiment $\mathcal{H}_1$, $\text{Adv}_\mathcal{A} = \frac{1}{2} + \text{negl}(n)$. Hence, for any adversary $\mathcal{A}$, its total advantage $\text{Adv}_\mathcal{A} = \frac{1}{2} + \text{negl}(n)$.

4   Conclusion

In this paper, we construct a two-round, statistical sender-private (in the semi-honest model) and 1-out-of-N OT from the MLWE assumption with sub-exponential noise-ratio. A simple and novel structure allows us to directly achieve 1-out-of-N OTs without the need for converting 1-out-of-2 OTs to 1-out-of-N OTs. We make the sender hide N messages in a packed way, thereby making our protocol more efficient. Furthermore, this item, which hides N messages, is statistically indistinguishable from uniform and guarantees sender's security against computationally unbounded and honest-but-curious adversaries.

Acknowledgement. We thank anonymous reviewers for their helpful comments very much. This work was supported in part by National Key Research and Development Project (No. 2020YFA0712300), National Natural Science Foundation of China (No. 62372445, 62032009, 12226006) and Innovation Program for Quantum Science and Technology under Grant 2021ZD0302902.

References

1. Beaver, D.: Precomputing oblivious transfer. In: Coppersmith, D. (ed.) CRYPTO 1995. LNCS, vol. 963, pp. 97–109. Springer, Heidelberg (1995). https://doi.org/10.1007/3-540-44750-4_8
2. Beaver, D.: Correlated pseudorandomness and the complexity of private computations. In: Proceedings of the Twenty-Eighth Annual ACM Symposium on Theory of Computing. STOC '96, pp. 479–488, Association for Computing Machinery, New York, NY, USA (1996). https://doi.org/10.1145/237814.237996
3. Bisheh-Niasar, M., Azarderakhsh, R., Mozaffari-Kermani, M.: High-speed NTT-based polynomial multiplication accelerator for post-quantum cryptography. In: 2021 IEEE 28th Symposium on Computer Arithmetic (ARITH), pp. 94–101 (2021). https://doi.org/10.1109/ARITH51176.2021.00028
4. Blum, M.: Coin flipping by telephone a protocol for solving impossible problems. SIGACT News **15**(1), 23–27 (1983). https://doi.org/10.1145/1008908.1008911
5. Boyle, E., et al.: Efficient two-round OT extension and silent non-interactive secure computation. In: Proceedings of the 2019 ACM SIGSAC Conference on Computer and Communications Security. CCS '19, pp. 291–308. Association for Computing Machinery, New York, NY, USA (2019). https://doi.org/10.1145/3319535.3354255

6. Boyle, E., Couteau, G., Gilboa, N., Ishai, Y., Kohl, L., Scholl, P.: Efficient pseudo-random correlation generators: silent OT extension and more. In: Boldyreva, A., Micciancio, D. (eds.) CRYPTO 2019. LNCS, vol. 11694, pp. 489–518. Springer, Cham (2019). https://doi.org/10.1007/978-3-030-26954-8_16

7. Brakerski, Z., Döttling, N.: Two-message statistically sender-private OT from LWE. In: Beimel, A., Dziembowski, S. (eds.) TCC 2018. LNCS, vol. 11240, pp. 370–390. Springer, Cham (2018). https://doi.org/10.1007/978-3-030-03810-6_14

8. de Castro, L., Juvekar, C., Vaikuntanathan, V.: Fast vector oblivious linear evaluation from ring learning with errors. In: Proceedings of the 9th on Workshop on Encrypted Computing & Applied Homomorphic Cryptography. WAHC '21, pp. 29–41. Association for Computing Machinery, New York, NY, USA (2021). https://doi.org/10.1145/3474366.3486928

9. Costa, B., Branco, P., Goulão, M., Lemus, M., Mateus, P.: Randomized oblivious transfer for secure multiparty computation in the quantum setting. Entropy **23**(8) (2021). https://doi.org/10.3390/e23081001, https://www.mdpi.com/1099-4300/23/8/1001

10. Dodis, Y., Ostrovsky, R., Reyzin, L., Smith, A.: Fuzzy extractors: how to generate strong keys from biometrics and other noisy data. SIAM J. Comput. **38**(1), 97–139 (2008). https://doi.org/10.1137/060651380

11. Gentry, C., Peikert, C., Vaikuntanathan, V.: Trapdoors for hard lattices and new cryptographic constructions. In: Proceedings of the Fortieth Annual ACM Symposium on Theory of Computing. STOC '08, pp. 197–206. Association for Computing Machinery, New York, NY, USA (2008). https://doi.org/10.1145/1374376.1374407

12. Gertner, Y., Ishai, Y., Kushilevitz, E., Malkin, T.: Protecting data privacy in private information retrieval schemes. J. Comput. Syst. Sci. **60**(3), 592–629 (2000). https://doi.org/10.1006/jcss.1999.1689, https://www.sciencedirect.com/science/article/pii/S0022000099916896

13. Goldreich, O.: How to play any mental game or a completeness theorem for protocols with honest majority. In: STOC'87, pp. 218–229 (1987)

14. Harn, L., Lin, H.-Y.: An oblivious transfer protocol and its application for the exchange of secrets. In: Imai, H., Rivest, R.L., Matsumoto, T. (eds.) ASIACRYPT 1991. LNCS, vol. 739, pp. 312–320. Springer, Heidelberg (1993). https://doi.org/10.1007/3-540-57332-1_26

15. Ishai, Y., Kilian, J., Nissim, K., Petrank, E.: Extending oblivious transfers efficiently. In: Boneh, D. (ed.) CRYPTO 2003. LNCS, vol. 2729, pp. 145–161. Springer, Heidelberg (2003). https://doi.org/10.1007/978-3-540-45146-4_9

16. Kalai, Y.T.: Smooth projective hashing and two-message oblivious transfer. In: Cramer, R. (ed.) EUROCRYPT 2005. LNCS, vol. 3494, pp. 78–95. Springer, Heidelberg (2005). https://doi.org/10.1007/11426639_5

17. Kolesnikov, V., Kumaresan, R.: Improved OT extension for transferring short secrets. In: Canetti, R., Garay, J.A. (eds.) CRYPTO 2013. LNCS, vol. 8043, pp. 54–70. Springer, Heidelberg (2013). https://doi.org/10.1007/978-3-642-40084-1_4

18. Langlois, A., Stehlé, D.: Worst-case to average-case reductions for module lattices. Des. Codes Cryptogr. **75**, 565–599 (2014). https://api.semanticscholar.org/CorpusID:1853632

19. Liu, M., Hu, Y.: Universally composable oblivious transfer from ideal lattice. Front. Comput. Sci. **13**, 879–906 (2019)

20. Lyubashevsky, V., Peikert, C., Regev, O.: A toolkit for ring-LWE cryptography. In: Johansson, T., Nguyen, P.Q. (eds.) EUROCRYPT 2013. LNCS, vol. 7881, pp. 35–54. Springer, Heidelberg (2013). https://doi.org/10.1007/978-3-642-38348-9_3

21. Micciancio, D., Peikert, C.: Trapdoors for lattices: simpler, tighter, faster, smaller. In: Pointcheval, D., Johansson, T. (eds.) EUROCRYPT 2012. LNCS, vol. 7237, pp. 700–718. Springer, Heidelberg (2012). https://doi.org/10.1007/978-3-642-29011-4_41

22. Micciancio, D., Regev, O.: Worstcase to averagecase reductions based on gaussian measures. SIAM J. Comput. **37**(1), 267–302 (2007). https://doi.org/10.1137/S0097539705447360

23. Naor, M., Pinkas, B.: Computationally secure oblivious transfer. J. Cryptol. **18**, 1–35 (2005)

24. Orrù, M., Orsini, E., Scholl, P.: Actively secure 1-out-of-N OT extension with application to private set intersection. In: Handschuh, H. (ed.) CT-RSA 2017. LNCS, vol. 10159, pp. 381–396. Springer, Cham (2017). https://doi.org/10.1007/978-3-319-52153-4_22

25. Peikert, C., Vaikuntanathan, V., Waters, B.: A framework for efficient and composable oblivious transfer. In: Wagner, D. (ed.) CRYPTO 2008. LNCS, vol. 5157, pp. 554–571. Springer, Heidelberg (2008). https://doi.org/10.1007/978-3-540-85174-5_31

26. Quach, W.: UC-secure OT from LWE, revisited. In: Galdi, C., Kolesnikov, V. (eds.) SCN 2020. LNCS, vol. 12238, pp. 192–211. Springer, Cham (2020). https://doi.org/10.1007/978-3-030-57990-6_10

27. RABIN, M.: How to exchange secrets by oblivious transfer. Tech. Memo TR-81, Aiken Computation Laboratory, Harvard University (1981)

28. Yadav, V.K., Verma, S., Venkatesan, S.: Linkable privacy-preserving scheme for location-based services. IEEE Trans. Intell. Transp. Syst. **23**(7), 7998–8012 (2021)

29. Yao, A.C.C.: How to generate and exchange secrets. In: 27th Annual Symposium on Foundations of Computer Science (SFCS 1986), pp. 162–167. IEEE (1986)

Acceleration of Core Post-quantum Cryptography Primitive on Open-Source Silicon Platform Through Hardware/Software Co-design

Emma Urquhart[(✉)] and Frank Stajano

University of Cambridge, Cambridge, UK
eu233@cam.ac.uk, frank.stajano@cl.cam.ac.uk

Abstract. Post-Quantum Cryptography (PQC) algorithms are currently being standardised and their early implementations are not as efficient as the well-established public key cryptography (PKC) algorithms that have benefited from decades of optimisations. We report on our efforts to accelerate the Number Theoretic Transform (NTT), the most computationally expensive primitive in the Kyber (ML-KEM) and Dilithium (ML-DSA) PQC algorithms selected by NIST for standardisation. Our target platform is the OpenTitan Big Number Accelerator (OTBN), part of the first open-source silicon root-of-trust chip. We implemented the Kyber NTT in OTBN assembly, using only the existing instructions, and identified its bottlenecks. We then restructured the code to exploit parallelism and defined additional assembly instructions for the open-source co-processor that would enable execution of our vectorised implementation. Our hardware/software co-design approach yielded a significant performance improvement: NTT ran 21.1 times faster than the baseline implementation which used only OTBN's existing instructions. Our approach fully leverages the potential for parallelism and maximally exploits the existing capabilities of OTBN. Some of our optimisations are fairly general and might be successfully applied to other contexts, including accelerating other algorithms on other platforms.

Keywords: OpenTitan · Open-Source Hardware · Post-Quantum Cryptography · Number Theoretic Transform · Kyber · ML-KEM · Performance Optimisation · Hardware/Software co-design

1 Introduction

In the realm of Internet of Things (IoT) security, the ever-increasing ubiquity and connectivity of mobile devices presents challenges and opportunities. Public Key Cryptography (PKC) algorithms such as Rivest-Shamir-Adleman (RSA)

Authors' preprint of 2024-07-11. To appear in *Proc. International Conference on Cryptology and Network Security (CANS 2024), Springer LNCS.*

[13] and Elliptic Curve Cryptography (ECC) [9] are used to ensure the confidentiality and integrity of communication channels. Execution of these algorithms can be expensive on resource-constrained devices and therefore many are equipped with specialized cryptographic co-processors. In February 2024, the first commercially-available open-source silicon root of trust was released by the OpenTitan [7] consortium stewarded by lowRISC. This chip marks a significant development in secure and transparent hardware. It incorporates the OpenTitan Big Number Accelerator (OTBN), a cryptographic co-processor specifically designed for use in IoT devices [8].

The advent of quantum computing poses an impending threat to the public-key cryptosystems that are integral to the security of communications between these devices. The mathematical problems on which algorithms such as RSA and ECC rely include factorization of large integers and the discrete logarithm problem. These tasks are computationally infeasible for classical computers, but can be solved in polynomial time by a quantum adversary, as proven by Shor [15]. To mitigate this threat, Post-Quantum Cryptography (PQC) provides solutions that can be implemented on classical hardware but are capable of withstanding quantum attacks. The US National Institute for Standards and Technology (NIST) is conducting a standardization process for post-quantum cryptosystems, currently in its fourth round.

Lattice-based cryptography is emerging as a promising approach to PQC, encompassing three of the four algorithms already selected for standardisation: CRYSTALS-Kyber (ML-KEM) [3], a key encapsulation mechanism, and two digital signature algorithms, CRYSTALS-Dilithium (ML-DSA) [4] and Falcon [5]. Implementation of these algorithms, particularly on resource-constrained devices, poses practical challenges as their core operations incur significant overheads on existing platforms. Modern cryptographic co-processors such as OTBN are optimised for execution of RSA and ECC, providing large integer arithmetic capabilities. However, lattice-based PQC algorithms do not involve such operations and therefore do not benefit from the capabilities of these co-processors. OTBN is not yet specialised for PQC. We propose realistic and low-cost hardware improvements to OTBN that can be leveraged to significantly enhance the performance of PQC on this platform.

Due to the predicted prevalence of ring-based lattice schemes, we focus on a characteristic bottleneck of such schemes: polynomial multiplication. We investigate acceleration of polynomial multiplication via the number theoretic transform (NTT) in Kyber. The target platform is OTBN. The proposed instructions and software implementations leverage OTBN's existing capabilities and incorporate viable architectural extensions. Our main contributions include:

- Baseline implementation of the NTT in Kyber using the existing OTBN instruction set, replicating the C reference implementation as closely as possible.
- Detailed analysis of the bottlenecks of the baseline implementation and current limitations of OTBN in the context of efficient execution of NTT.

- Set of 8 additional assembly instructions for acceleration of NTT on OTBN and estimations of cycle cost for each instruction.
- A novel, vectorized implementation of the NTT in Kyber for OTBN, which leverages the new instructions and achieves a reduction in cycle cost from 92,074 to 4,356 cycles compared to the baseline (21.1× improvement factor).

Our approach for identifying the bottlenecks and our ideas on how to speed them up might also serve as inspiration for researchers seeking to accelerate other algorithms on other platforms. Our code is publicly available at: https://github.com/emmau678/opentitan/tree/mphil_thesis_pqc_acceleration.

2   Background

2.1   OpenTitan Big Number Accelerator

OpenTitan is the first open-source silicon root of trust (RoT) project, aimed at creating a high-quality reference for transparent and secure silicon. The first OpenTitan chips, based on the Earl Grey discrete RoT, reached commercial availability in February 2024. OTBN, a co-processor for acceleration of asymmetric cryptography, serves as a fundamental hardware security primitive. Its large data path and specialized instruction set enhance the efficiency of classical PKC algorithms. However, OTBN is not yet optimised for PQC.

OTBN features a 32-bit wide control path and a 256-bit wide data path, each containing 32 registers. Its security-centric design incorporates a reduced instruction set which comprises a base subset for control flow and a big-number subset for wide-integer arithmetic in data flow. The separation of paths reduces the risk of data leakage. OTBN supports data integrity protection and secure wipe of internal states. Cryptographic security is further enhanced by its internal random number generation mechanism which is connected to the Entropy Distribution Network. OTBN implements two dedicated memories of 4 kiB: instruction memory (IMEM) and data memory (DMEM), separated to bolster security.

2.2   The Number Theoretic Transform

Polynomial multiplication is one of the most performance-critical implementation elements of lattice-based PQC schemes such as Kyber and Dilithium. The NTT is commonly adopted for this purpose, enabling a reduction in complexity of polynomial multiplication from $O(n^2)$ to $O(n)$. It is a specialised form of the Discrete Fourier Transform, which operates on the finite field $\mathbb{Z}_q$ instead of complex numbers. The NTT operates by transforming polynomials into a domain in which multiplication is highly efficient. The multiplications are performed within the NTT domain before the results are transformed back into the normal domain using the inverse number theoretic transform (INTT). The NTT transforms polynomials from their coefficient representation to their point-value form. Multiplication of two polynomials in their point-value form is a straightforward pointwise product. Given polynomials f and g, we compute their product according to Eq. 1, where ∘ denotes multiplication within the NTT domain:

$$f \cdot g = INTT(NTT(f) \circ NTT(g)) \tag{1}$$

The operation of the NTT is given in Eq. 2. This equation describes the transformation on a polynomial g of degree n, where $g = \sum_{i=0}^{n-1} g_i X^i$ and $g_i \in \mathbb{Z}_q$. In this equation, ω represents the primitive n-th root of unity, where $\omega^n \equiv 1 \mod q$ and, for any $1 \leq k < n$, $\omega^k \not\equiv 1 \mod q$. Values of ω^{ij} are known as twiddle factors. Multiplication by these values is equivalent to evaluating the polynomial at powers of the n-th root of unity. The INTT reverses this transformation.

$$\hat{g} = \text{NTT}(g) = \sum_{i=0}^{n-1} \hat{g}_i X^i, \quad \text{with} \quad \hat{g}_i = \sum_{j=0}^{n-1} g_j \omega_n^{ij} \pmod{q}. \tag{2}$$

2.3   Profiling the Reference Kyber C Implementation

After selecting Kyber as the focus of our optimisation efforts, we conducted an analysis of the reference C implementation to inform our choice of algorithmic components to target for acceleration. Two implementations of Kyber are available within the official repository [12]: a platform-agnostic implementation and an optimised AVX2 implementation. The optimised implementation may be run on processors that support the AVX2 instruction set. AVX2 offers capabilities for signed and unsigned processing of high and low parts of packed values within SIMD registers. These processors also offer out-of-order execution, meaning that instructions can be interleaved. Our target platform is OTBN, which has a restricted instruction set, does not support advanced extensions like AVX2 and does not support out-of-order execution. Therefore, the platform-independent implementation was the most suitable reference point for our work. Given that OTBN is not yet equipped with a compiler, the reference C code cannot be directly excuted on the platform. We obtained the profiling results by executing the reference code on a regular laptop (Core i7 processor). We assume an approximate equivalence in terms of distribution of computational effort within the Kyber algorithm between the reference C code and a full OTBN implementation.

Three executables are generated for each parameter set (512, 768 and 1024) by compiling the test program; `test_kyber$ALG`, `test_kex$ALG` and `test_vectors$ALG`, where `$ALG` identifies the parameter set. According to the repository documentation, `test_kyber$ALG` runs 1,000 tests which encompass key generation, encapsulation and decapsulation. We used `test_kyber$ALG` for profiling. The parameter sets correspond to the different security levels of Kyber. We obtained results for all three security levels. The algorithm remains the same for each security level; all that changes are parameter values. We generated a flat profile for each parameter set, i.e. a table that captured the total amount of time spent in the execution of each function. A visualisation of the percentage of execution time spent within each function is presented in Fig. 1.

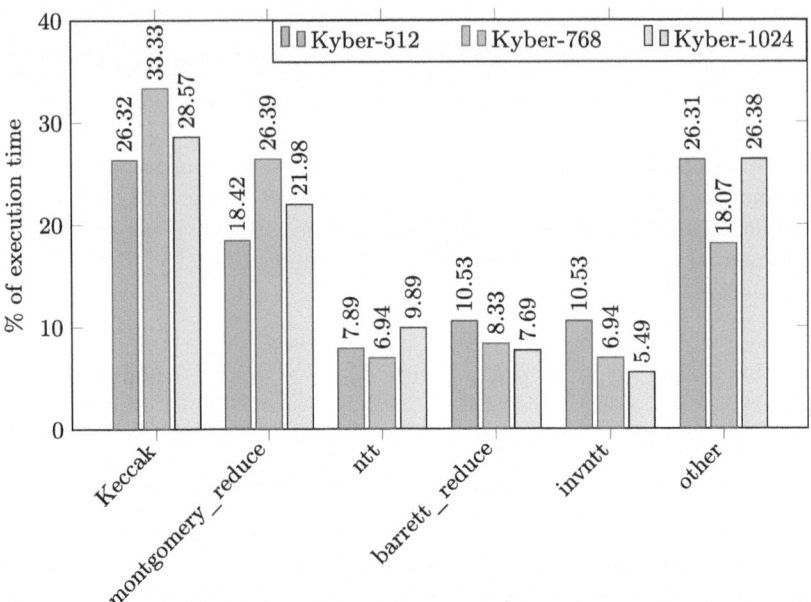

Fig. 1. Profiling results for reference Kyber implementations

From the data in Fig. 1, we firstly note that the distributions across the parameter sets are similar, which aligns with expectations given that the code is the same. The Keccak function is the most computationally intensive component of the algorithm. However, the Keccak core is most conducive to acceleration in pure hardware, as it was designed as a hardware-oriented implementation of the SHA-3 hashing algorithm [2]. The purpose of our research is to investigate acceleration of Kyber on OTBN through hardware/software co-design. Therefore, while a custom Keccak accelerator could likely be integrated as a hardware extension, it is not the ideal candidate for optimisation via instruction set extensions which do not aim to drastically alter the hardware architecture.

The four next most expensive functions are `montgomery_reduce`, `barrett_reduce`, `ntt`, and `invntt`. It is important to note that the `montgomery_reduce` function is called from both `ntt` and `invntt`, while the `barrett_reduce` function is called from the `invntt` function. Algorithmically, the `ntt` and `invntt` functions are closely (inversely) related and hence share a number of similarities. As a result, it appeared likely that it would be possible to design certain optimisations to target both functions. Because `montgomery_reduce` is a component of the `ntt` function, it was also targeted in our optimisation strategies. We implemented and accelerated the NTT using acceleration techniques and new instructions which we believe would contribute similar performance improvements to an implementation of the INTT.

3 Methodology

3.1 Development Environment and Testing Infrastructure

During our development work, OTBN was still being taped out as an engineering sample. A Python simulator for OTBN is available as part of the OpenTitan repository and this was used for development. The simulator is cycle-accurate for all existing OTBN instructions, which execute in either one or two CPU cycles. In the case of designing instruction set extensions, it was necessary to consider the required hardware modifications to estimate cycle counts. The instructions we propose are designed to maximally leverage OTBN's existing hardware components and require only minor modifications. This not only facilitates an easily implemented and low-cost solution that enhances performance, but ensures that cycle count estimates are aligned with the ground-truth performance of existing instructions. A C compiler is not yet available for OTBN, so all code was written in OTBN assembly.

Correctness of implementations was validated by extending the testing infrastructure within the simulator. The repository contains a simple testing framework for sample instructions. An input assembly file and a corresponding file containing expected output values is provided for each test case. We integrated a Python script that dynamically creates input and output files for customisable input ranges and the corresponding outputs generated by function prototypes. We created template files containing placeholders indicating the values to be dynamically overwritten for each input/output pair and used them to automatically create the files for processing. For simple subroutines and instruction tests, we wrote the function prototypes in Python. For increasingly complex implementations, we used `ctypes` to ensure absolute alignment with the reference C implementation of Kyber, as Python's type handling would lead to divergence of results. Once the full implementation of `ntt()` was complete, we implemented a black-box test to run NIST vector tests. We captured the input/output pairs to the `ntt` function by separately running the Kyber reference implementation and storing the state of the input/return array before and after invocation of `ntt()`.

3.2 Identifying the Bottlenecks in the Baseline Implementation

We first developed a baseline implementation of the NTT by porting the code in the Kyber reference implementation as directly as possible to OTBN assembly, using only the existing instructions. This process established the current performance of OTBN in execution of these functions and provided baseline performance benchmarks against which to compare optimisation efforts.

It should be noted that the Kyber reference implementation has not been optimised for any platform. However, the reduced instruction set of OTBN constrains the potential for optimisation without implementing instruction set extensions, so the baseline performance provides a reasonable estimate of its capabilities. Analysis of the baseline implementation on OTBN granted insights

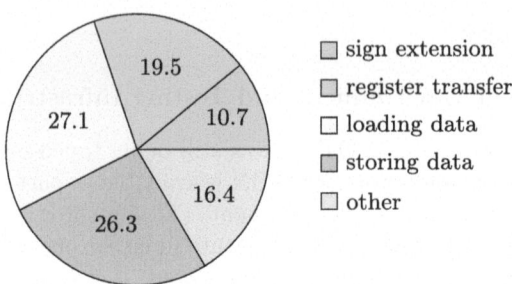

Fig. 2. % execution time spent on functionality types in NTT baseline

into performance bottlenecks and particularly inefficient operations, hence serving to motivate optimisations and inform the design of instruction set extensions. In Fig. 2, we present our analysis of the baseline implementation of NTT on OTBN. Performance bottlenecks are analysed in terms of percentage of overall cycle count.

The baseline implementation of NTT required 91,939 CPU cycles to execute. During the implementation process, the most significant performance impediment we noticed was the restriction to scalar computations on the wide data registers (WDRs) of 256 bits. These registers were designed to perform arithmetic on large integers; however, in the case of ntt, the integers involved in computation, including intermediate results, do not exceed 32 bits and hence the large register capacity is not utilised. The computational effort spent on these operations is not being exploited to its full potential and the same effects could be achieved by operating on much smaller units. We noted that vectorisation of operations could be maximised to enable full use of WDRs.

Although the majority of instructions in both subsets execute in a single clock cycle, in the context of the Big Number subset, additional operations are required to perform certain computations. OTBN only supports unsigned arithmetic and the NTT function operates on signed values. Two's complement is used to represent negative numbers. Although the values involved in multiplication operations are 16 bits in width, it was necessary to sign-extend these numbers to 64 bits before using BN.MULQACC, as it operates on 64-bit operands. This had to be done manually if this data had been transferred from GPRs. In the interest of maintaining a constant-time implementation, we adopted the following approach. The sign bit is isolated through a right shift of 15 bits and multiplied by a 64-bit mask with the upper 48 bits set. The result is then XORed with the original 16-bit value, resulting in sign-extension to 64 bits. This process costs 4 cycles for each of two operands, before a multiplication can be performed. Sign extension required 10.7% of the total cycle count of the ntt baseline (2). In order to enhance the efficiency of sign extension, we reduced the operand size in our vectorised implementation. For example, if lanes were 16 bits in length, this would align with the operand width and therefore sign extension beyond this width would not be necessary.

Another notable bottleneck was the requirement to transfer data between the register types to perform different operations. Certain instructions, such as multiplication, are only available in the Big Number subset. Conversely, other operations, such as left shift, are only available in the base subset. Given that the Big Number subset is designated for data flow, transferring data back and forth between WDRs and GPRs during the main computation is both inefficient and not compliant with standard practice. However, at certain points in the implementation this is necessary, for example, loading array values at fine granularity from data addresses. A resulting objective of our design of new instructions was to minimise the requirement for data transfer between register types. Transferring of data between register types cost 19.5% of the cycle count of the ntt baseline (2).

The array r, which is processed by the NTT function, consists of 256 16-bit elements which are stored contiguously in memory. Each element is processed individually and reads from memory to GPRs can only be performed on 32-bit-aligned boundaries. Therefore, data can only be loaded in fixed 32-bit blocks. This complicated the element loading and storage procedures. In order to load and operate on r[j], we floor-divide the index j by 2 by performing a right shift by 1 bit, in order to identify the index of the 32-bit block containing r[j]. We then shift the result right by 2 to compute the byte offset from the base address of r from which to load the block. We determine whether index j is even or odd by computing j AND 1. In the case of an even index, we isolate r[j] via an AND of the loaded block with a 16-bit mask. In the case of an odd index, we shift the loaded block right by 16 bits. However, this approach contains a conditional statement, which may lead to violation of constant-time properties. In the case of development of the baseline and optimised implementations, we avoided the use of conditional statements in order to retain constant-time properties.

Therefore, we require a single execution path for loads and stores of odd- and even-indexed values. To load and isolate an individual array value (of either odd or even index) in a GPR, we follow the process outlined in Fig. 3. We begin by loading a data block containing 2 contiguous array elements following the previous procedure, one of which is at the required index j. We compute j AND 1 and its inverse. We shift both values left by 4 so the non-zero remainder represents 16. We then shift the loaded block right by the former value ((j AND 1) << 16), shift left by the same value and finally shift right by the latter value ((NOT (j AND 1)) << 16). This method isolates the required element in the least significant position in the case of both odd and even indices, enabling subsequent computations. For storing the result, we only overwrite one element of r, leaving the other 16 bits of the 32-bit block unchanged. The opposite 16-bit value in the block is isolated in a similar way to r[j]. Before the final block is stored to memory, the two 16-bit components are shifted back to their original position and combined with an XOR. We noted the evidently large computational overhead introduced by replicating the elementwise loading procedure of the reference implementation. In the ntt baseline (2), loading of values into GPRs (including subsequent manipulation of loaded values) cost 27.1% of the

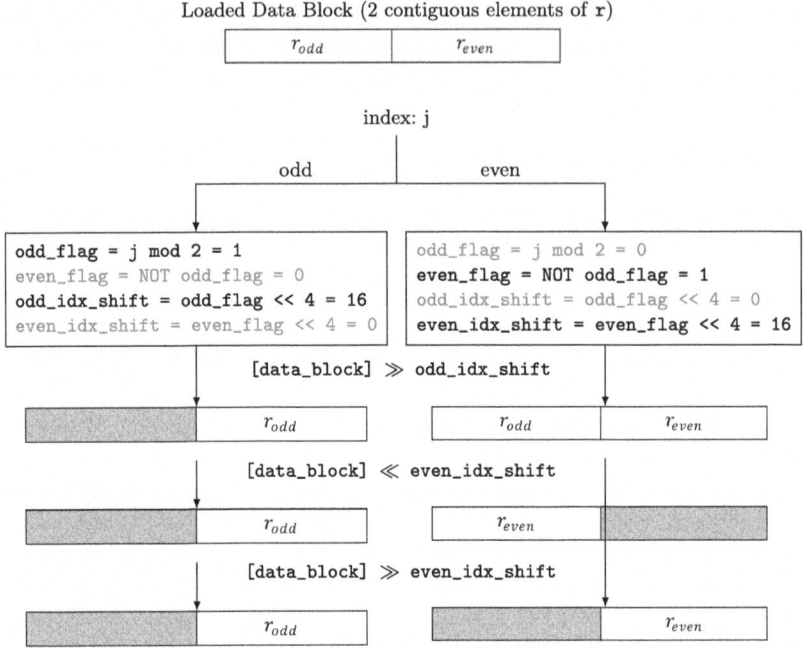

Fig. 3. Loading and isolating data elements in GPRs

total cycles. Meanwhile, constructing the resulting data blocks and storing them to memory cost 26.3% of the total cycles. We aimed to reduce the number of load and store operations, eliminate manipulation of loaded values and facilitate parallel computation on loaded values directly.

4   Vectorised Implementation Design

We designed the vectorised implementation of the `ntt()` function, outlined in pseudocode in Algorithm 1, with the aim of maximising parallelism, minimising load/store overhead, minimising data transfer between register types and more efficiently handling signed multiplication. We designed an implementation that maximises the vectorisation potential of OTBN and enables full usage of the capacity of the WDRs. To implement it, we designed new instruction set extensions that complement the existing capabilites of OTBN and incorporate some moderate hardware modifications, which could realistically be introduced to the platform. The optimised implementation loads and stores 16 polynomial coefficients at a time, significantly reducing the load/store overhead of the baseline. Array elements are operated on in-place using vectorised instructions, which enables us to avoid manipulation of loaded values. Explicit sign extension is no longer required due to the narrower lane widths.

Algorithm 1: Vectorized NTT Implementation

---

1 Masks[$mask\_len8$] ← [0 × 00000000] * 4 + [0xFFFFFFFF] * 4
2 Masks[$mask\_len4$] ← ([0 × 00000000] * 2 + [0xFFFFFFFF] * 2) * 2
3 Masks[$mask\_len2$] ← [0 × 00000000FFFFFFFF] * 4
4 **Function** mont_reduce_vec(a):
5   **for** i ← 0 **to** 7 **do**
6   t[i] ← a[i] × QINV
7   t[i] ← t[i] × KYBER_Q
8   t[i] ← a[i] - t[i]
9   t[i] ← t[i] ≫ 16
10   **return** t

11 **Function** fqmulvec(vec_a, vec_b):
12   **return** mont_reduce_vec($a[i]$&0xFFFF × $b[i]$&0xFFFF for i ← 0 **to** 7)

13 **Function** ntt_vec($r[256]$):
14   **for** len in {128, 64, 32, 16} **do**
15   **for** $start$ ← 0 **to** 255 **by** $2×len$ **do**
16   zetavec ← broadcast zeta[k++]
17   **for** i ← 0 **to** 15 **do**
18   idx ← i×16 + start
19   Vec[rj_vec] ← r[idx ... idx+15]
20   Vec[$rjlen\_vec$] ← r[idx+len ... idx+len+15]
21   Vec[$rjlen\_vec\_low$] ← rjlen_vec AND [0 × 0000FFFF] * 8
22   Vec[$rjlen\_vec\_upp$] ← rjlen_vec ≫ 16
23   t_low ← fqmulvec($zetavec, rjlen\_vec\_low$)
24   t_upp ← fqmulvec($zetavec, rjlen\_vec\_upp$)
25   t ← t_low XOR t_upp
26   rjlen_vec_new ← rj_vec - t
27   rj_vec_new ← rj_vec + t
28   store rjlen_vec_new, rj_vec_new to r[idx+len], r[idx]

29   **for** len in {8, 4, 2} **do**
30   **for** i ← 0 **to** 15 **do**
31   num_zetas ← 8 / len
32   zetavec ← 0
33   zeta_mask ← (1 ≪ (len ≪ 4)) - 1
34   **for** z ← 0 **to** num_zetas - 1 **do**
35   tmp ← broadcast zeta[k++]
36   tmp ← tmp AND zeta_mask
37   zetavec ← zetavec XOR tmp
38   zeta_mask ← zeta_mask ≪ (len ≪ 5)
39   idx ← i × 16
40   Vec[$rjvec$] ← r[idx ... idx+15]
41   Vec[$nextvec$] ← r[idx+16 ... idx+31]
42   Vec[$rjlen\_vec$] ← (nextvec ⊕ rjvec) ≫ (len ≪ 4)
43   Vec[$rjlen\_vec\_low$] ← rjlen_vec AND [0 × 0000FFFF] * 8
44   Vec[$rjlen\_vec\_upp$] ← rjlen_vec ≫ 16
45   t_low ← fqmulvec($zetavec, rjlen\_vec\_low$)
46   t_upp ← fqmulvec($zetavec, rjlen\_vec\_upp$)
47   t ← t_low XOR t_upp
48   Vec[$rjlen\_vec\_new$] ← rjvec - t
49   rjlen_vec_new ← rjlen_vec_new AND Masks[$mask\_len\{len\}$]
50   rjlen_vec_new ← rjlen_vec_new ≪ (len ≪ 4)
51   Vec[$rjvec\_new$] ← rjvec + t
52   rjvec_new ← rjvec_new AND Masks[$mask\_len\{len\}$]
53   res ← rjvec_new XOR rjlen_vec_new
54   store res to r[idx]

The values of `zeta` are broadcasted at 32-bit intervals across WDRs before entering the `fqmul` computation. Because the broadcast instruction replicates the value in a GPR across all lanes of a WDR, we must load `zeta` from memory directly into a GPR. We aimed to minimise the overhead of loading and isolating elements. We achieved this by unrolling two iterations of each loop which required a new value of `zeta` to be assigned. This enabled us to load two values at once, isolate them and retain the second one in a separate GPR instead of performing a second load. In the baseline implementation, loading and isolating two values of `zeta` cost 26 cycles, whereas this approach costs only 6 cycles.

The implementation is split into two parts: the first deals with values of `len` which are multiples of 16. This means that the number of elements between `r[j]` and `r[j+len]` can be stored in a distinct number of WDRs. Therefore the new values of `r[j]` and `r[j+len]` can be separately computed and written to memory in batches of 16 elements. Within the `fqmul` function, intermediate values can occupy up to 32 bits. At this point, the lane widths are effectively expanded from 16 to 32 bits. This process is illustrated in Fig. 4, where shaded sections of mask registers represent all 0 s and non-shaded sections all 1 s. Note that shifts applied are vectorised on 32-bit lanes. The lower and upper 16-bit elements in each 32-bit lane of the wide data register are extracted into two separate registers. We isolate the elements of even index by pre-loading a 256-bit mask with every even-indexed 16-bit element set and performing an `AND` operation between this register and the loaded values. Then, to isolate the values at odd indices, a vectorised right shift by 16 bits of each 32-bit lane is used to place them in the lower positions. The `fqmul` operations can then proceed in the same way for both vectors. The results of the two `fqmul` computations are then combined by reversing the shift and performing an XOR between the two registers.

The second part of the implementation deals with values of `len` which are factors of 16. The number of elements between `r[j]` and `r[j+len]` is less than the capacity of a WDR. As data elements are loaded contiguously, computations of the new values of `r[j]` and `r[j+len]` are combined within registers. Iteration levels are merged to maximise computational capacity. This part of the implementation has one less nested loop than the first, merging the loading of zetas into the innermost loop. Then `8/len` zetas are loaded into a single register, occupying equal proportions. Each iteration reads 16 consecutive elements as a vector of `r[j]`. Since loads to wide data registers are only permitted at 256-bit boundaries, OTBN's 512-bit barrel shifter, which produces a 256-bit output, is used to load `r[j+len]` at the required level of finer granularity. The subsequent block of 16 elements is then loaded, concatenated with the previous and shifted right by `len` elements, returning the low 256 bits as the corresponding vector of `r[j+len]`. This construction of the vectors of zetas, `r[j]` and `r[j+len]` allows the rest of the computation to proceed in the same way as the first part of the implementation. Once `fqmul` has been computed, however, the computations of the new values of `r[j]` and `r[j+len]` must be combined within the same resulting register. This is achieved using bitmasks and shifting to interleave the calculated values at offsets of length `len` within the register. Due to the direct operations on data in WDRs throughout the computation, the overhead of transferring data between register types in NTT is reduced to zero from a cycle count of 17,918 in the baseline (1).

Throughout the vectorised computation, elements are fully packed into the WDRs. The combination of the computation of new values of r[j] and r[j+len] within the same registers ensures that this potential remains maximised even for values of len that are less than the element capacity of a WDR. The expansion of lane widths from 16 to 32 bits is implemented for the smallest possible number of instructions. Once 32-bit precision is no longer required for intermediate computations, the implementation transitions back to the initial mode of operation on 16 elements in parallel. Minimisation of load/store overhead is achieved, as the optimised implementation loads and stores 16 elements at once. Additional pre-processing of loaded array values is eliminated as all loaded values are operated on directly in the positions within the register at which they were loaded. As shown in Table 1, the number of cycles spent on the loading of values and manipulation of loaded values was reduced from 24,947 to 1,196 cycles for NTT (1). Similarly, the cycles required for constructing and storing data blocks to memory was reduced from 24,192 to 592 for NTT. Loading of zeta values into GPRs before broadcasting is optimised by isolating and storing the two values that are loaded at once from memory. The multiplication process has been streamlined to eliminate the requirement for explicit sign extension in software. In the baseline implementation of NTT, 9,854 cycles were spent on sign extension, however this costs no additional cycles in the optimised implementations.

Table 1. Comparison of Cycle Count Distribution Between Implementations

Implementation	Sign Extension	Register transfer	Load	Store	Other	Total
ntt_baseline	9854	17918	24947	24192	15028	91939
ntt_optimised	0	0	1196	592	2568	4356

5 Instruction Set Extensions for OTBN

The new instruction set extensions are outlined in Table 2. This section describes the reasoning used to estimate cycle counts, including details of how existing hardware components are leveraged and hardware modifications required.

BN.LSHI: operates in the same way as the existing BN.RSHI instruction for OTBN which executes in one cycle, but performs a left shift instead of right.

BN.MULVEC: Existing 64-bit multiplication units would need to be reconfigured to operate independently on 32-bit segments and truncate results to 32 bits. Due to the shorter combinatorial path for 32-bit lanes, the critical path should execute within the single cycle required for current 64-bit operations.

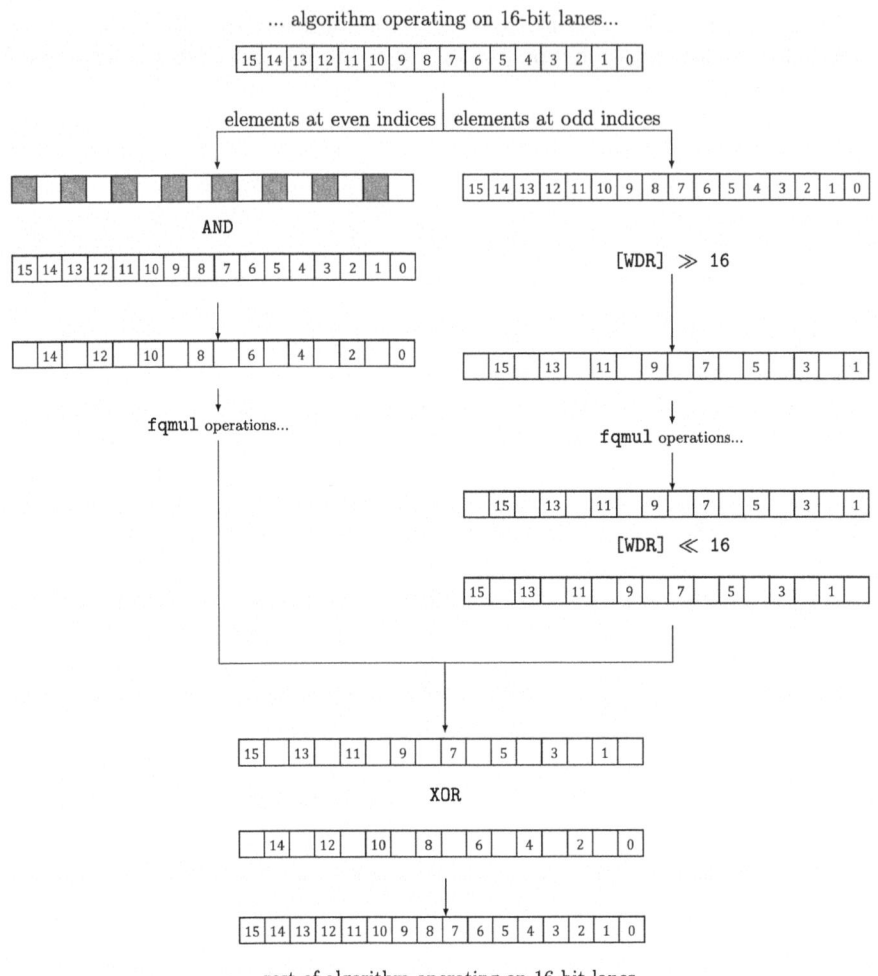

Fig. 4. Expansion of lane width from 16 to 32 bits

BN.MULVEC32: The sign bit of each 16-bit input should be isolated (using a simple shift) and replicated across bits 17–31 of each lane using a series of multiplexers. The same logic as in BN.MULVEC can then be followed. Given that the existing BN.MULQACC can multiply and add to an accumulator within a single cycle, it is reasonable to assume single-cycle latency in this case.

BN.ADDVEC and BN.SUBVEC: OTBN features a 256-bit adder, which add/subtract in one cycle. Therefore, it should be possible to perform vectorized addition/subtraction on a 256-bit register within a single cycle.

BN.RSHIFTVEC and BN.LSHIFTVEC: OTBN features a 512-bit barrel shifter that produces a 256-bit output within one cycle. This is more complex

Table 2. Instruction Set Extensions

Instruction	Description	Latency (Cycles)
BN.LSHI	Concatenates contents of 2 WDRs and shifts right by an immediate. Truncates to 256 bits.	1
BN.MULVEC	Vectorized signed multiplication on the low 16 bits of each 32-bit lane.	1
BN.MULVEC32	Vectorized multiplication on each 32-bit lane. Truncates to 32 bits.	1
BN.ADDVEC	Vectorized addition on each 16-bit lane.	1
BN.SUBVEC	Vectorized subtraction on each 16-bit lane.	1
BN.RSHIFTVEC	Vectorized right shift on each 32-bit lane.	1
BN.LSHIFTVEC	Vectorized left shift on each 32-bit lane.	1
BN.BROADCAST	Replicate value in selected GPR in each 32-bit lane of WDR.	1

than a 256-bit barrel shifter, which would be sufficient for this instruction. Vectorized shifts would be performed across 256-bit registers, in parallel lanes of 32 bits. The combinatorial path of each of these shifts would be much shorter than that of a full 256-bit shift as computations within each lane can be computed independently. Therefore it would execute in one cycle.

BN.BROADCAST: OTBN features a GPR selector multiplexer. The GPR value should be replicated 8 times across the destination WDR, which would require a simple fanout of wires. The existing WDR input multiplexer would need to be extended by one input to accept data from GPRs. The critical path requirements are relatively simple in the context of the existing instruction set, so this instruction should execute in one cycle.

6   Evaluation and Results

We extensively validated the correctness of our implementations using the gold-standard input/output value pairs generated by NIST test vectors. We captured the expected input and output value pairs upon entry to and exit from the NTT function during execution of the official reference implementation on a regular laptop. We used the `test_vectors$ALG` executable upon compiling the reference C code on Linux. This generates 10,000 sets of test vectors which contain keys, ciphertexts and shared secrets. The $ALG variable is used to identify the parameter set, which represents the security level in Kyber. We gathered values for all 3 parameter sets and for each set, tested our implementations in a black-box test setting, comparing expected and generated output values.

Our optimised implementation of NTT demonstrates a 21.1× speed-up over our OTBN baseline. It should be noted that the reference implementation that we translated to OTBN assembly was not optimised for any platform. We did not invest efforts into manual optimisation of the baseline OTBN implementation using the existing instruction set. This may be an avenue for further research, which may more precisely quantify the performance benefits added solely by our new instructions and the optimisations they enable. However, it is worth noting that the limited nature of the existing OTBN instruction set constrains optimisation potential without introducing new instructions.

Given that we implemented our baseline ourselves[1], we sought an additional benchmark to ensure an objective comparison. The most similar platform to OTBN on which we could execute the reference implementation directly was the RISC-V Ibex core. Our optimised OTBN implementation uses 10.7× fewer cycles.

To estimate the performance improvement for the entire Kyber algorithm, we profiled the reference implementation on a regular (Core i7) laptop. As a full implementation of Kyber was not available in OTBN assembly, we made the assumption that the distribution of computational effort within Kyber would be approximately equal across both platforms. Approximately 32% of execution time was spent in the ntt() and montgomery_reduce() functions. If our optimisations speed up these functions by 21.1×, their contribution will reduce to $32\%/21.1 = 1.5\%$ and the overall runtime will be dominated by the remaining non-accelerated 68%. Thus the overall speed-up for Kyber would be 1.43×, obtained as $T/T' = 100\%/(1.5 + 68)\% = 1.43$.

The cycle counts spent in the execution of each implementation are presented in Table 3. The performance improvement factors achieved by the optimised implementations over the baseline implementations are shown in Table 4. Because the new vectorised implementation required a complete redesign of the algorithm, incremental performance measurements would not have led to meaningful results. Therefore, only the final results are reported for implementations that had been fully functionally verified.

The montgomery_reduce() function is also invoked by the INTT, so our approach would need to be extended to encompass this function to fully exploit this acceleration. This would also lead to greater performance improvements in the overall algorithmic context.

---

[1] We had to manually translate the Kyber reference from C to OTBN assembly because a C compiler was not yet available for this new platform.

Table 3. Comparison of Implementation Cycle Counts

Implementation	Cycle Count
otbn_ntt_baseline	91939
ibex_ntt_baseline	46497
otbn_ntt_optimised	4356

Table 4. Performance Improvements over Baseline Implementation

Implementation	OTBN Baseline	Ibex Baseline
OTBN Optimised NTT	21.1x	10.7x

7 Related Work

Previous research has explored acceleration methods for lattice-based PQC in three categories: pure software, custom hardware and hardware/software co-design.

Software approaches leverage features of modern instruction sets such as fixed-point arithmetic in Armv8-A Neon (Becker et al. [1]) and blend/shuffle instructions in Intel-AVX2 (Seiler [14]). For more limited resource-constrained settings, there is increasing interest in hardware and co-design approaches to acceleration.

A custom polynomial multiplier using bitwise modular reduction is presented by Yaman et al. [16] as an embedded hardware accelerator. In other work, Yaman et al. [11] incorporate a combination of inter- and intra-module pipelining optimizations into a custom hardware module.

Hardware-software co-designs have proposed instruction set extensions for the acceleration of the NTT, with a strong emphasis on extensions to the RISC-V target architecture. Among these, Fritzmann et al. [6] embedded tightly-coupled hardware accelerators into a RISC-V processing pipeline. Nannipieri et al. [10] presented instruction set extensions based on a post-quantum arithmetic logical unit for acceleration of Kyber and Dilithium on RISC-V.

In contrast, our work tightly aligns with the architecture of OTBN and is designed to propose feasible extensions that could be incorporated without the requirement for custom hardware components.

8 Limitations

As mentioned, the OTBN chip was still being taped out during our development and therefore we could only measure performance through a cycle-accurate simulator. Other potentially useful measurements such as memory and power consumption were not reported by the simulator but it will be interesting to measure them on the physical chip once samples are available. It is possible that performance differences between the simulation and physical deployment may be observed. In addition, certain hardware-specific implementation challenges may arise during physical hardware development, which may not have been fully reflected in the simulated implementation. However, the simulator provided various advantages such as access to an accurate model of the entire OTBN block while the physical chip did not exist yet. It facilitated low-cost and efficient experimentation for early development. The flexibility afforded by the simulator facilitated relatively fast testing of different implementation strategies and enabled us to validate the functionality of our instructions and implementations without access to the physical chip.

9   Conclusions and Future Work

We documented and demonstrated how we achieved a substantial speed-up for the Number Theoretic Transform (an important primitive for lattice-based PQC algorithms including ML-KEM Kyber and ML-DSA Dilithium) by recasting the implementation in vectorized form and incorporating minor architectural modifications to our target processor to enable vectorized processing. Our instruction set extensions allow the programmer to make full use of OTBN's wide data path.

We have open-sourced our own contributions and made them publicly available at https://github.com/emmau678/opentitan/tree/mphil_thesis_pqc_acceleration.

Future work might investigate the general applicability of our techniques to other cryptographic contexts. Minor modifications to our implementation would enable straightforward translation to the INTT in Kyber and the (I)NTT in Dilithium, with the potential to serve as a foundation for optimisation of other PQC functions on modern cryptographic co-processors.

Acknowledgements. We are grateful to Robert Mullins and particularly Andreas Kurth at lowRISC C.I.C. for helping to define the project, offering access to relevant resources and supporting the implementation efforts of the first author.

References

1. Becker, H., Hwang, V., Kannwischer, M.J., Yang, B.-Y., Yang, S.-Y.: Neon NTT: faster Dilithium, Kyber, and Saber on Cortex-A72 and Apple M1. IACR Trans. Cryptographic Hardware Embedded Syst. **2022**(1), 221–244 (2021). https://doi.org/10.46586/tches.v2022.i1.221-244. URL https://eprint.iacr.org/2021/986
2. Bertoni, G., Daemen, J., Peeters, M., Van Assche, G.: Keccak. In: Johansson, T., Nguyen, P.Q. (eds.) EUROCRYPT 2013. LNCS, vol. 7881, pp. 313–314. Springer, Heidelberg (2013). https://doi.org/10.1007/978-3-642-38348-9_19
3. Bos, J., et al.: CRYSTALS - Kyber: a CCA-secure module-lattice-based KEM. In: 2018 IEEE European Symposium on Security and Privacy (EuroS&P), pp. 353–367. IEEE (2018). https://doi.org/10.1109/EuroSP.2018.00032, https://eprint.iacr.org/2017/634.pdf

4. Ducas, L., et al.: CRYSTALS-Dilithium: a lattice-based digital signature scheme. IACR Trans. Cryptographic Hardware Embedded Syst. **2018**(1), 238–268 (2018). https://doi.org/10.13154/tches.v2018.i1.238-268, https://eprint.iacr.org/2017/633.pdf

5. Fouque, P.-A., et al.: Falcon: fast-fourier lattice-based compact signatures over NTRU (2018). https://www.di.ens.fr/~prest/Publications/falcon.pdf. Submission to the NIST's post-quantum cryptography standardization process

6. Fritzmann, T., Sigl, G., Sepúlveda, J.: RISQ-V: tightly coupled RISC-V accelerators for post-quantum cryptography. IACR Trans. Cryptographic Hardware Embedded Syst. **2020**(4), 239–280 (2020). https://doi.org/10.13154/tches.v2020.i4.239-280

7. lowRISC. OpenTitan (2024). https://opentitan.org/

8. lowRISC. OTBN - OpenTitan Documentation (2024). https://opentitan.org/book/hw/ip/otbn/

9. Miller, V.S.: Use of elliptic curves in cryptography. In: Williams, H.C. (ed.) CRYPTO 1985. LNCS, vol. 218, pp. 417–426. Springer, Heidelberg (1986). https://doi.org/10.1007/3-540-39799-X_31

10. Nannipieri, P., Di Matteo, S., Zulberti, L., Albicocchi, F., Saponara, S., Fanucci, L.: A RISC-V post quantum cryptography instruction set extension for number theoretic transform to speed-up CRYSTALS algorithms. IEEE Access **9**, 150798–150808 (2021). https://doi.org/10.1109/ACCESS.2021.3126208

11. Ni, Z., Khalid, A., e Shahwar Kundi, D., O'Neill, M., Liu, W.: HPKA: a high-performance CRYSTALS-kyber accelerator exploring efficient pipelining. IEEE Trans. Comput. **72**(12), 3340–3353 (2023). ISSN 1557-9956. https://doi.org/10.1109/TC.2023.3296899, https://eprint.iacr.org/2022/1093

12. PQ-CRYSTALS. Kyber. GitHub (2022). https://github.com/pq-crystals/kyber

13. Rivest, R.L., Shamir, A., Adleman, L.: A method for obtaining digital signatures and public-key cryptosystems. Commun. ACM **21**(2), 120–126 (1978). ISSN 0001-0782. https://doi.org/10.1145/359340.359342

14. Seiler, G.: Faster AVX2 optimized NTT multiplication for Ring-LWE lattice cryptography. IACR Cryptology ePrint Archive (2018). http://eprint.iacr.org/2018/039

15. Shor,P.W.: Polynomial-time algorithms for prime factorization and discrete logarithms on a quantum computer. SIAM J. Comput. **26**(5), 1484-1509 (1997). ISSN 0097-5397. https://doi.org/10.1137/S0097539795293172

16. Yaman, F., Mert, A.C., Öztürk,E., Savaş, E.: A hardware accelerator for polynomial multiplication operation of CRYSTALS-KYBER PQC scheme. In: 2021 Design, Automation & Test in Europe Conference & Exhibition (DATE), pp. 1020–1025. IEEE (2021). https://doi.org/10.23919/DATE51398.2021.9474139, https://eprint.iacr.org/2021/485

Anonymity and Privacy

Taming Delegations in Anonymous Signatures: k-Times Anonymity for Proxy and Sanitizable Signature

Xavier Bultel[1] and Charles Olivier-Anclin[1,2,3(✉)]

[1] LIFO, Université d'Orléans, INSA Centre Val de Loire, Inria, Bourges, France
charlesolivier@outlook.fr
[2] Université Clermont Auvergne, LIMOS, CNRS, Clermont-Ferrand, France
[3] be ys Pay, Paris, France

Abstract. Fully traceable k-times anonymity is a security property concerning anonymous signatures: if a user produces more than k anonymous signatures, its identity is disclosed and all its previous signatures can be identified. In this paper, we show how this property can be achieved for delegation-supported signature schemes, especially proxy signatures, where the signer allows a delegate to sign on its behalf, and sanitizable signatures, where a signer allows a delegate to modify certain parts of the signed messages. In both cases, we formalize the primitive, give a suitable security model, provide a scheme and then prove its security under the DDH assumption. The size of the keys/signatures is logarithmic in k in our two schemes, making them suitable for practical applications, even for large k.

1 Introduction

Proxy signature [26], which enables the signer to delegate the ability to sign messages on its behalf to a delegate, is a standard cryptographic primitive that has attracted a great deal of interest in recent decades. In some contexts, it is preferable to hide the delegate's identity from the signature verifier. Such a signature is called an *anonymous proxy signature* [19]. A trivial way of achieving this property is to give the delegate the signing key directly, however, this technique allows the delegate to impersonate the signer without any constraint, which is clearly not desirable. The signer therefore needs a way of tracing its delegates if one of them abuses their power. This leads to two inherent issues: the signer must be active to manage the trace, and must have access to the signatures.

The concept of traceable k-times anonymity offers an alternative way to delegate tracing. Signature schemes following this paradigm allow users to create k signatures anonymously. If they exceed this limit, a verifier can then publicly link two signatures and trace the identity of the signer. This property has been defined for *ring signatures* [20], *group signatures* [2] and *anonymous authentication* [27]. Moreover, a k-times signature is said to be *fully traceable* when the verifier can retrieve all the signatures generated by the signer which has exceeded

M. Kohlweiss et al. (Eds.): CANS 2024, LNCS 14905, pp. 165–186, 2025.
https://doi.org/10.1007/978-981-97-8013-6_8

the k limit *a posteriori*. To the best of our knowledge, this more powerful property has only been defined for ring signatures [7].

However, k-times anonymity has never been applied directly to proxy signatures, even though they seem naturally suited to this property. This would enable a verifier, which has access to all signatures, to publicly trace dishonest proxies on its own, while preserving the anonymity of honest proxies, without the intervention of the signer. In this paper, we close this gap by modeling and instantiating the first fully traceable k-times anonymous proxy signature.

On the other hand, *sanitizable signatures* [1] are conceptually close to proxy signatures: in this primitive, the delegate (called the sanitizer) can no longer produce signatures by itself, but can modify certain parts of a signed message. When considering a setting where the sanitizer must remain anonymous, the same problems arise as with proxy signatures. Applying a similar approach, we propose the first fully traceable k-times anonymous sanitizable signatures.

Contributions and Technical Overview. We give a formal definition, a security model, and an efficient scheme (in term of size of the keys/signatures) for fully traceable k-times anonymous proxy signatures and fully traceable k-times anonymous sanitizable signatures. We give security proofs for these schemes. From a technical point of view, we rely on the method proposed in [7]: the delegate has k different public/secret keys; if it reuses the same key twice, then it is possible to link the two signatures to the user and extract an element that links all its other signatures. However, this method requires a number of keys linear in k; our main technical contribution is a method for generating k distinct and mutually unlinkable keys from $2\log_2(k)$ keys only. The idea is to compose, at the ith signature, the keys corresponding to the bits of i to obtain a new public/secret key pair. These keys must be certified by the delegator, but must be unlinkable. To achieve these two properties simultaneously, we use a signature on equivalence class [18], which allows the delegate to randomize the $2\log_2(k)$ keys while maintaining the validity of their certificate. This method requires the creation of an ad-hoc zero-knowledge proof ensuring the verifier that the delegate has correctly generated its key. For the special case where k is not a power of 2, we build another ad-hoc zero-knowledge proof to ensure that i is indeed less than k. Both of these proofs have logarithmic complexity in size, enabling us to obtain logarithmic complexity in size for both our keys and our signatures. This method is fairly generic, so we think it could be of independent interest in other primitives requiring the generation of several certified keys. Our sanitizable signature scheme uses the same technique as the one proposed in [3] combined with the method described above to make it k-times anonymous. The main technical challenge here is to adapt the signature to enable the signer to simulate the use of the $2\log_2(k)$ keys in the original signature, so that it is not possible to determine whether it has been sanitized or not.

For each signature primitive, we define the following properties in addition to unforgeability:

Anonymity: signatures are anonymous as long as the delegate does not exceed k signatures. In particular, they cannot be linked to each other.

Traceability: if the delegate exceeds the k signatures limit, it cannot prevent anyone from linking all its signatures and recovering its identity.

Non-framability: a delegate cannot produce a signature that can be traced back to someone else.

We also adapt the security properties of sanitizable signatures:

Immutability: it is not possible to modify parts of messages that are not intended to be modified.

Transparency: it is not possible to guess whether a signature has been sanitized or not. This property implies privacy: it is not possible to determine any information about the original message.

Unlinkability: it is not possible to link a sanitized signature to the original signature, or to link sanitized signatures from the same original signature. A few schemes such as [17] achieve this property. Note that unlinkability differs from anonymity, which ensures that it is not possible to link signatures from the same user. We provide more details about this on Sect. 6.

Invisibilty: it is not possible to identify which part of the message is modifiable. Note that designing schemes that are both unlinkable and invisible is challenging, and there are only two schemes in the literature that combine these properties [3, 8].

Motivations. Anonymous proxy signatures are used wherever an entity wishes to delegate the ability to sign on its behalf to others, without making the delegation policy transparent to the recipient of the messages. Anonymity can also protect proxies when their identity must remain secret, for example in legal proceedings where retaliation is possible. Conversely, anonymity provides a high level of protection for proxies who might be tempted to abuse their power. The fully traceable k-times anonymity property can significantly limit this, even in the absence of the delegate. Sanitizable signatures extend proxy signatures by adding a degree of control over the messages sent by delegates. For example, they can be used to force the use of message templates.

For instance, consider a manager who delegates the ability to sign and send emails on their behalf from their email address to multiple entities. These could be employees or servers that automatically send emails that contain, depending on their role, specific messages, appointments, contracts, payments, invoices, reminders, summonses or other legal or commercial documents. If too many emails are being sent from the same entity on behalf of the manager, the company's mail server can use the k-times mechanism to locate the offending entity, block the emails it is sending, list all its signatures and alert the manager and anyone else who has received emails from this entity in the past. Note that in our case the server is honest but curious: we trust it to check signatures and detect anomalies (it cannot be fully corrupted by an active attacker), but the information it processes does not allow it to learn anything about the identity of honest proxies or the delegation policy (a passive attacker can observe everything that passes through the server without compromising anonymity).

To control the content of messages, it is helpful to use sanitizable signatures that force delegates to use templates. For example, by setting the metadata it is possible to allow emails to be sent only to certain people, on certain dates, with certain subjects, or by forcing the addition of copy users who can check the content of the email. In the case of automatic emails, such as invoices, it is possible to impose a very precise template where only the customer's name, date and amount can be changed. Note that thanks to the security properites of our sanitizable signatures (transparency, anonymity, unlinkability, and invisibility), the company's delegation policy remains entirely private from the point of view of the verifiers and the mail server as long as the the k limit is not exceeded,

Related Works. Anonymous proxy signatures have been introduced by Fuchsbauer and Pointcheval [19]. Since then, several other anonymous proxy signature schemes have been proposed [28,29]. However, as mentioned above, they all consider active traceability management by the original signer or a dedicated semi-trusted proxy. Note that unlike our scheme, Fuchsbauer and Pointcheval's scheme allows hierarchical management of proxies (a delegate can allow a sub-delegate to sign in its place, etc.). This feature could naturally be achieved by extending our scheme, despite a linear growth in the number of delegations. This function is left outside of the scope of this work.

k-times anonymity has been introduced for authentication, group signature (where the group is managed by an authority that generates keys), and ring signature (where the group is chosen ad-hoc at the time of signing) in [2,27], and [20] respectively. In some schemes, the identity of the signer leaks if it produces more than k signatures. Fully traceable k-times anonymity [7] extends this concept by making it possible to trace all signatures produced a priori by the user that exceed the k signatures (and not just a pair of signatures). To the best of our knowledge, the only scheme that matches this property is the ring signature described in [7], and this at the cost of a signature size in $O(nk)$ where n is the number of users, and a secret key size in $O(k)$.

In [19], Fuchsbauer and Pointcheval mention that anonymous proxy signatures can be seen as group signatures: the delegator becomes the group manager and each delegate (*i.e.,* each group member) can sign anonymously on behalf of the manager (*i.e.,* within the group). We can therefore see our fully traceable k-times proxy signature as the first fully traceable k-times group signature. Since our aim is also to design sanitizable signatures, which have some similarities with proxy signatures (in both cases a delegator gives a delegate the power to create new signatures on his behalf), we have chosen to present our scheme as an anonymous proxy signature rather than as a group signature. In comparison with the only k-times group signature scheme [2] in the literature, our scheme achieves full traceability, in return the key/signature size is in $O(\log(k))$ whereas [2] claims a constant key/signature size (note, however, that in this scheme, the delegator must produce and share a public key of size linear in k, moreover if the limit k is different for each delegate, then this key must be kept secret by each delegate, which significantly restrains its practicability for large k).

Sanitizable signatures were introduced by Ateniese *et al.* in [1], who identified several security properties (unforgeability, immutability, privacy, transparency, and accountability) later formally defined in [4]. They show that privacy (the original message does not leak from the sanitized signature) is implied by transparency. Invisibility was also introduced in [1] but received formal treatment much later in [10]. Last but not least, unlinkability has been introduced and formalized in [5] and studied in [6,17]. Only two schemes guarantee all these properties at once [3,8]. In this paper, we adapt and prove all these properties on our scheme, with the exception of accountability, which consists in allowing the signer to reveal the author (*i.e.*, the original signer or the sanitizer) of a problematic signature, since this information leaks spontaneously if the sanitizer exceeds the limit of k sanitizations.

Traceable k-times anonymous proxy signatures should not be confused with the k-times (not anonymous) proxy signatures introduced by Liu *et al.* in [25], where if the (non-anonymous) proxy exceeds a limit of k signatures, then its secret key leaks. This primitive is close to ours, but differs in two crucial points: (i) the proxy is not anonymous, so there is no need to trace it or link signatures, thus full traceability makes no sense in [25], and (ii) unlike [25] we do not want to leak the proxy's secret key for security reasons. Indeed, if a verifier recovers a proxy secret key, it can sign messages as a proxy without the original signer having chosen to give it this power. As a result, users which have not had access to the $k + 1$ proxy signatures (including the original signer) are unaware that this verifier can impersonate the signer, which causes serious security problems in most applications. Similarly, one line of work, started in [23], aims to limit the sanitizer's power in various ways in sanitizable signatures [12]. In particular, in [12,23] the authors propose a scheme where if the (non-anonymous) sanitizer exceeds a limit of k signatures, then its secret key leaks, as in k-times (not anonymous) proxy signatures [25]. The differences between this primitive and ours are the same as those between k-times proxy signatures [25] and our k-times anonymous proxy signatures.

Finally, k-times anonymous sanitizable signatures should not be confused with γ-times sanitizable signatures [3], where γ bounds the number of blocks that can be modified instead of the number of times the signature can be sanitized. In the primitive introduced in [3], the sanitizer is not anonymous, and cannot (in the computational sense) sanitize a signature by modifying more than γ blocks. The mechanism is therefore very different, as there is no intention of triggering some secret information leak when the limit is exceeded.

2   Preliminaries

Notations. $r \leftarrow_\$ S$ means that r is chosen uniformly at random over the set S and $|S|$ is the cardinal of S. The operator $\xrightarrow{p}$ denotes the parsing of a tuple or a set of elements. We denote by $y \leftarrow \mathcal{A}(x)$ the execution of an algorithm $\mathcal{A}$ outputting y on input x. When $\mathcal{A}$ is probabilistic, $[\mathcal{A}]$ denotes the set of all its possible outputs. Considering a second algorithm $\mathcal{O}$, $\mathcal{A}^\mathcal{O}$ means that the algorithm $\mathcal{A}$ has access to $\mathcal{O}$ as a black-box oracle. PPT means *Probabilistic Polynomial Time*. $[\![n]\!]$ denotes the set $[\![n[\![$. For a vector $m = (m_1, \cdots, m_n)$ and an integer μ, m^μ denotes the vector $(m_1^\mu, \cdots, m_n^\mu)$. $\sqcup$ operates as the union $\cup$ while preserving the repetition of elements, hence producing a multi-set. Finally, $\eta[i]$ refers to the ith bit of some integer η.

Mathematical Background. Throughout this paper, we consider a bilinear group setting $(p, \mathbb{G}_1, \mathbb{G}_2, \mathbb{G}_t, e)$ where $\mathbb{G}_1$ $\mathbb{G}_2$, and $\mathbb{G}_t$ are multiplicative groups of prime order p, $g_1 \in \mathbb{G}_1$ and $g_2 \in \mathbb{G}_2$, and e is a type-3 bilinear pairing $e \colon \mathbb{G}_1 \times \mathbb{G}_2 \to \mathbb{G}_t$. We assume the *Decision Diffie-Hellman* (DDH) assumptions over these three groups: given $(g, g^a, g^b, g^z) \in \mathbb{G}^4$, there exists no PPT algorithm in $|p|$ able to decide whether $z = a \cdot b$ or not with non negligible probability[1]. This assumption implies hardness of the *Discrete Logarithm* (DL) problem: given $(g, g^x) \in \mathbb{G}^2$, there exists no PPT algorithm in $|p|$ able to return x with non-negligible probability. We also consider the relation $\mathcal{R}$ over $(p, \mathbb{G}_1, \mathbb{G}_2, \mathbb{G}_t, e)$ defined by $\mathcal{R} = \{(m, m') \in \mathbb{G}^l \times \mathbb{G}^l \mid \exists \mu \in \mathbb{Z}_p, m' = m^\mu\}$ defining equivalence classes $[M]_\mathcal{R} \subset \mathbb{G}$ for an element $M \in \mathbb{G}^l$.

In what follows, we recall the definitions of structure-preserving signatures for equivalent class, zero-knowledge proofs, and encryption scheme.

Definition 1 (Class-hiding). *Let $l > 1$ be an integer, and $\mathbb{G}$ be group. $(\mathbb{G}^*)^l$ is class-hiding if for all PPT adversaries $\mathcal{A}$, the following probability is negligible:*

$$\Pr \begin{bmatrix} b \leftarrow_\$ \{0,1\}, \ M \leftarrow_\$ (\mathbb{G}^*)^l, \ M^{(0)} \leftarrow_\$ (\mathbb{G}^*)^l, \\ M^{(1)} \leftarrow_\$ [M]_\mathcal{R}, \ b^* \leftarrow \mathcal{A}(M, M^{(b)}) \end{bmatrix} : b = b^* \ \Bigg].$$

Lemma 1 (Fuchsbauer *et al.* [18]). *Let $l > 1$ be an integer, and $\mathbb{G}$ be a group of prime order p. Then $(\mathbb{G}^*)^l$ is a class hiding message space if and only if the DDH assumption holds in $\mathbb{G}$.*

Definition 2 (SPS-EQ [18]). *A Structure-Preserving Signatures for Equivalence Classes $\mathcal{R}$ SPS-EQ over a group $\mathbb{G}$ is a tuple of algorithms:*

$\mathsf{KeyGen}_{\mathsf{SPS-EQ}}(1^\lambda, l; \mathcal{R})$: *given an integer $l > 1$, return a key pair $(\mathsf{pk}, \mathsf{sk})$.*

$\mathsf{Sign}_{\mathsf{SPS-EQ}}(\mathsf{sk}, m; \mathcal{R})$: *given a secret sk and a message m, return a signature σ.*

$\mathsf{ChgRep}_{\mathsf{SPS-EQ}}(m, \sigma, \mu, \mathsf{pk}; \mathcal{R})$: *given a representative m of an equivalent class, a signature σ, a scalar μ, and a public key pk, return an updated signature σ' for the message m^μ.*

$\mathsf{Verif}_{\mathsf{SPS-EQ}}(m, \sigma, \mathsf{pk}; \mathcal{R})$: *given a public key pk, a message m, a signature σ, return 0 or 1 (meaning reject or accept).*

We require that SPS-EQ meets Correctness, EUF-CMA, and Signature Adaptation (Sign$_{\mathsf{SPS-EQ}}$ and ChgRep$_{\mathsf{SPS-EQ}}$ outputs are identically distributed). We further describe these properties in the extended version of this work [9]. Since we always use the relation $\mathcal{R}$ defined above, we will no longer specify it in the input to the SPS-EQ algorithms.

---

[1] A function $\epsilon \colon \mathbb{N} \to \mathbb{R}^+$ is called *negligible*, if $\forall c > 0, \exists k_0 \in \mathbb{N}, \forall k > k_0, |\epsilon(k)| < \frac{1}{|k^c|}$.

Definition 3 (NIZK [13] and SoK [22]). *A* Non-Interactive Zero-Knowledge proof (NIZK) *for a relation* $\mathcal{R}$ *is a pair of* PPT *algorithms:*

ZK $\{w : (w, \phi) \in \mathcal{R}\}$: *given a witness* w *and a statement* ϕ, *return a proof* π,
ZK.Verif(ϕ, π): *given a statement and a proof, return a bit 0 or 1.*

A NIZK *requires* Completeness, Simulation-Extractability *and* Zero-Knowledge *properties to be secure. We recall the definition of these properties in the extended version of this work [9].*

A Signature of Knowledge (SoK) is similar to a NIZK *except that the proof algorithm* SoK$_m\{w : (w, \phi) \in \mathcal{R}\}$ *takes* m *as an additional parameter. As a consequence, the* Simulation-Extractability *of a SoK, similar to soudness of* NIZK *proofs, implies that it can be used as an EUF-CMA signature scheme, where* ϕ *is the public key,* w *is the secret key,* m *is the signed message, and* π *is the signature.* SoK *also achieve* Perfect Simulability *which is defined similarly to zero-knowledge for* NIZK *proofs. A signature of knowledge can be constructed from a non-interactive zero knowledge proof based on the Fiat-Shamir heuristic [11].*

Definition 4 (Asymmetric Encryption [21]). *An* asymmetric encryption scheme $\mathcal{E}$ *is a triple of* PPT *algorithms:*

KeyGen(1^λ): *return a key pair* (pk, sk).
Enc$($pk$, p)$: *given a public key* pk *and a message* p, *return a ciphertext* c.
Dec$($sk$, c)$: *given a secret key* sk *and a ciphertext* c, *return a message* p.

An encryption scheme $\mathcal{E}$ *has to achieve* Correctness *and* Indistinguishability under Chosen Ciphertext Attack *(IND-CCA). We recall this property in the extended version of this work [9].*

3 k-Times Anonymous Proxy Signature

In this section we give a formal definition and security model for *(fully traceable) k-times anonymous proxy signature*. In this primitive, a signer can delegate to a proxy the authority to anonymously produce at most k signatures. To do this, the signer generates a delegation certificate (denoted del) via the algorithm Delegate, using the proxy's public key and the limit k as input. To produce a proxy signature, the proxy uses this delegation with an integer $\eta \in \{0, \cdots, k-1\}$ that must be different for each k signature. Note that η must not appear in the signature to preserve anonymity (we will describe the corresponding security model in more detail later in this section), so it is not given as input to the verification algorithm. If the proxy decides to produce more than k signatures, it will be forced to use the same index η twice, triggering a mechanism that allows any user to link these two signatures using an algorithm Link, and to extract the identity of the proxy. The algorithm Link also returns a token w which, when used with a signature as input to the Trace algorithm, indicates whether or not the signature was generated by the same proxy, making it possible to find all signatures generated by the proxy in the past. Note that the signer can extend the limit by generating new delegations for the same proxy.

Definition 5 (k-APS). *A k-times Anonymous Proxy Signature scheme (k-APS)is a tuple of algorithms:*

Setup(1^λ): *given a security parameter, return a public parameter* params. *Note that* params *is considered as implicit input of all the following algorithms.*

KeyGen($1^\lambda, k$): *given a limit $k \in \mathbb{N}$, return the signer secret/public keys* (sk, pk).

PKeyGen(1^λ): *return the proxy secret/public keys* (psk, ppk).

Delegate(sk, ppk, l): *given the keys* sk, ppk *and $l \leq k$, return a delegation certificate* del.

Sign(pk, psk, m, del, η): *given the keys* pk, psk, *a message m, a certificate* del, *and an index η, return a signature σ.*

Verify(pk, m, σ): *given the key* pk, *a message m, and a signature σ, return 0 or 1 (for* reject *or* accept*).*

Link(pk, m, σ, m', σ'): *given a key* pk *and two pairs (m, σ), (m', σ'), return an identity* ppk *and a witness w or $\bot$ in case of failure.*

Trace(w, σ): *given a witness w and a signature σ, return 0 or 1.*

A k-APS is said to be *correct* if, using keys/certificateshonestly generated by the algorithms KeyGen, PKeyGen, and Delegate, (i) any signature produced by the algorithm Sign is verified by the algorithm Verify using the signer public key, (ii) 2 signatures are linked by the algorithm Link which outputs the corresponding public key if and only if they were produced with the same delegation certificate and the same η, and (iii) the algorithm Trace returns 1 on the token outputted by Link and any of the signatures produced from this delegation certificate.

Our security model is inspired both by that of anonymous proxy signatures [19] and that of k-times full traceability [7]. The security experiments and associated oracles are given in Fig. 1, with Fig. 2 providing a subroutine for the experiment associated to the traceability. For each oracle, the underlined inputs correspond to those chosen by the opponent. Experiments use multisets (sets that may contain the same element multiple times) that are considered to be global variables (and can therefore be accessed and modified in oracles): $\mathcal{U}$ stores the registered users, $\mathcal{D}$ stores the delegations, $\mathcal{S}$ stores the produced signatures, and $\mathcal{H}$ stores the signature indexes. The security properties required for k-APS are defined as follows:

Unforgeability. This property ensures that an adversary playing the role of proxies will not be able to produce a signature unless they have received a delegation certificate. For this property to hold, a PPT adversary $\mathcal{A}$ must forge a valid fresh message/signature pair (m^*, σ^*) for a message that has never been queried to the signature oracle. The adversary can request delegation certificates generated for non-corrupted proxies whose secret keys it does not know.

A k-APS is *Unforgeable* if for any probabilistic polynomial time algorithm $\mathcal{A}$, the probability $\mathsf{Adv}^{\mathsf{unf}}_{\mathsf{k\text{-}APS},\mathcal{A}}(1^\lambda) = \Pr[\mathsf{Exp}^{\mathsf{unf}}_{\mathsf{k\text{-}APS},\mathcal{A}}(1^\lambda) = 1]$ is negligible.

Anonymity. The anonymity ensures that the signatures do not disclose the identity of the proxy signer (given by its public key) and that signatures generated by the same proxy signer remain unlinkable. Note that in our model, anonymity only concerns the signature verifiers, and not the delegator; indeed,

$\mathsf{Exp}^{\mathsf{unf}}_{k\text{-APS},\mathcal{A}}(1^\lambda)$	$\mathsf{Exp}^{\mathsf{Ano}}_{k\text{-APS},\mathcal{A}}(1^\lambda)$
1 : $\quad \mathcal{D}, \mathcal{S} \leftarrow \emptyset$	1 : $\quad b \leftarrow_\$ \{0,1\}, \mathcal{D} \leftarrow \emptyset, \eta_0, \eta_1 \leftarrow 0, \gamma \leftarrow 1$
2 : $\quad \mathsf{params} \leftarrow \mathsf{Setup}(1^\lambda)$	2 : $\quad \mathsf{params} \leftarrow \mathsf{Setup}(1^\lambda)$
3 : $\quad (\mathsf{pk}, \mathsf{sk}) \leftarrow \mathsf{KeyGen}(1^\lambda, k)$	3 : $\quad (\mathsf{pk}, \mathsf{sk}) \leftarrow \mathsf{KeyGen}(1^\lambda, k)$
4 : $\quad (m^*, \sigma^*) \leftarrow \mathcal{A}^{\mathcal{O}^{\mathsf{unf}}_{\mathsf{Register}}, \mathcal{O}^{\mathsf{unf}}_{\mathsf{Delegate}}, \mathcal{O}^{\mathsf{unf}}_{\mathsf{Sign}}}(\mathsf{pk}, k)$	4 : $\quad \mathbf{for}\ j \in \{0,1\},$
5 : $\quad \mathbf{return}\ \mathsf{Verify}(\mathsf{pk}, m^*, \sigma^*) \wedge ((m^*, \cdot) \notin \mathcal{S})$	5 : $\quad\quad (\mathsf{ppk}_j, \mathsf{psk}_j) \leftarrow \mathsf{PKeyGen}(1^\lambda)$
$\mathsf{Exp}^{\mathsf{Trace}}_{k\text{-APS},\mathcal{A}}(1^\lambda)$	6 : $\quad t \leftarrow \mathcal{A}^{\mathcal{O}_{\mathsf{Delegate}}}(\mathsf{pk}, \mathsf{ppk}_0, \mathsf{ppk}_1)$
1 : $\quad \mathcal{D} \leftarrow \emptyset$	7 : $\quad \mathbf{if}\ t \notin [\![k]\!], \mathbf{return}\ b$
2 : $\quad \mathsf{params} \leftarrow \mathsf{Setup}(1^\lambda)$	8 : $\quad \mathbf{for}\ j \in \{0,1\},$
3 : $\quad (\mathsf{pk}, \mathsf{sk}) \leftarrow \mathsf{KeyGen}(1^\lambda, k)$	9 : $\quad\quad \mathsf{del}_j \leftarrow \mathsf{Delegate}(\mathsf{sk}, \mathsf{ppk}_j, t)$
4 : $\quad (m^*_i, \sigma^*_i)^{q_s}_{i=1} \leftarrow \mathcal{A}^{\mathcal{O}_{\mathsf{Delegate}}}(\mathsf{pk})$	10 : $\quad b^* \leftarrow \mathcal{A}^{\mathcal{O}_{\mathsf{Delegate}}, \mathcal{O}^{\mathsf{Ano}}_{\mathsf{Sign}}, \mathcal{O}^{\mathsf{Ano}}_{\mathsf{chal}}}(\mathsf{pk}, \mathsf{ppk}_0, \mathsf{ppk}_1)$
5 : $\quad b \leftarrow \mathsf{CheckTrace}(\mathsf{pk}, (m^*_i, \sigma^*_i)^{q_s}_{i=1})$	11 : $\quad \mathbf{return}\ b^* = b$
6 : $\quad \mathbf{return}\ b$	**Anonymity Oracle**
$\mathsf{Exp}^{\mathsf{no-Frame}}_{k\text{-APS},\mathcal{A}}(1^\lambda)$	Oracle $\mathcal{O}^{\mathsf{Ano}}_{\mathsf{chal}}(b, t, (\mathsf{psk}_i, \underline{\mathsf{del}_i})_{i \in \{0,1\}}, \underline{m})$
1 : $\quad \mathcal{U}, \mathcal{D}, \mathcal{S} \leftarrow \emptyset$	1 : $\quad \mathbf{if}\ \gamma = 0, \mathbf{return}\ \perp$
2 : $\quad \mathsf{params} \leftarrow \mathsf{Setup}(1^\lambda)$	2 : $\quad \gamma \leftarrow 0$
3 : $\quad (\mathsf{pk}, \mathsf{sk}) \leftarrow \mathsf{KeyGen}(1^\lambda, k)$	3 : $\quad \sigma \leftarrow \mathcal{O}^{\mathsf{Ano}}_{\mathsf{Sign}}(b, t, (\mathsf{psk}_i, \mathsf{del}_i)_{i \in \{0,1\}}, b, m)$
4 : $\quad (m^*_i, \sigma^*_i)^2_{i=1}$	4 : $\quad \mathbf{return}\ \sigma$
5 : $\quad \leftarrow \mathcal{A}^{\mathcal{O}^{\mathsf{no-Frame}}_{\mathsf{Register}}, \mathcal{O}_{\mathsf{Delegate}}, \mathcal{O}^{\mathsf{no-Frame}}_{\mathsf{Sign}}}(\mathsf{pk})$	$\mathcal{O}^{\mathsf{Ano}}_{\mathsf{Sign}}(b, t, (\mathsf{psk}_i, \underline{\mathsf{del}_i})_{i \in \{0,1\}}, \underline{j}, \underline{m})$
6 : $\quad (\mathsf{ppk}, w) \leftarrow \mathsf{Link}(\mathsf{pk}, m^*_1, \sigma^*_1, m^*_2, \sigma^*_2)$	1 : $\quad \mathbf{if}\ j = b \wedge \eta_j = t - \gamma, \mathbf{return}\ \perp$
7 : $\quad \mathbf{if}\ (\mathsf{ppk}, \cdot, \cdot, 1) \in \mathcal{U} \wedge |\mathcal{S}[\mathsf{ppk}]| \le k,$	2 : $\quad \mathbf{if}\ j = 1 - b \wedge \eta_j = t - 1, \mathbf{return}\ \perp$
8 : $\quad\quad \mathbf{return}\ 1$	3 : $\quad \sigma \leftarrow \mathsf{Sign}(\mathsf{pk}, \mathsf{psk}_j, m, \mathsf{del}_j, \eta_j)$
9 : $\quad \mathbf{return}\ 0$	4 : $\quad \eta_j \leftarrow \eta_j + 1$
General Oracle	5 : $\quad \mathbf{return}\ \sigma$
Oracle $\mathcal{O}_{\mathsf{Delegate}}(\mathsf{sk}, \underline{\mathsf{ppk}}, \underline{l \le k})$	**Unforgeability Oracles**
	$\mathcal{O}^{\mathsf{unf}}_{\mathsf{Register}}(\perp)$
1 : $\quad \mathsf{del} \leftarrow \mathsf{Delegate}(\mathsf{sk}, \mathsf{ppk}, l)$	1 : $\quad (\mathsf{ppk}, \mathsf{psk}) \leftarrow \mathsf{PKeyGen}(1^\lambda)$
2 : $\quad \mathcal{D} \leftarrow \mathcal{D} \sqcup \{(\mathsf{ppk}, \mathsf{del}, l)\}$	2 : $\quad \mathcal{U} \leftarrow \mathcal{U} \cup \{(\mathsf{ppk}, \mathsf{psk})\}$
3 : $\quad \mathbf{return}\ \mathsf{del}$	3 : $\quad \mathbf{return}\ \mathsf{ppk}$
Non-Frameability Oracles	Oracle $\mathcal{O}^{\mathsf{unf}}_{\mathsf{Delegate}}(\mathsf{sk}, \underline{\mathsf{ppk}}, \underline{l \le k})$
$\mathcal{O}^{\mathsf{no-Frame}}_{\mathsf{Register}}(\mathcal{U}, \underline{\mathsf{ppk}})$	1 : $\quad \mathbf{if}\ \nexists \mathsf{psk}, \mathrm{s.t.}(\mathsf{ppk}, \mathsf{psk}) \in \mathcal{U}, \mathbf{return}\ \perp$
1 : $\quad \mathbf{if}\ \mathsf{ppk} = \perp,$	2 : $\quad \mathsf{del} \leftarrow \mathsf{Delegate}(\mathsf{sk}, \mathsf{ppk}, l)$
2 : $\quad\quad (\mathsf{ppk}, \mathsf{psk}) \leftarrow \mathsf{PKeyGen}(1^\lambda)$	3 : $\quad \mathcal{D} \leftarrow \mathcal{D} \sqcup \{(\mathsf{ppk}, \mathsf{del}, l)\}$
3 : $\quad\quad \mathcal{U} \leftarrow \mathcal{U} \cup \{(\mathsf{ppk}, \mathsf{psk}, |\mathcal{U}|, 1)\}$	4 : $\quad \mathbf{return}\ \mathsf{del}$
4 : $\quad \mathbf{else}\ \mathcal{U} \leftarrow \mathcal{U} \cup \{(\mathsf{ppk}, \perp, |\mathcal{U}|, 0)\}$	Oracle $\mathcal{O}^{\mathsf{unf}}_{\mathsf{Sign}}(\mathsf{pk}, \underline{\mathsf{ppk}}, \underline{\mathsf{del}}, \underline{\eta}, \underline{m})$
5 : $\quad \mathbf{return}\ \mathsf{ppk}$	1 : $\quad \mathbf{if}\ \nexists \mathsf{psk}, \mathrm{s.t.}(\mathsf{ppk}, \mathsf{psk}) \in \mathcal{U}, \mathbf{return}\ \perp$
$\mathcal{O}^{\mathsf{no-Frame}}_{\mathsf{Sign}}(\mathsf{pk}, (\mathsf{psk}_i, \mathsf{del}_i)_{i \in \{0,1\}}, \underline{j}, \underline{\eta}, \underline{m})$	2 : $\quad \sigma \leftarrow \mathsf{Sign}(\mathsf{pk}, \mathsf{psk}, m, \mathsf{del}, \eta)$
1 : $\quad \mathbf{if}\ \eta \in \mathcal{S}[\mathsf{ppk}], \mathbf{return}\ \perp$	3 : $\quad \mathcal{S} \leftarrow \mathcal{S} \cup \{(m, \sigma)\}$
2 : $\quad \mathbf{if}\ \exists \mathsf{psk}, i\ \mathrm{s.t.}\ (\mathsf{ppk}, \mathsf{psk}, i, 1) \in \mathcal{U},$	4 : $\quad \mathbf{return}\ \sigma$
3 : $\quad\quad \mathcal{S}[\mathsf{ppk}] \leftarrow \mathcal{S}[\mathsf{ppk}] \cup \{\eta\}$	
4 : $\quad\quad \mathbf{return}\ \mathsf{Sign}(\mathsf{pk}, \mathsf{psk}_j, m, \mathsf{del}_j, \eta)$	
5 : $\quad \mathbf{else\ return}\ \perp$	

Fig. 1. Experiments and Oracles modeling the Security of k-Times Anonymous Proxy Signatures. (Oracles inputs provided by the adversary are underlined, the other are provided by the challenger. The sets $\mathcal{U}, \mathcal{D}, \mathcal{S}, \mathcal{H}$ are global parameters. Subroutine CheckTrace is defined in Fig. 2.)

CheckTrace(pk, $(m_i^*, \sigma_i^*)_{i=1}^{q_s}$)

---

1 :   **if** $\mathcal{D}$ is defined, $\mathcal{D} \xrightarrow{P} (\text{pk}_i, \text{del}_i, k_i)_{i=1}^{n}$ // For proxy signatures only.

2 :   **if** $\mathcal{S}$ is defined $\wedge \exists i \in [\![q_s]\!], (m_i^*, \sigma_i^*, *, *) \in \mathcal{S}$, **return** 0   // For sanitizable signatures only.

3 : $T \leftarrow 0, \mathsf{W}, \mathsf{ID} \leftarrow \emptyset, \text{diff} \leftarrow q_s - \sum_{1 \leq i \leq n} k_i$ // diff is required to be strictly positive.

4 :   **if** $(\exists i \in [\![q_s]\!], \mathsf{Verify}(\text{pk}, m_i^*, \sigma_i^*) = 0) \vee (\exists i, j \in [\![q_s]\!], j \neq i, (m_i^*, \sigma_i^*) = (m_j^*, \sigma_j^*)) \vee (\text{diff} \leq 0),$

5 :   **return** 0

6 :   **for** $1 \leq i < j \leq q_s$,

7 : $(\text{ppk}_{i,j}, w_{i,j}) \leftarrow \mathsf{Link}(\text{pk}, m_i^*, \sigma_i^*, m_j^*, \sigma_j^*)$ // Try linking any two signatures.

8 :   **if** $(\text{ppk}_{i,j}, w_{i,j}) \neq \perp \wedge \text{ppk}_{i,j} \notin \mathsf{ID}$,   // Identities for which signatures have been linked.

9 : $\mathsf{ID} \leftarrow \mathsf{ID} \cup \{\text{ppk}_{i,j}\}, W[\text{ppk}_{i,j}] \leftarrow W[\text{ppk}_{i,j}] \cup \{w_{i,j}\}$

10 : $T \leftarrow \sum_{\text{ppk} \in \mathsf{ID}} \left(\sum_{w \in W[\text{ppk}]} \left(\sum_{i=1}^{q_s} \mathsf{Trace}(w, \sigma_i) \right) \right)$ // Sum up traced signatures and compare it to the number of allowed signatures for these entities.

11 :   **if** $T < \sum_{\text{pk}_i \in \mathsf{ID}} k_i + \text{diff}$, **return** 1, **else**, **return** 0

Fig. 2. CheckTrace Subroutine for the Traceability Experiment.

in our application, there is no reason why the delegator should not know the identity of the proxy signing on its behalf, and it is even rather preferable that it should for accountability reasons. In the corresponding experiment, the adversary chooses a limit $t \leq k$, then it tries to distinguish the origin of a challenge signature produced by one of two honest proxies. The adversary can request to the oracles a maximum of $t - 1$ signatures for each of the proxies, and a single signature for one of the two proxies (the one chosen by the challenger), which guarantees that the adversary cannot obtain more than t signatures for one of the two proxies (it would trivially link these signatures to the challenge, which is an inherent property of our primitive). For each of the two proxies, the signature oracle increments the index η at each signature, which ensures that a η is not used twice for the same proxy. Our model therefore considers adversaries trying to link two signatures from two different proxies with the same η, which would allow the adversary to infer that two signatures are not from the same proxy, and thus generally ensures that η is not leaked from the signature.

A k-APS is *anonymous* if for any PPT $\mathcal{A}$, the probability $\mathsf{Adv}_{\text{k-APS}, \mathcal{A}}^{\text{Ano}}(1^\lambda) = |\Pr[\mathsf{Exp}_{\text{k-APS}, \mathcal{A}}^{\text{Ano}}(1^\lambda) = 1] - 1/2|$ is negligible.

Traceability. This property guarantees that the Trace algorithm leaks the identity of any adversary overpassing the delegation limit. In the corresponding experiment, the adversary's target is to produce more signatures than allowed by the delegator, without the Link and Trace algorithms being able to correctly link or trace the signatures. For that the adversary can obtain multiple delegation certificates for different limits and different public keys ppk. Since each delegation certificate allows it to produce k_i signatures, it is required to produce strictly more than $\sum_{i=1}^{n} k_i$ valid signatures. The adversary wins the experiment if the number of traced signatures is less than the number of signatures that would have been traced if they had been generated honestly. This test, which is described in Fig. 2, has to take account of all the delegations that have been exceeded in any execution scenario. First, note that if the limit of a delegation certificate for a public key is exceeded, then it must be possible to trace all signatures generated by the owner of that public key, even if they were generated using a different delegation certificate. Thus, the number of signatures traced T should be at least the sum of the limits k_i of each delegation produced for each public key traced (expressed as $\sum_{\mathsf{pk}_i \in \mathsf{ID}} k_i$ in Fig. 2), to which we add the number of signatures that exceed the global sum of the limits for all delegation certificate used by the adversary (expressed as $\mathsf{diff} = q_s - \sum_{i=1}^{n} k_i$ in Fig. 2, where q_s is the number of signatures outputted by the adversary). A k-APS is *traceable* if for any PPT algorithm $\mathcal{A}$, the probability $\mathsf{Adv}^{\mathsf{Trace}}_{\text{k-APS}, \mathcal{A}}(1^\lambda) = \Pr[\mathsf{Exp}^{\mathsf{Trace}}_{\text{k-APS}, \mathcal{A}}(1^\lambda) = 1]$ is negligible.

Non-frameability. This property prevents a PPT adversary from framing someone else by generating malformed yet valid signatures. More precisely, the goal of the adversary is to output two signatures traceable to a registered proxy who remains honest. To help it, the adversary has access to oracles that can be used to register users, obtain delegation certificates, and obtain signatures for honest users. The adversary must of course not have abused the signature oracle by producing more than k signatures for the proxy it wishes to trace. Note that in our model we implicitly assume that the linking of two signatures and the tracing are performed by the same user (we do not consider the case where an adversary only generates a tracing token w that traces an honest user without the linked signatures). In practice, this means that to delegate tracing, the delegate must be provided with the two linked signatures so that it can link them and produce its own token w. A k-APS is *Non-Frameable* if for any PPT algorithm $\mathcal{A}$, the probability $\mathsf{Adv}^{\mathsf{no-Frame}}_{\text{k-APS}, \mathcal{A}}(1^\lambda) = \Pr[\mathsf{Exp}^{\mathsf{no-Frame}}_{\text{k-APS}, \mathcal{A}}(1^\lambda) = 1]$ is negligible.

4   Our k-Times Anonymous Proxy Signature Scheme

In this section, we present our k-times anonymous proxy signature (Setup, KeyGen, PKeyGen, Delegate, Sign, Verify, Link, Trace), which uses a bilinear group setting $(p, \mathbb{G}_1, \mathbb{G}_2, \mathbb{G}_t, e)$ and a SPS-EQ scheme.

Construction Intuition The setup (algorithm Setup) of our construction returns several group elements and the description of a hash function. In particular, the group element g_1 will be used as a basis for the proxy public key $\mathsf{ppk} = g_1^{\mathsf{psk}}$ (where psk is the proxy secret key). The signer key pair (generated from based on KeyGen) is a SPS-EQ key pair supporting vectors of $4l + 1$ group elements in $\mathbb{G}_1$, where $l = \lceil \log_2(k) \rceil$.

To delegate (algorithm Delegate) the power to create k anonymous signatures, the signer will create two sets of l public/secret keys $(y_{i,0}, x_{i,0})_{i \in [\![l]\!]}$ and $(y_{i,1}, x_{i,1})_{i \in [\![l]\!]}$. The idea behind this technique is to be able to create k public/secret keys by composing the previous $2 \log_2(k)$ keys: given an integer $\eta < k$, the key corresponding to η will be composed of the keys corresponding to each of the bits in η. For each i, the signer also produce a Diffie-Hellman key

$\mathsf{ppk}_{i,j} = g_1^{\mathsf{psk} \cdot x_{i,j}}$ between $y_{i,j} = g_1^{x_{i,j}}$ and $\mathsf{ppk} = g_1^{\mathsf{psk}}$. This will enable us to link the keys produced by these elements to the ppk owner later on. Finally, all these public keys are signed with an SPS-EQ, acting as a certificate, so that they can be randomized. All these elements are stored in the delegation del. Thanks to del, we have already shown that the proxy can produce k distinct pairs of certified ElGamal public/secret keys. The idea of our signature algorithm (Sign) is to use one of its keys for each signature. If the same key is used several times, however, it will be possible to find its owner thanks to the mechanism introduced in [7] (this point will be discussed further in this section). However, to preserve anonymity, these keys must not be linkable, so they must be randomized (note that the SPS-EQ properties preserve their certification by the signer).

Assume that the delegate is using the algorithm for the ηth time. First, the delegate randomizes g_1 and all the elements $y_{i,j}$ and $\mathsf{ppk}_{i,j}$ using the same random r as an exponent, and adapts the SPS-EQ accordingly. The randomized version of g_1 is denoted $\widehat{g}_1$, and the keys are respectively denoted $\widehat{y}_{i,j}$ and $\widehat{\mathsf{ppk}}_{i,j}$. This first step randomizes all the elements in the delegation $y_{i,j}$ and $\mathsf{ppk}_{i,j}$, so that it is not possible to make the link between the randomized delegation $\widehat{y}_{i,j}$ and $\widehat{\mathsf{ppk}}_{i,j}$ and the original one. Then, the delegate chooses a new random s, randomize the basis $\widehat{g}_1$ in $\widetilde{g}_1$, and randomizes only the $\widehat{y}_{i,\eta[i]}$ and $\widehat{\mathsf{ppk}}_{i,\eta[i]}$ corresponding to the bits of η to obtain the keys $\widetilde{y}_i$ and $\widetilde{\mathsf{ppk}}_i$. The delegate uses a zero-knowledge proof to ensure that the randomization has been done correctly and with an integer η actually lower than k (the instantiation of this proof is rather technical and described in more details in the next section). In this way, it is possible to multiply the public keys $\widetilde{y} = \prod_{i=1}^{l} \widetilde{y}_i$ and add the corresponding secret keys $x = \sum_{i=1}^{l} x_{i,\eta[i]}$ to obtain a new public/secret key pair $(\widetilde{y}, x)$ that verifies $\widetilde{y} = \widetilde{g}_1^x$. This second step allows the proxy to hide its chosen η in the elements $\widetilde{y}_i$ and $\widetilde{\mathsf{ppk}}_i$ (by randomizing the $\widehat{y}_{i,\eta[i]}$ and $\widehat{\mathsf{ppk}}_{i,\eta[i]}$ again) while preserving the link between the randomized delegation $\widehat{y}_{i,j}$ and $\widehat{\mathsf{ppk}}_{i,j}$ and the generated key pair $(\widetilde{y}, x)$. Note that $\widetilde{\mathsf{ppk}} = \prod_{i=1}^{l} \widetilde{\mathsf{ppk}}_i$ is the Diffie-Hellman of $\widetilde{y}$ and ppk, which links $\widetilde{y}$ to the owner of ppk in a hidden way. It allows the delegate to prove in zero-knowledge that the identity revealed by the mechanism of [7] is indeed the identity of the delegate. This proof, denoted π_σ, also proves that the mechanism of [7] triggers correctly if the delegate signs more than k messages. The technical description of this proof is given in the extended version of this work [9].

The signature verification (algorithm Verify) consists of re-computing $\widetilde{y}$ and $\widetilde{\mathsf{ppk}}$ and checking that the proof π_σ is valid. Finally, the Link and Trace algorithms work in the same way as in [7]: each signature contains $\alpha_1 = h_1^x$, $\alpha_2 = g_2^t$, $\alpha_3 = h_2^x \cdot g_1^{u \cdot \mathsf{psk}}$, and $\alpha_4 = h_3^x \cdot h_4^{v \cdot \mathsf{psk}}$. Thus, if the same key x is used twice in signatures, they can be linked since they share the same $\alpha_1 = h_1^x$. Let's note $\alpha_3' = h_2^x \cdot g_1^{u' \cdot \mathsf{psk}}$ the element α_3 of the second signature. It is possible to find the identity of the delegate by computing $(\alpha_3/\alpha_3')^{1/(u-u')} = \mathsf{ppk}$. By a similar way, the token $\omega = h_4^{\mathsf{psk}}$ leaks from α_4 when two signatures are linked. Each signature has also the elements $\tau = e(\omega, \alpha_2)$. Without knowledge of ω, τ is indistinguishable from a random element under the DDH assumption, but a user which knows the delegate's token ω can retrieve its signatures by recomputing τ, thus achieving full traceability.

Formal Description. Below is the formal description of our scheme.

$\underline{\mathsf{Setup}(1^\lambda)}$: sample $g_1, h_1, h_2, h_3, h_4 \in \mathbb{G}_1$ and $g_2 \in \mathbb{G}_2$, choose a hash function $H : \{0,1\}^* \to \mathbb{Z}_p^*$, and return them as the common parameters.

$\underline{\mathsf{KeyGen}(1^\lambda, k)}$: set $l = \lceil \log_2(k) \rceil$, and return $(\mathsf{pk}, \mathsf{sk}) \leftarrow \mathsf{KeyGen}_{\mathsf{SPS\text{-}EQ}}(1^\lambda, 4l+1)$.

$\underline{\mathsf{PKeyGen}(1^\lambda)}$: sample $\mathsf{psk} \leftarrow\!\!\$\ \mathbb{Z}_q$ and set $\mathsf{ppk} = g_1^{\mathsf{psk}}$. Return the pair $(\mathsf{psk}, \mathsf{ppk})$.

$\underline{\mathsf{Delegate}(\mathsf{sk}, \mathsf{ppk}, k)}$: set $l = \lceil \log_2(k) \rceil$, abort if the SPS-EQ key sk does not support message of $4l+1$ elements. For all $(i,j) \in \llbracket l \rrbracket \times \{0,1\}$, sample $x_{i,j} \leftarrow\!\!\$\ \mathbb{Z}_p^*$, set $y_{i,j} = g_1^{x_{i,j}}$, $\mathsf{ppk}_{i,j} = \mathsf{ppk}^{x_{i,j}}$ and produce $\widehat{\sigma} \leftarrow \mathsf{Sign}_{\mathsf{SPS\text{-}EQ}}(\mathsf{sk}, g_1, y_{1,0},$ $\cdots, y_{l,1}, \mathsf{ppk}_{1,0}, \cdots, \mathsf{ppk}_{l,1})$. Return $\mathsf{del} = ((x_{i,j}, y_{i,j}, \mathsf{ppk}_{i,j})_{i \in \llbracket l \rrbracket; j \in \{0,1\}}, \widehat{\sigma})$.

$\underline{\mathsf{Sign}(\mathsf{pk}, \mathsf{psk}, m, \mathsf{del}, \eta)}$: set $l = \lceil \log_2(k) \rceil$. Sample $r, s \leftarrow\!\!\$\ \mathbb{Z}_p^*$, set $\widehat{g_1} = g_1^r$ and $\widetilde{g_1} = \widehat{g_1}^s$. For all $i \in \llbracket l \rrbracket$ and $j \in \{0,1\}$, compute $\widehat{y}_{i,j} = y_{i,j}^r$ and $\widehat{\mathsf{ppk}}_{i,j} = \mathsf{ppk}_{i,j}^r$, adapt the SPS-EQ signature $\widehat{\sigma} \leftarrow \mathsf{ChgRep}_{\mathsf{SPS\text{-}EQ}}((g_1, y_{1,0}, \cdots, y_{l,1}, \mathsf{ppk}_{1,0}, \cdots,$ $\mathsf{ppk}_{l,1}), \widehat{\sigma}, r, \mathsf{pk})$, compute $\widetilde{y}_i = \widehat{y}_{i,\eta[i]}^s$, and $\widetilde{\mathsf{ppk}}_i = \widehat{\mathsf{ppk}}_{i,\eta[i]}^s$. Generate a zero-knowledge proof $\Pi_{<k}$ of knowledge of s and η which proves that (i) $\widetilde{y}_i$ and $\widetilde{\mathsf{ppk}}_i$ are well formed according to s and some integer η of l bits and (ii) $\eta < k$. We defer the formalisation of this zero-knowledge proof to Sect. 5. Set $x = \sum_{i=1}^l x_{i,\eta[i]}$, $\widetilde{y} = \prod_{i=1}^l \widetilde{y}_i$, $\widetilde{\mathsf{ppk}} = \prod_{i=1}^l \widetilde{\mathsf{ppk}}_i$, sample $t \leftarrow\!\!\$\ \mathbb{Z}_p^*$ and compute $\alpha_1 = h_1^x$, $\alpha_2 = g_2^t$, $u = H(m, 0, \alpha_2)$ and $v = H(m, 1, \alpha_2)$. Generate the matching elements $\alpha_3 = h_2^x \cdot g_1^{u \cdot \mathsf{psk}}$ and $\alpha_4 = h_3^x \cdot h_4^{v \cdot \mathsf{psk}}$, and the tracing element $\tau = e(h_4, \alpha_2)^{\mathsf{psk}}$. Also generate:

$$\pi_\sigma \leftarrow \mathsf{ZK} \left\{ \mathsf{psk}, x, t : \begin{array}{l} \widetilde{y} = \widetilde{g_1}^x \wedge \widetilde{\mathsf{ppk}} = \widetilde{y}^{\mathsf{psk}} \wedge \alpha_1 = h_1^x \wedge \alpha_2 = g_2^t \\ \wedge \alpha_3 = h_2^x \cdot g_1^{u \cdot \mathsf{psk}} \wedge \alpha_4 = h_3^x \cdot h_4^{v \cdot \mathsf{psk}} \wedge \tau = e(h_4, \alpha_2)^{\mathsf{psk}} \end{array} \right\}.$$

Set $\sigma_{\mathsf{del}} = (\widehat{g_1}, ((\widehat{y}_{i,b}, \widehat{\mathsf{ppk}}_{i,b})_{b \in \{0,1\}}, \widetilde{y}_i, \widetilde{\mathsf{ppk}}_i)_{i \in \llbracket l \rrbracket}, \widehat{\sigma}, \Pi_{<k})$ and return the signature $\sigma = (\widetilde{g_1}, \alpha_1, \alpha_2, \alpha_3, \alpha_4, \tau, \pi_\sigma, \sigma_{\mathsf{del}})$.

$\underline{\mathsf{Verify}(m, \sigma, \mathsf{pk})}$: parse $\sigma \xrightarrow{p} (\widetilde{g_1}, \alpha_1, \alpha_2, \alpha_3, \alpha_4, \tau, \pi_\sigma, \sigma_{\mathsf{del}})$ and $\sigma_{\mathsf{del}} \xrightarrow{p} (\widehat{g_1}, ((\widehat{y}_{i,b}, \widehat{\mathsf{ppk}}_{i,b})_{b \in \{0,1\}}, \widetilde{y}_i, \widetilde{\mathsf{ppk}}_i)_{i \in \llbracket l \rrbracket}, \widehat{\sigma}, \Pi_{<k})$. Compute $u = H(m, 0, \alpha_2)$, $v = H(m, 1, \alpha_2)$, $\widetilde{y}_n = \prod_{i=1}^l \widetilde{y}_i$, and $\widetilde{\mathsf{ppk}} = \prod_{i=1}^l \widetilde{\mathsf{ppk}}_i$. Verify the signature $\widehat{\sigma}$ and the proofs $\Pi_{<k}$ and π_σ. If all checks are correct, returns 1, otherwise 0

$\underline{\mathsf{Link}(\mathsf{pk}, m, \sigma, m', \sigma')}$: verify that $\mathsf{Verify}(\mathsf{pk}, m, \sigma) = \mathsf{Verify}(\mathsf{pk}, m', \sigma') = 1$ and return 0 if $\alpha_1 \neq \alpha_1'$ or if one of the verification failed. Compute $u = H(m, 0, \alpha_2)$, $v = H(m, 1, \alpha_2)$, $u' = H(m', 0, \alpha_2')$, $v' = H(m', 1, \alpha_2')$, $\mathsf{ppk} = (\alpha_3/\alpha_3')^{1/(u-u')}$ and $w = (\alpha_4/\alpha_4')^{1/(v-v')}$. Return (ppk, w).

$\underline{\mathsf{Trace}(w, \sigma)}$: return 1 if and only if $\tau = e(w, \alpha_2)$.

In the following, we informally explain why each of the security properties presented in Sect. 3 holds in our scheme.

Unforgeability. Zero-knowledge proofs produced during the signing process ensure that the delegate has used its certificate correctly. This means that a user who has not been delegated cannot produce a valid fresh signature under the assumption that the proof is sound.

Anonymity. Since the elements of the certificate are randomized for each new signature, and since the delegate is able to create public keys $\widetilde{y}$ for k different secret keys x, it is not possible to link two signatures from the elements $\widehat{y}_{i,j}$ and $\widetilde{y}_i$ under the DDH assumption. Recall also that the $\widehat{\mathsf{ppk}}_{i,j}$ and $\widetilde{\mathsf{ppk}}_i$ do not allow the signature to be linked to ppk under the DDH assumption either. On the other hand, the element h_2^x (resp. h_3^x) is the Diffie-Hellman of h_2 (resp. h_3) and $\widetilde{y}$ (where $\widetilde{y}$ varies with each of the k signatures), and therefore hides the elements linked to the identity of the delegate composing α_3 (resp. α_4). Finally, τ hides the value of ppk under the DDH assumption on the elements h_4 and ppk. Assuming that the proofs are indeed zero-knowledge, it is not possible to link two signatures from the same honest user.

Traceability and Non-frameability. Zero-knowledge proofs ensure that the signature is correct and that the delegate knows the secret key corresponding to the public key used in the certificate. Thus, the delegate cannot bypass the mechanism for linking/tracing its signatures if it exceeds the limit, which ensures traceability, and the delegate can only use elements of its own delegation, which ensures non-frameability.

We therefore have the following theorem, the proofs are available in the extended version of this work [9].

Theorem 1. *Instanciated by a signature on equivalent classes that is unforgeable, class-hiding, and signature adaptable, by* NIZK *proofs which are zero-knowledge and sound, and by a collision-resistante hash function, our* k-APS *scheme is unforgeable, anonymous, traceable and non-frameable under the* DDH *assumption in* $\mathbb{G}_1$ *and* $\mathbb{G}_2$.

5   Zero-Knowledge Proof Instantiation

The proof $\Pi_{<k}$ requires several building blocks. In [14], Chaum and Pedersen introduce a zero-konwledge proof of knowledge for discrete logarithm equality ZK $\{x : y_1 = g_1^x \wedge y_2 = g_2^x\}$ in a group of prime order p. This proof is a sigma protocol: the prover sends a commitment, the verifier sends a challenge (chosen in $\mathbb{Z}_p^*$), and the prover sends a response. This proof can be extended to prove the equality of more than two discret logarithms equalities, in this case the size of the resulted transcript is linear in the number of statements. In general, if two sigma protocols for two instances ϕ_1 and ϕ_2 and two relations $\mathcal{R}_1$ and $\mathcal{R}_2$ use the same challenge space, it is possible to merge the proofs by using the same challenge in order to obtain an and-proof ZK $\{w_1, w_2 : (w_1, \phi_1) \in \mathcal{R}_1 \wedge (w_2, \phi_2) \in \mathcal{R}_2\}$. This method can also be extended to any number of instances. In [15], Cramer *et*

al. propose a zero-knowledge proof to prove the knowledge of the witness corresponding to one of two instances $\mathsf{ZK}\{w : (w, \phi_1) \in \mathcal{R}_1 \vee (w, \phi_2) \in \mathcal{R}_2\}$, under the hypothesis that $\mathsf{ZK}\{w : (w, \phi_1) \in \mathcal{R}_1\}$ and $\mathsf{ZK}\{w : (w, \phi_2) \in \mathcal{R}_2\}$ are sigma protocols that use the same challenge space. The challenge space of the resulting proof remains the same as that of the two combined proofs. The method can be extended to prove the knowledge of a witness in relation to one instance among n, in which case the transcript size is equal to the sum of the transcript sizes of the proofs of each instance.

The proof $\Pi_{<k}$ ensures that the prover knows s and η such that (i) $\widetilde{y}_i$ and $\widetilde{\mathsf{ppk}}_i$ are well formed according to s and some integer η of l bits, and (ii) $\eta < k$. Proving (i) is equivalent to prove $(\widetilde{g}_1 = \widehat{g}_1^s$ and $\widetilde{y}_i = \widehat{y}_{i,0}^s$ and $\widetilde{\mathsf{ppk}}_i = \widehat{\mathsf{ppk}}_{i,0}^s)$ or $(\widetilde{g}_1 = \widehat{g}_1^s$ and $\widetilde{y}_i = \widehat{y}_{i,1}^s$ and $\widetilde{\mathsf{ppk}}_i = \widehat{\mathsf{ppk}}_{i,1}^s)$ for all $i \in [\![0, l]\!]$. The tools introduced in the previous paragraph allow us to construct the following proof for such a statement: $\mathsf{ZK}\left\{s : \bigwedge_{i=0}^{l} \bigvee_{j=0}^{1}\left(\widetilde{g}_1 = \widehat{g}_1^s \wedge \widetilde{y}_i = \widehat{y}_{i,j}^s \wedge \widetilde{\mathsf{ppk}}_i = \widehat{\mathsf{ppk}}_{i,j}^s\right)\right\}$. The transcript of this proof is linear in l. On the other hand, proving (ii) consists in proving $\eta < k$, where each bit $\eta[i]$ of η is committed in $\widetilde{y}_i = \widehat{y}_{i,\eta[i]}^s$. So to prove that η is smaller than k, we need to compare k and η as binary words across commitments $\widetilde{y}_i$, by going through the bits from most to least significant. For instance, using $k = 1001101$, proving that $\eta < k$ consists in proving that $\eta[0] = 0$ or $(\eta[1] = 0$ and $\eta[2] = 0$ and $(\eta[3] = 0$ or $(\eta[4] = 0$ or $(\eta[5] = 0$ and $\eta[6] = 0)))$. In this case, the required proof is:

$$\mathsf{ZK}\left\{s : \begin{array}{l} (\widetilde{g}_1 = \widehat{g}_1^s \wedge \widetilde{y}_0 = \widehat{y}_{0,0}^s) \vee ((\widetilde{g}_1 = \widehat{g}_1^s \wedge \widetilde{y}_1 = \widehat{y}_{1,0}^s) \wedge (\widetilde{g}_1 = \widehat{g}_1^s \wedge \widetilde{y}_2 = \widehat{y}_{2,0}^s) \\ \wedge((\widetilde{g}_1 = \widehat{g}_1^s \wedge \widetilde{y}_3 = \widehat{y}_{3,0}^s) \vee ((\widetilde{g}_1 = \widehat{g}_1^s \wedge \widetilde{y}_4 = \widehat{y}_{4,0}^s) \\ \vee((\widetilde{g}_1 = \widehat{g}_1^s \wedge \widetilde{y}_5 = \widehat{y}_{5,0}^s) \wedge (\widetilde{g}_1 = \widehat{g}_1^s \wedge \widetilde{y}_6 = \widehat{y}_{6,0}^s))))) \end{array}\right\}.$$

This technique can be generalized as follows. Let $(i_j)_{0 \leq j \leq n}$ be the indices of the 1's in the binary word k. Note that i_0 is always 1. Proving that $\eta < k$ consists in the following proof:

$$\mathsf{ZK}\left\{s : \begin{array}{l} (\widetilde{g}_1 = \widehat{g}_1^s \wedge \widetilde{y}_{i_0} = \widehat{y}_{i_0,0}^s) \vee (\bigwedge_{i=i_0+1}^{i_1-1}(\widetilde{g}_1 = \widehat{g}_1^s \wedge \widetilde{y}_i = \widehat{y}_{i,0}^s) \wedge \\ ((\widetilde{g}_1 = \widehat{g}_1^s \wedge \widetilde{y}_{i_1} = \widehat{y}_{i_1,0}^s) \vee (\bigwedge_{i=i_1+1}^{i_2-1}(\widetilde{g}_1 = \widehat{g}_1^s \wedge \widetilde{y}_i = \widehat{y}_{i,0}^s) \wedge (\cdots \\ (\widetilde{g}_1 = \widehat{g}_1^s \wedge \widetilde{y}_{i_n} = \widehat{y}_{i_n,0}^s) \vee (\bigwedge_{i=i_n+1}^{l}(\widetilde{g}_1 = \widehat{g}_1^s \wedge \widetilde{y}_i = \widehat{y}_{i,0}^s)) \cdots)))) \end{array}\right\}$$

The relation of this proof is a boolean combination of l proofs of equality of discrete logarithms. Using the techniques presented above, we thus obtain a proof whose transcript size is l times the transcript size of a proof of equality of discrete logarithms. This may seem surprising, since the development of the boolean formula gives on the order of l^2 terms, however the generic transformations we use for the **and** and **or** proofs depend on how the formula is expressed, and the size of the proofs is linear in the number of termes in the formula. We detail an example to illustrate this point in the extended version of this work [9]. Finally, we use the Fiat-Shamir [16] transform to change these proofs into non-interactive ones. The proof $\Pi_{<k}$ is the composition of the two proofs presented above.

6   Extension to Sanitizable Signatures

Sanitizable signature schemes [1] enable a delegate called the *sanitizer* to modify specific sections of a signed message $m = m_1 \| \cdots \| m_n$ and update the signature consistently with these modifications. They can also be seen as a more restrictive variant of proxy signatures, in which the sanitizer receives delegations prescribing portions of the messages it can sign: the (sanitizable) signature algorithm produces both a signature and data enabling the delegate to produce new signatures using the sanitization algorithm (corresponding to the delegation certificate in proxy signature) as long as the restrictions chosen by the signer are respected.

In this section we formalise the notion of a *(fully traceable) k-times anonymous sanitizable signature* (k-SAN). Due to space limitations, we only briefly describe the formal definition and the security model for k-SAN (the full definitions are given in the extended version of this work [9]). We then extend our proxy signature scheme to the case of sanitizable signatures. Our formal definition combines the features of the k-times anonymous proxy signatures defined in Sect. 3 with the standard features of sanitizable signatures [3,4,12,24]. In particular, each sanitization requires the use of a delegation that can only be used k times, even if it is used for different signatures.

A k-SAN is composed by the algorithms Setup, KeyGen, SaKeyGen, Delegate, Sign, Sanitize, Verify, Link and Trace. With the exception of Sign and Sanitize, all these algorithms are defined in a similar way to k-APS (SaKeyGen correspond to PKeyGen and generate the sanitizer key pair (ssk, spk)). The algorithms Sign and Sanitize are defined as follows:

Sign(m, ADM, sk, spk): given a signer secret key sk, a sanitizer public key spk, a message m, a admissible set ADM (which describes the set of all modifications MOD that can be applied to the message), return a signature σ.

Sanitize(m, σ, MOD, ssk, pk, del, η): given the signer public key pk, the sanitizer secret key ssk, a message-signature pair (m, σ), a modification MOD, a delegation del, a signature index η, return a signature σ' (for the modified message MOD(m)).

A k-times Anonymous Sanitizable Signature scheme is required to achieve *Unforgeability, Immutability, Transparency, Invisibility, Unlinkability, Anonymity, Traceability* and *Non-Frameability*. After describing our scheme, we give some intuition on these requirement and set out how they are achieved.

Note that sanitizable signatures usually have two additional algorithms, Prove and Judge, which allow the delegating signer to reveal a posteriori that a given signature was produced by the sanitizer. In this case, an additional security property, accountability, is required to ensure that the signer cannot blame the sanitizer for a signature it did not produce, and that the sanitizer will not be able to produce a signature that cannot be traced by the signer. Since in this article we are considering a scenario where the tracing of dishonest users is not done by the signer, but by the verifier using the mechanism triggered when the sanitizer produces too many signatures, we have not provided our construction with these algorithms and have not adapted the accountability model.

Our k-times anonymous sanitizable signature combines the design of the sanitizable signatures in [3,8] with the mechanism we introduced in our k-times anonymous proxy signature. The signature contains commitements that allows the sanitizer to show that only admissible blocks are modified. More precisely, the sanitizer gives a proof that for every block within the altered message, the commitment corresponds to the hash of the index or the hash of the index combined with its content. If any unauthorized block is altered, then the sanitizer is unable to generate the proof. In addition, the sanitizer produces elements that enable our tracing mechanism to work if it exceeds its sanitization limit. In order to achieve transparency, we show how the signer can simulate these elements in the original signature. This results in two computationally identically distributed signatures outputed by Sign and Sanitize. In what follows, we describe our k-SAN scheme. The Setup algorithm is the same as in Sect. 4.

KeyGen($1^\lambda, k, n$): if $n > 1$, set $l = \lceil \log_2(k) \rceil$, and generate two SPS-EQ keys
pairs $(\mathsf{pk}^{\mathsf{del}}_{\mathsf{SPS\text{-}EQ}}, \mathsf{sk}^{\mathsf{del}}_{\mathsf{SPS\text{-}EQ}}) \leftarrow \mathsf{KeyGen}_{\mathsf{SPS\text{-}EQ}}(1^\lambda, 4l+1)$ and $(\mathsf{pk}^{\mathsf{MOD}}_{\mathsf{S}}, \mathsf{sk}^{\mathsf{MOD}}_{\mathsf{S}}) \leftarrow$
$\mathsf{KeyGen}_{\mathsf{SPS\text{-}EQ}}(1^\lambda, 2n)$. Sample $\mathsf{sk}_{\log} \leftarrow_\$ \mathbb{Z}_p^*$ and set $\mathsf{pk}_{\log} = g_1^{\mathsf{sk}_{\log}}$. Return $\mathsf{pk} = (\mathsf{pk}^{\mathsf{del}}_{\mathsf{SPS\text{-}EQ}}, \mathsf{pk}^{\mathsf{MOD}}_{\mathsf{SPS\text{-}EQ}}, \mathsf{pk}_{\log})$ and $\mathsf{sk} = (\mathsf{sk}^{\mathsf{del}}_{\mathsf{SPS\text{-}EQ}}, \mathsf{sk}^{\mathsf{MOD}}_{\mathsf{SPS\text{-}EQ}}, \mathsf{sk}_{\log})$.

SaKeyGen(1^λ): sample $\mathsf{ssk}_{\log} \leftarrow_\$ \mathbb{Z}_q$, set $\mathsf{spk}_{\log} = g_1^{\mathsf{ssk}_{\log}}$, run $(\mathsf{ssk}_e, \mathsf{spk}_e) \leftarrow \mathsf{KeyGen}_{\mathcal{E}}(1^\lambda)$ and return $\mathsf{ssk} = (\mathsf{ssk}_{\log}, \mathsf{ssk}_e)$ as the secret key and $\mathsf{spk} = (\mathsf{spk}_{\log}, \mathsf{spk}_e)$ as the public key.

Delegate($\mathsf{sk}, \mathsf{spk}, k$): set $l = \lceil \log_2(k) \rceil$, abort if the SPS-EQ key $\mathsf{sk}^{\mathsf{del}}_{\mathsf{SPS\text{-}EQ}}$ does not support messages of $4l + 1$ group elements. For all $(i, j) \in [\![l]\!] \times \{0, 1\}$, sample $x_{i,j} \leftarrow_\$ \mathbb{Z}_p^*$, set $y_{i,j} = g_1^{x_{i,j}}$, $\mathsf{spk}_{i,j} = \mathsf{spk}_{\log}^{x_{i,j}}$ and produce the SPS signature $\widehat{\sigma} \leftarrow \mathsf{Sign}_{\mathsf{SPS\text{-}EQ}}(\mathsf{sk}^{\mathsf{del}}_{\mathsf{SPS\text{-}EQ}}, g_1, y_{1,0}, \cdots, \mathsf{spk}_{l,1})$. Return $\mathsf{del} = ((x_{i,j}, y_{i,j}, \mathsf{spk}_{i,j})_{i \in [\![l]\!]; j \in \{0,1\}}, \widehat{\sigma})$.

Below, we describe the Sign and Sanitize algorithms, drawing parallels between their similarities and specifying their respective executions when they differ.

Both $\mathsf{Sign}(m, \mathsf{ADM}, \mathsf{sk}, \mathsf{spk})$ and $\mathsf{Sanitize}(m, \sigma, \mathsf{MOD}, \mathsf{ssk}, \mathsf{pk}, \mathsf{del}, \eta)$ set $l = \lceil \log_2(k) \rceil$. Then:

Sign: Parse $m \xrightarrow{p} m_1 \| \cdots \| m_n$, sample $\eta \leftarrow_\$ [\![0, k-1]\!]$, $s \leftarrow_\$ \mathbb{Z}_p^*$, and $\widehat{g}_1, \widehat{y}_{i,j}, \widehat{\mathsf{spk}}_{i,j} \leftarrow_\$ \mathbb{G}_1$ for all $(i, j) \in [\![l]\!] \times \{0, 1\}$. Simulate a delegation by singing $\widehat{\sigma} \leftarrow \mathsf{Sign}_{\mathsf{SPS\text{-}EQ}}(\mathsf{sk}^{\mathsf{del}}_{\mathsf{SPS\text{-}EQ}}, \widehat{g}_1, \widehat{y}_{1,0}, \cdots, \widehat{\mathsf{spk}}_{l,1})$. For all $i \in [\![l]\!]$ and $j \in \{0, 1\}$, set $\widetilde{y}_i = \widehat{y}_{i, \eta[i]}^s$, and $\widetilde{\mathsf{spk}}_i = \widehat{\mathsf{spk}}_{i, \eta[i]}^s$.

Sanitize: Parse $\mathsf{MOD}(m) \xrightarrow{p} m_1 \| \cdots \| m_n$, $\sigma \xrightarrow{p} (\mathsf{del}_\sigma, \mathsf{tra}, \pi_\sigma)$, $\mathsf{del}_\sigma \xrightarrow{p} (\widehat{g}_1, \widehat{g}_1, ((\widehat{y}_{i,b}, \widehat{\mathsf{spk}}_{i,b})_{b \in \{0,1\}}, \widetilde{y}_i, \widetilde{\mathsf{spk}}_i)_{i \in [\![l]\!]}, \widehat{\sigma}, \Pi_{<k})$ and $\mathsf{tra} \xrightarrow{p} ((u_i, v_i)_{i=1}^n, \widetilde{y}, \alpha_1, \alpha_2, \alpha_3, \alpha_4, \tau, \pi_{\mathsf{MOD}}, \sigma_{\mathsf{MOD}}, e)$ (Note that the values of most of these variables will be updated by reallocation during the algorithm). Then proceeds similarly to the initial steps of the Sign algorithm of the k-APS signature scheme, halting before the execution of the proof $\Pi_{<k}$.

Both algorithms generate the proof $\Pi_{<k}$ of knowledge of s and η which proves that (i) $\widetilde{y}_i$ and $\widetilde{\mathsf{spk}}_i$ are well formed according to s and some integer η of l bits

and *(ii)* $\eta < k$. This proof follows the same instantiation as before. To conclude this first part, set $\mathsf{del}_\sigma = (\widehat{g}_1, \widetilde{g}_1, ((\widehat{y}_{i,b}, \widehat{\mathsf{spk}}_{i,b})_{b \in \{0,1\}}, \widetilde{y}_i, \widetilde{\mathsf{spk}}_i)_{i \in \llbracket l \rrbracket}, \widehat{\sigma}, \Pi_{<k})$.

Both algorithms start the second phase by setting the message blocks:

<u>Sign:</u> To mandate the sanitizer for a set of modifiable blocks: sample $a \leftarrow\!\!\$ \, \mathbb{Z}_p^*$. For all $i \in \mathsf{ADM}$ let $u_i = H(m_i, i, 0)^a$ and $v_i = H(m_i, i, 1)^a$, otherwise let $u_i = H(i, 0)^a$ and $v_i = H(i, 1)^a$. Encrypt $e \leftarrow \mathsf{Enc}(\mathsf{spk}_e, a)$

<u>Sanitize:</u> Sample $b \leftarrow\!\!\$ \, \mathbb{Z}_p^*$, decrypt $a \leftarrow \mathsf{Dec}(\mathsf{ssk}_e, e)$ and update $e \leftarrow \mathsf{Enc}(\mathsf{spk}_e, a \cdot b)$. Set $\mathsf{ADM} = \emptyset$ and $\forall i \in \llbracket n \rrbracket$, let $u_i = H(m_i, i, 0)^{a \cdot b}$ and $v_i = H(m_i, i, 1)^{a \cdot b}$ when the signature contains $H(m_i, i, 0)^a$ and $H(m_i, i, 1)^a$, otherwise let $u_i = H(i, 0)^{a \cdot b}$ and $v_i = H(i, 1)^{a \cdot b}$. Check $\mathsf{MOD} \subset \mathsf{ADM}$ and set $a = a \cdot b$.

Both algorithms prove:

$$\pi_{\mathsf{MOD}} \leftarrow \mathsf{SoK}_e \left\{ a : \bigwedge_{1 \leq i \leq n} \begin{matrix} (u_i = H(m_i, i, 0)^a \wedge v_i = H(m_i, i, 1)^a) \\ \vee \, (u_i = H(i, 0)^a \wedge v_i = H(i, 1)^a) \end{matrix} \right\}.$$

<u>Sign:</u> execute $\sigma_{\mathsf{MOD}} \leftarrow \mathsf{Sign}_{\mathsf{SPS\text{-}EQ}} \left(\mathsf{sk}_{\mathsf{SPS\text{-}EQ}}^{\mathsf{MOD}}, u_1, v_1, \cdots, u_n, v_n \right)$. Set $\widetilde{y} = \prod_{i=1}^l \widetilde{y}_i$, $\widetilde{\mathsf{spk}} = \prod_{i=1}^l \widetilde{\mathsf{spk}}_i$, $u = \sum_{i=1}^n u_i$, $v = \sum_{i=1}^n v_i$ and sample the elements $\alpha_1, \alpha_3, \alpha_4 \leftarrow\!\!\$ \, \mathbb{G}_1$, $\alpha_2 \leftarrow\!\!\$ \, \mathbb{G}_2$ and a tracing element $\tau \leftarrow\!\!\$ \, \mathbb{G}_t$.

<u>Sanitize:</u> Adapt σ_{MOD} according to the randomness b: $\sigma_{\mathsf{MOD}} \leftarrow \mathsf{ChgRep}_{\mathsf{SPS\text{-}EQ}}((u_1, v_1, \cdots, u_n, v_n), \sigma_{\mathsf{MOD}}, b, \mathsf{pk}_{\mathsf{SPS\text{-}EQ}}^{\mathsf{MOD}})$. Set $x = \sum_{i=1}^l x_{i, \eta[i]}$, $\widetilde{y} = \prod_{i=1}^l \widetilde{y}_i$, $\widetilde{\mathsf{spk}} = \widetilde{y}^{\mathsf{ssk}_{\log}}$, and compute $\alpha_1 = h_1^x$. Let $u = \sum_{i=1}^n u_i$, $v = \sum_{i=1}^n v_i$ and sample $t \leftarrow\!\!\$ \, \mathbb{Z}_p^*$. Compute $\alpha_2 = g_2^t$, the matching elements $\alpha_3 = h_2^x \cdot g_1^{u \cdot \mathsf{ssk}_{\log}}$, $\alpha_4 = h_3^x \cdot h_4^{v \cdot \mathsf{ssk}_{\log}}$ and a tracing element $\tau = e(h_4, \alpha_2)^{\mathsf{ssk}_{\log}}$.

The vector of elements $\mathsf{tra} = ((u_i, v_i)_{i=1}^n, \widetilde{y}, \alpha_1, \alpha_2, \alpha_3, \alpha_4, \tau, \pi_{\mathsf{MOD}}, \sigma_{\mathsf{MOD}}, e)$ is set by both entities and embed in a signature of knowledge where the sanitizer proves the first part of the **or** statement and the signer the second part:

$$\pi_\sigma \leftarrow \mathsf{SoK}_{(\mathsf{del}, \mathsf{tra})} \{ \mathsf{sk}_{\log} : (\widetilde{y} = \widehat{g}_1^{x \cdot s} \wedge \widetilde{\mathsf{spk}} = \widetilde{y}^{\mathsf{ssk}_{\log}} \wedge \alpha_1 = h_1^x \wedge \alpha_2 = g_2^t \wedge$$
$$\alpha_3 = h_2^x \cdot g_1^{u \cdot \mathsf{ssk}_{\log}} \wedge \alpha_4 = h_3^x \cdot h_4^{v \cdot \mathsf{ssk}_{\log}} \wedge \tau = e(h_4, \alpha_2)^{\mathsf{ssk}_{\log}}) \vee (\mathsf{pk}_{\log} = g_1^{\mathsf{sk}_{\log}}) \}.$$

Finally **Sign** and **Sanitize** return the signature $\sigma = (\mathsf{del}_\sigma, \mathsf{tra}, \pi_\sigma)$.

The *signature verification* consists of re-computing the elements that are necessary for the verification of every **SPS-EQ** and signature of knowledge.

We will now informally describe the security properties of k-SAN (we recall that the formal definition can be found in the extended version of this work [9]) and explain why they hold on our scheme, except for anonymity, traceability and non-frameability that are reached in a similar way to our k-APS (Sect. 4).

Unforgeability. The users cannot generate a valid signature without knowing a secret key which has obtained a delegation. This property relies on the hardness of recovering the secret key of the signer or one of the sanitizers, which is ensured by the DDH assumption. Once this have been ruled out, we can reduce the ability of an adversary to forge a signature to its ability to forge SPS signatures.

Immutability. A sanitizable signature is *immutable* when no adversary is able to sanitize with unauthorized modification. This property relies on the collision resistance of the hash function, as well as the soundness and zero-knowledge properties of the signature of knowledge π_{MOD} (as they link the message to the signature). Moreover, the EUF-CMA security of the SPS-EQ and the DDH assumption prevent impersonation of the signer.

Transparency. The verifier cannot decide whether a given signature has been sanitized or not, which means that the outputs of Sign and Sanitize should be computationally indistinguishable. The randomised delegation encompassed in the signature is identically distributed to a newly produced one. All SoK can be produced by both the signer and the sanitizer, while the other elements are shown to computationally indistinguishable based on the DDH problem.

Invisibility. The invisibility property prevents an adversary which is not the signer nor the sanitizer of a signature from determining any information on the modifiable blocks. The difference between a modifiable block and a non-modifiable block is the input of the hash function serving as a commitment. The obtained hash is then elevated to a secret random power. Therefore, invisibility mainly relies on the class hiding property (Definition 1).

Unlinkability. Considering a fixed sanitizer assigned with two signatures, the verifier cannot link a sanitized signature with its original version. In the proposed signature scheme, all elements undergo randomization during sanitization or are entirely new, which ensures this property.

Anonymity Versus Unlinkability. We highlight the fact that, although conceptually close, the properties of unlinkability and anonymity capture independent attack scenarios. In unlinkability, the adversary tries to link signatures modified for a single known sanitizer, while in anonymity, the adversary has to guess the identity of an unknown sanitizer for a given message and can control the modifications this sanitizer makes to these signatures. Since in anonymity the adversary chooses for itself how and by whom signatures are modified via oracles, knowing how to link a sanitized signatures to its original gives it no advantage. Note that for signatures sanitized by the unknown sanitizer that the adversary has to determine, the sanitization oracle will always use the key of the unknown sanitizer, thus avoiding trivial attacks where the adversary tests whether the sanitization of its signature by a chosen sanitizer fails or not.

On the other hand, in unlinkability, the adversary receives a signature sanitized by a given user, and must determine the original signature used. As the original signature can only be sanitized by one sanitizer chosen *a priori* by the signer, guessing the identity of this sanitizer by attacking anonymity gives the adversary no advantage. So there is no implication between unlinkability and anonymity.

Note that when the k limit is exceeded, it is the identity of the sanitizer and the link between their signatures that are leaked, but it is still not possible to link the sanitized signatures to the original signatures; we link the signatures of a sanitizer, but the unlinkability property still holds for these signatures.

We therefore have the following theorem, the proofs are availablein the extended version of this work [9].

Theorem 2. *Instanciated by a signature on equivalent classes that is unforgeable, class-hiding, and signature adaptatable, by* NIZK *proofs which are zero-knowledge and sound, by a collision-resistant hash function, by a* SoK *that is perfectly-simulability and simulation-extractability, and by an* IND-CCA *public key encryption, our* k-SAN *is unforgeable, immutable, transparent, unlinkable, anonymity, invisible, k-traceable and non-frameable under the* DDH *assumption in* $\mathbb{G}_1$ *and* $\mathbb{G}_2$ *in the random oracle model.*

7   Conclusion

In this paper, we mitigate for practical purposes the delegations carried out through some signatures with anonymity. To this end, we define full traceable k-times anonymity for proxy signatures and sanitizable signatures. In both cases, we define a security model, give an efficient scheme (in the sense that the size of keys and signatures is logarithmic in k), and prove its security. In the future, we would like to address two problems that we leave open: the construction of k-times proxy/sanitizable signature schemes that produce signatures of constant size, and the construction of schemes that do not require the generic group model (required for equivalence class signatures).

Acknowledgments. The authors would like to thank Jan Bobolz and the anonymous reviewers for their valuable and insightful comments. Xavier Bultel's research was supported by the ANR project PRIV-SIQ (ANR-23-CE39-0008). Charles Olivier-Anclin's research was partially supported by the ANR projet MobiS5 (ARN-18-CE39-0019).

References

1. Ateniese, G., Chou, D.H., De Medeiros, B., Tsudik, G.: Sanitizable signatures. In: Computer Security–ESORICS 2005: 10th European Symposium on Research in Computer Security (2005)
2. Au, M.H., Susilo, W., Yiu, S.M.: Event-oriented k-times revocable-iff-linked group signatures. In: ACISP 2006 (2006)
3. Bossuat, A., Bultel, X.: Unlinkable and invisible γ-sanitizable signatures. In: International Conference on Applied Cryptography and Network Security (2021)
4. Brzuska, C., et al.: Security of sanitizable signatures revisited. In: Public Key Cryptography–PKC 2009: 12th International Conference on Practice and Theory in Public Key Cryptography (2009)
5. Brzuska, C., Fischlin, M., Lehmann, A., Schröder, D.: Unlinkability of sanitizable signatures. In: PKC 2010 (2010)
6. Brzuska, C., Pöhls, H.C., Samelin, K.: Efficient and perfectly unlinkable sanitizable signatures without group signatures. In: Public Key Infrastructures, Services and Applications: 10th European Workshop (2014)
7. Bultel, X., Lafourcade, P.: k-times full traceable ring signature. In: 2016 11th International Conference on Availability, Reliability and Security (2016)

8. Bultel, X., Lafourcade, P., Lai, R.W., Malavolta, G., Schröder, D., Thyagarajan, S.A.K.: Efficient invisible and unlinkable sanitizable signatures. In: 22nd IACR International Conference on Practice and Theory of Public-Key Cryptography (2019)

9. Bultel, X., Olivier-Anclin, C.: Taming delegations in anonymous signatures: k-times anonymity for proxy and sanitizable signature (2024). https://hal.science/hal-04644979

10. Camenisch, J., Derler, D., Krenn, S., Pöhls, H.C., Samelin, K., Slamanig, D.: Chameleon-hashes with ephemeral trapdoors. In: PKC 2017 (2017)

11. Camenisch, J., Stadler, M.: Efficient group signature schemes for large groups. In: Advances in Cryptology — CRYPTO '97 (1997)

12. Canard, S., Jambert, A.: On extended sanitizable signature schemes. In: Cryptographers' Track at the RSA Conference (2010)

13. Chase, M., Lysyanskaya, A.: On signatures of knowledge. In: Advances in Cryptology-CRYPTO: 26th Annual International Cryptology Conference (2006)

14. Chaum, D., Pedersen, T.P.: Wallet databases with observers. In: Brickell, E.F. (ed.) CRYPTO 1992. LNCS, vol. 740, pp. 89–105. Springer, Heidelberg (1993). https://doi.org/10.1007/3-540-48071-4_7

15. Cramer, R., Damgård, I., Schoenmakers, B.: Proofs of partial knowledge and simplified design of witness hiding protocols. In: Desmedt, Y.G. (ed.) CRYPTO 1994. LNCS, vol. 839, pp. 174–187. Springer, Heidelberg (1994). https://doi.org/10.1007/3-540-48658-5_19

16. Fiat, A., Shamir, A.: How to prove yourself: Practical solutions to identification and signature problems. In: CRYPTO' 86 (1987)

17. Fleischhacker, N., Krupp, J., Malavolta, G., Schneider, J., Schröder, D., Simkin, M.: Efficient unlinkable sanitizable signatures from signatures with re-randomizable keys. In: 19th IACR International Conference on Practice and Theory in Public-Key Cryptography (2016)

18. Fuchsbauer, G., Hanser, C., Slamanig, D.: Structure-preserving signatures on equivalence classes and constant-size anonymous credentials. J. Cryptology (2019)

19. Fuchsbauer, G., Pointcheval, D.: Anonymous proxy signatures. In: Security and Cryptography for Networks: 6th International Conference (2008)

20. Fujisaki, E., Suzuki, K.: Traceable ring signature. In: Public Key Cryptography – PKC 2007 (2007)

21. Goldwasser, S., Micali, S.: Probabilistic encryption. J. Comput. Syst. Sci. (1984)

22. Groth, J., Maller, M.: Snarky signatures: minimal signatures of knowledge from simulation-extractable snarks. In: Annual International Cryptology Conference (2017)

23. Klonowski, M., Lauks, A.: Extended sanitizable signatures. In: Proceedings of the 9th International Conference on Information Security and Cryptology, ICISC'06 (2006)

24. Krenn, S., Samelin, K., Sommer, D.: Stronger security for sanitizable signatures. In: International Workshop on Data Privacy Management (2015)

25. Liu, W., Yang, G., Mu, Y., Wei, J.: k-time proxy signature: formal definition and efficient construction. In: Provable Security: 7th International Conference, ProvSec 2013, Melaka, Malaysia, October 23-25, 2013. Proceedings 7 (2013)

26. Mambo, M., Usuda, K., Okamoto, E.: Proxy signatures for delegating signing operation. In: Proceedings of the 3rd ACM Conference on Computer and Communications Security. CCS '96 (1996). https://doi.org/10.1145/238168.238185

27. Teranishi, I., Furukawa, J., Sako, K.: k-times anonymous authentication (extended abstract). In: ASIACRYPT 2004 (2004)

28. Wei, J., Yang, G., Mu, Y.: Anonymous proxy signature with restricted traceability. In: 2014 IEEE 13th International Conference on Trust, Security and Privacy in Computing and Communications (2014)
29. Wei, J., Yang, G., Mu, Y., Liang, K.: Anonymous proxy signature with hierarchical traceability. Comput. J. (2015)

LARMix++: Latency-Aware Routing in Mix Networks with Free Routes Topology

Mahdi Rahimi[✉] [iD]

COSIC (KU Leuven), Leuven, Belgium
mahdi.rahimi@esat.kuleuven.be

Abstract. Mix networks (mixnets) enhance anonymity by routing client messages through multiple hops, intentionally delaying or reordering these messages to ensure unlinkability. However, this process increases end-to-end latency, potentially degrading the client experience. To address this issue, LARMix (NDSS, 2024) proposed a low-latency routing methodology specifically designed for stratified mixnet architectures. Our paper extends this concept to Free Routes mixnet designs, where, unlike stratified topologies, there are no restrictions on node connections. We adapt several state-of-the-art low-latency routing strategies from both mix and Tor networks to optimize the Free Routes topology. Despite the benefits, low-latency routing can cause certain mixnodes to receive disproportionate amounts of traffic. To overcome this challenge, we introduce a novel load-balancing algorithm that evenly distributes traffic among nodes without significantly compromising low-latency characteristics. Our analytical and simulation experiments demonstrate a considerable reduction in latency compared to uniform routing methods, with negligible loss in message anonymity, defined as the confusion an adversary experiences when correlating messages exiting the mixnet to an initially targeted input message. Additionally, we provide an analysis of adversarial strategies, revealing a balanced trade-off between low latency and adversary advantages.

Keywords: Mix network · Anonymity · Latency

1 Introduction

Anonymous communication systems, designed to conceal the identities of communicators within network infrastructures, can be implemented using various methodologies [24]. Among the most prominent is the Tor overlay network [11], which supports over two million daily users. In Tor, a client selects three intermediary nodes-termed Guard, Middle, and Exit relays-and sequentially encrypts the message with the public keys of these relays. Each relay, upon receiving the message, decrypts it with its private key and forwards it to the next relay, with knowledge limited only to the identities of the adjacent relays in the message path,

M. Kohlweiss et al. (Eds.): CANS 2024, LNCS 14905, pp. 187–211, 2025.
https://doi.org/10.1007/978-981-97-8013-6_9

thereby preserving anonymity. However, Tor's architecture has vulnerabilities to adversaries who observe both ends of the communication channel-specifically, the interactions between the client and the Guard relay, and between the Exit relay and the destination [27]. These vulnerabilities can be exploited through compromised Guard and Exit relays or by controlling Autonomous Systems (ASes) located between these communication points. Such exposures allow adversaries to conduct effective correlation attacks that can potentially deanonymize the communication endpoints [2].

The vulnerabilities of Tor to correlation attacks render it less secure and suboptimal for scenarios requiring high anonymity guarantees. To address these vulnerabilities and propose an anonymous system that not only mitigates Tor's weaknesses but is also immune to a global passive adversary (GPA) observing all network communications, the concept of a mix network (mixnet) has been followed in several studies [8, 16, 19, 28]. Mixnets enhance the anonymity provided by Tor through implementing traffic mixing at each intermediary node, known as a mixnode, a concept pioneered by Chaum [5]. This mixing process ensures that the output from each mixnode is not directly linkable to its input, thus preserving anonymity. Consequently, as long as one mixnode correctly performs this mixing along the message route, it can effectively thwart a GPA's attempts to correlate traffic [7].

This obfuscation (traffic mixing) provided by mixnodes can be achieved through various methods. The first method involves threshold mixes [5], which accumulate messages until a preset count is reached before forwarding them. The second method employs pool mixnodes [10], requiring both a threshold number of messages and a time limit before messages are forwarded. The third method, stop-and-go mixes [14], introduces a random, exponentially distributed delay to each message before release. Among these methods, stop-and-go mixing offers a high degree of anonymity due to the memoryless property of the exponential distribution and has been recently put into practice due to its manageable average latency [8].

Like mixnode types, mixnet topologies can also be implemented in several distinct ways to enhance security and anonymity [9]. For a mixnet consisting of L intermediary hops, a common configuration is the cascade topology, where mixnodes are organized into cascades, each containing L mixnodes. Clients select one of these cascades for message routing [4, 16, 28]. An alternative configuration, known as Free Routes, involves clients randomly selecting L distinct nodes from all available mixnodes to establish a message path [17].[1] Another approach is the stratified topology, which organizes mixnodes into L different layers. A message path is then formed by selecting one mixnode from each layer, ensuring diversified routing and enhanced anonymity due to the many possible routing paths compared to the cascade topology [8, 19].[2]

---

[1] The Tor network also employs a Free Routes topology for message routing.

[2] However, the stratified topology provides less anonymity compared to the Free Routes topology.

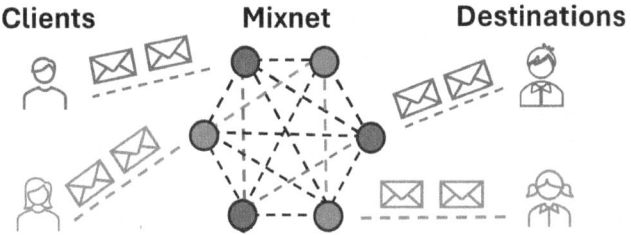

Clients   Mixnet   Destinations

Fig. 1. Clients communicating through a Free Route mixnet.

These topological choices significantly influence the network's anonymity and its handling of cover traffic. Cover traffic consists of dummy messages introduced by clients or mixnodes that do not have a designated destination and are eventually dropped. Cover traffic strategies are often designed to mislead the GPA and enhance anonymity. Typically, cover traffic is added based on the input traffic to ensure that all mixnodes handle nearly the same amount of traffic. As a result, when routing in the mixnet is more restricted, the input traffic for most nodes is similar due to fewer diverse routes. In contrast, less restricted routing results in mixnodes with diverse input traffic. Consequently, the cascade topology allows for substantial integration of cover traffic but generally provides lower levels of anonymity compared to other configurations. Free Routes offer the highest degree of anonymity but are less effective at incorporating cover traffic. The stratified topology, however, represents an optimal design that maximizes anonymity while minimizing overhead [9]. Due to these advantageous characteristics, the stratified network topology has recently gained in popularity [8].

Although the stratified topology is recognized as the optimal mixnet topology for anonymizing communications, this type often requires decentralized parties to decide on numerous aspects, such as the number of mixnodes at each layer, the specific layer each mixnode should occupy, and the protocols for how, when, and where cover traffic should be added and removed. This coordination is often managed by external entities involved in mixnets, like NYM[3], which necessitates that clients wishing to join the network must subscribe and be verified by these parties to ensure they are authorized to access the network [8]. Specifically, such a design can become prohibitive in cost for a local group of clients with few mixnodes that wish to establish a local mixnet. In these cases, the best option is the Free Routes topology, which offers the highest level of anonymity with a simpler structure, eliminating the need for an external party. However, as Free Routes are less effective for incorporating cover traffic, it is crucial to ensure sufficient traffic volume when using this structure.[4]

---

[3] https://nymtech.net.

[4] One pertinent example of this case is opportunistic social networks, where users utilize mobile devices to communicate and share data without a centralized control point. To achieve greater anonymity in these networks, the Free Routes topology of mixnet is recommended [6].

Design Goals. Despite the low-cost and easy deployment characteristics of Free Routes mixnets, there has been limited effort to optimize message routing within this framework. This paper aims to provide optimized routing for Free Routes mixnets, with a focus on reducing latency. Latency optimization is crucial in mixnets as any configuration of mixnets inherently increases latency. This is due to the forwarding of clients' messages through multiple mixnodes before reaching their final destinations, with additional delays incurred by mixnodes for mixing purposes. For example, Fig. 1 illustrates a Free Routes mixnet topology where clients first forward their messages to the mixnet, incurring client-mixnet link delay. The messages are then forwarded through mixnodes, incurring both mix-link delays and mixing delays. Finally, the messages are sent to the destination, leading to mix-destination link latency. To reduce latency in such scenarios, the selection of mixnodes within the mixnet can be strategically biased towards low-latency paths where most mixnodes are either close or at least not excessively far apart, thus facilitating faster connections. Therefore, our goal is to design a mixnet routing strategy that reduce link delays within mixnet while preserving a high degree of anonymity and ensuring balanced load distribution among mixnodes.

Related Works. Despite investigating latency optimization of Free Route mixnets in this work, significant efforts to reduce latency in anonymous communications have predominantly focused within Tor networks [1,13,23]. These studies, despite being centered on Tor, could potentially inform strategies for Free Routes mixnets, although the differences in threat models between Tor networks and mixnets make them only indirectly applicable. For example, Lastor [1] introduces low-latency methods that suggest partitioning the network into regions where each contains a few Tor relays. Clients successively select the closest region, and within it, they randomly choose their relay. However, this approach has two main issues. First, partitioning the network in such a manner, assuming dynamic changes, is not entirely realistic, especially for a mixnet where the primary threat is considered to be a GPA rather than AS-level adversaries. Secondly, their method could lead to an imbalance of traffic distributions in the mixnet, which should be addressed to maintain network efficiency.

In other research, ShorTor [13] investigates the inefficiencies of the Border Gateway Protocol (BGP) in optimizing for the shortest or lowest latency paths, suggesting that sometimes routing through intermediate nodes rather than direct transmission can accelerate connections. This principle, similar to methods used by Content Delivery Networks (CDNs) to reduce latency, implies forming a multi-hop overlay network atop the Tor network. Although potentially useful for mixnets, this approach would require significant infrastructure modifications for adaptation to mixnets. Moreover, the paper does not thoroughly address load balancing in such configurations.

Another particularly innovative approach, CLAPS [23], potentially can enhance location-aware schemes in Tor by employing linear programming to optimize routing for reduced latency, targeted reduction in ASes correlation attacks, or improved relay resilience against IP hijacking. While CLAPS can be adapted to mixnet applications with some changes and also provides load balancing, it faces high computational costs due to the nature of linear programming. In the best case, using Interior Point Methods, the complexity of linear programming is $O(n^3 b)$, where n represents the number of constraints, reaching up to a million in the case of Tor, and b represents the number of bits needed to represent numbers.[5]

Within mixnet research, LARMix [22] stands out as the only initiative that has explicitly targeted reducing end-to-end latency. LARMix investigates a stratified mixnet model and proposes a node selection scheme that ensures a diverse assignment of mixnodes across network layers, incorporating a sufficient number of nodes from varied jurisdictions. Additionally, their routing formula prioritizes proximity in node selection along the message paths, regulated by a tunable parameter $0 \leq \tau \leq 1$, which strategically balances latency reduction with anonymity and load balancing. However, this approach is specifically designed for stratified mixnets and does not directly translate to Free Route mixnets. Building upon these findings, our research aims to extend the results of LARMix to develop a low-latency Free Route mixnet, adapting the principles to fit a different network structure.[6]

Our Contributions. To develop low-latency routing for mixnets with a Free Routes topology, we consider a setup where there are N available mixnodes, and each client selects L distinct mixnodes to form message paths.[7] Building on this framework, we first adapt the LASTor [1] and LARMix [22] routing equations to our scenario, specifically by tuning the parameter $0 \leq \tau \leq 1$ to manage latency effectively. Applying these routing policies can result in some mixnodes receiving a higher traffic rate than normal. To counteract this, we have developed the Rebalancing Load Distribution (RLD) algorithm, which adjusts routing policies in mixnets to ensure traffic is fairly distributed among mixnodes while minimally impacting the low-latency property of the routing. Implementing RLD incurs a computational expense of $O(kN^2)$ when k is usually much less than N. On the other hand, it also curtails the advantage of adversaries who could potentially exploit the routing strategies from LARMix or LASTor to corrupt mixnodes in positions that receive a high proportion of traffic.[8]

Furthermore, we incorporate a linear programming approach inspired by the CLAPS framework [23] to derive a routing policy that prioritizes low-latency

---

[5] Other location-aware Tor strategies [18,26,29] primarily focus on limiting the visibility of ASes or ISPs, or strengthening the resilience of Tor relays against active IP hijacking. These considerations are less relevant to mixnets, given the assumption of a GPA and their non-applicability for low-latency routing in mixnets.

[6] CALM [21] is another similar work to LARMix, designed to extend LARMix's results to include low-latency message forwarding from clients to the mixnet.

[7] Note that clients can generally choose more or fewer than L hops; however, in practice, to ensure that the load received by mixnodes is balanced and that anonymity and latency are controlled, the number of hops is considered a fixed parameter.

[8] This type of attack is known as Guard Replacement Attacks in Tor [29].

paths. We make this linear programming tunable with the parameter τ, introducing a tunable load balancing option for CLAPS. Here, $\tau = 0$ represents the most biased routing with the least load balance, while $\tau = 1$ signifies a fully balanced approach, less biased towards low-latency paths. Although this approach is computationally demanding, it effectively reduces latency while maintaining balanced load distribution across mixnodes.

We evaluate the developed routing strategies in two phases. **Firstly**, we perform an analytical assessment, similar to the approach taken by LARMix, by measuring the entropy of the distinguishing likelihood of message paths as an indicator of analytical anonymity, and by measuring the average link delay caused by the mixnet as analytical latency. **Secondly**, we simulate a Free Route mixnet using the discrete event simulator *SimPy* [20] in *Python*, where we measure the end-to-end latency (caused by both link delays and mixing processes) and the entropy of messages based on the algorithm in [3]. Our experiments, under the constraint of a mixnet with 100 nodes and modeling the link delay between mixnodes using the RIPE Atlas dataset [25], show that using an adapted version of LARMix routing can reduce the link delay latency by up to 61% compared to uniform routing while compromising at most 1 bit of message entropy. Further, applying the RLD algorithm to balance the mixnet results in a 40% reduction of this latency while losing less than 0.5 bits of entropy and ensuring fair load distribution among the mixnodes. Additionally, experiments suggest that using CLAPS-based routing can achieve latency on par with LARMix while maintaining load balance, albeit at the cost of high computational demands and reducing anonymity dramatically.

Finally, we provide an analysis to ensure that our modifications do not significantly enhance the capabilities of mixnode adversaries who corrupt (own) some mixnodes in the mixnet and, in collaboration with GPA, attempt to de-anonymize client connections. This analysis considers random corruption of mixnodes as well as corruption of mixnodes from a particular location, as suggested by LARMix [22]. Furthermore, we have developed the Intelligent Corruption algorithm (IC), which allows adversaries to strategically control mixnodes to maximize their advantage, measured in terms of the fraction of fully corrupted paths (FCP). Our findings reveal that in the worst-case scenario, while maintaining a balanced mixnet, a mixnode adversary can corrupt paths at a rate twice as high as that observed with uniform routing.

2   Approach

This section details routing strategies aimed at reducing latency within a Free Routes mixnet. This involves a scenario where N mixnodes are available, and for each message route, L must be selected. To better understand this, consider an example depicted in Fig. 2. In this example, $N = 4$ and $L = 3$. A client willing to form a path for her message first picks the initial mixnode (1st hop) uniformly at random as M_1. Based on this choice, the client then selects the next mixnode (2nd hop) by considering the latency from the first mixnode M_1

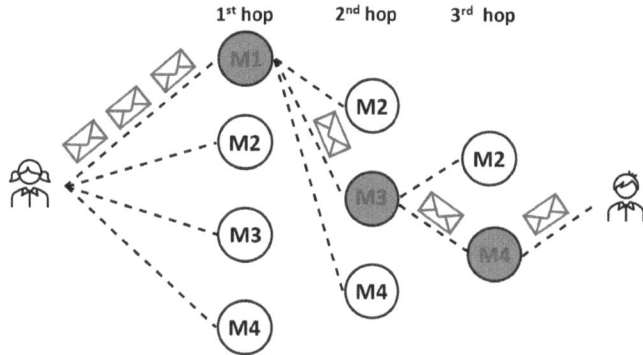

Fig. 2. Example of mixnode selection in a Free Routes mixnet.

to the unselected ones. If M_3 is chosen for the 2nd hop, this process is repeated for selecting the third mixnode (3rd hop) by evaluating the latency between M_3 and the two remaining mixnodes (M_2 and M_4). Considering such scenarios, we begin by adapting both LASTor [1] and LARMix [22] routing strategies for the Free Routes topology. We then enhance these strategies with load balancing by developing the RLD algorithm. Furthermore, we introduce a linear programming approach inspired by CLAPS [23] to optimize low-latency routing.

2.1 LASTor Routing

We adapt LASTor routing as shown in Eq. (1), defining the routing strategy from node i at hop k to any node j at hop $k + 1$. This formula specifically ties the selection of the next mixnode to the inverse of its latency (l_{ij} represents the latency between node i and j), implying that the closer the node, the higher the probability it will be selected. In other words, Eq. (1) specifies R_{ij}^k as the probability of forwarding a message from mixnode i at the kth hop to mixnode j at the $(k+1)^{th}$ hop, given that j belongs to S_k, where S_k is the set of available mixnodes for selection at hop $k+1$, excluding any mixnodes that were previously chosen for hop 1 to k.

In Eq. (1), the parameter τ moderates the level of bias: when $\tau = 0$, the routing is fully biased towards the inverse of latency, whereas increasing τ makes the routing more uniform. Specifically, when $\tau = 1$, the routing becomes uniformly random among all mixnodes that can be selected as the next hop. For instance, as depicted in Fig. 2, consider the latency between M_3 and M_2 is 10 ms, and between M_3 and M_4 is 5 ms; when $\tau = 0$, M_4 will be chosen twice as often as M_2 on average with LASTor routing.

$$R_{ij}^k = \frac{\frac{1}{l_{ij}}^{(1-\tau)}}{\sum_{j \in S_k} \frac{1}{l_{ij}}^{(1-\tau)}}. \tag{1}$$

2.2 LARMix Routing

LARMix routing formula can also be adapted for Free Routes mixnets as described in Eq. (2), showing R_{ij}^k for choosing mixnode j at hop $k + 1$. Similar to LASTor, LARMix prioritizes mixnodes with lower latency by considering the inverse of latency raised to the power of $1 - \tau$. Additionally, LARMix introduces a ranking function f_{ij}, which receives nodes i and j and assigns a rank indicating the closeness of j to i, starting from 0 for the closest mixnode to $|S_k| - 1$ for the farthest mixnode. This ranking mechanism ensures that as τ approaches 0, the selection of the closest mixnode occurs with a probability approaching 1, effectively tuning the routing from a fully deterministic choice of the closest mixnode to a uniform routing when $\tau = 1$. This flexibility allows for tuning bias in the network design according to specific requirements. For example, consider the scenario of routing from the 2nd to the 3rd hop in Fig. 2. If $\tau = 0$ and $f_{34} = 0$, M_4 would be selected with a probability of 1 as the 3rd hop.

$$
R_{ij}^k = \frac{\left(\frac{1}{e}\right)^{f_{ij}\frac{(1-\tau)}{\tau}} \cdot \left(\frac{1}{l_{ij}}\right)^{(1-\tau)}}{\sum_{j \in S_k} \left(\frac{1}{e}\right)^{f_{ij}\frac{(1-\tau)}{\tau}} \cdot \left(\frac{1}{l_{ij}}\right)^{(1-\tau)}}. \tag{2}
$$

2.3 Rebalancing Load Distributions (RLD)

After biasing the routing using either the LASTor or LARMix formulas in a mixnet, some mixnodes receive loads greater than those typically experienced under a uniform routing policy. If not addressed, this imbalance can confer an advantage to adversaries by allowing them to deploy high-capacity mixnodes capable of handling significant traffic, potentially leading to substantial de-anonymization of network traffic. This type of threat in the Tor network is known as Guard Replacement Attacks [29]. To mitigate this, the load distribution must be rebalanced.

The concept of balancing loads was first introduced in LARMix [22], using a Greedy approach to ensure network rebalancing while considering the prioritization of low-latency paths. However, this approach is specific to stratified mixnets and is not applicable to Free Routes mixnets. In this context, we introduce a Rebalancing Load Distributions (RLD) algorithm that effectively balances network load while still prioritizing low-latency routings.

Before explaining the RLD, it is important to note that clients are supposed to pick the first hop uniformly at random, similar to the assumption in LARMix [22]. Additionally, we suppose each node is equally likely to be in each position (each hop). Based on this, we balance the received load from each position by the mix nodes. To this end, we define $\mathbf{R}^k$ as the routing matrix from hop k to hop $k+1$, where $\mathbf{R}^k = \begin{bmatrix} R_{ij}^k \end{bmatrix}$. Initially, we start with balancing $\mathbf{R}^1$. For $\mathbf{R}^1$, as each mixnode should be used once in a message-route, we set $R_{ij} = 0$ if $i = j$. To rebalance this matrix, we begin by summing up each column, which shows the received loads by mixnodes at the second hop. Columns with a summation greater than 1 are considered overloaded, those with a summation less than 1 are underloaded, and those with a summation of 1 are balanced.

The RLD algorithm begins by addressing the overloaded columns, attempting to balance them by multiplying each entry in those columns by the inverse of the column's total summation. The surplus load from these columns is then redistributed to underloaded columns. This redistribution takes into account each entry individually and considers the proximity of overloaded mixnodes to underloaded ones. This ensures that the surplus load is distributed based on the probability of message forwarding from overloaded nodes to underloaded nodes. The process is iteratively repeated for all overloaded mixnodes until all columns sum to 1, achieving balanced routing from the first hop to the second hop. However, an exception to this process arises when there is only one underloaded mixnode remaining. In such scenarios, the rebalancing is adjusted to avoid loops or redundant paths. For example, consider that we have only the jth node underloaded at the second hop, while the ith node is overloaded. In this situation, any excess traffic from node i should not be redirected to node j if node j initially transferred this traffic to node i at the first hop, even if j is underloaded. This precaution prevents considering a node multiple times in the same message route, thereby preserving the integrity of the routing paths and avoiding loops.

As an example, consider Fig. 2, where we have four mixnodes at the first hop. Suppose after applying the low-latency formula, the initial routing matrix is described as:

$$\mathbf{R}^1 = \begin{bmatrix} 0 & 0.2 & 0.4 & 0.4 \\ 0.1 & 0 & 0.6 & 0.3 \\ 0.5 & 0.5 & 0 & 0 \\ 0.3 & 0.3 & 0.4 & 0 \end{bmatrix}.$$

The summation of columns in this matrix is [0.9, 1, 1.4, 0.7], indicating that the second mixnode in the second hop is balanced, the third is overloaded, and the first and fourth are underloaded. To begin balancing the matrix, we address the overloaded third column by multiplying each entry by $\frac{1}{1.4}$, adjusting the entries to $0.29, 0.42, 0$, and 0.29 respectively.

Now, we have an excess of 0.4 from the third column that should be distributed over the first and fourth columns. Starting with the first entry of the third column, which has a surplus of 0.11 (i.e., $0.4 - 0.29$), it cannot be transferred to the first column due to the diagonal constraint $R_{ij} = 0$ for $i = j$, so it is allocated to the fourth column. As for the second entry of the third column, it has a surplus of 0.18 (i.e., $0.6 - 0.42$), which will be distributed between the first and fourth columns, with the fourth column receiving three times more ($\frac{0.3}{0.1} = 3$) due to its higher probability. The third column's third entry has no surplus as it is a diagonal entry, and the fourth entry has a surplus of 0.11, which is allocated totally to the first column, also because of the diagonal constraint. After first iteration of rebalancing, the matrix looks as follows:

$$\mathbf{R}^1 = \begin{bmatrix} 0 & 0.2 & 0.29 & 0.51 \\ 0.145 & 0 & 0.42 & 0.435 \\ 0.5 & 0.5 & 0 & 0 \\ 0.41 & 0.3 & 0.29 & 0 \end{bmatrix}.$$

However, in the new matrix, the first column is slightly overloaded, and the fourth column is slightly underloaded. To further balance this, we note that the sum of the first column is 1.055. The elements of this column should be multiplied by $\frac{1}{1.055}$, but since we have only one underloaded column, we avoid distributing the surplus to the diagonal element of the fourth column. Instead, we do not touch the 0.41 entry, and we balance the other entries of the first column by a new balancing condition, which should be $1 - 0.41 = 0.59$. Therefore, all the other entries, except for the 0.41 entry, will be multiplied by $\frac{0.59}{0.145+0.5=0.645}$, and their leftovers will be transferred to the corresponding underloaded entries to achieve a fully balanced matrix.

$$\mathbf{R}^1 = \begin{bmatrix} 0 & 0.2 & 0.29 & 0.51 \\ 0.133 & 0 & 0.42 & 0.457 \\ 0.457 & 0.5 & 0 & 0.033 \\ 0.41 & 0.3 & 0.29 & 0 \end{bmatrix}.$$

Furthermore, we note that a similar process can be applied to $\mathbf{R}^k$ beyond the first hop. However, there are additional considerations for these subsequent matrices. For example, when balancing $\mathbf{R}^2$ (the same scenario as in Fig. 2), we must consider that there were four choices for the first hop. Thus, balancing the matrix $\mathbf{R}^2$ should take this into account. That is, if the first hop is M_1, then $\mathbf{R}^2$, the matrix that indicates probability distribution from the 2nd to the 3rd hop, should reflect this by having both diagonal and one additional entry at each row set to zero. This means that if M_1 is the first hop, the second, third, or fourth entries will be zeroed to prevent the repetition of sending messages through the same mixnodes multiple times, and the remaining balancing will proceed as before.

2.4 CLAPS Mix Routing

In this section, we introduce a linear programming approach tailored for designing low-latency routing in Free Routes mixnets. This methodology draws inspiration from the CLAPS framework, originally developed to enhance the resilience of Tor relays against attacks by malicious ASes [23]. Unlike CLAPS, our primary objective is to minimize end-to-end latency rather than improve resilience. Thus, we focus on minimizing the average latency between successive mixnodes, starting with the initial routing matrix, $\mathbf{R}^1$ (shown in Eq. (3)).

To achieve the low-latency routing, we iteratively optimize subsequent routing matrices, such as $\mathbf{R}^2$, enforcing constraints that ensure each matrix preserves the probability of node selection across the first and second hops. Additionally, we incorporate constraints to ensure that diagonal elements of $\mathbf{R}^k$ are zero (to prevent routing loops), and that the mixnet maintains balanced loading, modulated by the parameter τ. At $\tau = 1$, the routing within the mixnet achieves balance,[9] although not necessarily uniformity, diverging from approaches like LARMix and LASTor. Conversely, at $\tau = 0$, the routing is least balanced but potentially most optimized.[10]

$$\text{Minimize} \quad \frac{1}{N}\sum_{i=1}^{N}\sum_{j=1}^{N}R_{ij}^{1}l_{ij}, \tag{3}$$

$$\text{subject to} \quad \forall i,j, \quad 0 \le R_{ij}^{1} \le 1,$$

$$\forall i,j, \quad R_{ij}^{1} = 0 \text{ if } i = j,$$

$$\forall i, \quad \sum_{j=1}^{N}R_{ij}^{1} = 1,$$

$$\forall j, \quad \tau \le \sum_{i=1}^{N}R_{ij}^{1} \le N - \tau(N-1).$$

Finally, we note that the mentioned linear programming problem can be solved using Interior Point Methods, which operate in $O(n^3 b)$, where b is the number of bits required for the representation of the numbers and n is the number of constraints. Based on Eq. (3), $n = N^2 + 2N$, leading to a complexity of $O(N^6 b)$. However, the RLD algorithm is much more efficient than linear programming. In this algorithm, for each overloaded node, we need at most $O(N)$ operations to balance it, which should be done in the worst case for at most $N - 1$ nodes when only one node is underloaded. This process must be repeated K times, where K is generally much less than N, leading to a complexity of $O(N^2 K)$.

Furthermore, we note that clients executing routing algorithms and the RLD do not need to rely on a third party. Instead, through a decentralized and reliable approach proposed in Verloc [15], mixnodes measure their latency from one another. This data is collected and made publicly available, ensuring that clients only need to trust the majority of honest mixnodes. With these reliable latency measurements, clients with sufficient computational resources can run routing algorithms to derive the routing matrix.[11] However, in cases where the computational load exceeds the client's resources, the client can outsource the computations. In this scenario, a third party or a group of third parties, such as the network provider (like NYM) or some of the mixnodes themselves, compute the routing matrix and provide proof by employing a SNARK like Groth16 [12]. This is based on a circuit that receives the latency measurements as input and outputs the routing matrix. This ensures that the calculations derived by the

---

[9] Setting $\tau = 1$ actually obviates the need for using RLD algorithm.

[10] It is important to acknowledge that linear programming approaches are computationally intensive. However, investigating whether this computational effort can effectively reduce latency can be useful.

[11] Note that Verloc is deployed in NYM.

designated parties are valid. Importantly, this SNARK can be optimized since achieving zero-knowledge property is unnecessary; only the succinctness of proofs is required.

3   Evaluation

In this section, we evaluate the average link delay within a mixnet, which is promised to be reduced with the introduced routing methodologies discussed in Sect. 2. Additionally, we assess how much anonymity is compromised in terms of increasing the advantage of a GPA while employing low-latency routing methods.

3.1   Experimental Setup

We consider a Free Route mixnet topology with $N = 100$ mixnodes, where each client selects $L = 3$ mixnodes to form their message routes.[12] To model the link delay between network mixnodes, we utilize the RIPE Atlas dataset [25], as its globally scattered endpoints offer a representative model of latency.

To measure the average latency, we first compute all possible paths in the mixnet, which total $N(N - 1)(N - 2)$ considering $L = 3$. We then calculate the probability of each path using the routing matrix $\mathbf{R}^k$ and subsequently derive the average latency as the weighted sum of the latencies of these paths. Additionally, we consider the entropy of the probability distribution of these paths as $\mathsf{H}(P)$, representing the entropy of paths. This metric indicates how biased routing increases the advantage of a Global Passive Adversary (GPA). When the routing within the mixnet is uniformly random, the GPA has no better guess than a uniform distribution for the paths selected by the clients. However, biased routing can improve the GPA's guess.[13]

For instance, in the case of uniform routing, the entropy of paths $\mathsf{H}(P)$ equals $\log(N(N - 1)(N - 2))$, which approximates $3\log(N)$ for $L = 3$ and $N = 100$, giving $\mathsf{H}(P) = \log(10^6) \approx 20$. This metric allows us to quantify how anonymity is compromised using different routing bias approaches.

3.2   Latency

We initiate our analysis by examining the average link delay, as depicted in Fig. 3a. This figure illustrates the impact of varying τ on latency in mixnet link delays when employing different routing algorithms: LASTor, LARMix, and CLAPS Mix, under both balanced and imbalanced network conditions. Specifically, an increase in τ consistently results in higher latency across all strategies.

---

[12] Usually, in Tor [11] or the NYM network [8], the number of hops is set to 3 to manage latency while maintaining sufficient anonymity, and $N = 100$ as it is within the range of the number of nodes in each layer in deployed mixnets [8].

[13] A similar concept was used in LARMix to measure the advantage of such an adversary, albeit with an abstract consideration of the probability of connecting the entry mixnodes to the exit mixnodes.

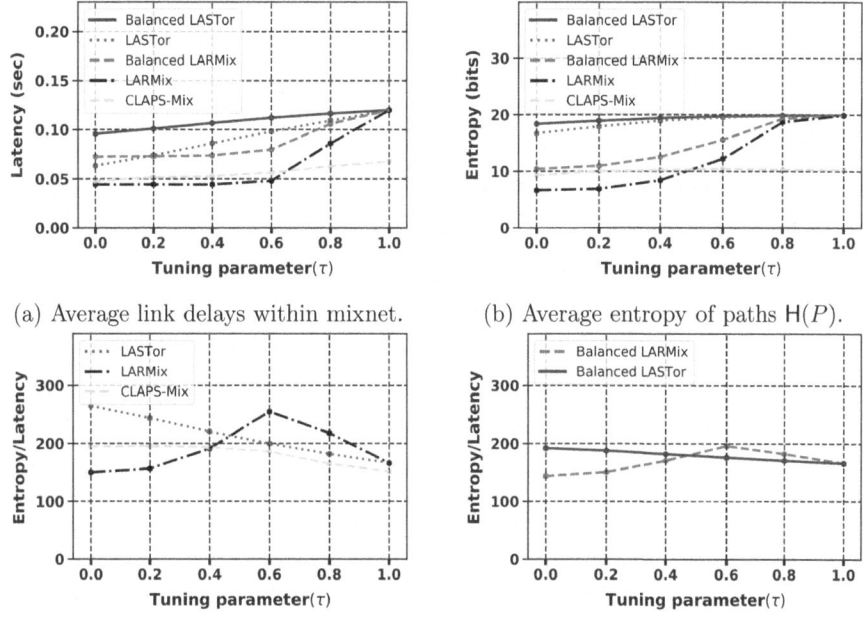

(a) Average link delays within mixnet.

(b) Average entropy of paths $H(P)$.

(c) Entropy/Latency for imbalance routings.

(d) Entropy/Latency for balanced routings.

Fig. 3. Analytical experiments

In LASTor and LARMix, τ acts as a tuning parameter that injects a varying amount of randomness into the routing policies. This randomness influences routing decisions by deprioritizing paths with lower latency, thereby increasing the average link delay. In contrast, in CLAPS Mix, τ primarily functions as a bias control factor, rather than a randomness factor. Adjusting τ in CLAPS Mix affects the network's balance rather than its randomness. As a result, higher τ values lead to a preference for more balanced paths, which naturally exhibit higher latencies compared to faster, less balanced alternatives. This trend also holds for balanced configurations in both LARMix and LASTor, where balanced setups tend to experience greater latencies than their imbalanced counterparts.

Additionally, when routing is uniform ($\tau = 1$) for LASTor and LARMix, the average link latency is approximately 120 ms. Utilizing LARMix can reduce this latency to 46 ms, representing a 61% reduction when $\tau = 0$. When LARMix is balanced, the latency is minimized to 73 ms, achieving a 40% reduction. In contrast, using LASTor in both imbalanced and balanced configurations results in latencies of 65 ms and 98 ms, respectively. Remarkably, CLAPS Mix matches the performance of an imbalanced LARMix with $\tau = 0$. Intriguingly, when CLAPS Mix is balanced ($\tau = 1$), the latency stabilizes at 65 ms, equivalent to LASTor in its imbalanced state with $\tau = 0$. This demonstrates the efficacy of linear programming in reducing latency across various configurations while ensuring a balanced distribution of traffic.

3.3   Anonymity

Figure 3b depicts the entropy of paths versus tuning parameter τ. In the uniform case, where $\tau = 1$ for LARMix or LASTor routing, the entropy is approximately 20 bits. Using CLAPS Mix, which provides very low latency, results in a dramatic decrease in entropy to about 10 bits for almost all values of the tuning parameter τ. This reduction could be detrimental as it increases the likelihood that an adversary can guess the paths selected by clients. In contrast, LARMix exhibits variable effects depending on the value of τ. For example, at $\tau = 0.6$, a balanced configuration of LARMix reduces the entropy to 16.5 bits while providing a latency of 75 ms. On the other hand, LASTor demonstrates the best overall performance; in both imbalanced and balanced configurations, it reduces entropy to 17 bits and 18.5 bits, respectively. For instance, with $\tau = 0$ in an imbalanced LASTor configuration, the latency is reduced to 65 ms and the entropy to 17 bits, which appears to be a favorable trade-off. Moreover, a balanced LASTor configuration offers very high entropy, but it does not reduce latency below 100 ms, which may not meet practical performance requirements.

3.4   Trade-Offs

To facilitate a better comparison of different approaches and to determine which one offers the optimal trade-off, we further explore the ratio of Entropy to Latency for both imbalanced and balanced routing configurations. These comparisons are depicted in Fig. 3c for imbalanced configurations and Fig. 3d for balanced configurations. Figure 3c illustrates the imbalanced configurations of LASTor, LARMix, and CLAPS Mix. Notably, CLAPS Mix is always considered imbalanced, except when $\tau = 1$.

It is observed that for $\tau < 0.43$, LASTor yields the highest Entropy/Latency ratio, suggesting a favorable trade-off. In this range, LASTor's latency varies from 65 ms to 80 ms, while its entropy ranges from 17 bits to 19 bits. However, for $\tau > 0.43$, LARMix leads in performance, particularly at $\tau = 0.6$ where it reduces latency to 50 ms and achieves an entropy of 12 bits. This suggests that LARMix tends to favor lower latency, whereas LASTor prioritizes higher entropy. Conversely, CLAPS Mix does not exhibit very high performance due to its consistent entropy of approximately 10 bits across all values of τ. Given this consistent performance, CLAPS Mix may be recommended when minimizing latency is more critical than maximizing the entropy of paths in the network.

On the other hand, Fig. 3d illustrates the Entropy/Latency ratio for the balanced approaches, including Balanced LARMix and Balanced LASTor. As observed, the trend between these two algorithms is similar to their imbalanced counterparts, although the Entropy/Latency ratio in balanced approaches is slightly lower. This suggests that achieving a fair distribution of loads across mixnodes comes at the expense of less favorable trade-offs. However, in balanced

Approaches	N = 50	N = 100	N = 200
LASTor	100 ms	88 ms	82 ms
Balanced LASTor	117 ms	109 ms	105 ms
LARMix	60 ms	45 ms	25 ms
Balanced LARMix	87 ms	75 ms	68 ms
CLAPS-Mix	71 ms	53 ms	45 ms

Approaches	N = 50	N = 100	N = 200
LASTor	16.2 bits	17.9 bits	21.8 bits
Balanced LASTor	16.5 bits	19 bits	22.3 bits
LARMix	7.6 bits	8.8 bits	9.6 bits
Balanced LARMix	11.3 bits	12.2 bits	13.8 bits
CLAPS-Mix	8.6 bits	10 bits	13.6 bits

(a) Average latency.   (b) Entropy of paths ($H(P)$).

Fig. 4. Effects of network size (N) on latency and anonymity.

cases when $\tau < 0.42$, LASTor exhibits the best performance, thanks to the highest entropy provided in this interval. Nevertheless, the balanced version of LASTor cannot provide latency lower than 100 ms, making LARMix a preferable option unless the reduction in entropy is not tolerable by the clients. For $\tau > 0.42$, Balanced LARMix consistently delivers better performance, with an optimal balance achieved at $\tau = 0.6$, where it offers a substantial reduction in latency to 75 ms while maintaining an entropy of 12 bits.[14] Lastly, it is noted that at $\tau = 1$, CLAPS Mix provides a balanced version which, compared to Balanced LASTor and Balanced LARMix, is not optimal; however, it can offer very low latency, which may be advantageous in scenarios where lower latency is favored while a reduction in entropy is tolerable.

3.5 Scaling the Mixnet

Up till now, the mixnet size was set to $N = 100$ and the number of hops to $L = 3$, specifically to align with real-world deployed mixnets such as NYM. However, in this section, we analyze how increasing the network size (N) and the number of hops (L) affect both latency and anonymity. To do so, considering all introduced routing strategies, we set the tuning parameter $\tau = 0.4$. Firstly, we fixed $L = 3$ and varied the network size, recording the average link delay and entropy of paths, as illustrated in Fig. 4.

More accurately, Fig. 4a delineates the effect of network size on latency. Increasing the network size across all routing strategies results in a reduced average link latency. Specifically, when the network size increases from $N = 50$ to $N = 200$, the latency induced by LARMix shows an approximate 58% reduction. This significant effect can be attributed to the fact that a larger number of nodes increases the likelihood of having geographically closer peers, enabling clients to select paths through the mixnet that minimize latency. Thus, augmenting the number of mixnodes can potentially reduce latency.

Conversely, Fig. 4b indicates that increasing the number of active mixnodes enhances the entropy of paths. This outcome arises because a greater number of

---

[14] Note that this entropy is sufficient for comparing different approaches, but will not reflect the exact impact of low-latency routing on anonymity. We will examine this impact in terms of message entropy in Sect. 4.

Approaches	L = 2	L = 3	L = 4
LASTor	40 ms	88 ms	130 ms
Balanced LASTor	50 ms	109 ms	163 ms
LARMix	21 ms	45 ms	67 ms
Balanced LARMix	38 ms	75 ms	114 ms
CLAPS-Mix	23 ms	53 ms	72 ms

Approaches	L = 2	L = 3	L = 4
LASTor	12.8 bits	17.9 bits	24.4 bits
Balanced LASTor	13 bits	19 bits	25.4 bits
LARMix	5.9 bits	8.8 bits	13.1 bits
Balanced LARMix	8.9 bits	12.2 bits	17.8 bits
CLAPS-Mix	7.2 bits	10 bits	14.6 bits

(a) Average latency.   (b) Entropy of paths ($H(P)$).

Fig. 5. Effects of number of hops (**L**) on latency and anonymity.

nodes provides more options for constructing a message route, thereby increasing the entropy values.[15]

Figure 5 illustrates the relationship between the number of hops (L) and the average link delay or entropy of paths, with the mixnet size fixed at $N = 100$. More specifically, Fig. 5a demonstrates that increasing the number of hops proportionally increases the average latency. Indeed, adding more hops necessitates longer travel distances for messages, resulting in heightened latency. Consequently, as the number of hops increases, the number of possible ways to create a message route also increases. Therefore, as depicted in Fig. 5b, increasing the number of hops consistently enhances anonymity. Hence, the number of hops is a crucial parameter that needs to be tuned to balance latency and anonymity. In networks such as Tor and NYM, this is typically fixed at $L = 3$.

4   Simulation of Free Routes Mixnet

In our analysis so far, we've examined the effects of low-latency routing on mixnet link delays and the entropy of paths ($H(P)$). While these metrics are sufficient for comparing different approaches, they may not fully capture the real effect of each approach on the anonymity of messages, which is primarily determined by the mixing process. Therefore, this section focuses on such analysis by simulating the action of mixnodes within a mixnet together with clients, and assessing anonymity measures based on message entropy while also recording end-to-end latency.

To conduct this analysis, we simulate a Free Routes mixnet using *SimPy* [20], a discrete event simulator implemented in Python. We employ the mixing process via the stop-and-go mixing strategy [14], which introduces delays to input messages based on an exponential distribution with an average delay parameter μ. For our simulation, we set μ at 50 ms to mirror NYM network conditions. Additionally, the input traffic is modeled to follow a Poisson distribution with a rate parameter $\lambda = 10000$, implying that, on average, 10,000 messages enter each mixnode in the network.

---

[15] It is important to note that increasing the number of nodes is advantageous only if there is sufficient traffic for each node. In a network with low traffic, adding more nodes can negatively impact message anonymity. If there are more mixnodes than necessary, the traffic will be distributed among more nodes, diminishing the chances of messages being mixed with a sufficient number of other messages.

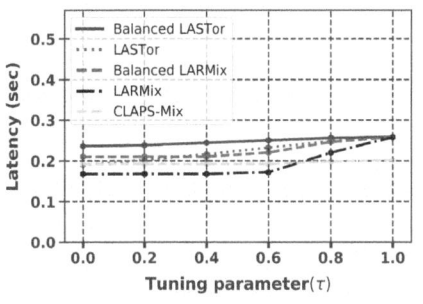

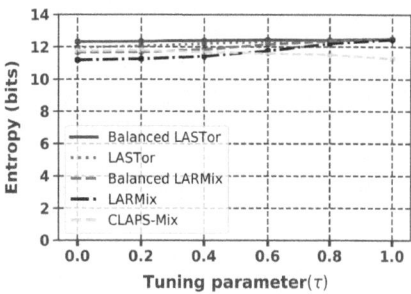

(a) Average end-to-end latency.   (b) Average entropy of messages H(m).

Fig. 6. Simulation experiments

We record the entering and exiting times of each message to compute end-to-end latency. Furthermore, we utilize a methodology outlined in [3] to quantify the anonymity of messages. This approach evaluates the probability that a message entering the mixnet, targeted by the adversary, can be correlated to its counterpart at the exit among other messages.[16]

4.1 Basic Results

In our mixnet simulator, we conducted two key experiments to evaluate **first**, the end-to-end latency, which encompasses both the link delay within the mixnet and the additional delay imposed by the mixing process at mixnodes; and **second**, message anonymity, quantified by H(m). We conducted around 100 iterations for each experiment, configuring a new mixnet each time to ensure the reliability of our results.

Figure 6a illustrates the end-to-end latency across all routing approaches, including LASTor, LARMix in both balanced and imbalanced cases, and CLAPS Mix. We adjusted the tuning parameter τ for all approaches and observed behavior almost identical to that seen for the average link delay within the mixnet versus varying τ, with the notable exception of higher average latency. In this context, latency includes delays from mixnodes, which, with an average contribution of $50 \times 3 = 150$ ms, can be further tuned according to network requirements but typically has a negative impact on the overall end-to-end latency. With a 50 ms average exponential delay, the minimum achievable latency through imbalanced LARMix or CLAPS Mix is 85 ms, marking a 44% reduction compared to the uniform routing ($\tau = 1$), which increases latency to 250 ms. Conversely, in this scenario, Balanced LASTor behaves almost like a uniform approach without substantial improvement in latency, while imbalanced LASTor and Balanced LARMix can reduce latency to as low as 200 ms, amounting to a 20% reduction in end-to-end latency.

---

[16] Further details of the simulation process are provided in Appendix A.

Figure 6b presents the entropy of messages across all routing approaches mentioned in this paper, analyzed against varying values of τ. The observations indicate that, irrespective of the τ values, the message entropy typically fluctuates around 12 bits. This consistency suggests that the real anonymity of the mixnet (specifically, the anonymity provided by the messages themselves) remains relatively stable despite the entropy of path selection showing dramatic decreases. This reveals that while $H(P)$ is useful for analyzing biased routing, it does not fully capture the nuances of message anonymity. In scenarios involving biased routing, both the LARMix imbalances and CLAPS Mix can lead to a reduction of up to 1 bit in message entropy ($H(m)$). Conversely, imbalanced LASTor and Balanced LARMix exhibit similar behavior, whereas Balanced LASTor slightly enhances the entropy of messages, benefiting from less biased routing toward low-latency paths. Overall, the approaches show a slight increase in message entropy as τ increases, likely due to the introduction of more randomness into the network.

4.2   Constraint on End-to-End Latency

In certain scenarios, clients utilizing mixnets may necessitate meeting an average end-to-end latency to ensure fast and reliable communication. In default mixnet configurations, this requirement can generally be addressed by adjusting the average latency induced by mixnodes (μ). However, this straightforward approach often leads to a significant reduction in anonymity, as the mixing delay directly influences message anonymity.

A more practical method to manage end-to-end latency involves the use of low-latency approaches introduced in this study. For instance, consider a scenario where the end-to-end latency is represented as l_{e2e}. One straightforward method to achieve this end-to-end latency is to set the mixing delay and subsequently adjust the tuning parameter for low-latency routing, seeking a combination that satisfies the end-to-end latency requirement. Although this trial-and-error method can be effective, it cannot fully optimize message anonymity while satisfying the end-to-end latency constraint. This limitation arises because increasing the tuning parameter τ improves the entropy of paths $H(P)$ but also heightens the link delay within the mixnet. Consequently, there is less room for mixing delays, leading to a reduction in message anonymity.

To attain a more optimized setting, we propose an approach wherein the parameter τ is first set, followed by measuring the link delays within the mixnodes in such settings. With this information, the mixing delay can be established as $\mu = \frac{l_{e2e} - \text{link delays}}{L}$. By adjusting the value of τ, one can identify the optimal combination of τ and μ that maximizes message anonymity while adhering to the average end-to-end latency constraints.

Following this approach, we performed an experiment considering the LARMix routing for a scenario where the average end-to-end latency is set to 150 ms. In this case, we first varied the value of τ and then measured the link delays and subsequently the mixing delays for the mixnodes, with a setting of

$N = 100$ and $L = 3$. The results are shown in Table 1. As illustrated, increasing τ increases the entropy of paths as well as link delays within the mixnet, consequently decreasing mixing delays. However, the anonymity of messages, influenced by both τ and mixing delays, demonstrates different behavior. When $\tau \leq 0.7$, message anonymity increases by increasing τ, but when $\tau \geq 0.7$, this metric started decreasing after further increasing τ. This suggests that the optimal combination for this end-to-end constraint is to set $\tau = 0.7$ and subsequently set the mixing delay $\mu = 27$ ms.

Table 1. Optimizing anonymity while meeting an end-to-end average latency.

Tuning parameter τ	0.0	0.1	0.2	0.3	0.4	0.5	0.6	0.7	0.8	0.9	1.0
Link delays ms	58.0	58.1	58.15	58.2	58.3	58.3	60	70	91	108.2	121
Mix delay (μ) **ms**	30	30	30	30	29.9	29.9	29.8	27	19	14	10
Entropy of Messages (H(m)) **bits**	10.1	10.2	10.21	10.42	10.8	11	11.4	11.6	11.5	11.2	10.8
Entropy of Paths (H(P)) **bits**	6.64	6.65	6.9	7.6	8.5	9.9	12.5	16.2	18.8	19.7	19.9

5 Adversarial Mixnodes

In this section, we broaden the scope of adversarial analysis in mixnets, shifting from a GPA to a more localized threat, the mixnode adversary. A GPA can observe all connections and transactions within the communication network but lacks the ability to inspect the internal operations of mixnodes or directly engage in the mixing process. Therefore, to render our analysis more practical, we explore scenarios in which the adversary is capable of corrupting parts of the mixnet by compromising specific mixnodes. Through these compromised nodes, the adversary can link input and output messages, effectively nullifying the anonymity of communications routed through these nodes. Consequently, it is crucial for client messages to pass through at least one uncorrupted mixnode to maintain anonymity.

Moreover, for an adversary to achieve comprehensive de-anonymization, control over at least L mixnodes is necessary to construct complete paths. To augment their capability to de-anonymize clients, adversaries must also increase the number of mixnodes under their control, ensuring their inclusion across numerous paths. This strategic positioning increases the probability of intercepting and compromising client communications. Within this context, we assess the adversary's effectiveness when routing preferences are skewed towards low-latency routers. In these scenarios, the primary objective for the adversary is to maximize the Fraction of Corrupted Paths (FCP), thereby ensuring a significant number of paths within the mixnet are fully compromised. In the next subsection, we will delineate some possible strategies that may be taken into account by adversaries for these purposes.

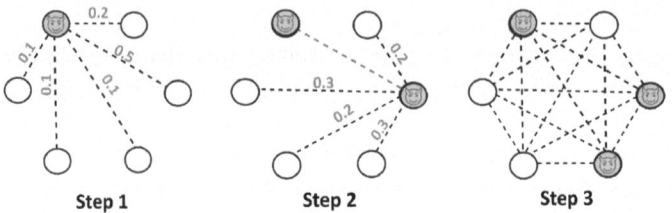

Fig. 7. Intelligent Corruption of mixnodes.

5.1 Adversarial Strategies

Random Strategy. The Random Strategy is the most basic approach to corrupting mixnodes within the mixnet. Here, the adversary controls C mixnodes selected at random. Depending on the dynamics of selection, this approach can occasionally yield a high probability of intercepting paths that frequently incorporate these mixnodes, while at other times, it may result in less optimal node placements, targeting paths with lower selection probabilities. For instance, in a Free Routes mixnet with uniform routing, if $L = 3$ and $C = \frac{3N}{10}$ (indicating that 30% of the nodes are corrupted), the FCP would be approximately 2.5%.

Single Location Strategy. Another tactical approach involves exploiting the clients' preference for low-latency routing, which often directs traffic through mixnodes located within the same jurisdiction or region. By identifying and corrupting mixnodes within these targeted regions, the adversary can significantly enhance their strategic advantage. This method is particularly effective as it raises the likelihood that messages will pass through adversarially controlled nodes, thus amplifying the potential for fully de-anonymizing clients.

Intelligent Corruption Strategy. To comprehensively analyze the capability of a mixnode adversary, we introduce a practical strategy termed Intelligent Corruption, assuming the adversary has complete information about the other active mixnodes in the network. This strategy begins by randomly corrupting a mixnode within the mixnet. The adversary then assesses the distance from this possessed mixnode to all others, selecting those closest or with the highest probability of being the next hop. This process continues, choosing subsequent mixnodes that are nearest to the most recently corrupted node or those most likely to be selected next, until C mixnodes are corrupted.

For example, as depicted in Fig. 7, consider a Free Route mixnet with $N = 6$ mixnodes and an adversary's budget of $C = 3$. Initially, the adversary corrupts a random mixnode. They then evaluate the likelihood of selecting any uncorrupted mixnodes from this node, aiming to maximize the probability of routing through corrupted paths. Subsequently, the adversary corrupts the mixnode with the highest selection probability (e.g., 0.5). Next, from the second corrupted node,

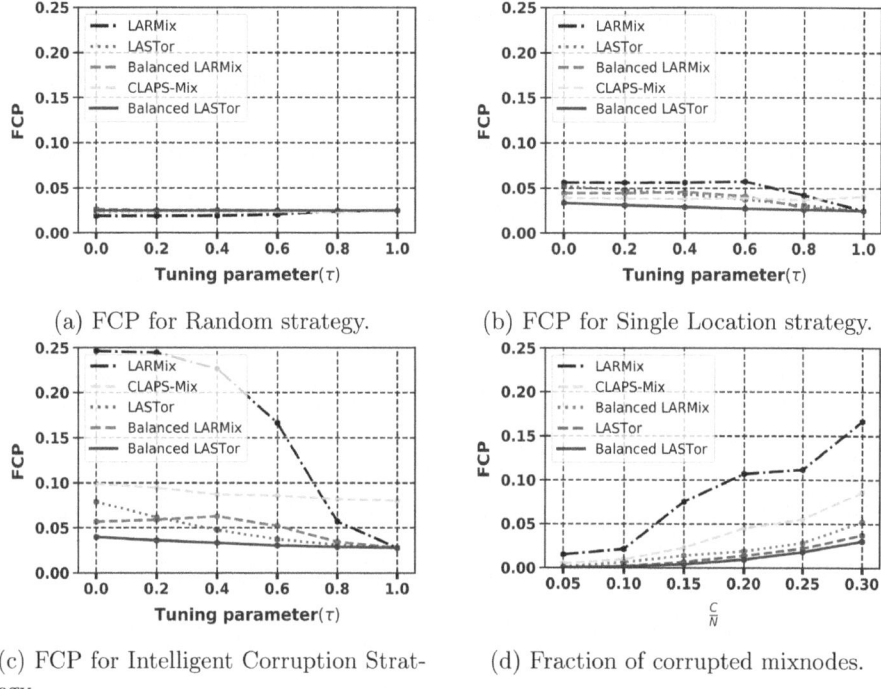

(a) FCP for Random strategy.

(b) FCP for Single Location strategy.

(c) FCP for Intelligent Corruption Strategy.

(d) Fraction of corrupted mixnodes.

Fig. 8. Adversarial experiments

they assess two mixnodes, each with a selection probability of 0.3, and corrupt one of them in the final step, completing the Intelligent Corruption of the mixnet.

5.2 Evaluation of Adversarial Strategies

To evaluate the adversarial strategy for maximizing the FCP, we considered all routing strategies-LARMix, LASTor, and CLAPs Mix-in both imbalanced and balanced cases. We then measured the FCP by varying the value of τ and setting the fraction of corrupted mixnodes as $\frac{C}{N} = 0.3$. Figure 8a illustrates the results of FCP derived from Random corruption of mixnodes. As observed, almost all the routing approaches yield similar results; even as τ varies, the results do not change dramatically. This consistency can be attributed to the nature of Random Corruption, where the adversary might corrupt mixnodes that are either on highly probable paths or, conversely, on paths with very low probability of selection. Therefore, on average, the amount of FCP should be comparable to that with uniform routing, previously described as 2.5%.

Figure 8b showcases the results of employing the Single Location strategy for corrupting mixnodes within low-latency routings approaches. As the value of τ increases, the FCP generally decreases across most routing configurations. The primary reason for this trend is that increasing τ introduces greater random-ness into the routing decisions of LASTor and LARMix, both in imbalanced and balanced scenarios. This increased randomness reduces the probability of select-ing low-latency paths that were previously chosen with higher likelihood, thus diminishing the adversary's advantage when the corruption of mixnodes adheres to the Single Location strategy for all routing approaches.

In the case of CLAPS Mix, since an increase in τ does not necessarily equate to enhanced randomness, the outcomes remain relatively consistent regardless of τ value adjustments. As depicted in Fig. 8b, LARMix under imbalanced con-ditions is notably more susceptible to the Single Location strategy, exposing up to a 6% FCP. Conversely, both Imbalanced LASTor and Balanced LARMix exhibit performances closely aligned with that of CLAPS Mix, particularly when $\tau < 0.6$. However, there is a marked reduction in FCP for these strategies rel-ative to CLAPS Mix once τ surpasses this threshold. Contrastingly, Balanced LASTor offers the least benefit to the adversary by maintaining a low FCP, comparable to outcomes derived from the Random Strategy. This observation underscores that the variance between low-latency and high-latency paths in this case is minimal, thereby limiting the adversary's leverage when utilizing the Single Location strategy.

In addition, applying the Intelligent Corruption strategy, as shown in Fig. 8c, reveals that, similar to the results from the Single Location strategy, increas-ing the value of τ generally leads to a reduction in FCP. However, this strat-egy results in a consistently higher FCP compared to the Single Location case. Specifically, when using Imbalanced LARMix, the FCP can reach up to 25% at $\tau = 0$, which is up to five times higher than the results observed from the Single Location strategy. This underscores the effectiveness of Intelligent Corruption, particularly when latency is a significant factor within Imbalanced LARMix sce-narios.

In contrast, for other routing approaches like CLAPS Mix, the increase in FCP using the Intelligent Corruption strategy does not exceed twice the baseline. Notably, for Balanced LARMix, unlike its imbalanced configuration, the FCP result is only marginally higher than that achieved through the Single Location strategy, and it aligns closely with the results of Imbalanced LASTor. Meanwhile, Balanced LASTor exhibits results nearly identical to those of the Single Location strategy. This suggests that even though balancing the mixnet using the RLD algorithm may potentially heighten end-to-end latency, it can effectively mitigate the impact of the Intelligent Corruption strategy. This is particularly significant when compared to the higher vulnerabilities observed in the Imbalanced LARMix configuration.

Furthermore, to assess the effect of adversary budget, Fig. 8d presents the results of Intelligent Corruption when we set $\tau = 0.6$ for all routing approaches in both balanced and imbalanced cases. We then vary the fraction of corrupted nodes ($\frac{C}{N}$) from 5% to 30%. As demonstrated, increasing the adversary's budget translates into corrupting more mixnodes, thereby increasing the likelihood that adversarial mixnodes will compromise complete paths. Consequently, as seen in Fig. 8d, the FCP increases. This behavior remains consistent across various approaches; specifically, the imbalanced LARMix configuration proves to be the most vulnerable approach to increasing adversary budgets. Conversely, CLAPS Mix is the second most susceptible. Meanwhile, Balanced LARMix and imbalanced LASTor exhibit similar trends, and Balanced LASTor shows the greatest resilience towards increasing the adversarial budget.

6   Conclusion

In this work, we introduced the first low-latency routing methodology tailored for mixnets with a Free Routes design. We began by adapting existing routing approaches from LASTor, LARMix, and CLAPS for use in mixnet environments. Additionally, we developed the RLD algorithm that ensures each mixnode, regardless of its position within the mixnet, receives an equal amount of traffic. Our comprehensive analytical and simulation experiments demonstrate substantial latency reductions, while only compromising a negligible amount of anonymity. Moreover, our adversarial analysis reveals no significant advantage for mixnode adversaries compared to a GPA. We anticipate that this framework will prove especially useful in scenarios requiring cost-effective (or low-latency) anonymity.

Acknowledgement. We would like to thank the anonymous reviewers for their valuable feedback. This research is partially supported by CyberSecurity Research Flanders with reference number VR20192203.

A   Expanding on Simulation of Free Routes Mixnet

Table 2. Detailed analysis of end-to-end latency.

Approaches	$\tau = 0$			$\tau = 0.6$			$\tau = 1$		
Statistics	Average	Variance	CI	Average	Variance	CI	Average	Variance	CI
LASTor	0.20	0.01	$[0.20, 0.204]$	0.24	0.01	$[0.240, 0.243]$	0.26	0.01	$[0.26, 0.267]$
Balanced LASTor	0.24	0.01	$[0.24, 0.242]$	0.25	0.01	$[0.25, 0.26]$	0.26	0.01	$[0.26, 0.266]$
LARMix	0.17	10^{-3}	$[0.165, 0.171]$	0.173	10^{-3}	$[0.163, 0.184]$	0.26	0.01	$[0.26, 0.27]$
Balanced LARMix	0.215	0.01	$[0.21, 0.22]$	0.228	0.01	$[0.227, 0.228]$	0.26	0.01	$[0.26, 0.27]$
CLAPS-Mix	0.202	10^{-3}	$[0.202, 0.203]$	0.206	10^{-3}	$[0.206, 0.207]$	0.212	10^{-3}	$[0.212, 0.213]$

In Sect. 4, we provided the results of end-to-end latency and entropy of messages, respectively, in Fig. 6a and Fig. 6b. However, we postponed the details of these results, such as the variance and confidence interval of the average results, to this subsection. To ensure the reliability of the results, we applied a 95% confidence interval with a confidence test. The data for the average end-to-end latency and the entropy of messages are presented in Table 2 and Table 3, respectively.

Table 3. Detailed analysis of message entropy.

Approaches	$\tau = 0$			$\tau = 0.6$			$\tau = 1$		
Statistics	Average	Variance	CI	Average	Variance	CI	Average	Variance	CI
LASTor	12.03	0.04	[11.99, 12.07]	12.38	0.02	[12.35, 12.41]	12.49	0.03	[12.26, 12.53]
Balanced LASTor	12.32	0.03	[12.28, 12.36]	12.43	0.02	[12.4, 12.47]	12.54	0.03	[12.5, 12.57]
LARMix	11.12	0.1	[10.96, 11.27]	11.79	0.07	[11.74, 11.85]	12.5	0.02	[12.47, 12.54]
Balanced LARMix	11.69	0.09	[11.64, 11.75]	12.12	0.04	[12.08, 12.17]	12.5	0.02	[12.47, 12.54]
CLAPS-Mix	11.71	0.35	[11.61, 11.85]	11.69	0.21	[11.6, 11.8]	11.37	0.18	[11.3, 11.46]

As observed, the variance in all cases is almost negligible, and the confidence interval is tight enough to conclude that the results in Fig. 6a and Fig. 6b are reliable.

References

1. Akhoondi, M., Yu, C., Madhyastha, H.V.: Lastor: a low-latency as-aware tor client. In: 2012 IEEE Symposium on Security and Privacy, pp. 476–490. IEEE (2012)
2. Bauer, K., McCoy, D., Grunwald, D., Kohno, T., Sicker, D.: Low-resource routing attacks against tor. In: Proceedings of the 2007 ACM Workshop on Privacy in Electronic Society, pp. 11–20 (2007)
3. Ben Guirat, I., Gosain, D., Diaz, C.: Mixim: Mixnet design decisions and empirical evaluation. In: Proceedings of the 20th Workshop on Workshop on Privacy in the Electronic Society, pp. 33–37 (2021)
4. Chaum, D., et al.: cMix: mixing with minimal real-time asymmetric cryptographic operations. In: Gollmann, D., Miyaji, A., Kikuchi, H. (eds.) ACNS 2017. LNCS, vol. 10355, pp. 557–578. Springer, Cham (2017). https://doi.org/10.1007/978-3-319-61204-1_28
5. Chaum, D.L.: Untraceable electronic mail, return addresses, and digital pseudonyms. Commun. ACM **24**(2), 84–90 (1981)
6. Chen, D., Borrego, C., Navarro-Arribas, G.: A privacy-preserving routing protocol using mix networks in opportunistic networks. Electronics **9**(11), 1754 (2020)
7. Diaz, C.: Anonymity and privacy in electronic services. Katholieke Universiteit Leuven. Faculteit Ingenieurswetenschappen, Heverlee (2005)
8. Diaz, C., Halpin, H., Kiayias, A.: The nym network (2021)
9. Diaz, C., Murdoch, S.J., Troncoso, C.: Impact of network topology on anonymity and overhead in low-latency anonymity networks. In: Privacy Enhancing Technologies: 10th International Symposium, PETS 2010, Berlin, Germany, July 21-23, 2010. Proceedings 10. pp. 184–201. Springer (2010)
10. Diaz, C., Preneel, B.: Taxonomy of Mixes and Dummy Traffic. In: Deswarte, Y., Cuppens, F., Jajodia, S., Wang, L. (eds.) SEC 2004. IIFIP, vol. 148, pp. 217–232. Springer, Boston, MA (2004). https://doi.org/10.1007/1-4020-8145-6_18
11. Dingledine, R., Mathewson, N., Syverson, P.F., et al.: Tor: the second-generation onion router. In: USENIX Security Symposium, vol. 4, pp. 303–320 (2004)
12. Groth, J.: On the size of pairing-based non-interactive arguments. In: Advances in Cryptology–EUROCRYPT 2016: 35th Annual International Conference on the Theory and Applications of Cryptographic Techniques, Vienna, Austria, May 8-12, 2016, Proceedings, Part II 35. pp. 305–326. Springer (2016). https://doi.org/10.1007/978-3-662-49896-5_11

13. Hogan, K., Servan-Schreiber, S., Newman, Z., Weintraub, B., Nita-Rotaru, C., Devadas, S.: Shortor: improving tor network latency via multi-hop overlay routing. In: 2022 IEEE Symposium on Security and Privacy (SP), pp. 1933–1952. IEEE (2022)

14. Kesdogan, D., Egner, J., Büschkes, R.: Stop- and- Go-MIXes providing probabilistic anonymity in an open system. In: Aucsmith, D. (ed.) IH 1998. LNCS, vol. 1525, pp. 83–98. Springer, Heidelberg (1998). https://doi.org/10.1007/3-540-49380-8_7

15. Kohls, K., Diaz, C.: {VerLoc}: verifiable localization in decentralized systems. In: 31st USENIX Security Symposium (USENIX Security 22), pp. 2637–2654 (2022)

16. Kwon, A., Lu, D., Devadas, S.: {XRD}: scalable messaging system with cryptographic privacy. In: 17th USENIX Symposium on Networked Systems Design and Implementation (NSDI 20), pp. 759–776 (2020)

17. Möller, U., Cottrell, L., Palfrader, P., Sassaman, L.: Mixmaster protocol-version 2 (2003)

18. Nithyanand, R., Starov, O., Zair, A., Gill, P., Schapira, M.: Measuring and mitigating as-level adversaries against tor. arXiv preprint arXiv:1505.05173 (2015)

19. Piotrowska, A.M., Hayes, J., Elahi, T., Meiser, S., Danezis, G.: The loopix anonymity system. In: 26th *USENIX* Security Symposium (*USENIX* Security 17), pp. 1199–1216 (2017)

20. Python: Event discrete, process based simulation for python (2013). https://pypi.org/project/simpy/

21. Rahimi, M.: CLAM: client-aware routing in mix networks. In: Pérez-González, F., Alfaro, P.C., Krätzer, C., Zhao, H.V. (eds.) Proceedings of the ACM Workshop on Information Hiding and Multimedia Security, IH&MMSec 2024, Baiona, Spain, June 24-26, 2024, pp. 199–209. ACM (2024). https://doi.org/10.1145/3658664.3659631

22. Rahimi, M., Sharma, P.K., Diaz, C.: Larmix: latency-aware routing in mix networks. In: The Network and Distributed System Security Symposium. Internet Society (2024)

23. Rochet, F., Wails, R., Johnson, A., Mittal, P., Pereira, O.: Claps: client-location-aware path selection in tor. In: Proceedings of the 2020 ACM SIGSAC Conference on Computer and Communications Security, pp. 17–34 (2020)

24. Shirazi, F., Simeonovski, M., Asghar, M.R., Backes, M., Diaz, C.: A survey on routing in anonymous communication protocols. ACM Comput. Surv. (CSUR) **51**(3), 1–39 (2018)

25. Staff, R.N.: Ripe atlas: a global internet measurement network. Internet Protocol J. **18**(3), 2–26 (2015)

26. Sun, Y., Edmundson, A., Feamster, N., Chiang, M., Mittal, P.: Counter-raptor: safeguarding tor against active routing attacks. In: 2017 IEEE Symposium on Security and Privacy (SP), pp. 977–992. IEEE (2017)

27. Sun, Y., et al.: {RAPTOR}: Routing attacks on privacy in tor. In: 24th USENIX Security Symposium (USENIX Security 15), pp. 271–286 (2015)

28. Van Den Hooff, J., Lazar, D., Zaharia, M., Zeldovich, N.: Vuvuzela: scalable private messaging resistant to traffic analysis. In: Proceedings of the 25th Symposium on Operating Systems Principles, pp. 137–152 (2015)

29. Wan, G., Johnson, A., Wails, R., Wagh, S., Mittal, P.: Guard placement attacks on path selection algorithms for tor. Proc. Privacy Enhancing Technol. **2019**(4) (2019)

On the Anonymity of Linkable Ring Signatures

Xavier Bultel[1] and Charles Olivier-Anclin[1,2,3]

[1] INSA Centre Val de Loire, LIFO, Université d'Orléans, Inria, Bourges, France
charlesolivier@outlook.fr
[2] Université Clermont Auvergne, LIMOS, CNRS, Clermont-Ferrand, France
[3] be ys Pay, Paris, France

Abstract. Security models provide a way of formalising security properties in a rigorous way, but it is sometimes difficult to ensure that the model really fits the concept that we are trying to formalise. In this paper, we illustrate this fact by showing the discrepancies between the security model of anonymity in linkable ring signatures and the security that is actually expected for this kind of signature. These signatures allow a user to sign anonymously within an ad hoc group generated from the public keys of the group members, but all their signatures can be linked together. Reading the related literature, it seems obvious that users' identities must remain hidden even when their signatures are linked, but we show that, surprisingly, almost none of the anonymity models guarantee this property. We illustrate this by presenting two counter-examples which are secure in most anonymity model of linkable ring signatures, but which trivially leak a signer's identity after only two signatures.

A natural fix to this model, already introduced in some previous work, is proposed in a corruption model where the attacker can generate the keys of certain users themselves, which seems much more coherent in a context where the group of users can be constructed in an ad hoc way at the time of signing. We believe that these two changes make the security model more realistic. Indeed, within the framework of this model, our counter-examples becomes insecure. Furthermore, we show that most of the schemes in the literature we surveyed appear to have been designed to achieve the security guaranteed by the latest model, which reinforces the idea that the model is closer to the informal intuition of what anonymity should be in linkable ring signatures.

Keywords: Linkable Ring Signature · Anonymity · Security Model

1 Introduction

Ring signatures [34] are amongst the most studied privacy-preserving signature schemes. Over the years, they have been used in many real-world applications, making them one, if not the most widely deployed type of privacy-preserving signatures. Their applications are numerous and include blockchains (Monero based on CryptoNote [39]), electronic voting [36], attestation [36], *etc.*. These applications regularly require a mitigation of the powerful property of anonymity brought by the original concept.

Anonymity Mitigation. To adapt to its use cases, variations of the original concept have been developed to mitigate its full anonymity. These mitigations, introduced as new properties, are, amongst others, *traceability* of the signer [23], *repudiability* for non-signers [32] and *revocability* of the signer's anonymity [43]. In this article, we focus on yet another property: *linkability* of the signature produced by the same signer, and its implications on anonymity. Introduced by Liu *et al.* [28], linkable ring signatures (LRS) have been the subject of many research papers (see Table 1 for a list of existing work), as it allows any verifier to link signatures produced by the same signer while concealing the signer's identity. This would allow a verifier to link the signatures of two electronic ballots from the same entity, in order to prevent multiple voting without manipulating voters' identities and to allow the vote to be modified during electronic elections (as in the Estonian electronic voting system [38]).

In their definition, linkable ring signatures, as such as ring signatures, include a key generation algorithm, a signature algorithm, and a verification algorithm. Unlike traditional ring signatures, they allow for the verification of whether two signatures were produced by the same signer based on a linking algorithm, while still concealing the signer's identity. This preservation of privacy for the signer is often referred to as *pseudonymity, partial anonymity*, or simply *anonymity*. In the existing literature, the term *anonymity* has been preferred, but we highlight that for linkable ring signatures it represents a weaker property than when applied to ring signatures.

Security Considerations. Four security properties have been defined to model what is expected from linkable ring signatures: *unforgeability* of signatures, *anonymity* of the signer, *linkability* of the signatures and *non-slanderability*, *i.e.*, the inability to maliciously link signatures. Of these properties, *unforgeability* and *anonymity* are derived from ring signatures, while the other two are necessary to guarantee the security of the linkability. Although supposedly adapted from ring signatures, the level of anonymity formalised by most of previous works, even the most recent ones, is insufficient. In fact, the associated constructions could suffer from a total lack of anonymity in real applications. What is more, where their are deployed this could lead to concrete breaches in the anonymity of entities. In recent works such as [9], anonymity is informally characterised by the following statement:

> *"Anonymity, demands that an adversary cannot tell which of a ring's secret keys was used to produce a signature."*

Despite the correct informal description, we demonstrate in this paper that the most widely adopted definitions essentially define anonymity as follows:

> *Anonymity, demands that an adversary cannot tell which of a ring's secret keys was used to produce **an entity's first signature**.*

Table 1. Existing Linkable Ring Signatures. ✗ → ✓ means that it seems possible to extend the existing proof. N.A. for "Not Applicable".

Reference	Assumption	One-time Anonymity	Anonymity	Model[a]
Liu et al. [28]	DL related[2]	Computational	✗ → ✓	ROM
Tsang et al. [37]	Strong RSA & DDH[b]	Computational	✗ → ✓	ROM
Liu and Wong [29]	DL related	Computational	✗ → ✓	ROM
Tsang and Wei [36]	DL related	Computational	N.A.	ROM
Liu et al. [27]	DL related	Unconditional	✗ → ✓ (Unconditional)	ROM
Yuen et al. [41]	DL related	Computational	✗ → ✓	Standard
Boyen and Haines [11]	CDL[c]	Unconditional	Non conclusive	ROM
Branco and Mateus [12]	GSD[3]	Computational	Non conclusive	ROM
Alberto et al. [1]	R-SIS	Unconditional	N.A., see Sect. 6	ROM
Baum et al. [5]	SIS, LWE	Computational	✗ → ✓	ROM
Lu et al. [31]	SIS	Computational	Non conclusive	ROM
Liu et al. [30]	M-SIS, D-MLWE	Computational	See Sect. 6	ROM
Backes et al. [3]	Generic construction	N.A.	✓ (already proven)	Standard
Beullens et al. [8]	SIDH, M-LWE	N.A.	✓ (already proven)	ROM
Zhang et al. [43]	DL related	Computational	✗ → ✓	ROM
Balla et al. [4]	DL related	Unconditional	✗ → ✓ (Unconditional)	ROM
Bootle et al. [9]	DL related	Computational	✗ → ✓	ROM
Xiangyu et al. [25]	DL related	Computational	✗ → ✓	ROM
Xue et al. [40]	Generic construction	Computational	✗ → ✓	ROM

[a]ROM, which stands for *Random Oracle Model*, is a paradigm for security proofs [26].
[b] DL: Discrete logarithm; DDH: Differential Diffie Hellman, distinguishing between (g^x, g^y, g^{xy}) and (g^x, g^x, g^z) for some generator g and random values $x, y, z \in \mathbb{Z}_p^*$.
[c] CDL: Central Decoding Problem; GSD: General Syndrome Decoding

And, while this may be a feature of some schemes, such as [36], this statement seems much weaker than the previous one in many scenarios. Indeed, there is no guarantee regarding what the second signature might reveal about the identity of the signer, as we elucidate below. This is why we refer to this definitions of anonymity as *one-time anonymity* in order to better reflect the actual guarantees provided by the formalisation of this property. In looking for the rationale behind such a definition, one might speculate that it is linked to a statement made in Bender *et al.*'s seminal paper [7], which provided a security framework for ring signatures. The statement in question is as follows:

> *"a weaker definition of anonymity whereby the adversary obtains only users' public keys and a single signature – but cannot obtain multiple other signatures via a signing oracle – does not imply unlinkability."*

At first glance, removing the right to obtain multiple signatures in the experiment may seem like a reasonable way of defining anonymity with linkability. However, upon closer examination, this statement actually discusses the fact that unlinkability is not considered when only one signature is issued to the adversary. We have not found any explicit explanation for the previous formalisation of the anonymity of linkable ring signatures. Therefore, all we can ascertain about the definition of anonymity is that this flaw appeared in the very first articles on linkable ring signatures and has persisted across most existing constructs. Only two existing works [3,8] have formalised the anonymity of LRS in a more realistic experiment. However, their model is left unconsidered in subsequent works.

Our Contributions. In this article, we argue the insecurity of the most widely used security model of linkable ring signature. We highlight the lack of usage of an appropriate formalism for anonymity, even in the most recent works. After recalling this model in Sect. 2.1, we propose two constructions which could have been considered as *"secure linkable ring signatures"*, in Sect. 3. These two constructions are artificial and serve as counter-examples. In particular, they do not realise the expected informal anonymity property described above. Following this discussion, we introduce an improved formalism for the notion of anonymity which has originally been proposed by Backes *et al.* [3] (see Sect. 4). We therefore push forward stronger notions of security. We discuss the insecurity of our counter-examples in this stronger model in Sect. 5 and review all existing work based on the weaker notion in Sect. 6. By that, we rule out a general lack of anonymity of existing constructions. Studying the proofs of existing schemes, we noticed that many of them follow the same proof pattern that can be extended by simple hybrid arguments. This results are summarised in Table 1.

Related Work. Since 2004, numerous works have focused on linkable ring signature. In Table 1 we provide, to the best of our knowledge, an exhaustive description of the existing linkable ring signatures in the literature while omitting signatures that have been shown to contain flaws. These primitives claim either computational or unconditional anonymity. Most of them they rely on discrete logarithm related assumptions, while only few schemes are based on lattice assumptions [1,5,8,30] and could achieve some post-quantum security. Some of these schemes achieves additional properties such as *threshold* [37] or *forward-security* [11]. Alberto *et al.* [1] proposed the only existing one-time linkable ring signature. However, their definition of anonymity is in fact the same as that of most linkable ring signatures. This should have given rise to concern.

All the signatures highlighted in the Table 1 are based on security models adapted for each individual purposes. However, their models consistently encompass flawed anonymity, apart for two works [3,8]. Branco and Mateus [12] have proposed a *Same Ring Linkable Ring signature* and Aranha *et al.* a *Same Message Linkable Ring Signature* [2], both with similar realistic models. Their signatures allow more anonymity than generally considered by the above schemes, as it limits the linkability of the signature when two signatures have been generated respectively for the same ring or the same message. Fujisaki and Suzuki introduced a security model for *Traceable Ring signatures* [23] that extends and is stronger than those considered for linkable ring signatures. Indeed, their model is similar to what was later proposed in [3] for linkable ring signatures, however, it includes additional failure conditions to prevent the adversary from trivially tracing the signer behind the challenges. All these related primitives are not strictly linkable ring signatures and their authors have not directly provided a model adapted to linkable ring signatures, even so the general idea behind their formalism is more accurate. In order to focus only on the existing model for linkable ring signatures, we leave aside their formalism and concentrate only on the definitions that aim to formalise the security of linkable ring signatures.

Other signatures with linking have been proposed, they are based on two types of privacy preserving signatures:

Group signatures: such as *linkable group signatures* [42], from which LRS originate, are its centralised version where an authority is responsible for managing
the group. There are also weaker linkability properties, for example *selective
linkability* [22,24] which means that all signature are unlinkable per default
and only when needed, a set of signatures can be linked through the central
authority. Unlike the case of ring signature, it is possible to use hybrid arguments showing that providing one or more signatures to the adversary leads
to the same property of anonymity, as the adversary has the secret signature keys of all the members of the group [6]. Their decentralised equivalent
also exists [21] and their anonymity is formalised in a realistic way. Diaz and
Lehmann [17] also introduced a *user-controlled Linkable Group Signature* for
which signers can provide proof of links in between their signatures. With
such a property, the model differs from linkable group or ring signatures as
the proof of a link must be produced by the signers before a connection can be
established by a verifier, and is therefore not de facto accessible. As a result,
the same flaw is not passed on to their model.

Attribute-based signatures: *Attribute-based Signatures* [18,19] have also been
proposed with user-controlled linkability. The same observation can be made
as for user-controled linkable group signature.

2   Review of Definitions

2.1   Linkable Ring Signature in the Honest Key Model

Definitions of *linkable ring signatures* vary across the literature (see reference given in Table 1). Despite that, the prescribed algorithms have been defined in the same way in almost all presented works. This is not always the case for their associated security definitions, even if they remain relatively similar.

Definition 1 (Linkable Ring Signature - LRS). *A* Linkable Ring Signature *scheme is composed of five algorithms defined as follows:*

Setup(1^λ): *is a* PPT *(probabilistic polynomial-time) algorithm that takes the security parameter 1^λ and produces the* public parameters pp.

We assume these parameters as common inputs to all the upcoming algorithms.

Gen(1^λ): *is a* PPT *algorithm that takes the security parameter 1^λ (and the public
parameters* pp*), it returns a pair of keys* (pk, sk).

$\mathsf{Sign}(m, \{\mathsf{pk}_j\}_{j \in \mathcal{R}}, \mathsf{sk}_i)$: *is a* PPT *algorithm that takes a* public key set $\{\mathsf{pk}_i\}_{i \in \mathcal{R}}$ *for a ring set* $\mathcal{R}$, *a signer secret key* sk_i *(with* $i \in \mathcal{R}$*) and a message* m, *it returns a ring signature* σ.

$\mathsf{Verify}(m, \sigma, \{\mathsf{pk}_j\}_{j \in \mathcal{R}})$: *is a deterministic polynomial-time algorithm that takes a public key set* $\{\mathsf{pk}_i\}_{i \in \mathcal{R}}$, *a signature* σ, *and a message* m, *if the signature* σ *is valid, it returns 1, otherwise it returns 0.*

$\mathsf{Link}(\sigma, \sigma')$: *is a deterministic polynomial-time algorithm that takes two signatures* σ *and* σ', *it returns 1, if they are linked, otherwise, returns 0.*

We now present the state-of-the-art definition (excluding the model from [3], which is described in the Sect. 4). As discussed in depth in [7], the security model of LRS, in particular the anonymity of the signer, can be based on different corruption setups [7], from the weakest to the strongest:

Honest Key Model. This model assumes that the keys are generated honestly, by the challenger, as part of the experiments. Consequently, no security is provided against keys generated maliciously.

Adversarially-chosen Keys Model. This model solves the previous problem by allowing maliciously generated keys within the model. However, it does not guarantee that the entities in the ring are unable to identify the signer if they all cooperate together.

Full key Exposure Model. This model solves the previous problem by assuming full disclosure of the secret key to the adversary. However, this level of security cannot be achieved for the linkable ring signature schemes because of the possibility of linking signatures made by the same signer.

Like in most previous models, the security of LRS is introduced here in the *honest key model*, *i.e.*, all keys must have been generated honestly by the challenger and can be corrupted based on a corruption oracle by the adversary. This lead to a rather weak security model, contradicting the ad hoc purpose of ring signatures. We first introduce the definition of *correctness* and the required oracles before presenting the four game-based security requirements for *secure linkable ring signatures*.

Correctness. Let $[\mathsf{Alg}(x)]$ be the set of possible outputs of an algorithm Alg for given inputs x. Honestly generated signatures should verify the equation:

$$\forall \lambda, \forall \mathcal{R} \subset \mathbb{N}, \forall i \in \mathcal{R}, \forall \mathsf{pp} \in [\mathsf{Setup}(1^\lambda)], \forall (\mathsf{pk}_j, \mathsf{sk}_j)_{j \in \mathcal{R}} \in [\mathsf{Gen}(1^\lambda)]_{j \in \mathcal{R}},$$
$$\forall \sigma \in [\mathsf{Sign}(m, \{\mathsf{pk}_j\}_{j \in \mathcal{R}}, \mathsf{sk}_i)], \mathsf{Verify}(m, \sigma, \{\mathsf{pk}_j\}_{j \in \mathcal{R}}) = 1.$$

It should be noted that the correctness of the linking algorithm Link is guaranteed by the upcoming properties of *linkability* and *non-slanderability*.

Oracles. The adversary has access to the following oracles when it attempts to break the security of a linkable ring signature scheme.

$\mathcal{JO}$. The *Joining Oracle.* Given the security parameter 1^λ, $\mathcal{JO}$ run $(\mathsf{pk}, \mathsf{sk}) \leftarrow \mathsf{Gen}(1^\lambda)$ and outputs the public key pk.

$\mathcal{CO}$. The *Corruption Oracle*. Given a public key pk which is the output of a previous query to $\mathcal{JO}$, $\mathcal{CO}$ returns its corresponding secret key sk.

$\mathcal{SO}$. The *Signature Oracle*. Given a public key vector $\{pk_i\}_{i \in \mathcal{R}}$, an insider public key pk_i, for $i \in \mathcal{R}$ previously generated by $\mathcal{JO}$, and a message m, $\mathcal{SO}$ returns the signature $\sigma \leftarrow \mathsf{Sign}(m, \{pk_i\}_{i \in \mathcal{R}}, sk_i)$ and keeps record of the signed messages m in the set $\mathcal{SO}$.

For the purposes of notation, in our security experiments, we also use the oracle to refer to the set of the public keys that have been inputted into them.

Security Model. A linkable ring signature must achieve *unforgeability, anonymity, linkability* and *non-slanderability*. To define these four properties we always consider experiments where an adversary $\mathcal{A}$ answers a challenger $\mathcal{C}$ executing the experiments. We denote by $\mathsf{Adv}^{\mathsf{prop}}_{\mathsf{LRS},\mathcal{A}}(1^\lambda)$ the advantage of $\mathcal{A}$ against the property prop of a linkable ring signature LRS for a given security parameter 1^λ.

Unforgeability (unf). Constructing a valid signature without using the secret key should be infeasible. Formally, the probability $\mathsf{Adv}^{\mathsf{unf}}_{\mathsf{LRS},\mathcal{A}}(1^\lambda)$ of a PPT adversary $\mathcal{A}$ winning (*i.e.*, making the challenger return 1) against the experiment $\mathsf{Exp}^{\mathsf{unf}}_{\mathcal{A}}(1^\lambda)$ should be negligible for the security parameter 1^λ. Note that we could instead require a stronger variation where a new signature on a signed messages would be accepted as a forge. For that a record of the messages inputed in the signature oracle and the outputed signature is kept in the set $\mathcal{SO}$, and line 5 of $\mathsf{Exp}^{\mathsf{unf}}_{\mathcal{A}}$ checks if $(m^*, \sigma^*) \in \mathcal{SO}$ instead.

$\mathsf{Exp}^{\mathsf{unf}}_{\mathcal{A}}(1^\lambda)$ - (Unforgeability Experiment)

$1:$ $pp \leftarrow \mathsf{Setup}(1^\lambda)$

$2:$ $(m^*, \sigma^*, (pk_i)_{i \in \mathcal{R}}) \leftarrow \mathcal{A}^{\mathcal{JO}, \mathcal{CO}, \mathcal{SO}}(pp)$

$3:$ **if** $(pk_i)_{i \in \mathcal{R}} \not\subseteq \mathcal{JO}$: **return** 0 // All of the public keys in $(pk_i)_{i \in \mathcal{R}}$ are outputs of $\mathcal{JO}$.

$4:$ **if** $(pk_i)_{i \in \mathcal{R}} \cap \mathcal{CO} \neq \varnothing$: **return** 0 // No public key in $(pk_i)_{i \in \mathcal{R}}$ has been queried to $\mathcal{CO}$.

$5:$ **if** $m^* \in \mathcal{SO}$: **return** 0 // The message m^* has not been an input of $\mathcal{SO}$.

$6:$ **return** $\mathsf{Verify}(m^*, \sigma^*, \{pk_i\}_{i \in \mathcal{R}}) = 1$

One-time Anonymity (1-ano) *(Previously Named Anonymity)*. It must be difficult to guess the public key corresponding to the secret key used to produce a signatory's first signature. Here we present the property generally provided in the literature and call it *One-time Anonymity* whereas the property was previously given as *Anonymity*. Formally, for any PPT adversary $\mathcal{A}$, the experiment $\mathsf{Exp}^{\mathsf{1\text{-}ano}}_{\mathcal{A}}(1^\lambda)$ should have a negligible probability

$$\mathsf{Adv}^{\mathsf{1\text{-}ano}}_{\mathsf{LRS},\mathcal{A}}(1^\lambda) = |\Pr[\mathsf{Exp}^{\mathsf{1\text{-}ano}}_{\mathcal{A}}(1^\lambda) = 1] - 1/2| \leqslant \mathsf{negl}(\lambda).$$

$\mathsf{Exp}_{\mathcal{A}}^{\text{1-ano}}(1^\lambda)$ - (One-time Anonymity Experiment)

---

1 : $\mathsf{pp} \leftarrow \mathsf{Setup}(1^\lambda)$

2 : $(m^*, (\mathsf{pk}_i)_{i \in \mathcal{R}^*}, i_0, i_1) \leftarrow \mathcal{A}^{\mathcal{JO},\mathcal{CO},\mathcal{SO}}(\mathsf{pp})$

3 : $b \leftarrow\$ \mathcal{R}^*$

4 : $\sigma \leftarrow \mathsf{Sign}(m^*, (\mathsf{pk}_i)_{i \in \mathcal{R}^*}, \mathsf{sk}_{i_b})$

5 : $b^* \leftarrow \mathcal{A}^{\mathcal{JO},\mathcal{CO},\mathcal{SO}}(\sigma)$

6 : **if** $\{\mathsf{pk}_i\}_{i \in \mathcal{R}^*} \not\subseteq \mathcal{JO}$: **return** 0 $/\!\!/$ All of the public keys in $(\mathsf{pk}_i)_{i \in \mathcal{R}^*}$ are outputs of $\mathcal{JO}$.

7 : **if** $\{\mathsf{pk}_i\}_{i \in \mathcal{R}^*} \cap \mathcal{CO} \neq \varnothing$: **return** 0 $/\!\!/$ No public key in $(\mathsf{pk}_i)_{i \in \mathcal{R}^*}$ has been queried to $\mathcal{CO}$.

8 : **if** $\mathcal{SO}$ was queried with pk_{i_0} or pk_{i_1} : **return** 0 $/\!\!/$ The oracle $\mathcal{SO}$ did not allow the link.

9 : **return** $b = b^*$

This property only allows the adversary $\mathcal{A}$ to obtain a single signature σ produced by the signer associated with the key pk_{i_b} and no signature from the signer associated with the key $\mathsf{pk}_{i_{(1-b)}}$. Consequently, the property offers no guarantees on the anonymity of the signer when several signatures are produced with the same keys. This formalism contradicts the intended use for LRS, which is designed for different use cases than one-time LRS. In particular, anonymity of the signer is expected to persist throughout the lifespan of the keys.

Some models, such as in [27], are even weaker and assume that none of the members of the challenge ring (*i.e.*, all entities associated with keys in $\{\mathsf{pk}_i\}_{i \in \mathcal{R}^*}$) have ever produced a signature with their keys. These definitions do not reflect the actual use of linkable ring signatures, as they were designed to allow multiple anonymous signatures. In the Sect. 3, we give further arguments and two counterexamples for obtaining the above property, but without what was informally described as *anonymity* (see Sect. 1).

Linkability (link). It must be difficult to generate two unlinked valid signatures from the same signer. To obtain linkability, the probability $\mathsf{Adv}_{\mathsf{LRS},\mathcal{A}}^{\mathsf{link}}(1^\lambda)$ of winning the experiment $\mathsf{Exp}_{\mathsf{LRS},\mathcal{A}}^{\mathsf{link}}(1^\lambda)$ must be negligible.

$\mathsf{Exp}_{\mathcal{A}}^{\mathsf{link}}(1^\lambda)$ - (Linkability Experiment)

---

1 : $\mathsf{pp} \leftarrow \mathsf{Setup}(1^\lambda)$

2 : $(m_0, \sigma_0^*, (\mathsf{pk}_{i_0})_{i_0 \in \mathcal{R}_0^*}), (m_1, \sigma_1^*, (\mathsf{pk}_{i_1})_{i_1 \in \mathcal{R}_1^*}) \leftarrow \mathcal{A}^{\mathcal{JO},\mathcal{CO},\mathcal{SO}}(\mathsf{pp})$

3 : **if** $(\mathsf{pk}_i)_{i \in \mathcal{R}_0^* \cup \mathcal{R}_1^*} \not\subseteq \mathcal{JO}$: **return** 0 $/\!\!/$ Public keys in $(\mathsf{pk}_i)_{i \in \mathcal{R}_0^* \cup \mathcal{R}_1^*}$ are honestly generated.

4 : **if** $\exists i, j \in \mathcal{R}_0^* \cup \mathcal{R}_1^*, i \neq j, \mathsf{pk}_i, \mathsf{pk}_j \in \mathcal{CO}$: **return** 0 $/\!\!/$ Max. one corrupted key in the rings.

5 : **if** $\mathcal{SO}$ was queried with pk_{i_0} or pk_{i_1} : **return** 0 $/\!\!/$ The oracle $\mathcal{SO}$ did not allow the link.

6 : **return** $\mathsf{Verify}(m_0^*, \sigma_0^*, \{\mathsf{pk}_{i_0}\}_{i_0 \in \mathcal{R}_0^*}) = \mathsf{Verify}(m_1^*, \sigma_1^*, \{\mathsf{pk}_{i_1}\}_{i_1 \in \mathcal{R}_1^*}) = 1 \wedge \mathsf{Link}(\sigma_0^*, \sigma_1^*) = 0$

Non-slanderability (slan). It should be infeasible to link two valid signatures correctly generated by different signers. To obtain non-slanderability, the probability $\mathsf{Adv}_{\mathsf{LRS},\mathcal{A}}^{\mathsf{slan}}(1^\lambda)$ of winning the experiment $\mathsf{Exp}_{\mathcal{A}}^{\mathsf{slan}}(1^\lambda)$ must be negligible.

$\mathsf{Exp}_{\mathcal{A}}^{\mathsf{slan}}(1^\lambda)$ - (Non-slanderability Experiment)

---

1 : $\mathsf{pp} \leftarrow \mathsf{Setup}(1^\lambda)$

2 : $\mathsf{pk}, m_0^*, \mathcal{R}_0^* \leftarrow \mathcal{A}^{\mathcal{JO}, \mathcal{CO}, \mathcal{SO}}(\mathsf{pp})$

3 :   **if** $\{\mathsf{pk}\} \cup \{\mathsf{pk}_i\}_{i \in \mathcal{R}_0^*} \not\subseteq \mathcal{JO}$: **return** 0   // Keys are generated honestly by the challenger.

4 : $\sigma \leftarrow \mathsf{Sign}(m_0^*, \{\mathsf{pk}\} \cup \{\mathsf{pk}_i\}_{i \in \mathcal{R}_0^*}, \mathsf{sk})$ // sk is the secret key associated to pk.

5 : $m_1^*, \sigma^*, \mathcal{R}_1^* \leftarrow \mathcal{A}^{\mathcal{JO}, \mathcal{CO}, \mathcal{SO}}(\sigma)$

6 :   **if** $\exists i \in \mathcal{R}_1^*, \mathsf{pk}_i \notin \mathcal{JO}$: **return** 0   // The set $\mathcal{R}_1^*$ only contains honestly generated keys.

7 :   **if** $\mathsf{pk} \in \mathcal{CO}$: **return** 0   // The public key pk has not been requested from $\mathcal{CO}$.

8 :   **if** $\mathcal{SO}$ was queried with pk : **return** 0   // The oracle $\mathcal{SO}$ did not produce the signature σ^*.

9 :   **return** $\mathsf{Verify}(m_1^*, \sigma^*, \{\mathsf{pk}_i\}_{i \in \mathcal{R}_1^*}) = 1 \wedge \mathsf{Link}(\sigma, \sigma^*) = 1$

Some definition of non-slanderability such as in [1] requires $\mathcal{A}$ to use specific keys to generate a signature. We deviate slightly from their definition by prohibiting corruption of the entity targeted by the attack, while following the main idea of their definition.

Unconditional Variant. We say that a property prop is obtained unconditionally if, for any unbounded probabilistic adversary $\mathcal{A}$, its advantage $\mathsf{Adv}_{\mathsf{LRS}, \mathcal{A}}^{\mathsf{prop}}(1^\lambda)$ is equal to 0. Amongst the existing scheme (see Table 1), only a few schemes, such as [1,4,11,27], have achieved unconditional one-time anonymity.

Adversarially-Chosen Keys Model. As stated above, most of the current work sets unusually low security requirements. All security experiment given in this section and in most previous works are modeled within the honest key model. The failure to consider the possibility of *adversarially-chosen keys* is inconsistent with the informal security expectations for LRS. We presents the definitions introduced by Backes *et al.* [3] in the adversarially-chosen keys model in Sect. 4. This stronger model directly encompasses an improve anonymity definition.

2.2   Other Cryptographic Background

This section introduce two cryptographic primitives used to demonstrate the weaknesses in the linkable ring signature model of Sect. 2.1. First, let us introduce a primitive, called *Secret Sharing scheme*, an example of which is the well-known Shamir secret sharing scheme [35].

Definition 2 (Secret Sharing). *A secret sharing scheme amongst n participants is given by:*

$\mathsf{Split}(m, n)$**:** *is a* PPT *algorithm that takes parameters n and a message m, it returns a vector of shares* $(s_i)_{1 \leqslant i \leqslant n}$.

$\mathsf{Recover}((s_i)_{1 \leqslant i \leqslant n})$**:** *is a deterministic polynomial-time algorithm that takes a vector of shares* $(s_i)_{1 \leqslant i \leqslant n}$, *it returns a message m.*

It must verify the *correctness* described by the equality $\mathsf{Recover}(\mathsf{Split}(m, n)) = m$ and achieve *perfect secrecy*.

Perfect Secrecy [35]. Recovering a message m split for a threshold of k with less than k shares is unfeasible. The experiment $\mathsf{Exp}_{\mathcal{A}}^{\mathsf{PS}}(\lambda)$ for an adversary $\mathcal{A}$ and for a secret sharing scheme is defined as:

$\mathsf{Exp}_{\mathcal{A}}^{\mathsf{PS}}(\lambda)$ - (Perfect Secrecy)

---

1 : $m_0, m_1, n, k \leftarrow \mathcal{A}(\lambda)$ // The value k must be contained in the set $\{1, \ldots, n\}$.

2 : $b \xleftarrow{\$} \{0, 1\}$

3 : $(s_i)_{1 \leqslant i \leqslant n} \leftarrow \mathsf{Split}(m_b, n)$ // Split one of the messages based on a uniform distribution.

4 : $b' \leftarrow \mathcal{A}((s_i)_{1 \leqslant i \leqslant n, i \neq k})$ // Here $\mathcal{A}$ must operate $\mathsf{Recover}$ with one less share than necessary.

5 : **return** $(b = b')$

and for any adversary it should lead to

$$\mathsf{Adv}_\lambda^{\mathsf{PS}}(\mathcal{A}) = \big| \Pr[\mathsf{Exp}_{\mathcal{A}}^{\mathsf{PS}}(\lambda) = 1] - 1/2 \big| = 0.$$

This scheme is used for our first counter-example introduced in Sect. 3. We also need to introduce *non-interactive zero-knowledge proofs* for further investigation of a counter-example based on previously published work.

Definition 3 (Non-Interactive Zero-Knowledge proof). *A Non-Interactive Zero-Knowledge proof (NIZK) for a relation $\mathcal{R}$ is a pair of* PPT *algorithms. We use the Camenisch and Stadler [14] notation to describe the algorithms and their associated arguments.*

ZK $\{w : (w, \phi) \in \mathcal{R}\}$: *is a* PPT *algorithm that takes a witness w, a statement ϕ, it returns a proof π.*

Ver(ϕ, π): *is a deterministic polynomial-time algorithm that takes a statement ϕ and a proof π, it returns a bit 0 or 1.*

A NIZK *requires* Completeness, Soundness *and* Zero-Knowledge. *A definition of these properties can be found in [15].*

3   A Counter-Example to the Previous Definition

We have outlined our main concerns about the modelisation of signer's anonymity in Sect. 2.1. Despite that it is the models used by almost all existing works. In this section, we present two counter-examples showing that these definitions lacks of anonymity. Our first counter-example is a dedicated construction, while the second comes from existing work [13] with a different purpose.

Dedicated Counter-Example. We start with a secure linkable ring signature LRS, such as the ones exposed in Table 1. From this LRS we instantiate a new linkable ring signature scheme by combining it with a secret sharing scheme.

Setup(1^λ): corresponds to the execution of LRS.Setup(1^λ).
Gen(1^λ): execute $(\mathsf{sk_{LRS}}, \mathsf{pk_{LRS}}) \leftarrow$ LRS.Gen(1^λ) and $s_1, s_2 \leftarrow$ Split$(\mathsf{pk_{LRS}}, 2)$. Set and return $\mathsf{sk} = (\mathsf{sk_{LRS}}, s_1, s_2)$, $\mathsf{pk} = \mathsf{pk_{LRS}}$.

Sign($m, \{pk_j\}_{j\in\mathcal{R}}, sk_i$): parse sk_i into (sk_{LRS}, s_1, s_2), randomly sample $b \leftarrow\!\!\$ \{1,2\}$ and return LRS.Sign($(m\|s_b), \{pk_j\}_{j\in\mathcal{R}}, sk_{LRS}$) and s_b as σ.

Verify($m, \sigma, \{pk_j\}_{j\in\mathcal{R}}$): parse σ into σ_{LRS} and s. Execute and return the result of LRS.Verify($(m\|s), \sigma_{LRS}, \{pk_j\}_{j\in\mathcal{R}}$).

Link(σ, σ'): parse σ into σ_{LRS} and s, and σ' into σ'_{LRS} and s'. Execute and return the result of LRS.Link($\sigma_{LRS}, \sigma'_{LRS}$).

The secret sharing share included in a single signature does not reveal any information about the signer's public key, since the secret sharing scheme is perfectly secret. On the other hand, we have considered a LRS scheme with one-time anonymity, which therefore does not reveal the identity of the signer. Nevertheless, a signer has a probability of at least $1/2$ of revealing its identity when it sends its second signature. Since one-time anonymity is modelled by a single signature disclosed to the adversary (see Sect. 2.1), this construction can still be proved secure as per property 1 and its proof. Moreover, the revelation of the identity of the signer when more signature can be claimed does not affect the other properties. This highlights the lack of anonymity of existing models.

Property 1. Consider a secure linkable ring signature LRS and a secret sharing scheme with perfect secrecy. Then, the above scheme is a linkable ring signature with correctness, unforgeability, one-time anonymity, linkability and non-slanderability under the definitions introduced in Sect. 2.1.

Proof. The correctness follows by investigation. We prove the other properties based on the security of the LRS scheme and the perfect secrecy of the secret sharing scheme.

Unforgeability. First, it should be noted that the LRS scheme is assumed to satisfy the (strong) unforgeability prescribed in Sect. 2.1, and that the share s_b is signed with the message. An adversary modifying s_b in the signature would cause the verification to fail because the wrong message would be introduced into the verification algorithm. Hence, the property follows from a direct reduction to the unforgeability of the LRS signature. A forge against the presented scheme for a message m would correspond to a forge for a message $m\|s$ for a random s.

One-time Anonymity (Unconditional if Unconditional for the LRS). This is a two step proof. As only one signature is provided to the adversary for the public identities pk_{i_0} and pk_{i_1}, the first step is to replace the element s embedded in the signature σ by a random element based on the perfect secrecy, this is possible as one of the shares is never disclosed during the experiment. From then on, the signature σ is just a LRS signature with a random elements concatenated to the signed message. The one-time anonymity of the LRS scheme guarantees that no identity related information would leak from the signature σ_{LRS}, hence from the signature σ provided to the adversary.

Linkability & Non-slanderability. As the linking algorithms only take into account the sub-signatures $\sigma_{LRS_0^*}, \sigma_{LRS_1^*}$, these experiments give the same answers for the supplied scheme and the LRS scheme used as its base. Hence, linkability and non-slanderability are both ensured under the hypothesis that the LRS scheme is secure.

Counter-Example from an Existing Construction. We present a second counter-example based on a construction which has been constructed with a different purpose: revealing the public identity of signers overpassing a limit of k signatures. Originally proposed in [13], this primitive is called *k-times full traceable ring signature*. It is a ring signature that becomes linkable when the signer exceeds its limit of k allowed signatures. Once this limit has been exceeded, any verifier is capable of tracing the identity of the signer using an algorithm pk $\leftarrow$ Trace(σ, σ').

We only consider *1-times full traceable ring signatures*, which allow a signer to produce one ring signature before disclosing their public key. Under the definition currently in use, we claim that this type of signature is also a linkable ring signature, even though a linkable ring signature should not reveal the identity of the signer, even after an arbitrary number of issued signatures. We now examine the instance of the scheme from [13] with $k = 1$.

Setup(1^λ): generate three groups $\mathbb{G}_1, \mathbb{G}_2, \mathbb{G}_t$ of prime order p with a pairing mapping $e\colon \mathbb{G}_1 \times \mathbb{G}_2 \to \mathbb{G}_t$ (a computable non-degenerated bilinear map). Pick up six generators $g_1, h_0, h_1, h_2, h_3 \in \mathbb{G}_1$ and $g_2 \in \mathbb{G}_2$ and a hash function H mapping to $\mathbb{Z}_p^*$.

Gen(1^λ): the keys come in two parts, two discrete logarithm secret x and y constitute the secret key sk and the two associated elements of $\mathbb{G}_1$, pk$_1 = g_1^x$ and pk$_2 = g_1^y$ constitute the public key pk.

Sign$(m, \{\text{pk}_i\}_{i\in\mathcal{R}}, \text{sk}_i)$: sample a random $r \leftarrow\$ \mathbb{Z}_p^*$ and compute $u = H(m, 0, g_2^r)$, $v = H(m, 1, g_2^r)$, $T_1 = h_1^y$, $T_2 = h_2^y \cdot g_1^{u\cdot x}$, $T_3 = h_3^y \cdot h_4^{v\cdot x}$, $T_4 = g_2^r$, $T_5 = e(h_4, T_4)^x$. Generate a zero-knowledge proof to wrap up all the elements:

$$\Pi \leftarrow \mathsf{ZK} \left\{ x, y, r \colon \begin{array}{l} \left(\bigvee_{(\text{pk}_1, \text{pk}_2)\in\{\text{pk}_i\}_{i\in\mathcal{R}}} (\text{pk}_1 = g_1^x \wedge \text{pk}_2 = g_1^y) \right) \\ \wedge T_1 = h_1^y \wedge T_2 = h_2^y \cdot g_1^{u\cdot x} \wedge T_3 = h_3^y \cdot h_4^{v\cdot x} \\ \wedge T_4 = g_2^r \wedge T_5 = e(h_4, T_4)^x \end{array} \right\}.$$

Return $\sigma = (T_1, T_2, T_3, T_4, T_5, \Pi)$ as the signature of the message m.

Verify$(m, \sigma, \{\text{pk}_i\}_{i\in\mathcal{R}})$: parse the signature, compute $u = H(m, 0, T_4)$, $v = H(m, 1, T_4)$ and verify the zero-knowledge proof.

Link(σ, σ'): parse the signatures, check if $T_1 = T_1'$ and return 1 if so, otherwise return 0. We assume that the signatures have been verified before.

Trace(σ, σ'): check the link between the two signatures by executing Link(σ, σ') and stop if it fails. On two signatures σ, σ' being linked, compute u, u' and id $= (T_2/T_2')^{1/(u-u')}$. Returns the identity id. A second element $w = (T_3/T_3')^{1/(v-v')}$ is also recovered in the construction presented in [13], this element is not useful in the case $k = 1$.

A k-times full traceable ring signature must be *unforgeable, anonymous* and *traceable*. A description of these properties is presented in [13]. We recall it, in the same formalism as our other definitions in Appendix B.

Property 2. The 1-times full traceable ring signature from Bultel and Lafourcade introduced in [13] and depicted above is a linkable ring signature and achieves correctness, unforgeability, one-time anonymity, linkability and non-slanderability under the definitions introduced in Sect. 2.1.

Proof. The correctness follows by investigation. Security proofs for the scheme are given for the associated model in [13], we rely on them to construct ours. Indeed, their model is directly inspired from linkable ring signatures.

Unforgeability. Both the model presented in Sect. 2.1 and in the EUF-CMA experiment in [13] matches each other: the adversary has to return a valid signature, *i.e.*, Verify$(m^*, \sigma^*, \{pk_i\}_{i \in \mathcal{R}}) = 1$, for a set of uncorrupted users with honestly generated key $\{pk_i\}_{i \in \mathcal{R}}$. Furthermore, this signature should not have been outputted by a call to the signature oracle. Thus, unforgeability is obtained directly from the proof of unforgeability given in [13]. It relies mainly on the soudness of the zero-knowledge proof Π.

One-Time Anonymity. The anonymity presented in the Anon experiment in [13] is stronger than the anonymity introduced for the LRS schemes and presented in Sect. 2.1. In their model, the authors of [13] made it possible for the adversary to obtain multiple signatures from the same designated signer, with a limit of k signatures per signer. The model from [13] works in a static framework: the number of public keys in the ring is fixed to an integer n. Reducing our case to the static environment implies the introduction of a polynomial factor in the reduction but remains feasible. Consequently, their anonymity implies one-time anonymity.

Linkability. We are looking at the construction proposed in [13] using the setup $k = 1$, where k denotes the number of signatures that can be produced without being traced (linkability of all the produced signature and identification of authors of the signatures). As the adversary can infer the identity of signers through its calls to the signing oracles, the ability to trace does not reveal any information. Hence, this property falls under the *traceability* of the 1-times full traceable ring signature as only one signature is queried for the challenger signers. Moreover, the proof Π is sound under the hardness of the DL problem (see [13] for the security proof). Since the adversary is unable to forge a signature for an honest and uncorrupted user under the soudness of π, linkability is an implication of the correctness of the Link algorithms.

Non-slanderability. In this experiment the condition Link$(\sigma, \sigma^*) = 1$ enforces that $T_1 = h_1^y = h_1^{y^*} = T_1^*$, hence $y = y^*$, where y and y^* are such that for $pk = (pk_1, pk_2)$ and $pk^* = (pk_1^*, pk_2^*)$, $pk_2 = g_1^y$ and $pk_2^* = g_1^{y^*}$. Under the soundness of the proof Π, the adversary must know y^* (thus y too). And under the zero-knowledge property of Π, we ultimately reduce the security against non-slanderability to the hardness of the DL problem.

Therefore, the full 1-time full traceable ring signature of [13] can also be considered as a linkable ring signature based on the model of Sect. 2.1. From these counter-examples, we have demonstrated the existence of a gap between the definition existing definition of anonymity provided in most of the literature and the informal and expected purposes of this property. We now provide the formalism which has only been used by [3,8]. Latter, in Sect. 5, we demonstrate that these definitions bridge the anonymity gap in the definition.

4   Anonymity of Linkable Ring Signatures

Security properties of ring signatures, originate from Bender *et al.* [7] where unforgeability and anonymity have been extensively studied. Their models encompass three levels of security: in the *honest key model*, in the *adversarially-chosen keys model* and in the *insider corruption model*, when even the challenger's signer can be corrupted after signing. The honest key model is the most considered one for linkable ring signature and always with the flawed one-time anonymity experiments. Only two works [3,8] stand out and consider the adversarially-chosen keys model. Moreover, their definition of anonymity, that of the second [8] resulting from the first [3], is the only one in the literature to consider a natural and stronger formalisation of anonymity for linkable ring signatures.

They take advantage of what is sometimes called a *Left-or-Right* ($\mathcal{L}o\mathcal{R}$) oracle. It acts as a challenge oracle providing signatures to the adversary for consistent unknown *left* and *right* signers. The adversary must uncover how the identity of the two signers are distributed in between the two challenger's signers. The signature oracles are defined as follow:

$\mathcal{SO}$. The oracle $\mathcal{SO}(\cdot, \cdot, \cdot)$ is such that for a call $\mathcal{SO}(i, m, \mathcal{R})$, it returns $\mathsf{Sign}(m, \{\mathsf{pk}_i\}_{i \in \mathcal{R}}, \mathsf{sk}_i)$, where sk_i must be known by the challenger and $i \in \mathcal{R}$.

$\mathcal{L}o\mathcal{R}$. For two honestly generated key pairs $(\mathsf{pk}_{i_0}, \mathsf{sk}_{i_0})$ and $(\mathsf{pk}_{i_1}, \mathsf{sk}_{i_1})$. The oracle $\mathcal{L}o\mathcal{R}_b(\cdot, \cdot)$ is such that for a call $\mathcal{L}o\mathcal{R}_b(m, \{\mathsf{pk}_i\}_{i \in \mathcal{R}})$, it returns a signature $\mathsf{Sign}(m, \{\mathsf{pk}_i\}_{i \in \mathcal{R}} \cup \{\mathsf{pk}_{i_0}, \mathsf{pk}_{i_1}\}, \mathsf{sk}_{i_b})$, where sk_b is know by the challenger.

The $\mathcal{L}o\mathcal{R}$ oracle can be queried for any arbitrary set of public keys $\{pk_i\}_{i \in \mathcal{R}}$. This set is always supplemented by the key of the two challengers, pk_{i_0} and pk_{i_1}, in order to avoid trivial identification attacks based on the failure of the oracles.

In these security experiment the registration and corruption oracles $\mathcal{JO}$ and $\mathcal{CO}$ are removed to better reflect the ad hoc ring construction. Instead, an arbitrary key input to the $\mathcal{SO}$ and $\mathcal{L}o\mathcal{R}$ oracles are allowed and provide alternatives to the corruption oracle. The same modification can be made for the other properties in a similar manner, we introduce the alternative experiments in Fig. 1.

Definition 4. *A* Linkable Ring Signature *scheme is defined with algorithms described in Definition 1 and achieves a security in the* adversarially-chosen key model *if it achieves the properties of* Unforgeability, Anonymity, Linkability *and* Non-slanderability, *described in Sect. 2.1 but, this time, on the basis of the experiments provided in Fig. 1.*

$\mathsf{Exp}_{\mathcal{A}}^{\mathsf{ano}}(1^\lambda, n)$ - (Anonymity w.r.t. adversarially-chosen keys experiment)

1 : $\mathsf{pp} \leftarrow \mathsf{Setup}(1^\lambda)$

2 : $\{\mathsf{pk}_i, \mathsf{sk}_i\}_{i=1}^n \leftarrow \mathsf{Gen}(1^\lambda)$

3 : $(i_0, i_1) \leftarrow \mathcal{A}^{\mathcal{SO}}(\mathsf{pp}, \{\mathsf{pk}_i\}_{i=1}^n)$ // The set $\mathcal{R}$ for which $\mathcal{SO}$ is queried can now also contain public keys pick arbitrarily by the adversary.

4 : $b \leftarrow_\$ \{0, 1\}$

5 : $b^* \leftarrow \mathcal{A}^{\mathcal{SO}, \mathcal{L}o\mathcal{R}_b}(1^\lambda)$

6 : **if** $\mathcal{SO}$ was queried with pk_{i_0} or pk_{i_1} : **return** 0   // The oracle $\mathcal{SO}$ did not allow any link.

7 : **return** $b = b^*$

$\mathsf{Exp}_{\mathcal{A}}^{\mathsf{unf}}(1^\lambda)$ - (Unforgeability experiment)

1 : $\mathsf{pp} \leftarrow \mathsf{Setup}(1^\lambda)$

2 : $\{\mathsf{pk}_i, \mathsf{sk}_i\}_{1 \leqslant i \leqslant n} \leftarrow \mathsf{Gen}(1^\lambda)$

3 : $(m^*, \sigma^*, \{\mathsf{pk}_i\}_{i \in \mathcal{R}}) \leftarrow \mathcal{A}^{\mathcal{SO}}(\mathsf{pp}, (\mathsf{pk}_i)_{1 \leqslant i \leqslant n})$

4 : **if** $\mathcal{R} \not\subseteq \{1, \ldots, n\}$: **return** 0   // No corrupted public key in the ring.

5 : **if** $m^* \in \mathcal{SO}$: **return** 0   // The message m^* has not been an input of $\mathcal{SO}$.

6 : **return** $\mathsf{Verify}(m^*, \sigma^*, \{\mathsf{pk}_i\}_{i \in \mathcal{R}}) = 1$

$\mathsf{Exp}_{\mathcal{A}}^{\mathsf{link}}(1^\lambda, n)$ - (Linkability experiment)

1 : $\mathsf{pp} \leftarrow \mathsf{Setup}(1^\lambda)$

2 : $\{\mathsf{pk}_i, \mathsf{sk}_i\}_{1 \leqslant i \leqslant n} \leftarrow \mathsf{Gen}(1^\lambda)$

3 : $(m_0, \sigma_0^*, \{\mathsf{pk}_i\}_{i \in \mathcal{R}_0^*}), (m_1, \sigma_1^*, \{\mathsf{pk}_i\}_{i \in \mathcal{R}_1^*}) \leftarrow \mathcal{A}^{\mathcal{SO}}(\mathsf{pp}, \{\mathsf{pk}_i\}_{1 \leqslant i \leqslant n})$

4 : **if** $\exists i \in \mathcal{R}_0^*, \exists j \in \mathcal{R}_1^*, \mathsf{pk}_i \neq \mathsf{pk}_j, \mathsf{pk}_i, \mathsf{pk}_j \notin \{\mathsf{pk}_i\}_{1 \leqslant i \leqslant n}$: **return** 0

   // Only one common corrupted key or many in the same ring.

5 : **if** (m_0, σ_0^*) or $(m_1, \sigma_1^*) \in \mathcal{SO}$: **return** 0   // The oracle $\mathcal{SO}$ did not produce the signatures.

6 : **return** $\mathsf{Verify}(m_0^*, \sigma_0^*, \{\mathsf{pk}_i\}_{i \in \mathcal{R}_0^*}) = 1 \wedge \mathsf{Verify}(m_1^*, \sigma_1^*, \{\mathsf{pk}_i\}_{i \in \mathcal{R}_1^*}) = 1 \wedge \mathsf{Link}(\sigma_0^*, \sigma_1^*) = 0$

$\mathsf{Exp}_{\mathcal{A}}^{\mathsf{slan}}(1^\lambda, n)$ - (Non-slanderability experiment)

1 : $\mathsf{pp} \leftarrow \mathsf{Setup}(1^\lambda)$

2 : $\{\mathsf{pk}_i, \mathsf{sk}_i\}_{1 \leqslant i \leqslant n} \leftarrow \mathsf{Gen}(1^\lambda)$

3 : $i^*, m_0^*, \mathcal{R}_0^* \leftarrow \mathcal{A}^{\mathcal{SO}}(\mathsf{pp}, \{\mathsf{pk}_i\}_{1 \leqslant i \leqslant n})$

4 : **if** $i^* \notin \{1, \ldots, n\}$: **return** 0   // The designated signer has been produced by the challenger.

5 : $\sigma \leftarrow \mathsf{Sign}(m_0^*, (\mathsf{pk}_i)_{i \in \mathcal{R}_0^*}, \mathsf{sk}_{i^*})$

6 : $m_1^*, \sigma^*, \mathcal{R}_1^* \leftarrow \mathcal{A}^{\mathcal{SO}}(\sigma)$

7 : **if** $\mathcal{SO}$ was queried with pk_{i^*} : **return** 0

   // The oracle $\mathcal{SO}$ did not allowed to produce the signature σ^* for the key pk_{i^*}.

8 : **return** $\mathsf{Verify}(m_1^*, \sigma^*, \{\mathsf{pk}_i\}_{i \in \mathcal{R}_1^*}) = 1 \wedge \mathsf{Link}(\sigma, \sigma^*) = 1$

Fig. 1. Experiments for anonymity, unforgeability, linlability and non-slanderability in the adversarially-chosen keys model. Similar to the one given in [3].

An alternative definition of anonymity in the *honest-keys model* is provided in Appendix A. Most linkable ring signatures have been proposed without regard to these models (see the other works in Table 1), although we believe that most linkable ring signatures could achieve this stronger properties, even in the adversarially-chosen key model, as it is not much more demanding on the design than the honest key model. Only two schemes in [3,8] stand out from the rest of the literature and have been shown to be secure within the framework of this model. Further work is needed to re-examine the security of existing systems in these scenarios. Considering it would provide more realistic guarantees by using this new model. See Table 1, column named *Anonymity* and Sect. 6 for a literature review.

Stronger anonymity setups such as the case where all entities can be corrupted, including the challenger, have been formalised for ring signatures. Bender *et al.* [7] named this setup as *Anonymity against full key exposure*. This property cannot be attained for linkable ring signatures. Indeed, linkable ring signature are always claimable, by making a signature for a given challenge and using the link algorithm. Hence, a corruption of one of the challenger's key would break the anonymity.

5 Review of Our Counter-Examples

In this section, we evaluate the anonymity of our counter-examples.

Since it is now possible to obtain multiple signatures of the challenger signer based on $\mathcal{LoR}$ oracle, our two counter-examples have become insecure for the new definition of anonymity. This is because a PPT adversary can claim more than one signature for one of the challenger signers when interacting with the challenger in one of the two $\mathsf{Exp}^{\mathsf{ano}}$ experiments. As shown in the Sect. 3, both schemes have non-negligible probabilities of revealing the identity of their signer after the second signature. For our counter-example construction, the probability of obtaining both secret sharing shares after the second signature is $1/2$, which allows identity recovery with a probability significantly different from $1/2$ (random guessing) even if we had obtained unconditional one-time anonymity based on an unconditionally anonymous LRS and a perfectly secret secret sharing scheme. This shows that even some schemes with unconditional one-time anonymity may not be secure.

Regarding Bultel and Lafourcade's construction [13], their primitive is specifically designed to reveal the identity of the signer after a given number of signatures. We have set this value to 2 in Sect. 3. Thus, given a polynomial number of accesses to the signature oracle, an adversary can always query the oracles twice and break the game by revealing the identity of the signer based on the Trace algorithm. As a result, our two counter-examples have become insecure in the definitions of anonymity of Sect. 4 and this holds even under the honest key model. Such as model is provided in Appendix A.

6 Literature Review

In this section, we provide a systematic review of all existing constructs in the literature in term of the experiment introduced in Sect. 4. Given the arguments of Sect. 3 and 5, it becomes apparent that the security of linkable ring signatures with one-time anonymity should be re-evaluated, even when one-time anonymity holds unconditionally. We offer insights into how the stronger security requirement of anonymity applies to existing schemes. Yet, we do not seek to prove the security of existing systems.

Given their design choices, it seems that the authors of the schemes in the literature aimed to offer the security described in the stronger model, when one-time anonymity was not considered to be a feature of the scheme. Indeed, this is reflected in the informal description of anonymity provided in previous works. We stress however that, even if the quoted schemes seem to have been designed to achieve our security, it would be necessary to re-analyse their security in the model of Sect. 4.

All linkable ring signatures include the ability to link signatures generated from the secret key sk. In general, these signatures can be divided into two parts: σ the "signature" itself and a *tag*. The purpose of the *tag* is to link valid signatures by their direct comparison while being bound to the "signature" part. The tags are usually in the form $tag = h^{\mathsf{sk}}$, for some fixed element h when relying on DL related hypothesis, or similarly when relying on other mathematical bases. The "signature" part wraps everything together to avoid modification of the tag, it can for example be a "OR" proof over the Schnorr NIZK proof [16,20] over all the public keys $\mathsf{pk} = g^{\mathsf{sk}}$. This construction has been studied in [37] with a proof in the model of Sect. 2.1. As part of the security reduction of the anonymity, these tag are being stripped of the signer's identity by applying decisional hypothesis, *e.g.*, the DDH hypothesis for tags formed as above, then, providing a random value g^z instead of $h^{\mathsf{sk}} = g^{x \cdot \mathsf{sk}}$ for some unknown x. The reduction for other parts of the signature is more specific to the design, we detail below existing lines of work and their methods.

General Idea of our Analysis. When investigating the anonymity proofs of existing signature schemes, it was common to be able to divide the proof into three parts: (1) an initial sequence of game hopes, *e.g.*, programming the ROM, (2) a sequence involving the modification of elements limited to the signature part σ of the challenge decorrelating all but the tag from the signer's secret key, *e.g.*, simulation of the NIZK proof wrapping up the signature, (3) a sequence of game hopes making it possible to decorrelate the signature tag of the signature σ from the signer's keys. For example the one based on the DDH and mentionned above. Now, given steps 2 (associated with the challenge signature) and 3 (associated with the label value), a hybrid argument seems to be possible most of the time to apply independently these parts of the proof to the multiple challenges generated by the $\mathcal{LoR}$ oracle. In particular, the proof of [8], which scheme is secure in the strong model of Sect. 4, mainly follows these steps. We therefore investigated whether it is possible to obtain a hybrid argument based on the provided reductions to decorrelate the multiple challenges of the signer's identity and summarised our results in Table 1.

Zero-Knowledge Based Schemes. As a prominent basis for LRS, the constructions from [9,12,25,29,36,37,40,41], are based on zero-knowledge proofs, zero-knowledge arguments or signature of knowledge are used to wrap up ring signatures and link them with tags. The reductions provided by the authors of the existing schemes are mainly based on the zero-knowledge security of their NIZK proofs. This leads us to believe that the security of the previous schemes can be extended to our stronger version of anonymity with adversarially-chosen keys. This is because the proofs corresponding to the signature can be simulated independently and, by virtue of the existing proof for one-time anonymity, it must be possible to decorrelated the tag from the signer's keys. This last reduction for the tag most likely applies to several signatures at the same time.

Pedersen Commitment Based Schemes for Unconditional Anonymity. The Pedersen commitment [33] where two secret values r and s are sampled and form a public commitment $c = g^r h^s$, for two generators g and h of a group, was used to obtain unconditional anonymity for LRS. The elements r and s usually form the secret key and c the public key. As multiple pairs (r, s) leads to the same public key pk, an unbounded adversary is unable to recover the secret from the public key. The anonymity reductions provided by the authors of these schemes [4,11,27] are essentially the same. For any signature, there is always a secret key pair leading to any public key involved and from which the same signature could results. Seen otherwise, whatever secret key is used, the statistical distribution of the signature remains unchanged. Given the independence of the signatures from the secret keys, we claim that the proof for all three schemes can be generalise to our new definition of anonymity, at least under the honest key model.

Remaining Schemes. Among the existing schemes, some do not fall into the previous two categories and their anonymity relies solely on decisional hypothesis, such as the DDH problem for [28,43] or the *Decisional Module-LWE problem* [10] for [5] and [30]. Another scheme [31] is based on the Chameleon hash function. For the first two schemes [28,43], each of the provided arguments only apply to a single element in the signatures and the associated reductions can be performed an arbitrary polynomial number of times. We therefore believe that their reductions can be generalised for any number of signatures. As for the scheme [30], we cannot verify how the reduction is performed for this scheme as we have been unable to find an obvious reference to the full proofs.

The security of the remaining scheme [1] does not need to be treated as their authors proposed a one-time linkable ring signature with one-time unforgeability and as such considering more signature for the anonymity is unnecessary.

The results of these investigations regarding expected security, obtained after a broad review of the literature, are summarized in Table 1. We are expecting that most schemes verify the stronger definitions of Sect. 4 as they were constructed with this idea in mind while schemes in [3] and [8] have already been proven secure by their authors in the model of Sect. 4. Furthermore, most security reduction of the existing schemes where provided based on arguments applied to one signature and decorrelating it from the keys of the signer. Their security proof, for most of them, can be generalised when these arguments can be applied independently using an hybrid argument. This is unlike the reduction we have provided for our counter-examples[1].

7   Conclusion and Further Work

We have demonstrated that most security analysis for existing linkable ring signatures lacked of any guarantee of anonymity, even for the most recent ones. To support our claim, we provided two constructions that can be proven secure under the most commonly used security model, despite clearly breaking the informal anonymity expected from such schemes. Indeed, these counter-examples leaked the identity of the signer after only two signatures.

Based on this observation, we highlighted the model proposed by Backes *et al.* [3] and subsequently used by Beullens *et al.* [8] which has been left out of subsequent works. We believe that the model presented, in the adversarially-chosen keys model, better reflects the use cases of linkable ring signatures unlike the currently used one. In particular, they leave out the two counter-example constructions as we demonstrate.

Finally, we reviewed the literature providing arguments in favor of existing schemes realising the new properties. Thus, we rule out a global lack of anonymity for existing schemes.

Acknowledgments. The authors would like to thank Octavio Perez-Kempner and the anonymous reviewers for their valuable and insightful comments. Xavier Bultel's research was supported by the ANR project PRIV-SIQ (ANR-23-CE39-0008). Charles Olivier-Anclin's research was partially supported by the ANR projet MobiS5 (ARN-18-CE39-0019).

A   Anonymity in the Honest-Keys Model

Section 4 highlight anonymity for linkable ring signatures in the adversarially-chosen keys model. In this section, we highlight the definition of anonymity for linkable ring signatures in the weaker *honest-key model*.

For the anonymity under the honest key model to hold against a PPT adversary $\mathcal{A}$, it should be computationally difficult to guess the public key corresponding to the secret key used during the production of the signatures of a signer. Formally, the experiment $\mathsf{Exp}_{\mathcal{A}}^{\mathsf{ano}}(1^\lambda)$ should have a negligible probability $\mathsf{Adv}_{\mathcal{A}}^{\mathsf{ano}}(1^\lambda)$ given by:

$$\mathsf{Adv}_{\mathcal{A}}^{\mathsf{ano}}(1^\lambda) = |\Pr[\mathsf{Exp}_{\mathcal{A}}^{\mathsf{ano}}(1^\lambda) = 1] - 1/2| \leqslant \mathsf{negl}(\lambda).$$

And this for the following experiment.

---

[1] Our counter-examples where purposely lacking security when more signature needed to be produced, but their reduction involved arguments that were not limited to a single signature each time (*e.g.*, the perfect secrecy of the Sharmir secret sharing apply to $k-1$ shares but does not holds anymore when the kth shared is revealed).

$\mathsf{Exp}_{\mathcal{A}}^{\mathsf{ano}}(1^\lambda, n)$ - (Anonymity in the honest keys model)

1 : $\mathsf{pp} \leftarrow \mathsf{Setup}(1^\lambda)$

2 : $\{\mathsf{pk}_i, \mathsf{sk}_i\}_{i=1}^n \leftarrow \mathsf{Gen}(1^\lambda)$

3 : $(m^*, i_0, i_1) \leftarrow \mathcal{A}^{\mathcal{SO}}(\mathsf{pp}, \{\mathsf{pk}_i\}_{i=1}^n)$ // Requests $\mathcal{SO}$ must be made using the provided keys.

4 : $b \leftarrow\!\!\$\ \{0, 1\}$

5 : $b^* \leftarrow \mathcal{A}^{\mathcal{SO}, \mathcal{LoR}_b}(\sigma)$

6 : **if** $\mathcal{SO}$ was queried with pk_{i_0} or pk_{i_1} as a signer : **return** 0   // The $\mathcal{SO}$ oracle did not allow any link.

7 : **if** $\mathcal{SO}$ was queried for a ring $\mathcal{R}$ with a public key which is not in $\{\mathsf{pk}_i\}_{i=1}^n$: **return** 0

8 : **if** $\mathcal{LoR}$ was queried for a ring $\mathcal{R}$ with a public key which is not in $\{\mathsf{pk}_i\}_{i=1}^n$: **return** 0

9 : **return** $b = b^*$

In this experiment, the challenge is not directly sent to the adversary, but is deported to the answers of the $\mathcal{LoR}$ oracle which provides challenges as output when called by the adversary. Therefore, when proving the anonymity of LRS under this model, every execution of the oracle $\mathcal{LoR}$ would have to be considered by the reduction instead of just the first signature, which could lead to less tight reduction when these reductions are not unconditional. However, it does more accurately formalise the anonymity of the linkable ring signature than has previously been achieved in the literature.

Despite this, this model remains too weak for many use cases, as it assumes honest generation of signature keys. The above definition of honest key anonymity assumes that it is either (1) possible to prove the honesty of key generations of the keys, or (2) that all ring members are honest. While this assumption may be realistic for some threat models, ring signatures are, by their very nature, intended for use in contexts where there is no central authority responsible for verifying the validity of public keys. Therefore, this definition this does not always reflect the actual security needs for linkable ring signatures, especially when used in decentralised scenarios such as blockchains [1]. This model leaves open possible attack scenarios in which (1) an adversary generates public keys arbitrarily (which may possibly depend on the public keys of honest users), and then (2) a legitimate signer generates a signature for a ring containing some of these adversary-generated public keys. The above definition offers no protection under these scenarios. This motivates the usage of the stronger definition in the adversarially-chosen keys model presented in Sect. 4.

B   k-Times Full Traceable Ring Signatures Model

This section presents the model for *k-Times Full Traceable Ring Signature* originally introduced by Bultel and Lafourcade [13].

Definition 5 (*k*-Times Full Traceable Ring Signature (k-FTRS). *A k-Times Full Traceable Ring Signature scheme is composed of five algorithms defined as follows:*

$\mathsf{Setup}(1^\lambda)$: *is a* PPT *(probabilistic polynomial-time) algorithm that takes the security parameter* 1^λ *and produces the* public parameters pp.

We assume these parameters as common inputs to all the upcoming algorithms.

Gen($1^\lambda, k$): *is a* PPT *algorithm that takes the security parameter* 1^λ *and a threshold value* k *denoting the maximum number of anonymous signatures authorized, it returns a pair of keys* (pk, sk).

Sign($m, \{pk_j\}_{j \in \mathcal{R}}, sk_i, l$): *is a* PPT *algorithm that takes a vector* $\{pk_i\}_{i \in \mathcal{R}}$ *of public keys for a ring set* $\mathcal{R}$, *a signer secret key* sk_i *(with* $i \in \mathcal{R}$), *a the witness* $l \in \{1, \ldots, k\}$ *and a message* m. *It outputs a ring signature* σ.

Verify($m, \sigma, \{pk_i\}_{i \in \mathcal{R}}$): *is a deterministic polynomial-time algorithm that takes a public key vector* $\{pk_i\}_{i \in \mathcal{R}}$, *a signature* σ, *and a message* m, *if the signature* σ *is valid, it returns 1, else it returns 0.*

Link(σ, σ'): *is a deterministic polynomial-time algorithm that takes two signatures* σ *and* σ', *it returns 1, if they are linked, otherwise, returns 0. Before running this algorithm, both signatures must be verified.*

Match(σ, σ'): *is a deterministic polynomial-time algorithm that takes two signatures* σ *and* σ', *if* Link(σ, σ') = 1, *it return the public key of the signer* pk *and a tracing element* ω, *else* $\bot$.

Trace(σ, ω): *is a deterministic polynomial-time algorithm that takes a signature* σ *and a tracing element* ω, *it return 1 if the signature* σ *has been produced by the signer associated to the tracer* ω, *else 0.*

A k-times full traceable ring signature k-FTRS must achieve the following properties.

Unforgeability: Constructing a valid signature without using the secret key should be infeasible. The probability $\mathsf{Adv}^{k-unf}_{k\text{-FTRS}, \mathcal{A}}(1^\lambda, k, n)$ of a PPT adversary $\mathcal{A}$ winning against the experiment $\mathsf{Exp}^{k-unf}_{\mathcal{A}}(1^\lambda, k, n)$ should be negligible for any integer $n \in \mathbb{N}$, any $k \leqslant n$ and any security parameter 1^λ.

$\mathsf{Exp}^{k-unf}_{\mathcal{A}}(1^\lambda, k, n)$ - (Unforgeability experiment for k-FTRS)

---

1 : $pp \leftarrow \mathsf{Setup}(1^\lambda)$

2 : $\{pk_i, sk_i\}_{1 \leqslant i \leqslant n} \leftarrow \mathsf{Gen}(1^\lambda, k)$

3 : $(m^*, \sigma^*, (pk_i)_{i \in \mathcal{R}}) \leftarrow \mathcal{A}^{\mathcal{SO}}(pp, (pk_i)_{1 \leqslant i \leqslant n})$

4 : **if** $\mathcal{R} \not\subseteq \{1, \ldots, n\}$: **return** 0   // No corrupted public key in the ring.

5 : **if** $\sigma^* \notin \mathcal{SO}$: **return** 0   // The signature σ^* has not been an output of $\mathcal{SO}$.

6 : **return** Verify($m^*, \sigma^*, \{pk_i\}_{i \in \mathcal{R}}$) = 1

Where $\mathcal{SO}$ is a signing oracle that takes $(pk_i, \{pk_j\}_{j \in \mathcal{R}}, m, l)$ as input to sign the message m. If $pk_i \notin \{pk_i, sk_i\}_{1 \leqslant i \leqslant n}$ then it returns $\bot$, else it computes $\sigma \leftarrow \mathsf{Sign}(m, \{pk_j\}_{j \in \mathcal{R}}, sk_i, l)$ and returns σ.

Anonymity: Guessing the public key corresponding to the secret key used to produce less than $(k + 1)$ signatures should be hard. For any PPT adversary $\mathcal{A}$, the experiment $\mathsf{Exp}^{k-ano}_{\mathcal{A}}(1^\lambda)$ should have a negligible probability

$$\mathsf{Adv}^{k-ano}_{k\text{-FTRS}, \mathcal{A}}(1^\lambda, k, n) = |\Pr[\mathsf{Exp}^{k-ano}_{\mathcal{A}}(1^\lambda, k, n) = 1] - 1/2| \leqslant \mathsf{negl}(\lambda),$$

for any integer $n \in \mathbb{N}$, any $k \leqslant n$ and any security parameter 1^λ.

$\mathsf{Exp}_{\mathcal{A}}^{\mathsf{k-ano}}(1^\lambda, k, n)$ - (Anonymity experiment for k-FTRS)

---

1 : $b \leftarrow\$ \{0, 1\}$

2 : $\mathsf{pp} \leftarrow \mathsf{Setup}(1^\lambda)$

3 : $\{\mathsf{pk}_i, \mathsf{sk}_i\}_{i=1}^n \leftarrow \mathsf{Gen}(1^\lambda, k)$

4 : $(m^*, i_0, i_1) \leftarrow \mathcal{A}^{\mathcal{SO}}(\mathsf{pp}, \{\mathsf{pk}_i\}_{i=1}^n)$

5 : $\sigma_0 \leftarrow \mathcal{SO}(m, \{\mathsf{pk}_j\}_{j \in \mathcal{R}}, \mathsf{sk}_{i_0}, l)$

6 : $\sigma_1 \leftarrow \mathcal{SO}(m, \{\mathsf{pk}_j\}_{j \in \mathcal{R}}, \mathsf{sk}_{i_1}, l)$

7 : $b^* \leftarrow \mathcal{A}^{\mathcal{SO}}(\sigma_b)$

8 :   **return** $b = b^*$

Where $\mathcal{SO}$ is a signing oracle that takes $(\mathsf{pk}_i, \{\mathsf{pk}_j\}_{j \in \mathcal{R}}, m, l)$ as input to sign the message m. If $l > k$ or $\mathsf{pk}_i \notin \{\mathsf{pk}_j, \mathsf{sk}_j\}_{j=1}^n$ then it returns $\perp$ and aborts. If $l \in \{1, \dots, k\}$ was already queried for pk_i, it also returns $\perp$. Else it computes $\sigma \leftarrow \mathsf{Sign}(m, \{\mathsf{pk}_j\}_{j \in \mathcal{R}}, \mathsf{sk}_i, l)$ and returns σ.

Traceability: More then k signatures coming from the same signers are always (linkable and then) traceable. The probability $\mathsf{Adv}_{\mathsf{k-FTRS},\mathcal{A}}^{\mathsf{k-trace}}(1^\lambda, k, n)$ of a PPT adversary $\mathcal{A}$ winning against the experiment $\mathsf{Exp}_{\mathcal{A}}^{\mathsf{k-trace}}(1^\lambda, k, n)$ should be negligible for any integer $n \in \mathbb{N}$, any $k \leqslant n$ and any security parameter 1^λ.

$\mathsf{Exp}_{\mathcal{A}}^{\mathsf{k-trace}}(1^\lambda, k, n)$ - (Traceability experiment for k-FTRS)

---

1 : $\mathsf{pp} \leftarrow \mathsf{Setup}(1^\lambda)$

2 : $\{\mathsf{pk}_i, \mathsf{sk}_i\}_{1 \leqslant i \leqslant n} \leftarrow \mathsf{Gen}(1^\lambda)$

3 : $i^* \leftarrow \mathcal{A}^{\mathcal{SO}}(\mathsf{pp}, \{\mathsf{pk}_i\}_{1 \leqslant i \leqslant n})$

4 : $(\{\mathsf{pk}_j\}_{j \in \mathcal{R}_i^*}, m_i^*, \sigma_i^*)_{1 \leqslant i \leqslant l} \leftarrow \mathcal{A}^{\mathcal{SO}}(\mathsf{sk}_{i^*})$

5 :   **if** $l \geq k \wedge (\forall i \in \{1, \dots, k\}, \mathsf{Verify}(m_i^*, \sigma_i^*, \{\mathsf{pk}_j\}_{j \in \mathcal{R}_i^*}) = 1 \wedge (\{\mathsf{pk}_j\}_{j \in \mathcal{R}_i^*}, m_i^*, \sigma_i^*) \notin \mathcal{SO})$

   $\wedge \big((\forall 1 \leqslant a < b \leqslant k, \mathsf{Link}(\sigma_a, \sigma_b) \neq 1) \vee (\exists a, b, i, \mathsf{Match}(\sigma_a, \sigma_b) = (\mathsf{pk}, \omega), \mathsf{pk} \neq \mathsf{pk}_{i^*}$

   $\vee\ \mathsf{Trace}(\sigma_i, \omega_i) \neq 1))$

6 :   **return** 1

7 :   **return** 0

Wher the $\mathcal{SO}$ oracle operate similarly to the signing oracle defined for the unforgeability of k-FTRS.

References

1. Alberto Torres, W.A., et al.: Post-quantum one-time linkable ring signature and application to ring confidential transactions in blockchain (Lattice Ringct v1. 0). In: Information Security and Privacy: 23rd Australasian Conference, ACISP (2018)
2. Aranha, D.F., Hall-Andersen, M., Nitulescu, A., Pagnin, E., Yakoubov, S.: Count me in! extendability for threshold ring signatures. In: IACR International Conference on Public-Key Cryptography (2022)
3. Backes, M., Döttling, N., Hanzlik, L., Kluczniak, K., Schneider, J.: Ring signatures: logarithmic-size, no setup—from standard assumptions. In: Ishai, Y., Rijmen, V. (eds.) EUROCRYPT 2019. LNCS, vol. 11478, pp. 281–311. Springer, Cham (2019). https://doi.org/10.1007/978-3-030-17659-4_10

4. Balla, D., Behrouz, P., Grontas, P., Pagourtzis, A., Spyrakou, M., Vrettos, G.: Designated-verifier linkable ring signatures with unconditional anonymity. In: International Conference on Algebraic Informatics (2022)
5. Baum, C., Lin, H., Oechsner, S.: Towards practical lattice-based one-time linkable ring signatures. In: Naccache, D., et al. (eds.) ICICS 2018. LNCS, vol. 11149, pp. 303–322. Springer, Cham (2018). https://doi.org/10.1007/978-3-030-01950-1_18
6. Bellare, M., Micciancio, D., Warinschi, B.: Foundations of group signatures: formal definitions, simplified requirements, and a construction based on general assumptions. In: Advances in Cryptology-EUROCRYPT 2003: International Conference on the Theory and Applications of Cryptographic Techniques (2003)
7. Bender, A., Katz, J., Morselli, R.: Ring signatures: Stronger definitions, and constructions without random oracles. In: Theory of Cryptography Conference (2006)
8. Beullens, W., Katsumata, S., Pintore, F.: Calamari and Falafl: logarithmic (linkable) ring signatures from isogenies and lattices. In: Moriai, S., Wang, H. (eds.) ASIACRYPT 2020. LNCS, vol. 12492, pp. 464–492. Springer, Cham (2020). https://doi.org/10.1007/978-3-030-64834-3_16
9. Bootle, J., Elkhiyaoui, K., Hesse, J., Manevich, Y.: DualDory: logarithmic-verifier linkable ring signatures through preprocessing. In: European Symposium on Research in Computer Security (2022)
10. Bos, J., et al.: Crystals-Kyber: a CCA-secure module-lattice-based KEM. In: 2018 IEEE European Symposium on Security and Privacy (2018)
11. Boyen, X., Haines, T.: Forward-secure linkable ring signatures. In: Information Security and Privacy: 23rd Australasian Conference, ACISP (2018)
12. Branco, P., Mateus, P.: A code-based linkable ring signature scheme. In: Provable Security: 12th International Conference, ProvSec 2018 (2018)
13. Bultel, X., Lafourcade, P.: k-times full traceable ring signature. In: 2016 11th International Conference on Availability, Reliability and Security (ARES) (2016)
14. Camenisch, J., Stadler, M.: Efficient group signature schemes for large groups. In: Annual international cryptology conference (1997)
15. Chase, M., Lysyanskaya, A.: On signatures of knowledge. In: Advances in Cryptology-CRYPTO: 26th Annual International Cryptology Conference (2006)
16. Cramer, R., Damgård, I., Schoenmakers, B.: Proofs of partial knowledge and simplified design of witness hiding protocols. In: CRYPTO 1994 (1994)
17. Diaz, J., Lehmann, A.: Group signatures with user-controlled and sequential linkability. In: IACR International Conference on Public-Key Cryptography (2021)
18. El Kaafarani, A., Chen, L., Ghadafi, E., Davenport, J.: Attribute-based signatures with user-controlled linkability. In: Cryptology and Network Security: 13th International Conference, CANS 2014 (2014)
19. El Kaafarani, A., Ghadafi, E.: Attribute-based signatures with user-controlled linkability without random oracles. In: Cryptography and Coding: 16th IMA International Conference, IMACC 2017 (2017)
20. Fiat, A., Shamir, A.: How to prove yourself: practical solutions to identification and signature problems. In: CRYPTO 1986 (1987)
21. Fiore, D., Garms, L., Kolonelos, D., Soriente, C., Tucker, I.: Ring signatures with user-controlled linkability. In: European Symposium on Research in Computer Security (2022)
22. Fraser, A., Garms, L., Lehmann, A.: Selectively linkable group signatures-stronger security and preserved verifiability. In: International Conference on Cryptology and Network Security (2021)
23. Fujisaki, E., Suzuki, K.: Traceable ring signature. In: International Workshop on Public Key Cryptography (2007)

24. Garms, L., Lehmann, A.: Group signatures with selective linkability. In: Public-Key Cryptography–PKC 2019: 22nd IACR International Conference on Practice and Theory of Public-Key Cryptography (2019)

25. Hui, X., Chau, S.C.K.: LLRing: logarithmic linkable ring signatures with transparent setup. Cryptology ePrint Archive, Paper 2024/421 (2024)

26. Koblitz, N., Menezes, A.J.: The Random Oracle Model: A Twenty-Year Retrospective. Designs, Codes and Cryptography (2015)

27. Liu, J.K., Au, M.H., Susilo, W., Zhou, J.: Linkable ring signature with unconditional anonymity. IEEE Trans. Knowl. Data Eng. (2013)

28. Liu, J.K., Wei, V.K., Wong, D.S.: Linkable spontaneous anonymous group signature for ad hoc groups. In: Information Security and Privacy: 9th Australasian Conference, ACISP (2004)

29. Liu, J.K., Wong, D.S.: Linkable ring signatures: security models and new schemes. In: International Conference on Computational Science and Its Applications–ICCSA 2005 (2005)

30. Liu, Z., Nguyen, K., Yang, G., Wang, H., Wong, D.S.: A lattice-based linkable ring signature supporting stealth addresses. In: Computer Security–ESORICS 2019: 24th European Symposium on Research in Computer Security (2019)

31. Lu, X., Au, M.H., Zhang, Z.: Raptor: a practical lattice-based (linkable) ring signature. In: Deng, R.H., Gauthier-Umaña, V., Ochoa, M., Yung, M. (eds.) ACNS 2019. LNCS, vol. 11464, pp. 110–130. Springer, Cham (2019). https://doi.org/10.1007/978-3-030-21568-2_6

32. Park, S., Sealfon, A.: It wasn't me! In: Annual International Cryptology Conference (2019)

33. Pedersen, T.P.: Non-interactive and information-theoretic secure verifiable secret sharing. In: Annual International Cryptology Conference (1991)

34. Rivest, R.L., Shamir, A., Tauman, Y.: How to leak a secret. In: International Conference on the Theory and Application of Cryptology and Information Security (2001)

35. Shamir, A.: How to share a secret. Commun. ACM (1979)

36. Tsang, P.P., Wei, V.K.: Short linkable ring signatures for e-voting, e-cash and attestation. In: International Conference on Information Security Practice and Experience (2005)

37. Tsang, P.P., Wei, V.K., Chan, T.K., Au, M.H., Liu, J.K., Wong, D.S.: Separable linkable threshold ring signatures. In: Progress in Cryptology-INDOCRYPT 2004: 5th International Conference on Cryptology in India (2005)

38. Valimised: internet voting in Estonia (2024). https://www.valimised.ee/en/internet-voting-estonia. Accessed 18 June 2024

39. Van Saberhagen, N.: Cryptonote v 2.0 (2013)

40. Xue, Y., Lu, X., Au, M.H., Zhang, C.: Efficient linkable ring signatures: new framework and post-quantum instantiations. Cryptology ePrint Archive, Paper 2024/553 (2024)

41. Yuen, T.H., Liu, J.K., Au, M.H., Susilo, W., Zhou, J.: Efficient linkable and/or threshold ring signature without random oracles. Comput. J. (2013)

42. Zhang, L., Li, H., Li, Y., Yu, Y., Au, M.H., Wang, B.: An efficient linkable group signature for payer tracing in anonymous cryptocurrencies. Future Generation Computer Systems (2019)

43. Zhang, X., Liu, J.K., Steinfeld, R., Kuchta, V., Yu, J.: Revocable and linkable ring signature. In: Information Security and Cryptology: 15th International Conference, Inscrypt 2019 (2020)

Blockchain Technology

Mithril: Stake-Based Threshold Multisignatures

Pyrros Chaidos[1]([✉]) and Aggelos Kiayias[2]

[1] National and Kapodistrian University of Athens & IOG, Athens, Greece
pchaidos@di.uoa.gr
[2] University of Edinburgh & IOG, Edinburgh, Scotland
akiayias@inf.ed.ac.uk

Abstract. Stake-based multiparty cryptographic primitives operate in a setting where participants are associated with their stake, security is argued against an adversary that is bounded by the total stake it possesses —as opposed to number of parties— and we are interested in *scalability*, i.e., the complexity of critical operations depends only logarithmically in the number of participants (who are assumed to be numerous).

In this work we put forth a new stake-based primitive, *stake-based threshold multisignatures* (STM, or "Mithril" signatures), which allows the aggregation of individual signatures into a compact certificate provided the stake that supports a given message exceeds a stake threshold. This is achieved by having for each message a pseudorandomly sampled subset of participants eligible to issue an individual signature; this ensures the scalability of signing, communicating the signatures, aggregating them to a certificate and verifying it.

We formalize the primitive in the universal composition setting and propose efficient constructions for STMs in the unstructured reference string model. We also showcase that STMs are eminently useful in the blockchain setting by providing three applications: (i) stakeholder decision-making for Proof of Work (PoW) blockchains, specifically, Bitcoin, (ii) fast bootstrapping for Proof of Stake (PoS) blockchains, and (iii) proofs of data availability for consensus scaling.

1 Introduction

A wide class of multiparty cryptographic protocols is currently considered in the *stake-based* setting, where a public-key directory of N keys associates each key mvk_i with a real number s_i,—the key's stake. In the stake-based setting, the adversary has a corruption bound which is expressed in terms of total stake controlled—rather than number of keys or identities—and the complexity metrics of the protocol aim to scale with $\log N$ rather than N.

While any standard "key-based" multiparty protocol can be trivially ported to the stake-based setting by "flattening" out the stake distribution and associating each unit of stake (aka coin) to a distinct cryptographic key, the resulting constructions are typically extremely inefficient. Motivated by advances in

© The Author(s), under exclusive license to Springer Nature Singapore Pte Ltd. 2025
M. Kohlweiss et al. (Eds.): CANS 2024, LNCS 14905, pp. 239–263, 2025.
https://doi.org/10.1007/978-981-97-8013-6_11

blockchain technology, an array of recent protocol design efforts have focused on the topic of native stake-based design, with prominent examples in the area of consensus protocols, e.g., Algorand [11] and the Ouroboros protocols [15,24,26], and more recently secure multiparty computation [12].

Pushing the state of the art forward in this direction, this work puts forth stake-based threshold multisignatures (STM).

- In an STM, as in a threshold signature, a quorum of signers is required to engage in order for a signature to be produced. However, the threshold is expressed in terms of stake rather than a number of keys or identities.
- Second, in an STM, contrary to a multisignature, not all signers are eligible to sign all messages—this is necessary in order to match the communication scalability requirement. On the other hand, when they are eligible, similar to a multisignature, they can act independently producing (pre-)signatures that can be individually verified.
- Third, in an STM, in line with the scalability objective of the stake-based setting, we want the operations of issuing a signature, aggregation of individual signatures, verification *as well as total communication* to depend logarithmically in N. Furthermore, we allow for the verifier to operate using a concise verification key.

STMs can have profound implications in the topic of blockchain governance, (e.g., it is possible for all Bitcoin holders to ratify a particular software upgrade) but also other applications such as fast blockchain bootstrapping of cryptocurrency wallets. Specifically, to articulate the latter application, in a proof-of-stake blockchain like Cardano, Algorand or Tezos, using an STM, it is possible to certify the state of the ledger efficiently at regular intervals by creating certified checkpoints. This can facilitate a fast bootstrapping process for a wallet application joining the system: instead of the wallet acting as a "full node" and processing all ledger transactions to sync up to the recent state, it can "hop" across checkpoints from checkpoint to checkpoint starting from the genesis block (or the most recently known trusted block) until the latest checkpoint is reached from which point it can process transactions normally.

Our Contributions. In more detail, our contributions are as follows:

- *Formalization of the Stake-based Threshold Multisignature primitive.* The fundamental concept in achieving a scalable STM is to pseudorandomly associate with each message a sufficiently large committee drawn from the stakeholder distribution. For this reason, we introduce the notion of an eligibility check before signing. At the same time, we also use the notion of an index, iterating over the available seats in the committee. We present our modeling as an ideal functionality in the universal composition (UC) setting.
- *A scalable instantiation.* We instantiate our primitive in a modular way, by building a proof system around a core relation. We provide a concatenation-based instantiation in the text and also outline a Bulleproof based instantiation [7] with improved proof size.

– *Efficiency Considerations and Applications.* We compare the space efficiency of our construction with that of similar primitives and describe three potential applications in which our design is readily applicable. First, we describe how STM functionality can be integrated into bitcoin by using pay-to-script-hash P2SH to facilitate registration. Second, we describe how STMs can facilitate bootstrapping in Proof of Stake (PoS) blockchains. Finally, we comment on how STMs can play a role in the design of high performance permissionless distributed ledger protocols.

1.1 System Overview and Design Challenges

The operation of our primitive, Stake-based Threshold Multisignatures (detailed in Sect. 4) is as follows: the semantics are similar to those of a standard threshold signature scheme, with the addition of an eligibility predicate based on user stake. The purpose of the predicate is to pre-emptively filter the number of users signing each message to a quantity independent of the number of total users, and independent of the particulars of the stake distribution.

In typical stake-based blockchain constructions, blocks are produced by turning to a verifiable or distributed randomness generation to select the users responsible for block production, and then by having the selected users sign the blocks. Our construction (Sect. 5) aims to instantiate our primitive by combining this random selection with the signature. To extend the lottery analogy, in our construction the individual signatures will also serve as eligibility tickets. The odds of a ticket winning are proportional to the signer's stake.

From Stake to Tickets. Potential signers can check eligibility locally leading to clear efficiency gains: non-winning tickets incur no communication, storage or aggregation costs. On top of this, we will also need a mechanism that checks that a particular message is in fact supported by stakeholders of a sufficient amount of stake—a form of signature aggregation. To accomplish this, we run m lotteries (signing sessions) in parallel and require that at least k of them are won (produce a successful signature), for suitable choices of the parameters k, m. Subsequently we facilitate signature aggregation by using them as witnesses in a properly crafted aggregation relation. A particular challenge in our setting is to ensure that the adversary cannot bias the lotteries to its advantage, especially given the fact that our constructions cannot always rely fully on idealized abstractions such as the random oracle model.

Verifying signatures in this system would require verifiers to know the public keys and stake held by each user, which can often be cost-prohibitive in large user sets. We formalize this requirement by requiring a key registration functionality that organizes the participants' stake; to minimize the assumptions placed on the setup of the primitive, we assume the functionality is aware of the stake of participants and invites them to register their cryptographic keys. Upon termination of this phase, the parties can retrieve those keys and organize them in a Merkle tree (note that this Merkle tree organization can take place as part of setup and hence need not encumber the parties computationally).

In this way, verifiers only need to be made aware of the tree root rather than the entirety of the contents. In turn, this implies that signatures need to contain the path to their key and stake alongside their signature and session index(es) for which they claim they are eligible. This is still a net gain, as the length of the Merkle tree path is only logarithmic with regard to the number of users.

A natural tool for concisely aggregating Merkle proofs as well as signatures, are proofs of knowledge. Interestingly, even as we only require compactness and not secrecy, our tools are derived from zero knowledge protocols. Even so, we face a number of design challenges: the hash function in the Merkle tree needs to be optimized for use inside a proof system, as well as the signature and mapping verification. Furthermore, we cannot directly encapsulate a random oracle inside the proof system as that would swap the oracle for a concrete function [2]; calls must be avoided or externalized. We lay out the groundwork for a circuit-based approach by utilizing a modular approach for our design, and elaborate on a Bulletproof based construction describing the necessary components and an Elligator-based mapping function.

1.2   Comparisons to Related Work

Ad-hoc threshold multisignatures (ATMS) were put forth in [21]. ATMS is like a threshold signature, in the sense that a quorum of signers need to issue "signature shares" that are subsequently combined. Signature shares however are verifiable as signatures. Key generation is ad-hoc without participant coordination. This allows a maximal committee to be fixed ahead of time whilst allowing for individual members to abstain or be unavailable. The multisignature-based construction in [21] operates by first committing the verification keys of all users to a Merkle tree and also producing an aggregate verification key for the entire user set. Signing operates by producing a multisignature representing all the users who *did* participate, as well as a list of all the verification keys of users who did not. The list is supported by Merkle tree proofs verifying their membership in the set. This results in a size linear to the number of abstaining users (regardless of their amount of stake).

In contrast, our notion of a "threshold" is predicated by the stake held by each user and additionally involves random eligibility sampling to keep participation requirements manageable. Essentially, whereas in an ATMS scheme selecting a committee is an external operation, in STM it is (implicitly) performed internally. This is beneficial to security (as there is no need to identify committee members) as well as liveness: a (partly) inactive committee stops progress in an ATMS scheme, but an STM scheme can recover by signing an alternative message (as eligibility is pseudorandomly redistributed per message).

More recently, Micali et al. [29] introduced compact certificate schemes (CCCK) which can be seen as the stake-based version of ATMS. Compared to our primitive, they lack the concept of eligibility. As a result, depending on the stakeholder distribution, a significant percentage of the user base needs to produce and transmit their individual signatures in order for the protocol to succeed. They do utilize sampling during aggregation however, something that enables them to only reveal a small number of signatures as proof of a certificate's validity. The construction of [29], uses a Merkle tree for registration, similar to ATMS and Mithril. For signing, it first commits to the set of collected signatures, and then uses random sampling to determine which of the committed signatures will be revealed to the verifier.

Interestingly, in terms of efficiency, this adaptive sampling enables the use of a more aggressive quorum parameter, producing certificates that are 2–3 times smaller than our concatenation-based instantiation, with similar asymptotics. However, this comes at the expense of a centralized aggregator that needs to collect all signatures making the communication of the approach unattractive.

Table 1. Comparison to previous work for N users with sizes in kilobytes (KB) unless noted. Communication costs are the sum of all individual signatures produced by signers. We assume a flat (uniform) stake distribution, $\frac{1}{3}$ adversarial stake and full adversarial abstention (bottom subtable) or participation (top). This leads to numreveals = 128/80 for CCCK when the adversary is abstaining/participating. We use $k = 424$ for $\mathsf{PS}^B, \mathsf{PS}^C$. Signature and hash bit lengths are 512/256 for the baseline and CCCK systems, 384/256 for ATMS, Telescope and PS^C and 446/446 for PS^B respectively. In all cases aggregation must be performed by a full node. CH indicates a concurrent hybrid of $k = (286, 769), m = (1747, 6654)$, see Sect. 6. For PS^B we have included the cost to avoid complexity leveraging. For an abstaining adversary, we calculate the expected communication cost including retries. We optimize all Merkle tree proofs using Merkle caps. The parenthesised values correspond to the "empty body" variant in Sect. 7.

System	$\log N = 10$		$\log N = 13$		$\log N = 20$		$\log N = 30$	
	comms	size	comms	size	comms	size	comms	size
Baseline - Participation	64	42	512	335	64 MB	42 MB	64 GB	42 GB
ATMS [21]	48	.05	384	.05	48 MB	.05	48 GB	.05
CCCK [29]	64	34	512	49	64 MB	84	64 GB	134
Telescope, Cent. [10]	102 (54)	17	816 (432)	25	102 (54) MB	44.5	102 (54) GB	72
Telescope, Dec. [10]	102 (54)	18	816 (432)	26.5	102 (54) MB	47	179 (97) MB	76.5
PS^C [Sect. 5.2]	61 (32)	102	61 (32)	141	61 (32)	234	61 (32)	367
PS^C CH [Sects. 5.2, 6]	132 (70)	69	132 (70)	96	132 (70)	158	132 (70)	248
PS^B [Sect. 5.3]	70 (37)	4.5	70 (37)	4.7	70 (37)	5.1	70 (37)	5.6
PS^B CH [Sects. 5.3, 6]	153 (80)	4.3	153 (80)	4.4	153 (80)	4.6	153 (80)	4.9
Baseline - Abstention	43	42	341	335	43 MB	42 MB	43 GB	42 GB
ATMS [21]	32	64	256	512	32 MB	64 MB	32 GB	64 GB
CCCK [29]	43	46	341	70	43 MB	126	43 GB	206
Telescope, Cent. [10]	68 (36)	24	544 (288)	37.5	68 (36) MB	68	68 (36) GB	112
Telescope, Dec. [10]	68 (36)	25.5	544 (288)	39.5	68 (36) MB	72.5	311 (165) MB	120
PS^C [Sect. 5.2]	88 (47)	102	88 (47)	141	88 (47)	234	88 (47)	367
PS^C CH [Sects. 5.2, 6]	92 (49)	161	92 (49)	232	92 (49)	401	92 (49)	641
PS^B [Sect. 5.3]	102 (54)	4.5	102 (54)	4.7	102 (54)	5.1	102 (54)	5.6
PS^B CH [Sects. 5.3, 6]	106 (56)	5.5	106 (56)	5.9	106 (56)	6.6	106 (56)	7.6

The contemporary work on the Telescope [10] family of protocols is also applicable to our setting. Though the authors frame their design as a framework to prove knowledge of elements satisfying a predicate, it is straightforward to adapt it in a signature setting by means of a unique signature scheme. For a certain message m, an element satisfies the predicate iff it correctly verifies against on of the verification keys in a fixed set. The authors offer a centralized version where every signer needs to contact the aggregator, and a decentralized version where eligibility sampling is performed beforehand, though the protocol exhibits a very high lower bound in the number of transmitted signatures. This is visible in Table 1 as the decentralized version tracks the centralized one even for 2^{20} users. To adapt their scheme to our setting, we need to enable certificate recipients to verify signatures: in the Telescope setting this functionality is a given. Towards this, we assume the set of verifier keys is stored in a Merkle Tree, and include costs for the Merkle paths in the certificate size only. We also provide costs were the signed message is split in two parts, (topic, body) which are signed separately with only topic determining eligibility as in Sect 4.

Our construction instead is scalable in terms of communication costs and aggregation effort as only a small subset of users is involved in signature production. We can also implement STMs using bulletproofs for the proof system, something that squashes the proof length (at the cost of higher computation). We note that the constructions of [10, 29] could possibly similarly be augmented with a more compact proof system but has not been explored in the corresponding works.

We provide a comparison with concrete numbers between the schemes in Table 1, showcasing the scalability of Mithril against a naive base scheme, the ATMS construction of [21] the compact certificates of [29] and Telescope [10]. The naive baseline system polls all users and produces a certificate by fully revealing enough signatures to overtake the presumed adversarial stake, as described in [29]. The PS^B instantiations of Mithril make use of bulletproofs to reduce the proof size. The security proof for the bulletproof based instantiation, PS^B requires an optional leveraging argument. If we eschew leveraging, we will need to also add the leaf index corresponding to each of the k contained signatures. This adds $k \cdot \log N$ bits to the proof size, and has no effect to the other metrics. In the most extreme case, this will add 2.7KiB to the concurrent hybrid (CH) proof sizes for 2^{30} users, and as little as .6KiB for 1024 users. For convenience, we include these costs in the table.

In short, ATMS is best-suited for a small number of parties, whereas Mithril, CCCK and Telescope scale better. Mithril best "compresses" the signer set before transmission and thus wins on communication. On the other hand, CCCK performs that compression after the fact, and Telescope at both ends, with both revealing fewer signatures than the concatenation version of Mithril, PS^C.

Blockchains and Proof of Stake. In terms of client bootstrapping, proof of Work blockchains admit simple solutions like Simple Payment Verification (SPV), where bootstrapping can be performed by verifying only the headers of the chain [30]. Further optimizations such as Non-interactive proofs of proof-of-work (NIPoPoWs) [25] and flyclient [8] drastically reduce the number of headers required by attaching additional significance to blocks with a specific, rare property. This critically hinges on the ability to verify headers without the need to establish a stakeholder distribution.

Turning to PoS blockchains, the works of [2,19] are orthogonal to our work: they describe how a single user can privately prove eligibility, whilst we tackle eligibility over multiple users. Vault [27] uses a construction similar to ours as a component in an efficient bootstrapping and storage solution for Algorand. In comparison, by using the notion of a dense mapping, we obtain greater flexibility in terms of size-time tradeoffs by choosing the appropriate proof system.

Plumo [18] uses a two layer solution tailored to blockchain bootstrapping, where one layer proves epoch transitions and the other aggregates over multiple epochs. Their system is highly efficient, but requires stronger setup assumptions to utilize SNARKS. Similarly, the subsequent works of Das et al. [14] and Garg et al. [20] make use of customized snarks to produce weighted threshold signatures with a trusted setup. Agrawal et al. [1] introduce an efficient interactive bootstrapping solution with some online requirements. It is orthogonal to (and compatible with) our work: e.g. their solution can be applied to a chain of Mithril certificates (Table 2).

Table 2. Notation used in this work

Numbering	
N	Number of users registered.
m	Number of lotteries to be held.
k	Number of lotteries to be won for a certificate to be accepted.
Registration	
mvk_i	Verification key of user i.
$stake_i$	Stake held by user i.
AVK	Aggregate key of N users, defined as the root of a Merkle Tree with $reg_i = (mvk_i, stake_i)$ as leaves.
Messages	
mesg	A message for the STM, in the form of mesg = (topic, body)
topic	Part of a mesg, used to determine eligibility.
body	Part of a mesg, not used to determine eligibility.
msg	The message passed to the underlying unique signature primitive, as a function of mesg and AVK.
Sampling	
$\phi(stake_i)$	A function mapping the stake $stake_i$ of an individual user, or set of users to the probability of wining one of the lotteries.

2   Preliminaries

Notation. We use λ as the security parameter. When S is a set, the assignment operator $x \leftarrow S$ stands for x being sampled from the set S uniformly at random. We use bold characters to denote vectors of variables i.e. $\boldsymbol{b} := (b_1, \ldots, b_n)$. We require the Discrete Log (DL) and co-computational Diffie-Hellman (co-CDH) problems to be difficult in this setting.

Group Setting. We require a pairing-friendly elliptic curve E on $\mathbb{F}_p$, forming groups $\mathbb{G}_1, \mathbb{G}_2$ of order q, with pairing function $e : \mathbb{G}_1 \times \mathbb{G}_2 \to \mathbb{G}_T$. We use g_1, g_2 to refer to generators of $\mathbb{G}_1, \mathbb{G}_2$ respectively.

Common setup. We use $\mathsf{Setup}(1^\lambda)$ to refer to the group generator function which generates a group setting with the above requirements. $\mathsf{Setup}(1^\lambda)$ generates groups $\mathbb{G}_1 = \langle g_1 \rangle, \mathbb{G}_2 = \langle g_2 \rangle$ of order q, as well as $e : \mathbb{G}_1 \times \mathbb{G}_2 \to \mathbb{G}_T$, and returns system parameters $\mathsf{Param} = (\mathbb{G}_1, \mathbb{G}_2, g_1, g_2, q, e, \mathbb{G}_T)$.

We optionally require a group $\mathbb{G}_H$ of order p so that E can be embedded in $\mathbb{G}_H$, and additionally that the structure of E is compatible with the Elligator [4] or Elligator squared [34] representation functions. We require E to be pairing-friendly due to our choice of signature scheme. Compatibility with Elligator depends on our choice of dense mapping. In that case, we set $\mathsf{Param} = (\mathbb{G}_1, \mathbb{G}_2, g_1, g_2, q, e, \mathbb{G}_T, \mathbb{G}_H, g_h, p)$.

Hash Functions. We need hash functions $H_{\mathbb{G}_1} : \{0,1\}^* \to \mathbb{G}_1$, $H_q : \{0,1\}^* \to \mathbb{Z}_q$ modeled as random oracles, producing group elements in the corresponding groups for use with our unique signature scheme and mapping. For batching, we also use a truncated version of H_q, $H_\lambda : \{0,1\}^* \to \mathbb{Z}_{2^\lambda}$.

We also require a collision resistant hash function H_p on $\mathbb{F}_p$ to produce Merkle trees. Depending on our choice of a proof system (see Sect. 5.1), we can opt to use a prime p and an arithmetic friendly hash that is believed to be collision resistant, such as Poseidon [23] to instantiate H_p when using an arithmetic proof system that is efficient for $\mathbb{F}_p$. If the proof system evaluates H_p only natively, we can set p to a large power of 2 and opt to use any collision resistant hash.

Merkle Trees. A Merkle tree is a well-used data structure based on hash functions that allows one to represent N items[1] of arbitrary size by one hash value. We have that $\mathsf{MT.Create}(v)$ for a vector v_i of length N creates a tree with the values v_i as leaves and root T, and $\mathsf{MT.Check}(T, N, v, i, p)$ checks if value v is contained in leaf i of a size N tree with root T across path p. For simplicity, we write that $v \in T$, for a fixed N if there exist i, p such that $\mathsf{MT.Check}(T, N, v, i, p)$ is 1. In this work we will rely on the fact that Merkle trees are binding.

Weighting Function. Looking forward, we will use the concept of weights to randomly assign eligibility to participants. As we want eligibility to be calculated independently, a simple linear weighting is not desirable. Take 2 parties of equal weight x_0, each with an assigned 10% probability of eligibility. Between them, they will have a 19% probability of at least one of them being eligible, rather than 20% if they merge. Like Ouroboros [15], we use the function $\phi(x) = 1 - (1 - f)^x$ to assign success probabilities to weights $x \in [0, 1]$. The value $\phi(1) = f$ is a tuning parameter, representing the success probability of the total weight.

---

[1] For ease of exposition, we assume N to be a power of 2.

The end result is to make the probability of success for a given party irrespective of the exact distribution in virtual identities: i.e. an adversary controlling weight x has the same chance of success if she keeps the weight under a single identity or splits it in various ways. More concretely, we have that $\phi(a + b) = 1 - (1 - \phi(a)) \cdot (1 - \phi(b))$, that is, the probability of success assigned to one party with stake $a + b$ is equal to the probability that at least one of two independent parties with stakes a, b respectively achieves success.

Non Interactive Proof Systems. In our construction, we use a proof system to allow a prover to prove statement x is true by demonstrating she knows a witness w such that $R(x, w)$ is true. We refer to the reference string setup, prover and verifier algorithms as $\mathsf{PS.RS} \leftarrow \mathsf{PS.S(Param)}$, $\pi_C \leftarrow \mathsf{PS.P(PS.RS}, x, w)$, $0/1 \leftarrow \mathsf{PS.V(PS.RS}, x, \pi_C)$, where x, w refer to the statement and witness respectively.

3   Unique Signature Scheme with Dense Mappings

Unique signature schemes [16,22,28] guarantee that for any given message m, a user associated with a verification key vk is only able to produce exactly one *valid* signature σ. This enables predicating eligibility by evaluating our dense mapping on σ.

We use a variant of MSP-PoP, a multisignature based on Boneh Lynn Shacham (BLS) signatures [6] with proofs of possession (PoPs) as described in [5,31].

- $\mathsf{MSP.Gen(Param)}$: $sk \leftarrow \mathbb{Z}_q$; $mvk \leftarrow g_2^{sk}$;
  $\kappa_1 \leftarrow H_{\mathbb{G}_1}(\text{"PoP"} \| mvk)^{sk}$; $\kappa_2 \leftarrow g_1^{sk}$. Return secret key sk, verification key mvk and proof of possession $\boldsymbol{\kappa} = (\kappa_1, \kappa_2)$
- $\mathsf{MSP.Check}(mvk, \boldsymbol{\kappa})$: If $e(\kappa_1, g_2) = e(H_{\mathbb{G}_1}(\text{"PoP"} \| mvk), mvk)$ and $e(g_1, mvk) = e(\kappa_2, g_2)$ are both true, return 1, otherwise return 0.
- $\mathsf{MSP.Sig}(sk, msg)$: Return $\sigma \leftarrow H_{\mathbb{G}_1}(\text{"M"} \| msg)^{sk}$.
- $\mathsf{MSP.Ver}(msg, mvk, \sigma)$: Return 1 if $e(\sigma, g_2) = e(H_{\mathbb{G}_1}(\text{"M"} \| msg), mvk)$. Otherwise return 0.
- $\mathsf{MSP.AKey}(\mathbf{mvk})$: Takes a vector $\mathbf{mvk}$ of (previously checked) verification keys and returns an intermediate aggregate public key $ivk = \prod mvk_i$.
- $\mathsf{MSP.ASig}(\boldsymbol{\sigma})$: Takes as input a vector $\boldsymbol{\sigma}$ and returns $\mu \leftarrow \prod \sigma_i$.
- $\mathsf{MSP.BKey}(\mathbf{mvk}, e_{\boldsymbol{\sigma}})$: Takes a vector $\mathbf{mvk}$ of (previously checked) verification keys and weighting seed $e_{\boldsymbol{\sigma}}$, and returns an intermediate aggregate public key $ivk = \prod mvk_i^{e_i}$, where $e_i \leftarrow H_\lambda(i, e_{\boldsymbol{\sigma}})$.
- $\mathsf{MSP.BSig}(\boldsymbol{\sigma})$: Takes as input a vector of signatures $\boldsymbol{\sigma}$ and returns $(\mu, e_{\boldsymbol{\sigma}})$ where $\mu \leftarrow \prod \sigma_i^{e_i}$, where $e_i \leftarrow H_\lambda(i, e_{\boldsymbol{\sigma}})$ and $e_{\boldsymbol{\sigma}} \leftarrow H_p(\boldsymbol{\sigma})$.

The MSP scheme has been shown to be *complete* and *unforgeable* in [31] and [6]. We will redo the unforgeability proof as a number of differences are important for out application. First, in the definition of Boneh et al. [6], there exists only a single honest user so there is no possibility of the adversary issuing a signing query on the message targeted by the forgery: if a message has been queried, it becomes ineligible for the adversary to win with. With multiple honest users however, it becomes possible that the adversary has honest user a sign a message and produces a forgery on account of honest user b. Second, instead of the ψ isomorphism between $\mathbb{G}_1$ and $\mathbb{G}_2$ used by [31] and [6], we instead add a second element to the Proof of Possession. We present our security definition and corresponding unforgeability proof for our variant of MSP in the full version [9].

The MSP.Check function is used to verify that the proofs of possession κ attached to a public key mvk are correct. The scheme operates as a standard multisignature, aggregating keys via MSP.AKey and signatures via MSP.ASig.

We also use the MSP.BKey and MSP.BSig functions, which enforce more stringent checking than that of standard multisignatures by utilizing the short random exponent batching of Bellare et al. [3]. The difference from standard multisignature aggregation (via MSP.AKey and MSP.ASig), is that the randomized check will fail with overwhelming probability if any of the individual signatures is invalid, whereas standard aggregation allows for spurious individual signatures as long as they sum up to the correct aggregate. Furthermore, MSP.BKey uses a weighting seed e_σ as input; in practice this is produced by the signature set to be verified and cannot be run ahead of time. In our use case, this can be overcome by having MSP.BKey be evaluated inside a proof system.

3.1   Dense Mappings for Unique Signatures

Being able to deterministically attach a regularly-sampled value to signatures enables us to flag a small subset of signatures as eligible by requiring their values under the mapping for a sequence of indexes to be under a given threshold.

Definition 1. *A deterministic function* $M : \mathbb{G}_1 \to \mathbb{Z}_p \cup \{\bot\}$ *is a dense mapping if, for some negligible* ϵ, *it holds that for any* $y \in \mathbb{Z}_p$, $|Pr[M(x) = y|M(x) \neq \bot] - 1/p| \leq \epsilon$ *and* $Pr[M(x) \neq \bot]$ *is non-negligible, when* x *is uniform over* $\mathbb{G}_1$.

Given a family $M_{msg,\mathsf{index}}$ of dense mappings indexed by index, we can add a new operation to a unique signature scheme as follows.

– MSP.Eval($msg, \mathsf{index}, \sigma$): Return $ev \leftarrow M_{msg,\mathsf{index}}(\sigma)$.

For the concatenation proof system PS^C in Sect. 5.2 we use a random oracle $H : \{0,1\}^* \to \mathbb{Z}_p$ for the mapping as: $M^R_{msg,\mathsf{index}}(\sigma) := H(\text{“map”}\|msg\|\mathsf{index}\|\sigma)$.

In the full version we also show how to construct a dense mapping $M^E_{msg,\mathsf{index}}(\sigma)$ based on Elligator Squared, which avoids oracle calls on witness-specific data.

4   Ideal Functionality for Stake Based Threshold Multisignatures

We will now describe a stake based threshold multisignature functionality similar to the PoS Anonymous Selection of [2]. The messages mesg to be signed are of the form mesg = (topic, body), where the eligibility of a signer is a function of their stake and topic, but not body.

The STM functionality $\mathcal{F}^{\phi}_{\text{STM}}(\mathcal{P}, m, k)$. Initialisation phase

$\mathcal{F}^{\phi}_{\text{STM}}(\mathcal{P}, m, k)$ initializes the variable Allow to 1, and table K to be empty and proceeds as follows:

- Upon receiving (Register, sid) on behalf of party P_i:
  1. If Allow is 0, $P_i \notin \mathcal{P}$, or $K(P_i)$ is already defined, ignore the request.
  2. Otherwise, set $K(P_i) = 1$ send (Registered, sid, P_i) to $\mathcal{A}$ and output (Registered, sid) to P_i.
- Upon receiving (Start, sid) from the adversary $\mathcal{A}$:
  1. Set Allow to 0.

Fig. 1. The Stake Based Threshold Multisignature functionality $\mathcal{F}^{\phi}_{\text{STM}}(\mathcal{P}, m, k)$ in the Initialisation phase interacting with the adversary $\mathcal{A}$.

Separation of Topic, and Body. This distinction can be used to limit the feasibility of an adversary trying to "grind" by trying different messages in the hope they are indeed eligible for one. By prescribing that topic must follow a narrowly defined format the adversary's options are limited. Alternatively, body may be left blank, simplifying the construction and also making it harder for adversaries to leverage dynamic corruptions: a user who is eligible to sign for (topic=President, body=Alice) can be corrupted to sign for (topic=President, body=Bob) as eligibility will persist. By mandating that the body is blank, a user who signs (topic=President,Alice) is not more or less likely to be able to sign (topic=President,Bob). We revisit this distinction and tradeoffs in the full version [9] of this work.

The functionality maintains a list $\mathcal{L}$ of signatures produced by itself, and a list $\mathcal{E}$ storing the eligibility of the various parties. The functionality operates on a fixed player list $\mathcal{P} = (P_i, \text{stake}_i)$, where $|\mathcal{P}| = n$, a scaling function $\phi(x)$, security parameter $m \geq log^2\lambda$ and quorum parameter $k = m \cdot \phi(\frac{1}{2})$. The functionality operates on a static corruption model where the adversary is allowed to corrupt up to $\frac{1}{2} - a$ of the total stake.

The functionality works by sampling eligibility over m indices. Users are made eligible in proportion to their stake and independently of each other. Producing an aggregate signature requires individual signatures over k different indices.

The STM functionality $\mathcal{F}_{\mathsf{STM}}^{\phi}(\mathcal{P}, m, k)$, operation phase.

- Upon receiving (EligibilityCheck, sid, mesg, index) from a party P_i:
  1. If $K(P_i)$ is undefined, or $P_i \notin \mathcal{P}$ ignore the request.
  2. If flag(topic) is empty, send (EligibilityCheck, sid, topic, $\mathcal{P}$) to $\mathcal{A}$. Else, goto 5.
  3. On receiving (Eligible, sid, topic, $\mathcal{B}, t$) parse $\mathcal{B}$ as a $n \times m$ bit matrix and let $\mathcal{E}$(topic, P_i, index) $\leftarrow \mathcal{B}(i, \text{index})$, and let flag(topic) $\leftarrow 1$.
  4. If $\mathcal{B}$ assigns eligibility to corrupted users on k or more indices, abort.
  5. Output (EligibilityCheck, sid, $\mathcal{E}$(topic, P_i, index)) to P_i.
- Upon receiving (CreateSig, sid, mesg, index) from a party P_i:
  1. If $K(P_i)$ is undefined, ignore the request. If flag(topic) is undefined, send (EligibilityCheck, sid, topic, $\mathcal{P}$) to $\mathcal{A}$. Else, goto 4.
  2. On receiving (Eligible, sid, topic, $\mathcal{B}, t$) parse $\mathcal{B}$ as a $n \times m$ bit matrix and let $\mathcal{E}$(topic, P_i, index) $\leftarrow \mathcal{B}(i, \text{index})$, and let flag(topic) $\leftarrow 1$.
  3. If $\mathcal{B}$ assigns eligibility to corrupted users on k or more indices, abort.
  4. Check $\mathcal{E}$(topic, P_i, index). If it is 0, send (Declined, sid, mesg) to P_i. Otherwise if it is 1, send (Prove, sid, P_i, mesg, index) to $\mathcal{A}$.
  5. When receiving (Done, sid, P_i, π, mesg, index) from $\mathcal{A}$, store $(1, P_i, \pi, \text{mesg}, \text{index})$ in $\mathcal{L}$. Send (Proof, sid, π, mesg, index) to P_i.
- Upon receiving (Verify, sid, P_i, π, mesg, index) from a party P':
  1. If $K(P_i)$ is undefined, ignore the request.
  2. If $(v, P_i, \pi, \text{mesg}, \text{index}) \in \mathcal{L}$ send (Verified, sid, $(P_i, \pi, \text{mesg}, \text{index}), v$) to P'.
  3. Else, if $\mathcal{E}$(topic, P_i, index) is 0 or P_i is honest, send (Verified, sid, $(P_i, \pi, \text{mesg}, \text{index}), 0$) to P'.
  4. Else, send (Verify, sid, (P_i, π, mesg)) to $\mathcal{A}$, and wait for (Verified, sid, $(\pi, \text{mesg}), v$) from $\mathcal{A}$. If $v \notin \{0, 1\}$: $v \leftarrow 0$. Store $(v, P_i, \pi, \text{mesg}, \text{index})$ in $\mathcal{L}$ and reply (Verified, sid, $(P_i, \pi, \text{mesg}, \text{index}), v$) to P'.
  5. Else, send (Verified, sid, $(P_i, \pi, \text{mesg}, \text{index}), 0$) to P'.

Fig. 2. The Stake Based Threshold Multisignature functionality on the operation phase $\mathcal{F}_{\mathsf{STM}}^{\phi}(\mathcal{P}, m, k)$ interacting with the adversary $\mathcal{A}$. EligibilityCheck, CreateSig and Verify.

The functionality is split in two phases. It starts in the initialisation phase which we present in Fig. 1. The decision to move to the operation phase, presented in Figs. 2 and 3 is left to the adversary.

At a high level, the ideal functionality allows users to call EligibilityCheck and CreateSig to check whether they are able to sign, and if so, produce signatures. Both calls are parametrized by an index value representing which of the m parallel lotteries the user is referring to. In practice, users will check all lotteries. Eligibility is decided by the adversary under the condition that corrupt users cannot form a quorum (i.e. eligibility over at least k indices).

Since corruptions are static, this implies that corrupt users can never succeed in producing an aggregate signature. Aggregate will only produce an aggregate signature if there exist k individual signatures for the same mesg over different index values, and VerifyAggregate requires that an aggregate signature came from Aggregate, or that enough individual signatures have or could have been

---

The STM functionality $\mathcal{F}_{\mathsf{STM}}^\phi(\mathcal{P}, m, k)$, *operation phase. [Continued]*

- Upon receiving (Aggregate, sid, $\boldsymbol{P}, \boldsymbol{\pi}$, **index**, mesg) from a party P' :
  1. Parse $\boldsymbol{P}, \boldsymbol{\pi}$, **index** as vectors of length k containing P_i, π_i, index$_i$.
  2. If $K(P_i)$ is undefined for any i, ignore the request.
     Run (Verify, sid, P_i, π_i, mesg, index$_i$) for each i.
  3. If any produce 0, or if index$_i$ = index$_j$ for $i \neq j$, reply (Aggregation, sid, $(\boldsymbol{P}, \boldsymbol{\pi}$, mesg$), 0)$.
  4. Otherwise, send (Aggr, sid, $\boldsymbol{P}, \boldsymbol{\pi}$, **index**, mesg) to $\mathcal{A}$.
  5. When (AggrDone, sid, $\boldsymbol{P}, \boldsymbol{\pi}$, **index**, ρ, mesg) is received from $\mathcal{A}$, let $\tau = \rho$, store $(1, m, \tau$, mesg) in $\mathcal{L}$.
  6. Send (Aggr, $\tau, \boldsymbol{P}, \boldsymbol{\pi}$, mesg) to P'.
- Upon receiving (VerifyAggregate, sid, τ, mesg) from a party P' :
  1. If $(v, \tau$, mesg) exists in $\mathcal{L}$, then send (Verified, sid, m, τ, mesg), v) to P'.
  2. Else, send (AVerify, sid, $(\tau$, mesg)) to $\mathcal{A}$, and wait for (Verified, sid, $(\tau$, mesg), v) from $\mathcal{A}$.
  3. If $v = 1$, count the indexes with either (1) a previously produced signature for (mesg) in $\mathcal{L}$ or (2) a corrupted player eligible to sign on topic. If the total is k or more, store $(1, \tau$, mesg) in $\mathcal{L}$ and output (Verified, sid, $(m, \tau$, mesg), 1) to P'.
  4. Else, store $(0, \tau$, mesg) in $\mathcal{L}$, and send (Verified, sid, $(m, \tau$, mesg), 0) to P'.

Fig. 3. The Stake Based Threshold Multisignature functionality on the operation phase $\mathcal{F}_{\mathsf{STM}}^\phi(\mathcal{P}, m, k)$ interacting with the adversary $\mathcal{A}$. Interfaces Aggregate and VerifyAggregate.

produced to support it. That is, we allow that aggregation can be performed by any party as there is no private information required.

In Figs. 4 and 7 we present a protocol $\Pi.\mathsf{STM}$ realizing $\mathcal{F}_{\mathsf{STM}}^\phi(\mathcal{P}, m, k)$ in the $\mathcal{F}_{\mathsf{RS}}(\mathcal{P}), \mathcal{F}_{\mathsf{Kr}}^{\psi_0}(\mathcal{P})$-hybrid model. The functionality $\mathcal{F}_{\mathsf{RS}}(\mathcal{P})$ provides access to a reference string, whereas $F_{\mathsf{Kr}}^{\psi_0}(\mathcal{P})$ provides key registration so that a key can only be used by one party. Both hybrid functionalities we use are practical to realize in common applications. For $\mathcal{F}_{\mathsf{RS}}$, the group can be realistically hardcoded, leaving only the proof system reference string. We present functionality $\mathcal{F}_{\mathsf{Kr}}^\psi(\mathcal{P})$ in Fig. 5. The parameter ψ is a function that checks public keys by calling MSP.Check. Functionality $\mathcal{F}_{\mathsf{RS}}(\mathcal{P})$ is presented in Fig. 6.

A trivial realization. If we assume uniform stake distribution, we can realize the above using only signatures: we set $m = N$, and fix the eligibility function to $\mathcal{E}(\mathsf{topic}, P_i, \mathsf{index}) = 1$ iff $i = \mathsf{index}$ and 0 otherwise. CreateSig is implemented by signing. Verification only accepts signatures for index i from user P_i. Aggregate is implemented by concatenating signatures and signer identities. VerifyAggregate then consists of parsing, and counting the number of valid signatures.

While simple, the aggregate signatures have size linear in the number of users which is cost-prohibitive in practice. Assuming uniform stake is also problematic in general. One could argue that a user holding s units of stake could be simulated

---

Protocol Π.STM. Initialisation phase

- **Setup:** Users start in the initialisation phase. Each user locally sets Reg $\leftarrow \emptyset$, and sends (GetRS, sid) to $\mathcal{F}_{RS}(\mathcal{P})$. Upon receiving (GetRS, sid, RS), store RS.
- **Register:** Each user P_i gets their keys by running $(msk_i, mvk_i, \kappa_i) \leftarrow$ MSP.Gen(Param). They set $(vk_i, sk_i) := ((mvk_i, \kappa_i), msk_i,)$. A user then sends (Register, sid, vk_i) to $\mathcal{F}_{Kr}^{\psi_0}(\mathcal{P})$.
- **Startup:** When a user receives (RetrieveAll, sid, K), from $\mathcal{F}_{Kr}^{\psi_0}(\mathcal{P})$ it sets Reg $:= (K(P_i), \text{stake}_i)$ for $P_i \in \mathcal{P}$, and Reg is padded to length N, using null entries of stake 0. Let AVK $\leftarrow$ MT.Create(Reg). The user moves to the operation phase.

Fig. 4. The STM Protocol Π.STM in the initialisation phase.

by s users each holding 1 unit, but this only exacerbates the size issue. In the next Section we expand our treatment to cover the more general case, and use dense mappings as a form of lottery so that only a few stakeholders need to participate at any one time.

Our notion of lottery based sampling alleviates both of these concerns: stake is used to determine the odds of wining with no need of duplication. Additionally, it operates as a filter, reducing both the number of signatures communicated to the aggregator as well as the size of the certificate.

5   A Stake Based Threshold Multisignature Scheme

The key registration functionality, $\mathcal{F}_{Kr}$ can be realized by means of a broadcast channel which can be implemented via a blockchain.

As with the ideal functionality, the protocol operates in two phases. The initialisation phase is presented in Fig. 4 and the operation phase in Fig. 7. The

---

The Key Registration functionality $\mathcal{F}_{Kr}^{\psi}(\mathcal{P})$.

$\mathcal{F}_{Kr}^{\psi}(\mathcal{P})$ initializes the variable Allow to 1 and proceeds as follows:

- Upon receiving (Register, sid, vk) on behalf of party P_i:
    1. If Allow is 0, $P_i \notin \mathcal{P}$, $K(P_i)$ is already defined, or $vk \in K$, ignore the request.
    2. If $\psi(vk) = 1$, let $K(P_i) \leftarrow vk$, and output (RegKey, sid, 1) to P_i.
- Upon receiving (Retrieve, sid, P_i) on behalf of party P_j:
    1. $P_j \notin \mathcal{P}$, or $K(P_i)$ is not defined, output (Retrieve, $sid, P_i, \perp$) to P_j.
    2. Otherwise, output (Retrieve, $sid, P_1, K(P_i)$) to P_j
- Upon receiving (CloseRegistration, sid) on behalf of the adversary $\mathcal{A}$:
    1. Set Allow to 0.
    2. For each $P_i \in \mathcal{P}$, send (RetrieveAll, sid, K) to P_i.

Fig. 5. The Key Registration functionality $\mathcal{F}_{Kr}^{\psi}(\mathcal{P})$, with key checking function ψ.

The Reference String functionality $\mathcal{F}_{RS}(\mathcal{P})$.

- Upon Initialization, let Param $\leftarrow$ Setup(1^λ); PS.RS $\leftarrow$ PS.S(Param);
  Set RS := (Param, PS.RS), and send (GetRS, sid, RS) to $\mathcal{A}$.
- Upon receiving (GetRS, sid) on behalf of party P_i:
  1. If $P_1 \in \mathcal{P}$ Output (GetRS, sid, RS) to P_i.

Fig. 6. The Reference String functionality $\mathcal{F}_{RS}(\mathcal{P})$ interacting with the adversary $\mathcal{A}$.

protocol operates on a fixed player list $\mathcal{P} = (P_i, \text{stake}_i)$, where $|\mathcal{P}| = n$, a scaling function $\phi(x)$, a lottery parameter $m \geq \log^2 \lambda$ and quorum parameter $k = m \cdot \phi(\frac{1}{2} + a)$, where $\psi_0(mvk, \boldsymbol{\kappa}) := \text{MSP.Check}(mvk, \boldsymbol{\kappa})$.

Our scheme requires two main components: a unique signature scheme with a dense mapping, and a proof system to produce proofs of multiple signatures with specific mapping constraints, i.e. each signature must map to a value smaller than the target value implied by the signer's stake.

The simplest option would be to construct aggregate proofs by simply concatenating individual signatures. This allows for simple and efficient choices in the other parameters but produces a large aggregate proof. On the other hand, we can use a circuit-based proof system such as Bulletproofs, which will produce much smaller proofs. However, this choice requires careful selection of the other primitives, as we need to e.g. avoid evaluating random oracles in the circuit. We will further explore the instantiation options in Sects. 5.3 and 5.2, and compare their efficiency in Sect. 6.

5.1 The Relation $\mathcal{R}_{avk}$

Our proof systems operate on language $\mathcal{L}_{avk}$, i.e. we prove knowledge of a witness w such that statement x holds, i.e. $\mathcal{R}_{avk}(x, w) = 1$. Concretely, statements are $x = (\text{AVK}, ivk, ivk_{\text{body}}, \mu, e_\sigma, \text{mesg})$ and witnesses are of the form $w = (mvk_i, \text{stake}_i, \boldsymbol{p}_i, ev_i, \sigma_i, \text{index}_i)$ for $i \in \{1 \ldots k\}$. The relation $\mathcal{R}_{avk}$ is parametrized on $N, m, k, \phi()$, which are public. $R_{avk}(x, w) = 1$ if and only if the following hold:

- $ivk = \text{MSP.BKey}(\mathbf{mvk}, e_\sigma)$ and $ivk_{\text{body}} = \text{MSP.AKey}(\mathbf{mvk})$.
- $(\mu, e_\sigma) = \text{MSP.BSig}(\boldsymbol{\sigma})$.
- $\forall i : \text{index}_i \leq m$ and $\forall i \neq j : \text{index}_i \neq \text{index}_j$.
- For $i \in \{1 \ldots k\}$: (mvk_i, stake_i) lies in Merkle tree AVK, N following path $\boldsymbol{p}_i$.
- For $i \in \{1 \ldots k\}$: MSP.Eval(topic, $\text{index}_i, \sigma_i) = ev_i$
- For $i \in \{1 \ldots k\}$: $ev_i \leq \phi(\text{stake}_i)$

Contradictions for $\mathcal{R}_{avk}$. Due to the use of Merkle trees in the avk relation, there may exist numerous "alternative" openings for given a root, enabling the adversary to produce a proof by means of using such an opening as part of the witness. Obviously, any such witness combined with our known opening of the

Merkle tree would contradict the collision resistance of H_p. However, it might not be possible to extract that witness from a proof in the UC setting. For this reason, we will define a class of statements to be *contradictory* if they are not consistent with our known opening of the Merkle tree. We then need to show for our proof system, that proofs of such statements can only be produced with negligible probability. We defer a formal definition to the full version as the property is trivial when the witness is part of the proof, as in PS^C in the following.

5.2   An Instantiation via Concatenation Proofs

The proof system PS^C consists of releasing the witness w and letting the verifier check if $R(x, w) = 1$. Looking forward, w will be a concatenation of individual signatures, hence the name. Contradiction soundness is trivial for PS^C, as the full witness is present without rewinding. We use mapping $M = M^R$ for PS^C.

5.3   An Instantiation Based on Bulletproofs

We have ensured that the overall design is modular so that the proof system can be changed with relatively few changes. Nonetheless, some issues require attention. Specifically, for the bulletproof based system PS^B, we need to (a) ensure performance by matching the arithmetic of the proof system to the curve arithmetic of signatures, (b) ensure no oracle calls are required inside the circuit and (c) establish contradiction soundness because standard soundness is inadequate (due to spurious hash preimages), and rewinding cannot be invoked by the simulator. Due to size, we present the technical details in the full version [9] of this work.

5.4   Adversarial Eligibility

A core component in the security argument is proving that the adversary has a negligible probability of achieving eligibility across enough lotteries, and thus any success by the adversary would involve breaking at least one of the other underlying primitives. Towards that, we argue that if the adversary has probability p' of winning a single lottery, he will win an average of $m \cdot p'$ lotteries. We therefore set $k = mp$ high enough that the adversary will only win k lotteries with negligible probability. Let the adversary's stake be $\frac{1}{2} - a$. We now need to calculate the probability p' of the adversary wining a single lottery.

For honest parties, this would be simple to compute due to the properties of the weighting function: take for example two parties A, B with stakes a,b, their individual probability of wining a lottery will be by definition $p_a = \phi(a)$ and $p_b = \phi(b)$. The probability that either party wins will then be $1 - (1-p_a)\cdot(1-p_b)$ which is $1 - (1 - \phi(a)) \cdot (1 - \phi(b))$. However, the latter term is exactly equal to $\phi(a+b)$. A crucial requirement for this to hold is that the probabilities of A and B wining the lottery are independent. For honest users, this is true as their keys

---

Protocol Π.STM. Operation phase

- EligibilityCheck: On input (mesg, index), user P_i runs: Let $\overline{\text{topic}}$ ← "0"||AVK||topic, σ ← MSP.Sig(msk, $\overline{\text{topic}}$); ev ← MSP.Eval($\overline{\text{topic}}$, index, σ). Return 1 if $ev < \phi$(stake), else return 0.
- CreateSig: On input (mesg, index): If EligibilityCheck(mesg, index) is 1, then let $\overline{\text{topic}}$ ← "0"||AVK||topic; σ ← MSP.Sig(msk, $\overline{\text{topic}}$); σ_{body} ← MSP.Sig(msk, "1"||$\overline{\text{topic}}$||body) and produce an individual signature $\pi = (\sigma, \sigma_{\text{body}}, reg_i, i, \boldsymbol{p}_i)$, where $\boldsymbol{p}_i$ is the user's path inside the Merkle tree AVK and reg_i is (mvk_i, stake$_i$).
- Verify: On input a party P_i, a signature π, index index, and message (mesg), parse $\pi = (\sigma, \sigma_{\text{body}}, reg_i, i, \boldsymbol{p}_i)$. Parse reg_i as (mvk_i, stake$_i$). Check that reg_i corresponds to party P_i, let $\overline{\text{topic}}$ ← "0"||AVK||topic; ev ← MSP.Eval($\overline{\text{topic}}$, index, σ) check that $ev < \phi$(stake$_i$) and check MT.Check(AVK, N, (vk_i, stake$_i$), i, $\boldsymbol{p}_i$) = 1. If parsing or checking fails, return 0. Otherwise, return MSP.Ver($\overline{\text{topic}}$, mvk_i, σ) $\wedge$ MSP.Ver("1"||$\overline{\text{topic}}$||body, mvk_i, σ_{body}).
- Aggregate: On input vectors $\boldsymbol{P}$, $\boldsymbol{\pi}$, **index** and message (mesg), parse $\boldsymbol{P}$, $\boldsymbol{\pi}$ and **index** as a vector P_j, π_j, index$_j$ of size k, let $\overline{\text{topic}}$ ← "0"||AVK||topic and run Verify(P_j, index$_j$, mesg, π_j).
  If parsing or checking fails, return $\perp$. If any index$_j$ = index$_i$ for $j \neq i$ return 0. Otherwise, parse $\pi_j = (\sigma_j, \sigma_{\text{body},j}, reg_j, i_j, \boldsymbol{p}_j)$ and reg_j as (mvk_j, stake$_j$). Let ivk ← MSP.BKey($\mathbf{mvk}$, $\boldsymbol{\sigma}$), ivk_{body} ← MSP.AKey($\mathbf{mvk}$), μ ← MSP.BSig($\boldsymbol{\sigma}$), μ_{body} ← MSP.ASig($\boldsymbol{\sigma}_{\text{body}}$), set $x = (\text{AVK}, ivk, \mu, e_\sigma, \text{mesg})$ and $\boldsymbol{w} = (mvk_j, \text{stake}_j, \boldsymbol{p}_j, ev_j, \sigma_j, \text{index}_j)$ for $j \in \{1 \ldots k\}$. Then, π_{avk} ← PS.P(PS.RS, x, $\boldsymbol{w}$). Return $\tau = (ivk, \mu, e_\sigma, ivk_{\text{body}}, \mu_{\text{body}}, \pi_{avk})$.
- VerifyAggregate: On input (τ, mesg), parse $\tau \rightarrow (ivk, \mu, e_\sigma, ivk_{\text{body}}, \mu_{\text{body}}, \pi_{avk})$, check that PS.V(PS.RS, (AVK, ivk, μ, e_σ, mesg), π_{avk}) is true. If parsing and checking is successful, let $\overline{\text{topic}}$ ← "0"||AVK||topic and return MSP.Ver($\overline{\text{topic}}$, ivk, μ) $\wedge$ MSP.Ver("1"||$\overline{\text{topic}}$||body, ivk_{body}, μ_{body}).

Fig. 7. The STM Protocol Π.STM in the operation phase.

are independent, and their signatures are deterministic functions of the message and their key.

Adversarial parties however, may try to produce correlated keys in the hope of increasing the odds of an adversarial party wining the lottery (one winer per lottery is sufficient so multiple wins are in effect "wasted"). For this reason, we require that either the mapping function enforces independence even if the keys are somehow correlated, or that the gain to the adversary is minimal.

Adversarial Eligibility for Concatenation Proofs. For the concatenation proof system PS^C, our mapping of signatures to eligibility is a simple random oracle, so the eligibility of different users is independent across the same lottery, even if the adversarial keys themselves are related, so that $p' = \phi(\frac{1}{2} - a)$.

Lemma 1. *For the mapping $M_{msg,index}^R(\sigma) := H(\text{"map"}\|msg\|index\|\sigma)$, the eligibility of each potential signer for any of the lotteries is independent of that of others, as long as the public keys of users are not repeated.*

Proof. The eligibility predicate for a potential signer with stake s_a is calculated by checking iff $\phi(s_a) > H(\text{"map"}\|msg\|index\|\sigma)$. Due to the signature scheme being unique, the signatures of different voters cannot be equal[2], the value of each random oracle call is independent of all others, and thus the eligibility predicates of different users are always independent.

Adversarial Eligibility for Bulletproofs. For PS^B, we show a weaker result: evaluations are independent across lotteries (Lemma 2), but correlated keys (and by extension, correlated signatures) may potentially produce correlated values. The reason for this is that for PS^B, the used mapping does not pass signatures through a random oracle: we cannot instantiate the oracle inside a circuit, and do not wish to send the signatures to the verifier. Instead, we pass $H_q(msg, index)$ through the oracle and use it as a "randomizer" for σ.

In theory, this allows the adversary to gain a slight advantage by stake splitting and exploiting the subadditivity of ϕ. However, in Lemma 3 we show that we can bound the Adversary's gain by a small value.

Lemma 2. *For the mapping $M_{msg,index}^E(\sigma) := R(msg, \sigma^{H_q(msg,index)}, index)$, adversarial eligibility is independent across lotteries.*

Proof. We allow the adversary to control various parties each with stake s_i such that the keys of adversarial users may somehow be correlated. We consider the adversary to be eligible for a given index idx_0 iff at least one of the parties she controls is eligible for that index, i.e. $R(msg, \sigma^{H_q(msg,index)}, index) < \phi(s_i)$. Consider a fixed message msg_0, and also fix the set of adversarial keys and stakes (the second restriction is implied in our application as the AVK of all public keys is appended to the message).

The eligibility of each adversarial party (and therefore the eligibility of the adversary in general) is then completely determined by the value of $H_q(msg_0, index)$, its stake and public key. We also observe, that the eligibility of the adversary in general can also be expressed as a (slightly more complex function) of $H_q(msg_0, index)$ and the set of adversarial keys and corresponding stakes.

As H_q is modelled to be a random oracle, the distribution of $H_q(msg_0, index)$ is independent across different values of index, therefore the adversary's eligibility is also independent across different values of index, as it is a fixed function of $H_q(msg_0, index)$.

Lemma 3. *For the mapping $M_{msg,index}^E(\sigma) := R(msg, \sigma^{H_q(msg,index)}, index)$, and for fixed values of msg, idx, the probability of an adversary controlling a a fraction of the stake winning the lottery is bounded by $\phi(a) \cdot (1 + c))$, where c is $f \cdot \ln\left(\frac{1}{1-f}\right) - 1$.*

---

[2] Apart from a negligible fraction of pathological messages hashing to $1_{\mathbb{G}_1}$.

Proof. We know that the probability of a potential signer controlling a percentage s of stake is $\phi(s)$, where $\phi(s) = 1 - (1 - f)^s$ and $f = \phi(1)$. An adversary controlling a a share can therefore split into n parties of stake s_i such that $\sum_{i=1}^{n} s_i = a$, so that party i succeeds with probability $\phi(s_i)$. We do not know that probabilities of the adversarial parties are indeed independent, but we can initially bound their joint probability by $\sum_{i=1}^{n} \phi(s_i)$. One difficulty here is that the value of this bound depends on the exact split chosen by the adversary.

As ϕ is subadditive (i.e. $\phi(a + b) < \phi(a) + \phi(b)$), we can further bound our initial bound by the limit $\lim_{n\to\infty} n \cdot \phi(a/n)$, which does not depend on the exact split.

We have that $\phi(x) = 1 - (1 - f)^x$. Let $\kappa = (1 - f)^a$. Then $\phi(a) = 1 - \kappa$ and $\phi(a/n) = 1 - \kappa^{1/n}$. Our limit is thus

$$\lim_{n\to\infty} n \cdot (1 - \kappa^{1/n}) = -\ln(\kappa)$$

We know that $\phi(a) = 1 - \kappa$, so $\frac{n \cdot \phi(a/n)}{\phi(a)}$ is bounded by $\frac{-\ln(\kappa)}{1-\kappa} = \frac{-a\ln(1-f)}{\phi(a)} \leq f \cdot \ln\left(\frac{1}{1-f}\right)$ as $\phi(x) \geq x \cdot f$ in $(0,1)$. Thus $\frac{n \cdot \phi(a/n)}{\phi(a)}$ is bounded by $\phi(a) \cdot (1+c)$, where $c = f \cdot \ln\left(\frac{1}{1-f}\right) - 1$.

In practical terms, the advantage of an adversary that can create correlations amongst keys is not large. Let $\phi_{\max}(a) := a \cdot \ln\left(\frac{1}{1-f}\right)$. Then, for $f = .2$ we have that $\phi_{\max}(.3) \approx \phi(.31)$ and $\phi_{\max}(.4) \approx \phi(.419)$. For $f = .1$ we have that $\phi_{\max}(.3) \approx \phi(.305)$ and $\phi_{\max}(.4) \approx \phi(.409)$. In plain terms, for $f = .1$ we can replace a (potentially) corelating 40% adversary by a non-corelating 41% one.

Adversarial Eligibility Over. k Lotteries In the following lemma, we calculate the probability that an adversary with probability $p' = \phi(\frac{1}{2} - a)$ to win a single lottery, manages to be eligible over enough lotteries to form a certificate by winning at least k out of m different lotteries. Looking forward to Theorem 1, this would cause our simulation to fail as the ideal functionality will abort.

Let $\phi(\frac{1}{2}) = p$. Then $k = mp$. First, we point out that for $f \leq \frac{1}{4}$ and $a \leq \sqrt{1 - f}$, it holds that for $p' = \phi(\frac{1}{2} - a)$ we have $\frac{p}{p'} = \frac{\phi(1/2)}{\phi(1/2-a)} \geq 1 + a$.

Lemma 4. *[Sampling Property] Let p' be the probability that the adversary succeeds in any single lottery, and $\phi(\frac{1}{2}) = p$. When $\frac{p}{p'} \geq 1+a$, the eligibility matrix sampled by the simulator causes the functionality to abort with probability negligible in m. Furthermore, for $m = -(2+a)/(a^2 \cdot \phi(\frac{1}{2} - a)) \ln(\varsigma)$, the probability of failure is at most ς.*

Proof. Each of the m columns of the matrix represents an independent trial in which the adversary has a probability p' of being eligible via at least one corrupted user. Thus, the expected number of successes is the mean, i.e. $p'm \leq \frac{k}{1+a}$. The functionality will thus abort only if the actual number of successes, X is greater than $1 + a$ times the mean.

By Chernoff bounds, the probability of aborting is: $\Pr[X > k] \leq \Pr[X > p'm \cdot (1 + a)] \leq e^{\frac{-a^2 \cdot p'm}{2+a}}$. As $p' \neq 0$ by the definition of the ϕ function, the chance of aborting is negligible in m.

For the second part, rewriting m as $m = -(2+a)/(a^2 \cdot \phi(\frac{1}{2}-a)) \ln(\varsigma)$, directly produces the required bound.

As a corollary, for $m \geq \log^2 \lambda$, the above probability is negligible in λ.

5.5 Security Proof

In this section we show that our protocol realizes the ideal functionality of an STM. A core property is that the adversary is unable to create a valid certificate.

In the previous section we showed that the probability of an adversary with stake $\frac{1}{2} - a$ to achieve a quorum is negligible for appropriate values of k, m. To complete the proof we also need to show that the adversary cannot gain an advantage by means of breaking one of the primitives used in the protocol, or otherwise cause the simulation to fail.

Theorem 1. *Let $a < \frac{1}{2}$, $m \geq \log^2 \lambda$ and quorum parameter $k = m \cdot \phi(\frac{1}{2} + a)$. The protocol Π.STM of Sect. 5 realizes $\mathcal{F}_{\mathsf{STM}}^{\phi}(\mathcal{P}, m, k)$ against adversaries with stake at most $\frac{1}{2} - a$ in the $\mathcal{F}_{\mathsf{RS}}(\mathcal{P}), \mathcal{F}_{\mathsf{Kr}}^{\psi_0}(\mathcal{P})$-hybrid model, under the leveraged[3] co-CDH assumption, if H_p is collision resistant and $H_{\mathbb{G}_1} : \{0,1\}^* \to \mathbb{G}_1$, $H_q : \{0,1\}^* \to \mathbb{Z}_q$ are modeled as random oracles.*

Proof (Sketch). The simulator operates by using the programmability of the random oracle to (effectively) obtain the signing keys of all users via the proofs of possession. This enables it to calculate the eligibility for any message. The ideal functionality will reject if the table contains a dishonest quorum, but that happens with only negligible probability. Collision resistance implies that the adversary cannot use an opening of the AVK that differs from the registered one, and the unforgeability of the signature scheme prevents the adversary from utilizing the keys belonging to honest users.

We defer the complete proof and supporting lemmas to the full version [9].

6 Efficiency and Parameter Selections

Quorum Parameters. Due to Lemma 4, the probability of an adversarial minority achieving a quorum is negligible, while the probability of the honest majority forming one is overwhelming. For a probability of an adversarial quorum bounded by 2^{-128}, we use the lemma to obtain initial values of k, m and reduce them until they are tight, whilst maintaining $k = m \cdot \phi(\frac{1}{2})$. However, we are able to perform additional fine tuning: in many applications a forgery may be catastrophic whilst an isolated failure to sign may be recoverable (via retries, or

---

[3] PS^C does not require leveraging, we include the assumption for uniformity with PS^B.

redundancy in the application using the primitive). Towards this, we may vary the relation between k and m. Intuitively, $k = m \cdot \phi(\frac{1}{2})$ implies that a group holding $\frac{1}{2}$ fraction of the stake has a significant probability of signing with that probability quickly rising (or respectivelly falling) if the amount of stake held is more (or less) than $\frac{1}{2}$. By setting $k = m \cdot \phi(\frac{1}{2+\beta})$ for a positive safety margin $\beta \leq \frac{1}{2}$, we are able to sacrifice liveness in favor of smaller parameters. Following the above intuition, when we set $\beta > \alpha$, the honest majority cannot reliably sign without the adversary being involved: the honestly held stake is $(\frac{1}{2} + \alpha)$ whereas the baseline is $(\frac{1}{2} + \beta)$ which is higher.

Table 3. Required values of k, m so that an adversarial quorum is formed with probability at most 2^{-128}. L-Abs and L-Par represent the probabilities to form a quorum (before any retries) when the adversarial stake abstains or participates respectively. LL describes probabilities $< 1\%$. The parameters can be meaningfully used in conjunction with an incentive scheme or as an auxiliary opportunistic parametrization where a less aggressive parametrization is used as a fallback. Values of ≈ 1 indicate a chance of failure $< 10^{-30}$.

	Adversarial Stake							
	40%				33%			
$\frac{k}{m}$	k	m	L-Abs	L-Par	k	m	L-Abs	L-Par
$\phi(.50)$	3684	34891	99.99 %	≈ 1	1129	10690	$1 - 2^{-30}$	≈ 1
$\phi(.55)$	1865	16144	99.99 %	≈ 1	769	6654	$1 - 2^{-30}$	≈ 1
$\phi(.60)$	1182	9433	48.67 %	≈ 1	576	4593	99.59 %	≈ 1
$\phi(.67)$	755	5434	LL	≈ 1	414	3050	47.75 %	≈ 1
$\phi(.75)$	526	3411	LL	$1 - 3 \cdot 10^{-12}$	326	2113	1.98%	$1 - 3 \cdot 10^{-8}$
$\phi(.80)$	441	2695	LL	$1 - 7 \cdot 10^{-7}$	286	1747	LL	99.99%

In Table 3, we calculate values for combinations of adversarial stake and quorum percentage $\frac{k}{m}$ and fixed $\phi(1) = \frac{1}{5}$. Reducing $\phi(1)$ would allow one to very slightly decrease k for a significant increase in m.

From the table, liveness can be challenging in certain parametrizations. This can be addressed in a number of ways: First, the probability of an honest quorum can be boosted by allowing retries (e.g. by attaching a short counter to the message). Second, if an incentive structure is in place, rational adversaries who cannot directly subvert the protocol will choose to participate in signing honest messages. Ideally, we would like to be able to use the more compact parameters until such time as liveness is at risk, and then fall back to higher (k, m) values. In the following paragraph, we describe a way to achieve this :

Concurrent Hybrids. Our protocol is amenable to running parametrizations of multiple (k, m) concurrently with minimal impact to the adversary's chance of success. Thus, individual signatures are produced according to the maximal pair of (k, m) values, and aggregation chooses the smallest ones that form a quorum. This will increase communication costs by transmitting potentially unneeded individual signatures, but will choose the smallest feasible quorum size.

7   Dynamic Adversaries and Forward Security

We have modeled our functionality and scheme in a static corruption model. In proof of Stake applications, dynamic corruption greatly enhances the power of the adversary: the adversary waits to see which users are eligible for an action (e.g. to produce the next block) and then corrupts them. In our functionality, it is possible to make a tradeoff between security against dynamic adversaries and grinding: mandating the body field of each message to be empty (and the entire message be used as the topic) implies that eligibility is predicated on the message, and is independently distributed across different messages. That is, user P_1 being eligible for message mesg$_1$ is independent of user P_1 being eligible for message mesg$_2$. This defeats the strategy of corrupting a user after they have demonstrated their eligiblity on a particular topic.

Nevertheless, in the ideal world, the adversary is able to set eligibility before performing corruptions, and would thus be able to assign eligibility to users before corrupting them. We defer further discussion to the full version [9].

8   Applications

In this section we delve into some applications of Mithril (STM) signatures in the blockchain setting. In general, STMs could be applied in any setting where we can associate an amount of stake to a set of public-keys. Given such arrangement, stakeholders can produce certificates for any given message mesg of interest. Before we proceed, we remark that some care needs to be applied to ensure the integrity of STM sampling based on our security model, namely that user public-keys are fixed prior to messages being proposed for signing. Even though grinding attacks have a negligible probability to produce a forgery, cf. Lemma 4, an attacker who knows topic prior to the keys being finalized, can attempt to grind the probability of signing topic by trying multiple keys. In this way the attacker will boost somewhat the number of lottery tickets it wins, something undesirable in practice (since e.g., we would need to take this opportunity into account when selecting the number of lotteries m).

In a blockchain setting, this attack can be averted by storing the public-keys on chain and then including an unpredictable fresh nonce drawn from the blockchain itself as part of the message while also verifying this nonce during verification. For simplicity, we assume this is implemented by default.

Bitcoin Referendums. We first consider using Mithril in the context of a proof-of-work cryptocurrency such as Bitcoin as a decision-making tool. Using STM it is possible to probe the population of Bitcoin holders (as opposed to, say, the miners) regarding a particular topic or action.

In Bitcoin, balances are sent to a SCRIPTPUBKEY and are spendable by revealing a corresponding SCRIPTSIG. The SCRIPTPUBKEY value can be either of the form pay to public-key (P2PK) or pay-to-script-hash (P2SH). Payments of the latter form are made to SCRIPTPUBKEY = OP_HASH160 <scripthash> OP_EQUAL where <scripthash> is the hash of a "redeem script" that needs to be provided when the UTXO is spent. Using P2SH it is possible to receive payments and associate the resulting UTXO with an STM public-key. Specifically we can use the redeem script: OP_HASH160 <STMpkhash> OP_EQUALVERIFY OP_HASH160 <pkhash> OP_EQUALVERIFY OP_CHECKSIG which contains the hashes of the STM public-key and of the ECDSA key controlling the balance; spending requires opening both keys & a signature for the ECDSA key. Such a P2SH can be spent with the following SCRIPTSIG <Sig> <pk> <STMpk> <RedeemScript>. Evaluating this script by itself, will verify <STMpkhash>, <pk> and the ECDSA signature. Subsequently it is also checked that <RedeemScript> verifies correctly with regard to <scripthash>.

Fast bootstrapping in PoS Blockchains. In this scenario we want to facilitate the expedient synchronization of a client for a proof of Stake blockchain. The problem is similar to the problem of simplified payment verification (SPV) as in [30], with the challenge that in a PoS blockchain, e.g., [26], there is no way to verify blocks just by looking at the headers (as in the case of a PoW-based blockchain); some transactional information is essential to establish the stakeholder distribution that is eligible to issue blocks.

In order to facilitate the use of Mithril in this setting, we first have to expand the blockchain accounting model so that each account is also associated with an STM key. We assume a synchronous system operation and divide time into periods sufficient to allow ledger settlement. Let SD_i be a settled stakeholder distribution (i.e. all honest parties agree on it) during period i. SD_0 is the stakeholder distribution embedded at genesis; we assume parties agree on SD_0.

When the distribution SD_i is derived from the blockchain, the message $\mathsf{mesg}_i = (i, C_i)$ is formed where C_i is a Merkle tree commitment to SD_i. Subsequently the stakeholders in SD_{i-1} attempt to issue an STM on mesg_i. Whenever a stakeholder is eligible, they release the individual signature over the peer-2-peer network. If sufficient individual signatures are collected with respect to the given stake threshold, the resulting signature, denoted by chp_i can be computed and disseminated. The triple (i, C_i, chp_i) is the i-th checkpoint of the blockchain.

In this way, the system continuously issues checkpoints. When a new client joins for the first time with only knowledge of the genesis block, it queries and verifies the sequence of checkpoints starting from the genesis block and arriving up to the most recent one SD_n. Subsequently blocks can be verified w.r.t. SD_n.

Proofs of Data Availability. High performance consensus protocol design in the permissioned setting (e.g., [13,17,33]) heavily exploits a decoupling between the data that are to be agreed on and the consensus protocol itself which is running on short references to that data. Such decoupling naturally carries a potential risk: running consensus on references for which the corresponding data does not exist. It follows that proving such optimizations secure may require resolving this *data availability* consideration. Even though this problem is easy to tackle in the permissioned setting (as e.g., we may require a sufficient number of signatures so we ensure at least one honest party has seen the data) it is much more challenging to solve in the permissionless setting [32]. Mithril provides an immediate solution: if the underlying consensus protocol is run on references for which a Mithril signature exists, data availability is (cryptographically) guaranteed.

References

1. Agrawal, S., Neu, J., Tas, E.N., Zindros, D.: Proofs of proof-of-stake with sublinear complexity. In: Bonneau, J., Weinberg, S.M. (eds.) Advances in Financial Technologies (AFT 2023), pp. 14:1–14:24. Schloss Dagstuhl (2023)
2. Baldimtsi, F., Madathil, V., Scafuro, A., Zhou, L.: Anonymous lottery in the proof-of-stake setting. In: CSF (2020)
3. Bellare, M., Garay, J.A., Rabin, T.: Fast batch verification for modular exponentiation and digital signatures. In: EUROCRYPT (1998)
4. Bernstein, D.J., Hamburg, M., Krasnova, A., Lange, T.: Elligator: elliptic-curve points indistinguishable from uniform random strings. In: CCS (2013)
5. Boneh, D., Drijvers, M., Neven, G.: Compact multi-signatures for smaller blockchains. In: ASIACRYPT (2018)
6. Boneh, D., Lynn, B., Shacham, H.: Short signatures from the weil pairing. In: ASIACRYPT (2001)
7. Bünz, B., Bootle, J., Boneh, D., Poelstra, A., Wuille, P., Maxwell, G.: BulletProofs: short proofs for confidential transactions and more. In: Security and Privacy (2018)
8. Bünz, B., Kiffer, L., Luu, L., Zamani, M.: FlyClient: super-light clients for cryptocurrencies. In: Security and Privacy (2020)
9. Chaidos, P., Kiayias, A.: Mithril: Stake-based threshold multisignatures. Cryptology ePrint Archive, Paper 2021/916 (2021). https://eprint.iacr.org/2021/916
10. Chaidos, P., Kiayias, A., Reyzin, L., Zinovyev, A.: Approximate lower bound arguments. In: EUROCRYPT, pp. 55–84. Springer, Cham (2024). https://doi.org/10.1007/978-3-031-58737-5
11. Chen, J., Micali, S.: Algorand: a secure and efficient distributed ledger. Theor. Comput. Sci. **777**, 155–183 (2019)
12. Malkin, T., Peikert, C. (eds.): CRYPTO 2021. LNCS, vol. 12826. Springer, Cham (2021). https://doi.org/10.1007/978-3-030-84245-1
13. Danezis, G., Kokoris-Kogias, L., Sonnino, A., Spiegelman, A.: Narwhal and tusk: a DAG-based Mempool and efficient BFT consensus. In: EuroSys (2022)
14. Das, S., Camacho, P., Xiang, Z., Nieto, J., Bünz, B., Ren, L.: Threshold signatures from inner product argument: succinct, weighted, and multi-threshold. In: Proceedings of the 2023 ACM SIGSAC Conference on Computer and Communications Security, pp. 356–370 (2023)
15. David, B., Gaži, P., Kiayias, A., Russell, A.: Ouroboros Praos: an adaptively-secure, semi-synchronous proof-of-stake blockchain. In: Nielsen, J.B., Rijmen, V. (eds.) EUROCRYPT 2018. LNCS, vol. 10821, pp. 66–98. Springer, Cham (2018). https://doi.org/10.1007/978-3-319-78375-8_3
16. Dodis, Y., Yampolskiy, A.: A verifiable random function with short proofs and keys. In: Public Key Cryptography (2005)

17. Fitzi, M., Hirt, M.: Optimally efficient multi-valued byzantine agreement. In: PODC (2006)
18. Gabizon, A., et al.: Plumo: towards scalable interoperable blockchains using ultra light validation systems (2020)
19. Ganesh, C., Orlandi, C., Tschudi, D.: Proof-of-stake protocols for privacy-aware blockchains. In: EUROCRYPT (2019)
20. Garg, S., Jain, A., Mukherjee, P., Sinha, R., Wang, M., Zhang, Y.: hinTS: threshold signatures with silent setup. In: 2024 IEEE Symposium on Security and Privacy (SP), pp. 57–57. IEEE Computer Society (2023)
21. Gaži, P., Kiayias, A., Zindros, D.: Proof-of-stake sidechains. In: Security and Privacy (2019)
22. Goldwasser, S., Ostrovsky, R.: Invariant signatures and non-interactive zero-knowledge proofs are equivalent. In: CRYPTO (1992)
23. Grassi, L., Khovratovich, D., Rechberger, C., Roy, A., Schofnegger, M.: Poseidon: a new hash function for zero-knowledge proof systems. In: USENIX Security (2021)
24. Kerber, T., Kiayias, A., Kohlweiss, M., Zikas, V.: Ouroboros crypsinous: privacy-preserving proof-of-stake. In: Security and Privacy (2019)
25. Kiayias, A., Miller, A., Zindros, D.: Non-interactive proofs of proof-of-work. In: Bonneau, J., Heninger, N. (eds.) FC 2020. LNCS, vol. 12059, pp. 505–522. Springer, Cham (2020). https://doi.org/10.1007/978-3-030-51280-4_27
26. Kiayias, A., Russell, A., David, B., Oliynykov, R.: Ouroboros: a provably secure proof-of-stake blockchain protocol. In: Katz, J., Shacham, H. (eds.) CRYPTO 2017. LNCS, vol. 10401, pp. 357–388. Springer, Cham (2017). https://doi.org/10.1007/978-3-319-63688-7_12
27. Leung, D., Suhl, A., Gilad, Y., Zeldovich, N.: Vault: fast bootstrapping for the algorand cryptocurrency. In: NDSS (2019)
28. Lysyanskaya, A.: Unique signatures and verifiable random functions from the DH-DDH separation. In: Yung, M. (ed.) CRYPTO 2002. LNCS, vol. 2442, pp. 597–612. Springer, Heidelberg (2002). https://doi.org/10.1007/3-540-45708-9_38
29. Micali, S., Reyzin, L., Vlachos, G., Wahby, R.S., Zeldovich, N.: Compact certificates of collective knowledge. In: Security and Privacy (2021)
30. Nakamoto, S.: Bitcoin: A peer-to-peer electronic cash system. Tech. rep. (2008)
31. Ristenpart, T., Yilek, S.: The power of proofs-of-possession: Securing multiparty signatures against rogue-key attacks. In: EUROCRYPT (2007)
32. Smith, C., Beckett, A., Wackerow, P., AlehN: Data availability. https://ethereum.org/en/developers/docs/data-availability/
33. Spiegelman, N.G., Giridharan, N., Sonnino, A., Kokoris-Kogias, L.: Bullshark: DAG BFT protocols made practical. CCS (2022)
34. Tibouchi, M.: Elligator squared: uniform points on elliptic curves of prime order as uniform random strings. In: Financial Cryptography (2014)

Scalable and Lightweight State-Channel Audits

Christian Badertscher[1], Maxim Jourenko[3], Dimitris Karakostas[2(✉)],
and Mario Larangeira[3]

[1] IOG, Zurich, Switzerland
christian.badertscher@iohk.io
[2] University of Edinburgh, Edinburgh, UK
dkarakos@ed.ac.uk
[3] Tokyo Institute of Technology & IOG, Tokyo, Japan
jourenko.m.ab@m.titech.ac.jp, mario.larangeira@iohk.io,
mario@c.titech.ac.jp

Abstract. Payment channels are one of the most prominent off-chain
scaling solutions for blockchain systems. However, regulatory institutions
have difficulty embracing them, as the channels lack insights needed for
Anti-Money Laundering (AML) auditing purposes. Our work tackles the
problem of a formal reliable and controllable inspection of off-ledger payment channels, by offering a novel approach for maintaining and reliably
auditing statistics of payment channels. We extend a typical trustless
Layer 2 protocol and provide a lightweight and scalable protocol s.t.:
(i) every state channel is provably auditable w.r.t. a configurable set of
policy queries, s.t. a regulator can retrieve reliable insights about the
channel; (ii) no information beyond the answers to auditing queries is
leaked; (iii) the cryptographic operations are inexpensive, the setup is
simple, and storage complexity is independent of the transaction graph's
size. We present a concrete protocol, based on Hydra Isomorphic State
Channels (FC'21), and tie the creation of a state channel to real-world
identifiers, both in a plain and privacy-preserving manner. For this, we
employ verifiable credentials for decentralized identifiers, specifically verifiable Legal Entity Identifiers (vLEI) that increasingly gain traction for
financial service providers and regulated institutions.

1 Introduction

Layer 2 protocols enable interactions between parties without the immediate
aid of a public ledger [21,26]. This family of protocols includes payment [20],
state [16], and multiplayer channels [10,15] which require only an initial step that
locks the funds of the parties in the Layer 1 ledger, as well as networks [31].
Off-chain protocols ease the burden of a blockchain system and enable the generation, and verification of transactions in a low-cost and fast manner, which

This work was supported by Input Output Global and JST CREST JPMJCR2113,
Japan.

depends exclusively on the network delays instead of the ledger's confirmation time. As a consequence, payment channels are often the go-to scalability solution in large-scale deployments of cryptocurrencies.

Notably, the main efficiency benefit of Layer 2 protocols, namely the ability to transact in bulk off-chain, also makes them opaque. It is known that the Layer 1 ledger is oblivious to the Layer 2 transactions since none of them is registered in public. This feature introduces a significant burden to regulated institutions and service providers, like banks and government bodies in the presence of auditing according to Anti-Money Laundering (AML) policies.

For a more concrete example, consider that a typical question that authorities ask is whether two parties transacted during a certain period of time and whether the exchanged funds were above some legal threshold. It is trivial to answer such questions in centralized systems and, thus they are part of everyday activities of a compliance department. In practice, AML, Know-Your-Costumer (KYC), and Anti-Terror regulation techniques crucially rely on transaction monitoring. The discussion around Central Bank Digital Currencies (CBDC) [17,18,24] strongly suggests that regulation is a major concern and a current topic of discussion in the industry and academia. Here, the off-chain setting poses a significant gap in addressing such concerns, especially regarding privacy and regulatory compliance, and the topic is currently actively discussed [6].

Evidently, in the presence of digital currencies and smart contracts, new tools are required to answer questions a regulator might pose. Without such tools, an auditor would need to reliably obtain essentially all off-chain transactions which is not only impractical, but goes against the scalability improvements offered by Layer 2 protocols for its users. To the best of our knowledge, selective disclosure capabilities, which are able to answer policy queries, have not been suggested for Layer 2 protocols. Consequently, it is unclear how off-chain protocols can be used efficiently and effectively in a regulatory compliant manner. The existing gap was further identified in a joint report of the ECB and the Bank of Japan [36, §4.2.3], as well as recent Systematization of Knowledge (SoK) work [11] as follows: *"Is auditing of transactions that do not appear in the ledger (or happen "off the chain") possible?"* To the best of our knowledge, our work is the first attempt to formalize the problem statement and close this gap with a positive result.

While our solution puts forth a generic approach to the problem that can be applied to most Layer 2 systems, we offer a first formal result by enhancing the Hydra Protocols [10,27,28]. The Hydra Protocol [10] is a recent generalization of multiparty state channels with smart contract capabilities. In Hydra, a group of parties initiate an *isomorphic* off-chain channel, the "head". Isomorphism ensures that the head's state is enforceable in the Layer 1 ledger, s.t. the head can be used as a ledger on its own, i.e., detached from the consensus protocol. Eventually, a head is closed by replicating the head's state to the ledger seamlessly, thus Hydra puts forth a computational layer that allows the concurrently creation of multiple heads with a well defined computational model, i.e., a state machine.

State-Channel Audit Basic Requirements. State channel audits are an extremely broad goal, but the general approach is to allow regulated institutions to (1) perform bookkeeping efficiently and (2) interact with (potentially) identifiable participants in a way that the obtained statistics are provably sound. *Relevant statistics and policies.* In the context of transaction systems, an individual participant (such as a financial service provider) will be subject to audits of several types, where an authority or regulator $\mathcal{R}$ defines the set of statistics that a participant is required to maintain. We call those statistics "policies" and denote the *policy set* by $\mathfrak{S}$. Typically, a regulated institution needs to identify other participants or be assured they are identifiable (KYC). There are also additional prototypical statistics, e.g., that have been identified as relevant in the context of Central Bank Digital Currencies (CBDCs) [5,17,25]: (1) Have parties (P_1, P_2) transacted directly? (2) Have (P_1, P_2) transacted more than T_{tx} assets in one transaction? (3) Within a window of N consecutive transactions, have (P_1, P_2) transacted more than T_{tx} assets on aggregate? (4) Did the balance of party P exceed T_{bal} at any point in time? (5) Within a window of t minutes, has P sent/received more than T_{send}/T_{recv} assets on aggregate?

Requirements for an audit protocol. An audit protocol is a cryptographic protocol which needs to satisfy several security-relevant features: (1) *Soundness*: no malicious party (incl. the auditor) can forge a response to an audit query w.r.t. the public execution trail of the audit protocol; (2) *Termination*: the audit process should terminate even if either $\mathcal{R}$ or the audited party abort; (3) *Availability*: $\mathcal{R}$ can query any supported policy at any point in time; (4) *Audit Privacy (* [36]*)*: an audit request should not leak more than the answer to the query.

Aside of the above main properties, one might be interested in further requirements (cf. [11]). First, in certain use-cases the audit trail should be *publicly verifiable*, i.e., $\mathcal{R}$ cannot dispute an honest-party's audit results and a malicious user cannot deny how their interactions with an honest authority. Second, at least a subset of the parties should be *identifiable* and connected to a real-world entity. Finally, auditing should not impose high costs, e.g., blockchain fees.

The audit procedure should ideally introduce very little overhead and complexity to existing transaction protocols. Thus, as a design principle, we aim at a solution where any piece of information that is to be additionally published, for the sake of an audit, needs to be succinct (as some data is expected to be on chain). Furthermore, the storage requirement of honest participants should be less than linear on the number of all transactions created in the Hydra head.

Related Work. Auditability of distributed ledgers has been a point of interest for many years. zkLedger [34], PRCash [39], Garman *et al.* [19], PGC [12] are examples of ledgers that, to some degrees, support auditing by design, i.e., they are designed with auditing capabilities in mind. A relevant line of work concerns efficiently proving the ownership of cryptocurrency assets in a privacy-preserving manner. These works, like Provisions [13], are termed "proofs of solvency" and are primarily used by exchanges. Further, in the context of CBDCs, as mentioned above, extensive auditing capabilities are a core design element and has in fact gained a lot of traction recently [30,40]. The setting and the corresponding solutions however depart heavily from simple peer-to-peer transaction systems since a bank is needed to settle transactions, so they do not provide a (lightweight) solution or drop-in replacement for existing payment channel systems to enable auditing capabilities for decentralized currencies.

Contributions and Roadmap. Our work presents an auditability extension to Layer 2 ledgers and introduces a concrete construction based on the Hydra protocol [10]. The extension is lightweight and requires only small additional values to be published on the main chain. First, Sect. 3 introduces our proposed auditing framework in a generic Layer 2 model. Then Sect. 4 focuses on the Hydra protocol [10] to make it auditable. We provide formal definitions of the main goals by extending Hydra's security experiment. Our construction enables identifiability of parties via decentralized identifiers (DIDs) [1], which are integrated in a plain and privacy-preserving manner. To connect our design with practice, we explore the verifiable credentials for Legal Entity Identifiers (LEI) issued by GLEIF [3], a widely accepted way to identify regulated institutions or financial service providers in traditional settlement layers. This integrated real-world identification allows to make the realistic assumption that at least one participant (is obliged to) perform the audit reliably. Specifically, if at least one participant is identifiable [36] in a legal jurisdiction accepted by the auditor, where accessibility to crucial information can be achieved through enforcement, they risk legal implications if valid (in the cryptographic sense) but inconsistent audit information about a state channel are observed, i.e., if parties equivocate. Finally, Sect. 4.3 presents our main result, a Hydra protocol that enables audits between a regulating authority and the users. Our protocol achieves the main requirements of correctness, soundness, and privacy, as well as public verifiability, identifiability, and efficient auditing. Also it is scalable for policies that can be computed by a Turing machine executing an online algorithm in sub-linear space, where each input is evaluated in sub-linear time.

2   Preliminaries

Before we introduce our construction, it is convenient to briefly recall a state channel protocol, the Hydra construction, and decentralized identifiers which are crucial to ground the identity of the protocol players.

2.1   Hydra: Isomorphic State Channels

Hydra [10] is an isomorphic state channel developed for the Cardano [7]. Briefly, it allows any set of parties to move part of the ledger's state off-chain,i.e., the "Hydra head" where participants interact directly. The state machine model is inspired by the Extended UTxO model [9] and Chimeric Ledgers [41].

Hydra employs a multi-signature scheme ⟨MS-Setup, MS-KG, MS-AVK⟩, to generate the global setup parameters, key pairs, and aggregate public key. While the Hydra head operates, there exist two core data types. First, a snapshot $\mathcal{U} = \langle s, U, h, T, S, \hat{\sigma} \rangle$, where: i) s is its number which is generated sequentially;

ii) U is its corresponding UTxO set; iii) h is the hash value of the UTxO set; iv) T is the set of transactions that relates this snapshot to the previous one; v) S is its array of signatures (a signature accumulator); vi) $\hat{\sigma}$ is the all participants multi-signature of the snapshot.

Second, a transaction $\tau = \langle i, \mathsf{tx}, h, S, \hat{\sigma} \rangle$, where: i) i is the index of the party issuing it; ii) tx is the transaction's information; iii) h is the hash value of tx; iv) S is its array of signatures; v) $\hat{\sigma}$ is its multi-signature. $\mathcal{U}.s$ denotes the snapshot's number (similar for all other parameters of a snapshot and transaction).

The Hydra protocol proceeds in phases. Initially, each party generates their key pair and collects their UTxOs. The keys will form the head's aggregate public key, while the UTxOs form the initial UTxO set. After the parties gather, the Hydra Protocol comprises the actions in Table 1.

Table 1. The parameters are: (i) initial is a state identifier; (ii) h_{MT} is the root of a Merkle tree for the verification keys of all parties; (iii) n is the number of head members; (iv) T is the length of the contestation period; (v) v_{com} is a validating script, which ensures that the outputs are locked to the right instance of the state machine; (vi) π_{MT} the head's identifier; (vii) ξ is information about the head's state (e.g., a snapshot).

	Action	Object/State Identifier
Onchain	Initialize	$\mathsf{init} = \langle \mathsf{initial}, vk_{\mathrm{agg}}, h_{\mathsf{MT}}, n, T \rangle$
	Commit	$\mathsf{commit} = \langle v_{\mathrm{com}}, \mathcal{O}_i \rangle$
	Abort	$\mathsf{abort} = \langle \pi_{\mathsf{MT}} \rangle$
	Open head	$\mathsf{collectCom} = \langle \mathsf{initial}, vk_{\mathrm{agg}}, h_{\mathsf{MT}}, n, T \rangle$
	Close head	$\mathsf{close} = \langle \pi_{\mathsf{MT}}, \xi \rangle$
	Contest	$\mathsf{cont} = \langle \pi_{\mathsf{MT}}, \xi \rangle$
	Finalize	$\mathsf{fanout} = \langle \pi_{\mathsf{MT}} \rangle$
Offchain (in-head)	Request	$\mathsf{reqTx} = \langle \tau \rangle$
	Acknowledge	$\mathsf{ackTx} = \langle \tau.h, \sigma_j \rangle$
	Confirm	$\mathsf{confTx} = \langle \tau.h, \hat{\sigma} \rangle$
	Request	$\mathsf{reqSn} = \langle \mathcal{U}.s, \mathcal{U}.T \rangle$
	Ack. snapshot	$\mathsf{ackSn} = \langle \mathcal{U}.s, \sigma_j \rangle$
	Conf. snapshot	$\mathsf{confSn} = \langle \mathcal{U}.s, \hat{\sigma} \rangle$

The head is initialized when one of the parties publishes on Layer 1 the state identifier, which establishes the head's initial state and parameters. Each party acknowledges this, s.t. the initiator collects the commitments and opens the head. To create a transaction τ, a party P multicasts τ to all head participants, who validate and sign it. State changes are completed with a new *snapshot*, where a "leader" collects all not-yet-snapshot transactions and multicasts them, each party validates and signs them, and the leader broadcasts a multi-signature.

A head is closed by publishing on Layer 1 a confirmed snapshot that parties may contest, e.g., if incorrect. After the contesting period ends, a finalizing transaction on Layer 1 allows each party to redeem their assets from the head.

Finally, the EUTxO model was extended in the multi-asset EUTxO_{ma} ledger [8], which enables token bundles. These bundles store both a ledger's native currency and fungible and non-fungible tokens. A relevant application for our setting is state thread tokens, that is non-fungible tokens stored within a state machine's assets, which we will use in the context of vLEIs.

2.2 Decentralized Identifiers and vLEIs

Decentralized Identifiers (DIDs), which recently achieved the status of W3C recommendation [1], are reminiscent of traditional digital certificates, e.g., X.509. They aim to be highly dynamic, configurable objects, suited for decentralized applications. In its basic form, a DID structure contains information associated to an entity that enables performing cryptographic operations like signing. A DID is always connected to a particular *method* protocol, that defines how a DID is created, where the associated cryptographic material (DID document) is stored, how it is updated or revoked, and how to retrieve the document given an identity. Our work assumes a prototypical and minimal set of features. A DID object did has the form `did:method:id`, that is a pointer to access public key material relevant to this DID. `method` specifies the method and `id` is typically the hash of the DID's (master) verification key; did.vk denotes the result of resolving did to obtain its verification key.

A verifiable credential (VC) [2], vc, is a signed statement by a (trusted) credential issuer, that asserts certain claims about a subject vc.sub identified by a did. Here, we are interested in a VC called vLEI [3] that is of a particular simple type. The claim appearing in a vLEI is just the LEI, the Legal Entity Identifier, issued by GLEIF [3]. Recall that the LEI is not a new invention [4], but the initiative to cast it as VC is very recent. In more detail, a vLEI can be abstracted as the tuple vc = (sub, n, σ) denoting the subject (the DID of the organization for which the LEI is issued), the LEI-number, and the signature of the GLEIF-accredited LEI issuer, respectively. We assume that such an accreditation happens within a smart contract maintained by GLEIF for example.

3 Auditable State Channels

This section reviews UTxO ledgers and Layer 2 protocols and formally presents the audit extension framework and its security properties.

The UTxO Ledger. In the Unspent Transaction Output (UTxO) model of blockchains, such as Bitcoin [33], the ledger's state Σ is a set of UTxO which are tuple of form (b, ν, δ) where $b \in \mathbb{N}$ is an amount of coins, $\delta \in \{0,1\}^*$ and $\nu \in \{0,1\}^*$ is a verification script such that the UTxO can be spent by a transaction if presented a witness $w \in \{0,1\}^*$ where $\nu(w, \delta) = 1$. A transaction tx of form (In, Out) can be used to change the ledger's state by specifying a set of UTxO Out as well a list of UTxO In. A transaction can only modify a ledger's state if all UTxO in In are within Σ, i.e. In $\subseteq \Sigma$, and otherwise is called *invalid*. Two transactions tx_0 and tx_1 are *conflicting* if $\text{tx}_0.\text{In} \cap \text{tx}_1.\text{In} \neq \varnothing$. We denote following state transition function $\circ$ on sets of UTxO $\mathcal{O}$ where $\circ : \mathcal{O}, \mathcal{X} \rightarrow \mathcal{O}$ where $\mathcal{O} \circ X = \mathcal{O} \cup (\bigcup_{tx:\mathcal{X}} tx.\text{Out}) \setminus (\bigcup_{tx:\mathcal{X}} tx.\text{In})$ or $\mathcal{O} \circ X = \bot$ if $\mathcal{X}$ contains either conflicting or with respect to $\mathcal{O}$ invalid transactions. Then, when the transaction $tx = (\text{In}, \text{Out})$ is applied to the ledger, it's state changes to $\Sigma' = \Sigma \circ \{tx\}$. Note that while the Extended UTxO model [9] (EUTxO) explicitly include δ in its definition, Bitcoin's [33] UTxO can embed δ within their script ν.

Layer 2 Ledgers. Similar to Jourenko et al. [27] we assume the existence of a family of protocols that construct Layer 2 ledgers $\mathcal{L}^2$. Moreover, we define their security properties analogous to Hydra [10]. Layer 2 Ledgers are structures created on a physical ledger $\mathcal{L}$, such as Bitcoin, are executed by $n \geq 2$ parties $\mathcal{H}$ where $H_{cont} \subseteq \mathcal{H}$ are honest parties. It function as follows: (1) A Layer 2 ledger maintains a set of UTxOs as state Σ^2, (2) UTxO can be moved in-between the physical ledger's state Σ and Σ^2, (3) the parties operating $\mathcal{L}^2$ have means to modify Σ^2 through a set of – potentially implicit – transactions $\mathcal{X}$ and (4) when performing m transactions on $\mathcal{L}^2$ at most a sublinear amount of transactions are committed on $\mathcal{L}$. Note that concrete implementations can restrict moving UTxO between $\mathcal{L}$ and $\mathcal{L}^2$ to setup and tear-down of the protocol. Moreover, transactions on $\mathcal{L}^2$ can have lower expressiveness than those on $\mathcal{L}$. We observe that a wide variety of protocols fall into this family of constructions such as Bitcoin's Lightning payment channels [35] where $n = 2$ parties lock some of their UTxO on $\mathcal{L}$, effectively moving them to $\mathcal{L}^2$ during the opening of the channel to perform a potentially arbitrary amount of transactions, which are limited to payments, using the coins locked in these UTxOs. Lastly the parties will retrieve their coins by closing the channel and moving two UTxO into $\mathcal{L}$ that represent the channels latest balance distribution. On the other side, the Hydra protocol [10] allows for the creation of a multi-party state channel among an arbitrary amount of parties that holds a set of UTxO as state explicitly and where transactions can modify the Hydra channel's state with the same expressiveness as on the physical ledger $\mathcal{L}$.

A Protocol Framework for Trustless Layer 2 Ledgers. We assume that any transaction that modifies the state of $\mathcal{L}^2$ has to be acknowledged by all parties $\mathcal{H}$, so we consider the following framework. At any point, a party can broadcast (reqTx, tx) to all other parties requesting confirmation of transaction tx. If a party $\mathcal{P}_i$, $0 \leq i \leq n$ receives (reqTx, tx) then $\mathcal{P}_i$ acknowledges it if it is neither invalid nor conflicting with any previously acknowledged transactions. If tx is acknowledged, $\mathcal{P}_i$ broadcasts (ack, tx) to all parties in $\mathcal{H}$. In the following, let $\hat{S}_i$ be the set of all transactions for which party $\mathcal{P}_i$ broadcasts (ack, tx) and let $\hat{C}_j$ be the set of all transactions for which party $\mathcal{P}_j$, $0 \leq j \leq n$ received (ack, tx) from all parties in $\mathcal{H}$. This framework does not limit existing protocols and instead covers what – potentially implicitly – is already done in existing trustless Layer 2 ledger constructions like Payment Channels or Hydra [10].

The extension to an auditable Layer 2 ledger can be simply formalized at this abstract layer: given a designated auditor $\mathcal{R}$ and the set of admissible policy queries $\mathfrak{I}$, a set of functions on the (confirmed) transaction $\bar{C}$, the auditor is allowed to ask queries of the form (query, Q) upon which it is allowed to interact with a participant P_i of its choice, and the auditor finally produces the functional output (auditRes, Q, v). Furthermore, the auditable Layer 2 ledger must support a validity predicate $\mathcal{V}$ to judge the validity of an auditor's output in an execution. **Security Properties.** We define security of Layer 2 ledgers analogous to Hydra [10]. In the following let the UTxO set $\mathcal{O}_0$ be the initial state of $\mathcal{L}^2$, i.e. Σ^2 and $\mathcal{O}_{\mathsf{final}}$ be the final state of $\mathcal{L}^2$ upon its tear-down. For audits, we state the most fundamental property, soundness, and defer the definition of further properties (including privacy) directly to our concrete Hydra realization.

A *trustlessly* secure Layer 2 ledger has following properties [10].

- Consistency ($\mathcal{L}^2$): For all, i, j, $\mathcal{O}_0 \circ (\bar{C}_i \cup \bar{C}_j) \neq \perp$, i.e., no two uncorrupted parties see conflicting transactions confirmed;
- Liveness ($\mathcal{L}^2$): For any transaction tx input via (NEW, sid, tx), the following eventually holds: $tx \in \cap_{i \in [n]} \bar{C}_i \vee \forall i : \mathcal{O}_0 \circ (\bar{C}_i \cup \{tx\}) = \perp$, i.e., every party will observe the transaction confirmed or every party will observe the transaction in conflict with his confirmed transaction;
- Soundness ($\mathcal{L}$): $\exists \tilde{S} \subseteq \cap_{i \in \mathcal{H}} \hat{S}_i : \mathcal{O}_{final} = \mathcal{O}_0 \circ \tilde{S}$, i.e., the final UTxO set results from a set of seen transactions;
- Completeness ($\mathcal{L}$): For $\tilde{S}$ as above, $\cup_{P_i \in H_{cont}} \bar{C}_i \subseteq \tilde{S}$, i.e., all transactions seen as confirmed by an honest party at the end of the protocol are considered;
- Audit Soundness: For any request (query, Q) by $\mathcal{R}$ towards any party P_j holding confirmed transaction set $\bar{C}_j$ as above, the auditor's output (auditRes, Q, v) satisfies $v.val = Q(\bar{C}_j)$ whenever $\mathcal{V}(v, \bar{C}_j) = 1$;
- Audit Correctness: For any request (query, Q) by $\mathcal{R}$ towards any honest party P_j holding confirmed transaction set $\bar{C}_j$ as above, the auditor's output (auditRes, Q, v) satisfies $\mathcal{V}(v, \bar{C}_j) = 1$;
- Audit Privacy: This is defined through a game played by two adversaries $\mathcal{A}_\tau$ and $\mathcal{A}_{Aud}$ that do not share any private information and a challenger $\mathcal{C}$. Let $\mathcal{O}^0$ and $\mathcal{O}^1$ be two UTxO sets generated by two executions of a trustless Layer 2 ledger $\mathcal{L}_0^2$ and $\mathcal{L}_1^2$ on a common initial UTxO set $\mathcal{O}_0$ chosen by $\mathcal{A}_\tau$. The game is executed by having $\mathcal{C}$ pick $b_C \in \{0,1\}$ and $\mathcal{A}_\tau$ submit a sequence of tuples (b_A, τ) upon which τ is applied on $\mathcal{L}_{b_A}^2$. At any point $\mathcal{A}_{Aud}$ can submit (query, Q) upon which $\mathcal{C}$ responds with (auditRes, Q, v_b) for both $\mathcal{L}_b^2$, $b \in \{0, 1\}$ respectively, if $v_0.val = v_1.val$ and with $\perp$ otherwise. Finally, $\mathcal{A}_{Aud}$ submits b_{Aud} and wins if $b_{Aud} = b_C$. The advantage of the attacker is defined as $|\mathsf{Pr}(b_{Aud} = b_C) - \frac{1}{2}|$ and a protocol has audit privacy if the advantage of any efficient adversary is negligible.

4   Auditable Hydra Isomorphic State Channels

In this section we provide a concrete instantiation of an auditable Layer 2 protocol. Our proposal extends Hydra [10] (cf. Sect. 2.1), to introduce audit capabilities, and makes use of Decentralized Identifiers (DID) (Sect. 2.2), to enable meaningful auditing based on real-world identities.

4.1 Auditable Hydra

We now describe the auditing extension to the Hydra Protocol (Table 2). Auditing is performed between a special party, the regulating authority $\mathcal{R}$, and the set of the Hydra head's participants $\mathbb{P}$.

Table 2. In addition to the parameters of Table 1, the auditable Hydra protocol is parameterized by the following: (i) $\mathfrak{I}$ is a set of auditable policies Q; (ii) $vk_{\mathcal{R}}$ is the public key of the auditing authority $\mathcal{R}$; state thread token $\mathsf{t}_{\mathsf{lei}}$ via which the smart contract of the vLEI issuer(s) can be referenced to verify credentials; (iii) C_G is a commitment to a representation of the transaction graph G, honestly-generated by function $\mathsf{Com}(\cdot)$; (iv) π_P is a proof of a party's response to an auditing request, honestly-generated by function $\mathsf{ProofGen}(\cdot)$ (given a policy in $\mathfrak{I}$ and a transaction graph G); The verification generates two values, a bit b_π^P and the information d_Q^P.

	Action	Object/State Identifier
Auditing onchain	Initialize	auditInit =
	Commit snapshot	$\langle \mathfrak{I}, vk_{\mathcal{R}}, \mathcal{T}, \mathsf{t}_{\mathsf{lei}} \rangle$
	Close head	commitSn = $\langle C_G \rangle$
		closeHead = $\langle C_G \rangle$
Auditingoffchain	Request	reqAudit = $\langle Q, \mathbb{P}_Q \rangle$
	Respond	resAudit = $\langle \pi_P \rangle$
	Validate	valAudit = $\langle b_\pi^P, d_Q^P \rangle$

Parameters. The auditing protocol supports a set of policies $\mathfrak{I}$, each of which takes as input a transaction graph, given by any participant, or subset of $\mathbb{P}$, in the head. Each request can be addressed, from the $\mathcal{R}$, to any head participant even after the head is already closed. Moreover, the protocol requires pre-negotiated timing parameters $\mathcal{T}$ that specify an upper limit on the rate of transactions, which is used to implement time based policies as further described in Sect. 4.5. Finally, the Hydra participants must agree on the vLEI credential issuer, in the form of the unique state token associated to the issuer-maintained contract on the main chain $\mathsf{t}_{\mathsf{lei}}$. That is, the issuer-governed list of accredited public keys that certify verifiable credentials (in this case simple vLEI identifiers).

Initializing. We extend the initialization procedure in a non-trivial way, to achieve query support as well as building trust in the form of identification. When the head is initialized, each participant $P \in \mathbb{P}$ is given a set of policies $\mathfrak{I}$ and the public key of $\mathcal{R}$ $vk_{\mathcal{R}}$. These parameters are used for auditing requests, when $\mathcal{R}$ queries a head participant about policies in $\mathfrak{I}$. This step can be combined with the original Hydra's initializing process, i.e., init, in a straightforward manner.

Recall that each party acknowledges and verifies the initialization by posting a transaction which locks their outputs to head. In an auditable Hydra head, committing UTxOs is extended to give the participant two options: either submit an ordinary commit-transaction or an audit-commit-transaction.

An audit-commit is richer as it contains additional elements. First, aside of the referenced locked UTxO set $\mathcal{O}_i$, a party P_i specifies, in the data field of the transaction's output, a DID identifier did_i and a verifiable credential vc_i. A valid commit transaction must satisfy the property of the standard commit transaction regarding the validity of $\mathcal{O}_i$. Second, the transaction is signed w.r.t. $\mathsf{did}_i.vk$. Third, vc_i is a vLEI credential s.t. $\mathsf{vc}_i.\mathsf{sub} = \mathsf{did}_i$ the credential's signature verifies as valid w.r.t. a public key identified via a valid reference into the data field of an unspent output identified via state-thread token $\mathsf{t}_{\mathsf{lei}}$. That is, the state machine maintained by the trusted LEI issuer. In summary, an audit-commit binds a UTxO set not only to one particular Hydra-head, but additionally presents a real-world credential via which the participant can be identified. A natural extension can make this process privacy-preserving, where the party reveals the credential only to the regulator and proves publicly that the regulator can identify them.[1]

As before, the head's initiator collects the commitments and formally opens the head by publishing a transaction with collectCom in the main ledger. The only change here is that this state transition is only successful if at least one committed output is from an audit-commit transaction.

Snapshot commitment and head closing. The head participants regularly commit publicly to the head's snapshot. In this way, the authority gains access to a commitment of the transaction graph. In effect, in this step the participants commit to the version of the transaction history that $\mathcal{R}$ can query. The final such commitment is published upon closing the head, which again can be part of the close step of the original Hydra protocol.

Main chain and on-chain verification. The head's status is kept by the variable η which is part of the state of the state machine (SM), and it is updated by the *onchain verification (OCV) algorithms*, namely Initial, Close and Contest and Final, as in the original Hydra protocol. Here, we add the audit related algorithm ProofGen. Each head participant runs the Prot algorithm representing the head SM, hence the auditable head protocol AHP is the tuple (Prot, Initial, Close, Contest, Final, ProofGen). Note that the participants can be asked audit queries, so they are equipped with ProofGen, while only the $\mathcal{R}$ is requested to execute ProofVal, thereby AHP does not contain ProofVal.

Auditing. Each participant is equipped with the algorithm ProofGen, while the $\mathcal{R}$ can execute ProofVal. Respectively for answering audit queries, and checking the validity of the proof. The auditing proceeds in three phases. First, $\mathcal{R}$ makes a request by sending a policy $Q \in \Im$ to a subset of participants $\mathbb{P}_Q \subseteq \mathbb{P}$. Second, each queried participant constructs a response π. If the participant is honest, it constructs the response π by running their respective ProofGen algorithm. Third, $\mathcal{R}$ verifies the responses. Specifically, for every response π it obtains two bits $\langle b_\pi, d_Q \rangle$ by running ProofVal on each reply. If, for some party, the proof bit is false, that is $b_\pi = 0$, then $\mathcal{R}$ outputs this party, signifying that its response was

---

[1] The privacy-preserving variant is deferred to Sect. 5.1.

invalid. Additionally, the authority outputs the policy query response d_Q, which corresponds to a response with a valid proof bit.[2]

Smart contracts and addresses. Smart contracts are a challenge for auditability, as party interactions through smart contracts strongly depend on their code. Storing the code and all interactions for auditability would result in a memory cost linear to head's transactions, violating our efficiency requirements. However, not tracking this information would allow parties to trivially avoid auditability by using a smart contract with the sole purpose of forwarding coins to a recipient. Similarly, tracking all newly created addresses within a Hydra head would result in high memory costs, but not tracking them would enable audit evasion. Note that this issue only applies to addresses and smart contracts that are active. Addresses that do not spend coins, e.g., belong to parties external to the Hydra head, are visible on-chain when the respective UTxOs are decommitted. Note that smart contracts can be made uniquely distinct via non-fungible thread tokens [8]. So, to resolve these issues, we employ the following simplification. For each smart contract interaction, one party declares ownership of that contract by signing its thread token. We model the smart contract as a black box s.t. all interactions with it are considered as interactions that its owner party helped to facilitate. This results in a memory cost linear in the number of parties that execute the Hydra head. Similarly, each address is claimed by one party as its alias, s.t. interactions with that address are attributed to that party.

4.2   Security Experiment

We now instantiate the generic security properties outlined in the previous section for the specific case of Auditable Hydra Protocol. Prior to describing the security experiment for AHP and the implied security notions, we present the more detailed execution.

General Setup. To analyze security we can consider an experiment similar to the original Hydra [10]. Once the main chain machine arrives in the final state, the adversary wins if certain conditions are not satisfied. Consider the following random variables in an execution of the auditable head protocol AHP = (Prot, Initial, Close, Contest, Final, ProofGen):

- The set of n parties P_i running the auditable head protocol with the parameters from the setup phase and an initial UTxO set $\mathcal{O}_0$;
- The adversary $\mathcal{A}$ who can see the messages exchanged by the participants P_i and chooses the initial UTxO set $\mathcal{O}_0$;
- The regulator $\mathcal{R}$ which can choose a single policy $Q \in \mathfrak{S}$ and submit it to any P_i with $i \in [n]$;
- The set of (at the time) uncorrupted parties H_{cont} who produced ξ upon close/contest request and ξ was applied to correct the information η;
- The set of corrupted participants $\mathcal{C}$;

---

[2] As we will show in the security analysis, audit soundness guarantees that, if the proof bit is 1, then the policy response data is correct.

- Every party P_i's and performs $\langle vk_i, sk_i \rangle \leftarrow$ MS-KG($\mathcal{S}$), and computes the aggregate signature $vk_{\mathrm{agg}} \leftarrow$ MS-AVK($\mathcal{S}, \underline{vk}$), for the local verification key vector $\underline{vk}$ of the i-th party.

The head-protocol machine Prot has the following environment interface:

- On input of (INIT, $sid, i, vk_{\mathrm{agg}}, sk_i, \mathcal{O}_0$), P_i initializes Prot;
- On input of (NEW, sid, τ), P_i submits a new transaction τ;
- When the party output (SEEN, sid, τ), it announces it has seen τ;
- When the party output (CONF, sid, τ), it announces that in its local view τ has been confirmed;
- On input of (CLOSE, sid), it starts head closure and outputs a certificate ξ;
- On input of (CONT, sid, η), it contests closure and outputs a certificate ξ.

The Experiment. Now, consider the following experiment for the protocol AHP and its OCV functions with audit algorithms.

1. Global Parameters $\mathcal{S} \leftarrow$ MS-Setup, and $\mathcal{S}$ is passed to adversary $\mathcal{A}$ along with the set of policies $\mathfrak{I}$ and the regulator public key $vk_{\mathcal{R}}$;
2. For each party P_i, key material $\langle vk_i, sk_i \rangle \leftarrow$ MS-KG($\mathcal{S}$) is generated, and the vector $\underline{vk}$ of all parties' public keys and vk_{agg} are passed to $\mathcal{A}$, which returns the initial set $\mathcal{O}_0$;
3. Each party P_i's protocol machine is initialized with (INIT, $sid, i, vk_{\mathrm{agg}}, sk_i, \mathcal{O}_0$), where $\mathcal{O}_0$ was chosen by $\mathcal{A}$;
4. The adversary now controls inputs to the parties, (e.g., new transactions, close/contest requests) and sees outputs (e.g., seen and confirmed transactions). The following bookkeeping takes place:
   - when an uncorrupted party p_i outputs ξ upon command (CLOSE, sid), record (CLOSE, i, ξ), for the certificate ξ;
   - when an uncorrupted party p_i outputs ξ upon command (CONT, sid, η), record (CONT, i, η, ξ), such that η is the context information.
5. In "parallel" to the above, the experiment sets $\mathcal{C}, H_{cont} \leftarrow \emptyset$, and does the following to simulate the main chain:
   - Initialize $\eta \leftarrow (\mathcal{O}_0, 0, \emptyset)$;
   - When $\mathcal{A}$ supplies (i, ξ') : If i is uncorrupted, ξ' gets replaced by the ξ record in (CLOSE, i, ξ) and $H_{cont} \leftarrow H_{cont} \cup \{i\}$. Then $\eta \leftarrow$ Close($vk_{\mathrm{agg}}, \eta, \xi$) and $\mathcal{C} \leftarrow \mathcal{C} \cup \{i\}$ is computed. If Close rejects, everything in this step is discarded and the step is repeated;
   - The adversary gets to repeatedly supply (i, ξ) for $i \notin \mathcal{C}$; if i is uncorrupted, ξ gets replaced by the ξ recorded in (CONT, i, ξ) and $H_{cont} \leftarrow H_{cont} \cup \{i\}$. Then, $\eta \leftarrow$ Contest($vk_{\mathrm{agg}}, \eta, \xi$) and $\mathcal{C} \leftarrow \mathcal{C} \cup \{i\}$ is computed. If Contest rejects, everything in this step is discarded.
   - When $\mathcal{A}$ supplies $\mathcal{O}_{final}$, $b \leftarrow$ Final($\eta, \mathcal{O}_{final}$) is computed.
6. $\mathcal{A}$ can submit (AUDIT, $sid, i, $ reqAudit) s.t. reqAudit $= \langle Q, \mathbb{P} \rangle$ for $Q \in \mathfrak{I}$ and the participants subset $\mathbb{P}$, and receives the reply (AUDITREPLY, $sid,$ resAudit) for resAudit $= \langle \pi_{\mathbb{P}} \rangle$, s.t. $\pi_{\mathbb{P}}$ is computed by each participant's ProofGen execution, i.e., $\pi_{\mathbb{P}}$ is the $|\mathbb{P}|$-long π proofs tuple;

7. The experiment ends when $\mathcal{A}$ sends (HALT, sid).

Collusion and listener participant. A significant technical challenge is to formally define the properties of audit security properties to cope with the case of total collusion of the head participants. In order to better illustrate this scenario, assume the existence of at least *one single* honest participant. In such a case, any regulator can cross check the replies from all the participants and potentially pinpoint the set of cheaters given their inability to properly reply to the regulator queries. On the other hand, in the case where all the participants of the head are malicious, then they can collude to generate a correct and consistent pair (G^*, C_G^*), of an artificial transaction graph that satisfies all the expectations of the auditor. In such challenging scenario, the regulator/auditor cannot distinguish it from an honest execution of the protocol. The honest participant assumption is a strong guarantee, which does not exist in this case.

Security events. As in the original Hydra, security is captured by a number of events, which correspond to each outlined security property. All events hold in the presence of an *active adversary*. We use the standard notation that a transaction τ is valid for a set of UTxO $\mathcal{O}$ if $\mathcal{O} \circ \tau \neq \bot$.

Each participant P_i stores a short representation C_{G_i} and auditing statistics of the graph G throughout the head's life cycle. For every honest P_i, statistics about G_i and C_{G_i} are correct audit information the auditor can expect from an audit query. The existence of an honest participant provides an execution description (G, C_G), which is assumed to be correct and honest. Our formalization assumes a special protocol participant, $P_{\mathcal{L}}$, that is not part of the protocol, i.e., is a "virtual participant", who observes the protocol's execution and records all transactions. Thus, $P_{\mathcal{L}}$ keeps $(G_{\mathcal{L}}, C_{G_{\mathcal{L}}})$ which is considered the true execution of the protocol. Note that such participant does not exist in reality, however it allows us to correctly define and capture the desired audit security properties.

Following, we outline the security properties for the audit hydra head with respect to the *listener participant* $P_{\mathcal{L}}$. Intuitively, correctness guarantees that any honest user's response will be valid, i.e., $\mathcal{R}$ will accept its proof ($b_\pi^{P_i} = 1$). Also soundness guarantees that, if the regulator accepts a party P_i's proof as correct ($b_\pi^{P_i} = 1$), then it should be infeasible for another participant to also present an acceptable proof for a contradictory response to the same policy query.

Definition 1 (Audit Correctness). *Given policy $Q \in \mathfrak{S}$, let $\langle b_\pi^{P_i}, d_Q^{P_i} \rangle$ be the bits output by $\mathcal{R}$ for the response of an honest party P_i; it should hold that $b_\pi^{P_i} = b_\pi^{P_{\mathcal{L}}} = 1$, for the replies with respect to the listener participant $P_{\mathcal{L}}$.*

Definition 2 (Audit Soundness). *Given policy $Q \in \mathfrak{S}$, let $\langle b_\pi^{P_i}, d_Q^{P_i} \rangle$ be the bits output by $\mathcal{R}$ for the response of a party P_i; it should hold that, if $b_\pi^{P_i} = b_\pi^{P_{\mathcal{L}}} = 1$, then $d_Q^{P_i} = d_Q^{P_{\mathcal{L}}}$, for the replies with respect to the listener participant $P_{\mathcal{L}}$.*

Finally, privacy ensures that $\mathcal{R}$ gains no additional information about the transaction graph, beyond what is revealed by the query answer. We assume $\mathcal{R}$ is an external party to the channel, only observing its public footprint. This assumption is required as Layer 2 transactions are not private by default [22].

Although transaction privacy has been researched extensively for Layer 1 protocols, in Layer 2 some proposals only try to increase unlinkability [23,37], but they are still susceptible side-channel attacks and collusion between certain trusted parties. Therefore, our work aims to maintain the level of privacy that Layer 2 solutions offer while enabling auditing.

Definition 3 (Audit Privacy). *Assume two adversaries that share no private state, but both observe the public trace of the execution, denoted $\mathcal{A}_\tau$ and $\mathcal{A}_{Aud}$. $\mathcal{A}_\tau$ drives the generation of the transaction graph, by submitting transactions and choosing an initial UTxO set, while $\mathcal{A}_{Aud}$ submits audit queries. A challenger $\mathcal{C}$ carries the security experiment described above for two executions w.r.t. two different UTxO sets, $\mathcal{O}_0^0$ and $\mathcal{O}_0^1$. $\mathcal{C}$ picks a random bit b which corresponds to the execution subject to audits.*

The execution proceeds as described above, where $\mathcal{A}_\tau$ controls the UTxO set and transaction generation. For every action $\mathcal{A}_\tau$ performs, it specifies to which UTxO set it corresponds. At any moment $\mathcal{A}_{Aud}$ submits audit queries to $\mathcal{C}$. If the functional output of the query w.r.t. to both $\mathcal{O}_0^0$ and $\mathcal{O}_0^1$ is the same, $\mathcal{C}$ replies to $\mathcal{A}_{Aud}$ with it; otherwise, if the functional output is different, $\mathcal{C}$ outputs a special value $\perp$. Finally, $\mathcal{A}_{Aud}$ submits a bit b_{Aud}, and wins if $b_{Aud} = b$.

Privacy is violated if the adversary $\mathcal{A}_{Aud}$ in the above game wins with probability $\frac{1}{2} + \epsilon$ for non-negligible values of ϵ.

4.3   Snapshots and Audit Protocol

We now implement the auditable Hydra protocol following Sect. 4.1. Our construction assumes that at least one head participant is honest and all policies, for which $\mathcal{R}$ might query the parties, are known beforehand.

Our implementation supports queries with *aggregatable values*. Specifically, consider a transaction graph G and the value v of a specific policy w.r.t. G. Given a new transaction τ that is applied on G, the new policy value should be computable given only v and τ, that is without needing to access G.

Protocol idea. The main idea of our construction (Fig. 1) is that participants maintain a set of statistics about the transaction graph, which are sufficient to answer $\mathcal{R}$'s queries. Abstractly speaking, the protocol needs two primitives. First, it needs a (binding and hiding) commitment function, which gets as input a set of values (the statistics maintained about a transaction graph) and outputs a succinct value C_G. Second, it needs a proof scheme. Intuitively, proof generation takes two inputs, a policy $Q \in \Im$ and some witness (the maintained statistics), and outputs a proof π, which contains also the answer to the query. For verification, one must know the commitment C_G, a policy Q, and a proof value π, and the output is a bit indicating the validity of π w.r.t. C_G. From a security perspective, the scheme should guarantee that every honestly-generated proof is valid and that no wrong claims can be proven w.r.t. the committed values.

Construction. The construction relies on a zero-knowledge set (ZKS) [32]. A ZKS is a tuple of algorithms $\langle$SetupZKS, CommitZKS, QueryZKS, VerifyZKS$\rangle$.

Intuitively, a ZKS enables a party to create (via CommitZKS) a succinct commitment to a set of values $\mathbb{S}$, s.t. they can later prove efficiently (via QueryZKS) inclusion ($k \in \mathbb{S}$) or non-inclusion ($k \notin \mathbb{S}$) statements. Crucially, a ZKS reveals no additional information about the committed set beyond the proven statement. This property is important as the auditor $\mathcal{R}$ should not obtain data about the transaction graph, beyond the information revealed as part of the auditing process (cf. Definition 3). For this reason, primitives like Merkle trees or some accumulators [14] are not suitable, as they don't guarantee the ZK property.

In our construction, each element of the set corresponds to a possible answer to all supported policies, for any subset of parties to which the policy can apply. Note that each policy and each party is uniquely identifiable, so the elements can be ordered in a deterministic manner. We note that a property of ZKS is hiding the size of the committed set. In our application this property is not needed, since the number of parties and the policies are known to $\mathcal{R}$. Therefore, we use the relaxed notion of *nearly* ZKS [29], which preserves the ZKS properties but only leaks the committed set's size. Specifically, we use a nearly ZKS scheme based on polynomial commitments [29]

For each policy $Q \in \mathfrak{F}$ exists a function q. This function outputs the answer to the policy query, given a previous answer and a transaction. For example, for the policy "Have P, P' transacted?", $q(b, \tau)$ is 1 if either $b = 1$ or τ transfers funds between P, P'.[3] When a transaction τ is added in the head, each party P updates affected elements of their set. For each element l with a policy function q, P updates its value with $\langle q(l, \tau), Q, \tau.h \rangle$, where $\tau.h$ is the hash of τ. Since transactions are broadcast to all parties, honest parties maintain the same set.

Note on updatable Commitments: In the standard KZG setting, each new transaction requires an update on the information kept by the participants, including the regeneration of the commitment. A more efficient alternative is to use updatable variants, e.g., a recent concrete construction by Tas and Boneh [38] which allows efficient updates.

When evaluating policies, the parties involved in τ are looked up in $\mathcal{U}.I$, where addresses and state thread tokens are substituted with parties. Policies have access to both τ and $\mathcal{U}.I$, so they can differentiate whether a party was involved directly through a transaction or facilitated a transaction as owner of a state machine. State machine owners are considered intermediaries of a transaction, s.t. they are always considered to be both sender and receiver of the transaction. While this holds true for transactions that perform a state transition of a state machine where a state thread token is in both the transaction's inputs and outputs, this is not the case for initial and final states. Respectively, when evaluating the policies of transactions that create and close a state machine, the owner is implicitly considered to be both sender and receiver.

When $\mathcal{R}$ makes a policy query Q, an honest participant P retrieves the element l which corresponds to the query's answer,[4] constructs an inclusion proof π_l for l w.r.t. the latest published commitment C_G, and responds with

---

[3] Section 4.5 offers more examples of relevant policies.

[4] For ease of notation, Q contains both the policy query and the parties under question.

$\pi_P = (l, \pi_l)$. $\mathcal{R}$ then validates the element corresponds to the correct policy and verifies the inclusion proof w.r.t. the latest commitment C_G. If the checks pass, it sets a bit $b = 1$, otherwise it sets $b = 0$, and outputs $\langle b, l \rangle$.

4.4   Security Analysis

We now show that the auditable Hydra protocol (Fig. 1) satisfies the properties of Sect. 4.2.

Since our state-machine extension (Table 2) preserves Hydra's structure and merely includes additional values in initializations and snapshots, Hydra's security guarantees are preserved, providing the assurance of safety and liveness for snapshots that now also include the audit-related commitment.

Therefore, we can proceed to prove the main audit guarantees. First, Theorem 1 proves that the auditable Hydra protocol satisfies audit correctness. This property is directly inherited from the properties of the original Hydra. Second, Theorem 2 focuses on audit soundness. Our proof relies both on Hydra's properties, namely that all parties observe all transactions, and the binding property of the used ZKS primitive. Third, Theorem 3 proves our protocol satisfies audit privacy. The main idea here is that, due to the zero-knowledge property of the ZKS, the auditor $\mathcal{R}$ cannot obtain information about the transaction graph or its statistics, beyond the information revealed by each answered policy query.

Auditable Hydra Protocol π_{Audit}

π_{Audit} keeps the initially empty variables $\mathcal{T}$, which is an array of policy answers, and C, a commitment to $\mathcal{T}$.

Initialize: Upon receiving auditInit for some set of policies $\mathfrak{I}$, wait for array $\mathcal{T}_L$ from P_L. Then set $\mathcal{T} = \mathcal{T}_L$.

Graph Update: Upon receiving confTx for some transaction τ, do the following. For each element l of $\mathcal{T}$, which corresponds to a policy Q with function q, replace l with $\langle q(l, \tau), Q, \tau.h \rangle$, where $\tau.h$ is τ's hash. Then run *Commit Snapshot* as below.

Commit Snapshot: Upon receiving commitSn, compute $\mathcal{T}$'s commitment C and output $\langle C \rangle$.

Close Head: Upon receiving closeHead, output $\langle C \rangle$.

Audit request: Upon receiving reqAudit for policy Q, which corresponds to element l of $\mathcal{T}$, create an inclusion proof π_l for l and output $\pi = (l, \pi_l)$.

Audit validation: Upon receiving resAudit with a proof $\pi = (l, \pi_l)$ for policy Q, do the following checks: (i) verify that the response corresponds to Q; (ii) validate the inclusion proof π_l w.r.t. C. If both checks pass, set $b = 1$, otherwise set $b = 0$. Finally output $\langle b, l \rangle$.

Fig. 1. The Auditable Hydra Protocol.

Theorem 1 (Audit Correctness). *Given a secure implementation of the Hydra state-machine [10], the auditable Hydra protocol of Fig. 1 satisfies audit correctness (Definition 1).*

Proof. By assumption, a correct and secure realization of the Hydra state machine implies consistency and liveness of the head operations [10]. Specifically, an honest user only accepts confirmed transactions, which are (i) non-conflicting (due to safety) and (ii) the same for all parties (due to liveness). So all honest parties, including the listener participant, construct locally the same set of policy answers and each honest party's response is consistent with the published commitment.   □

Theorem 2 (Audit Soundness). *Given a secure implementation of the Hydra state-machine [10], the auditable Hydra protocol of Fig. 1 satisfies audit soundness (Definition 2).*

Proof. Audit soundness follows similarly to consistency. Specifically, since honest parties accept only confirmed transactions and all such transactions are available to all parties, honest parties answer with the same value as the listener in the security experiment (Sect. 4.2). Additionally, due to the binding property of the ZKS which is used in the protocol, an adversary cannot present a forged inclusion proof for a given snapshot's commitment.   □

Theorem 3 (Audit Privacy). *Given a secure implementation of the Hydra state-machine [10], the auditable Hydra protocol of Fig. 1 satisfies audit privacy (Definition 3).*

Proof. First, by assumption the adversary $\mathcal{A}_{Aud}$ (Definition 3) that submits audit queries does not know the transaction graph. This implies that no party that is in the Hydra head colludes with $\mathcal{A}_{Aud}$ (that is, with $\mathcal{R}$), otherwise privacy cannot be guaranteed, since all parties observe all transactions.

Consequently, $\mathcal{A}_{Aud}$ has access only to the following information: i) the sequence of published commitments; ii) the inclusion proof for each answered query; iii) the answer to specific policy queries. First, due to the zero-knowledge (hiding) property of the ZKS commitment, $\mathcal{A}_{Aud}$ cannot infer any information about the values in the set given the published commitment or an inclusion proof. Second, the answer to a policy query is not sufficient to violate audit privacy by definition (cf. Definition 3). Therefore, audit privacy is guaranteed by the construction in Fig. 1.   □

4.5   Implementation Considerations

Our construction opens various practicality questions.

Termination. The auditing protocol should terminate. This can be achieved via timeouts, so if a party fails to respond within reasonable time then it fails the audit. Similarly, the protocol can define a time period during which the authority can issue policy queries, akin to real-world document retention policies.

Disputes. A dispute resolution mechanism could help in case $\mathcal{R}$ tries to reject an honest party's response. This is enabled via the DID features, by requiring the user to sign their responses, s.t. a corrupted authority could not challenge an honest party's response unless forging their DID signature.

Storage. The storage complexity is proportional to the size of the array. Therefore, for a set of policies $\mathfrak{S}$, each pertaining to a pair of parties, the complexity is $O(|\mathfrak{S}| \cdot n^2)$, where n is the number of the head's participants. Note that the authority $\mathcal{R}$ can make a query for any supported policy at any point in time, after the head's creation. This requirement forces each party to indefinitely keep a local copy of the array. In addition, a party's response contains an inclusion proof, so it is logarithmic on the number of elements.

Costs. The cost of auditing for each participant should be upper-bounded and excess costs, e.g., blockchain fees, should be paid by $\mathcal{R}$. This guarantees that a malicious authority cannot impose heavy costs on a head's participants albeit it limits $\mathcal{R}$, since its budget needs to cover the extra fees for auditing queries. In practice, this can again be guaranteed by using a blockchain, where the authority reimburses the transaction fees that a user pays for replying to a query.

Time Parameter. The protocol requires pre-negotiated timing parameters $\mathcal{T} = (n_t, t_l, t_\epsilon)$, where $n_t, t_l, t_\epsilon \in \mathbb{N}$ Here n_t is number of transactions, t_l is a time duration and t_ϵ is the drift of a party's local clock. The value $\mathcal{T}$ is chosen s.t. less than t_n transactions are issued in the head within any time window t_l. This is not intended to limit transaction throughput, but instead an estimate provided by the parties to enable implementation of timing based parameters with time and space complexity independent of the transaction graph's size.

Adjustments to Snapshot Generation. Let $\mathcal{T} = (n_t, t_l, t_\epsilon)$ be the timing parameter provided during protocol setup. We require that each snapshot that is created offchain in a Hydra Head contains a timestamp $t_s \in \mathbb{N}$ and parties reject the snapshot if $|t_s - t_c| \geq t_\epsilon$. Parties maintain a list T which contains entries of form (τ, t) where τ is a transaction and $t \in \mathbb{N}$ is a point in time where $t_c - t_l \leq t \leq t_c$ where t_c is the party's local time. For each new transaction τ to be issued in the head parties refuse including τ in the Hydra head if $|T| = n_t$. Moreover, we modify Hydra's snapshot request from $\mathsf{reqSn} = \langle \mathcal{U}.s, \mathcal{U}.T \rangle$ into $\mathsf{reqSn} = \langle \mathcal{U}.s, \mathcal{U}.T, \mathcal{U}.I \rangle$ where $\mathcal{U}.I = (A, C)$. In the following, let $P_i, 1 \leq i \leq n$ be any party that participates in the auditable Hydra head. Then $A = \{(\alpha, P_i, \sigma_i) | \forall \alpha$ where $\langle \alpha, \theta, H(D) \rangle \in \tau.\mathcal{O}_o \vee \langle \alpha, \theta, H(D) \rangle \in \tau.\mathcal{O}_i$ where $\tau \in \mathcal{U}.T, \tau = \langle [\mathcal{I}], [\mathcal{O}_o] \rangle, \langle \mathcal{O}_i, \mathsf{S}, D, w \rangle \in \tau.[\mathcal{I}] : \exists!(\alpha, P_i, \sigma_i) \in A\}$ specifies the aliases of all parties, i.e. informally for each address α that is in a transaction's inputs or outputs within a snapshot $\mathcal{U}$, there exists exactly one tuple (α, P_i, σ_i) in A that includes a signature σ_i of P_i and declares α to be an address of P_i. Analogously $C = \{(t_s, P_i, \sigma_i) | \forall$ state thread token $t_s \in \theta$ where $\langle \alpha, \theta, H(D) \rangle \in \tau.\mathcal{O}_o \vee \langle \alpha, \theta, H(D) \rangle \in \tau.\mathcal{O}_i$ where $\tau \in \mathcal{U}.T, \tau = \langle [\mathcal{I}], [\mathcal{O}_o] \rangle, \langle \mathcal{O}_i, \mathsf{S}, D, w \rangle \in \tau.[\mathcal{I}] : \exists!(t_s, P_i, \sigma_i) \in C\}$ declares ownership of CEMs, i.e. informally for each state thread token t_s that is in a transaction's inputs or outputs within a snapshot $\mathcal{U}$, there exists exactly one tuple (t_s, P_i, σ_i) in C that includes a signature σ_i of P_i and declares the CEM that is uniquely identified through t_s to be owned by P_i.

Aggregatable Policy Values. Our scheme only supports policies with aggregatable values, s.t. users only keep the array of policy answers, instead of the entire transaction graph. In the following we briefly describe how auditable properties as mentioned in Sect. 1 can be computed and analyze their computational and memory costs. Note that the aim of utilizing aggregatable values is to render the memory and computational requirements of updating these properties to be independent of the amount of transactions performed. Recall that a party, upon receiving confTx for some transaction τ, updates each element l of $\mathcal{T}$, which corresponds to a policy Q with function q, with $\langle q(l,\tau), Q, \tau.h \rangle \in \{0,1\}$ where the response to a policy Q is 1 if and only if the answer to that policy is true.

From now we deem that two parties P_i, $i \in \{0,1\}$ transact directly with a transaction $\tau = \langle [\mathcal{I}], [\mathcal{O}] \rangle$ if it contains a UTxO $\mathcal{O} \in [\mathcal{O}]$ where $\mathcal{O} = \langle \alpha, \theta, H(D) \rangle$ and an transaction input $\mathcal{I} \in [\mathcal{I}]$, $\mathcal{I} = \langle \mathcal{O}, \mathsf{S}, D, w \rangle$ where $\mathcal{I}.\mathcal{O}\alpha$ contains one of P_i's addresses (or $\mathcal{I}.\mathcal{O}.\theta$ contains a thread token associated with P_i) and $\mathcal{O}.\alpha$ has an address of P_{1-i} (or $\mathcal{O}.\theta$ contains a thread token associated with P_{1-i}) .

Have parties (P_1, P_2) transacted directly? This can be done by storing one bit value for each pair of parties which is initialized with 0. As soon as P_1 and P_2 are observed to have transacted directly, the value is flipped to 1, i.e., parties have transacted. The computational requirement is constant and the total memory requirements to store this for all party pairs is $\mathcal{O}(n^2)$.

Have parties (P_1, P_2) transacted directly an amount of more than T_{tx} coins in one transaction? This is done analogous to computing whether P_1 and P_2 transacted directly, however, in addition an auxiliary value $c \in \mathbb{N}$ is stored which is initialized with 0 and set to $c' \in \mathbb{N}$ if P_1 and P_2 transact directly an amount of coins $c' > c$. Once $c > T_{\mathsf{tx}}$ is observed, a bit value storing the answer to this property is set to 1. As above the computational requirement for updating this value is constant and the total memory requirements to store this for all pairs of parties is $\mathcal{O}(n^2)$.

Within every window o N consecutive transactions, have parties (P_1, P_2) transacted an aggregate amount of more than T_{tx} coins? This is done analogous to computing whether P_1 and P_2 transacted directly, however, in addition an auxiliary list of numbers $c_0, \ldots, c_N$ are stored, together with a pointer value $p \in \{0, 1, \ldots, N\}$. The entries in the list as well as p are initialized to 0. Once two parties are observed to transact directly a value of $c \in \mathbb{N}$ coins the value c_p is set to c and p is set to $(p+1) \mod N$. If $\sum_0^N \geq T_{\mathsf{tx}}$ is observed, a bit value storing the answer to this property is set to 1. The computational cost of updating this value is $\mathcal{O}(N)$ and the total memory requirements to store this for all pairs of parties is $\mathcal{O}(n^2 N)$.

Did the balance of party P exceed T_{bal} at any point in time? This can be done by storing a bit value for each pair of parties which is initialized to 0 if their initial balance at the start of the protocol is T_{bal} and 1 otherwise. If at any point in time the observed total balance of a party exceeds T_{bal} the respective bit value is set to 1.

Does there exist a path of length N and value T_{tx} between P_1 and P_2 in the transaction graph? This can be done by storing a graph with n nodes where each party P is represented by a node v_P and there exists an edge between nodes v_{P_1} and v_{P_2} if parties P_1 and P_2 have transacted directly with another. Note that the amount of edges is up to $\mathcal{O}(n^2)$. Moreover, we store a list D of form $\{d_{P_i,P_j} | i,j \in \mathbb{N}, 0 \le i, j \le n, i \neq j\}$ which stores the shortest path length between nodes v_{P_i} and v_{P_j}. The graph is initialized to have no edges and D is initialized correspondingly. Once P_1 and P_2 are observed to have transacted directly with another and no edge between v_{P_1} and v_{P_2} exists, we proceed as follows. An edge between v_{P_1} and v_{P_2} is created and Dijkstra's shortest path algorithm is executed twice, to compute the shortest paths from v_{P_1} and v_{P_2} respectively to all reachable nodes and we update D correspondingly for parties v_{P_1} and v_{P_2}. Note that the weight of each edge is implicitly set to 1. Afterwards, for each pair of parties v_{P_i} and v_{P_j} in the graph we evaluate if $d_{\{P_i,P_j\}} \ge d_{\{P_i,P_k\}} + d_{\{P_k,P_j\}}$ where $k \in \{1,2\}$ and update D if a shortest path is found in the process. The computational cost is $\mathcal{O}(n^2)$ and the storage requirements to store all required auxiliary data is $\mathcal{O}(n^2)$.

Within any window of t minutes, has party P sent more than T_{send} assets on aggregate? Recall that parties limit the transaction throughput based on the timing parameter $\mathcal{T} = (n_t, t_l)$ such that within any time window t_l at most n_t transactions are included in the Hydra head. Let $t_c \in \mathbb{N}$ be a party's local time at moment of evaluating this policy. Then for each party P we store a list $T_{P,s}$ with entries of form (t, b) where $t \in \mathbb{N}$ is the time stored for the snapshot in which a transaction τ was included in the Hydra head in which P sent $b \in \mathbb{N}$ assets and $t_c - t \le t \le t_c$. When evaluating this policy the value $\sum_{(t,b) \in T_{P,s}} b \ge T_{\mathsf{send}}$ the respective bit value is set to 1. Note that the required storage for this policy is $\mathcal{O}(\frac{t n_t n}{t_l})$, i.e. it depends on the timing parameter $\mathcal{T} = (n_t, t_l)$ and the computational complexity is analogous.

Within any window of t minutes, has party P received more than T_{recv} assets on aggregate? This is analogous to the above question on whether P has sent more than T_{send} with the difference of storing how much assets a party has received within a time window T_{recv}.

5   Enhancements

In this section we propose enhancements to the auditable protocol of Sect. 4. Specifically, we detail how the protocol can support auditing in a privacy-preserving manner, such that parties can be audited without revealing their real-world identity. Next, we discuss how the protocol can be expanded to guarantee consistency even under a setting where all participants in the Hydra head collude.

5.1   Privacy-Preserving Audit-Commits

In the simple version, verifying the statement that a credential vc_i is issued for a DID did_i is based purely on signatures. While this gives an extremely efficient implementation, a financial service provider identified by a LEI does not always want to reveal its presence publicly. For this case, one can validate a non-interactive zero-knowledge argument or proof of knowledge (NIZK). More precisely, we need a NIZK for the following relation that turns the vLEI into an anonymous credential. The statement is given by $x = (vk_{\text{lei}}, \tau, \text{com}, C, pk_{\mathcal{R}}, \text{method})$ and the witness is $w = (vk, \text{vc}_{\text{lei}} = (\text{sub}, n, \sigma_{\text{lei}}), \sigma_{\tau}, r_1, r_2)$. The relation must assert that each of the following equations hold:

- $\text{com} = \text{Com}((\text{sub}, n); r_1)$
- $C = \text{Enc}_{pk_{\mathcal{R}}}((\text{sub}, n); r_2)$
- $\text{Verify}(vk_{\text{lei}}, (\text{sub}, n), \sigma_{\text{lei}}) = 1$
- $\text{Verify}(vk, \tau, \sigma) = 1$
- $\text{sub} = \text{did:method:id}$ with $\text{id} = H(vk)$ (where H is a public hash function).

The equations express that the party controls a valid DID of a given method by a signature on the transaction, and for which a valid credential has been issued by the vLEI issuer. Using this NIZK, the validity is determined in the expected way.[5] First, aside of the referenced locked UTxO set $\mathcal{O}_i$, a party P_i specifies, in the data field of the output of the transaction, the two party specific elements of the statement (com, C) and the proof π of the above relation. Second, a valid commit transaction must satisfy the property of the standard commit transaction regarding the validity of $\mathcal{O}_i$. Additionally, π_i must be a valid proof for the statement $x = (vk_{\text{lei}}, \tau, \text{com}_i, C_i, pk_{\mathcal{R}}, \text{method})$, composed of the two values (com_i, C_i) and the public parameters $pk_{\mathcal{R}}$, vk_{lei} (obtained via reference to state machine identified by t_{lei}). The remaining actions remain the same, in particular, collecting those commitments is now done as described in Sect. 4.1.

5.2 Consistency in Case of Full Corruption

A design goal of our audit protocol is simplicity, in particular easy deployment on top of any Hydra head implementation. A crucial assumption, backed with real-world identification, is that identified parties are disincentivized to fake the reporting due to legal enforcement. It is still worthwhile to investigate what guarantees we could still obtain if all Hydra head participants colluded.

In that setting it is not clear anymore what the "true" transaction graph looks like, because this notion is not well-defined anymore. The best we can do here is to have parties publicly commit to the transaction graph and prove it, using a SNARK type of proof that the committed statistics in the form of the ZKS is formed correctly based on the committed transaction graph. We further need a sequence of such snapshots on the mainchain for security purposes in order to avoid any sort of equivocation later. Those snapshots are further required to be valid continuations of the state of the state channel and therefore, akin to typical

---

[5] We assume that the CRS required for the NIZK is part of the parameter set of the Hydra protocol, and part of the initial agreement of participants. Likewise, we assume that the accepted DID method is publicly known, such as KERI for vLEI.

rollup systems, need a second SNARK to prove their validity. We observe that such a solution is much more involved, both in design and deployment, as well as with respect to the cost of performing consistent checkpoints.

6 Conclusion

Our work proposes the first auditable Layer 2 protocol, where a regulator can audit a wide range of policies in a scalable and privacy-preserving manner. We instantiate the protocol as an extension of Hydra state channels [10]. Our scheme is very lightweight and the storage complexity depends only on the number of supported policies and participants and not on the channels' transaction graph.

Our work poses various questions for future work. First, our instantiation assumes a set of pre-defined audit policies. Adding policies on the fly, after the channel is opened, would be particularly useful. Additionally, one could consider other policies, beyond aggregatable (cf. Sect. 4.5), that could be supported, e.g., via storing a partial graph, and which policies require access to the full graph, thus being impractical. Second, regarding privacy, there are two paths for future work. First, a thorough exploration of audit commits could enhance the scheme's guarantees, as discussed briefly in Sect. 5.1. Second, existing Layer 2 solutions offer minimal to no privacy guarantees w.r.t. participants in the protocol. An interesting direction is defining auditable privacy-preserving state channel protocols, that maintain a high level of privacy while also being efficient. Third, our scheme assumes at least one honest participant. We briefly discuss (Sect. 5.2) if auditing is possible when all participants collude, but a more thorough analysis could investigate concrete implementations with such guarantees. Finally, Hydra was recently enhanced with head merging [27], s.t. two groups of participants can join a single head. This introduces auditing challenges, e.g., if the heads support different policies, that merit further consideration.

References

1. W3c recommendation on decentralized identifiers (2022). https://www.w3.org/TR/did-core/. Accessed 15 Sep 2023
2. W3c recommendation on verifiable credentials (2022). https://www.w3.org/TR/vc-data-model/. Accessed 15 Sept 2023
3. Global legal entity identifier foundation (gleif) (2023). https://www.gleif.org/en/about/this-is-gleif. Accessed 15 Sept 2023
4. Legal identity identifier lookup service (2023). https://www.lei-lookup.com/. Accessed 15 Sept 2023
5. Bank, E.C.: Exploring anonymity in central bank digital currencies (2019). https://www.ecb.europa.eu/paym/intro/publications/pdf/ecb.mipinfocus191217.en.pdf
6. Buterin, V., Illum, J., Nadler, M., Schär, F., Soleimani, A.: Blockchain privacy and regulatory compliance: Towards a practical equilibrium. Available at SSRN (2023)
7. Cardano: Cardano (2023). https://cardano.org/. Accessed 7 Mar 2023

8. Chakravarty, M.M.T., Chapman, J., MacKenzie, K., Melkonian, O., Müller, J., Peyton Jones, M., Vinogradova, P., Wadler, P.: Native custom tokens in the extended utxo model. In: Margaria, T., Steffen, B. (eds.) Leveraging Applications of Formal Methods, Verification and Validation: Applications. pp. 89–111. Springer International Publishing, Cham (2020)

9. Chakravarty, M.M., Chapman, J., MacKenzie, K., Melkonian, O., Jones, M.P., Wadler, P.: The extended utxo model. In: 4th Workshop on Trusted Smart Contracts (2020)

10. Chakravarty, M.M.T., Coretti, S., Fitzi, M., Gaži, P., Kant, P., Kiayias, A., Russell, A.: Fast isomorphic state channels. In: Borisov, N., Diaz, C. (eds.) FC 2021. LNCS, vol. 12675, pp. 339–358. Springer, Heidelberg (2021). https://doi.org/10.1007/978-3-662-64331-0_18

11. Chatzigiannis, P., Baldimtsi, F., Chalkias, K.: SoK: auditability and accountability in distributed payment systems. In: Sako, K., Tippenhauer, N.O. (eds.) ACNS 2021. LNCS, vol. 12727, pp. 311–337. Springer, Cham (2021). https://doi.org/10.1007/978-3-030-78375-4_13

12. Chen, Yu., Ma, X., Tang, C., Au, M.H.: PGC: decentralized confidential payment system with auditability. In: Chen, L., Li, N., Liang, K., Schneider, S. (eds.) ESORICS 2020. LNCS, vol. 12308, pp. 591–610. Springer, Cham (2020). https://doi.org/10.1007/978-3-030-58951-6_29

13. Dagher, G.G., Bünz, B., Bonneau, J., Clark, J., Boneh, D.: Provisions: privacy-preserving proofs of solvency for bitcoin exchanges. In: Ray, I., Li, N., Kruegel, C. (eds.) ACM CCS 2015, pp. 720–731. ACM Press, October 2015. https://doi.org/10.1145/2810103.2813674

14. Damgård, I., Triandopoulos, N.: Supporting non-membership proofs with bilinear-map accumulators. Cryptology ePrint Archive, Report 2008/538 (2008). https://eprint.iacr.org/2008/538

15. Dziembowski, S., Eckey, L., Faust, S., Hesse, J., Hostáková, K.: Multi-party virtual state channels. In: Ishai, Y., Rijmen, V. (eds.) EUROCRYPT 2019. LNCS, vol. 11476, pp. 625–656. Springer, Cham (2019). https://doi.org/10.1007/978-3-030-17653-2_21

16. Dziembowski, S., Eckey, L., Faust, S., Malinowski, D.: PERUN: Virtual payment channels over cryptographic currencies. Cryptology ePrint Archive, Report 2017/635 (2017). https://eprint.iacr.org/2017/635

17. of England, B.: Central bank digital currency opportunities, challenges and design (2020). https://www.bankofengland.co.uk/-/media/boe/files/paper/2020/central-bank-digital-currency-opportunities-challenges-and-design.pdf

18. G7-UK2021: Public policy principles for retail central bank digital currencies (2021). https://www.mof.go.jp/english/policy/international_policy/convention/g7/g7_20211013_2.pdf

19. Garman, C., Green, M., Miers, I.: Accountable privacy for decentralized anonymous payments. In: Grossklags, J., Preneel, B. (eds.) FC 2016. LNCS, vol. 9603, pp. 81–98. Springer, Heidelberg (2017). https://doi.org/10.1007/978-3-662-54970-4_5

20. Green, M., Miers, I.: Bolt: Anonymous payment channels for decentralized currencies. Cryptology ePrint Archive, Report 2016/701 (2016). https://eprint.iacr.org/2016/701

21. Gudgeon, L., Moreno-Sanchez, P., Roos, S., McCorry, P., Gervais, A.: SoK: Off the chain transactions. Cryptology ePrint Archive, Report 2019/360 (2019). https://eprint.iacr.org/2019/360

22. Gudgeon, L., Moreno-Sanchez, P., Roos, S., McCorry, P., Gervais, A.: SoK: layer-two blockchain protocols. In: Bonneau, J., Heninger, N. (eds.) FC 2020. LNCS, vol. 12059, pp. 201–226. Springer, Cham (2020). https://doi.org/10.1007/978-3-030-51280-4_12

23. Heilman, E., Alshenibr, L., Baldimtsi, F., Scafuro, A., Goldberg, S.: Tumblebit: An untrusted bitcoin-compatible anonymous payment hub. In: Network and Distributed System Security Symposium (2017)

24. of International Settlements, B.: Central bank digital currencies: foundational principles and core features (2020). https://www.bis.org/publ/othp33.htm

25. of International Settlements, B.: Central bank digital currencies: foundational principles and core features (2020). https://www.bis.org/publ/othp33.pdf

26. Jourenko, M., Kurazumi, K., Larangeira, M., Tanaka, K.: SoK: a taxonomy for layer-2 scalability related protocols for cryptocurrencies. Cryptology ePrint Archive, Report 2019/352 (2019). https://eprint.iacr.org/2019/352

27. Jourenko, M., Larangeira, M.: State machines across isomorphic layer 2 ledgers (2023)

28. Jourenko, M., Larangeira, M., Tanaka, K.: Interhead hydra: Two heads are better than one. In: Pardalos, P., Kotsireas, I., Guo, Y., Knottenbelt, W. (eds.) Mathematical Research for Blockchain Economy, pp. 187–212. Springer, Cham (2023). https://doi.org/10.1007/978-3-031-18679-0_11

29. Kate, A., Zaverucha, G.M., Goldberg, I.: Constant-size commitments to polynomials and their applications. In: Abe, M. (ed.) ASIACRYPT 2010. LNCS, vol. 6477, pp. 177–194. Springer, Heidelberg (2010). https://doi.org/10.1007/978-3-642-17373-8_11

30. Kiayias, A., Kohlweiss, M., Sarencheh, A.: PEReDi: privacy-enhanced, regulated and distributed central bank digital currencies. In: Yin, H., Stavrou, A., Cremers, C., Shi, E. (eds.) ACM CCS 2022, pp. 1739–1752. ACM Press, November 2022. https://doi.org/10.1145/3548606.3560707

31. Kiayias, A., Litos, O.S.T.: A composable security treatment of the lightning network. Cryptology ePrint Archive, Report 2019/778 (2019). https://eprint.iacr.org/2019/778

32. Micali, S., Rabin, M.O., Kilian, J.: Zero-knowledge sets. In: 44th FOCS, pp. 80–91. IEEE Computer Society Press, October 2003. https://doi.org/10.1109/SFCS.2003.1238183

33. Nakamoto, S.: Bitcoin: A peer-to-peer electronic cash system (2008)

34. Narula, N., Vasquez, W., Virza, M.: zkLedger: privacy-preserving auditing for distributed ledgers. Cryptology ePrint Archive, Report 2018/241 (2018). https://eprint.iacr.org/2018/241

35. Poon, J., Dryja, T.: The bitcoin lightning network: Scalable off-chain instant payments (2016). See https://lightning.network/lightning-network-paper.pdf

36. Stella, P.: Balancing confidentiality and auditability in a distributed ledger environment (2020). https://www.ecb.europa.eu/paym/intro/publications/pdf/ecb.miptopical200212.en.pdf

37. Tairi, E., Moreno-Sanchez, P., Maffei, M.: A^2L: Anonymous atomic locks for scalability and interoperability in payment channel hubs. Cryptology ePrint Archive, Report 2019/589 (2019). https://eprint.iacr.org/2019/589

38. Tas, E.N., Boneh, D.: Vector commitments with efficient updates. Cryptology ePrint Archive, Paper 2023/1830 (2023). https://doi.org/10.4230/LIPICS.AFT.2023.29, https://eprint.iacr.org/2023/1830, https://eprint.iacr.org/2023/1830

39. Wüst, K., Kostiainen, K., Čapkun, V., Čapkun, S.: PRCash: fast, private and regulated transactions for digital currencies. In: Goldberg, I., Moore, T. (eds.) FC 2019. LNCS, vol. 11598, pp. 158–178. Springer, Cham (2019). https://doi.org/10.1007/978-3-030-32101-7_11

40. Wüst, K., Kostiainen, K., Delius, N., Capkun, S.: Platypus: A central bank digital currency with unlinkable transactions and privacy-preserving regulation. In: Yin, H., Stavrou, A., Cremers, C., Shi, E. (eds.) ACM CCS 2022, pp. 2947–2960. ACM Press, November 2022. https://doi.org/10.1145/3548606.3560617

41. Zahnentferner, J.: Chimeric ledgers: Translating and unifying UTXO-based and account-based cryptocurrencies. Cryptology ePrint Archive, Report 2018/262 (2018). https://eprint.iacr.org/2018/262

PARScoin: A Privacy-preserving, Auditable, and Regulation-friendly Stablecoin

Amirreza Sarencheh[1,2]([⊠]), Aggelos Kiayias[1,2], and Markulf Kohlweiss[1,2]([⊠])

[1] The University of Edinburgh, Edinburgh, UK
{amirreza.sarencheh,aggelos.kiayias,markulf.kohlweiss}@ed.ac.uk
[2] IOG, Edinburgh, UK

Abstract. Stablecoins are digital assets designed to maintain a consistent value relative to a reference point, serving as a vital component in Blockchain, and Decentralized Finance (DeFi) ecosystem. Typical implementations of stablecoins via smart contracts come with important downsides such as a questionable level of privacy, potentially high fees, and lack of scalability. We put forth a new design, PARScoin, for a Privacy-preserving, Auditable, and Regulation-friendly Stablecoin that mitigates these issues while enabling high performance both in terms of speed of settlement and for scaling to large numbers of users as our performance analysis demonstrates. Our construction is blockchain-agnostic and is analyzed in the Universal Composition (UC) framework, offering a secure and modular approach for its integration into the broader blockchain ecosystem.

Keywords: Stablecoin · Privacy · Regulation · Auditing ·
Decentralized Finance · Cryptography · Transaction Fee · Scalability ·
Universal Composition

1 Introduction

Stablecoins are digital assets engineered to uphold a consistent valuation against a designated reference point. They have surfaced as a foundational element in Decentralized Finance (DeFi) and the cryptocurrency ecosystem in general. They play a crucial role in addressing the volatility risks associated with cryptocurrencies, which can hinder their functionality as global currencies. The stablecoin market has witnessed substantial growth, with a total market capitalization of over $127 billion as of July 2023 [9].

Stablecoins can be categorized into three types based on how they maintain their peg: (i) fiat-backed (e.g., USDT [24], and USD Coin [26]), (ii) crypto-backed

---

The author order follows the Blockchain Technology Laboratory policy with junior (and corresponding) author Amirreza Sarencheh and senior authors Aggelos Kiayias and Markulf Kohlweiss.

M. Kohlweiss et al. (Eds.): CANS 2024, LNCS 14905, pp. 289–313, 2025.
https://doi.org/10.1007/978-981-97-8013-6_13

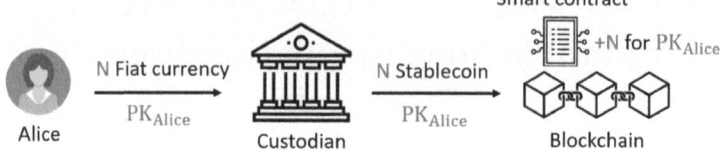

Fig. 1. Canonical Fiat-Backed Stablecoin Mechanism (e.g., USDC [26] and USDT [24]).

(e.g., MakerDAO's DAI [17]), and sUSD [23], and (iii) algorithmic stablecoins (e.g., Ampleforth AMPL [3]).

In this work, our emphasis is on fiat-backed stablecoins. It is by far the largest class in terms of market capitalization [10] and the one for which it is easiest to argue how it can maintain its peg to its underlying reference point as it is feasible (in principle) to perform an audit of the fiat currency and other assets that are held on custody vis-à-vis the amount of stablecoins issued.

We abstract fiat-backed stablecoins as follows: an *issuer* offers a way to digitize an amount of fiat currency that is deposited by a *user* to a *custodian*. Subsequently, users can exchange any amount of stablecoin they possess for services or other functions. Further, at any time a user can request to withdraw her stablecoin funds by "burning" them and creating a claim (we call this a "proof of (stablecoin) burn") that enables the user to withdraw the funds from the custodian in the form of fiat currency. An *auditor* is capable of monitoring the total amount of stablecoin issued by the issuer so that it can verify with the custodian that a sufficient amount of fiat currency (or equivalent assets) is available to cover the issuer's liabilities to all stablecoin holders. Finally, a *regulator* may impose additional regulatory constraints such as Know Your Customer (KYC), Anti-Money Laundering (AML), and Combating the Financing of Terrorism (CFT) to be performed by the issuer.

The canonical way to implement a fiat-backed stablecoin is to have the issuer create a smart contract on a blockchain such as Ethereum [11] and partner with a custodian such as a bank that can accept user deposits and maintain fiat reserves serving as the stablecoin's collateral, see Fig. 1.

Due to the transparency of the underlying blockchain, the amount of stablecoin issued (and the associated public key) are always available to the auditor who can subsequently investigate the reserves held by the custodian to ensure the matching funds exist. Users can transfer stablecoin to each other by sending transactions to the issuing contract, an operation whose integrity is provided by the underlying blockchain platform.

There are several shortcomings associated with the aforementioned approach for realizing fiat-backed stablecoins:

1. There is no **privacy** offered to participating users; indeed, users are typically assigned a pseudonym within the smart contract, and each time they perform a transaction their pseudonym can be associated with other attributes of their

identity. Due to the transparency of the underlying blockchain, this lack of privacy seems like an inherent problem.

2. There are **transaction fees** due for each stablecoin transfer between users; contrary to standard user-to-user fiat transfers, engaging with the issuing smart contract requires paying a transaction fee, typically in the underlying cryptocurrency of the platform. This has two important downsides; first, it imposes a requirement that each user should have a reserve of such cryptocurrency in addition to the stablecoin in order to be able to use their stablecoin wallet. Second, it puts users to compete for blockchain processing capacity with other applications; in case other blockchain participants (e.g., DeFi users) wish to issue large numbers of transactions they can push the system to increase its transaction fees making it hard to engage with the issuing smart contract for stablecoin operations. This also seems like an inherent problem, since it is infeasible to engage with a blockchain contract without incurring a transaction fee in a "layer 1" blockchain.

3. Finally, the **performance and scalability** of the construction is questionable as it directly relies on a L1 for settling all transactions.

Our Results. Motivated by the above issues, we propose a new design for a (fiat-based) stablecoin that, as far as our understanding goes, for the first time mitigates the shortcomings we described above together with other important properties. In detail, our construction **PARScoin** (**P**rivacy-preserving, **A**uditable, and **R**egulation-friendly **S**table**coin**), offers the following.

1. **Privacy-preserving operation**. Stablecoins are issued to users who can transfer them to other users without revealing their identities, the transaction value, or even linking these actions to any past transactions.

2. **Auditability & Regulation-friendliness**. The backing of the stablecoin can be audited without hurting the privacy of users. Furthermore, being issued stablecoin or transferring it between users can be subject to regulatory checks such as KYC, AML, and CFT that can be integrated into the system without hurting the privacy-preserving operation and in an efficient way.

3. **Blockchain independent fees**. Stablecoin transfers are executed *user-to-user* via the certification of a quorum of issuers and they do not require to be settled "on chain." This decouples stablecoin transfers from any underlying blockchain settlement mechanism and hence any fees incurred can be decided independently of other applications.

4. **Blockchain-agnosticism & Interoperability**. The system operates purely independently of any underlying blockchain. Moreover, it can interoperate with any number of them, by enabling the custodian to deploy standard (non-private) smart contract-based withdrawals (e.g. as ERC-20 tokens).

5. **UC security**. We formulate a Universal Composition (UC) functionality [8] for (fiat-based) stablecoins and realize it. This facilitates for our protocol secure composition with other systems – an important consideration in the blockchain and DeFi setting.

6. **Distributed operation.** The issuance, burning, and transfer operations of the stablecoin together with ensuring regulatory compliance are distributed among a set of independent entities in a threshold cryptographic manner.
7. **Efficiency & Scalability.** Based on our performance analysis, our design demonstrates practical real-world efficiency through the usage of suitable protocol techniques and efficient building blocks.
8. **Self-custody.** Users possess complete control and ownership of their stablecoin, marking a departure from the usual fiat-backed stablecoins where a user's stablecoin balance is documented within a smart contract, subjecting it to potential restrictions such as address blacklisting or coin destruction.

Related Works. Due to page restrictions, we present a summary of related works here; a detailed elaboration is available in the full version of the paper [21].

Each stablecoin type offers unique advantages and challenges in achieving price stability. Fiat-backed stablecoins like USDT [24], and USD Coin (USDC) [26] rely on traditional fiat currency reserves (note that in practice this includes assets that supposedly easily translate to fiat), while crypto-backed stablecoins like MakerDAO's DAI [17], and sUSD [23] use cryptocurrencies for backing and smart contracts for stability. Algorithmic stablecoins, like Ampleforth (AMPL) [3], depend on algorithms to regulate supply and demand dynamics. However, their stability remains a subject of scrutiny due to their (in)ability to absorb shocks during adverse macroeconomic conditions as exemplified by the Terra-Luna collapse [20]. All three types of stablecoins, as mentioned earlier, have privacy, transaction fee and scalability problems. Furthermore, both USDT and USDC tokens are administered by centralized issuers (stablecoins within the last two classifications offer the advantage of decentralization). Additionally, the regulation-friendliness of all these stablecoins remains unclear.

Zerocash [5], Monero [19], Quisquis [13], Zether [6], Platypus [27], and PEReDi [15] are cryptographic schemes for anonymous payments. In those schemes a sender generates a Zero-Knowledge Proof (ZKP) to demonstrate the well-formedness of transaction information. The transaction conceals the transferred value within a commitment or encryption. The sender in their ZKP provides a proof of knowledge of secret values, including the used randomness in commitments/encryptions. Additionally, the sender proves they possess adequate funds for the transaction (e.g., ensuring the balance remains non-negative posttransaction) or the sum of input coins equals sum of output coins (no money is generated/destructed) and that the value sent is positive and within a defined range.

Platypus [27], and PEReDi [15] offer privacy-preserving operations combined with various levels of regulation-friendliness. While we share some architectural similarities with PEReDi which is also distributed there are important differences: In Platypus and PEReDi, both the sender and receiver must interact to complete transactions, meaning that offline receivers cannot access funds. This is sharply different from PARScoin, which supports non-interactive payments.

In PEReDi, both the sender and receiver must actively participate in completing transactions, thereby preventing offline receivers from accessing funds. This contrasts with PARScoin, which facilitates payments where the receiver is offline. The transition to such "non-interactive" transactions presents several technical challenges which we describe below.

In PEReDi, account information is concealed, and only the account holder possesses the necessary witness to submit a Zero-Knowledge Proof (ZKP) for advancing the account state in a privacy-preserving manner. This implies that the sender cannot advance the receiver's account state if the receiver is not available during payment. Consequently, the system mandates the receiver's continuous online presence to receive funds. Our work overcomes this challenge. In our approach, the sender advances their account state, and the sender's ZKP leaves a cryptographic element as a footprint on the system's global state maintained by distributed issuers. This allows the offline receiver to later claim the funds once they come online with the help of issuers by proving certain conditions.

The mechanism that solves this problem must be carefully designed to guarantee the funds transfer without requiring maintaining a complete ledger. Additionally, the funds should be claimable only once by the associated receiver to prevent malicious receivers from executing replay attacks. This requires implementing checks within the distributed protocol to efficiently detect and thwart any attempts at reusing transaction elements fraudulently.

Moreover, the construction must ensure the integrity of the transaction, guaranteeing that no additional money is generated and that no funds are destroyed. It must also be designed to safeguard privacy. Specifically, it must obscure the receiver's identity, the transaction value, and its creator's identity (which is the sender). The sender must also efficiently prove the well-formedness of the cryptographic object in relation to their own account state transition. This requirement ensures that system validators (issuers) can verify that the transaction is legitimate-namely, that the value has been appropriately deducted from the sender's account and correspondingly reflected in the cryptographic element.

Whenever the receiver comes online, they must be able to identify the objects that belong to them and subsequently submit an efficient ZKP demonstrating that each cryptographic object belongs to them. This proof must not reveal any information about their identity, but merely confirm their ownership. This ownership confirmation is necessary to transfer the funds embedded within the cryptographic object to the receiver's account.

Furthermore, we should meet the privacy requirements associated with making payments non-interactive (as described above) by relying solely on sigma-protocols for both sender and receiver ZKPs. This makes our approach suitable for real-world applications. We highlight that in privacy-preserving schemes, general-purpose ZKPs can be trivially used to conceal sensitive information. However, these proofs are inefficient in terms of proof generation time (for discrete logarithm-based relations) compared to sigma-protocols. Our construction is based on sigma protocols.

Regarding auditability, the auditability functionality of our work is fundamentally different from PEReDi's. PEReDi's auditability pertains to privacy revocation and tracing users. However, in our work, auditability, as formally defined via our ideal functionality, ensures that the stablecoin in circulation is backed by sufficient off-chain funds, which is important for price stability. This is not relevant to the setting of [15] where the central bank is fully trusted in terms of the money supply and is not accountable to anyone in terms of its reserves.

Specifically, our stablecoin issuance and stablecoin burn protocols ensure that the amount of stablecoin in circulation is accurately adjusted in a distributed and privacy-preserving manner whenever a new stablecoin is issued or burned. This guarantees that the system always maintains a correct and accountable state.

Moreover, our approach addresses the non-trivial challenge of integrating auditability within a privacy-preserving framework. Our protocol ensures that the issuance and burning of stablecoins occur without revealing the amount of the coin or the identity of the user involved. Additionally, stablecoin burning facilitates interoperability by allowing users to exchange stablecoins for fiat currency or digital assets across different blockchains, ensuring seamless interaction with diverse blockchain networks. To sum it up, privacy-preserving stablecoin issuance and burning, ensuring the stablecoin in circulation is correctly and efficiently updated in both these schemes, and facilitating interoperability is another novelty of our approach compared to [15].

Aztec [1] is a layer two zk-Rollup on Ethereum that uses succinct arguments and ZKP to offers scalability and privacy for smart contracts. While a step in the right direction with respect to our problem, implementing a stablecoin via an Aztec wrapping of ERC-20 (or similar contract) comes with important downsides compared to our approach. First, Aztec necessitates resolution in L1, incurring time-related expenditures (and fees for submission to L1). Second, Aztec uses a generalized ZK programming language, Noir, that employs zk-SNARKs, and this proof generation can become too costly for stablecoin transfers.

2   Desiderata and Formal Modeling

2.1   Stablecoin Entities

1. The Custodian: The custodian plays a critical role in maintaining the stablecoin's value by managing and safeguarding assets like USD and EUR, and controlling the issuance and redemption of stablecoins based on collateral deposits and burns.
2. Issuers: Issuers, who are authorized and independent entities, manage user onboarding, stablecoin transactions, and regulatory compliance, allowing the

custodian and regulator minimal involvement except in fiat currency transactions, and are accountable for maintaining system integrity[1].

3. The Auditor: The auditor regularly evaluates the custodian to ensure that the reserve assets are sufficient and well-managed, including the enforcement of strong security measures to protect against theft, cyberattacks, and other risks.
4. The Regulator: The task of validating transactions for regulatory compliance is assigned to a consortium of issuers to reduce the risk of a single point of failure, allowing the regulatory body to operate minimally or remotely.
5. Users: Participants can assume roles as either the sender or the recipient of stablecoins. They can encompass both individuals and organizations.

Security and Privacy Desiderata. In terms of privacy, we aim to protect privacy by hiding *all transaction metadata* in user-to-user transactions even against an adversary who controls *all entities* in the system who are not counterparties in a transaction. Operations such as issuing stablecoin and burning stablecoin are visible to the auditor (but not to other parties) so it is possible to keep track of the amount of stablecoin circulating in the system (which is necessary for the stability of the price). Finally, in terms of the integrity of transactions, we assume that the adversary controls a number of issuer entities that is below a given a threshold (which is a system parameter).

2.2   Stablecoin Requirements

In this section, we informally describe the security requirements of stablecoin systems.

1. **Auditing:** Auditing custodians is crucial for confirming fiat currency backing, increasing transparency, and establishing trust among users, investors, and regulators, thus preventing risks like insolvency and ensuring stablecoin stability through regular, independent reviews. [4,16].
2. **Regulatory Compliance:** The term includes facets like KYC, which verifies user identities to prevent fraud and enhance transparency and credibility in digital currencies, and AML/CFT measures, which are essential for preventing money laundering and terrorist financing, thus maintaining regulatory compliance and strengthening stablecoin integrity [18,25].
3. **Full Privacy:** This property encompasses four aspects [12,15]. (i) *Account Privacy:* Protects the confidentiality of user accounts, preventing exposure of financial balances and other sensitive data within user accounts to network participants. (ii) *Identity Privacy:* Maintains the anonymity of senders and receivers in transactions, and makes tracing their transaction participation impossible. (iii) *Transaction Privacy:* Ensures the amount transferred

---

[1] Our focus in this work is on fiat-backed stablecoins. We are already in a scenario where an off-chain, possibly distributed, entity is trusted for stablecoin issuance. Given this, we can rely on a group of issuers for off-chain fast settlement in a privacy-preserving manner.

remains hidden. (iv) *Unlinkability:* Stops connections between transactions and real-world identities, and prevents tracing the source of funds in subsequent transactions.

4. **Avoiding Single Point of Trust/Failure:** In Decentralized Finance (DeFi) and blockchain technology, designing stablecoin systems without a single point of trust or failure is critical. This vulnerability could compromise decentralization, security, and stability. Distributing trust and responsibility across a network enhances system robustness and resilience, reducing risks from attacks and failures.

5. **Blockchain Agnosticism:** A stablecoin system that is blockchain agnostic has the advantage of broader adoption and enhanced sustainability within the diverse blockchain landscape. This approach allows the system to adapt to new technologies without being tied to the developments of any single blockchain platform, reducing risks and ensuring flexibility.

6. **Interoperability:** Blockchain agnosticism facilitates interoperability, allowing different blockchain networks to work together seamlessly. This interoperability is crucial as it promotes inclusivity and liquidity across various blockchain ecosystems.

7. **Integrity:** This requirement ensures that user states cannot be modified by unauthorized entities. It includes mechanisms to prevent double-spending, guaranteeing that each transaction updates the user's account balance accurately.

2.3   Notations

In this paper, we employ diverse notations, which are summarized in Table 1 and Table 2.

Table 1. Table of Notations

Symbol	Description	Symbol	Description
U, v	User, Transacting value	$\mathcal{D}_i$	Local database of the i-th issuer
I, I_i	Issuer, The i-th issuer	$\mathcal{I}$, acc	Set of all issuers, User's account
N	Total number of issuers	U_s, U_r	Sender, Receiver
CUS, AUD	Custodian, Auditor	(pk_A, sk_A)	Auditor's key pair
$\tilde{\chi}$	ElGamal Encryption	$(pk, sk), B$	User's key pair, its Balance
x	User's transaction counter	com	Pedersen commitment
$\mathcal{A}, \mathcal{Z}$	Adversary, Environment	RB.Sig	Randomizable-Blind Signature
TRB.Sig, Γ	Threshold Randomizable-Blind Signature, its threshold	π	Non-Interactive Zero Knowledge proof
sn, tag	Serial number, Tag (for double-spending prevention)	x, w	Statement, Witness (of proof)

2.4 Formal Model

We define a privacy-preserving, auditable, and regulation-friendly stablecoin system in the form of an ideal functionality $\mathcal{F}_{\mathsf{PARS}}$, which formally captures the relevant security properties. $\mathcal{F}_{\mathsf{PARS}}$ is parameterized by the set of identifiers of issuers $\mathcal{I}$, the custodian CUS, and the auditor AUD. Also it is parameterized by a threshold Γ. In the Universal Composition setting, we allow the adversary $\mathcal{A}$ to drive communication and potentially block messages.

1. **Initialization.** Session identifiers are of the form $\mathtt{sid} = (\{\mathcal{I}, \mathsf{CUS}, \mathsf{AUD}\}, \mathtt{sid}')$. Initially, $\mathsf{init} \leftarrow 0$. At the end of *Initialization* init is set to 1.[2]
2. **User Registration.** Each user U must have their account approved by the system. If issuers have already registered U, it cannot be registered again. Initially, $\mathbb{R}(\mathsf{U}) = \perp$, and once U is registered, $\mathbb{R}(\mathsf{U})$ is set to 0 denoting initial user balance $\mathsf{B} = 0$.
3. **Stablecoin Issuance.** CUS possesses the authority to confirm the identity U and v by providing (U, v) to $\mathcal{F}_{\mathsf{PARS}}$.[3] Initially, $\mathcal{F}_{\mathsf{PARS}}$ verifies whether the recipient of stablecoin U, is a registered user. Following each stablecoin issuance,

Table 2. Table of Notations

Symbol	Description	Symbol	Description
$\sigma_i^{\mathsf{blind}}$	Blind signature of the i-th issuer	σ_i	Unblinded signature of the i-th issuer
$\sigma_{\mathcal{I}}$	Aggregated signature of issuers	$\sigma_{\mathcal{I}}^{\mathsf{RND}}$	Randomized aggregated signature of issuers
$\sigma_{\mathsf{CUS}}^{\mathsf{blind}}$	Blind signature of the custodian	σ_{CUS}	Unblinded signature of the custodian
$\sigma_{\mathsf{CUS}}^{\mathsf{RND}}$	Randomized signature of the custodian	TV	Total value of stablecoin in circulation
$\mathcal{F}_{\mathsf{KeyReg}}$	Key registration functionality	$\mathcal{F}_{\mathsf{RO}}$	Random oracle functionality
$\mathcal{F}_{\mathsf{Ch}}^{\mathsf{SSA}}$	Secure and sender anonymous channel	$\mathcal{F}_{\mathsf{Ch}}^{\mathsf{SRA}}$	Secure and receiver anonymous channel
$\mathcal{F}_{\mathsf{Ch}}^{\mathsf{ISAS}}$	Insecure, sender anonymous to adversary, and sender known to recipient channel	$\mathcal{F}_{\mathsf{Ch}}^{\mathsf{IRAS}}$	Insecure, receiver anonymous to adversary, and sender known to recipient channel
$\mathcal{F}_{\mathsf{NIZK}}$	Non-Interactive Zero Knowledge functionality	$\mathcal{F}_{\mathsf{B}}^{\mathsf{SA}}$	Sender anonymous broadcast functionality
$\mathcal{F}_{\mathsf{PARS}}$	PARScoin functionality	$\mathcal{F}_{\mathsf{B}}^{\mathsf{S}}$	Standard broadcast functionality

---

[2] Afterward at the beginning of all parts of the functionality (namely *User Registration*, *Stablecoin Issuance*, *Stablecoin Transfer*, *Stablecoin Claim* , *Stablecoin Burn*, *Proof of Burn*, and *Reserve Audit*) it is checked whether init has been set to 1. If it has not been set to 1, $\mathcal{F}_{\mathsf{PARS}}$ ignores the received message. For the sake of simplicity, we have omitted the inclusion of these particulars within the functionality description.

[3] This signifies that CUS has conducted its own verifications to ensure that U has indeed made a deposit of fiat currency equivalent to v into the account maintained by CUS.

the state of the recipient's account is updated. $\mathcal{A}$ has the potential to obstruct the progression. U and v are concealed from $\mathcal{A}$. A successful issuance operation results in an increase in the recipient's balance by v: $\mathbb{R}(\mathsf{U}) \leftarrow (\mathsf{B} + v)$, and an increase in the total value of stablecoin in circulation $\mathsf{TV} \leftarrow (\mathsf{TV} + v)$ (which is not revealed to $\mathcal{A}$). $\mathcal{A}$ is also required to submit a *unique* identifier $\tilde{\chi}$ which is assigned to each updated TV (by recording $(\tilde{\chi}, \mathsf{TV})$). $\tilde{\chi}$ is output to $\mathcal{I}$.[4]

Public-delayed output means $\mathcal{F}_{\mathsf{PARS}}$ lets $\mathcal{A}$ know the output and decide its delivery.

4. **Stablecoin Transfer.** The sender $\mathsf{U_s}$ submits $(\mathsf{U_r}, v)$ to $\mathcal{F}_{\mathsf{PARS}}$. After some verification (e.g., $\mathsf{U_s}$ has sufficient funds) $\mathcal{F}_{\mathsf{PARS}}$ informs $\mathcal{A}$. $\mathcal{A}$ provides a *unique* identifier ϕ, which serves as a means to document an entry. This entry takes the shape of $(\phi, \mathsf{U_s}, \mathsf{U_r}, v, b)$, signifying that $\mathsf{U_s}$ has transmitted a quantity of v stablecoins to $\mathsf{U_r}$. The inclusion of $b = 0$ signifies that this payment has not yet been claimed by $\mathsf{U_r}$ (payments are non-interactive) thereby averting double-spending.

5. **Stablecoin Claim.** Upon the receipt of ϕ from $\mathsf{U_r}$, $\mathcal{F}_{\mathsf{PARS}}$ checks whether the entry $(\phi, \mathsf{U_s}, \mathsf{U_r}, v, b)$ has been previously recorded or not. In the event that it is indeed registered, the $\mathcal{F}_{\mathsf{PARS}}$ proceeds to verify whether it has already been claimed by $\mathsf{U_r}$ (via checking b). Assuming all checks pass successfully, upon receiving ϕ from honest issuers, $\mathcal{F}_{\mathsf{PARS}}$ proceeds to augment the balance of $\mathsf{U_r}$. The condition $|f_h| < \Gamma$ signifies that fewer than Γ honest issuers are actively engaged in the protocol, thus the protocol remains incomplete (the function f_h gets as input a set of issuer identifiers and outputs the same set where malicious issuer identifiers are removed). The transmission of ϕ by issuers to $\mathcal{F}_{\mathsf{PARS}}$ signifies that they have conducted their own verifications pertaining to the identifier ϕ. This method represents a means to conceptualize the process by which for instance, issuers ascertain the presence/absence of the value ϕ within the public blockchain ledger by conducting checks.

6. **Stablecoin Burn.** The user U submits a value v to $\mathcal{F}_{\mathsf{PARS}}$ along with a label ℓ. The purpose of this label, ℓ, is to specify the type of asset against which U intends to initiate the burning process for withdrawal. U has the option to burn their stablecoins in exchange for fiat currency withdrawal or any other digital asset (that can be confirmed by CUS). The latter option allows the user to obtain digital assets on any particular blockchain, the selection of which is determined exclusively by the label ℓ. This operational approach facilitates interoperability within our model. After burning the stablecoin, the total value in circulation TV is updated, and, similar to the *Stablecoin Issuance* protocol, an $\tilde{\chi}$ value is assigned to the newly updated amount. It's important to note that the amount that has been burned has not yet been withdrawn from the custodian. However, our focus here is not on micromanaging this procedure on the custodian side, as it is beyond our formal modeling scope. The burning process is a private operation to ensure that a potentially malicious

---

[4] In order to make this accessible to $\mathcal{Z}$. Note that more precisely, $\mathcal{F}_{\mathsf{PARS}}$ lets $\mathcal{A}$ decide: message delivery and the order of issuers receiving the message.

Functionality: $\mathcal{F}_{\mathsf{PARS}}$ – Part I

1 Initialization. (a) Upon input $(\mathtt{Int}, \mathtt{sid})$ from party $P \in \{\mathcal{I}, \mathsf{CUS}, \mathsf{AUD}\}$: (i) Ignore if $\mathtt{sid} \neq (\{\mathcal{I}, \mathsf{CUS}, \mathsf{AUD}\}, \mathtt{sid}')$. (ii) Else, output $(\mathtt{Int.End}, \mathtt{sid}, P)$ to $\mathcal{A}$. (iii) Once all parties have been initialized, set $\mathsf{init} \leftarrow 1$.

2 User Registration. (a) Upon receiving a message $(\mathtt{Rgs}, \mathtt{sid})$ from some party U: (i) If $\mathbb{R}(\mathsf{U}) = \bot$, output $(\mathtt{Rgs}, \mathtt{sid}, \mathsf{U})$ to $\mathcal{A}$. (ii) Else, ignore. (b) Upon receiving $(\mathtt{Rgs.Ok}, \mathtt{sid}, \mathsf{U})$ from $\mathcal{A}$: (i) Ignore if $\mathbb{R}(\mathsf{U}) \neq \bot$. (ii) Else, set $\mathbb{R}(\mathsf{U}) \leftarrow 0$.

3 Stablecoin Issuance. (a) Upon receiving a message $(\mathtt{Iss}, \mathtt{sid}, \mathsf{U}, v)$ from CUS: (i) Ignore if $\mathbb{R}(\mathsf{U}) = \bot$. (ii) Else, generate a new $\mathsf{SI.idn}$ and set $\mathbb{O}(\mathsf{SI.idn}) \leftarrow (\mathsf{U}, v)$. (iii) If U is honest (resp. malicious) output $(\mathtt{Iss}, \mathtt{sid}, \mathsf{SI.idn})$ (resp. $(\mathtt{Iss}, \mathtt{sid}, \mathsf{SI.idn}, (\mathsf{U}, v))$) to $\mathcal{A}$. (b) Upon receiving $(\mathtt{Iss.Ok}, \mathtt{sid}, \mathsf{SI.idn}, \tilde{\chi})$ from $\mathcal{A}$: (i) Ignore if $\mathbb{O}(\mathsf{SI.idn}) = \bot$ or there exists $(\tilde{\chi}, \cdot)$. (ii) Else, retrieve $\mathbb{O}(\mathsf{SI.idn}) = (\mathsf{U}, v)$, and $\mathbb{R}(\mathsf{U}) = \mathsf{B}$. (iii) Set $\mathbb{R}(\mathsf{U}) \leftarrow (\mathsf{B} + v)$, $\mathbb{O}(\mathsf{SI.idn}) \leftarrow \bot$, and $\mathsf{TV} \leftarrow (\mathsf{TV} + v)$. (iv) Record $(\tilde{\chi}, \mathsf{TV})$. (v) Output $(\mathtt{Iss.End}, \mathtt{sid}, \tilde{\chi})$ to $\mathcal{I}$ via public-delayed output.

4 Stablecoin Transfer. (a) Upon receiving a message $(\mathtt{Gen.ST}, \mathtt{sid}, \mathsf{U}_r, v)$ from some party U_s: (i) Ignore if $\mathbb{R}(\mathsf{U}_s) = \bot$ or $v < 0$. (ii) Else, generate a new $\mathsf{ST.idn}$ and set $\mathbb{V}(\mathsf{ST.idn}) \leftarrow (\mathsf{U}_s, \mathsf{U}_r, v)$. (iii) Output $(\mathtt{Gen.ST}, \mathtt{sid}, \mathsf{ST.idn})$ to $\mathcal{A}$. (b) Upon receiving $(\mathtt{Gen.ST.Ok}, \mathtt{sid}, \mathsf{ST.idn}, \phi)$ from $\mathcal{A}$: (i) Ignore if $\mathbb{V}(\mathsf{ST.idn}) = \bot$ or there exists $(\phi, \cdot, \cdot, \cdot, \cdot)$. (ii) Else, retrieve $\mathbb{V}(\mathsf{ST.idn}) = (\mathsf{U}_s, \mathsf{U}_r, v)$, and $\mathbb{R}(\mathsf{U}_s) = \mathsf{B}_s$. (iii) Ignore if $\mathsf{B}_s < v$. (iv) Else, set $\mathbb{R}(\mathsf{U}_s) \leftarrow (\mathsf{B}_s - v)$, and $\mathbb{V}(\mathsf{ST.idn}) \leftarrow \bot$ (v) Record $(\phi, \mathsf{U}_s, \mathsf{U}_r, v, 0)$. (vi) Output $(\mathtt{Gen.ST.End}, \mathtt{sid}, \mathsf{U}_r, v, \phi)$ to U_s via private-delayed output.

5 Stablecoin Claim. (a) Upon receiving a message $(\mathtt{Clm.ST}, \mathtt{sid}, \phi)$ from some party U_r: (i) Ignore if $\mathbb{R}(\mathsf{U}_r) = \bot$ or there does not exist $(\phi, \cdot, \mathsf{U}_r, \cdot, 0)$. (ii) Else, retrieve $\mathbb{R}(\mathsf{U}_r) = \mathsf{B}_r$. (iii) Generate a new $\mathsf{SC.idn}$ and set $\mathbb{C}(\mathsf{SC.idn}) \leftarrow (\phi, \mathsf{U}_s, \mathsf{U}_r, v, b)$. (iv) Output $(\mathtt{Clm.ST}, \mathtt{sid}, \mathsf{SC.idn})$ to $\mathcal{A}$. (b) Upon receiving $(\mathtt{Clm.ST.Ok}, \mathtt{sid}, \mathsf{SC.idn})$ from $\mathcal{A}$: (i) Ignore if $\mathbb{C}(\mathsf{SC.idn}) = \bot$. (ii) Else, retrieve $\mathbb{C}(\mathsf{SC.idn}) = (\phi, \mathsf{U}_s, \mathsf{U}_r, v, b)$, and ignore if $b = 1$. (iii) Else, retrieve $\mathbb{R}(\mathsf{U}_r) = \mathsf{B}_r$. (c) Upon receiving $(\mathtt{Clm.ST.Issuer.Ok}, \mathtt{sid}, \phi)$ from $f_h(\{\mathsf{I}_1, \ldots, \mathsf{I}_N\})$: (i) Ignore if $|f_h(\{\mathsf{I}_1, \ldots, \mathsf{I}_N\})| < \Gamma$. (ii) Else, output $(\mathtt{Clm.ST.Issuer.Ok}, \mathtt{sid}, \mathsf{SC.idn})$ to $\mathcal{A}$. (d) Upon receiving $(\mathtt{Clm.ST.Issuer.Ok}, \mathtt{sid}, \mathsf{SC.idn})$ from $\mathcal{A}$: (i) Retrieve $\mathbb{C}(\mathsf{SC.idn}) = (\phi, \mathsf{U}_s, \mathsf{U}_r, v, b)$, and ignore if $b = 1$. (ii) Else, set $\mathbb{R}(\mathsf{U}_r) \leftarrow (\mathsf{B}_r + v)$, and $b \leftarrow 1$ in $(\phi, \mathsf{U}_s, \mathsf{U}_r, v, b)$.

6 Stablecoin Burn. (a) Upon receiving a message $(\mathtt{Brn}, \mathtt{sid}, v, \ell)$ from some party U: (i) Ignore if $\mathbb{R}(\mathsf{U}) = \bot$ or $v < 0$. (ii) Else, generate a new $\mathsf{SB.idn}$ and set $\mathbb{B}(\mathsf{SB.idn}) \leftarrow (\mathsf{U}, v, \ell, \mathsf{B})$. (iii) Output $(\mathtt{Brn}, \mathtt{sid}, \ell, \mathsf{SB.idn})$ to $\mathcal{A}$. (b) Upon receiving $(\mathtt{Brn.Ok}, \mathtt{sid}, \mathsf{SB.idn}, \eta, \tilde{\chi})$ from $\mathcal{A}$: (i) Ignore if $\mathbb{B}(\mathsf{SB.idn}) = \bot$ or there exists $(\eta, \cdot, \cdot, \cdot, \cdot)$ or there exists $(\tilde{\chi}, \cdot)$. (ii) Else, retrieve $\mathbb{B}(\mathsf{SB.idn}) = (\mathsf{U}, v, \ell, \mathsf{B})$, and $\mathbb{R}(\mathsf{U}) = \mathsf{B}$. (iii) Ignore if $\mathsf{B} < v$. (iv) Else, set $\mathbb{R}(\mathsf{U}) \leftarrow (\mathsf{B} - v)$, $\mathsf{TV} \leftarrow (\mathsf{TV} - v)$, and $\mathbb{B}(\mathsf{SB.idn}) \leftarrow \bot$. (v) Record $(\eta, \mathsf{U}, v, \ell, q)$ where $q = 0$, and $(\tilde{\chi}, \mathsf{TV})$. (vi) Output $(\mathtt{Brn.End}, \mathtt{sid}, \eta, \ell, \tilde{\chi})$ to $\mathcal{I}$ via public-delayed outputs.

Functionality: $\mathcal{F}_{\mathsf{PARS}}$ – Part II

---

7 **Proof of Burn.** (a) Upon receiving a message $(\mathsf{PoB}, \mathsf{sid}, \eta, \ell)$ from some user U: (i) Ignore if $\mathbb{R}(\mathsf{U}) = \perp$ or there does not exist $(\eta, \mathsf{U}, \cdot, \ell, \cdot)$ or there exists $(\eta, \mathsf{U}, \cdot, \ell, 1)$. (ii) Else, retrieve $(\eta, \mathsf{U}, v, \ell, 0)$, generate a new PB.idn and set $\mathbb{V}(\mathsf{PB.idn}) \leftarrow (\eta, \mathsf{U}, v, \ell, 0)$. (iii) Output $(\mathsf{PoB}, \mathsf{sid}, \ell, \mathsf{PB.idn})$ to $\mathcal{A}$. (b) Upon receiving $(\mathsf{PoB.Ok}, \mathsf{sid}, \mathsf{PB.idn})$ from $\mathcal{A}$: (i) Ignore if $\mathbb{V}(\mathsf{PB.idn}) = \perp$. (ii) Else, retrieve $\mathbb{V}(\mathsf{PB.idn}) = (\eta, \mathsf{U}, v, \ell, q)$. (c) Upon receiving $(\mathsf{PoB.CUS}, \mathsf{sid}, \eta, \ell)$ from CUS: (i) Output $(\mathsf{PoB.CUS.Ok}, \mathsf{sid}, \mathsf{PB.idn})$ to $\mathcal{A}$. (d) Upon receiving $(\mathsf{PoB.CUS.Ok}, \mathsf{sid}, \mathsf{PB.idn})$ from $\mathcal{A}$: (i) Retrieve $\mathbb{V}(\mathsf{PB.idn}) = (\eta, \mathsf{U}, v, \ell, q)$ and ignore if $q = 1$. (ii) Else, output $(\mathsf{PoB.End}, \mathsf{sid}, \eta, \mathsf{U}, v, \ell)$ to CUS via private-delayed output, and set $q \leftarrow 1$ in $(\eta, \mathsf{U}, v, \ell, q)$.

8 **Reserve Audit.** (a) Upon receiving a message $(\mathsf{Audit}, \mathsf{sid}, \tilde{\chi}, \mathsf{RV})$ from AUD: (i) Ignore if there does not exist $(\tilde{\chi}, \cdot)$. (ii) Else, retrieve $(\tilde{\chi}, \mathsf{TV})$, and if $\mathsf{RV} \geq \mathsf{TV}$, set $b \leftarrow 1$. (iii) Else, set $b \leftarrow 0$. (iv) Output $(\mathsf{Audit.End}, \mathsf{sid}, b)$ to AUD via public delayed output.

---

custodian does not have visibility into the burned value. Furthermore, users have the option to immediately withdraw from the custodian upon burning. $\mathcal{A}$ provides η that serves as a proof of burn. It is crucial to emphasize that $\mathcal{F}_{\mathsf{PARS}}$ ensures the freshness of η before proceeding further. $\mathcal{F}_{\mathsf{PARS}}$ maintains a record of $(\eta, \mathsf{U}, v, \ell, q)$, which demonstrates that U has executed the burning of stablecoins amounting to v in association with a particular label, ℓ, while utilizing q for the prevention of double-spending.

7. **Proof of Burn.** U is required to provide evidence to CUS, indicating that they have successfully conducted a burn operation amounting to v for a specific label, ℓ. Upon receipt of CUS's instruction in the form of $(\mathsf{PoB.CUS}, \mathsf{sid}, \eta, \ell)$, $\mathcal{F}_{\mathsf{PARS}}$ proceeds to inform CUS about the user's identity U and the burned value, v, if U has already submitted a message to $\mathcal{F}_{\mathsf{PARS}}$ that confirms both η and ℓ.

8. **Reserve Audit.** As explained above each unique $\tilde{\chi}$ value has been recorded, along with the corresponding total stablecoin supply TV at the time of $\tilde{\chi}$ submission. AUD supplies both $\tilde{\chi}$ and RV to $\mathcal{F}_{\mathsf{PARS}}$ where RV is the total value of reserves held in custody. Consequently, $\mathcal{F}_{\mathsf{PARS}}$ retrieves the corresponding TV value associated with the provided $\tilde{\chi}$ and verifies whether the condition $\mathsf{RV} \geq \mathsf{TV}$ is satisfied. Here, RV represents the reserves held by CUS, provided by $\mathcal{Z}$.[5]

3   Our Construction

Our construction Π_{PARS} employs various cryptographic primitives, including ElGamal encryption, threshold randomizable-blind signature TRB.Sig, and Ped-

---

[5] In a real-world implementation, it is imperative for AUD to diligently ensure the validity of RV through their due diligence efforts.

ersen commitment (see full version of the paper [21] for formal definitions and associated security properties). Additionally, it uses the following ideal sub-functionalities: $\mathcal{F}_{\mathsf{KeyReg}}, \mathcal{F}_{\mathsf{RO}}, \mathcal{F}_{\mathsf{Ch}}, \mathcal{F}_{\mathsf{B}}$, and $\mathcal{F}_{\mathsf{NIZK}}$ (see Table.2 for their full names and full version of the paper [21] for their formal definitions). In the following, verifiers, maintainers, and issuers are interchangeably used.

3.1   High-Level Technical Summary

In Π_{PARS}, inspired by PEReDi [15], users enjoy self-sovereignty over their accounts, with the account state being controlled by the user's secret key. User accounts are of the form: $\mathsf{acc} = (\mathsf{B}, \mathsf{sk}, \mathsf{sk}^x, \mathsf{sk}') \in \mathbb{Z}_p^4$ wherein the user balance B and transaction counter x are updated in each transaction. The selection of sk^x is motivated by the necessity of incorporating a transaction counter x for preventing double-spending. This counter assures system's verifiers that users are not utilizing their previous account. However, employing just x is insufficient, as we aim to hide this value[6] while demonstrating, through (efficient, Sigma protocol-based) Non-Interactive Zero Knowledge (NIZK) proof π, that in the new account, x has been precisely incremented by 1. Users prove that the third element in their account (sk^x) is accurately updated (sk^{x+1}) without revealing sk and x. Simultaneously, the user discloses a deterministically defined double-spending prevention tag, a function of sk^x. Double-spending is prevented by forcing users to disclose $\mathsf{tag} = g^{(\mathsf{sk}^{x+1})}$ associated with the new account. The disclosed tags are retained by issuers and ensure that only the updated account can be used in the future. This tag aids verifiers in recognizing a valid account update as for each account state update the user has to increment x by 1 (given the current state of the account tag is uniquely defined).

The balance B ($\in \mathsf{acc}$) of the user is updated by themselves (so it is privacy-preserving). As an example, once U_r receives value v, she updates her account as follows: $\mathsf{acc}_r^{\mathsf{old}} = (\mathsf{B}_r^{\mathsf{old}}, \mathsf{sk}_r, \mathsf{sk}_r^x, \mathsf{sk}_r') \dashrightarrow \mathsf{acc}_r^{\mathsf{new}} = (\mathsf{B}_r^{\mathsf{old}} + v, \mathsf{sk}_r, \mathsf{sk}_r^{x+1}, \mathsf{sk}_r')$. Each transaction updates the account state. The user provides a NIZK proof π ensuring the integrity of account update by themselves, and well-formedness of tag.

Π_{PARS} achieves four aspects of privacy outlined in Sect. 2.2 for all transactions between an honest sender and honest receiver. This entails users maintaining the confidentiality of their account information vis-à-vis all network participants (including issuers who are verifying transactions), while efficiently proving via NIZK π, the accuracy of account updates. Through π, users prove the possession of a validly signed account by the issuers $\sigma_{\mathbb{I}}$ (which is a threshold signature of issuers on $\mathsf{acc}^{\mathsf{old}}$), affirming that the proposed account update $\mathsf{acc}^{\mathsf{new}}$ is based on their previously approved account $\mathsf{acc}^{\mathsf{old}}$ while keeping both $\mathsf{acc}^{\mathsf{old}}$, and $\mathsf{acc}^{\mathsf{new}}$ hidden by blinding them. Issuers verify π, which proves that the new blinded account $\mathsf{acc}^{\mathsf{new,blind}}$ is consistent with the signature of issuers on the old blinded

---

[6] As x reveals the number of times the user has been a counterparty in a transaction either as a sender or receiver.

account $\text{acc}^{\text{old,blind}}$. If π is verified, issuers sign $\text{acc}^{\text{new,blind}}$ and record the double-spending tag tag, advancing the user's account state by one step so that the user is ready for the next transaction. Additionally, to achieve efficient unlinkability[7] the user employs signature randomization $\sigma_{\text{I}}^{\text{RND}}$. In addition to transactions among users, Π_{PARS} offers privacy in the *Stablecoin Issuance*, and *Stablecoin Burn* protocols, thereby preventing any malicious issuer from learning the identity of the user or the quantity of stablecoin being issued/burned[8].

We emphasize that the system's public parameters are integrated into NIZK statements. For simplicity, we have not explicitly addressed these parameters in statements.

3.2 Our PARScoin Protocol

We provide a detailed explanation of our construction in the full version of the paper [21].

In the subsequent protocols, whenever there is a need for user-issuer communication, U engages in such interactions by leveraging the threshold randomizable-blind signature protocol (which is the modification of Coconut [22], see full version of the paper [21] for more details). In order to enhance simplicity within the UC framework, we let $\mathcal{Z}$ provide instructions to entities carrying relevant values. Consequently, we have refrained from addressing a publicly accessible blockchain ledger in our formal modelling. When an environment $\mathcal{Z}$ sends a message to an honest party, if that party is already in a state transition, they will ignore the message.

Initialization. The following public keys are registered calling $\mathcal{F}_{\text{KeyReg}}$.

1. **The Auditor.** AUD runs KeyGen algorithm of ElGamal encryption and gets $(\text{pk}_{\text{A}}, \text{sk}_{\text{A}})$ as output[9].
2. **Each Issuer.** I_i engages in the distributed key generation protocol TRB.Sig.KeyGen of threshold randomizable-blind signature and gets sk_i, and pk_i as outputs. Signature's public key $\text{Sig.pk} = (\text{par}, \tilde{\alpha}, \{\beta_\kappa, \tilde{\beta}_\kappa\}_{\kappa=1}^4)$ is publicly announced where $\text{par} = (p, \mathbb{G}, \tilde{\mathbb{G}}, \mathbb{G}_t, e, g, \tilde{g}, \{h_\kappa\}_{\kappa=1}^4, g_1, W)$; and $(g_1, W) \in \mathbb{G}$ with unknown discrete logarithm base g.
3. **The Custodian.** CUS runs RB.Sig.KeyGen algorithm of non-threshold randomizable-blind signature and gets $\bar{\text{par}} = (\bar{p}, \bar{\mathbb{G}}, \bar{\tilde{\mathbb{G}}}, \bar{\mathbb{G}}_t, \bar{e}, \bar{g}, \bar{\tilde{g}}, \{\bar{h}_\kappa\}_{\kappa=1}^4)$, $\bar{\text{sk}}$, and $\bar{\text{pk}} = (\bar{\text{par}}, \bar{\tilde{\alpha}}, \{\bar{\beta}_\kappa, \bar{\tilde{\beta}}_\kappa\}_{\kappa=1}^4)$ as outputs.

---

[7] In principle, one could prove the full signature in zero-knowledge also achieving unlinkability.

[8] This level of privacy can persist even in scenarios where (malicious) CUS collaborates with malicious issuers. CUS engages with U in a coin flipping protocol to generate sn. Hence issuers will be incapable of establishing any linkage between U's interactions with them and fiat currency deposits via U on CUS's side. It is worth mentioning that the system will be vulnerable to front-running attack by a malicious U if the protocol lets U choose sn as sn is revealed to issuers.

[9] We note that it is possible to "thresholdize" in a straightforward way the key generation for the auditor if so desired.

4. The User. U chooses $(\mathsf{sk}, \mathsf{sk}') \xleftarrow{\$} \mathbb{Z}_p^*$ and computes $\mathsf{pk} = g^{\mathsf{sk}'}$.

User Registration. Issuers undertake user enrollment process within the system by generating a TRB.Sig signature for the user's initial account. Subsequently, U utilizes this signature for conducting transactions. Users obtain the signature of issuers for their initial account which is $\mathsf{acc} = (0, \mathsf{sk}, 1, \mathsf{sk}')$ where balance B and transaction counter x are 0. However, users are unwilling to disclose their secret keys to issuers, so that they blind their initial accounts $\mathsf{acc}^{\mathsf{blind}}$. Subsequently, the user proves, through a NIZK proof π, the validity of the blinded information (e.g., $\mathsf{B} = x = 0$). π proves knowledge of secret keys and proves that the secret key associated with the registered public key pk (in $\mathcal{F}_{\mathsf{KeyReg}}$) has indeed been blinded. The user U initiates the *User Registration* protocol with issuers upon receiving $(\mathsf{Rgs}, \mathsf{sid})$ from $\mathcal{Z}$ as follows:

User Registration: U

---

1 Parse $\mathsf{acc} = (0, \mathsf{sk}, 1, \mathsf{sk}')$. Compute $\mathsf{acc}^{\mathsf{blind}}$.

2 Call $\mathcal{F}_{\mathsf{NIZK}}$ with $(\mathsf{Prove}, \mathsf{sid}, \mathsf{x}, \mathsf{w})$ for the relation:
$R(\mathsf{x}, \mathsf{w}) = \mathsf{NIZK}\{(\text{well-formedness of } \mathsf{acc}^{\mathsf{blind}}) \wedge \mathsf{pk} = g^{\mathsf{sk}'}\}; \mathsf{x} = (\mathsf{acc}^{\mathsf{blind}}, \mathsf{pk});$
$\mathsf{w} = (\mathsf{sk}, \mathsf{sk}', \text{randomness}).$

3 Upon receiving $(\mathsf{Proof}, \mathsf{sid}, \pi)$ from $\mathcal{F}_{\mathsf{NIZK}}$, set $\mathfrak{R} \leftarrow (\mathsf{x}, \pi)$.

4 Call $\mathcal{F}_{\mathsf{B}}^{\mathsf{S}}$ with $(\mathsf{Broadcast}, \mathsf{sid}, \mathfrak{R})$.

Each issuer checks whether the user has been previously registered. In case U is new and NIZK proof π is valid, the issuer proceeds to record the user's identifier in its local database $\mathcal{D}_i$ as the registered user. Note that $\mathcal{D}_i$ is confidential to the i-th issuer and can be updated only by the i-th issuer. Subsequently, the issuer provides a blind signature $\sigma_i^{\mathsf{blind}}$ for the user's initial blinded account $\mathsf{acc}^{\mathsf{blind}}$ and transmits the blind signature share back to U. I_i upon receiving $(\mathsf{Broadcasted}, \mathsf{sid}, \mathsf{U}, \mathfrak{R})$ from $\mathcal{F}_{\mathsf{B}}^{\mathsf{S}}$ acts as follows.

User Registration: I_i

---

1 Ignore $\mathfrak{R}$ if $(\mathsf{U}, \cdot) \in \mathcal{D}_i$. Else, parse $\mathfrak{R} = (\mathsf{x}, \pi)$, and ignore if upon calling $\mathcal{F}_{\mathsf{NIZK}}$ with $(\mathsf{Verify}, \mathsf{sid}, \mathsf{x}, \pi)$, $(\mathsf{Verification}, \mathsf{sid}, 0)$ is received.

2 Else, parse $\mathsf{x} = (\mathsf{acc}^{\mathsf{blind}}, \mathsf{pk})$, and save $(\mathsf{U}, \mathsf{pk})$ in $\mathcal{D}_i$.

3 Compute blind signature share $\sigma_i^{\mathsf{blind}}$ for the message $\mathsf{acc}^{\mathsf{blind}}$.

4 Call $\mathcal{F}_{\mathsf{Ch}}^{\mathsf{ISAS}}$ with $(\mathsf{Send}, \mathsf{sid}, \mathsf{U}, \sigma_i^{\mathsf{blind}})$.

U performs the unblinding process on the received blind signature share $\sigma_i^{\mathsf{blind}}$ to get σ_i. U disregards it if found to be invalid. Upon accumulating a sufficient number (Γ) of valid signature shares from several issuers, U combines them to generate a single aggregated signature $\sigma_{\mathbb{I}}$ (so that once the user would like to prove the validity of its account instead of providing several signatures it provides one aggregated signature which results in better efficiency).

U upon receiving $(\mathsf{Received}, \mathsf{sid}, \mathsf{I}_i, \sigma_i^{\mathsf{blind}})$ from $\mathcal{F}_{\mathsf{Ch}}^{\mathsf{ISAS}}$ unblinds the received signature share $\sigma_i^{\mathsf{blind}}$ to obtain σ_i. Computes aggregated signature $\sigma_{\mathbb{I}}$.

Stablecoin Issuance. After obtaining the unique identifier of the user U and the value v from the environment $\mathcal{Z}$, the custodian CUS randomly chooses a serial number sn. This serial number serves the purpose of preventing the occurrence of double-spending, and it is subsequently transmitted to U. Upon receiving $(\mathtt{Iss}, \mathtt{sid}, \mathsf{U}, v)$ from $\mathcal{Z}$, CUS picks $\mathsf{sn} \xleftarrow{\$} \mathbb{Z}_p$ and calls $\mathcal{F}_{\mathsf{Ch}}^{\mathsf{SRA}}$ with $(\mathtt{Send}, \mathtt{sid}, \mathsf{U}, (\mathsf{sn}, v))$.

The user U is required to obtain CUS's signature confirming the value v for the stablecoin that is to be issued. However, due to privacy requirements concerning both v and identity, U cannot simply procure CUS's signature on its identity and v. U needs to present the signature of CUS to the issuers in order to obtain the stablecoins, and it is imperative to conceal both the identity of the user and the value of the stablecoin from all issuers. We use blind version of Pointcheval-Sanders signature (see full version of the paper [21]) as the underlying signature between U and CUS. U binds the received serial number sn, its secret keys $(\mathsf{sk}, \mathsf{sk}')$, and v to each other generating an account $\mathsf{a\bar{c}c}$ to get the signature of CUS. The user U blinds $\mathsf{a\bar{c}c}$ to get $\mathsf{a\bar{c}c}^{\mathsf{blind}}$ and demonstrates in ZK the well-formedness of $\mathsf{a\bar{c}c}^{\mathsf{blind}}$ (e.g., sk' is the associated secret key of U's registered public key, and the statement of NIZK reveals v, and sn so that CUS makes sure that those are correct). Note that while v, and sn are revealed to CUS, CUS remains blind to $(\mathsf{sk}, \mathsf{sk}')$. U acts as follows upon receiving $(\mathtt{Received}, \mathtt{sid}, \mathsf{CUS}, (\mathsf{sn}, v))$ from $\mathcal{F}_{\mathsf{Ch}}^{\mathsf{SRA}}$:

Stablecoin Issuance: U

1 Compute $\mathsf{a\bar{c}c}^{\mathsf{blind}}$ for $\mathsf{a\bar{c}c} = (\mathsf{sn}, \mathsf{sk}, v, \mathsf{sk}')$.
2 Call $\mathcal{F}_{\mathsf{NIZK}}$ with input $(\mathtt{Prove}, \mathtt{sid}, \mathsf{x}, \mathsf{w})$, for the relation:
  $\mathsf{R}(\mathsf{x}, \mathsf{w}) = \mathsf{NIZK}\{(\text{well-formedness of } \mathsf{a\bar{c}c}^{\mathsf{blind}}) \wedge \mathsf{pk} = g^{\mathsf{sk}'}\}$; $\mathsf{x} = (\mathsf{a\bar{c}c}^{\mathsf{blind}}, \mathsf{pk}, v, \mathsf{sn})$; $\mathsf{w} = (\mathsf{sn}, \mathsf{sk}, \mathsf{sk}', \text{randomness})$.
3 Upon receiving $(\mathtt{Proof}, \mathtt{sid}, \pi)$ from $\mathcal{F}_{\mathsf{NIZK}}$, set $\bar{\mathfrak{J}} \leftarrow (\mathsf{x}, \pi)$.
4 Call $\mathcal{F}_{\mathsf{Ch}}^{\mathsf{SSA}}$ with $(\mathtt{Send}, \mathtt{sid}, \mathsf{CUS}, \bar{\mathfrak{J}})$.

CUS signs $\mathsf{a\bar{c}c}^{\mathsf{blind}}$ (encompassing the user's secret keys $(\mathsf{sk}, \mathsf{sk}')$, serial number sn, and stablecoin value v) to generate $\sigma_{\mathsf{CUS}}^{\mathsf{blind}}$. Subsequently, CUS transmits $\sigma_{\mathsf{CUS}}^{\mathsf{blind}}$ back to U, so that U can acquire their stablecoins through the collaboration of distributed issuers by using CUS's signature as we will see. CUS acts as follows upon receiving $(\mathtt{Received}, \mathtt{sid}, \mathsf{U}, \bar{\mathfrak{J}})$ from $\mathcal{F}_{\mathsf{Ch}}^{\mathsf{SSA}}$:

Stablecoin Issuance: CUS

1 Parse $\bar{\mathfrak{J}} = (x, \pi)$, and $x = (\overline{acc}^{blind}, pk, v', sn')$.
2 Ignore $\bar{\mathfrak{J}}$ if at least one of the following conditions holds: (i) $v' \neq v$ or $sn' \neq sn$. (ii) Upon calling $\mathcal{F}_{NIZK}$ with $(\text{Verify}, sid, x, \pi)$, $(\text{Verification}, sid, 0)$ is received. (iii) Upon calling $\mathcal{F}_{KeyReg}$ with $(\text{Key.Retrieval}, sid, U)$, $(\text{Key.Retrieved}, sid, U, pk')$ is received where $pk' \neq pk$.
3 Upon receiving a message $(\text{Iss}, sid, U', v')$ from $\mathcal{Z}$, proceed if $U' = U$ and $v' = v$.
4 Compute blind signature σ_{CUS}^{blind} for the message $\overline{acc}^{blind}$.
5 Call $\mathcal{F}_{Ch}^{IRAS}$ with $(\text{Send}, sid, U, \sigma_{CUS}^{blind})$.

U first of all unblinds σ_{CUS}^{blind}, to get σ_{CUS}. Then, for preventing possible linkage randomizes the signature σ_{CUS}^{RND} (note that the message of the signature which is (sn, sk, v, sk') is kept secret). Note that we use blind Pointcheval-Sanders signature between U and CUS, and threshold blind Pointcheval-Sanders signature between U and issuers (see full version of the paper [21] for more details). U should update their account in a way that it is consistent with CUS's signature (σ_{CUS}^{RND}). Consequently, U sets $B^{new} = B^{old} + v$ and increments the transaction counter by 1 (sk^{x+1}). U blinds acc^{new} and proves in ZK that $acc^{new,blind}$ is consistent with σ_{CUS}^{RND} and with $acc^{old,blind}$ for which the user has signature of issuers $\sigma_{\mathbb{I}}$.

$\sigma_{\mathbb{I}}$ represents the (threshold) signature of issuers on acc^{old}, and it undergoes randomization by U to yield $\sigma_{\mathbb{I}}^{RND}$ (that is verified without revealing the message of the signature itself acc^{old}). The purpose of randomization is to preclude any potential linkage by a malicious issuer between the moment of signing acc^{old} and the subsequent submission of that signature for account update.

U calculates the double-spending tag $g^{(sk^{x+1})}$, a value deterministically derived from the user's account. It's important to highlight that sn is specifically utilized to prevent double-spending on the custodian's message, while tag serves the purpose of averting double-spending regarding the user's account.

Regarding privacy-enhanced auditing, for stablecoin issuance (and as we will see for stablecoin burn), users encrypt v under the public key pk_A of the auditor AUD, generating $\tilde{\chi}_t$. Note that users (efficiently) prove the consistency of v in $\tilde{\chi}_t$ with their account update via π. Notably, we use the homomorphic property of ElGamal encryption in pivotal role here: the i-th issuer multiplies the newly generated ciphertext by the user, the provided $\tilde{\chi}_t$, with the previously-stored ciphertext $\tilde{\chi}_i$ by themselves in their local database $\mathcal{D}_i$. This operation is executed without the issuer knowing v. The result of this operation represents an updated ciphertext, signifying the adjusted total value of stablecoins within the system. Ultimately, this updated ciphertext is then made available within the system (it is output to $\mathcal{Z}$). Hence, $\tilde{\chi}_t$ facilitates private issuance (and burn) by keeping value hidden while providing auditability (note that underlying broadcast functionality guarantees that honest issuers always have the same view). Whenever AUD wants, they can decrypt the ciphertext, thereby starting the auditing protocol in collaboration with CUS as we are about to see. U acts as follows upon receiving $(\mathtt{Received}, \mathsf{sid}, \mathsf{CUS}, \sigma_{\mathsf{CUS}}^{\mathsf{blind}})$ from $\mathcal{F}_{\mathsf{Ch}}^{\mathsf{IRAS}}$:

Stablecoin Issuance: U

1. Unblind the received signature $\sigma_{\mathsf{CUS}}^{\mathsf{blind}}$ to obtain σ_{CUS}. Compute $\sigma_{\mathsf{CUS}}^{\mathsf{RND}}$.
2. Parse $\mathsf{acc}^{\mathsf{old}} = (\mathsf{B}^{\mathsf{old}}, \mathsf{sk}, \mathsf{sk}^x, \mathsf{sk}')$. Compute
   $\mathsf{acc}^{\mathsf{new}} = (\mathsf{B}^{\mathsf{old}} + v, \mathsf{sk}, (\mathsf{sk}^{x+1}), \mathsf{sk}')$, and $\mathsf{acc}^{\mathsf{new},\mathsf{blind}}$. Compute $\sigma_{\mathbb{I}}^{\mathsf{RND}}$ (on $\mathsf{acc}^{\mathsf{old},\mathsf{blind}}$), and $\mathsf{tag} = g^{(\mathsf{sk}^{x+1})}$.
3. Pick $z \xleftarrow{\$} \mathbb{Z}_p$ and set $\tilde{\chi}_t = (\tilde{C}_1, \tilde{C}_2) = (g^z, \mathsf{pk}_{\mathsf{A}}^z \cdot g_1^v)$.
4. Call $\mathcal{F}_{\mathsf{NIZK}}$ with input $(\mathtt{Prove}, \mathsf{sid}, \mathsf{x}, \mathsf{w})$, for the relation:
   $R(\mathsf{x}, \mathsf{w}) = \mathsf{NIZK}\{(\text{well-formedness of } \sigma_{\mathsf{CUS}}^{\mathsf{RND}} \wedge \mathsf{acc}^{\mathsf{new},\mathsf{blind}} \wedge \sigma_{\mathbb{I}}^{\mathsf{RND}}) \wedge \mathsf{tag} = g^{(\mathsf{sk}^{x+1})} \wedge \tilde{C}_1 = g^z \wedge \tilde{C}_2 = \mathsf{pk}_{\mathsf{A}}^z \cdot g_1^v \wedge \mathsf{B}^{\mathsf{old}} + v \in [0, \mathsf{B}_{\mathsf{max}}]\}$;
   $\mathsf{x} = (\mathsf{sn}, \mathsf{acc}^{\mathsf{new},\mathsf{blind}}, (\text{commitments related to } \sigma_{\mathsf{CUS}}^{\mathsf{RND}} \text{ and } \sigma_{\mathbb{I}}^{\mathsf{RND}}), \mathsf{tag}, \tilde{\chi}_t, \mathsf{pk}_{\mathsf{A}})$; $\mathsf{w} = (\mathsf{B}^{\mathsf{old}}, \mathsf{sk}, \mathsf{sk}^x, \mathsf{sk}', v, z, \text{randomness})$.
5. Upon receiving $(\mathtt{Proof}, \mathsf{sid}, \pi)$ from $\mathcal{F}_{\mathsf{NIZK}}$, set $\mathfrak{I} \leftarrow (\sigma_{\mathsf{CUS}}^{\mathsf{RND}}, \sigma_{\mathbb{I}}^{\mathsf{RND}}, \mathsf{x}, \pi)$.
6. Call $\mathcal{F}_{\mathsf{B}}^{\mathsf{SA}}$ with $(\mathtt{Broadcast}, \mathsf{sid}, \mathfrak{I})$.

Each issuer verifies $\sigma_{\mathsf{CUS}}^{\mathsf{RND}}$, $\sigma_{\mathbb{I}}^{\mathsf{RND}}$, and NIZK proof π. Additionally, each issuer examines its local database $\mathcal{D}_i$ to ensure the absence of any double-spending occurrences. If all these checks pass, the encryption of the total value in circulation of the stablecoin is updated by multiplying the received ciphertext $\tilde{\chi}_t$ with the existing one $\tilde{\chi}_i$ recorded locally. This update occurs seamlessly due to the homomorphism property of the underlying ElGamal encryption, allowing for the modification of the total value without the need to reveal the specific value v. The updated ciphertext then is output to the environment $\mathcal{Z}$. Also, the issuer records tag and sn, and signs $\mathsf{acc}^{\mathsf{new},\mathsf{blind}}$ to get $\sigma_i^{\mathsf{new},\mathsf{blind}}$ which is sent back to U. I_i acts as follows upon receiving $(\mathtt{Broadcasted}, \mathsf{sid}, \mathfrak{I}, \mathsf{mid})$ from $\mathcal{F}_{\mathsf{B}}^{\mathsf{SA}}$:

Stablecoin Issuance: I_i

1. Parse $\mathfrak{I} = (\sigma_{\mathsf{CUS}}^{\mathsf{RND}}, \sigma_{\mathbb{I}}^{\mathsf{RND}}, \mathsf{x}, \pi)$, and
   $\mathsf{x} = (\mathsf{sn}, \mathsf{acc}^{\mathsf{new},\mathsf{blind}}, (\text{commitments related to } \sigma_{\mathsf{CUS}}^{\mathsf{RND}} \text{ and } \sigma_{\mathbb{I}}^{\mathsf{RND}}), \mathsf{tag}, \tilde{\chi}_t, \mathsf{pk}_{\mathsf{A}})$.
2. Ignore $\mathfrak{I}$ if at least one of the following conditions holds: (i) sn or tag already exists in $\mathcal{D}_i$, (ii) $\sigma_{\mathsf{CUS}}^{\mathsf{RND}}$ or $\sigma_{\mathbb{I}}^{\mathsf{RND}}$ is not verified, (iii) Upon calling $\mathcal{F}_{\mathsf{NIZK}}$ with $(\mathtt{Verify}, \mathsf{sid}, \mathsf{x}, \pi)$, $(\mathtt{Verification}, \mathsf{sid}, 0)$ is received.
3. Else, save tag and sn in $\mathcal{D}_i$.
4. Compute $\tilde{\chi}_i \leftarrow \tilde{\chi}_i \cdot \tilde{\chi}_t$. Record $\tilde{\chi}_i$, and output $(\mathtt{Iss.End}, \mathsf{sid}, \tilde{\chi}_i)$ to $\mathcal{Z}$.
5. Compute $\sigma_i^{\mathsf{new},\mathsf{blind}}$ for the message $\mathsf{acc}^{\mathsf{new},\mathsf{blind}}$.
6. Call $\mathcal{F}_{\mathsf{B}}^{\mathsf{SA}}$ with $(\mathtt{Send.Back}, \mathsf{sid}, \sigma_i^{\mathsf{new},\mathsf{blind}}, \mathsf{mid})$.

U upon receiving $(\mathtt{Received}, \mathsf{sid}, \mathsf{I}_i, \sigma_i^{\mathsf{new},\mathsf{blind}})$ from $\mathcal{F}_{\mathsf{B}}^{\mathsf{SA}}$ unblinds the received $\sigma_i^{\mathsf{new},\mathsf{blind}}$ to get σ_i^{new}. U disregards it if found to be invalid. Upon accumulating a sufficient number Γ of valid signatures, U combines them to generate a single aggregated signature $\sigma_{\mathbb{I}}^{\mathsf{new}}$.

Stablecoin Transfer. The sender U_s encrypts v under the receiver U_r's public key pk_r, generating χ_1, while keeping pk_r secret (for privacy concerns) by generating χ_2 (which is used in NIZK proof); U_s encrypts pk_r under public value W, generating χ_2. U_s encrypts its public key pk_s under pk_r, generating χ_3 (to help U_r identify U_s by decrypting χ_3). Additionally, U_s encrypts the constant 0 under pk_r, generating χ_4.[10] χ_2 and χ_4 are used in the proofs of the sender and receiver respectively to provide a reference to pk_r.

U_s initiates *Stablecoin Transfer* protocol with issuers upon receiving $(\texttt{Gen.ST}, \texttt{sid}, U_r, v)$ from $\mathcal{Z}$ as follows:

Stablecoin Transfer: U_s

---

1 Parse $\texttt{acc}^{\texttt{old}} = (B^{\texttt{old}}, sk_s, sk_s^x, sk_s')$. Compute $\texttt{acc}^{\texttt{new}} = (B^{\texttt{old}} - v, sk_s, (sk_s^{x+1}),$ $sk_s')$, and $\texttt{acc}^{\texttt{new,blind}}$. Compute $\sigma_{\mathbb{I}}^{\texttt{RND}}$ (on $\texttt{acc}^{\texttt{old,blind}}$), and $\texttt{tag} = g^{(sk_s^{x+1})}$.

2 Call $\mathcal{F}_{\texttt{KeyReg}}$ with $(\texttt{Key.Retrieval}, \texttt{sid}, U_r)$. Upon receiving

$(\texttt{Key.Retrieved}, \texttt{sid}, U_r, pk_r)$, pick $(z, y, q, t) \xleftarrow{\$} \mathbb{Z}_p$; and set:
(i) $\chi_1 = (C_1, C_2) = (g^z, pk_r^z \cdot g_1^v)$. (ii) $\chi_2 = (C_1', C_2') = (g^y, W^y \cdot pk_r)$.
(iii) $\chi_3 = (C_1'', C_2'') = (g^q, pk_r^q \cdot pk_s)$. (iv) $\chi_4 = (C_1''', C_2''') = (g^t, pk_r^t)$.

3 Call $\mathcal{F}_{\texttt{NIZK}}$ with input $(\texttt{Prove}, \texttt{sid}, x, w)$, for the relation:
$R(x, w) = \texttt{NIZK}\{(\text{well-formedness of } \texttt{acc}^{\texttt{new,blind}} \wedge \sigma_{\mathbb{I}}^{\texttt{RND}}) \wedge \texttt{tag} = g^{(sk_s^{x+1})}$
$\wedge C_1 = g^z \wedge C_2 = (C_2'/W^y)^z \cdot g_1^v \wedge C_1' = g^y \wedge C_1'' = g^q \wedge C_2'' =$
$(C_2'/W^y)^q \cdot g^{sk_s'} \wedge C_1''' = g^t \wedge C_2''' = (C_2'/W^y)^t \wedge v \in [0, B^{\texttt{old}}]\};$
$x = (\texttt{acc}^{\texttt{new,blind}}, (\text{commitment related to } \sigma_{\mathbb{I}}^{\texttt{RND}}), \texttt{tag}, \chi_1, \chi_2, \chi_3, \chi_4, W);$
$w = (B^{\texttt{old}}, sk_s, sk_s^x, sk_s', v, z, y, q, t, \text{randomness}).$

4 Upon receiving $(\texttt{Proof}, \texttt{sid}, \pi)$ from $\mathcal{F}_{\texttt{NIZK}}$, set $\mathfrak{T} \leftarrow (\sigma_{\mathbb{I}}^{\texttt{RND}}, x, \pi)$.

5 Call $\mathcal{F}_B^{\texttt{SA}}$ with $(\texttt{Broadcast}, \texttt{sid}, \mathfrak{T})$.

Similar to *Stablecoin Issuance* protocol each issuer verifies $\sigma_{\mathbb{I}}^{\texttt{RND}}$, and π. Additionally, each issuer searches its local database $\mathcal{D}_i$ for double-spending checking. If all these checks pass, the issuer signs $\texttt{acc}^{\texttt{new,blind}}$ to get $\sigma_i^{\texttt{new,blind}}$ which is sent back to U. I_i upon receiving $(\texttt{Broadcasted}, \texttt{sid}, \mathfrak{T}, \texttt{mid})$ from $\mathcal{F}_B^{\texttt{SA}}$ acts as follows.

Stablecoin Transfer: I_i

---

1 Parse $\mathfrak{T} = (\sigma_{\mathbb{I}}^{\texttt{RND}}, x, \pi)$, and
$x = (\texttt{acc}^{\texttt{new,blind}}, (\text{commitment related to } \sigma_{\mathbb{I}}^{\texttt{RND}}), \texttt{tag}, \chi_1, \chi_2, \chi_3, \chi_4, W).$

2 Ignore if at least one of the following conditions holds: (i) $\texttt{tag}$ already exists in $\mathcal{D}_i$, (ii) $\sigma_{\mathbb{I}}^{\texttt{RND}}$ is not verified, (iii) Upon calling $\mathcal{F}_{\texttt{NIZK}}$ with $(\texttt{Verify}, \texttt{sid}, x, \pi)$, $(\texttt{Verification}, \texttt{sid}, 0)$ is received.

3 Else, save $\texttt{tag}$, and $\phi = (\chi_1, \chi_3, \chi_4)$ in $\mathcal{D}_i$. Compute $\sigma_i^{\texttt{new,blind}}$ for the message $\texttt{acc}^{\texttt{new,blind}}$. Call $\mathcal{F}_B^{\texttt{SA}}$ with $(\texttt{Send.Back}, \texttt{sid}, \sigma_i^{\texttt{new,blind}}, \texttt{mid})$.

---

[10] The usage of χ_4 in *Stablecoin Transfer* (resp. χ_2 in *Stablecoin Burn*) protocol is to prevent malicious sender and receiver (resp. malicious user) from breaking the integrity of currency transfer (resp. burn) e.g., by generating fake money, without relying on any security assumption e.g., hardness of discrete logarithm.

U_s upon receiving $(\texttt{Received}, \texttt{sid}, I_i, \sigma_i^{\text{new,blind}})$ from $\mathcal{F}_B^{\text{SA}}$ unblinds $\sigma_i^{\text{new,blind}}$ to get σ_i^{new}, and generates a single aggregated signature $\sigma_{\mathbb{I}}^{\text{new}}$ (as described in earlier protocol). U_s outputs $(\texttt{Gen.ST.End}, \texttt{sid}, U_r, v, \phi)$ to $\mathcal{Z}$ where $\phi = (\chi_1, \chi_3, \chi_4)$.

Stablecoin Claim. The receiver U_r decrypts χ_1, and χ_3 to identify v, and U_s respectively. U_r updates their balance with respect to v, and proves ownership of (χ_1, χ_4) (by proving decryption via NIZK – see the relation $\mathsf{R(x,w)}$) so that with the confirmation of issuers (who receive ϕ from $\mathcal{Z}$) the balance is increased by v. U_r initiates *Stablecoin Claim* protocol with issuers upon receiving $(\texttt{Clm.ST}, \texttt{sid}, \phi)$ from $\mathcal{Z}$ as follows.

Stablecoin Claim: U_r

1. Parse $\phi = (\chi_1, \chi_3, \chi_4)$, $\chi_1 = (C_1, C_2)$, $\chi_3 = (C_1'', C_2'')$, and $\chi_4 = (C_1''', C_2''')$.
2. Compute $g_1^v = C_2/(C_1)^{\mathsf{sk}_r'}$ and $\mathsf{pk}_s = C_2''/(C_1'')^{\mathsf{sk}_r'}$. Extract v from g_1^v.
3. Parse $\mathsf{acc}^{\text{old}} = (\mathsf{B}^{\text{old}}, \mathsf{sk}_r, \mathsf{sk}_r^x, \mathsf{sk}_r')$. Compute $\mathsf{acc}^{\text{new}} = (\mathsf{B}^{\text{old}} + v, \mathsf{sk}_r, (\mathsf{sk}_r^{x+1}), \mathsf{sk}_r')$, and $\mathsf{acc}^{\text{new,blind}}$. Compute $\sigma_{\mathbb{I}}^{\text{RND}}$ (on $\mathsf{acc}^{\text{old,blind}}$), and $\mathsf{tag} = g^{(\mathsf{sk}_r^{x+1})}$.
4. Call $\mathcal{F}_{\text{NIZK}}$ with input $(\texttt{Prove}, \texttt{sid}, \mathsf{x}, \mathsf{w})$, for the relation:
   $\mathsf{R(x,w)} = \mathsf{NIZK}\{(\text{well-formedness of } \mathsf{acc}^{\text{new,blind}} \wedge \sigma_{\mathbb{I}}^{\text{RND}}) \wedge \mathsf{tag} = g^{(\mathsf{sk}_r^{x+1})}$
   $\wedge\ C_2 = C_1^{\mathsf{sk}_r'} \cdot g_1^v \wedge C_2''' = (C_1''')^{\mathsf{sk}_r'} \wedge \mathsf{B}^{\text{old}} + v \in [0, \mathsf{B}_{\max}]\}$;
   $\mathsf{x} = (\mathsf{acc}^{\text{new,blind}}, (\text{commitment related to } \sigma_{\mathbb{I}}^{\text{RND}}), \mathsf{tag}, \chi_1, \chi_4)$;
   $\mathsf{w} = (\mathsf{B}^{\text{old}}, \mathsf{sk}_r, \mathsf{sk}_r^x, \mathsf{sk}_r', v, \text{randomness})$.
5. Upon receiving $(\texttt{Proof}, \texttt{sid}, \pi)$ from $\mathcal{F}_{\text{NIZK}}$, set $\mathfrak{D} \leftarrow (\sigma_{\mathbb{I}}^{\text{RND}}, \mathsf{x}, \pi, \chi_3)$.
6. Call $\mathcal{F}_B^{\text{SA}}$ with $(\texttt{Broadcast}, \texttt{sid}, \mathfrak{D})$.

Each issuing entity operates akin to prior protocols, with the exception that it checks its database for ϕ. Subsequently, it awaits an instruction from the environment $\mathcal{Z}$, which should include the identical ϕ, and then proceeds to sign $\mathsf{acc}^{\text{new,blind}}$. I_i upon receiving $(\texttt{Broadcasted}, \texttt{sid}, \mathfrak{D}, \texttt{mid})$ from $\mathcal{F}_B^{\text{SA}}$ act as follows.

Stablecoin Claim: I_i

1. Parse $\mathfrak{D} = (\sigma_{\mathbb{I}}^{\text{RND}}, \mathsf{x}, \pi, \chi_3)$, and
   $\mathsf{x} = (\mathsf{acc}^{\text{new,blind}}, (\text{commitment related to } \sigma_{\mathbb{I}}^{\text{RND}}), \mathsf{tag}, \chi_1, \chi_4)$
2. Ignore $\mathfrak{D}$ if at least one of the following conditions holds: (i) tag or χ_1 already exists in $\mathcal{D}_i$. (ii) Upon calling $\mathcal{F}_{\text{NIZK}}$ with $(\texttt{Verify}, \texttt{sid}, \mathsf{x}, \pi)$, $(\texttt{Verification}, \texttt{sid}, 0)$ is received. (iii) $\sigma_{\mathbb{I}}^{\text{RND}}$ is not verified. (iv) There does not exist $\phi = (\chi_1, \chi_3, \chi_4)$ recorded in $\mathcal{D}_i$
3. Upon receiving $(\texttt{Clm.ST.Ok}, \texttt{sid}, \phi^*)$ from $\mathcal{Z}$, parse $\phi^* = (\chi_1^*, \chi_3^*, \chi_4^*)$. Proceed if $\chi_1^* = \chi_1$, $\chi_3^* = \chi_3$, and $\chi_4^* = \chi_4$.
4. Save tag, and χ_1 in $\mathcal{D}_i$.
5. Compute $\sigma_i^{\text{new,blind}}$ for the message $\mathsf{acc}^{\text{new,blind}}$.
6. Call $\mathcal{F}_B^{\text{SA}}$ with $(\texttt{Send.Back}, \texttt{sid}, \sigma_i^{\text{new,blind}}, \texttt{mid})$.

U_r upon receiving $(\texttt{Received}, \texttt{sid}, I_i, \sigma_i^{\text{new,blind}})$ from $\mathcal{F}_B^{\text{SA}}$ acts similar to the *Stablecoin Issuance* protocol to unblind $\sigma_i^{\text{new,blind}}$, and generate a single aggregated signature on their new account $\sigma_{\mathbb{I}}^{\text{new}}$.

Stablecoin Burn. The user U receives the value of stablecoin that is burned v and label ℓ from $\mathcal{Z}$. As described in Sect. 2.4, ℓ is to specify the type of asset against which U intends to initiate the burning process for withdrawal which facilitates interoperability within our model. For instance, user can burn v stablecoin to get another digital asset in a blockchain system (specified via ℓ) with the help of custodian (as we will see in the *Proof of Burn* protocol).

U employs encryption to hide the value v that is burned, resulting in the creation of a ciphertext χ_1 under their public key. Moreover, U utilizes their public key to encrypt the value 0 (that will be used in the *Proof of Burn* protocol). Additionally, to facilitate privacy-enhanced auditing, $\tilde{\chi}_t$ is generated as an encryption of v under the public key of AUD (pk_A), serving the same purpose as outlined in the *Stablecoin Issuance* protocol.

Subsequently, U proceeds to update their account and provides a NIZK proof, demonstrating the consistency among all ciphertexts, the signature on the old account, and the new blinded account. U initiates *Stablecoin Burn* protocol with issuers upon receiving $(\texttt{Brn}, \texttt{sid}, v, \ell)$ from $\mathcal{Z}$ as follows.

Stablecoin Burn: U

---

1 Parse $\text{acc}^{\text{old}} = (B^{\text{old}}, \text{sk}, \text{sk}^x, \text{sk}')$. Compute
  $\text{acc}^{\text{new}} = (B^{\text{old}} - v, \text{sk}, (\text{sk}^{x+1}), \text{sk}')$, and $\text{acc}^{\text{new,blind}}$.

2 Compute $\sigma_{\mathbb{I}}^{\text{RND}}$ (on $\text{acc}^{\text{old,blind}}$), and $\text{tag} = g^{(\text{sk}^{x+1})}$.

3 Pick $(z, q, t) \xleftarrow{\$} \mathbb{Z}_p$, set (i) $\chi_1 = (C_1, C_2) = (g^z, \text{pk}^z \cdot g_1^v)$,
  (ii) $\chi_2 = (C_1', C_2') = (g^t, \text{pk}^t)$, (iii) $\tilde{\chi}_t = (\tilde{C}_1, \tilde{C}_2) = (g^q, \text{pk}_A^q \cdot g_1^v)$.

4 Call $\mathcal{F}_{\text{NIZK}}$ with input $(\texttt{Prove}, \texttt{sid}, \text{x}, \text{w})$, for the relation:
  (i) $R(\text{x}, \text{w}) = \text{NIZK}\{(\text{well-formedness of } \text{acc}^{\text{new,blind}} \wedge \sigma_{\mathbb{I}}^{\text{RND}}) \wedge \text{tag} = g^{(\text{sk}_s^{x+1})} \wedge C_1 = g^z \wedge C_2 = g^{\text{sk}' \cdot z} \cdot g_1^v \wedge \tilde{C}_1 = g^q \wedge \tilde{C}_2 = \text{pk}_A^q \cdot g_1^v \wedge C_1' = g^t \wedge C_2' = g^{\text{sk}' \cdot t} \wedge v \in [0, B^{\text{old}}]\}$,
  (ii) $\text{x} = (\text{acc}^{\text{new,blind}}, (\text{commitment related to } \sigma_{\mathbb{I}}^{\text{RND}}), \text{tag}, \chi_1, \chi_2, \tilde{\chi}_t, \text{pk}_A, \ell)$,
  (iii) $\text{w} = (B^{\text{old}}, \text{sk}, \text{sk}^x, \text{sk}', v, z, q, t, \text{randomness})$.

5 Upon receiving $(\texttt{Proof}, \texttt{sid}, \pi)$ from $\mathcal{F}_{\text{NIZK}}$, set $\mathfrak{B} \leftarrow (\sigma_{\mathbb{I}}^{\text{RND}}, \text{x}, \pi)$.

6 Call $\mathcal{F}_B^{\text{SA}}$ with $(\texttt{Broadcast}, \texttt{sid}, \mathfrak{B})$.

Similar to previous protocols each issuer verifies signature, NIZK proof, and double-spending tag. If all these checks pass, similar to the *Stablecoin Issuance* protocol the encryption of the total value in circulation of the stablecoin is updated by dividing the existing ciphertext $\tilde{\chi}_i$ recorded locally by the received ciphertext $\tilde{\chi}_t$. Finally, the issuer outputs $(\eta, \ell, \tilde{\chi}_i)$ to $\mathcal{Z}$ showing that $\eta = (\chi_1, \chi_2)$ is associated to ℓ and updated total value in circulation of stablecoin is handled via $\tilde{\chi}_i$. I_i upon receiving $(\texttt{Broadcasted}, \texttt{sid}, \mathfrak{B}, \text{mid})$ from $\mathcal{F}_B^{\text{SA}}$ acts as follows.

Stablecoin Burn: I_i

1 Parse $\mathfrak{B} = (\sigma_{\mathbb{I}}^{\text{RND}}, x, \pi)$, and
$x = (\text{acc}^{\text{new,blind}}, (\text{commitment related to } \sigma_{\mathbb{I}}^{\text{RND}}), \text{tag}, \chi_1, \chi_2, \tilde{\chi}_t, \text{pk}_A, \ell)$.

2 Ignore $\mathfrak{B}$ if at least one of the following conditions holds: (i) tag already exists in $\mathcal{D}_i$, (ii) Upon calling $\mathcal{F}_{\text{NIZK}}$ with $(\text{Verify}, \text{sid}, x, \pi)$, $(\text{Verification}, \text{sid}, 0)$ is received, (iii) Parse $\sigma_{\mathbb{I}}^{\text{RND}} = (h', s')$ and if $h' = 1$ or if $e(h', \varkappa) \neq e(s', \tilde{g})$.

3 Compute $\tilde{\chi}_i \leftarrow \tilde{\chi}_i / \tilde{\chi}_t$. Record $\tilde{\chi}_i$, and output $(\text{Brn.End}, \text{sid}, \eta, \ell, \tilde{\chi}_i)$ to $\mathcal{Z}$ where $\eta = (\chi_1, \chi_2)$.

4 Save tag in $\mathcal{D}_i$, compute $\sigma_i^{\text{new,blind}}$ for the message $\text{acc}^{\text{new,blind}}$.

5 Call $\mathcal{F}_B^{\text{SA}}$ with $(\text{Send.Back}, \text{sid}, \sigma_i^{\text{new,blind}}, \text{mid})$.

The user U upon receiving $(\text{Received}, \text{sid}, I_i, \sigma_i^{\text{new,blind}})$ from $\mathcal{F}_B^{\text{SA}}$ unblinds $\sigma_i^{\text{new,blind}}$ to get σ_i^{new}, and generates a single aggregated signature $\sigma_{\mathbb{I}}^{\text{new}}$.

Proof of Burn. The user U receives $\eta = (\chi_1, \chi_2)$ and ℓ from $\mathcal{Z}$. U proves to CUS that both ciphertexts belongs to them and also proves the value of encryption is v. U initiates *Proof of Burn* protocol upon receiving $(\text{PoB}, \text{sid}, \eta, \ell)$ from $\mathcal{Z}$ as follows.

Proof of Burn: U

1 Parse $\eta = (\chi_1, \chi_2)$, $\chi_1 = (C_1, C_2)$, and $\chi_2 = (C_1', C_2')$.

2 Compute $g_1^v = C_2 / (C_1)^{\text{sk}'}$. Extract v from g_1^v.

3 Call $\mathcal{F}_{\text{NIZK}}$ with input $(\text{Prove}, \text{sid}, x, w)$, for the relation:
(i) $R(x, w) = \text{NIZK}\{C_2 = C_1^{\text{sk}'} \cdot g_1^v \wedge C_2' = (C_1')^{\text{sk}'}\}$, (ii) $x = (\eta, v, \ell)$, (iii) $w = \text{sk}'$.

4 Upon receiving $(\text{Proof}, \text{sid}, \pi)$ from $\mathcal{F}_{\text{NIZK}}$, set $\mathfrak{V} \leftarrow (x, \pi)$.

5 Call $\mathcal{F}_{\text{Ch}}^{\text{SSA}}$ with $(\text{Send}, \text{sid}, \text{CUS}, \mathfrak{V})$.

CUS verifies the NIZK proof, also checks if η has already been claimed or not. If checks pass, and upon receiving the same values of η, and ℓ from $\mathcal{Z}$, CUS accepts user's proof of burn (of v stablecoins) and outputs (η, U, v, ℓ) to $\mathcal{Z}$. CUS upon receiving $(\text{Received}, \text{sid}, U, \mathfrak{V})$ from $\mathcal{F}_{\text{Ch}}^{\text{SSA}}$ acts as follows.

Proof of Burn: CUS

1 Parse $\mathfrak{V} = (x, \pi)$, and $x = (\eta, v, \ell)$.

2 Ignore $\mathfrak{V}$ if upon calling $\mathcal{F}_{\text{NIZK}}$ with $(\text{Verify}, \text{sid}, x, \pi)$, $(\text{Verification}, \text{sid}, 0)$ is received or η already exists.

3 Upon receiving $(\text{PoB.CUS}, \text{sid}, \eta^*, \ell^*)$ from $\mathcal{Z}$, proceed if $\eta^* = \eta$, and $\ell^* = \ell$.

4 Record η, and output $(\text{PoB.End}, \text{sid}, \eta, U, v, \ell)$ to $\mathcal{Z}$.

Reserve Audit. The environment $\mathcal{Z}$ instructs the auditor AUD to audit total value of stablecoin in circulation TV with respect to reserves RV. At any given point in time, AUD can decrypt the most recent encryption of total value of stablecoin in circulation $\tilde{\chi}$ to get TV and compare it with RV given by $\mathcal{Z}$. AUD initiates *Reserve Audit* upon receiving $(\mathtt{Audit}, \mathtt{sid}, \tilde{\chi}, \mathsf{RV})$ from $\mathcal{Z}$.

Reserve Audit: AUD

1 Parse $\tilde{\chi} = (\tilde{C}_1, \tilde{C}_2)$. Compute $g_1^{\mathsf{TV}} = \tilde{C}_2 / \tilde{C}_1^{\mathsf{sk_A}}$. Extract TV from g_1^{TV}.[a]
2 If $\mathsf{RV} \geq \mathsf{TV}$, set $b \leftarrow 1$. Else, set $b \leftarrow 0$.
3 Output $(\mathtt{Audit.End}, \mathtt{sid}, b)$ to $\mathcal{Z}$.

---

[a]Considering realistic values for TV, we emphasize that the auditor possesses the necessary capabilities to effectively calculate TV.

Discussions on regulation-friendliness, account recovery, blockchain agnosticism, interoperability, and self-custody of PARScoin are provided in the full version of the paper [21].

4 PARScoin Security

Due to page limits, in this section, we provide our main *Theorem 1.*, for full security analysis of PARScoin see full version of the paper [21].

Theorem 1. *Given two polynomials* max_1 *and* max_2, *in the* $\{\mathcal{F}_{\mathsf{KeyReg}}, \mathcal{F}_{\mathsf{RO}}, \mathcal{F}_{\mathsf{Ch}}, \mathcal{F}_{\mathsf{B}}, \mathcal{F}_{\mathsf{NIZK}}\}$-*hybrid model, under the binding property of Pedersen commitments, the* IND-CPA *security of ElGamal encryption, the* EUF-CMA *security of Pointcheval-Sanders signatures in the random oracle model, and the hardness of the d-strong Diffie-Hellman problem, no (PPT) environment* $\mathcal{Z}$ *can distinguish the real-world execution* $\mathsf{EXEC}_{\Pi_{\mathsf{PARS}}, \mathcal{A}, \mathcal{Z}}$ *from the ideal-world execution* $\mathsf{EXEC}_{\mathcal{F}_{\mathsf{PARS}}, \mathcal{S}, \mathcal{Z}}$ *with advantage better than* $\mathsf{Adv}_{\mathcal{A}}^{\mathsf{Bind\text{-}com}} + \mathsf{max}_1 \cdot \mathsf{Adv}_{\mathcal{A}}^{\mathsf{IND\text{-}CPA}} + \mathsf{max}_2 \cdot \mathsf{Adv}_{\mathcal{A}}^{\mathsf{d\text{-}SDDH}} + \mathsf{Adv}_{\mathcal{A}}^{\mathsf{EUF\text{-}CMA}}$ *with static corruptions in the presence of an arbitrary number of malicious users, and up to t malicious issuers that are all colluding.*

We prove the statistical proximity between the random variables $\mathsf{EXEC}_{\Pi_{\mathsf{PARS}}, \mathcal{A}, \mathcal{Z}}$ and $\mathsf{EXEC}_{\mathcal{F}_{\mathsf{PARS}}, \mathcal{S}, \mathcal{Z}}$ through a series of games.

5 PARScoin Performance

In the section, we provide the computation and communication costs associated with PARScoin's stablecoin transfer and claim processes, for both the user (sender and receiver) and the issuers; for more information see full version of the paper [21]. This analysis illustrates the system's efficiency for real-world implementation. For example, the generation of zero-knowledge proofs by senders or receivers can be efficiently performed.

In our evaluation we use the Charm cryptographic framework [2] and bilinear pairings implemented over the Barreto-Naehrig curve [14]. Experiments were conducted on a system equipped with an Intel Core i7-9850H CPU operating at 2.60 GHz and 16 GB of RAM. We define the upper bound on user balance as $\mathsf{B}_{\mathsf{max}} = 2^n - 1$ and utilize bulletproofs [7] for range proofs.

- In the *Stablecoin Transfer* protocol, the sender requires $(0.05941 + 0.00712n)$ seconds to generate $\mathfrak{T} = (\sigma_{\mathbb{I}}^{\mathsf{RND}}, \mathsf{x}, \pi)$, with a resulting data size of $2.8711\mathsf{KB} + 2\log_2(n)$. Additionally, $(0.03409\Gamma + 0.02332)$ seconds are needed for the sender to unblind Γ signature shares and aggregate them into a consolidated signature.
- In the *Stablecoin Claim* protocol, the receiver spends $(0.04784 + 0.00712n)$ seconds to generate $\mathfrak{D} = (\sigma_{\mathbb{I}}^{\mathsf{RND}}, \mathsf{x}, \pi, \chi_3)$, with a data size of $1.793\mathsf{KB} + 2\log_2(n)$. The process of unblinding Γ signature shares and aggregating them into a consolidated signature takes $(0.03409\Gamma + 0.02332)$ seconds.
- For each issuer in both protocols, verification of the sender/receiver proof requires $(0.08816 + 0.00356n)$ seconds, and computing the blind signature share takes 0.00445 seconds.

Acknowledgements. This work has been supported by Input Output (iohk.io) through their funding of the University of Edinburgh Blockchain Technology Lab.

References

1. Aztec. https://aztec.network/
2. Akinyele, J.A., et al.: Charm: a framework for rapidly prototyping cryptosystems. J. Cryptogr. Eng. **3**, 111–128 (2013)
3. Ampleforth: Ampleforth documents. https://docs.ampleforth.org/
4. Bains, P., Ismail, A., Melo, F., Sugimoto, N.: Regulating the Crypto Ecosystem: The Case of Stablecoins and Arrangements. International Monetary Fund (2022)
5. Ben-Sasson, E., et al.: Zerocash: decentralized anonymous payments from bitcoin. In: 2014 IEEE Symposium on Security and Privacy, SP 2014, Berkeley, CA, USA, May 18-21, 2014, pp. 459–474. IEEE Computer Society (2014). https://doi.org/10.1109/SP.2014.36
6. Bünz, B., Agrawal, S., Zamani, M., Boneh, D.: Zether: towards privacy in a smart contract world. In: Bonneau, J., Heninger, N. (eds.) Financial Cryptography and Data Security, pp. 423–443. Springer, Cham (2020). https://doi.org/10.1007/978-3-030-51280-4_23
7. Bünz, B., Bootle, J., Boneh, D., Poelstra, A., Wuille, P., Maxwell, G.: Bulletproofs: short proofs for confidential transactions and more. In: 2018 IEEE Symposium on Security and Privacy (SP), pp. 315–334. IEEE (2018)
8. Canetti, R.: Universally composable security: a new paradigm for cryptographic protocols. In: Proceedings 42nd IEEE Symposium on Foundations of Computer Science, pp. 136–145. IEEE (2001)
9. CCData: Stablecoins and CBDCS report (2023). https://ccdata.io/reports/stablecoins-cbdcs-report-july-2023
10. CoinMarketCap: Top stablecoin tokens by market capitalization. https://coinmarketcap.com/view/stablecoin/
11. Ethereum whitepaper (2022). https://ethereum.org/en/whitepaper/
12. European Central Bank (ECB): ECB digital euro consultation ends with record level of public feedback (2021)
13. Fauzi, P., Meiklejohn, S., Mercer, R., Orlandi, C.: Quisquis: a new design for anonymous cryptocurrencies. In: Galbraith, S.D., Moriai, S. (eds.) ASIACRYPT 2019, pp. 649–678. Springer, Cham (2019). https://doi.org/10.1007/978-3-030-34578-5_23

14. Kasamatsu, K., Kanno, S., Kobayashi, T., Kawahara, Y.: Barreto-Naehrig curves, Internet-Draft. Network Working Group (2014)
15. Kiayias, A., Kohlweiss, M., Sarencheh, A.: PEReDI: privacy-enhanced, regulated and distributed central bank digital currencies. In: Proceedings of the 2022 ACM SIGSAC Conference on Computer and Communications Security, pp. 1739–1752 (2022)
16. Liao, G.Y., Caramichael, J.: Stablecoins: growth potential and impact on banking (2022)
17. MakerDAO: The maker protocol: Makerdao's multi-collateral Dai (MCD) system. https://makerdao.com/en/whitepaper/#abstract
18. Moin, A., Sekniqi, K., Sirer, E.G.: SoK: a classification framework for Stablecoin Designs. In: Bonneau, J., Heninger, N. (eds.) Financial Cryptography and Data Security, pp. 174–197. Springer, Cham (2020). https://doi.org/10.1007/978-3-030-51280-4_11
19. Noether, S., Mackenzie, A., et al.: Ring confidential transactions. Ledger 1, 1–18 (2016)
20. Q.ai: What really happened to LUNA crypto? (2022). https://www.forbes.com/sites/qai/2022/09/20/what-really-happened-to-luna-crypto/
21. Sarencheh, A., Kiayias, A., Kohlweiss, M.: PARScoin: a privacy-preserving, auditable, and regulation-friendly stablecoin. Cryptology ePrint Archive (2023)
22. Sonnino, A., Al-Bassam, M., Bano, S., Meiklejohn, S., Danezis, G.: Coconut: threshold issuance selective disclosure credentials with applications to distributed ledgers. In: NDSS 2019. The Internet Society (2019)
23. Synthetix: Whitepaper (2022). https://docs.synthetix.io/synthetix-protocol/readme
24. Tether: Whitepaper. https://tether.to/en/whitepaper
25. US Department of the Treasury: Report on stablecoins, Technical report (2021). https://home.treasury.gov/system/files/136/StableCoinReport_Nov1_508.pdf
26. USDCoin: Centre whitepaper (2021). https://whitepaper.io/coin/usd-coin
27. Wüst, K., Kostiainen, K., Delius, N., Capkun, S.: Platypus: a central bank digital currency with unlinkable transactions and privacy-preserving regulation. In: Proceedings of the 2022 ACM SIGSAC Conference on Computer and Communications Security, pp. 2947–2960 (2022)

Author Index

GPSR Compliance

The European Union's (EU) General Product Safety Regulation (GPSR) is a set of rules that requires consumer products to be safe and our obligations to ensure this.

If you have any concerns about our products, you can contact us on ProductSafety@springernature.com

In case Publisher is established outside the EU, the EU authorized representative is:

Springer Nature Customer Service Center GmbH
Europaplatz 3
69115 Heidelberg, Germany

The manufacturer's authorised representative in the EU is Springer
Nature Customer Service Centre GmbH, Europaplatz 3, 69115 Heidelberg,
Germany. If you have any concerns regarding our products, please
contact ProductSafety@springernature.com

Printed and bound by CPI Group (UK) Ltd, Croydon, CR0 4YY

29/04/2026

02099537-0005